Celibate and Childless Men in Power

This book explores a striking common feature of pre-modern ruling systems on a global scale: the participation of childless and celibate men as integral parts of the elites. In bringing these two different groups of ruling men together, this collection shows that the integration of men who were normatively or physically excluded from biological fatherhood offered pre-modern dynasties the potential to use different reproduction patterns. The shared focus on ruling eunuchs and bishops also reveals that these men had a specific position at the intersection of four fields: power, social dynamics, sacredness and gender/masculinities. The 13 chapters present case studies on clerics in Medieval Europe and court eunuchs in the Middle East, Byzantium, India and China. They analyse how these men in their different frameworks acted as politicians, participated in social networks and provided religious authority, and discuss their masculinities. Taken together, this collection sheds light on the political arena before the modern nation-state excluded these unmarried men from the circles of political power.

Almut Höfert is Professor for Medieval Transcultural History at the University of Zürich.

Matthew M. Mesley is a Visiting Fellow at the University of Huddersfield.

Serena Tolino is Junior Professor for Islamic Studies at the University of Hamburg.

Celibate and Childless Men in Power

Ruling Eunuchs and Bishops in the Pre-Modern World

Edited by Almut Höfert, Matthew M. Mesley and Serena Tolino

Routledge
Taylor & Francis Group
LONDON AND NEW YORK

First published 2018
by Routledge
2 Park Square, Milton Park, Abingdon, Oxon OX14 4RN

and by Routledge
711 Third Avenue, New York, NY 10017

Routledge is an imprint of the Taylor & Francis Group, an informa business

British Library Cataloguing-in-Publication Data
A catalogue record for this book is available from the British Library

Library of Congress Cataloging-in-Publication Data
Names: Höfert, Almut, editor.
Title: Celibate and childless men in power: ruling eunuchs and bishops in the pre-modern world / edited by Almut Höfert, Matthew M. Mesley, and Serena Tolino.
Description: 1st [edition]. | New York: Routledge, 2017. | Includes bibliographical references and index.
Identifiers: LCCN 2017015830 (print) | LCCN 2017028967 (ebook) | ISBN 9781315566658 (ebook) | ISBN 9781472453402 (alk. paper)
Subjects: LCSH: Eunuchs–History. | Power (Social sciences)–History. | Childlessness–History.
Classification: LCC HQ449 (ebook) | LCC HQ449 .C45 2017 (print) | DDC 303.309–dc23
LC record available at https://lccn.loc.gov/2017015830

ISBN: 978-1-4724-5340-2 (hbk)
ISBN: 978-1-315-56665-8 (ebk)

Typeset in Sabon
by Deanta Global Publishing Services, Chennai, India

Contents

List of contributors vii
Preface xiii

Introduction: Celibate and childless men placed into a *Shared Focus*: Ruling eunuchs and bishops between the intersections of power, networks, sacredness and gender 1
ALMUT HÖFERT

PART I
Bishops and eunuchs as parts of the ruling elites 41

1 The bishop in the Latin West 600–1100 43
JULIA BARROW

2 Guarding the harem, protecting the state: Eunuchs in a fourth/tenth-century Abbasid court 65
NADIA MARIA EL CHEIKH

3 Mu'nis al-Muẓaffar: An exceptional eunuch 79
HUGH KENNEDY

4 Harem and eunuchs: Liminality and networks of Mughal authority 92
RUBY LAL

PART II
Networks and kinships 109

5 Celibate, but not childless: Eunuch military dynasticism in medieval China 111
MICHAEL HOECKELMANN

6 Spiritual heirs and families: Episcopal relatives in early medieval Francia 129
RACHEL STONE

7 Eunuchs and the East India Company in north India 149
JESSICA HINCHY

PART III
Religious authority and sacredness 175

8 Physical and symbolic castration and the Holy Eunuch in late antiquity, third to sixth centuries CE 177
MATHEW KUEFLER

9 Monastic superiority, episcopal authority and masculinity in Caesarius of Heisterbach's *Dialogus Miraculorum* 192
MATTHEW M. MESLEY

10 The chief harem eunuch of the Ottoman empire: Servant of the sultan, servant of the Prophet 211
JANE HATHAWAY

PART IV
Gender and masculinities 227

11 Byzantine court eunuchs and the Macedonian dynasty (867–1056): Family, power and gender 229
SHAUN TOUGHER

12 Eunuchs in the Fatimid empire: Ambiguities, gender and sacredness 246
SERENA TOLINO

13 Under pressure: Secular–mendicant polemics and the construction of chaste masculinity within the thirteenth-century Latin church 268
SITA STECKEL AND STEPHANIE KLUGE

Bibliography 297
Index of eunuchs 345
Index of bishops 347
General index 350

Contributors

Julia Barrow studied at St Andrews University and at Oxford University, where she received her Ph.D. with a thesis on *The Bishops of Hereford and their Acta (charters) 1163–1219*. She held many positions, including a British Academy Postdoctoral Fellowship at Birmingham. She spent one year working for the Victoria County History of Cheshire, before she got a permanent lectureship at the University of Nottingham, where she taught until 2012. She is currently Professor and Director of the Institute of Medieval Studies at Leeds University. Her main research interest is church history (700–1300), especially English episcopal charters and administration (1000–1300) and the career structure of the medieval clergy in western Europe (800–1250). She has published extensively, most recently "Way-stations on English Episcopal Itineraries, c.700–c.1300", *English Historical Review*, 127 (2012); and *English Episcopal Acta*, 35: *Hereford 1234–1275* (Oxford, 2009).

Nadia Maria El Cheikh is Professor of History at the American University of Beirut (AUB). She received her B.A. in History and Archeology at AUB and her Ph.D. degree in History and Middle Eastern Studies from Harvard University in 1992. She has served as Director of the Center for Arab and Middle Eastern Studies and as Chair of the Department of History and Archaeology. She received the New York University Global Affair's International Visitors Program Grant in 2004 and in 2007 was the Shawwaf Visiting Professor of Arabic and Islamic Studies at the Department of Near Eastern Languages and Civilizations at Harvard University. Her book, *Byzantium Viewed by the Arabs*, was published by the Harvard Middle Eastern Monographs in 2004 and translated into Turkish and Greek. She has co-authored a book entitled *Crisis and Continuity at the Abbasid Court. Formal and Informal Politics in the Caliphate of al-Muqtadir (295–320/908–932)* (Leiden: Brill, 2013). Her most recent book, *Women, Islam and Abbasid Identity*, was published in 2015 by Harvard University Press. In 2016, she was appointed Dean of the Faculty of Arts and Sciences at the American University of Beirut.

Jane Hathaway received her Ph.D. from the Department of Near Eastern Studies, Princeton University, in 1992; she was a student of Cemal Kafadar. She is currently Professor of History at Ohio State University. Her expertise is the early modern Ottoman Empire, particularly the Arab provinces (Egypt in particular) and the eunuchs of the imperial harem. She has published numerous books and articles related to these topics, including *The Politics of Households in Ottoman Egypt: The Rise of the Qazdağlıs* (Cambridge, 1997); *A Tale of Two Factions: Myth, Memory, and Identity in Ottoman Egypt and Yemen* (State University of New York Press, 2003); *Beshir Agha, Chief Eunuch of the Ottoman Imperial Harem* (Oneworld, 2006); and *The Arab Lands under Ottoman Rule, 1500–1800* (Pearson/Longman, 2008). She is currently completing a book on the office of chief harem eunuch, to be published by Cambridge.

Jessica Hinchy is Assistant Professor of History at Nanyang Technological University in Singapore. In 2013, she obtained her Ph.D. in South Asian History from the Australian National University. Her research interests include gender, sexuality, domesticity and colonialism in late eighteenth and nineteenth-century north India. She has particularly examined the colonial regulation of peoples classified as "eunuchs", such as *khwāja-sarā'ī* eunuch slaves and the transgender *hijra* community. Her publications include "Enslaved Childhoods in Eighteenth Century Awadh" in *South Asian History and Culture* 6, no. 3 (2015); "The Sexual Politics of Imperial Expansion: Eunuchs and Indirect Colonial Rule in Mid-Nineteenth-Century North India" in *Gender & History* 26, no.3 (2014); and "Obscenity, Moral Contagion and Masculinity: Hijras in Public Space in Colonial North India" in *Asian Studies Review* 38, no. 2 (2014).

Michael Hoeckelmann studied Sinology, Linguistics and Political Science at Westfälische Wilhelms-Universität (WWU) in Münster. From 2005 to 2007, he studied Modern Chinese and Chinese Philosophy at Sun Yat-sen University in Guangzhou, PRC. He obtained his Ph.D. in Sinology in 2013 at the graduate school of the Cluster of Excellence "Religion and Politics in Pre-Modern and Modern Cultures" at WWU Münster. After holding a British Academy Postdoctoral Fellowship at King's College London and the University of Cambridge from 2013 to 2015, he now is Assistant Professor at the Department of History at Hong Kong Baptist University. His research interests include Classical Chinese philology, the intellectual and religious history of China, and eunuchs and elite formation in medieval China. His publications include *Li Deyu (787–850). Religion und Politik in der Tang-Zeit* (Wiesbaden: Harrassowitz, 2016) and "Gerechte Waffen und die Kunst des Strafens", in *Monumenta Serica* 58 (2010).

Almut Höfert studied History and Islamic Studies at the Universities of Bonn, Cairo and Freiburg im Breisgau. She obtained her Ph.D. at the European

University Institute of Florence in 2001. She worked as Assistant Professor at the University of Basel (2001–2005; 2007–2011), and she has been Visiting Fellow at the American University in Cairo (2005–6) and at the Wissenschaftskolleg zu Berlin (2006–7). Since 2011, she has been a Swiss National Science Foundation Professor in Transcultural History of the Latin and Arabic Middle Ages at the Department of History of the University of Zürich, where she is leading a project on *Hermaphrodites, Eunuchs, Priests: Gender Ambiguities and Masculinities in the Arab and Latin Middle Ages.* Her research interests include empire and caliphate, cultural and religious history in Latin, Arabic and Byzantine Middle Ages, methods of transcultural and gender history. Her publications include *Den Feind beschreiben. "Türkengefahr" und europäisches Wissen über das Osmanische Reich, 1450–1600* (Frankfurt a. M., 2003) and *Kaisertum und Kalifat. Der imperiale Monotheismus in Früh- und Hochmittelalter* (Frankfurt 2015). She also co-edited *Geschlechtergeschichte global (L'homme. Europäische Zeitschrift für feministische Geschichtswissenschaft* 23, 2) (Köln, Weimar, 2012) and *Between Europe and Islam. Shaping Modernity in a Transcultural Space* (Brüssel, Bern, Berlin, 2000).

Hugh Kennedy studied Arabic, Persian and History at Pembroke College (Cambridge) and obtained his Ph.D. in 1977 from the Faculty of Oriental Studies, Cambridge, with a thesis on the "Politics and the Political Elite in the Early Abbasid Caliphate". He taught at St Andrews University, where he also acted as Deputy Head of the School of History and then as Dean of the Faculty of Arts. He was Professor of Middle Eastern History at the University of St Andrews from 1997 to 2007. Since 2007, he has been Professor of Arabic at the School of Oriental and Asian Studies in London. His research topics include History of the Islamic Middle East, Islamic Archaeology and Muslim Spain. He has published several books on the history of the Middle East, like *The Great Arab Conquests* (London, 2007); in 2004, a revised edition of his *Prophet and the Age of the Caliphates, 600–1050* (London, 2004), first published in 1986; and, most recently, *The Caliphate: The History of an Idea* (2016). He has edited several volumes, including the *Historical Atlas of Islam* (Leiden, 2002), and he has published numerous articles.

Stephanie Kluge studied History and German Philology at the University of Münster and obtained her M.Ed. degree in 2013. Since 2014, she has been a doctoral researcher in the Volkswagen Foundation Dilthey project *Diversitas religionum. Thirteenth-century Foundations of European Discourses of Religious Diversity*, led by Sita Steckel. She is currently working on a dissertation studying polemical and didactic discourses of purity, chastity and masculinity among thirteenth-century Franciscans and Dominicans. Forthcoming publications concern debates about chastity in various thirteenth-century genres such as historiography and exempla literature.

Mathew Kuefler studied at the University of Alberta and at Yale University, where he obtained his Ph.D. in 1995. He has taught at several universities, including Yale University, Rice University, University of Alberta, University of British Columbia and finally at the San Diego State University, where he is now a Professor of History. His main research interests are medieval gender and sexuality, as well as the history of childhood and the family and LGBTQ history. He is the author of *The Manly Eunuch: Masculinity, Gender Ambiguity, and Christian Ideology in Late Antiquity* (Chicago, 2001) and *The Making and Unmaking of a Saint: Hagiography and Memory in the Cult of Gerald of Aurillac* (Pennsylvania, 2014); editor of *The History of Sexuality Sourcebook* (Toronto, 2007) and *The Boswell Thesis: Essays on Christianity, Social Tolerance, and Homosexuality* (Chicago, 2006); and author of numerous academic articles. From 2004 to 2014, he was director of the *Journal of the History of Sexuality*.

Ruby Lal is Professor of South Asian Studies in the Department of Middle Eastern and South Asian Studies at Emory University, Atlanta. She holds an M.Phil in History from the University of Delhi and a D.Phil from the University of Oxford. Before Emory, she taught at the Johns Hopkins University, Baltimore. She is the author of *Domesticity and Power in the Early Mughal World* (Cambridge University Press, New York, 2005), which won much acclaim, including more than 15 reviews in major international journals and magazines, such as *The New York Review of Books*, *The Economic and Political Weekly*, *Revue Historique* and *The Times Literary Supplement*. Her recent book entitled *Coming of Age in Nineteenth Century India: The Girl-Child and the Art of Playfulness* (Cambridge University Press, New York, 2013) has been reviewed extensively in academic journals and magazines with wider intellectual concerns. She is currently finalizing a narrative history of Mughal Empress Nur Jahan, titled *Uncrowned Empress* (W. W. Norton, 2017).

Matthew M. Mesley was awarded a BA [Hons, 1st] History at the University of Exeter in 2004; an MPhil in Medieval History at Corpus Christi College, Cambridge (2005); and an Arts and Humanities Research Council PhD at the University of Exeter (2009). In 2009, he was awarded a six-month Scouloudi Foundation Research Fellowship at the Institute of Historical Research, London. Between 2011 and 2016 he undertook a postdoctorate at the University of Zürich, working on a research project entitled *Die Männlichkeit der Kirchenfürsten* – directed by Almut Höfert and financed by the Swiss National Science Foundation. In 2014, he was awarded Medieval Fellow status at the Center of Medieval Studies, Fordham University, New York. He is currently a Visiting Fellow at the

University of Huddersfield (UK) and an Associate Lecturer at Bath Spa University (UK). Forthcoming publications include a chapter entitled "Chivalry, Masculinity, and Sexuality" in the *Cambridge Companion to the Literature of the Crusades* and a contribution to Palgrave MacMillan's *Handbook of Masculinity and Political Culture in Europe*. He has also reviewed for the journals *Early Medieval Europe*, the *Journal of British Studies*, *The Medieval Review*, *English Historical Review* and *Speculum*.

Sita Steckel obtained her doctoral degree from Ludwig-Maximilians-Universität in Munich in 2006, after training in Medieval History, Modern History and English Philology/Medieval Literature. She has held positions at Munich and at Harvard University, Cambridge, MA, but since 2004 she has mainly worked at the University of Münster and is currently Junior Professor at Münster's Historical Seminar. Her current research project, based on a Dilthey Fellowship granted by the Volkswagen Foundation, is titled *Diversitas religionum. Thirteenth-century Foundations of European Discourses of Religious Diversity*, and it primarily deals with religious polemics between different Christian groups such as monks/nuns, friars, clerics and laypeople. Recent publications concern not only religious polemics and conflicts within Christianity but also theoretical issues concerning the history of medieval religion.

Rachel Stone obtained a first degree in Mathematics; she then trained as a librarian and worked in a variety of specialist and academic libraries. She obtained a MPhil in Medieval History at Cambridge University and completed her Ph.D. at King's College London in 2005. Since then, she has researched and taught in London and Cambridge and has also worked as a librarian. She is currently a Visiting Research Associate at King's College London. Her research interests include Carolingian gender and women's history and the development of the early medieval clergy. Her recent publications include *Morality and Masculinity in the Carolingian Empire* (2012), *Hincmar of Rheims: Life and Work* (2015) (co-edited with Charles West) and *The Divorce of King Lothar and Queen Theutberga: Hincmar of Rheims's De Divortio* (2016) (jointly translated with Charles West).

Serena Tolino is currently Junior Professor for Islamic Studies at the Asia and Africa Institute of the University of Hamburg. She studied Arabic and Islamic Studies at the University of Naples *L'Orientale*, at Cairo University and at Dar Comboni for Arabic Studies (Cairo). In 2012, she was awarded a Ph.D. in Islamic Studies from the University of Naples *L'Orientale* and the Martin Luther University Halle-Wittenberg (co-tutelle). From 2012 to 2016, she worked as Postdoctorate Fellow of the Swiss National Science Foundation at the University of Zurich in a project on *Hermaphrodites, Eunuchs, Priests: Gender Ambiguities and Masculinities in the Arab and Latin Middle Ages*, directed by Almut

Höfert. In Winter Semester 2013, she was Visiting Fellow at the Islamic Legal Studies Program at Harvard Law School. She is particularly interested in Islamic law, gender in Islamic countries and sexuality in Islamic history. She has published a number of articles on homosexuality in Islamic law and in Islamic countries and the monograph *Omosessualità e atti omosessuali tra diritto islamico e diritto positivo: il caso egiziano con alcuni riferimenti all'esperienza libanese* (Homosexuality and Homosexual Acts between Islamic Law and Positive Law. The Egyptian Case with Some Notes on the Lebanese Case) (Naples, 2013).

Shaun Tougher studied at Queen's University of Belfast and obtained his Ph.D. from the University of St Andrews with a dissertation on the reign of Leo VI, 886–912. He subsequently taught at Queen's and at the University of St Andrews. He is a Reader in Ancient History in the School of History, Archaeology and Religion at Cardiff University. His main research interests include the history of the later Roman and Byzantine empires, Byzantium's Macedonian dynasty, eunuchs in the Byzantine empire and in general and the family in Byzantium. His publications include *The Eunuch in Byzantine History and Society* (Abingdon and New York, 2008), *Julian the Apostate* (Edinburgh, 2007) and *The Reign of Leo VI (886–912): Politics and People* (Leiden, 1997). He also co-edited *Emperor and Author: The Writings of Julian the Apostate* (Swansea, 2012), and he edited *Eunuchs in Antiquity and Beyond* (London, 2002).

Preface

Eunuchs and bishops appear to be so different that it might come as a surprise to see a collection that brings these two groups of men together. Whereas bishops in the pre-modern world have been for some time the subject of historical studies, scholars only began to be interested in eunuchs from the 1970s onwards, and thereafter an increasing number of studies have been published, many in the last decade. Although the history of eunuchs is still relatively new, scholars have demonstrated that the image of the eunuch as the avaricious and manipulative guardian of the harem is an ancient stereotype, but one that fails to appreciate their many roles and functions. Indeed, court eunuchs were an integral part of pre-modern ruling elites, whose manifold responsibilities went far beyond the harems' borders. With this scholarly appreciation of eunuchs as powerful figures in pre-modern dynasties, a striking parallel is evident: both eunuchs and bishops were either physically unable or normatively forbidden to father children, yet they still wielded significant social, political and cultural power in their respective societies. Our collection addresses this phenomenon. Without aiming at a strict comparison, it explores a variety of pre-modern cultures and analyses the ways in which both groups of men were excluded from legitimate or physical reproduction yet still remained an important feature of political dynastic systems.

In the introduction and first chapter, Almut Höfert sets out the analytical framework for the volume. She proposes the *Shared Focus* as an experimental comparative shapshot for transcultural collaborative projects and applies this approach to our topic. In so doing, she presents four interrelated fields in which both eunuchs and bishops held a special position: (1) their role as part of the ruling elites; (2) their involvement in kinship and networks; (3) their role in religion and their associations to sacredness; and (4) the understanding and representation of their masculinities and gender. As Höfert points out, the masculinities of eunuchs and bishops were particularly complex, conflicting and, one could say, "kaleidoscopic".

The case studies on bishops and eunuchs are themselves presented in four parts, which correspond to the four fields above. This placement reflects the main focus of the various case studies, although the boundaries are not strict. We have tried to reach a balance, in so far as contributions relate to different times periods and world regions; the collection covers the Late Antiquity to the nineteenth century, with chapters on the Middle East, Europe, China and India.

The contributions in the first part on "Bishops and eunuchs as parts of the ruling elites" provide a broader picture of bishops and eunuchs as political and military actors. Julia Barrow begins with a wide-ranging survey of the bishop and his roles in the Latin West between the seventh and twelfth centuries. Following this, she explores the importance that bishops had in fostering uncle–nephew relationships and providing education, patronage and institutional continuity for their charges. The contributions of Nadia Maria El Cheikh and Hugh Kennedy explore the significance of eunuchs in the Abbasid empire during the tenth century. Nadia Maria El Cheikh analyses the multiple roles and functions that court eunuchs held and the way they used their proximity to their masters as a way of acquiring authority. Hugh Kennedy presents a case study of the eunuch commander Muʾnis al-Muẓaffar, whose military successes resulted in him having a particularly powerful position in Abbasid politics. Ruby Lal explores the ways in which the ideology of the Mughal empire intersected with ideas about court eunuchs in the sixteenth and seventeenth centuries. In their manifold tasks, court eunuchs were part of a liminal zone, in which they were both loyal servants and officers of the empire.

The second part on "Networks and kinships" begins with Michael Hoeckelmann, who shows the crucial roles court eunuchs held in the late Tang dynasty (618–907) in China. Court eunuchs were often married and they could also adopt sons as successors – a practice that has been described as *eunuch dynasticism*. Rachel Stone analyses inheritance and succession patterns of Carolingian bishops in ninth- and tenth-century Europe. She explores how noble families tried to monopolise bishoprics, both before and after celibacy became the norm. Jessica Hinchy investigates high-ranking eunuch slaves, called *khwāja-sarāʾī*, in the North Indian province of Awadh. She suggests that their social and political roles were shaped by three factors: master–slave proximity, networks of adopted kin and disciples and adherence to hegemonic codes of masculinity. With the British annexation of Awadh and the historical transformations of colonial modernity in South Asia, the *khwāja-sarāʾī* were excluded from the political arena.

In the third part on "Religious authority and sacredness", Mathew Kuefler shows that despite the Christian church's theological condemnation of physical castration, some Christian believers thought self-castration was an appropriate choice. He explores how the relationship between eunuchs and sacredness remained a complex area of dispute. Matthew M. Mesley analyses the early thirteenth-century Cistercian text *Dialogus Miraculorum*, composed by Caesarius of Heisterbach. The ambiguous nature of episcopal authority is explored, as is the degree to which the medieval secular church was held up as the antithesis of monastic ways of living. Jane Hathaway analyses the involvement of Ottoman high-ranking court eunuchs in imperial religious politics in the seventeenth and eighteenth centuries. She highlights the rise of the black chief eunuchs of the harem, who would endow charitable and educational foundations and were often appointed as head of the eunuchs of the Prophet, who guarded the prophet's tomb in Medina. Being entrusted with one of the most sacred spaces in Islam, Ottoman chief harem eunuchs appear as pious servants to both sultan and the prophet.

In the fourth part on "Gender and masculinities", Shaun Tougher investigates the court eunuchs in the Byzantine empire under the Macedonian dynasty (867–1056). He argues that eunuchs should be analysed vis-à-vis other Greek men. Byzantine court eunuchs were not only recruited from slave markets but also came from families of ruling elites and even had family connections to the emperor. Serena Tolino examines the position of eunuchs in the shiʿa Fatimid Empire (297/909 until 567/1171). She analyses a variety of genres, including medical and legal texts, and demonstrates how different sources throw a distinct light on the eunuchs' gender. She also focuses on the ways in which sacredness was implicated in the relationship between eunuchs and the figure of the Fatimid imam–caliph. Sita Steckel and Stephanie Kluge demonstrate how, with the emergence of the mendicant orders in the thirteenth-century Latin church, several groups of celibate men competed within the arena of religious authority and gender. In the conflicts with secular clergymen, Franciscan and Dominican monks chose different strategies to represent and defend their chastity.

*

This collection is part of a larger research project based at the University of Zürich on "Hermaphrodites, Eunuchs and Priests: Gender Ambiguities and Masculinities in the Arab and Latin Middle Ages", conducted by Almut Höfert and financed by the Swiss National Science Foundation (SNSF). In this project, Matthew M. Mesley examines the figure of the medieval bishop; bishops' representation in English, German and Crusading contexts; and the relationship between their political authority and gender. Serena Tolino has worked on eunuchs in the Islamic Middle Ages, focusing on their role as political actors in the Fatimid Empire and the construction of eunuch identities and gender discourses.

The collection is a product of a conference held in Zürich in August 2013. Our thanks go to the contributors to this volume for the hard work they have put into preparing their separate chapters. We are grateful to the SNSF as well as to the following departments of the University of Zürich for their financial support at the conference: the University Research Priority Program (URPP) Asia and Europe, the Kompetenzzentrum Zürcher Mediävistik and the Universitätsverein Zürich. We are indebted to a number of people, including Roman Benz from the URPP Asia and Europe, who helped throughout the process with graphics, images, fliers and posters; Antje Flüchter, who accepted the difficult assignment of giving a final comment at the end of the conference; Michele Bernardini, Aldo Colucciello, Ashraf Hassan, Lisa Indraccolo, Marco Lauri and Nicola Verderame, who helped us with particularly complex transliterations in different languages; Matthew M. Mesley, who went through the challenging and meticulous work of editing all the chapters for an English-speaking academic audience; and his partner Christopher Bonfield, who helped so much with formatting the volume and provided much-needed technical and scholarly support. Serena Tolino would also like to thank the Islamic Legal Studies Program at the Faculty of Law, Harvard University, for its support during the Fall Semester 2013, which allowed her to carry on research on eunuchs in Islamic Law; and Ashraf, Sofia and Elias Hassan, for their patience, their support and their love. Almut Höfert (chapters) and Serena Tolino (bibliography) were responsible for finalizing the manuscript. Finally, we would especially like to thank Routledge, our publishers, who enthusiastically accepted our book proposal; and our editors, who have been patient, open and helpful throughout.

Almut Höfert, Matthew M. Mesley and Serena Tolino

Introduction

Celibate and childless men placed into a *Shared Focus*: Ruling eunuchs and bishops between the intersections of power, networks, sacredness and gender[1]

Almut Höfert

Ruling eunuchs and bishops: To our modern eye, these two groups of men have nothing in common. Why would one make a connection between bishops, noble princes of the Christian church who crowned and counselled mighty kings, with eunuchs, the slaves and treacherous schemers in Oriental harems? As it happens, both groups converge upon the boundary between the European world (which had bishops, but not eunuchs) and non-European societies in Asia (which had eunuchs, but not bishops). Byzantium, where eunuchs served in high offices at the imperial court, but were also accepted into the priesthood, and could become powerful patriarchs of the Constantinopolitan church, acts as an intermediate zone if we were to draw a line between the "European" and the "Oriental" world.

In the first instance, there might seem to be little reason to bring together a collection of articles investigating ruling eunuchs and bishops – both groups have been much discussed in their respective areas of study. With this collection, however, we intend to demonstrate that, despite the fact that (or maybe because) eunuchs and bishops were very different kinds of men, it is useful to bring European and non-European history together and to look at them in a shared perspective on a global horizon.

Comparative perspectives in global history

In recent decades, historians have tried to overcome, or at least problematise, the practice of their academic discipline, which often considers "Europe" as the normative sphere of pre-modern history, whereas "non-European" history is dealt with in specific area studies – Middle Eastern Studies, Indology, Sinology and so forth.[2] Furthermore, new studies of global history have sought to transgress academic and historiographical partitioning of different "civilisations" with their separate histories. In particular, the historiographical wall between "the West" and "the rest" has come under scrutiny, together with the inherent Eurocentric nature of much historical analysis. In theory, most scholars agree that we lose much of the complexity and entangled nature of the pre-modern world when the historical agenda, its fields, methods and "universal categories", are drawn solely from European material. The practice, however, of a history going beyond Europe proves to be more difficult. Most studies of global history have focussed upon modern history, with certain themes such as globalisation, colonisation and nation states being used to frame an analysis. Pre-modern history, on the other hand, is less prominent in recent methodological debates,[3] although it was certainly extensively treated in twentieth-century studies on *world history* (for example, Arnold Toynbee and Oswald Spengler, but also Max Weber and Immanuel Wallerstein) or *axial civilisations* (Shmuel Eisenstadt).[4] These approaches, however, utilised the category of "separated civilisations" and have been since criticised for reifying historiographical civilizational borders.[5]

If we identify recent attempts to analyse different phenomena explicitly in a global context,[6] several labels and approaches apart from global history have been proposed: transnational, transcultural, translocal, imperial, entangled, connected and shared history and so forth.[7] Notwithstanding the differences (although there are some overlaps) between these approaches, there are two basic methodological ways of analysing different regions/areas jointly, which may or may not have had contact with each other: (1) by comparison; and/or (2) by investigating relationships, interactions, exchanges, transfers and entanglements.[8] For the pre-modern era, however, historians have fewer choices: Before the modern inventions of mass communication and globalised transport, the extent and frequency of entanglements between different world regions were considerably less. Together with the limited survival of sources, especially for medieval history, there are fewer entanglements and interactions a historian can use to supplement his or her comparative perspective. Comparisons are also notorious for being challenging, precarious and time consuming, even more so on a transcultural level, if one wants to avoid the methodological traps of both civilisational approaches and Eurocentric analytical categories.[9]

In theoretical discussions on historical comparisons, some historians like William Sewell have made a distinction between a "comparative method" (the different kinds of historical comparisons that can be divided into different categories such as *parallel/cross-comparison*, *generalizing/contrasting comparison*, *reciprocal comparison*, etc.) and a "comparative perspective" (contextualising a concrete case within a broader context without a thoroughly executed comparison).[10] The common ground for our collection is not a comparison but another kind of a comparative perspective.

The contributions in this volume present individual case studies on bishops or eunuchs in the Middle East, Europe, India, China and Byzantium. Taken together and complemented by further material, one can create what I would like to call a "Shared Focus" that points to structural similarities between both groups of men beyond their obvious differences. This introduction presents the Shared Focus on eunuchs and bishops. In so doing, I am not proposing that comparing bishops and eunuchs should be a new vast field of research. I understand our Shared Focus rather as an experimental comparative snapshot that benefits from the possibilities of a comparative perspective. The Shared Focus has the advantage of not being a holistic enterprise that addresses the grand narratives of global history. It serves, instead, as an experimental way for finding new analytical directions concerning topics of different scales, large or small, and it is particularly well suited for collaborative research projects.[11]

The Shared Focus is carried out in three phases. In the first stage, two (or more) historical phenomena (A and B) are connected in a preliminary comparison through one or more common features. In does not matter whether A and B differ substantially in many other aspects – one is free to follow Marcel Etienne's plea to *comparer l'incomparable!* and to take advantage of the distancing effect (*Verfremdungseffekt*) that deprives both A and B of being self-evident. By comparing A with B, the results are then organised into an (always flexible) analytical agenda – be it a hierarchical or interdependent set of different fields or a simple list with more and less important questions. These questions of *why actually do we have A (or B)*, and *why in this specific form* shed new perspectives on both A and B, which tend to be not so clear (or even hidden) when A and B are examined in isolation.

In phase two, this analytical agenda is applied to various case studies of A and B. The author of each case study can apply the analytical agenda with different priorities in mind, emphasising certain aspects more substantially and leaving other points to different contributors. Every case study is free to shift their focus in whichever direction is most appropriate for their topic and to respond to particular questions that they are confronted with. If the analytical agenda of the Shared Focus has proven to be too daring during this process, the enterprise could finish there by providing different case studies of A and B. Indeed, at the very least, the case studies present further insights and understandings of their specific topics, even if our analytical agenda might be rejected. However, if the analytical agenda has proven to be fruitful, we can move onto stage three. In this phase, the new findings of the Shared Focus can be synthesised, and further questions on a global or transcultural scale can be addressed in one or various fields.

I intend to demonstrate that our example, of ruling eunuchs and bishops, is a case in which a Shared Focus can be successfully applied in all its three stages. Whereas the obvious differences between court eunuchs and bishops coincide with the academic and historiographical borders between different "civilisations", I hope to show that our Shared Focus sheds light on a transculturally common feature of pre-modern history: Celibate and childless men emerge as an integral part of the ruling elites in different societies and regions. By examining these groups together, we can appreciate how these men were embedded in a closely interconnected set of power positions, social patterns, understandings of sacredness, and gender. The analysis of celibate and childless men within this intersected set provides further insights into pre-modern rule. It also allows us to entangle the analysis of both bishops and eunuchs in a mutually conducive way: Thus, some questions that have been already considered in respect to eunuchs could prove to be of value in investigating bishops, as well as vice versa.

Similarities and differences between ruling eunuchs and bishops

The point of departure for our Shared Focus on ruling eunuchs and bishops consists of three similarities. Both groups of men:

1 were implicated in dynastic patterns of pre-modern rule, wielding significant social, political, economic and cultural power;
2 were either physically or normatively unable to father children;
3 from the nineteenth century, had either lost much of their political influence (the bishops) or had entirely lost such power (the eunuchs).

Both groups of men were heterogeneous within their categories, of course, yet there are three fundamental differences that can be applied to a majority of court eunuchs and bishops:

1 *Their social origin and mobility*
Whereas bishops were often of noble descent and pursued their careers in the political–geographical ambit of their aristocrat families, eunuchs were mostly from the lower social strata of society and, before they were made slaves, they had often been uprooted far from their place of birth. In their various positions, however, bishops and eunuchs were both quite mobile – and both groups of men could and did travel over long distances in order to fulfil their many tasks.
2 *Their institutional framework*
Bishops played prominent and powerful roles within the church; eunuchs were an integral part of a royal court infrastructure and were often recruited and educated within a military or imperial hierarchy.
3 *Their body*
In the Latin Christian church (leaving Byzantium aside for a moment), priests and bishops had to be physically complete, whereas eunuchs underwent castration, a radical physical alteration that brought the eunuch into being.

In respect to academic research, there is still one general point to be mentioned that reveals a typical difference between research on European and non-European history: We have countless studies on bishops but far fewer studies on eunuchs. In the last two decades, however, studies on eunuchs have increased.[12]

In our project and during the work on this collection, we set up four fields for our historical analysis that proved to be intersected: (1) bishops and court eunuchs as part of the ruling elites, (2) their kinships relations and networks, (3) their position as regards religious authority and sacredness and (4) the understanding and representations of their masculinity and gender. In this introduction, I shall present these four fields with one important addition after the presentation of the first field: I will also touch upon the point of how, in late antiquity, not only spiritual but also physical castration was discussed as a way to practice celibacy. Being myself trained in the history of Europe and the Middle East, these regions receive more attention than others. The examples used in relation to our Shared Focus, therefore, privilege some areas within its global horizon. I will draw upon the chapters of this volume, but I have also added relevant research from other studies and sources. Due to the analytical profile of the Shared Focus, however, I do not summarise each chapter in this volume; each contribution has its own independent analytical agenda.

In respect to the bishops, some words should be said about the category of celibacy. It has been a major achievement of recent scholarship on clerical masculinities that the former "trajectory ... which underscored the centrality of celibacy as the most vital component of a cleric's gender identity" has been abandoned: Clerical masculinities were defined by many factors indeed.[13] With this collection, we do not intend to go back in time and claim that celibacy should be the primordial category with which to analyse medieval priests and bishops. My goal of presenting bishops and eunuchs between the intersections of power, networks, sacredness and gender hopefully shows that both eunuchal and episcopal masculinities were defined by a complex set of different factors. However, although celibacy was not the *primordial* category used to define these men's lives, it was a *persisting* element that shaped the institutional and cultural framework for the medieval clergy. The same thing can be said about the childlessness of eunuchs. It is due to the comparative perspective of the Shared Focus that both celibacy and childlessness appear as the common feature of eunuchs and bishops and are thus singled out.

Bishops and court eunuchs in power

Eunuchs appear as court officials in the first millennium BC in both the Middle East and China.[14] From this point until the nineteenth century, court eunuchs were employed in the service of numerous monarchies and dynastic households. Although they were not a universal feature, and their numbers and significance varied, on the whole the institution of court eunuchs was an important and persistent characteristic of pre-modern monarchic rule. The office of the bishop, on the other hand, developed later from the second century of the early Christian church. By the fifth century, the "monarchical bishop" was the leader of his local church, a potential imperial actor and a prominent political leader of his city – if not the ruler of the city.[15] Around 1000, bishoprics were "small states, with almost everything which corresponds to our conception of a state: rulers, governments, central places, citizenship, legislation, taxation"; they were thus a central part of the European political landscape.[16] In the late Middle Ages, the term *prelate* was increasingly used to define a group that placed bishops, archbishops, cardinals and high-ranking male monastic superiors together and defined them as powerful political actors who lived in great splendour and acted as cultural patrons.[17] Even with these significant changes over time, throughout, bishops continued to play a crucial role in European politics until the end of the Ancien Régime.

In contrast to bishops, court eunuchs were not leaders of "small states". Yet at court, their tasks varied widely and might go far beyond the role of guarding the harem that has inspired modern stereotypes. Eunuchs often ran various offices of the imperial household, but they could be employed in any imperial office and served also as military commanders and governors. The eunuch general Narses, for example, defeated the Ostrogoths in 551, reclaiming large parts of Italy under the Byzantine rule of emperor Justinian. In Fatimid Cairo (973–1171), the two most important offices in the capital were the commandment of the local military force (*shurṭa*) and the market supervisor (*ḥisba*) – which were usually run by castrated men. All in all, eunuchs in service of a dynasty can be found in four different sectors: They were responsible for the (1) female and (2) male spheres of the imperial household, and they were employed – alongside non-castrated men – in (3) the imperial administration and (4) the military.

Since they could have access to all areas of the court, including the politically important harem, some eunuchs gained extraordinary political power and could often determine a dynasty's fate. The following examples of exceptionally powerful eunuchs are partly drawn from the various contributions in this volume: In China, the eunuch commander Yu Chaoʾen led the imperial army against a rebellion in 763, thus saving the emperor and earning himself a central position in the empire (Michael Hoeckelmann). The Abbasid eunuch Muʾnis al-Muẓaffar (d. 933), having prevented a coup against the new caliph in 908, became the military commander of Baghdad and was one of the leading figures in the Abbasid empire (Hugh Kennedy, Nadia Maria El Cheikh). Two eunuch regents would rule Egypt – first Kāfūr (946–968) and subsequently Barjawān (997–1000). In the Byzantine empire, where eunuchs were to a large extent not imported slaves but instead came from native families, chief court eunuch John Orphanotrophos (d. 1043) managed to obtain the imperial throne first for his brother Michael and then later his nephew Michael (emperors Michael IV, 1034–1041; and Michael V, 1041–1042) (Shaun Tougher). In eighteenth-century Awadh, a North Indian principality, the eunuch Almās ʿAlī Khān was a commercial magnate and commander of a vast army; he also had one-third of Awadh under his power, much to the irritation of the British East Indian Company, which later managed to exclude eunuchs from Awadh's political scene (Jessica Hinchy). These cases demonstrate that, under certain circumstances, eunuchs could become exceptionally powerful and leading players in their empires or regimes.

However, the vast majority of court eunuchs were integrated into an imperial hierarchy of offices. In Byzantium, for example, court eunuchs who were in direct contact with the emperor were called chamberlains (*cubiculari*) and were directed by a chief eunuch, the *praepositus sacri cubiculi.* As we will see below, a special ritual was required for a court eunuch to become a member of the *cubiculari.* All in all, there was a wide range of Byzantine court offices for eunuchs, starting with guardians of the palace doors (*papiai*) and including positions like the *deuteros* (responsible for imperial furniture, ceremonial clothing and the imperial insignia), the *pinkerēs* (cupbearer), the master of the table, the *protovestiarios* (first dresser) and the *parakomonenos* ("one who sleeps beside the bed").[18]

This kind of court hierarchy illustrates the main difference between bishops and eunuchs. Bishops were the heads of their sees and directed the administration of their diocese through their subordinates, whereas court eunuchs were part of a hierarchy with different levels of power, but they could potentially attain a high office, one that might lead to a prominent political role in the empire. Furthermore, the institution of court eunuchs was more fluid than the episcopate. The presence of court eunuchs was often bound to the life cycle of a dynasty. Once the court was fixed at one place for a lengthy period of time and consolidated its structures (often together with a more elaborated court ceremonial), the number of eunuchs usually increased. In some (and perhaps most) cases, one can also observe that the establishment of an elaborate eunuch hierarchy at court coincided with a decrease in eunuch military commanders, who tend to be more prominent in the early stages of a dynasty.

Celibacy, eunuchs and priests in late antiquity

Although the institutions of court eunuchs and bishops took very different paths, there is a short, but significant, overlap during the time when the episcopal office took its shape in the early Christian church. As Peter Brown has shown in his famous study, the perception of the body changed in late antiquity. In the Christian ascetic movement, sexual desires were no longer considered to be a part of needs and feelings that had to be moderated and controlled as with excessive appetite, drinking habits, rage and passion. According to Brown, sexual lust was placed within a central position in which Christians viewed the weak, earthly human body in opposition to the immortal soul. The sexual body was no longer neutral but marked as carnally sinful. As Jesus Christ was delivered by virgin birth, a life lived in chastity and without sexual desire prepared the believers for the heavenly kingdom.[19] Among early Christians, physical castration was one option for leading a chaste life and was discussed and practiced more often than it is generally believed.[20] In the long run, however, the church fathers prevailed by declaring that human sexual desire should be overcome through willpower rather than castration: Spiritual, not physical, eunuchism was promoted.

In order to grasp this transitional and diverse field of sexual renunciation in early Christianity, it is useful to look at the terms that were used for eunuchs. One of the main features of eunuch history is that we cannot always be confident that certain men were in fact eunuchs. Court eunuchs had the titles of their office and often specific designations (for example, in Arabic, there is *khādim,* "servant" and *ustādh,* "master"), but these terms were not exclusively applied to eunuchs.[21] It is telling that Arab chroniclers usually do not use the explicit term *khāṣī* ("castrated person") when commenting upon court eunuchs; although to our modern eye, we might consider castration to be the central feature of eunuchism, their physical condition was just one factor among others that determined their ranks and roles.

In late antique Greek and Latin, there were several terms for castrated men: *tomias*, *ektomias*, *praecisus* and *spado* (all designations mean "cut man", referring to eunuchs whose genitalia had been partly or entirely been removed); *thlibias* ("pressed hard": eunuchs whose scrotum had been tied up); and *thlasia* ("crushed": eunuchs whose testicles had been crushed).[22] In Roman law, the definition of the jurist Ulpian (ca. 170–223) was preserved in the *Digesta* (50.16.128), which uses *spado* as the main term for eunuchs: "The designation *spandones* is a general one: it contains those who are *spadones* by nature, as well as the *thlibiae thlasiae* but also any other kind of *spadones*".[23] With these words, Ulpian distinguished three categories of eunuchs. (1) "Eunuchs by nature" were probably males without fully developed sexual organs.[24] (2) *Thlibiae* and *thlasiae* were put into a second category, probably because both types of eunuchs did not suffer any amputation. (3) Techniques that involved cutting off the testicles and, in the most extreme cases, even the penis, were then included in Ulpian's third category. *Galli* were the eunuch priests in the cult of the goddess *Magna Mater*.[25] The Greek term *eunuchos* means literally "guardian of the bedchamber (*eunē* – "bed", *echō* – "to guard"). In the twelfth century, Byzantine authors added another meaning to the etymology of the term, claiming that *eunuchos* was a derivate of *eunoos,* the "well-minded".[26] *Eunuchos* was used for castrated men, often as a synonym for the above-mentioned terms, but it also had a much broader meaning. In the second century CE, *eunuchos* could refer to "any non-reproductive man, whether he was castrated, born without adequate reproductive organs, or had suffered injury that rendered him sterile".[27] Celibate monks and even nuns could be described as eunuchs too.[28] In the famous words of Matthew 19:12, *eunuchos* was the designation for a man living without a wife. After being questioned about whether a man is allowed to leave his wife, Jesus first stated, "What therefore God hath joined together, let not man put asunder", but he also concedes that some men might not be suitable for a married life:

> For there are some eunuchs, which were so born from their mother's womb: and there are some eunuchs, which were made eunuchs of

> men: and there be eunuchs, which have made themselves eunuchs for the kingdom of heaven's sake.
>
> [Matt. 19.12, King James Version]

Whereas the King James Version translates the term *eunuchos* of the Greek original text literally (as did Jerome in the Latin Vulgate), most German versions follow Luther's translation, which rendered "eunuch" in its broader meaning as "being unsuitable for marriage".

In discussing sexual renunciation, Christian theologians often referred to Matthew 19:12 and gave different explanations as to how these three categories of eunuchs should be understood.[29] In the third century, Clement of Alexandria (d. 215) reported the attitudes of a Gnostic school that distinguished on the basis of Matthew 19:12 three categories of *eunuchoi*: (1) men who had by birth a disinclination towards women and therefore should not marry; (2) men who had been physically emasculated by misfortune and are unfit for marriage; and (3) those "who eunuchize themselves for the sake of the heavenly kingdom" and therefore renounce marriage.[30] Gregory of Nanzianz (d. 390), an eminent theologian and bishop of Constantinople, interpreted the three kinds of eunuchs in Matthew 19:12 differently and thought it unlikely that Jesus had physical eunuchs in mind when he spoke these words:

> It seems to me that this word is not related to the bodies, but hints through the figure of the bodies towards something loftier. For it might be little, very feeble and unworthy of the [divine] word if one was to understand it in respect to the physical eunuchs [*tōn sōmatikōn eunouchōn*] only. We have to think about something worthy of the Spirit![31]

According to Gregory, the (1) "eunuchs which were so born from their mother's womb" were eunuchs by nature and thus should not be proud of their disposition, because they had not chosen their chaste fate. Moreover, those (2) "which were made eunuchs of men" were actually not physical eunuchs but Christians who have been instructed by a teacher to distance themselves from evil. Finally, the (3) "eunuchs which have made themselves eunuchs for the kingdom of heaven's sake" are those Christians who have not been instructed by anybody – be it a mother, a father, a priest, a bishop or any other teacher – but have found the way to become ready for God's kingdom by themselves: "you have amputated [*exetemes*] yourself, you have eunuchized [*eunouchisas*] yourself, you have amputated the root of evil".[32]

Ambrose of Milan (339–397) praised the "eunuchs [*spadones*] who have castrated themselves by will, not by necessity" and did not "restrain guilt with a knife".[33] As Mathew Kuefler has shown, the symbol of the eunuch was assimilated into the ideals of Christian perfection and masculinity. Through spiritual castration, the Christian monk became a "manly eunuch" and a spiritual warrior for Christ. In so doing, he left his wife and family behind him, for, as Jerome stated, "the love of Christ and the fear of hell easily break such bonds as these".[34]

As spiritual castration became an established ideal for the Christian monk, physical castration was increasingly less accepted. In 325, the first canon of the council of Nicaea excluded from the clergy any man who castrated himself but admitted those who have been castrated "by barbarians" or for health reasons.[35] In practice, eunuchs were admitted as priests and bishops in the Eastern church, whereas in the Latin West, a priest had to be physically intact. It was only in the sixteenth century, when the popes employed *castrati* as singers in the *cappella palatina*, that we see something comparable to eunuchs in the Latin church. However, it is significant that between the second and fourth century, the history of eunuchs and bishops intersect in a number of ways. Physical castration was discussed as an option for leading a chaste life. Furthermore, Roman Christianity modulated their ideals of sanctity by aligning gender and the body in the figures of the saints, monks, nuns and bishops. It is not a coincidence that in this complex *fabrique*, the eunuch as the embodiment of sexual castration and a potential symbol for gender ambiguity was a central point of reference. It is also a consequence of this development that bishops who became ecclesiastical princes, as part of the secular clergy, were often challenged by the ascetic and celibate life of the monastic orders.[36] In the early church, bishops could even marry. From the fourth century onwards, however, the popes tried to establish the criteria for future bishops, which would restrict clerical marriage: Candidates for the episcopal office should marry a virgin (not a widow or a divorced woman), they should live in strict monogamy and, if they were to have a family, they must do so while they were still in the lower ranks of the clerical hierarchy. If they decided that they could live with their wife in a chaste marriage, they were allowed to pursue the higher orders.[37]

Although we have important studies on how pre-modern conceptions of gender and masculinity shaped ideals of clerical celibacy and chastity, large parts of the scholarly literature on bishops appear to have ignored the fact that gender history might provide a valuable contribution and open up new research questions and avenues of investigation. The history of the church reforms and the investiture conflict in the eleventh and twelfth century, for example, has been considered to be a struggle for clerical identities according to an apostolic ideal, as an attempt to bring the church under papal control and as a conflict between the twin swords of priesthood and kingship where the political power of each was negotiated. Megan McLaughlin, however, has re-evaluated the gendered language of the debates: The *ecclesia* was the bride of Christ, simony (the acquisition of ecclesiastical offices through money) was condemned as prostitution, disobedience towards the pope was branded as contempt towards the mother – the language of this time marked immoral actions as rape, incest and fornication, whereas right actions were embedded in discussions about love, kisses and tender embracing. As McLaughlin has shown, it was not by coincidence that questions about authority and political order were negotiated in these terms. The highly gendered and sexualised representations of the church, bishops, popes, kings and laymen, and the relationships between them, incorporated the late antique discourse on sex and gender and were interwoven with new questions about family, marriage and sexual norms.[38]

One can, therefore, still argue with good reason, to quote the seminal article of Joan Scott, that "gender is a primary way of signifying relationships of power",[39] and that it is also integral to any position of power. With ruling eunuchs and bishops, we have two groups of men who were integrated within the ruling elites and were singled out by their position within the gender order – in being deprived (at least in theory) of sexual intercourse through spiritual or physical castration. Although in the early church, bishops were not at first expected to live the celibate life of monks, the late antique ideal of sexual continence and renouncement of a family life was an increasingly challenging model that prescribed celibacy for bishops *in officio*. In the long run, Latin bishops could not father any legitimate children, whereas in the Eastern church, married bishops had to separate from their wives.[40] The late antique model of spiritual castration was incorporated into the eleventh and twelfth-century reform movement debates concerning how the clergy should be distinguished from the laity.

Celibacy thus became one of the important norms that were linked to the episcopal office, whereas eunuchs usually could not procreate. In our Shared Focus, bishops and eunuchs are put together under the umbrella category of *celibate and childless men* because they usually could not be part of a father–son succession. As will be demonstrated, this norm resulted in alternative reproduction patterns and offered pre-modern societies opportunities to utilise celibate and childless men with specific functions.[41] Both eunuchs and bishops acted in similar ways to that of other men in the ruling elites, but they were distinct in that they were supposed to lead a celibate life. The late antique overlap in the history of eunuchs and bishops demonstrates that this common feature was linked to the fields of religious purity and family life.

Kinship relations and networks: Social dynamics of celibate and childless men

By the fifth century, bishops often came either from the municipal elite or the senatorial aristocracy, which provided these groups with a close ally who held a wealthy and powerful position.[42] In the seventh century, most bishops in the Frankish empire were recruited from an aristocratic background, and this continued to be the case in the following centuries.[43] However, bishops did not always derive from local aristocracies. Throughout the Middle Ages in England, for example, incumbents for the episcopal office tended not to be recruited from the higher nobility.[44] Even in the Merovingian empire (fifth–eighth century), where it has normally been assumed that bishops were of an aristocratic origin, this understanding has been questioned.[45] Since the position of the bishop was always embedded in different social-political contexts and connected to a wide array of clerical and royal settings and institutions, the aristocratic bishop was but one – although certainly an eminent type – among others. Further, the establishment of episcopal celibacy differed throughout Western Europe. As the contributions of Julia Barrow and Rachel Stone make clear, episcopal dynasties were common in Ireland, England, Brittany and Normandy until the eleventh and twelfth centuries. In most parts of the Carolingian empire (750–900), on the other hand, the married bishop who ideally lived in a chaste marriage with his wife had become an exception, notwithstanding that this model was still upheld in contemporary canonical theories. In France, the number of both married bishops and priests decreased in the sixth and seventh century as the clergy was mostly recruited at a young age. While father–son successions were practiced to a lesser degree, the uncle–nephew relationship became increasingly important. In this volume, Julia Barrow demonstrates that, until the eleventh century, young boys who were expected to embark upon a clerical career were taken into the care of a clergyman who was often their maternal or paternal uncle. Bishops also participated in uncle–nephew fosterage; they acted as paternal figures, supervised their nephews' education and paved the path for their ordination and further advancement in the church. Bishop Hincmar of Reims (d. 882), for instance, claimed that he had taken his nephew (later Bishop Hincmar of Laon) from his cradle into his house, even washing his nappies.[46]

As Rachel Stone points out in her contribution, the end of father–son direct inheritance of the episcopal office in the Frankish empire created both losers and winners. Noble families might no longer be sure that their preferred candidate would occupy a bishopric. However, although an episcopal see might be no longer the fixed prerogative of one family, the ruler might have more opportunities to choose an episcopal successor (among different families) that suited his needs. With the episcopal succession open to a wider circle of potential candidates, some aristocratic families could also accumulate several bishoprics in different parts of the empire, expanding their area of influence if they were fortunate. Because competition for the episcopal office increasingly became more intense, with no inevitable outcome, the uncle–nephew patronage proved to be more flexible and therefore more suited to the new dynamics in the empire – a son has only one father but might have several uncles. When the Carolingian kings lost power in West Francia at the end of the ninth century, however, a number of aristocratic families managed to regain their control over certain bishoprics. At the same time, the geographical landscape for episcopal candidates narrowed in the now politically fragmented landscape; the number of married clerics and bishops started to increase again.

The example of the Carolingian empire shows that, although canonical theory still accepted married bishops and priests who lived chastely with their wives, a number of social-political factors influenced, and sometimes determined, whether this model was practised or not. The appointment of unmarried bishops, together with the system of uncle–nephew fosterage, was evidence of both the impact of the Carolingian reforms in the empire and an increasingly competitive aristocracy that sought power and influence through the episcopal office. It is not a coincidence that Carolingian bishops started to confidently express their collective role as imperial actors in the ninth century: As guardians of the divine law, representing the church and the priesthood, they claimed, in concert with the king, to guarantee the wellbeing of the empire.[47]

All in all, one has to be careful when assessing the question whether or not bishops practised celibacy, which had been greatly advocated for by the church fathers, by investigating how families adjusted their strategies and how ecclesiastical networks developed.[48] The episcopal office could not have succeeded as a prominent position of power for more than a millennium if it had not adapted to very different conditions. It is, however, important for our Shared Focus that celibacy as a theoretical requirement for the episcopal office was a constant throughout and that it offered an alternative to the father–son succession of former episcopal dynasties that could be drawn upon when social-political dynamics made such an alternative opportune.

In the eleventh century, clerical and monastic lifestyles changed in an increasingly populated Europe, and new monastic orders such as the Cluniacs and Cistercians were established. In the cities, communities of regular canons like the Premonstratensians and the Canons Regular of Saint Augustine arose, standing between the secular clergy and monastic orders. The popes endeavoured to challenge episcopal power and make the church more centralised, with the apostolic see in Rome on top of an institutionally effective hierarchy. In this process, reformers stressed the distinctions between the laity and the clergy by promoting for the latter celibacy and cultic purity. Reformers like the papal legate Peter Damian (1007–1072) lamented the unchaste lives of clerics:

> O bishop (*sacerdos*), you whose name means to make sacred, that is, that you should offer sacrifice to God, why are you not terrified to offer yourself in sacrifice to the evil spirit? By committing fornication you cut yourself off from the members of Christ, and make yourself physically one with a harlot .... Are you unaware that the Son of God was so dedicated to the purity of the flesh that he was not born of conjugal chastity, but rather from the womb of a virgin?[49]

The reformers spoke with many voices, stressing different points.[50] However, the late antique concept of the holy church as manned by celibate officials was a recurrent topic that was adapted to the world of the eleventh and twelfth centuries. As Peter Brown has put it:

> The church was based, ideally, on the ethereal, nonphysical continuities of teaching and baptism administered by the clergy. Birth alone did not guarantee salvation. By insisting that its leaders no longer beget children, the Catholic Church in the West made plain that it enjoyed a supernatural guarantee of continuity that no ancient city could claim. If they were to be respected as the leaders of a "holy" institution, bishops and priests had to remain anomalous creatures.[51]

To conclude: Bishops added a specific dynamic to medieval society, offering alternatives to family reproduction patterns. Like other men, bishops were integral to kinship and familial structures; whether they acted as fathers or primarily as uncles in promoting their kin was due to many factors. As the institutional framework of the church developed and distinctions between the clergy and the laity were increasingly stressed, particularly so in the eleventh and twelfth centuries, so bishops increasingly did not father legitimate children. But even before this time, bishops, along with other high-ranking clergymen, were singled out in being simultaneously part of political and ecclesiastical networks. They were positioned between the reproduction patterns of kinship and the institutional continuity of the church that was viewed as holy and eternal.

If one looks at the recruitment paths and networks of court eunuchs, the picture is at least as complex and multifaceted as in the bishops' case. Eunuchs belonged to the "slave elites". Whereas research on slavery has been dominated for a long time by studies that explore the oppressive nature of slavery, recent general approaches have taken into account the powerful positions that slaves might hold in the Middle East and beyond.[52] This perspective sheds light on the high social and geographical mobility of the Middle Eastern ruling elites. Female slaves for the court harem, who were exchanged as gifts in diplomatic exchanges, might have come from an even more diversified horizon – transforming the harem of the Fatimid caliphs (909–1171), for example, into a "multi-ethnic, multi-cultural and religiously and linguistically diversified feminine universe".[53] It is often repeated that eunuchs, as slaves of foreign origin and thus with no ties to their home families and no possibility of producing offspring, were the ideal servants for a dynasty in which ultimate loyalty to a master was prized.[54] But despite this assumption, we see that eunuchs were part of many different kinds of social and political networks.

As Michael Hoeckelmann demonstrates in his chapter, Chinese eunuchs married and adopted children. During the Tang dynasty (618–907), the number of court eunuchs increased significantly. Court eunuchs came mainly from the lower strata of society, and so their recruitment complemented Tang nepotism with a more open social dynamic. Court eunuchs were also considered to be favourable marriage candidates for families who sought to move up the social ladder. As was also a custom in the military, eunuchs adopted sons and thus contributed to a mixed system of meritocratic and inherited court offices. Surviving tomb inscriptions from the Tang era show that eunuchs were buried as family men, beside their spouses and children – a practice that scholars have labelled "eunuch dynasticism".

If we turn to the Mediterranean, it seems at first that the concept of the "alien eunuch" is confirmed. Roman law prohibited castration – eunuchs had to be imported, at least in theory. This notion of the alien eunuch was continued in Byzantium and the Muslim empires – in the latter because Islamic law prohibited castration. As Ezgi Dikici has argued, each imperial tradition had its "favourite barbaric lands" located at the imperial borders (like Abyssinia and the Caucasus), which provided the empire with eunuchs. In the Byzantine empire from the ninth century onwards, however, eunuchs were also recruited from domestic families: "Unlike the first strategy that relied on the exploitative and hegemonic relationship established with an external and subordinate region, the second strategy created an additional path of upward social mobility for the imperial subjects in the empire's core territories".[55]

In the sixteenth-century Ottoman empire, this twofold pattern was further developed. The Ottoman empire is also a valuable example because it is only from the sixteenth century onwards that imperial Middle Eastern archives are preserved. With archival sources becoming available in the early modern period, family ties and networks of court eunuchs are much easier to trace. In the new Topkapı Palace in Istanbul, there were two different corps of eunuchs: the white eunuchs of the inner court and the black eunuchs who guarded the sultan's harem. Whereas the white chief eunuch was in charge of the male sphere, the black chief harem eunuch supervised the harem. Foreign visitors compared the strict discipline of both the male and female spheres that these two chief eunuchs supervised with monasteries.[56]

According to Dikici's stimulating hypothesis, one might speak of three different recruiting paths for Ottoman eunuchs in the sixteenth and seventeenth century: (1) the black eunuchs, who originated mostly from sub-Saharan castration centres in the Sudan, Abyssinia and Nubia; (2) white eunuchs, who were war prisoners that were brought into the Ottoman empire and served in the palace and were castrated there for a eunuch carrier; and (3) *devşirme*-eunuchs, who were recruited with other slaves within the Ottoman *devşirme* system. In the Ottoman *devşirme*, young boys, mainly from the Balkans, were taken from their families as part of a tax payment; they would convert to Islam and were trained in military or administrative skills. The practice of *devşirme* was disputed among Ottoman lawyers because it could be considered as the enslavement of freeborn Ottoman subjects. The castration of some of these enslaved boys was an even more delicate subject and is perhaps why there are very few sources on castration within the Ottoman Empire. One example of a *devşirme*-eunuch is the white eunuch ʿAlī Pasha (d. 1511), who was twice grand vizier and was recruited from a village near Sarajevo. As with other white eunuchs, whether they were recruited among war prisoners or within the *devşirme* system, he continued to have relationships with his family and his homeland. Ismāʿīl Ağa, to use another example, served in 1621–1623 as chief eunuch and founded and endowed a mosque in his hometown of Malatya in East Anatolia. He managed to arrange for his brother Süleymān to be brought to Istanbul and to become a court page; this brother was later promoted to the grand vizierate and was married to the sultan's daughter.[57]

Whereas white eunuchs, like other Ottoman officials, served as an intermediary between the palace and their homelands, black eunuchs were less likely to maintain relationships with their original families. However, black eunuchs did maintain important networks beyond the imperial capital. The first eunuch in the newly created office of the Baabűsaade Ağası (chief eunuch of the harem) was the black eunuch Mehmed Ağa (appointed in 1574). Mehmed, who was supposedly an Ethiopian and had been castrated in East Africa, came at first to the court of the Ottoman governor in Cairo, who then sent him to Istanbul, where he pursued a brilliant career.[58] As Jane Hathaway has shown, black eunuchs often maintained lifelong relations with Cairo and Egypt. In the recruitment pattern for black eunuchs, the Ottoman governor in Cairo selected suitable, already castrated candidates from slave caravans arriving from sub-Saharan Africa. Those few of them who managed to become chief eunuchs of the harem were also responsible for supervising the imperial endowments for holy foundations in Mecca and Medina. These endowments received substantial parts of their income from Egyptian villages. Ottoman chief eunuchs of the harem were also interested in maintaining relationships with Egypt, because they were usually exiled to Cairo when they were dismissed from their office. From the late seventeenth century, this retirement–exile pattern was turned into a prelude for their final post, the honourable appointment as guardian of the Prophet's tomb in Medina.[59] For the Ottoman dynasty, the establishment of the office of the harem's chief eunuch would turn out to be a valuable strategy in overcoming the dynastic crisis of 1600, when several sultans died young. This situation resulted in the increasing political significance of the harem; the sultan's mother, his concubines and the harem's chief eunuch became powerful figures, whereas the white eunuchs lost their influence over time.[60]

If we turn to North India in the eighteenth and nineteenth century and the case study presented by Jessica Hinchy, we see once more that eunuchs were not isolated individuals who depended entirely on their – albeit important – relationship with their masters and mistresses. In Awadh, a former province of the Mughal empire, court eunuchs (called *khwāja-sarāʾīs*) came either from abroad (mostly Ethiopia) or from the Indian subcontinent and were enslaved through war, kidnapping or sale by their own families. After their training at court, *khwāja-sarāʾīs* were employed in the administration of the household and of the state; they collected land revenues and acted as diplomats and military commanders. Whereas it is possible that some *khwāja-sarāʾīs* maintained a relationship to their natal family, their main kinship relations were built at court. Child *khwāja-sarāʾīs* became the brothers of their fellow boy eunuchs. As adults, they adopted sons, whose right to inherit, however, was often not accepted by the eunuchs' owners. Since adoption was disputed or even forbidden in Islamic traditions,[61] Awadh is an example of the differences between legal prescriptions and practices in Indian Islamic politics. These networks of adoptive kinship were complemented by teacher–disciple ties that were an important feature in pre-modern India. The submission of disciples to specific legal, moral and disciplinary practices has been labelled "monastic governmentality".[62] *Khwāja-sarāʾīs* teachers were responsible for their disciples (both eunuchs and non-eunuchs) who could also inherit their teachers' administrative position. The *khwāja-sarāʾīs*, on the other hand, expanded their political influence with an increased number of disciples.

These examples demonstrate that eunuchs broadened the spectrum of social reproduction as bishops did. As bishops, eunuchs could act as fathers and husbands, as brothers and uncles. But more often, they did not. As imported slaves from "the barbaric lands" outside the empire, they provided particular dynasties with a specific form of personnel, suited for the needs for courts that were organised into segregated female and male spheres. The career paths of eunuchs were also attractive for a second recruitment strategy that brought eunuchs from within the empire to the court, thus offering imperial subjects the possibility of social mobility. Eunuchs maintained a broad spectrum of biological and adoptive kinship as well as networks both at court and beyond the capital. The institution of court eunuchs, therefore, provided dynasties with different options of staff recruitment and added to the social dynamic within the empires. Both eunuchs and bishops were parts of both kinship and institutional networks – like other men. But the position of celibate and childless men was special insofar as they offered opportunities for a particularly broad spectrum of social relationships.

Religious authority and sacredness: Celibate and childless men between sacred and profane spheres

In order to unite ruling eunuchs and bishops in our third field of the Shared Focus, we must apply the concept of religion and sacredness more broadly, so as to encompass celibate and childless men.[63] Eunuchs and bishops played a number of roles in Christian, Islamic and other religious practices, but both groups were also connected to the sacredness of pre-modern monarchies; indeed, in claiming a religious standing in the divine order, pre-modern rulers relied on both eunuchs and bishops.

The most visible link between bishops and sacred kingship was the ritual of coronation. From the sixth century, archbishops and patriarchs of Western Europe (Byzantium is more problematic[64]) increasingly crowned and anointed their Christian rulers. In crowning kings, queens, emperors and empresses, (arch)bishops and popes bestowed upon these rulers a kind of religious legitimacy – an arrangement that could prove either advantageous or problematic for the ruler. Bishops could also be venerated as saints – St Nicholas of Myra and St Martin of Tours are two of the best-known examples. Whereas in the early Christian church, the common model of sainthood was martyrdom, the figure of the episcopal saint would increasingly become more prevalent throughout the Middle Ages.[65] Furthermore, although most bishops would never be elevated to sainthood, as ecclesiastical princes, their office was still associated in part with sacredness.

However, as has been argued, the religious authority that bishops wielded did not remain uncontested. There was a wide spectrum of opinions on the episcopate, and contemporaries both praised and bitterly criticised bishops, individually and collectively. Around 935, Bishop Rather of Verona would write gushingly of those men who held the office:

> They are gods, they are lords, they are Christians, they are heavens, they are angels, they are patriarchs, they are prophets, they are apostles, they are evangelists, they are martyrs, they are anointed, they are kings, they are princes, they are judges not only of men, but also of angels ... they are scholars, they are preachers of the Last Judge, they are guardians, they are the eyeball of the Lord, they are friends of the living God, they are sons of God, they are fathers, they are the lights of the world, they are the stars in the sky ... they carry the keys of heaven, it is in their power to open and close heaven.[66]

On the other hand, bishops were often targeted for failing to live up to the standards of their position within the church. William de Montibus (ca. 1140–1213), who served as a chancellor under the bishops of Lincoln, found not only bishops but also all the secular clergy to be more than wanting:

> Satan and all demons give thanks to archbishops, bishops, archdeacons, deacons, and parish priests because by their examples Christians are entirely turned to evil so that daily and without any impediment they are seized for the confinements of hell.[67]

Indeed, as part of the secular clergy (even if they were monks themselves), bishops were constantly challenged by monastic lifestyles. Matthew Mesley explores in his chapter the writings of Caesarius of Heisterbach (ca. 1180–after 1240), a Cistercian monk who sought to disseminate the proper way of living to Cistercian novices. Caesarius often focussed on the failings of the secular clergymen rather than upon the laity. At the same time, he also pointed to examples of episcopal misuse of authority and power. Bishops in medieval Germany often acted in similar ways to the secular princes of the Empire. For example, Archbishop Engelbert of Cologne (reigning 1216–1225), in whose diocese Caesarius' monastery was located, was one of the powerful political figures of his time. He acted as an imperial administrator for the mostly absent emperor Frederic II and took part in securing former royal rights (like coin minting, levying taxes and holding markets) for the ecclesiastical princes of the empire. He also consolidated the rights and territories of his archdiocese, to the disadvantage of the local aristocracy. After Engelbert was murdered by one of these competing aristocrats, he was venerated as a saint. Caesarius of Heisterbach was given the task of writing a saint's life for a man that he likely considered "a good duke, but not a good bishop".[68] In his *vita*, Caesarius presented Engelbert as a powerful, peacemaking prince who secured the ecclesiastical rights of his diocese. But he did not deny that Engelbert's life did not reflect the image of an ideal bishop:

> His precious death made up for the sanctity that was missing in his life. Although he was hardly perfect in his way of life, he was nevertheless sanctified through his martyrdom.[69]

It was only through his death as a martyr that Engelbert was freed of his worldly sins. Indeed, Caesarius portrayed in meticulous detail how Engelbert had been stabbed 47 times by his murderers and attributed the many wounds on every part of his body to every sin that Engelbert had committed in his life:

> For he was punished in every member through which he had sinned. He was multiply punished at his head, as it was apparent from his cap, namely at the top of his head, at front and back of his head, at his temples, lips and teeth. He was wounded so heavily that streams of blood flooded and streamed down. They flowed into the cavities of his eyes, his ears, his nose and his mouth and filled them. He was also punished at his throat and his neck, at his shoulders and his back, at his chest and his heart, his belly and his hips, his legs and his feet so that you, reader, might realize the kind of baptism by which Christ dignified his martyr in dissolving everything that he had [sinfully] assembled by boasting, looking, hearing, smelling, tasting, thinking, by being luxurious and busy, by touching, striding, as well as through lightness, omissions and negligence in respect to discipline.[70]

Unlike secular princes and kings, bishops were constantly challenged by monastic ideals and the demands that were placed upon them by the various medieval reform movements. The model of episcopal leadership included roles within both the ecclesiastical and secular spheres and offered considerably more opportunities for contemporaries to critique bishops, than that of the model of royal and princely leadership. Kings might be accused of being not pious or unjust tyrants, but they were judged as rulers, not as spiritual leaders. Monks and eremitical saints gained religious authority when they renounced the world and lived an ascetic life. Bishops, on the other hand, stood between the spiritual and worldly sphere – they were religious, but they lived and performed their roles within the world. As princes and leaders of the church, they had to pay the price of their priestly superiority by being responsible for their subordinates and the laity. They were expected "to render an account for even kings of men in the divine judgment", as Pope Gelasius (492–496) put it in his famous statement on spiritual and temporal power.[71] How would they be judged by God when they had to live up to spiritual standards that were often not compatible with their worldly responsibilities? For contemporaries, and for bishops themselves, episcopal sacredness and religious authority was often genuinely ambiguous.

Whereas bishops gained religious authority and sacredness *in officio,* the dangerous and painful procedure of castration, which marked a court eunuch, implied nothing of the sort. In comparison to the great number of holy bishops, there were only a few eunuchs who were venerated as saints, and most of these were in Byzantium. The sanctity of these holy eunuchs, however, was not a result of their physical castration. Holy eunuchs fulfilled many of the same requirements for sanctity as other saints, and their hagiographers mentioned their castration often only briefly.[72] Likewise, Byzantine priests and bishops who were also eunuchs were not considered more saintly for having been castrated. On the contrary, it was believed that as they were eunuchs, they did not need to master their sexual appetites or strive for chastity, and as such were not afforded any further spiritual merit. Between the ninth and twelfth centuries, however, models of Byzantine sanctity did change; sainthood was made more accessible for eunuchs, whose chaste, angelic life was increasingly prized.[73]

Byzantine court eunuchs, on the other hand, were different from Byzantine clerical eunuchs. As Kathryn Ringrose has shown, the emperor was always surrounded by eunuchs, who marked the "imperial *numen*" that had to be protected from external pollution.[74] Almost every object the emperor was given came from a eunuch's hand. In ceremonies, the emperor seldom spoke but instead used signals, which were translated by the chief eunuch; indeed, outsiders seldom heard the emperor's actual voice. In processions, the emperor moved amongst a group of eunuchs, who thus created a moving space that shielded the emperor from his surroundings. Eunuchs also controlled access to both emperor and empress.[75] Since the chamberlains (*cubiculari*) – all of them high-ranking court eunuchs – were the only people in the palace that could enter the quarters of the emperor and empress, they were in a privileged position in terms of procuring and transmitting information. The chief eunuch, for example, played a crucial role in imperial successions, as he was often the first person to know of an emperor's death. A candidate for the imperial office might fail at the first hurdle if the court chamberlains refused to present him with the imperial regalia, which was essential for any legitimate coronation.[76] Byzantine court eunuchs, therefore, marked the sacred sphere that surrounded the emperor and empress – and they acquired political power by controlling access to the imperial office.[77]

Court eunuchs, who were promoted into the ranks of chamberlains, did so through the performance of a specific accession ritual. The report of the so-called *Book of Ceremonial* gives us a frozen but nonetheless interesting picture of this ritual. According to this source, the chief eunuch brought the future chamberlain to the enthroned emperor in the main reception hall (*Chrysotriklinos*) of the palace. The candidate was then to be brought into the nearby oratory of St Theodor (which housed the imperial crown and holy relics) in front of its "holy doors". After giving the future chamberlain ethical instructions about his new office, the chief eunuch stated the following:

> Observe whence comes this dignity which now you have received. It is completely clear that it comes from these holy doors. Recognize that you have received your dignity from the hand of the Lord. Guard yourself diligently that so long as you live you maintain these precepts and keep them close to your heart. Displaying and ornamenting yourself with the greatest virtues, you will achieve the highest levels of honors by dispensing our wealth and [from] the holy emperor, and you will be glorified among the members of the holy *cubiculum*.[78]

Thereafter, the eunuch lay on the ground and gave thanks to God. Next, the chief eunuch dressed him with a golden robe, after which he and the other chamberlains kissed their new colleague. The new chamberlain was then led outside the oratory and returned to the emperor, where he prostrated himself. As Ringrose observes, it appears significant that the new chamberlain receives his new dignity not from the emperor but directly from God, in the oratory of a saint, orchestrated by the chief eunuch.[79] This accession ritual also bears some similarities with the consecration of priests and bishops – particularly, the use of clothes to signify their new rank, the candidate's position on the ground near an altar and how a higher-ranking figure officiates the ritual.

As Serena Tolino shows in her chapter, eunuchs played an equally important role at the court of the Fatimid caliphs (Maghreb and Egypt, 909–1171). The Fatimid caliphs were Shiʿi imams, who claimed an extraordinary high spiritual position – not only as direct descendants of the prophet Muḥammad but also as imams who possessed divine knowledge and *baraka* (divine charisma). In the early Fatimid period, court eunuchs served their imams in a number of high-ranking offices, such as chamberlains, chiefs of the public treasury, governors or intendants. With the Fatimid Shiʿi imams ruling over a mostly non-Shiʿi population, court eunuchs are represented in the sources as loyal servants, powerful commanders and fervent believers in their imams. When the second imam-caliph al-Qāʾim died in 946, and conflicts arose between the imam's male relatives about the succession, court eunuch al-Jawdhar, who was part of the harem's faction, managed to obtain the throne for his candidate, caliph al-Manṣūr (one of the sons of al-Qāʾim).[80] In a later report written by al-Jawdhar's secretary,[81] it is claimed that, before his death, al-Qāʾim had secretly designated al-Manṣūr as his heir, only informing al-Jawdhar of his plans. The early Fatimid-Shiʿi theology held that the living imam would tell only one person which of his sons would be his successor. This person was called the *ḥujja*.[82] Because God knows all future imams, the acting *ḥujja* was sharing divine knowledge of immense significance. In terms of Fatimid theology, therefore, the *ḥujja* was the most sacred position, apart from the imam himself; even the Fatimid chief theologian could not claim to be a conduit for divine knowledge. It is not likely that this lofty claim about al-Jawdhar being the *ḥujja* of al-Qāʾim was either known or shared during his lifetime. But al-Jawdhar's secretary – himself a eunuch, loyal to his master al-Jawdhar beyond death – saw al-Jawdhar's role in the imam succession as the rightful action of the *ḥujja*. The report of al-Jawdhar's secretary comes close to a "first person's writing"[83], in that we have a rare view of how eunuchs perceived their offices. Al-Jawdhar's claim (or that of his secretary) about his associations with sacredness are similar to the Byzantine eunuch's investiture ritual of a new chamberlain. Court eunuchs, who surrounded their divinely appointed ruler, were not only aware that their role marked the ruler's sacred status but also that they themselves might perceive this dignity as a direct connection to God. In 973, the Fatimid caliphs moved to a newly built palace in Cairo, and it was there that an elaborated court ceremonial was developed. As part of this process, a new corpus of court eunuchs was established, consisting of the so-called *muḥannakūn* eunuchs, who were in many ways similar to the Byzantine *cubiculari*. As Serena Tolino argues, the *muḥannakūn* eunuchs served in different ranks in close proximity to the imam, and this included important processions in which they surrounded him. They thus marked the imam's sacred sphere.

The institution of court eunuchs would continue in Egypt under the Sunni Mamluk sultanate (1250–1517). According to Shaun Marmon's study *Eunuchs and Sacred Boundaries in Islamic Societies*, the two highest ranks among Mamluk court eunuchs were the *zimāmdār*, the chief harem eunuch; and the *muqaddam al-mamālik al-ṣulṭanīya*, the commander of the sultan's military "family", the Mamluk military slaves. We see here a similar division between the female and male spheres of the court, each with its own chief eunuch, which was found later in the Ottoman Empire. Both the *zimāmdār* and the *muqaddam al-mamālik al-sulṭāniyya* were seen as guardians of moral and sacred boundaries. The *zimāmdār* guarded the royal women in the harem against sexual transgressions, whereas the *muqaddam al-mamālik al-sulṭāniyya* did the same for the adolescent boys under his command, who were also regarded as potential objects of sexual temptation and disorder.[84] The Cairo Citadel, where the Mamluk sultans resided, was compared to holy places like Jerusalem and perceived as a sanctuary with the sultan at its centre. To Muslim eyes, this comparison was also quite plausible because from the twelfth century onwards, the great sanctuaries of Islam were guarded by eunuchs: the tombs of the Patriarchs (including Abraham) in Hebron, the Dome of the Rock in Jerusalem, the Kaʿba in Mecca and the prophet's tomb in Medina. The eunuchs who safeguarded the prophet's tomb were called the "eunuchs of the prophet", a prestigious and wealthy "cultic organization … [that] can best be described as a powerful and deeply symbolic 'priesthood' of some forty eunuchs".[85] At this time, Medina was still dominated by Shiʿi Muslims. The eunuchs of the prophet – sent by the Sunni sultan in Egypt – helped to establish a Sunni presence in the city and were accordingly venerated for this role in Sunni hagiographies as being beautiful, pious, ascetic, compassionate and generous towards the poor. For Sunni Muslims, the chief eunuch in Medina inspired those in his presence with *hayba* – a strong emotion of fear and reverence that was also evoked by rulers and God himself.[86] A fourteenth-century diploma of investiture associated the new (black) chief eunuch in Medina with the Companions of the prophet, in describing him as

> the ascetic who prefers living in proximity [*jiwār*] to his Prophet to all else, the humble one who intends by his service [to the Prophet] to be included among the group [*zumra*] of those who served him [the Prophet] in his lifetime.[87]

The eunuchs of the prophet, therefore, appear outside secular time. Being deprived of contributing to the succession of their descendants through the fathering of children, as the fifteenth-century historian al-Maqrīzī has put it,[88] they were connected to the sacred time of Islam. According to an interview with the Saudi official in Mecca in 1990, there were still 14 eunuchs in Mecca and 17 serving at the prophet's tomb in Medina. As the official stated:

> God has deprived them [the eunuchs] of sensual pleasure in the world but he has enriched them with material possessions and, before that, with the honor of serving the Sacred House.[89]

We have already discussed how, in Ottoman times, the office of the chief eunuch in Medina became the honorary retirement place for the former chief harem eunuch in Istanbul. This career trajectory reinforced the networks of black eunuchs between Istanbul, Cairo and Medina. But the role of Ottoman chief harem eunuchs in Sunni Islam was not restricted to acting as guards to the Islamic sacred sanctuaries in Mecca and Medina. The aforementioned first chief harem eunuch Mehmed Ağa was "one of the pioneers in building a critical mass of public religious structures" in sixteenth-century Istanbul.[90] As Jane Hathaway shows in her chapter in this volume, the Ottoman chief harem eunuch also supported the Ḥanafī law school, which was promoted by the Ottoman dynasty in order to give a confessional Sunni coherence to the empire. The most powerful chief harem eunuch in Ottoman history, Beşir Ağa (term 1717–46) founded a religious school in Medina, donated Ḥanafī books to the al-Azhar mosque in Cairo and endowed a large religious-educational complex in Istanbul.[91] These endowments are just one example of a more general policy in which chief harem eunuchs provided young boys with religious training in the Ḥanafī legal rite. In their death, chief harem eunuchs were rewarded with tombs in close proximity to either the prophet or his companions – and this was also the case when they died before becoming chief eunuch in Medina: Chief harem eunuchs who died in Istanbul were buried in the Eyüb Cemetery in Istanbul. This cemetery was founded around a grave that was ascribed to Abū Ayyūb al-Anṣārī (576–ca. 670), the standard bearer of the prophet. The two most powerful Ottoman chief harem eunuchs, Muṣṭafā Ağa (term 1605–20) and Beşir Ağa (term 1623–24), were buried alongside Abū Ayyūb and were associated with him: As Abū Ayyūb once had converted to Islam and had loyally served the prophet, so had Muṣṭafā and Beşir Ağa. Even today, numerous pilgrims visit this mausoleum complex. As Jane Hathaway puts it: "serving the sultan and serving the Prophet were intertwined and mutually reinforcing … components of the Chief Harem Eunuch's office".[92]

To conclude: Unlike bishops, court eunuchs did not assume religious leadership or take responsibility in front of God for the spiritual wellbeing of their subordinates. Instead, court eunuchs were intrinsically linked to royal sacredness. In surrounding and shielding emperors and empresses, caliphs and sultans, in guarding the royal women in the harems, court eunuchs both created and performed royal sacredness. In so doing, they were loyal and pious servants to their masters and contributed to the religious coherence of the empire. Also in the Chinese empire, eunuchs took part in the emperor's sacredness and acted as patrons of religion, in donating Buddhist temples, for instance.[93] But there are also cases in which eunuchs derived their authority through a direct connection to God. For example, under the Sunni rule of the Mamluk and Ottoman sultanate (1250–1922), eunuchs guarded the most important sanctuaries of Islam. As guardians of the prophet's tomb in Medina, eunuchs were joined in unity to the sacred time of the prophet and his companions.

Their high position as power brokers, which resulted from the eunuchs' exclusive access to their ruler and their control over the royal harem, could evoke harsh criticism from their political opponents. However, whereas bishops were attacked for failing to live up to the standards of ideal priestly conduct, the main reason for attacking eunuchs was not connected to their supposed lack of religious purity but was rather a consequence of their intermediary position between men and women.

Gender: Clerical and eunuchal masculinities

Criticisms directed at eunuchs could be as harsh and bitter as those that were aimed at bishops. Since antiquity, there have been authors who express their disgust at castrated eunuchs, often representing them as not proper (or less than) men. As Mathew Kuefler shows in this volume, Christian authors adapted earlier Pagan and Jewish judgements regarding eunuchs.

The church father Basil the Great (ca. 330–379) thought the eunuchs of a rich household were

> a disgraceful and detestable set ... neither woman nor man, lustful, envious, ill-bribed, passion-filled, effeminate, slaves of the belly, mad for gold, ruthless, grumbling about their dinner, inconstant, stingy, greedy, insatiable, savage, jealous. What more need I say? At their very birth they were condemned to the knife. How can their mind[s] be right ...? They are lecherous to no purpose, of their own natural vileness.[94]

This quotation summarises the kind of polemical discourse that was representative of a certain viewpoint regarding eunuchs. To a certain degree, this discourse still today influences cultural understandings of eunuchs as wicked and greedy schemers of the harem. This discourse was certainly reflected in many different periods and places. In China, the image of the vicious and treacherous eunuch was a frequently used *topos* in medieval historical texts.[95] The image of the effeminate eunuch was bolstered by the belief that eunuchs prefer to have sex with other men.[96] Some chroniclers did also draw upon the more critical discourse on eunuchs, either in depicting them in a negative vein or in presenting them as an exception to the rule. The famous Greek historian Procopius (ca. 500–562), for instance, reported that the victorious general Narses, who had defeated the Ostrogoths in 552, was "keen and more energetic than would be expected of a eunuch".[97] In the main, however, when eunuchs were mentioned in historical narratives, they were mostly presented according to their different tasks (i.e. military commander, financial supervisor, chamberlain, chief eunuch, etc.) while their castrated status was not made explicit.

In non-narrative texts, Arab writers might perceive the eunuchs' position between the male and the female spheres in royal and rich households as a problem. The Muslim jurist al-Subkī (1284–1355) listed all sorts of offices and professions in fourteenth century Muslim society (like the caliphal office, the military, the civilian bureaucracy, religious scholars, craftsmen, shoemakers and beggars) and placed the eunuchs in one group (*ṭawāshiya*). Although al-Subkī prized some valuable qualities in eunuchs (like kindness, devotion and obedience to their masters and firm leadership), he also found that they had more questionable characteristics (like a harsh manner, a tendency towards jealousy and a lack of rational thought) that he attributed to the eunuchs' similarity with women. Since a eunuch moved within both male and female spheres, it was thought that he might become confused regarding his gender identity: "when he mixes with women, he tells himself that he is a man, when he is with men, he tells himself that he is a woman".[98]

As Serena Tolino shows in her chapter, polymath al-Jāḥiẓ (ca. 776–869) stated that the eunuch's "nature is divided between the one of the male and the one of the female. His behaviour will be neither pure nor clear, not that of a man or a woman, but mixed".[99] Statements like these tempt us to conclude that medieval eunuchs could be categorised as a "third gender", standing somewhere between men and women. Kathryn Ringrose has suggested as such in respect to Byzantine eunuchs.[100]

Abdallah Cheikh-Moussa, in a brilliant article from 1982 – doing gender history *avant la lettre* – has made another suggestion. Cheikh-Moussa pointed out that al-Jāḥiẓ ascribes a variety of the eunuchs' characteristics (jealousy, envy, weepiness, insatiable appetite and lust, frivolity, greed, revengeful scheming, etc.) to their proximity to women, children and old men. The underlying conception, therefore, is not a binary between men and women. The normative model is rather that of the adult (not a boy or old man) uncastrated man (for whom there exists an Arabic term that al-Jāḥiẓ uses, the *faḥl*), who is also a sophisticated urban citizen of sound mind. This adult, urban male is contrasted with women, children, old men, eunuchs and even adult male nomads, farm workers, Abyssinians or Indians.[101] The eunuch's hybridity, therefore, is not a hybridity between two genders. There are instead many factors that determine al-Jāḥiẓ's idea of an ideal human being, categories such as age, gender, lifestyle, race and male fertility. The ideal human being is judged according to these different factors. Insofar as it is gendered as *faḥl*, this quality appears not as binary (male versus female) but as unique. Through effemination and hybridisation, this pure, male gender is then polluted and degraded. This reflects, but only to a certain degree, Thomas Laqueur's findings, in which he concluded that before the modern, biological female–male binary, scholars operated with a one-sex model that was embodied by men, whereas women were considered to be imperfect men.[102] But al-Jāḥiẓ's text (which deserves a prominent place in source books on gender history but, unfortunately, has not yet been translated from the Arabic) is very much an example where we have to think of gender as a "multi-relational category" that is intertwined with other factors such as "age, religion, ethnos, race or even class".[103]

Whereas Kathryn Ringrose has proposed the "third gender" category to analyse eunuchs, Shaun Marmon has classified eunuchs as "a category of nongendered individuals who both defined and crossed highly charged boundaries of moral and physical space in the world of the living and in the world of the dead".[104] *Third gender* or *non-gendered* – it appears significant that scholars have thought about these two notions also in respect to clergymen. Robert Swanson has argued that there were cultural tensions between the "maleness" of clergymen and his suggested concept of "emasculinity" – in which, through celibacy, the clergy became like angels and thus could be perceived as a third gender.[105] Jo Ann McNamara has stated that until the twelfth century, the monastic chastity that was required of both monks and nuns, and was considered a superior lifestyle to that of the laity, tended to erase gender differences between men and women and ultimately led to a crisis of masculine identity.[106] *Third gender* or *no gender*, *one* or *two sexes*: what category do we use? And what do we do with debates concerning the concepts of *sex* and *gender*?

Especially from the late 1990s onwards, a further category was introduced into gender history: the concept of masculinity. Until recently, one can observe a striking asymmetry among historians, who use the category of masculinity much more often than the concept of femininity. For the novice in gender history, this may come as a surprise – if historians have worked so hard in order to show that not only women but also men have to be analysed as gendered beings, why do historians talk a lot about masculinities but much less about femininities? This asymmetry is partly due to the historical development of gender history: The subject evolved in the 1980s from women's history, whose main aim was to bring women as historical actors into focus (writing "her-story" instead of "his-story"). Within women's history, gender emerged then as a "useful category of historical analysis".[107] It was through the concept of masculinity that historians started to also analyse how men are gendered – while gender remains the general category in order to study both "men" and "women" (as well as persons and practices that transgress male–female binaries).[108] Within this process, the categories of *third gender* or *non-gendered* for Christian religious men were rather left to the side. Perhaps, this was partly just an analytical by-product of what appears to be a scholarly consensus in using the category of *masculinity* for studying the gender history of men. However, such a consensus proved useful insofar as it opened up perspectives on plural and competing masculinities, which avoided the danger of reproducing modern essentialist assumptions concerning male–female binaries.

In his chapter, Matthew Mesley points out how the study of clerical masculinities has shown that medieval clerics were "powerful figures of authority in their own right". But clerical masculinities were not simply an amalgamation of the different masculine characteristics of laymen. As noted above, secular clergymen and bishops were constantly challenged by monastic standards of asceticism, religious purity and celibacy. Mesley's analysis shows how Caesarius of Heisterbach propagated a particular form of Cistercian masculinity in which he not only often evoked the differences between laymen, secular clergy and monks but also sometimes drew upon alternatives, such as the concept of the spiritual warrior and knight.

The contribution from Sita Steckel and Stephanie Kluge demonstrates that conceptions of monastic masculinities were never monolithic. When the mendicant orders (the Franciscans and Dominicans) developed as orders in the late Middle Ages, they built their monasteries not in the countryside but in the cities, where they preached to laymen. Mendicant preachers were popular with large parts of the urban population and competed with the secular clergy in providing pastoral care. They were much more exposed to those living in the world and were in daily contact with women who might still be considered as "rotten food, a stinking rose, a sweet poison" or deemed to be "evil from the origin, a portal to death, a disciple of the snake, counselled by the devil, a fount of deception".[109] Being in contact with women and consequently always fearful of temptations, mendicants had to prove that they lived chaste lives and were superior to both the secular clergy and the older monastic orders. The sample of sources examined by Steckel and Kluge suggests that Franciscans solved this problem rather traditionally by practising a superior masculinity of discipline, chastity and piety, which they contrasted to the undisciplined, carnal and irreligious secular priests. Dominicans, on the other hand, did not create a dichotomy in which the secular clergy was conceived of as the enemy. Incontinence was rather seen as a normal human weakness that could be mastered through learning about worldly dangers. Using didactic texts, young Dominican novices might move from a naïve understanding of the world to a more nuanced view about sexuality and women, and thus they could acquire a "shield of knowledge" against the world's carnal temptations. Advocates of the secular clergy, on the other hand, proposed that contact with women should be either avoided or submitted to social control. As Steckel and Kluge point out, the competition for chastity as a legitimate basis for religious authority took on a new dynamic in the second half of the thirteenth century as the mendicant orders emerged as new players in the religious scene. Since the scholarly texts that were authored at this time were the first to be printed in the fifteenth and sixteenth century, these different notions of masculinity, which grounded clerical claims for religious authority, had an impact beyond the Late Middle Ages.

If we adapt the concept of masculinity as it has been analysed for secular and monastic clergy in our Shared Focus to eunuchs, we can abandon the notion of eunuchs as either a *third gender* or as *non-gendered individuals.* Instead, we can place eunuchal and clerical masculinities together and consider the results. Eunuchal and clerical masculinities stood in opposition to the masculinities of laymen and non-castrated men (Arabic *fuḥūl,* sg. *faḥl*). This opposition was crucial (although not absolute – e.g. reproductive men could also be accused of being effeminate).[110] As celibate and childless men, eunuchs and clerics were singled out in respect to reproduction patterns and marked the boundary between profane and sacred spheres. This specific position shaped clerical and eunuchal masculinities in a similar way.

Exploring the notion of eunuchal masculinities, there are two points that seem to be particularly significant. Although the polemical discourse on eunuchs as a reprehensible kind of being is striking, it was less powerful and omnipresent than one might first think. As mentioned above, we can often not be sure whether certain generals, governors and other high court officials outside the harem were actually eunuchs or not. Individual eunuchs often appear in the chronicles *in officio* without any distinction from their non-castrated colleagues. In these instances, their status as eunuchs was obviously not considered worth mentioning by chroniclers. But this is not the case in other sources. In her contribution, Serena Tolino looks at Islamic legal sources, medical texts and religious traditions. In the former, eunuchs were mostly treated in similar ways to other men, with rights to marry and divorce and even, in cases where their testicles had not been cut, the ability to father children. In so doing, Islamic jurists did not comment upon the gender status of eunuchs but viewed them as men, notwithstanding their castration. This is an interesting difference to hermaphrodites, whose legal status as either women or men, or as something in between, was debated at length.[111] Medical texts, on the other hand, operated on the basis of a continuum between male and female, with eunuchs located closer to the masculine pole.

Eunuchal masculinities, therefore, were like pictures produced in a kaleidoscope: They appeared like different shapes depending on particular historical contexts, as well as the different genres and discourses in which they featured and the perspectives of those who discussed or represented them (eunuchal or non-eunuchal voices). Missing from the historiography however, are in-depth sustained studies of eunuchal masculinities; these could draw inspiration from works on clerical masculinities, with their emphasis on the competition between the secular clergy, monastic orders and mendicants. We do have preliminary findings (for example, in Ringrose's study, which considers both ecclesiastical and court eunuchs)[112] and some hints here and there. Hugh Kennedy and Nadia Maria El Cheikh, for instance, have noticed the competition between Mu'nis, the powerful eunuch military commander in Baghdad, and the eunuchs at the Abbasid court.[113] We could therefore ask, in a more systematic way, whether the masculinities of different groups of eunuchs (for example, black versus white eunuchs, eunuchs in the imperial household versus military eunuchs, harem eunuchs versus eunuchs serving the ruler) differed in certain times and places. Since we have very few instances where we can grasp the self-representations of eunuchs, in contrast to the many clerical voices we can listen to, such an enterprise, however, might be rather limited. It would prevent us nonetheless from taking our modern concept of "eunuchs" – which implies a homogeneous group of men, notwithstanding the many different historical designations for eunuchs – as a guarantee that all eunuchs shared the same gender identity.

However, it seems to me that even if we knew more about different, and perhaps competing, eunuchal masculinities, my hypothesis of kaleidoscopic eunuchal masculinities might still stand and be worth considering also in discussions of clerical masculinities. By *kaleidoscopic masculinity*, I mean that the one and same eunuch was submitted to different degrees and ways of gendering in different contexts, no matter whether he was a harem eunuch or a military commander. One could describe these fluctuations as "fluent", "ambiguous" or "liminal", but the concept of kaleidoscopic masculinity expresses more clearly that a eunuch could be seen as *either* fully male *or* a dubious hybrid being *or* almost male *or* non-gendered, depending on the context. A victorious eunuch general might be perceived (and see himself) as a fine example of military manhood, but political opponents of the eunuch might in their criticism draw upon the polemical discourse on eunuchs, depicting him as effeminate, treacherous and scheming.[114] Eunuchal masculinities could take the shape of non-castrated manhood in chronicles, being almost male in legal texts, partly male in medical tracts, a despised hybridity in the polemical discourse and a kind of non-gendered identity at the prophet's tomb.[115]

Furthermore, the very existence of eunuchs was embedded within a deep contradiction in these societies: Castration was often legally forbidden and not supposed to occur, and yet, castrated men were needed. This contradiction resulted in either outsourcing castration beyond the imperial borders or in delicate concealment and silent tolerance of castration within the empire. Sometimes, these contradictions came to the surface. Ruby Lal points out that Mughal emperor Jahāngīr (reigned 1605–1627) forbade the castration of children in the province of Sylhet, where families sent castrated boys as tax payments to the province headquarters. As Jahāngīr proudly noted in his memoirs for the year 1608:

> I issued an order that hereafter no one should follow this abominable custom .... [The governors of Bengal] received firmans that whoever should commit such acts should be capitally punished and that they should seize eunuchs of tender years who might be in anyone's possession. No one of the former kings had obtained this success. Please Almighty God ... no one shall venture on this unpleasant and unprofitable proceeding.[116]

Jahāngīr did not pursue this policy, however. According to his own memoirs, he would in later years receive eunuchs from Sylhet, and he never again discussed his attempt to end this practice.

With this example in mind, we touch upon a significant difference between bishops and eunuchs: Whereas the recruitment of bishops from the priesthood was seen as an honourable career path, the physical castration of eunuchs was legally banned and considered to be a cruel mutilation. However, eunuchs and bishops were similar insofar as both groups were faced with deep contradictions concerning their position. As we have seen above, bishops were torn between spiritual standards and worldly responsibilities, making it almost impossible to be both a good bishop and a good duke, as Caesarius of Heisterbach remarked. Clergymen had to conceive of their masculinity in ways that confirmed their manhood, notwithstanding their abstinence from reproduction. Clerical and eunuchal masculinities, therefore, operated between different understandings of gender and between different social contexts and discourses. While one might concede that non-castrated men and women also had multifaceted gender identities, clerical and eunuchal masculinities were particularly complex and embedded in various societal contradictions.

Conclusion

Celibate and childless men in power were a common feature of pre-modern dynastic rule, embedded in very different social, economic, institutional, religious and cultural frameworks. Like other men and women, they stood between their original families and institutions such as monasteries, bishoprics, harems, court hierarchies and military corps. By being excluded (usually) from a father–son succession, however, bishops and eunuchs offered societies the potential to use different reproduction patterns, thus providing flexibility and presenting alternatives that other social groups could not offer to this degree. Eunuchs were recruited from within and outside the territories in which they lived, and although they could be cut off from or remain in contact with their original families, in their new roles they developed networks and engaged in adoptive kinships that acted as a mechanism for social mobility. Before the eleventh–twelfth century, bishops could be married and have children, or they might act as fathers in other ways by providing care and training for their nephews. But even after episcopal marriages were no longer considered acceptable, bishops were still useful to the reproduction patterns of their aristocratic families. An aristocratic family needed enough children to ensure the survival of their dynasty, but not too many – a bishop was an ideal backup for their family in case a succession was endangered by the death of a brother.[117] Celibate and childless men, therefore, broadened in different but particular ways the social dynamics of their environments.

Among gender historians, it has become a consensus that gender should not be analysed as an isolated element but in relation to other factors like religion, class, race and age. Although this principle should be applied to all historical actors, celibate and childless men are a specific and unique group that proves this approach is indeed appropriate: Their masculinities were particularly complex, multifaceted, conflicting and kaleidoscopic. As celibate and childless men, they stood at the very intersection of power, social dynamics, sacredness and gender. All these factors were deeply intertwined with each other, but the combination of such could differ from time and place. As Nadia Maria El Cheikh points out in her chapter, eunuchs had a privileged position because they could move between the female and male spheres at court. Bishops grounded their superiority over worldly leaders in certain debates by their spiritual responsibility towards God. Their religious authority, on the other hand, was constantly challenged by monastic orders. Bishops had a hybrid identity as secular and ecclesiastical leaders (as Matthew Mesley has phrased it), which put them in an ambiguous position in the light of their worldly and religious requirements. Eunuchs were embedded in an even bigger societal contradiction: Empires required their services, but their castration was considered illegal. Celibacy and castration singled bishops and eunuchs out among other men, at times associating them with the sacred sphere. But they could also fall from a much further height than other men and be charged with being worldly, effeminate or overrun with sexual lust. Among all the social roles of pre-modern societies, celibate and childless men had an outstandingly complex position in relation to men and also between men and women, family and network patterns and, finally, sacred and profane spaces.

In the nineteenth century, bishops lost much of their influence in modern politics. At the same time, the number of eunuchs decreased dramatically. The main reason for this disappearance was not that castration of boys and men was suddenly judged to be cruel – as we have seen, castration had been long considered illegal and was often viewed as a terrible mutilation. Eunuchs and priests in their long garments were marginalised altogether. In the political arena of the modern nation state, politicians were mostly married and started to wear suits, thus conforming to modern globalised standards of bodily practice, as the late Christopher Bayly has suggested.[118] If one wanted to explore why bishops and eunuchs disappeared from the political stage of modern nation states, one has to take into consideration how an entire set of factors – political system, family networks, sacredness and gender – changed. The Shared Focus on celibate and childless men in power, therefore, points to some of the big questions about both modern and pre-modern rule and societal patterns.

Notes

1 I thank Matthew Mesley, Serena Tolino, Claudia Ulbrich and the anonymous peer-reviewer for their careful reading and helpful suggestions for this chapter.

2 The literature on this topic is vast. See, for example, Dipesh Chakrabarty, *Provincializing Europe: Postcolonial Thought and Historical Difference* (2000; repr. Princeton: Princeton University Press, 2008); Sebastian Conrad, Shalini Randeria and Regina Römhild, eds., *Jenseits des Eurozentrismus: Postkoloniale Perspektiven in den Geschichts- und Kulturwissenschaften,* 2nd ed. (Frankfurt: Campus, 2013); Dominic Sachsenmaier, *Global Perspectives on Global History: Theories and Approaches in a Connected World* (Cambridge: Cambridge University Press, 2011); Birgit Schäbler, ed., *Area Studies und die Welt: Weltregionen und neue Globalgeschichte* (Vienna: Mandelbaum Verlag, 2007).

3 But for a recent work, see Peter Frankopan, *The Silk Roads: A New History of the World* (New York: Bloomsbury, 2015).

4 Arnold Toynbee, *A Study of History,* 10 vols, (Oxford: University Press, 1934–1979); Oswald Spengler, *Der Untergang des Abendlandes: Umrisse einer Morphologie der Weltgeschichte,* 2 vols, (Munich: Beck, 1922–1923); Immanuel Wallerstein, *The Modern World-System* (vols 1–3: New York, London, San Diego: Academic Press, 1974–1989; vol. 4: Berkeley: University of California Press, 2011); Max Weber, *Wirtschaft und Gesellschaft: Grundriß der verstehenden Soziologie,* ed. Johannes Winckelmann (Tübingen: Mohr, 1972); Shmuel N. Eisenstadt, ed., *The Origins and Diversity of Axial Age Civilizations* (Albany: State University of New York Press, 1986).

5 Sebastian Conrad and Andreas Eckert, "Globalgeschichte, Globalisierung, multiple Modernitäten: Zur Geschichtsschreibung in der modernen Welt," in *Globalgeschichte*, ed. Sebastian Conrad, Andreas Eckert and Ulrike Freitag (Frankfurt, New York: Campus, 2007), 19.

6 Sebastian Conrad, *Globalgeschichte: Eine Einführung* (Munich: C. H. Beck, 2013), 11.

7 Magrit Pernau, *Transnationale Geschichte* (Stuttgart: Vandenhoeck & Ruprecht, 2011). See also Patrick O'Brien, "Historiographical Traditions and Modern Imperatives for the Restoration of Global History," *Journal of Global*

History 1 (2006): 3–39; Lynn Hunt, *Writing History in the Global Era* (New York, London: Norton & Company, 2015).

8 Conrad, *Globalgeschichte*, 11.

9 Almut Höfert, "Europa und der Nahe Osten: Der transkulturelle Vergleich in der Vormoderne und die Meistererzählungen über den Islam", *Historische Zeitschrift* 287 (2008): 561–597.

10 William Sewell, "Marc Bloch and the Logic of Comparative History," *History and Theory* 6 (1967): 208–218. For the comparative method in history, see also Heinz-Gerhard Haupt and Jürgen Kocka, eds., *Geschichte und Vergleich: Ansätze und Ergebnisse international vergleichender Geschichtsschreibung* (Frankfurt/Main, New York: Campus 1996); Hartmut Kaelble, *Der historische Vergleich: Eine Einführung zum 19. und 20. Jahrhundert* (Frankfurt/Main: Campus 1999); Matthias Midell, "Kulturtransfer und Historische Komparatistik," *Comparativ* 10 (2000): 7–41; Deborah Cohen, "Comparative History: Buyer Beware", *Bulletin of the German Historical Institute* 29 (2001): 23–33; Deborah Cohen and Maura O'Connor, eds., *Comparison and History: Europe in Cross-National Perspective* (New York, London: Routledge, 2004); Michael Werner and Bénédicte Zimmermann, "Beyond Comparison: *Histoire Croisée* and the Challenge of Reflexivity," *History and Theory* 45 (2006): 30–50; Gareth Austin, "Reciprocal Comparison and African History: Tackling Conceptual Eurocentrism in the Study of Africa's Economic Past", *African Studies Review* 50, no. 3 (2007): 1–28; Benjamin Z. Kedar, "Outlines for Comparative History Proposed by Practicing Historians," in *Explorations in Comparative History,* ed. Benjamin Z. Kedar (Jerusalem: The Hebrew University Press, 2009), 1–28.

11 My idea of the Shared Focus is a follow-up of my comparative and transcultural research: Almut Höfert, *Kaisertum und Kalifat: Der imperiale Monotheismus im Früh- und Hochmittelalter*, Globalgeschichte 23 (Frankfurt/Main: Campus, 2015); Wolfram Drews, Antje Flüchter, Almut Höfert et al., *Monarchische Herrschaftsformen der Vormoderne in transkultureller Perspektive* (Berlin: De Gruyter, 2015); Almut Höfert, "Grenzüberschreitungen für das Mittelalter. Transkulturelles Forschen mit einer aussereuropäischen Quellensprache zwischen Geschichtswissenschaft und den Area Studies," *Schweizerische Zeitschrift für Geschichte* 64 (2014): 210–223. These studies made me think about approaches that give more methodological leeway. I do not want to claim that my idea of the Shared Focus is particularly original – it refers to modes of reflection, problem solving and brainstorming that are part of any comparative work (cf. Kedar, *Outlines for Comparative History*). In my experience, however, studies using the concepts of "comparison/comparative perspective" often evoke much harsher criticism than, for example, research under the label *Entangled History.* I propose the Shared Focus as a small, practical tool mainly for transcultural collaborative projects in order to explore new perspectives: a cooking recipe that belongs to the kitchen of *histoire croisée* (Werner / Zimmermann, *Beyond Comparison*).

12 General studies include Richard Millant, *Les eunuches à travers les âges* (Paris: Vigot Frères, 1908); Piotr O. Scholz, *Der entmannte Eros: Eine Kulturgeschichte der Eunuchen und Kastraten* (Düsseldorf and Zürich: Artemis & Winkler, 1997). For antiquity and late antiquity, see Shaun Tougher, ed., *Eunuchs in Antiquity and Beyond* (London: Classical Press of Wales and Duckworth, 2002); Mathew Kuefler, *The Manly Eunuch: Masculinity, Gender Ambiguity, and Christian Theology in Late Antiquity* (Chicago: Chicago University Press, 2001); Kathryn M. Ringrose, *The Perfect Servant: Eunuchs and the Social Construction of Gender in Byzantium* (Chicago: University of Chicago Press,

2003); Shaun Tougher, *The Eunuch in Byzantine History and Society* (London: Routledge, 2008). For China, see Jennifer W. Jay, "Another Side of Chinese Eunuch History: Castration, Marriage, Adoption, and Burial," *Canadian Journal of History/Annales canadiennes d'histoire* 28 (1993): 459–478; Jay, "Song Confucian Views on Eunuchs," *Chinese Culture: A Quarterly Review* 35, no. 3 (1994): 45–51; Henry Tsai Shih-Shan, *The Eunuchs in Ming Dynasty* (Albany: State University of New York Press, 1996). For the Middle East, see Shaun Marmon, *Eunuchs and Sacred Boundaries in Islamic Society* (New York: Oxford University Press, 1995); David Ayalon, *Eunuchs, Caliphs and Sultans: A Study in Power Relationships* (Jerusalem: Magnes Press, Hebrew University, 1999); Mohamed Meouak, *Ṣaqāliba, eunuques et esclaves à la conquête du pouvoir: Géographie et histoires des élites politiques "marginales" dans l'Espagne umayyade* (Helsinki: Academia Scientiarum Fennica, 2004); Jane Hathaway, *Beshir Agha: Chief Eunuch of the Ottoman Imperial Harem* (London: Oneworld, 2005).

13 Jennifer D. Thibodeaux, "Introduction: Rethinking the Medieval Clergy and Masculinity," in *Negotiating Clerical Identities: Priests, Monks and Masculinity in the Middle Ages*, ed. Jennifer D. Thibodeaux (Basingstoke, New York: Palgrave Macmillan, 2010), 1–15, at 3.

14 For the antique Middle East, see A. K. Grayson: "Eunuchs in Power: Their Role in the Assyrian Bureaucracy," in *Vom Alten Orient zum Alten Testament: Festschrift Wolfram von Soden zum 85. Geburtstag*, ed. Oswald Loretz and Manfried Dietrich (Neukirchen-Vluyn: Neunkirchener Verlag, 1995), 85–98; Raija Mattila, *The King's Magnates: A Study of the Highest Officials of the Neo-Assyrian Empire* (Helsinki: The Neo-Assyrian Text Corpus Project, 2000); J. D. Hawkins, "Eunuchs among the Hittites," in *Sex and Gender in the Ancient Near East: Proceedings of the 47th Rencontre Assyriologique Internationale, Helsinki, July 2–6, 2001*, ed. Simo Parpola and Robert M. Whiting (Helskinki: The Neo-Assyrian Text Corpus Project, 2002), 217–233; Claus Ambos, "Eunuchen als Thronprätendenten und Herrscher im alten Orient," in *Of God(s), Trees, Kings, and Scholars: Neo-Assyrian and Related Studies in Honour of Simo Parpola*, ed. Mikko Luukko, Saana Svärd and Raija Mattila (Helsinki: The Finnish Oriental Society, 2009), 1–7; Reinhard Pirngruber, "Eunuchen am Königshof. Ktesias und die altorientalische Evidenz," in *Die Welt des Ktesias: Ctesias' World*, ed. Josef Wiesehöfer, Robert Rollinger and Giovanni B. Lanfranchi (Wiesbaden: Harrassowitz, 2011), 279–312.

15 Victor Saxer, "Die kirchliche Organisation im 3. Jahrhundert," in *Das Entstehen der einen Christenheit (250–430)*, vol. 2 of *Geschichte des Christentums*, ed. Charles and Luce Piétri (Freiburg: Herder, 1996), 23–54; Claudia Rapp, *Holy Bishops in Late Antiquity: The Nature of Christian Leadership in an Age of Transition* (Berkeley: University of California Press, 2004); David Gwynn, "Episcopal Leadership," in *The Oxford Handbook of Late Antiquity*, ed. Scott Fitzgerald Johnson (Oxford: Oxford University Press, 2012), 876–915.

16 Timothy Reuter, "A Europe of Bishops: The Age of Wulfstan of York and Burchard of Worms," in *Patterns of Episcopal Power: Bishops in 10th and 11th Century Western Europe/Strukturen bischöflicher Herrschaft im westlichen Europa des 10. und 11. Jahrhunderts*, ed. Ludger Körntgen and Dominik Waßenhoven (Berlin and Boston: de Gruyter, 2011), 23. For other studies, see, for example, *The Bishop Reformed: Studies of Episcopal Power and Culture in the Central Middle Ages*, ed. John S. Ott and Anna Trumbore Jones (Aldershot: Ashgate, 2007); Angelo Silvestri, *Power, Politics and Episcopal Authority: The Bishops of Cremona and Lincoln in the Middle Ages (1066–1340)* (Cambridge: Cambridge Scholars Publishing, 2015).

17 Martin Heale, ed., *The Prelate in England and Europe* (York: Boydell & Brewer, 2015); Charles Tracy and Andrew Budge, *British Medieval Episcopal Thrones* (Oxford: Oxbow Books, 2015).
18 Ringrose, *The Perfect Servant,* 166–173; see also John Bagnell Bury, *The Imperial Administrative System in the Ninth Century* (London: Franklin, 1911); Nicolas Oikonomidès, ed., *Les listes de préséance byzantines des IXe et Xe siècles* (Paris: Editions du Centre National de la Recherche Scientifique, 1972).
19 Peter Brown, *The Body and Society: Men, Women, and Sexual Renunciation in Early Christianity* (1998; rev. ed. New York: Columbia University Press, 2008). See also Kim M. Phillips and Barry Reay, *Sex Before Sexuality: A Premodern History* (London: Polity Press, 2011).
20 Walter Stevenson, "Eunuchs and early Christianity," in *Eunuchs in Antiquity and Beyond,* ed. Shaun Tougher (Oakville: The Classical Press of Wales, 2002), 123–142; Kuefler, *The Manly Eunuch,* 260–273.
21 A. Cheikh Moussa, "Ǧāḥiẓ et les Eunuques ou la confusion du même et de l'autre," *Arabica* 29, fasc. 2 (1982): 184–214; Ayalon, *Eunuchs, Caliphs and Sultans*; Michael Jursa, "'Höflinge' (*ša rēši, ša rēš šarri, ustarbaru*) in babylonischen Quellen des ersten Jahrtausends," in Josef Wiesehöfer, Robert Rollinger and Giovanni Lanfranchi, eds., *Die Welt des Ktesias,* 159–174; Ilan Beled, "Eunuchs in Hatti and Assyria: A Reassessment," in *Time and History in the Ancient Near East: Proceedings of the 56th Rencontre Assyriologique Internationale at Barcelona,* ed. Lluis Feliu et al. (Winona Lake: Eisenbrauns, 2013), 785–797. See also Serena Tolino's chapter.
22 Ringrose, *The Perfect Servant*, 15; Kuefler, *The Manly Eunuch,* 33.
23 Dig. 50.16.128: "Spadonum generalis appellatio est: quo nomine tam hi, qui natura spadones sunt, item thlibiae thlasiae, sed et si quod aliud genus spadonum est, continentur." *Digesta Iustiniani Augusti,* ed. Theodor Mommsen and Paul Krueger (Berlin: Weidmann, 1870), 2:944.
24 Kuefler, *The Manly Eunuch,* 33.
25 Ibid., 247–282.
26 Ringrose, *The Perfect Servant,* 16.
27 Ibid., 14.
28 Ibid.
29 Ibid., 114–116; Kuefler, *The Manly Eunuch,* 243–282.
30 Clement of Alexandria, *Stromata I–IV,* ed. Ursula Treu (Berlin: Akademie Verlag, 1985), book 3, cap. 1.
31 Gregor of Nanzianz, *Discours 32–37,* ed. Claudio Moreschini, trans. into French Paul Gallay (Paris: Les Éditions du cerf, 1985), disc. 37, 20, pp. 310–313.
32 Ibid., disc. 37, 21, pp. 304–317, quotation at 314.
33 Kuefler, *The Manly Eunuch,* 268; Ambrose of Milan, *Verginità e vedovanza,* ed. Franco Gori (Milan: Biblioteca Ambrosiana, 1989), *De viduis,* cap. 13, 75ff (= *Patrologia Latina* 16, col. 257f).
34 Translated by Kuefler, *The Manly Eunuch,* 279; Jerome, *Epistulae*, ed. Joseph Jabourt, 8 vols. (Paris: Belles Lettres, 1949–1963), epistle 14.2–3.
35 Giuseppe Alberigo, ed., *Conciliorum oecumenicorum generalium decreta* (Turnhout: Brepols, 2006), 1:1–34.
36 Rapp, *Holy Bishops.*
37 David G. Hunter, "Clerical Marriage and Episcopal Elections in the Latin West: From Siricius to Leo I," in *Episcopal Elections in Late Antiquity,* ed. Johan Leemans (Boston: de Gruyter, 2011), 183–202.
38 Megan McLaughlin, *Sex, Gender, and Episcopal Authority in an Age of Reform, 1000–1122* (Cambridge: Cambridge University Press, 2010); Kuefler, *The Manly Eunuch.*

39 Joan Scott, "Gender: A Useful Category of Historical Analysis," *American Historical Review* 91 (1986): 1051–1075.
40 Helen L. Parish, *Clerical Celibacy in the West, c. 1100–1700* (Farnham: Ashgate 2009), 59–86. See also Johannes Preiser-Kapeller, *Der Episkopat im späten Byzanz. Ein Verzeichnis der Metropoliten und Bischöfe des Patriarchats von Konstantinopel in der Zeit von 1204 bis 1453* (Saarbrücken: Verlag Dr. Müller, 2008).
41 For another perspective, Gadi Algazi has shown that the erosion of celibacy for scholars resulted in a specific habitus of scholars and their families in continental Europe. Gadi Algazi, "Habitus, familia and forma vitae: Die Lebensweisen mittelalterlicher Gelehrter in muslimischen, jüdischen und christlichen Gemeinden – vergleichend betrachtet," in *Beiträge zur Kulturgeschichte der Gelehrten im späten Mittelalter*, ed. Frank Rexroth (Ostfildern: Thorbecke, 2010), 185–217.
42 Rapp, *Holy Bishops*; Ralph Mathisen, *Roman Aristocrats in Barbarian Gaul: Strategies for Survival in an Age of Transition* (Austin: University of Texas Press, 1993).
43 See Julia Barrow's Chapter, n. 33.
44 Julia Barrow's chapter, n. 35.
45 Steffen Patzold, "Bischöfe, soziale Herkunft und die Organisation sozialer Herrschaft," in *Chlodwigs Welt: Organisation von Herrschaft um 500*, ed. Mischa Meier and Steffen Patzold (Stuttgart: Franz Steiner Verlag, 2014), 523–544.
46 Julia Barrow's chapter, n. 37.
47 Steffen Patzold, *Episcopus: Wissen über Bischöfe im Frankenreich des späten 8. bis frühen 10. Jahrhunderts* (Ostfildern: Jan Thorbecke Verlag, 2008).
48 Anne Llewellyn Barstow, *Married Priests and the Reforming Papacy: The Eleventh Century Debates* (New York: Edwin Mellen Press, 1982); Parish, *Celibacy*; Antje Flüchter, *Der Zölibat zwischen Devianz und Norm: Kirchenpolitik und Gemeindealltag in den Herzogtümern Jülich und Berg im 16. und 17. Jahrhundert* (Cologne: Böhlau, 2006).
49 Petrus Damiani, *Letters 61–90,* trans. Owen J. Blum (Washington: The Catholic University of America Press, 1992), no. 61, 3:9f.; *Die Briefe des Petrus Damiani, Teil 2: Nr. 41–90,* ed. Kurt Reindel (Monumenta Germaniae Historica, Briefe der deutschen Kaiserzeit 4, 2, Munich, 1988), no. 61, 214.
50 See, for example, Giles Constable, *Reformation of the Twelfth Century* (Cambridge: Cambridge University Press, 1996); Michael Frassetto, ed., *Medieval Purity and Piety: Essays on Medieval Clerical Celibacy and Religious Reform* (New York and London: Garland Publishing, 1998); Hugh M. Thomas, *The Secular Clergy in England, 1066–1216* (Oxford: Oxford University Press, 2014); Jennifer D. Thibodeaux, *The Manly Priest: Clerical Celibacy, Masculinity, and Reform in England and Normandy, 1066–1300* (Philadelphia: University of Pennsylvania Press, 2015).
51 Brown, *Body and Society,* 443.
52 See, for example, Miura Toru and John Edwards Philips, eds., *Slave Elites in the Middle East and Africa* (London and New York: Kegan Paul International, 2000); Stefan Hanß and Juliane Schiel, eds., *Mediterranean Slavery Revisited (500–1800)* (Zurich: Chronos, 2014).
53 Delia Cortese and Simonetta Calderini, *Women and the Fatimids in the World of Islam* (Edinburgh: Edinburgh University Press, 2006), 78.
54 See, for example, Keith Hopkins, *Conquerors and Slaves* (Cambridge: Cambridge University Press, 1978).
55 Ezgi Dikici, "The Making of Ottoman Court Eunuchs: Origins, Recruitment Paths, Family Ties and Domestic Production," *Archivium Ottomanicum* 30 (2013): 105–136.
56 Leslie Pierce, *The Imperial Harem: Women and Sovereignty in the Ottoman Empire* (New York and Oxford: Oxford University Press, 1993), 141.

57 All examples are taken from Dikici, "*The Making of Ottoman Court Eunuchs*".
58 Ibid.
59 Jane Hathaway, "The Role of Kislar Ağası in 17th–18th Century Ottoman Egypt," *Studia Islamica* 75 (1992): 141–158.
60 Jane Hathaway, "Ḥabešī Meḥmed Agha: The First Chief Harem Eunuch (darüssaada ağası) of the Ottoman Empire," in *The Islamic Scholarly Tradition: Studies in History, Law, and Thought in Honor of Professor Michael Allan Cook*, ed. Asad Q. Ahmed, Behnam Sadeghi and Michael Bonner (Leiden: Brill, 2011), 179–195, 191ff.
61 David S. Powers, *Encyclopedia of Islam Online*, 3rd ed., s.v. "Adoption," accessed October 13, 2015, http://referenceworks.brillonline.com/entries/encyclopaedia-of-islam-3/adoption-SIM_0304?s.num=0&s.f.s2_parent=s.f.cluster.Encyclopaedia+of+Islam&s.q=Adoption .
62 Indrani Chatterjee, "Monastic Governmentality, Colonial Misogyny, and Postcolonial Amnesia in South Asia," *History of the Present* 3 (2013): 57–98.
63 I have explored the problems posed by the Eurocentric concepts of religion and sacredness for a thorough transcultural comparison in Höfert, *Kaisertum und Kalifat,* 24–28, 69–84.
64 Gilbert Dagron, *Emperor and Priest: The Imperial Office in Byzantium* (Cambridge: Cambridge University Press, 2003); Kai Trampedach, "Kaiserwechsel und Krönungsritual im Konstantinopel des 5. bis 6. Jahrhunderts," in *Investitur- und Krönungsrituale: Herrschaftseinsetzungen im kulturellen Vergleich*, ed. Marion Steinicke and Stefan Weinfurter (Cologne: Böhlau, 2005), 275–290.
65 André Vauchez, *Sainthood in the Late Middle Ages* (Cambridge: Cambridge University Press, 1997), 257; Thomas Wünsch, "Der heilige Bischof. Zur politischen Dimension von Heiligkeit im Mittelalter und ihrem Wandel," *Archiv für Kulturgeschichte* 82 (2000): 261–302; Robert Bartlett, *Why Can the Dead Do Such Great Things? Saints and Worshippers from the Martyrs to the Reformation* (Princeton: Princeton University Press, 2013).
66 Rather of Verona, *Praeloquia,* ed. Peter L. D. Reid, Corpus Christianorum: Continuatio mediaevalis 46 A (Turnhout: Brepols, 1984), cap. III, 12, 86 (quotation from Steffen Patzold, *Episcopus*, my translation): "Dii sunt, Domini sunt, Christi sunt, celi sunt, angeli sunt, patriarchae sunt, prophetae sunt, apostoli sunt, evangelistae sunt, martyres sunt, uncti sunt, reges sunt, principes sunt, iudices sunt, non tantum hominum, sed et angelorum, ... doctores sunt, precones uenturi Iudicis sunt, speculatores sunt, pupilla oculi Domini sunt, amici Dei uiuentis sunt, filii Dei sunt, patres sunt, luminaria mundi sunt, stellae celi sunt ... claues celi portant, reserare et claudere celum ualent ...."
67 Thomas, *Secular Clergy,* 17 (quotation from British Library, Cotton MS Vespasian E X, fos. 183r–v).
68 Quotation is referenced in Matthew Mesley's chapter.
69 Caesarius of Heisterbach, "*Vita et Miracula Engelberti,*" ed. Fritz Zschaeck in *Die Wundergeschichten des Caesarius von Heisterbach,* ed. Alfons Hilka (Bonn: Peter Hanstein Verlagsbuchhandlung, 1937), distinctio I, cap. 2, p. 236: "Sanctitatem, que vite defuit, mors pretiosa supplevit, et si minus perfectus erat in conversatione, sanctus tamen effectus est in passione."
70 Caesarius of Heisterbach, *Vita et Miracula Engelberti,* ed Zschaeck, distinctio II, cap. 8, p. 265: "In omnibus siquidem membris, in quibus peccaverat, punitus est. Punitus est in capite multipliciter, sicut apparet in eius pillio, scilicet in vertice, in fronte et occipite, in tymporibus, labiis et dentibus, et tam graviter, ut rivuli sanguinis inundantes et decurrentes fossas oculorum aurium narium orisque influerent et replerent. Punitus est etiam in gutture et collo, in humeris et dorso, in pectore et corde, in vetre et coxis, in cruribus et pedibus, ut cognoscas, lector, quali baptismo Christus in martire suo diluere dignatus sit, quidquid culpe

contraxerat superbiendo, videndo, audiendo, olfaciendo, gustando, cogitando, luxuriando, operando, tangendo, gradiendo sive aliis quibuscumque levitatibus, omissionibus et negligentiis circa disciplinam."

71 Gelasius, "Letter to emperor Anastasius in 494," in *Epistolae Romanorum pontificum genuinae et quae ad eos scriptae sunt a S. Hilaro usque ad Pelagium II* (Braunsberg, 1867), epistula 12, pp. 350ff. English translation in J. H. Robinson, *Readings in European History* (Boston: Ginn, 1905), 72ff.

72 Shaun Tougher, "Holy Eunuchs! Masculinity and Eunuch Saints in Byzantium," in *Holiness and Masculinity in the Middle Ages,* ed. P. H. Cullum and Katherine J. Lewis (Cardiff: Cardiff University Press, 2004), 93–108. See also Mathew Kuefler's chapter.

73 Ringrose, *The Perfect Servant*, 117–163. See also Lynn E. Roller, "The Ideology of the Eunuch Priest," in *Gender and the Body in the Ancient Mediterranean,* ed. Maria Wyke (Oxford: J. C. Gieben, 1998), 118–135; Pascal Poulhol and Isabelle Cochelin, "La rehabilitation de l'eunuque dans l'hagiography antique (IIe–VIe siècles)," in *Memoriam Sanctorum Venerantes: Miscellanea in onore de Monsignor Victor Saxer* (Vatican City: Pontificio Istituto di Archeologia Cristiana, 1992), 49–73.

74 Ringrose, *The Perfect Servant,* 163–183.

75 Ibid.

76 Trampedach, *Kaiserwechsel,* 288.

77 Whereas Kathryn Ringrose is "reluctant to label this surrounding area 'sacred space'" (Ringrose, *The Perfect Servant,* 169), I think this label is appropriate to a wider concept of sacredness, which I will apply to our third field of the Shared Focus.

78 Ringrose, *The Perfect Servant,* 180 (quoting Constantine VII Porphygenitus, *Le livre des cérémonies,* ed. Albert Vogt [Paris: Les Belles Lettres, 1935–40], book 2, cap. 25, 624).

79 Ringrose, *The Perfect Servant,* 179–181.

80 Heinz Halm, *The Empire of the Mahdi: The Rise of the Fatimids* (Leiden: Brill, 1996), 310ff.

81 Hamid Haji, *Inside the Immaculate Portal: A History from Early Fatimid Archives* (London: I. B. Tauris, 2012).

82 Vladimir Ivanow, *Ismaili Tradition Concerning the Rise of the Fatimids* (London: H. Milford, 1942).

83 François-Joseph Ruggiu, ed., *The Uses of First Person Writings: Africa, America, Asia, Europe*, Comparatism and Society 25 (Brussels: PIE Peter Lang, 2013).

84 Shaun Marmon, *Eunuchs and Sacred Boundaries in Islamic Society* (New York and Oxford: Oxford University Press, 1995), 12.

85 Ibid., 14.

86 Ibid., 55–61.

87 Ibid., 81 (quoting al-Qalqashandī, *Ṣubḥ al-aʿshā fī ṣināʿat al-inshāʾ* [Cairo: al-Maṭbaʿa al-Amīriyya, 1913–1920], 12:262).

88 Marmon, *Eunuchs and Sacred Boundaries,* 87.

89 Ibid., 111 (quoting Sālim Farīd, cited in an interview by Tawfīq Naṣr Allāh in the Saudi magazine *al-Yamāma,* February 7, 1990). Although the eunuchs of the prophet are dying out, there is a group of "effeminate men" around the prophet's tomb – to quote an Iranian who told me this in 2014. Some gay Muslims believe that these men stand in the tradition of the eunuchs of the prophet and that they might be gay. They take their presence at the prophet's tomb as a sign that God accepts homosexuality. See Scott Kugle, *Living Out Islam: Voices of Gay, Lesbian, and Transgender Muslims* (New York: New York University Press, 2014), 208.

90 Hathaway, *Role of Kislar Ağası*, 191.

91 See also Hathaway, *Beshir Aga*.
92 See the penultimate paragraph in Jane Hathaway's chapter.
93 See Michael Hoeckelmann's chapter.
94 See Matthew Kuefler's chapter, quoting Basil, *Epist.*, Patrologia Graeca 32 (Paris: J.-P. Migne, 1857), ed. and trans. Philip Schaff and Henry Wace, Nicene and Post-Nicene Fathers, 2nd. ser., vol. 8 (Edinburgh: T. and T. Clark, 1885), 191.115.
95 See Michael Hoeckelmann's chapter.
96 Shaun Tougher, "Images of Effeminate Men: The Case of Byzantine Eunuchs", in *Masculinity in Medieval Europe*, ed. Dawn M. Hadley (London, New York: Longman, 1999), 89–100; Hans Peter Pöckel, *Der unmännliche Mann: Zur Figuration des Eunuchen im Werk von al-Ǧāḥiẓ* (Würzburg: Ergon Verlag, 2014).
97 Procopius, *History of the Wars*, trans. H. B. Dewing, Loeb Classical Library 107 (1916; repr. Cambridge, MA: Harvard University Press, 1993), 3:403, par. 6.13.16. Quotation taken from Shaun Tougher's chapter.
98 Marmon, *Eunuchs and Sacred Boundaries,* 61–63, quotation at 63, quoting Tāj al-Dīn ʿAbd al-Wahhāb Ibn ʿAlī al-Subkī, *Muʿīd al-niʿam wa mubīd al-niqam*, ed. David W. Myhrman (London: Luzac, 1908; repr. New York: AMS Press, 1978), 56. See also the edition by Muḥammad ʿAlī al-Najjār (Cairo: Dār al-Kitāb al-ʿArabī, 1367/1948) and the abbreviated German translation by Oskar Rescher, "Tâǵ eddîn Es Subki's Muʿîd en-niʿam wa mubîd en-niqam: Über die moralischen Pflichten der verschiedenen islamischen Bevölkerungsklassen," in Rescher, *Gesammelte Werke*, part 2, vol. 2, 2nd ed. (Osnabrück: Biblio Verlag, 1980), 691–855.
99 See Serena Tolino's chapter (quoting al-Jāḥiẓ, *Kitāb al-ḥayawān,* [Cairo: Muṣṭafā al-bābī al-ḥalabī, 1938], 1:108).
100 Ringrose, *The Perfect Servant.*
101 Cheikh-Moussa, "Ǧāḥiẓ et les Eunuques".
102 Thomas Laqueur, *Making Sex: Body and Gender from the Greeks to Freud* (Cambridge, MA: Harvard University Press, 1990).
103 Andrea Griesebner, "Geschlecht als mehrfach relationale Kategorie: Methodologische Anmerkungen aus der Perspektive der Frühen Neuzeit," in *Geschlecht hat Methode: Ansätze und Perspektiven in der Frauen- und Geschlechtergeschichte,* ed. Veronika Aegerter (Zürich: Chronos, 1999), 130. See also Cordelia Beattie, "Introduction: Gender, Power, and Difference," in *Intersections of Gender, Religions and Ethnicity in the Middle Ages,* ed. Cordelia Beattie and Kirsten A. Fenton (New York: Palgrave, 2010), 1–11.
104 Marmon, *Eunuchs and Sacred Boundaries,* preface.
105 Robert N. Swanson, "Angels Incarnate: Clergy and Masculinity from Gregorian Reform to Reformation," in Hadley, ed., *Masculinity in Medieval Europe,* 160–177.
106 Jo Ann McNamara, "The *Herrenfrage*: The Restructuring of the Gender System, 1050–1150," in *Medieval Masculinities: Regarding Men in the Middle Ages,* ed. Clare A. Lees, Thelma S. Fenster and Jo Ann McNamara (Minneapolis and London: University of Minnesota Press, 1994), 3–30.
107 Scott, "Gender as a Useful Tool of Historical Analysis". For an intriguing recent proposal of how to use the category of *gender*, see Monika Mommertz, "Theoriepotentiale 'ferner Vergangenheiten': Geschlecht als Markierung/Ressource/Tracer." in *L'homme: Europäische Zeitschrift für feministische Geschichtswissenschaft* 26, no. 1 (2015): 79–97.
108 There are some exceptions, as the concept of *femininity* is used in Literature Studies. See Frederick Kiefer, ed., *Masculinities and Femininities in the Middle*

Ages and Renaissance (Turnhout: Brepols, 2009); Karina Marie Ash, ed., *Conflicting Femininities in Medieval German Literature* (Farnham: Ashgate, 2012). For studies on medieval masculinities and gender, see Jeffrey Cohen and Bonnie Wheeler, eds., *Becoming Male in the Middle Ages* (New York, London, 1997); Lees, Fenster, McNamara, eds., *Medieval Masculinities*; Hadley, ed., *Masculinity in Medieval Europe*; Ruth Mazo Karras, *From Boys to Men: Formations of Masculinity in Late Medieval Europe* (Philadelphia: University of Pennsylvania Press, 2003); Leslie Brubaker and Julia M. H. Smith, eds., *Gender in the Early Medieval World: East and West, 300–900* (Cambridge: Cambridge University Press, 2004); Cullum, Lewis, eds., *Holiness and Masculinity in the Middle Ages*; Elizabeth L'Estrange and Alison More, eds., *Representing Medieval Genders and Sexualities in Europe: Construction, Transformation and Subversion, 600–1530* (Farnham: Ashgate, 2011); P. H. Cullum and Katherine J. Lewis, eds., *Religious Men and Masculine Identity in the Middle Ages* (Woodbridge: Boydell and Brewer, 2013); Lisa M. Bitel and Felice Lifshitz, eds., *Gender and Christianity in Medieval Europe: New Perspectives* (Philadelphia: University of Pennsylvania Press, 2008); Rachel Stone, *Morality and Masculinity in the Carolingian Empire* (Cambridge: Cambridge University Press, 2012).

109 See the chapter by Sita Steckel and Stephanie Kluge (quoting the thirteenth-century Franciscan Salimbene de Adam, who cited the words of Augustine. See Salimbene de Adam, *Chronica*, ed. Giuseppe Scalia, Corpus Christianorum: Continuatio Medievalis 125 [Turnhout: Brepols, 1994], 199).

110 Effeminacy could indeed be linked to excessive sexual appetites. Furthermore, although it could be associated with sodomy, it was not necessarily directed at same-sex desires. As Robert Mills states, citing criticisms of the effeminate fashions of courtiers in Orderic Vitalis's twelfth-century *Ecclesiastical History*, "Effeminacy, represented as a mode of aesthetic as well as social transgression, is characterised as a sodomitic 'way of life', yet this is not linked definitively with homoerotic pursuits. Indeed the discussion of Fulk's pointy shoes makes clear that one of the reasons courtiers adopted this fashion was so they could 'seek the favours of women with every kind of lewdness'". Robert Mills, *Seeing Sodomy in the Middle Ages* (Chicago: The University of Chicago Press, 2015), 82–83. I thank Matthew Mesley for this reference.

111 Paula Sanders, "Gendering the ungendered body: Hermaphrodites in Medieval Islamic Law," in *Women in Middle Eastern History: Shifting Boundaries in Sex and Gender,* ed. Nikki R. Keddie and Beth Baron (New Haven: Yale University Press, 1991), 74–95.

112 Ringrose, *The Perfect Servant.*

113 See Hugh Kennedy's chapter, before footnote 12; also see Nadia Maria El Cheikh's chapter, footnote 55.

114 See, for example, the polemic of ʿAbd Allāh b. Ḥamdān against the eunuch commander Muʾnis in Hugh Kennedy's chapter.

115 I am not the first to consider the metaphor of a kaleidoscope as useful. See, for example, Liesbeth Geevers and Mirella Marini, "Introduction: Aristocracy, dynasty and identity in early modern Europe, 1520–1700," in *Dynastic Identity in Early Modern Europe. Rulers, Aristocrats and the Formation of Identities,* ed. Liesbeth Geevers and Mirella Marini (Farnham: Ashgate, 2014), 1–24, esp. 16ff.

116 See Ruby Lal's chapter (quoting Alexander Rogers, trans., Henry Beveridge ed., *Tūzuk-i-Jahāngīrī, or, Memoirs of Jahāngīr* [New Delhi: Atlantic Publishers and Distributors, 1989], 1150–151).

117 Flüchter, *Zölibat.*

118 Christopher Bayly, *The Birth of the Modern World 1780–1914* (Oxford: Blackwell, 2004), 12.

Part I

Bishops and eunuchs as parts of the ruling elites

1 The bishop in the Latin West 600–1100[1]

Julia Barrow

At first sight, there might seem little in common between medieval bishops and the eunuchs who played such prominent roles in Arab, Indian, Chinese and Ottoman courts. Church law was cautious about admitting castrated men to ordination: From the Council of Nicaea (325) onwards, those who had had themselves castrated in order to live lives of greater asceticism were rejected for ordination, and while those who had been castrated against their will were not prevented from being ordained, in practice it was relatively unusual for castrated men to be ordained in either the Western or the Eastern church.[2] Furthermore, unlike many of the court eunuchs featuring in other chapters in this volume, very few bishops spent any time as slaves. Instead, they were almost always freeborn and, indeed, were often of noble birth;[3] furthermore, they were usually not exiles, though some had left their homelands as a form of voluntary asceticism (*peregrinatio*).[4]

These important differences apart, however, there were ways in which bishops in the medieval west did resemble court eunuchs further to the east in the Eurasian land-mass. First of all, from the end of the fourth century onwards, bishops were supposed to renounce sexual relations within marriage on being elevated to the episcopate, and by the end of the sixth century, it was becoming usual for the clergy (including future bishops) to be recruited in boyhood, making it easier for their superiors to discourage them from marriage.[5] There were exceptions to this: In Ireland and England, for example, clerical dynasties were a common feature of society down to the twelfth century. However, in most of western Europe for most of the period 600–1100 (and beyond) it was relatively unusual for bishops to have legitimate offspring. Episcopal celibacy was also a requirement in the Eastern church, which, unlike the Western church, did not reject marriage for priests. Like eunuchs, bishops often drew on their family relationships to create surrogate father-son bonds, and the relatives most likely to be drawn into these surrogate bonds were their nephews.

The role of the bishop in the medieval West

Before embarking on an examination of how medieval bishops built up uncle–nephew relationships, it would be useful to supply some background information about the activities, functions and *raison d'être* of bishops in the medieval west.[6] Their roles were varied, spanning politics, law, cultural patronage and the supervision of education as well as their principal role, the spiritual oversight of the Christian faithful in the territories (dioceses) for which they were responsible.[7] Bishops in the Western church in the Middle Ages were part of a much longer tradition. Much of their role is only explicable in terms of the history of the church over the *longue durée*, though some of it was conditioned by the political and social circumstances of their time and place; we can start with the longer-term characteristics and then turn to the features specific to the 600–1100 period.

Bishops trace their origins to the apostles, Christ's disciples after the Crucifixion.[8] As the spiritual successors to the apostles, chosen by members of the church, at least in theory, and consecrated by the laying on of hands, bishops have overall responsibility for the spiritual health of Christian believers; the term *bishop*, which derives from the Greek *episkopos* or overseer, conveys a sense of this duty. From early on, bishops were based in individual cities, each responsible for a single community;[9] since each city within the Roman empire (where most though not all of the early church was situated) exercised political authority over a fixed territory, this pattern came to be replicated in ecclesiastical organisation, and by the later fourth century the term *dioikesis*, which originated as a term in civil administration, had begun to be used to mean an ecclesiastical territory, a diocese.[10] Bishops were supposed to respect each other's territories and not intervene unless invited by the local diocesan or unless commanded to do so by a group of bishops acting as a council. Certain cities, notably Rome, had a particular seniority as patriarchates, and their bishops had especial authority; because Rome was the only patriarchate in the Western church, the pattern of ecclesiastical authority in the west became more monarchical than in the east, though this took some time to evolve fully.[11]

Bishops had disciplinary authority over all the clergy of their diocese, who were theoretically supposed to remain within the diocese in which they had been ordained unless they received written permission to travel from their diocesan.[12] Their authority over lay people was more limited, since with respect to the laity, the law of the church (canon law) chiefly concerned sexual behaviour and questions of religious belief.[13] By the middle of the third century, bishops had begun to meet in councils to decide disciplinary and theological problems, and councils, some held within single provinces and some with a much wider geographical base, continued to provide a forum for debate for centuries to come.[14] Bishops thus often had chances to travel widely, and even if they did not necessarily get as far as Rome (and many did), they would be in frequent contact with their neighbours.[15] On a more local level, diocesan synods, which emerged early in the Middle Ages but were much developed in the Carolingian church in the ninth century, gave bishops the opportunity to exercise jurisdiction within their sees more effectively.[16]

In the second and third centuries, bishops were the only clerics able to celebrate the Eucharist, and the term *sacerdotes* (priests) was reserved for them. The early expansion of Christian communities within and beyond the cities in which they were originally established necessitated the foundation of many churches, and by the fourth century, it meant that the ability to celebrate the Eucharist and baptism had to be devolved to a wider group of clergy. Hence *presbyteroi* or elders were allowed to share this duty with bishops and acquired sacerdotal functions too.[17] Some rites came to be reserved for bishops alone; these were the ordination of clergy, the confirmation of baptized members of the Christian community and the consecration of churches.[18] These remained episcopal monopolies, and medieval bishops derived considerable authority from them: The right to bestow ordination and to consecrate churches gave them some control over the recruitment of the clergy and the positioning of new churches. Some further rites also came to be reserved to bishops. The most important of these in the medieval west was the anointing of kings: When in 751 the Carolingian dynasty usurped the Frankish throne, removing the original ruling dynasty, the Merovingians, from office, the new ruler, Pippin, adopted anointing as a royal inauguration ritual, in imitation of the Jewish kings. Pippin's anointing was carried out by bishops (and was repeated soon afterwards by the pope), and royal unction remained an episcopal monopoly from the start, not only for Carolingian rulers but also among their successors and more widely among Christian rulers across western Europe.[19]

So far, we have concentrated on the sacramental and disciplinary aspects of the bishop's office, but the pastoral role of the bishop, that is the bishop acting as teacher and preacher, was also vital. By the fourth century, bishops found that they had to devolve much of this rôle to other clergy in the diocese, especially priests, but they retained the right to license (and thus choose) preachers and were supposed to assess the learning and general suitability of clerical candidates for ordination by a short examination.[20] Bishops were supposed to ensure that education was available to clergy within their dioceses, and many went further, acting as patrons of literary works, theological and historical writings, art and music.[21]

From the fourth century, when Christianity became the official religion of the Roman empire, bishops began to have significant political roles, both in the service of rulers and also locally in their dioceses, in which, for example, they often acted as civic leaders and organisers of defences in the fifth and sixth centuries.[22] By ca. 600, bishops were powerful figures in royal assemblies in the Frankish kingdoms. Within their cities and dioceses, they rivalled local royal officials (counts) in influence.[23] This power was partly based on the landed endowments of bishoprics, which grew steadily throughout the earlier Middle Ages.[24] By the eighth century, many bishops were, thanks to their office, very wealthy landowners, and as a result of this were lords over large numbers of unfree and semi-free peasants; the freeborn were also increasingly drawn into their clientages. As a result, kings expected bishops to help organise defence, for although they were not expected to fight themselves (a few did, in breach of canon law),[25] they had to ensure that their tenants did. As members of the political elite, they were also expected to attend royal courts and advise on legislation; several of them helped to draft royal laws, and many supervised the copying of such texts.[26] In the Carolingian empire, bishops were among those chosen to act as *missi*, royal commissioners who had the task of ensuring that locally based royal officials acted as they were supposed to.[27] Although bishops in the Carolingian empire and its successor states were not supposed to act as judges in secular courts, their counterparts in Anglo-Saxon England (where public and ecclesiastical courts were not separated) helped to preside in locally based courts (shire courts).[28] In France and Germany, bishops often developed considerable jurisdictional rights over the inhabitants of their landed estates and (especially in Germany) of their see-cities, even though jurisdiction itself might be exercised by lay deputies.[29] Some of these powers can be seen in the law-code drawn up by Bishop Burchard of Worms (1000–25) for his ministerials (unfree tenants performing administrative roles).[30] As Tim Reuter remarked, "bishoprics c. 1000 were small states, with almost everything which corresponds to our conception of a state: rulers, governments, central places, citizenship, legislation, taxation".[31]

Because of these responsibilities and also because of their resources, bishops were powerful and wealthy. Unsurprisingly, kings and also the aristocratic elite were interested in their appointment. For rulers, it was most desirable to appoint clerics of ability who had spent time in royal service, for example as court chaplains.[32] From the mid-fifth century onwards in Gaul, though slowly to start with, aristocratic families began to ensure that bishops were drawn from their ranks.[33] From the seventh century, aristocratic backgrounds for bishops in Francia were normal, and this continued to be the case in the Frankish successor-states.[34] Quite often, as in Ottonian Germany, it was possible to keep both sets of demands satisfied: the Ottonians (919–1024) and the early Salians (1024–1125), while keeping control of most episcopal appointments, nonetheless paid heed to the views of their magnates.[35] In England, where connections between bishops and the higher aristocracy were rare from the tenth century to beyond the end of the Middle Ages, kings had more power over patronage.[36] In all areas, bishops were aware of what they owed to their patrons and to their families, and when they themselves exercised patronage, they would try to repay their debts to their lords and to their relatives. The remainder of this chapter examines an important duty of bishops towards their kin: support for their nephews.

Bishops and the uncle–nephew relationship: A case study

When, in 869, Archbishop Hincmar of Rheims fell out with his nephew and namesake Bishop Hincmar of Laon, who had been disobedient to him and also to their ruler, Charles the Bald (born 823; reigned 840–877), what particularly upset him was the memory of all that he had accomplished for his young kinsman:

> For you know well, if you discern reason, that you offer no sacrifice of a good work to God for just as long as you quarrel with the love of your neighbours, and much less indeed [do you offer sacrifice] if you quarrel with my affection, I who received you kindly to be fostered, I who with sweet affection fostered you as an orphan, I who tonsured you as a clerk, I who taught you in your letters myself and by whomsoever I could [afford], I who promoted you through each grade of ordination to the rank of the episcopate, I who obtained for you the intimate acquaintance [*familiaritatem*] and the sweetness of the affection of the lord our king.[37]

Hincmar the elder had done everything for his nephew that an episcopal uncle could do: fostering, tonsure, education, ordination and obtaining familiarity with the ruler, through whom patronage could be secured. His task had begun very early in his nephew's life; elsewhere, he says that the church of Rheims had taken in the young Hincmar "as I might say" from his cradle and had changed and washed young Hincmar's "cloths of infancy" (which presumably means nappies).[38] This is probably hyperbole, but not necessarily by very much; ecclesiastical careers in the Middle Ages began in childhood, with first tonsure often, as here, preceding the start of education in letters.

Hincmar was not alone. Historians have noticed many examples of bishops, and other members of the clergy, advancing the careers of their young nephews, especially those destined for the church, but there has until recently been curiously little attempt to put the examples together and look for patterns.[39] Examination of charter material, especially post-obit grants, makes it possible to see that in many churches there was an elaborate uncle–nephew dynastic succession system.[40] Uncles were generally important; uncles who remained laymen could be figures of power in the lives of their young nephews and nieces, so clerical uncles were not exceptional, but nonetheless there were services that they alone could provide because of their position in the church, and Hincmar's complaint lists these – fostering or *nutritio* within an ecclesiastical context; tonsure; education; ordination; assistance with patronage. In what follows, I will examine each of them in turn.

The episcopal career path

Biographical and canon law sources suggest that there had been two types of ecclesiastical career path in the fourth and fifth centuries.[41] Following the first path, clergy would start young, as boys, and work their way slowly through the grades of ordination, arriving at the priesthood at 30 or later. The total number of grades of ordination was not absolutely fixed at this point, but popes were already urging that ordination should follow a sequence, with appropriate time spent in each grade.[42] On the second path, adult laymen, often after prominent careers in the world, would become clerics in mid-life; quite often, high-ranking laymen might be elected bishop (for example, Sidonius Apollinaris as bishop of Clermont, ca. 470–85) and then have to work through all the grades of ordination within a year before their actual consecration as bishop.[43] By 600, the first type of progression had become normal for bishops. In the family of Gregory, bishop of Tours (573–94), we can see that this was how he himself had made his career, whereas in earlier generations we find examples of both sorts of advancement.[44] Examples of adult laymen being elected bishop in mid-life are much rarer after 600: Audoenus of Rouen and Eligius of Noyon were both consecrated in 641 after a year of being trained up through the canonical grades, but more often, accounts of Merovingian bishops, where they survive, show the gradualist approach.[45] And the main reason for the change was probably to do with schooling: by the sixth century, churches were becoming active in providing schooling, even at elementary level (where schools accepted boys irrespective of their future careers). Beyond that level, schools associated with bishops restricted themselves to teaching young clerics, but only a select few, while monastic schools probably concentrated on young monks.[46] In the cases of Audoenus and Eligius, we do not know about their early education, because it is not mentioned in their *Lives*. Audoenus must have received an education, since although he entered the king's military service, he became the king's referendary (the official at the Merovingian court in charge of producing royal charters); Eligius would have had time for elementary schooling in boyhood, before his apprenticeship to Abbo the goldsmith and mint-master, but we can only speculate on this.[47] They marked the end of the line, however; later bishops, where we have details, had become clerics or monks in childhood or at least in their teens. Adult entry into a clerical career with no schooling was hard work and was attempted only by a few: Saint Guthlac (674–714) had to undergo a two-year crash course at Repton at the age of 24 in order to provide himself with the necessary education to become a hermit, and there seems to have been no question of him becoming a bishop.[48]

The gradualist approach also made the question of celibacy more acute. Celibacy seems to have begun to be a real issue in the Western church in the later fourth century, as masses began to be celebrated on a daily rather than a weekly basis.[49] Weekly celebration had presumably meant abstaining from sexual intercourse one night in seven; daily celebration necessitated complete abstinence, at least in theory. In canon law, it was acceptable for married men to seek ordination provided that they agreed to give up sexual intercourse with their wives (in practice, they and their wives would be encouraged to live separately, preferably with their wives being encouraged to become nuns), but officially it was not possible to be ordained deacon or priest and then get married.[50] Some authorities insisted that this applied to subdeacons too, but this was not generally agreed upon until the eleventh century.[51] At all events, boys and young men who became clerics early knew that they could get married while still in minor orders but would find it easier to progress in the clerical grades if they remained single. Probably the chance of becoming a bishop was the principal inducement for encouraging clergy to remain celibate, that is, among those clerics who had a hope of rising that far – those with the right family background, a reasonable level of education and, vitally, the right contacts at court. The number of clerics hoping that they might possibly become bishop would be considerably greater than the number who actually achieved that rank. In addition, it might well have appeared a good thing to many aristocratic parents to encourage celibacy among some of their offspring, because this would simplify the problem of dividing up the family inheritance among ever-increasing groups of descendants and would also put members of the family in positions where they could help relatives in the next generation.[52] As Godding notes, the silence of Merovingian church councils from the later sixth century onwards on the subject of clerical continence suggests that celibacy was not disputed.[53] There were, however, areas of Europe where this was not the case: Britain and Ireland, Brittany and, in the tenth and eleventh centuries, also Normandy were much more relaxed; we will consider them later.

At all events, the most powerful groups within the church had accepted celibacy a long time before the Gregorian Reform. This was the movement, spearheaded by the papacy from the middle of the eleventh century, that demanded an end to marriage for priests and to lay involvement in appointments to ecclesiastical offices, and while it has been credited with marking a sharp caesura in attitudes towards clerical marriage, the picture is slightly more nuanced.[54] Abstinence from marriage for clergy with hopes, however faint, of becoming bishop was the framework within which clerical uncle–nephew relationships flourished.

Ecclesiastical uncles and nephews

Terminology for family relationships in medieval Latin can be slippery, so some discussion of vocabulary is necessary before we can identify ecclesiastical uncles and nephews. The term *nepos* is especially tricky; although "nephew" is one of its meanings, it can also mean "grandson", and Thietmar (bishop of Merseburg 1009–18) used it in his *Chronicle* to mean both "nephew" and "cousin".[55] *Sororius* (sister's son) and *fratruelis* (brother's son), however, are more likely to refer to nephews but can sometimes be used of cousins. Terms meaning "uncle" refer only to uncles, but here there can be some ambiguity, since *avunculus*, technically the mother's brother, was used promiscuously for either sort of uncle. However, *patruus* is used specifically for the father's brother, and sources quite often go to some pains to specify whether the relationship was maternal or paternal.

Among uncles who were laymen, those on the father's side of the family would be more powerful as guardians and would have greater rights. It is noticeable, for example, that Thietmar's *patrui*, his father's brothers (laymen), figure prominently in his life; even when Thietmar tried to obtain the provostship of Walbeck, on the grounds that it was his inheritance from his mother, it was his paternal uncle, Liuthar, Count of the Nordmark, who controlled appointment to this office. In 1002, Liuthar made his nephew pay a large sum to the cleric to whom he had sold the provostship.[56] By contrast, clerical uncle–nephew relationships seem to have operated with equal force regardless of whether the kinship was on the sister's side or the brother's. Indeed, it is possible that in clerical circles, the sister's brother may have had a special role, perhaps as the provider of extra inheritance or extra career-advancing pull, for those sister's sons intended for the church. Since the term *avunculus* was used fairly loosely, we have to look out for specific references to sisters, but they certainly occur. In the ninth century, Bishop Liudger of Münster's four clerical nephews, all future bishops, were the sons of his sisters, as Altfrid (one of the nephews in question, and an eventual successor of Liudger) is careful to point out, though without naming names.[57] Hincmar of Laon was the son of the older Hincmar's sister.[58] Uodalrich of Augsburg (923–73) took great care over the upbringing and career of his sister's son (*filio sororis suae*) Adalbero, who he hoped would succeed him.[59] Imad (1051–76), eventual successor of Meinwerk (1009–36) as bishop of Paderborn, is described as the latter's *sororius*, his sister's son, in the twelfth-century *Vita Meinwerci*, and although the *Vita* is too late to be necessarily reliable on this point, the fact that it stresses this relationship suggests that this is what its audience would have expected.[60] Brihtheah, bishop of Worcester 1033–8, was the sister's son (*filius sororis*) of Archbishop Wulfstan of York (1002–23), who had been bishop of Worcester (1002–16).[61] And mother's kin were important from early on: Gregory of Tours' elder brother Peter was entrusted to his maternal uncle Tetricus, bishop of Langres (539/40–72), whereas Gregory's clerical training was largely carried out at Clermont, where his father's brother Gallus had been bishop 525–51.[62] But there are plenty of references to bishops caring for brothers' sons too. Onomastic evidence suggests that the Bavarian uncle and nephew who were bishops of Auxerre in the later ninth century, Angelelm (812–29) and Heribald (d. perhaps 857), were probably linked on the father's side, because Heribald's father was Antelm and Angelelm's father was Obtelm.[63] Byrhtferth, in his *Vita Oswaldi*, describes Archbishop Oda of Canterbury as the *patruus* of Oswald (later bishop of Worcester and also archbishop of York).[64] Bishop Thierry (or Dietrich) I of Metz (965–84) educated his young nephew (*fratruelis*, brother's son) Everard.[65] The family trees constructed by Michel Parisse for various Lotharingian families show how the numerous Adalberos who were bishops of Metz and neighbouring sees in the tenth and eleventh centuries were connected in the paternal line. The two bishops and one bishop-elect of Metz, uncle (929–62), nephew

(984–1005) and great-nephew (elected 1005), belonged to the Luxemburger family (the dukes of Lotharingia); Archbishop Adalbero of Rheims (969–89) was a nephew (brother's son) of the first Adalbero, bishop of Metz (929–62); and Adalbero, bishop of Verdun (984–988/9), was the son of the archbishop's brother Godfrey, count of Verdun.[66]

Parents often began to plan for their children's futures while they were in their cradles. Naming patterns are striking here; although obviously only a minority of bishops' nephews were named after them, the number of clerical nephews who were namesakes of their uncles (and who often became bishops themselves) is noticeable: Hildigrim (d. 827) and Hildigrim (d. 886), brother and nephew of Bishop Liudger of Münster and both bishops themselves, of Châlons and Halberstadt respectively;[67] Hincmar and Hincmar; the three Salomos (great-uncle, uncle and nephew) who were bishops of Constance in the ninth and early tenth centuries;[68] the three Adalberos (great-uncle, uncle and nephew) who were bishops (the last one only bishop-elect) of Metz in the tenth and early eleventh centuries; Thierry, bishop of Verdun (1046–89), and his nephew Thierry the *primicerius* (head of the cathedral chapter) of Verdun;[69] Adalbert I and Adalbert II, both archbishops of Mainz in the first half of the twelfth century;[70] and, also in the first half of the twelfth century, John of Lisieux and John of Sées.[71] Although information about baptismal sponsorship is lacking in these cases, we know from other instances that parents could choose, as baptismal sponsors, clerics who could promote the futures of their children,[72] and it is possible that some of the namesake nephews were also godsons of their uncles.

Fosterage (*nutritio*)

When they were quite young, boys intended for a clerical career would be handed over (the verb used is usually *tradere*) to a senior cleric, often a kinsman and very often an uncle. This event, often termed *traditio*, "handing over", or *commendatio*, "commendation", is often described in lives of bishops as occurring after weaning. For aristocratic boys, weaning probably often occurred late, but even so mentioning weaning may be a poetic way of saying that infancy had ended. The handing-over ceremony marked the beginning of a process of fosterage (*nutritio*), and the terms *nutrire* (to nourish, to foster), *nutritor* (foster-father) and *nutritus* (foster-son) occur frequently in accounts of the upbringing of boys of good birth, for example in Hincmar's description of his nephew and in the account of how Uodalrich of Augsburg brought up his nephew Adalbero.[73] The foster-fathers might become very fond of their charges; a verse epitaph notes the "paternal affection" with which Bishop Thierry I of Metz had undertaken the education of his young nephew Everard "from his cradle"; on the young Everard's death in 978, the bishop had to organise his funeral.[74] Until about the ninth century in Francia and the tenth century in England, there was some overlap with royal fosterage, though the latter did not start until a boy's early teens, leaving time earlier in boyhood for some clerical training.[75] From the sixth century to the ninth century, and to some extent beyond, boys of very high birth were normally fostered by kings in their teenage years, irrespective of whether they were heading for a secular or an ecclesiastical career.[76] This was the case with Aldric, later bishop of Le Mans, nourished by Charles the Great and Louis the Pious; and Herifrid, later bishop of Auxerre, 887–909, brought up at the court of Charles the Bald. Both had previously been supervised by bishops, in Herifrid's case his kinsman Bishop Walter of Orléans.[77] In Anglo-Saxon England, royal fosterage of clerics continued even later, down to the mid-tenth century.[78] But royal fosterage, however useful socially, was disruptive to education, and bishops doubtless preferred their young charges, including their nephews, to remain in a stable environment where they could be sure of getting on with their studies. By the later eleventh century, *nutritio* was beginning to come to an end, particularly in France (it died more slowly in Germany); educational patterns were becoming looser as young clerics moved in search of different schools. The extent of the mobility can doubtless be exaggerated, but the fact that it could happen was decisive. Even so, the ending of *nutritio* did not stop episcopal uncles from taking a strong interest in the careers of their nephews; they continued to do this, as far as education and preferment were concerned, but in a more informal way.

Education

Uncles did not necessarily undertake the job of teaching their nephews themselves. In the case of bishops, direct involvement would have been difficult, though many of them were keen to ensure the education of their clerics.[79] However, they were well-placed to supervise it, usually in their own cathedral schools, but occasionally in another church in their lordship[80] or by paying to send their charges to school elsewhere. Gregory of Tours' uncle, Gallus, bishop of Clermont, took charge of him when his father died;[81] in the seventh century, Dido, bishop of Poitiers (ca. 628–67), ensured that his nephew Leudegar (bishop of Autun ca. 662–76) received a good education;[82] in the tenth century, Archbishop Oda of Canterbury (942–58) employed a Frankish tutor, Frithegod (Fredegaud) to teach his nephew Oswald;[83] in the early twelfth century, Archbishop Adalbert I of Mainz (1111–37) sent his young nephew (1138–41) to finish his education in Rheims, Paris and Montpellier.[84] Bishops who were their nephews' *nutritores* would also have the task of supervising their nephews' ordination, which would involve them in conducting examinations of the candidates' knowledge, at least for the higher grades (the archdeacon would examine the lower grades). As bishops, they would also be able to have their nephews installed as cathedral canons, which might happen on entry in childhood, though in these cases the status of the young canons might be confirmed more formally when they were ordained subdeacon, which usually marked the start of full adulthood for clerics. For example, at the age of 19, Thietmar was still under the authority of the *scholasticus* of Magdeburg cathedral, meaning that he had not yet become a subdeacon.[85] Most dignities (especially provostships) were also in the episcopal gift, so nephews might also count on getting one or more of those.

Help with career advancement

The support bishops gave to their nephews went well beyond education and first preferment. Although they were not supposed to arrange for their own succession, this was of course not unknown. The number of bishops who were succeeded by their nephews (not always immediately – sometimes there was another candidate in between) is striking. In the seventh century, for example, we find Agilbert, driven out of the see of Dorchester in 660, refusing to return but instead persuading the king of Wessex to accept his nephew Leuthere as bishop of Winchester (670–6).[86] Angilramn, successor of Bishop Chrodegang of Metz in the eighth century, may have been the latter's nephew;[87] Liudger, the first bishop of Münster, was succeeded by his brother and then by two of his nephews;[88] Angelelm was succeeded by Heribald at Auxerre 828 or 829;[89] Arnold, bishop of Toul (872–94), was the nephew of his immediate successor Arnulf (847–72);[90] the successor of Bernard, bishop of Verdun, 870–9 was his sister's son Dado (880–923);[91] the Salomos occupied the see of Constance for most of the period 838–920 (Salomo I was particularly instrumental in helping the career of his great-nephew Salomo III);[92] Poppo I (941–61) was succeeded by Poppo II (961–84) of Würzburg, and later, in the same diocese, we find the uncle and nephew Meinhard (1085–8) and Erlung (1106–21);[93] Lietbert (1051–76) was succeeded by his nephew Gerard II (1076–92) at Cambrai in 1076.[94] This is a scattering of examples only; there are more.[95] The failed succession attempts are also of interest. Uodalric spent time persuading Otto I and his fellow bishops to promote Adalpero after his death and had some success;[96] unfortunately for him, Adalpero died just ahead of him (24 April 973), apparently as the result of a faulty blood-letting.[97] Otto, *vicedominus* of Bremen, "gloried in" his uncle Archbishop Adaldag of Hamburg-Bremen (937–88) and hoped to succeed him, but Libentius (Liawizo) became archbishop instead (988–1013); on his deathbed, Libentius tried to promote Otto's case, but without success.[98] Royal wishes were almost always stronger than those of a dying bishop, but the succession of many nephews suggests that rulers, especially in Germany, paid some attention to the ambitions of the families of bishops.

Equally of interest are the instances of uncle and nephew bishops holding different sees. Here we can guess (in some cases we know) that the uncles helped bring their nephews to the notice of rulers and other influential forces; more importantly, perhaps, they would have helped provide them with the ecclesiastical training and social polish that made them acceptable. Hincmar introduced his nephew to Charles the Bald. The Salomo family did not only supply bishops for Constance but also bishops of Freising (883–906) and Chur (920–49; both called Waldo, also an uncle–nephew pair);[99] Geoffrey, bishop of Auxerre (1052–76) was nephew of Hugh I, bishop of Nevers (1016–69), and uncle of Hugh II, also bishop of Nevers (1074–96);[100] the counts of Saarbrücken supplied bishops for Worms (Winither, bishop-elect 1085–8), Mainz (Adalbert I and Adalbert II) and Speyer (Bruno, 1107–23) in three different generations across the late eleventh and early twelfth centuries.[101] Again, this is just a tiny scattering of examples.

A contrast: Father–son relationships in the church

To provide a point of comparison for our uncle–nephew pairings, it might be useful to look at a rather different society in which uncle–nephew links were less strong: England in the period before ca. 1100. It does not provide a complete contrast with the Frankish successor-states because there was some effort to keep the episcopate celibate. This was not wholly successful: Bishop Ælfsige of Winchester (951–9) had a son who became a powerful thegn;[102] Bishop Ealdhun of Durham (990–1018) had a daughter and used her marriages to create political connections for himself in the north of England;[103] Stigand, pluralistically bishop of Winchester (1043–70) and archbishop of Canterbury (1052–70), had a son, and so did his brother Æthelmaer, bishop of Elmham (1047–70).[104] However, on the whole, there is little evidence for episcopal marriage; moreover, from the mid-tenth century onwards, there were always some bishops who had been monks. Slightly lower down the scale, however, there is extensive evidence for clerical marriage among the wealthier clergy – royal clerics, clerics controlling minster churches and members of cathedral communities.[105] It is likely that many of these positions were hereditary throughout the final two centuries of Anglo-Saxon England; certainly, when some of them were recorded in sources of the eleventh and twelfth centuries, they were treated as such. Hereditary succession continued for at least one generation following the Norman Conquest, because many incoming Norman clerics were used to a similar system in their homeland. The chapter of St Paul's Cathedral, London, contained numerous Anglo-Saxon and Norman clerical dynasties in the late eleventh and early twelfth centuries.[106]

Clerical fathers, therefore, had a big role to play in their sons' training; outside patronage, especially from kings, was vital, but fathers may have helped their sons acquire this too, by introducing them to rulers.[107] In the case of Dunstan, archbishop of Canterbury (959–88), it is likely that his father was a clerk with royal connections, based in Winchester, either at the Old Minster (Winchester Cathedral) or the New Minster, a royal collegiate church until 964, when it was converted into a monastery.[108] Dunstan's contemporary, Æthelwold, bishop of Winchester (963–84), who was responsible for converting Old Minster and New Minster into Benedictine communities, was born in Winchester, possibly also into a clerical family.[109] Clerical uncles might also be important, as Archbishop Oda was in the case of his nephew Oswald; other clerical kinsmen were also useful (Cynesige, bishop of Lichfield 949–963/4, was a kinsman (*consanguineus*) of Dunstan) but less vital.[110] It is noteworthy that whereas the earliest *Life of Dunstan* says that his parents helped him to enter Glastonbury in his adolescence,[111] Adalard of Ghent says that Dunstan entered the household of his uncle Athelm (Æthelhelm, archbishop of Canterbury 923/5–926) and was helped by him. Adalard was probably trying to fit Dunstan into what he saw as the uncle–nephew succession he would have been more familiar with, and he probably created the relationship between Dunstan and Athelm (not attested earlier) to link Dunstan with his future see.[112] Family relationships were as important in Anglo-Saxon England as they were in the Frankish successor states, but they operated in a different way: clerics married each other's daughters or sisters, creating a more tightly-meshed clerical community, which, although forming an elite, was not closely linked with the high aristocracy. Very few bishops can be shown to be the sons of ealdormen.[113]

Conclusion

Although in canon law, it was always theoretically possible for married men to seek ordination in western Europe in the Middle Ages, provided that they and their wives agreed to separate and to lead celibate lives, this practice had in much of western Christendom been sidelined by recruiting boys into the clergy and then discouraging them from marriage. Although the observance of clerical celibacy in western Europe in the earlier Middle Ages was uneven, to say the least, it was usually observed by bishops. In Francia and its successor states, those clerics who had any hope of becoming bishops were encouraged to remain celibate not only by the churches to which they belonged but also by their relatives. Families benefited enormously from having kinsmen who were bishops because of the patronage the latter could exercise as major landholders, as powerful political figures and within the church itself.[114] Clerical kinsmen who failed to become bishops (the vast majority) also had their uses, though on a much smaller scale. Among the useful actions bishops could perform, perhaps the one most appreciated by their kinsmen was the upbringing of selected members of the next generation, those of their nephews who were handed over by their parents to become clerics. Although all members of the clergy could undertake this duty, bishops were best-placed to do it well, because they had authority over cathedral schools and could insist on their nephews being accepted into them, and furthermore they had the best opportunities to introduce their nephews to kings. Child entry into the clergy and the need for celibate bishops encouraged clerical uncles to act as foster-fathers and was one of the factors encouraging cathedrals and other major churches to develop good schools. It could often lead to nephews succeeding their uncles in office, though more often pressure from rival families or a wish on the part of rulers to favour close supporters would prevent this. Weaker support from rulers for clerical celibacy (as in Anglo-Saxon England, for example) could allow father–son clerical dynasties to flourish; this could co-exist with a largely celibate episcopate because the clergy who produced sons would not necessarily seek further advancement and probably often remained in minor orders. Although bishops continued to support clerical nephews throughout the Middle Ages, the end of the eleventh century marks a turning point, since the fosterage system faded away and more informal patterns of support became the norm.

Notes

1 Many of the quoted sources have been edited in various series of the Monumenta Germaniae Historica (abbreviated as MGH). Further abbreviations of the MGH-series can be found online at www.dmgh.de, together with the digitalised editions (open access).
2 Robert Muth, "Kastration," in *Reallexikon für Antike und Christentum*, ed. Franz-Joseph Dölger et al. (Stuttgart: Hiersemann, 2004) 20:285–342, esp. 325–326.
3 From early on, canon law was opposed to the ordination of slaves, but ordaining slaves freed by their masters was permitted: Robert Godding, *Prêtres en Gaule mérovingienne* (Brussels: Société des. Bollandistes, 2001), 85–90. On the noble origins of many bishops, see footnote 22 below.
4 Cf. James T. Palmer, *Anglo-Saxons in a Frankish World, 690–900* (Turnhout: Brepols, 2009), 59–76, and Rachel Stone, "Spiritual heirs and families: episcopal relatives in early medieval Francia," in this volume.
5 Godding, *Prêtres en Gaule mérovingienne*, 110–154; see also Stone, this volume.
6 For modern re-examination of these roles, see especially Timothy Reuter, "Ein Europa der Bischöfe: Das Zeitalter Burchards von Worms," in *Bischof Burchard von Worms 1000–1025*, ed. Wilfried Hartmann, Quellen und Abhandlungen zur mittelrheinische Geschichte 100 (Mainz: Gesellschaft für mittelrheinische Kirchengeschichte, 2000), 1–28. This article has been translated into English as "A Europe of Bishops: The Age of Wulfstan of York and Burchard of Worms," in *Patterns of Episcopal Power: Bishops in Tenth and Eleventh Century Western Europe*, ed. Ludger Körntgen and Dominik Waßenhoven, Prinz-Albert-Forschungen 6 (Berlin: De Gruyter, 2011), 17–38. See also Stephan Patzold, *Episcopus: Wissen über Bischöfe im Frankenreich des späten 8. bis frühen 10. Jahrhunderts*, Mittelalter-Forschungen 25 (Ostfildern: Thorbecke, 2008); John S. Ott and Anna Trumbore Jones, eds., *The Bishop Reformed: Studies in Episcopal Power and Culture in the Central Middle Ages* (Aldershot: Ashgate, 2007); Maureen C. Miller, *Clothing the Clergy: Virtue and Power in Medieval Europe, c. 800–1200* (Ithaca, NY: Cornell University Press, 2014).
7 On dioceses as territorial spaces in the Middle Ages, see Florian Mazel, *L'espace du diocèse: Genèse d'un territoire dans l'Occident médiéval (Ve-XIIIe siècle)* (Rennes: Presses universitaires de Rennes, 2008).
8 The emergence of the *episkopos* as the leading figure in each local church largely occurred in the second century: Wayne A. Meeks, "Social and Ecclesial Life of the Earliest Christians," in *Origins to Constantine*, vol. 1 of *The Cambridge History of Christianity*, ed. Margaret M. Mitchell and Frances M. Young (Cambridge: Cambridge University Press, 2006), 145–173, and particularly 153–154; Stuart

George Hall, "Institutions in the Pre-Constantinian *Ecclesia*," ibid., 415–433, especially 417–421. In general see Claudia Rapp, *Holy Bishops in Late Antiquity: The Nature of Christian Leadership in an Age of Transition* (Berkeley: University of California Press, 2005).

9 Raymond van Dam, "Bishops and Society," in *Constantine to c. 600*, vol. 2 of *The Cambridge History of Christianity*, ed. Augustine Casiday and Frederick W. Norris (Cambridge: Cambridge University Press, 2007), 343–366, especially 344–357.

10 Pierre Fourneret, "Diocèse," in *Dictionnaire de théologie catholique*, ed. Alfred Vacant, Joseph-Eugène Mangenot and Émile Amann (Paris: Letouzey et Ané, 1930–1950), 4:1362–1363.

11 Judith Herrin, *The Formation of Christendom* (Oxford: Princeton University Press, 1987), 103–106.

12 Carine van Rhijn, *Shepherds of the Lord: Priests and Episcopal Statutes in the Carolingian Period*, Cultural Encounters in Late Antiquity and the Middle Ages 6 (Turnhout: Brepols, 2007), 175–176, 179–180; Richard Fletcher, "An *Epistola Formata* from León," *Bulletin of the Institute of Historical Research* 45 (1972): 122–128.

13 Janet L. Nelson, "Law and its Applications," in *Early Medieval Christianities c.600-c.1100*, vol. 3 of *The Cambridge History of Christianity*, ed. Thomas F. X. Noble and Julia M. H. Smith (Cambridge: Cambridge University Press, 2008), 299–326.

14 On church councils, see Hall, "Institutions in the Pre-Constantinian *Ecclesia*," 428–433; Mark Edwards, "Synods and Councils", in *Origins to Constantine*, vol. 1 of *The Cambridge History of Christianity*, 367–385; Herrin, *Formation of Christendom*, 98–101; Wilfried Hartmann, *Die Synoden der Karolingerzeit im Frankenreich und Italien* (Paderborn: Ferdinand Schöningh, 1989); Catherine Cubitt, *Anglo-Saxon Church Councils c. 650-c. 850* (London: Leicester University Press, 1995).

15 Rosamond McKitterick, *Charlemagne: The Formation of a European Identity* (Cambridge: Cambridge University Press, 2008), 299–301; Veronica Ortenberg, "Archbishop Sigeric's Journey to Rome in 990," *Anglo-Saxon England* 11 (1990): 197–246.

16 Wilfried Hartmann, *Kirche und Kirchenrecht um 900: Die Bedeutung der spätkarolingischen Zeit für Tradition und Innovation im kirchlichen Recht* (Hanover: MGH, 2008), 78–80; Martina Stratmann, *Hinkmar von Reims als Verwalter von Bistum und Kirchenprovinz*, Quellen und Forschungen zum Recht im Mittelalter 6 (Sigmaringen: Thorbecke, 1991), 35–38; Rhijn, *Shepherds of the Lord*, 24–33.

17 Franz Pototschnig, "Priester," in *Lexikon des Mittelalters* (Munich: Artemis, 1995), 7:204.

18 On pre-Constantinian ordination, see Pierre van Beneden, *Aux origines d'une terminologie sacramentelle: Ordo, ordinare, ordinatio dans la littérature chrétienne avant 313*, Spicilegium Sacrum Lovaniens, Études et Documents 38 (Leuven: Spicilegium Sacrum Lovaniense, 1974), 93–139, and Bruno Kleinheyer, *Die Priesterweihe im römischen Ritus: Eine liturgiehistorische Studie*, Trierer Theologische Studien 12 (Trier: Paulinus, 1962), 12–25, 63–74; see also William Hugh Clifford Frend, *The Rise of Christianity* (London: Fortress Press, 1984), 404–406; Rapp, *Holy Bishops*, 98; for consecration of churches, see Susan Wood, *The Proprietary Church in the Medieval West* (Oxford: Oxford University Press, 2006), 12–14; for confirmation, see L. Hödl and J. Neumann, "Firmung," in *Lexikon des Mittelalters* (Munich: Artemis, 1989), 4:490–493.

19 Janet L. Nelson, "Carolingian Royal Ritual," in *Rituals of Royalty: Power and Ceremonial in Traditional Societies*, ed. David Cannadine and Simon Price (Cambridge: Cambridge University Press, 1987), 137–180.

20 Ernest Vykoukal, "Les examens du clergé paroissial à l'époque carolingienne," *Revue d'histoire ecclésiastique* 14 (1913): 81–96.

21 See, for example, Godefroid Kurth, *Notger de Liège et la civilisation au Xe siècle* (Paris: Picard, 1905), 1:130–169; 251–331; Michael Brandt and Arne Eggebrecht, ed., *Bernward von Hildesheim und das Zeitalter der Ottonen: Katalog der Ausstellung*, 2 vols, (Hildesheim: Bernward, 1993); Michel Sot, *Gesta episcoporum, gesta abbatum*, Typologie des sources du Moyen Age occidental 37 (Turnhout: Brepols, 1981), 22–23.

22 The position of bishops was "considerable" by ca. 450: Chris Wickham, *Framing the Early Middle Ages: Europe and the Mediterranean, 400–800* (Oxford: Oxford University Press, 2005), 159.

23 Raymond van Dam, "Merovingian Gaul and the Frankish Conquests," in *The New Cambridge Medieval History 1: c.500-c.700*, ed. Paul Fouracre (Cambridge: Cambridge of University Press, 2005), 214–222; Paul Fouracre, "Francia in the Seventh Century," ibid., 383–384; Georg Scheibelreiter, *Der Bischof in merowingischer Zeit* (Vienna: Böhlau, 1983), 172–180; Martin Heinzelmann, "Bischof und Herrschaft vom spätantiken Gallien bis zu den karolingischen Hausmeiern. Die institutionellen Grundlagen," in *Herrschaft und Kirche: Beiträge zur Entstehung und Wirkungsweise episkopaler und monastischer Organisationsformen*, ed. Friedrich Prinz (Stuttgart: Hiersemann, 1988): 23–82, esp. 37–54, 68–73.

24 Cf. Edward Roberts, "Flodoard, the Will of St Remigius and the See of Reims in the Tenth Century," *Early Medieval Europe* 22 (2014): 204; Nicholas Brooks, *The Early History of the Church of Canterbury* (Leicester: Leicester University Press, 1984), 100–107, 114–117, 129–149, 175–206.

25 E.g. Bishop Arn of Würzburg, *The Annals of Fulda*, trans. and ed. Timothy Reuter (Manchester: Manchester University Press, 1992), 95 (s. a. 884); *Reginonis abbatis Prumiensis chronicon cum continuatione Treverensi*, ed. Friedrich Kurze, MGH SS rer. Germ 50 (Hanover: Hahn, 1890), 140 (s. a. 892); for a translation of Regino, see *History and Politics in Late Carolingian and Ottonian Europe: the Chronicle of Regino of Prüm and Adalbert of Magdeburg*, trans. Simon MacLean (Manchester: Manchester University Press, 2009), 215.

26 Janet L. Nelson, "Literacy in Carolingian Government," in *The Uses of Literacy in Early Medieval Europe*, ed. Rosamond McKitterick (Cambridge: Cambridge University Press, 1990), 286–289; on the copying of Carolingian capitularies, see Rosamond McKitterick, *Charlemagne*, 232, and literature cited. On Wulfstan the Homilist, archbishop of York, who drafted laws for Æthelred the Unready and Cnut in early eleventh-century England, see Patrick Wormald, "Archbishop Wulfstan: Eleventh-Century State-Builder," in *Wulfstan, Archbishop of York*, ed. Matthew Townend (Turnhout: Brepols, 2004), 9–27.

27 McKitterick, *Charlemagne*, 259–260.

28 Richard Sharpe, "The Use of Writs in the Eleventh Century," *Anglo-Saxon England* 32 (2003): 251–252; Julia Barrow, "Wulfstan and Worcester: Bishop and Clergy in the Early Eleventh Century," in Townend, ed., *Wulfstan, Archbishop of York*, 143–144.

29 Reinhold Kaiser, *Bischofsherrschaft zwischen Königtum und Fürstenmacht: Studien zur bischöflichen Stadtherrschaft im westfränkisch-französischen Reich im frühen und hohen Mittelalter*, Pariser Historische Studien 17 (Bonn: Röhrscheid, 1981); Olivier Guyotjeannin, *Episcopus et comes: Affirmation et déclin de la seigneurie épiscopale au nord du royaume de France (Beauvais-Noyon, Xe – début XIIIe siècle)* (Geneva and Paris: Librairie Droz, 1987), esp. 3–66; Geneviève Bührer-Thierry, *Évêques et pouvoir dans le royaume de Germanie: Les Églises de Bavière et de Souabe, 876–973* (Paris: Picard, 1997), 206–224.

30 For Burchard of Worms' Hofrecht, see Lorenz Weinrich, ed., *Quellen zur deutschen Verfassungs-, Wirtschafts- und Sozialgeschichte bis 1250* (Darmstadt: Wissenschaftliche Buchgesellschaft, 1977), 88–105, and for discussion see Knut Schulz, "Das Wormser Hofrecht Bischof Burchards," in Hartmann, ed., *Bischof Burchard von Worms*, 251–278.

31 Reuter, "A Europe of Bishops," 23 (this model works best for Germany, somewhat less well for France and less well again for England).

32 For royal control over the appointment of bishops in the Île de France and northern Burgundy, see Marcel Pacaut, *Louis VII et les elections épiscopales dans le royaume de France* (Paris: Librairie Philosophique J. Vrin, 1957), 63–82; W. M. Newman, *Le domaine royal sous les premiers Capétiens (987–1180)* (Paris: Librairie du Recueil Sirey, 1937), 67–69, 216–224; Jörg Peltzer, *Canon Law, Careers and Conquest: Episcopal Elections in Normandy and Greater Anjou, c. 1140–c. 1230* (Cambridge: Cambridge University Press, 2008), 238–252. For the appointment of bishops in England see Catherine Cubitt, "Bishops and Succession Crises in Tenth- and Eleventh-Century England," in Körntgen and Waßenhoven, eds., *Patterns of Episcopal Power*, 124–125; Everett U. Crosby, *The King's Bishops: The Politics of Patronage in England and Normandy 1066–1216* (New York and Basingstoke: Palgrave Macmillan, 2013). For Germany, see n. 34.

33 Aristocrats in Gaul (but not Italy) began to be interested in becoming bishops from the mid-fifth century: S. Barnish, "Transformation and Survival in the Western Senatorial Aristocracy, c. A.D. 400–700," *Papers of the British School at Rome* 66 (1988): 138. However, even in Gaul, many bishops came from lower social ranks: Steffen Patzold, "Zur Sozialstruktur des Episkopats und zur Ausbildung bischöflicher Herrschaft in Gallien zwischen Spätantike und Frühmittelalter," in *Völker, Reiche und Namen im frühen Mittelalter*, ed. Matthias Becher and Stefanie Dick (Munich: Wilhelm Fink, 2010): 121–140, esp. 138. On Frankish aristocratic families in general from the seventh century onwards, see Régine Le Jan, *Famille et pouvoir dans le monde franc (VIIe-Xe siècle)* (Paris: Publications de la Sorbonne, 1995); Julia M. H. Smith, *Europe after Rome: A New Cultural History 500–1000* (Oxford: Oxford University Press, 2005), 115–147; Rachel Stone, *Morality and Masculinity in the Carolingian Empire* (Cambridge: Cambridge University Press, 2012), 247–310.

34 Patzold, *Episcopus*, 27–30 and literature cited; Steffen Patzold, "L'épiscopat du haute Moyen Âge du point de vue de la médiévistique allemande," *Cahiers de civilisation médiévale Xe-XIIe siècles* 48 (2005): 341–358; Herbert Zielinski, *Der Reichsepiskopat in spätottonischer und salischer Zeit (1002–1125)* (Stuttgart: Steiner Franz, 1984), 1:19–66; Constance B. Bouchard, *Sword, Miter, and Cloister: Nobility and the Church in Burgundy, 980–1198* (Ithaca, NY: Cornell University Press, 1987), 65–86 (noting that episcopal recruitment in Burgundy shifted from the higher to the lower nobility after ca. 1100); Bernard Guillemain, "Les origines des évêques en France aux XIe et XIIe siècles," in *Le istituzioni ecclesiastiche della "Societas Christiana" dei secoli XI–XII: Papato, cardinalato ed episcopato*, Miscellanea del Centro di studi medioevali 7 (Milano: Pubblicazioni dell'Università Cattolica del Sacro Cuore, 1974): 374–402.

35 Zielinski, *Der Reichsepiskopat*, esp. 187–198; note also Joseph Fleckenstein, *Die Hofkapelle der deutschen Könige*, Schriften der MGH 16, 1/2 (Stuttgart: Hiersemann, 1959–1966), 2:175–176; for comment on historiography, see Patzold, *Épiscopat du haut Moyen Âge,* 344–348.

36 Julia Barrow, *The Clergy in the Medieval World: Secular Clerics, their Families and Careers in North-Western Europe* (Cambridge: Cambridge University Press, 2015), chap. 4, nn. 141–142.

37 Rudolf Schieffer, ed., *Die Streitschriften Hinkmars von Reims und Hinkmars von Laon 869–871*, MGH Concilia 4, Suppl. 2 (Hanover: Hahn, 2003), 303, lines 12–18. Hincmar the elder was archbishop of Rheims from 845 until 882 (for further details see Stone, this volume); Hincmar the younger was bishop of Laon from 858 until his deposition in 871.

38 Schieffer, *Streitschriften*, 195: "Remensis ecclesia ... ut ita dicam, cunabulis dulci benignitate nutrivit et pannis infantie eluit atque exuit".

39 Crosby, *The King's Bishops*, 51–58, notes but does not analyse the phenomenon.

40 Barrow, *Clergy in the Medieval World*, chapters 4 and 9 examine these succession patterns among cathedral canons.

41 Godding, *Prêtres en Gaule mérovingienne*, 32–49.

42 John St H. Gibaut, *The Cursus Honorum: A Study of the Origins and Evolution of Sequential Ordination* (Bern: P. Lang, 2000), 85–91; Julia Barrow, "Grades of Ordination and Clerical Careers, c. 900-c. 1200," in *Anglo-Norman Studies XXX, Proceedings of the Battle Conference 2007*, ed. Christopher P. Lewis (Woodbridge: Boydell Press, 2008), 41–61.

43 Jill Harries, *Sidonius Apollinaris and the Fall of Rome, AD 407–485* (Oxford: Clarendon Press, 1994), 169–179; see also Godding, *Prêtres en Gaule mérovingienne*, 32–35, 45.

44 Martin Heinzelmann, *Gregor von Tours (538–594): Zehn Bücher Geschichte. Historiographie und Gesellschaftskonzept im 6. Jahrhundert* (Darmstadt: Wissenschaftliche Buchgesellschaft, 1994), 12. Translated by Christopher Carroll as *Gregory of Tours: History and Society in the Sixth Century* (Cambridge: Cambridge University Press, 2001), 10, Fig. 1.

45 Godding, *Prêtres en Gaule mérovingienne*, 41–45.

46 Ibid., 55–67.

47 Bruno Krusch, ed., "Vita Eligii," in *Passiones vitaeque sanctorum aevi Merovingici*, MGH SS rer. Merov. 4 (Hanover and Leipzig: Hahn, 1902), 2:671; Bruno Krusch and Wilhelm Levison, eds., "Vita Audoini," in *Passiones vitaeque sanctorum aevi Merovingici*, MGH SS rer. Merov. 5 (Hanover and Leipzig: Hahn, 1910), 3:555.

48 Bertram Colgrave, ed. and trans., *Felix's Life of Saint Guthlac* (Cambridge: Cambridge University Press, 1956), 82 for Guthlac's entry into Repton, 84–87 for Felix's tonsure and training, 144–147 for his ordination as priest once he had become a hermit and 193 for the date of his death.

49 Raymund Kottje, "Das Aufkommen der täglichen Eucharistiefeier in der Westkirche und die Zölibatsforderung," *Zeitschrift für Kirchengeschichte* 82 (1971): 218–228.

50 Godding, *Prêtres*, 119.

51 Roger E. Reynolds, "The Subdiaconate as a Sacred and Superior Order," in Reynolds, *Clerics in the Early Middle Ages: Hierarchy and Image*, Variorum Collected Studies 669 (Aldershot: Ashgate, 1999), 9–15.

52 Similarly, Régine Le Jan notes (*Famille et pouvoir*, 306–310, 316–318) that Frankish aristocratic families were happy to accept the very stringent rules of the church against incestuous marriage (forbidding marriage between sixth cousins).

53 Godding, *Prêtres*, 131–135.

54 For some examples of authors seeing the Gregorian reform as marking a sharp caesura, see Dyan Elliott, *Fallen Bodies: Pollution, Sexuality and Demonology in the Middle Ages* (Philadelphia: University of Pennsylvania Press, 1999), 81–106; Robert I. Moore, *The First European Revolution, c. 970–1215* (Oxford: Blackwell, 2000), 10–11, 15–16, 62, 88; Maureen Miller, "Masculinity, Reform and Clerical Culture: Narratives of Episcopal Holiness in the Gregorian Era," *Church History* 72 (2003): 25–52; Henrietta Leyser, "Clerical Purity and the

Re-Ordered World," in *Christianity in Western Europe c. 1100-c.* 1500, vol. 4 of *The Cambridge History of Christianity,* ed. Miri Rubin and Walter Simons (Cambridge: Cambridge University Press, 2009), 11–21; Megan McLaughlin, *Sex, Gender, and Episcopal Authority in an Age of Reform, 1000–1122* (Cambridge: Cambridge University Press, 2010).

55 Robert Holtzmann, ed., *Die Chronik des Bischofs Thietmar von Merseburg*, MGH SS rer. Germ. N.S. 9 (Berlin: Weidmann, 1935), 156, 432, 434 (= Book 4, 21; 7, 27, 30) for *nepos* meaning nephew (lay nephews in each case), and (among several instances of cousins), 321, 356, 362, 370, 406, 410 (= Book 6, 38, 66, 67, 74, 81; 7, 7, 10–11: Thietmar's cousin Dietrich, who became bishop of Münster). Translated and annotated by David A. Warner, *Ottonian Germany: The Chronicon of Thietmar of Merseburg* (Manchester: Manchester University Press, 2001), 50, 341–343, 379.

56 Holtzmann, *Die Chronik des Bischofs Thietmar*, 328–331 (= Book 6, 44); Warner, *Ottonian Germany*, 268.

57 Wilhelm Diekamp, ed., *Vita Sancti Liudgeri auctore Altfrido* (Münster: Theissing, 1881), 11; see also p. xv.

58 Jean Devisse, *Hincmar, archevêque de Reims 845–882* (Geneva: Librairie Droz, 1975–1976), 2:1096–1097; Heinrich Schrörs, *Hinkmar, Erzbischof von Reims. Sein Leben und seine Schriften* (Freiburg im Breisgau: Herder, 1884), 10. On Hincmar the younger (born between 835 and 838; died 879), see Rolf Grosse, "Hinkmar, Bischof von Laon," in *Lexikon des Mittelalters* (Munich: Artemis, 1991), 5:29.

59 Gerhard von Augsburg, *Vita Sancti Uodalrici: Die älteste Lebensbeschreibung des heiligen Ulrich*, ed. and trans. Walter Berschin and Angelika Häse (Heidelberg: Winter, 1993), 246–262 (Book 1, 21–24); for further discussion, see Miller, *Masculinity, Reform and Clerical Culture,* 28–45.

60 Franz Tenckhoff, ed., *Vita Meinwerci episcopi Patherbrunnensis*, MGH SS rer. Germ. 59 (Hanover: Hahn, 1921), 6 (= cap. 2 on Meinwerk's siblings); 84 (= cap. 160 on Imad). Imad may not necessarily have been a son of one of Meinwerk's sisters but was almost certainly a relative, and he was educated at Paderborn: Gabriele Meier, *Die Bischöfe von Paderborn und ihr Bistum im Mittelalter*, Paderborner theologische Studien 17 (Paderborn: F. Schöningh, 1987), 10–11.

61 N. P. Brooks, "Introduction: How Do We Know about St Wulfstan?" in *St Wulfstan and his World*, ed. Julia S. Barrow and N. P. Brooks (Aldershot: Asghate, 2005), 20, citing Reginald R. Darlington and Patrick McGurk, ed. and trans. *The Chronicle of John of Worcester* (Oxford: Clarendon Press, 1995), 2:518.

62 Martin Heinzelmann, *Gregory of Tours*, 10–11, 30–31.

63 Michel Sot, Guy Lobrichon, and Monique Goullet, eds., *Les gestes des évêques d'Auxerre* (Paris: Les Belles Lettres, 2002–2009), 1:142–143, 148–149 (= capitula 35–36).

64 Byrhtferth of Ramsey, *The Lives of St Oswald and St Ecgwine*, ed. and trans. Michael Lapidge (Oxford: Oxford University Press, 2009), 8–11, 32–29, 54–57.

65 Sigebert of Gembloux, *Vita Deoderici episcopi Mettensis*, in *Annales, chronica et historiae aevi Carolini et Saxonici,* ed. Georg Heinrich Pertz, MGH SS 4 (Hanover: Hahn, 1841), 461–483, here 480 (= cap. 19). Everard bore the same name as Thierry's father, Eberhard of Hamaland.

66 Michel Parisse, *La noblesse lorraine XIe-XIIIe siècle* (Lille and Paris: Université Nancy-II, 1976), 2:844–847; see also John Nightingale, *Monasteries and their Patrons in the Gorze Reform, c.850–1000* (Oxford: Clarendon Press, 2001), 71–77, 276.

67 Diekamp, *Vita Sancti Liudgeri auctore Altfrido*, xi, xv, 38, 265.

68 Helmut Maurer, *Das Bistum Konstanz 2: Die Konstanzer Bischöfe vom Ende des 6. Jahrhunderts bis 1206*, Germania Sacra, Neue Folge 42, 1 (Berlin: De Gruyter, 2003), 67–78, 84–119; Joseph Riegel, "Bischof Salomo I. von Konstanz und seine Zeit," *Freiburger Diözesan-Archiv* 42 (1914): 111–188, at 128, 188; Bührer-Thierry, *Évêques et pouvoir*, 122–125, 171–172.

69 Laurence of Liège, *Gesta episcoporum virdunensium*, in *Annales et chronica aevi Salici. Vitae aevi Carolini et Saxonici*, ed. Georg Waitz, MGH SS 10 (Hanover: Hahn, 1852), 489–516, here 503.

70 Anselm of Havelberg, *Vita Adelberti Maguntini Archiepiscopi*, in *Monumenta Moguntina*, ed. Philipp Jaffé, Bibliotheca Rerum Germanicarum 3 (Berlin: Weidmann, 1866), 565–603, esp. 569–571 (on p. 571 the elder Adalbert is referred to as *patruus* and the younger as *nepos* and *patruelis*).

71 David Spear, *The Personnel of the Norman Cathedrals during the Ducal Period, 911–1204* (London: Institute of Historical Research, 2006), 170, 273.

72 E.g. Halinard of Sombernon (Archbishop of Lyon 1046–52, born probably ca. 990), committed to his godfather and probable kinsman, Bishop Walter of Autun: "Vita venerabilis Halinardi," in *Patrologia Latina* (Paris: Garnier frères et J.-P. Migne, 1880), 142:1337–1339). For the identification of Halinard's parents (Warner of Sombernon and Istisburgis) see François Grignard, "Conjectures sur la famille d'Halinard, abbé de Saint-Bénigne," *Bulletin d'histoire et d'archéologie religieuses du diocèse de Dijon* 2 (1884): 202–206.

73 On *nutritio*, see Barrow, *Clergy in the Medieval World*, chap. 5; for Hincmar, see footnote 36 above; for Uodalric, see footnote 58.

74 Sigebert of Gembloux, *Vita Deoderici episcopi Mettensis*, MGH SS 4, 479–480 (= Book 1, 19).

75 Barrow, *Clergy in the Medieval World*, chap. 5.

76 Le Jan, *Famille et pouvoir*, 342–343, and Matthew Innes, "'A Place of Discipline': Carolingian Courts and Aristocratic Youth," in *Court Culture in the Early Middle Ages*, ed. Catherine Cubitt (Turnhout: Brepols, 2003), 61–66.

77 Margarete Weidemann, ed., *Geschichte des Bistums Le Mans von der Spätantike bis zur Karolingerzeit: Actus pontificum cenomannis in urbe degentium und Gesta Aldrici*, Römisch-Germanisches Zentralmuseum Monographien 56, 1–3 (Mainz and Bonn: Römisch-Germanisches Zentralmuseum, 2002), 1:118–119: *Gesta Domni Aldrici*, capitula 1–2; Sot, Lobrichon and Goullet, eds., *Les gestes des évêques d'Auxerre*, 1:169.

78 Wulfstan of Winchester, *The Life of St Æthelwold*, ed. Michael Lapidge and Michael Winterbottom (Oxford: Oxford University Press, 1991), 10–12 (= cap. 7); Michael Winterbottom and Michael Lapidge, eds. and trans., *The Early Lives of St Dunstan* (Oxford: Oxford University Press, 2012), 18–22 (= B, *Vita Dunstani*, capitula 5–6); see Barrow, *Clergy in the Medieval World*, chap. 5.

79 For examples of bishops encouraging education, see Kurth, *Notger de Liège*, 251–99; Henry Mayr-Harting, *Church and Cosmos in Early Ottonian Germany: The View from Cologne* (Oxford: Oxford University Press, 2007), 59–63, 131–144; C. Stephen Jaeger, *The Envy of Angels: Cathedral Schools and Social Ideals in Medieval Europe, 950–1200* (Philadelphia: University of Pennsylvania Press, 1994), 44–77. Meinhard, later bishop of Würzburg 1085–8, taught his nephew Erlung while Meinhard was *scholasticus* and Erlung was a canon at Bamberg; Erlung became bishop of Würzburg 1106–21:Alfred Wendehorst, *Das Bistum Würzburg, 1:Die Bischofsreihe bis 1254*, Germania Sacra Neue Folge 1 (Berlin: De Gruyter, 1962), 117–19 and 126–32, esp. 126.

80 Archbishop Ebo of Rheims had his nephew Ebo educated not in his cathedral but in the abbey of Saint-Rémy in Rheims and made him abbot there: Flodoard von Reims, *Die Geschichte der Reimser Kirche*, ed. Martina Stratmann, MGH SS 36 (Hanover: Hahn, 1998), 244.

81 Heinzelmann, *Gregory of Tours*, 13. *Passiones vitaeque sanctorum aevi Merovingici*, MGH SS rer. Merov. 4 (Hanover and Leipzig: Hahn, 1902).
82 "Passio Leudegarii episcopi Augustodunensis," cap. 1, in *Passiones vitaeque sanctorum aevi merovingici*, Krusch and Levison, eds., 3:283. Translated in English in Paul Fouracre and Richard A. Gerberding, eds. *Late Merovingian France* (Manchester: Manchester University Press, 1996), 217. Dido was Leudegar's *avunculus*.
83 Michael Lapidge, "A Frankish Scholar in Tenth-Century England: Frithegod of Canterbury/ Fredegaud of Brioude," *Anglo-Saxon England* 17 (1988): 46–65.
84 Anselm of Havelberg, *Vita Adelberti*, 575–586.
85 Holtzmann, *Die Chronik Thietmars von Merseburg*, 158–161 (= Book 4, capitula 24–25); Warner, *Ottonian Germany*, 168–169.
86 Bede, *Ecclesiastical History of the English People*, ed. and trans. Bertram Colgrave and R. A. M. Mynors (Oxford: Clarendon Press, 1969), 236 (= Book 3, cap. 7).
87 M. A. Claussen, *The Reform of the Frankish Church: Chrodegang of Metz and the Regula Canonicorum in the Eighth Century* (Cambridge: Cambridge University Press, 2004), 22.
88 Diekamp, *Vita Sancti Liudgeri auctore Altfrido*, 38, 265.
89 Sot, Lobrichon and Goullet, eds., *Les gestes des évêques d'Auxerre*, 1:142–143, 148–149.
90 Georg Waitz, ed., *Gesta episcoporum Tullensium*, in *Chronica et gesta aevi Salici*, MGH SS 8 (Hanover: Hahn, 1848), 631–648, here 637–638 (cap. 27).
91 Georg Waitz, ed., *Gesta episcoporum Virdunensium*, *Annales, chronica et historiae aevi Carolini et Saxonici*, MGH SS 4 (Hanover: Hahn, 1841), 36–51, here 37 (an autobiographical fragment by Bishop Dado).
92 Maurer, *Das Bistum Konstanz* 2, 67–78, 84–119: Salomo I was bishop from 838/839 till 871; Salomo II from 875/876 till 889; Salomo III from 890 till 919/920.
93 Wendehorst, *Das Bistum Würzburg 1*, 59–67, 117–119 and 126–132.
94 *Gesta Episcoporum Cameracensium Continuatio*, ed. Ludwig Konrad Bethmann, in *Chronica et gesta aevi Salici*, MGH SS 7 (Hanover: Hahn, 1846), 393–525, here 497.
95 See, for example, Bouchard, *Sword, Miter and Cloister*, 296 (Letbald II and Walter, bishops of Mâcon, 993–1016 and 1031–1061 respectively), 320–322 (Gibuin and Gibuin, bishops of Châlons-sur-Marne in the late tenth century), 400 (Hugh I and Hugh II, bishops of Nevers 1016–69 and 1074–96, great-uncle and great-nephew). See also Stone, this volume.
96 Gerhard, *Vita Sancti Uodalrici*, ed. Berschin, 110–113 (= Book 1, cap. 3), 246–259 (= Book 1, capitula 21–23).
97 Ibid., 258–261 (= Book 1, cap. 24). For the bloodletting story, see *Herimanni Augiensis Chronicon*, ed. Georg Pertz, in *Annales et chronica aevi Salici*, MGH SS 5 (Hanover: Hahn, 1844), 67–133, here 116 (Hermann of Reichenau's Chronicle, s.a. 973).
98 *Magistri Adam Bremensis Gesta Hammaburgensis Ecclesiae Pontificum*, ed. Bernhard Schmeidler, MGH SS Rer. Germ. 2, 3rd ed. (Hanover and Leipzig: Hahn, 1917), 89–90 and n.; see also Thietmar VI, cap. 89 (p. 380 in Holtzmann; pp. 296–297 in Warner).
99 On Bishop Waldo of Freising, brother of Salomo III, see Josef Fleckenstein, *Grundlegung: Die karolingische Hofkapelle,* MGH Schriften, 16,1 (Stuttgart: Hiersemann, 1959), 190n, 192–194, 202; for Bishop Waldo of Chur see ibid., 216; Bührer-Thierry, *Évêques et pouvoir*, 171–172 (and see ibid., 172–173, for another tenth-century uncle–nephew pair, Archbishop Frederick of Salzburg and Bishop Pilgrim of Passau).

100 Bouchard, *Sword, Miter, and Cloister*, 388, 400.

101 Peter Acht, "Adalbert I., Erzbischof von Mainz," in *Neue Deutsche Biographie* (Berlin: Duncker & Humblot, 1953), 1:44; Hans-Werner Hermann, "Saarbrücken, Grafen v.," in *Neue Deutsche Biographie*, 22:318.

102 Dorothy Whitelock, ed. and trans., *Anglo-Saxon Wills* (Cambridge: Cambridge University Press, 1930), 16–17, no. 4, with notes, pp. 114–116; discussion by Linda Tollerton, *Wills and Will-Making in Anglo-Saxon England* (Woodbridge: Boydell & Brewer, 2011), 117–118, and Barrow, *The Clergy in the Medieval World*, chap. 4, n. 148.

103 Thomas Arnold, ed., *Symeonis Monachi Opera Omnia*, Rolls Series 75 (London: Cambridge University Press, 1882–1885), 1:216–217; for discussion, see Barrow, *Clergy in the Medieval World*, chap. 4, n. 140.

104 The evidence for Stigand's son Robert is discussed by Alexander R. Rumble, "From Winchester to Canterbury: Ælfheah and Stigand – Bishops, Archbishops and Victims," in *Leaders of the Anglo-Saxon Church from Bede to Stigand*, ed. Alexander R. Rumble (Woodbridge: Boydell & Brewer, 2012), 175; for Æthelmær and his son Sæman see ibid., and for his wife see *Domesday Book 33, Norfolk*, ed. Philippa Brown, 2 parts (Chichester: Phillimore, 1984), 1, 10.28, and comment by Frank Barlow, *The English Church 1000–1066*, 2nd ed. (London and New York: Longman, 1979), 78, n. 1.

105 For discussion, see Barrow, *Clergy in the Medieval World*, chap. 4; Julia Barrow, *Who served the Altar at Brixworth? Clergy in English Minsters c.800–c.1200* (28th Brixworth Lecture, Leicester, 2013), 5–7.

106 Christopher Brooke, *The Medieval Idea of Marriage* (Oxford: Clarendon Press, 1989), 84–89; Barrow, *Who Served the Altar?*, 6, n. 17.

107 Julia Barrow, "The Clergy in English Dioceses c. 900–c. 1066," in *Pastoral Care in Late Anglo-Saxon England*, ed. Francesca Tinti (Woodbridge: Boydell & Brewer, 2005), 20–21; Barrow, *Who Served the Altar*, 5–7.

108 Barrow, *Clergy in the Medieval World*, chap. 4, n. 144.

109 Wulfstan of Winchester, *Life of St Æthelwold*, ed. and trans. Michael Lapidge and Michael Winterbottom (Oxford: Clarendon Press, 1991), 3 (*Vita Æthelwoldi*, cap. 1).

110 For Oda, see n. 58 above; for Cynesige, see Winterbottom and Lapidge, *The Early Lives of St Dunstan*, 68–69.

111 Winterbottom and Lapidge, *The Early Lives of St Dunstan*, 17–21 (= cap. 5).

112 Ibid., 118.

113 Æthelnoth of Canterbury (archbishop 1020–1038) was the son of Æthelmær the Stout, probably identifiable with ealdorman Æthelmær (John of Worcester, *Chronicle*, 2:506–507) says Æthelnoth was the son of the *nobilis viri* Æthelmær; Simon Keynes, "Cnut's Earls," in *The Reign of Cnut: King of England, Denmark and Norway*, ed. Alexander R. Rumble (London: Cassell,1994), 43–88, at 67–68 argues for Æthelmaer the Stout being ealdorman; Byrhthelm, bishop of Winchester, was a royal kinsman and may also have been related to the ealdorman Byrhtnoth: Shashi Jayakumar, "Eadwig and Edgar: Politics, Propaganda, Faction," in *Edgar, King of the English 959–975: New Interpretations*, ed. Donald Scragg (Woodbridge: Boydell Press, 2008), 86–87, and see also Patrick Wormald, "The Strange Affair of the Selsey Bishopric, 953–963," in *Belief and Culture in the Middle Ages: Studies Presented to Henry Mayr-Harting*, ed. Richard Gameson and Henrietta Leyser (Oxford: Oxford University Press, 2001), 128–141.

114 For the wider political and social implications of this phenomenon, see Stone, this volume.

2 Guarding the harem, protecting the state

Eunuchs in a fourth/tenth-century Abbasid court

Nadia Maria El Cheikh

The death of the Abbasid caliph al-Muktafī in 295/908 led to the proclamation as caliph of his 13-year-old brother, Jaʿfar (d. 320/932), who took the name "al-Muqtadir" on ascending the throne. On account of Jaʿfar's youth, a handful of personalities at court acquired undue influence, most notably, his mother Shaghab, the chamberlain Sawsan and two eunuchs, Mu'nis al-Muẓaffar, leader of the Baghdad forces; and Ṣāfī, the chief of eunuchs. Such circumstances gave eunuchs the opportunity to play a significant role in the palace and in government, as the evidence reveals that they became trusted political advisers and powerful administrators of the caliph. They also appeared in important positions in the army and police. This chapter analyses the variety of roles that eunuchs assumed in the Abbasid establishment during the early fourth/tenth century. It starts with some comparative remarks on eunuchs in the Byzantine and Abbasid empires and then proceeds to outline the various functions that eunuchs had in the Abbasid state, notably that of guarding the Abbasid courtly harem. Their political influence will then be investigated by examining the careers of three eunuchs, each of whom played leading roles at the court of the Abbasid caliph al-Muqtadir. This chapter will also refer to the competition that ensued among the leading eunuchs.

Eunuchs in the Byzantine and Abbasid empires: Some comparative remarks

In order to pinpoint the specific features of the eunuch institution in the Abbasid state, it is instructive to contrast it with that of eunuchs in the Byzantine empire of roughly the same period, namely in the fourth/tenth century.[1] This is especially pertinent given that the most obvious source of influence for the eunuch institution in Islam is Byzantium.[2] The third/ninth-century prose writer and humanist al-Jāḥiẓ claims that every castration in the world had its origin in Byzantium: "The *Rūm,* together with the *Ṣaqāliba* (Slavs) are the only nations to practice castration, a most odious crime and a sign of their pitiless natures and corrupt hearts".[3] Judge ʿAbd al-Jabbār b. Aḥmad al-Hamadhānī (d. 415/1024) also points out that when Byzantines capture Muslims, they take the children, castrating many of the boys, a number of whom die as a result. They claim to have compassion and mercy, even though castration was not prescribed in canonical law or the Torah.[4]

A major difference between the two cultures with regard to eunuchism is the fact that while in the Byzantine empire, eunuchs could be supplied from the native population, a factor that made them more integrated in Byzantine society, eunuchs in the Abbasid state were imported, castration being forbidden in Islamic law.[5] A total stranger, uprooted from his homeland and with no familial ties, the eunuch served his patron with particular devotion; it was a condition that facilitated relations of loyalty and trust. Existing outside of the dominant social values that promoted family, offspring and procreation, eunuchs in the Islamic context were ideally suited to be servants, agents and proxies for their masters.

One peculiarity of Byzantine eunuchs was the practice of voluntary castration for the sake of Christian ideals of celibacy and sanctity. There was a strong link, in Byzantium, between the practice of castration and the church, and many prominent tenth-century Byzantine churchmen were eunuchs.[6] The Byzantine custom of castrating children who were destined to be consecrated to the service of the church did not apply to the Abbasid Muslim context because no member of the Muslim religious establishment is required to be celibate. The centrality of marriage in Islam is in fact enunciated in the foundational Islamic texts. In the Quran, marriage appears in many verses as one of the most important human relationships,[7] and *ḥadīth* literature (the sayings of the prophet Muhammad) also includes many statements by the Prophet on the subject of marriage, one of which states: "If you are a Christian monk, then join them; if you are one of us, marriage is our *sunna*".[8] Marriage was thus considered the norm for all. The Prophet's own example established marriage as *sunna* (the generally approved practice introduced by the Prophet Muhammad, which includes not only *ḥadīth,* but also the Prophet's deeds and what he tacitly approved).

The nature of the Abbasid and Byzantine documentation regarding eunuchs is also different. Byzantinists benefit from surviving precedence lists, which provide a register of functionaries in the imperial administration, most importantly the *Kleterologion* produced by the court official Philotheos in AD 900, wherein a summary of titles reserved to eunuchs is provided. They are arranged in ascending order of prestige, the lowest being the holder of the washing bowl and the highest being the chief of the corps of eunuch household servants, who was responsible for financial, administrative and ceremonial matters.[9] Other than the titles, there were also clearly functional offices reserved to eunuchs, most notably the *papiai,* who acted as guardians of the doorway, controlling access to the imperial palace. Philotheos lists ten offices that were reserved for eunuchs, and all of them seem to convey the need for close physical proximity to the emperor and empress. However, as Nicholas Oikonomides notes, the rules prescribed for each duty are not clearly defined, and thus eunuchs could have other financial and juridical responsibilities, particularly in matters related to their administrative position or their rank at court.[10]

There are no such precedence lists for the Abbasid context. To complicate matters further, the very terms that refer to eunuchs in the Arabic sources in general are rather vague. In his study of eunuchs, David Ayalon argued that the term *khādim,* which in its original meaning signified servant, also meant eunuch and should in fact be regularly translated as the latter: "Of all the euphemisms of *khaṣī* (pl. *khiṣyān*) by far the commonest is *khādim* (pl. *khadam*, and, at a later period, *khuddām*), which, as everybody knows, originally meant 'servant'".[11] Following a challenge to this reading, Ayalon set out to prove his case by what he termed "a super-overkill". In so doing, he insisted that he had succeeded "in establishing beyond any reasonable doubt overwhelming predominance of that last meaning".[12] In addition to the term *khādim*, which seems indeed to have been used to refer to eunuchs, *ustādh* and *fatā* were also terms used in sources to refer to eunuchs. Certain eunuchs carried the title *al-ḥuramī*, that is, a person who is connected with the harem; *al-ḥuramī* was also taken to mean chief eunuch and keeper of the harem.[13]

Overview of the functions of eunuchs in the Abbasid state

Well-defined roles for eunuchs do not seem to have existed in the Abbasid caliphate, where there was little distinction between eunuchs serving the court and harem on the one hand, and those eunuchs who fulfilled administrative and military duties on the other. The same eunuchs could have connections and influence in both camps. Their occupations included those of acting as arresters, beaters and torturers, as well as those who handled money and salaries and guarded property.[14] They were also emissaries who carried vital messages at critical junctures and were sometimes entrusted with the caliphal insignia. The eunuch Ṣāfī al-Ḥuramī, for instance, removed the caliphal seal from the dying al-Muktafī (289–295/902–908) and handed it over to the vizier al-ʿAbbās b. al-Ḥasan (d. 296/908).[15]

One major development that ensured eunuchs would become increasingly important was the establishment of ceremonial practices at the Abbasid court. This was a gradual development, linked to architectural advances, specifically a new conceptual palatine model that was entirely innovative in Islam.[16] In this new schema, the caliphs were increasingly hidden from the public, and their appearances became theatrically staged events. By the time of al-Muqtadir's rule, the caliph's residence at Dār al-Khilāfa had expanded into a vast complex of palaces, public reception and banqueting halls, residential quarters, mosques, baths, pavilions, sports grounds, pleasure and vegetable gardens, orchards and the like. It occupied an area nearly a square mile in extent, surrounded by a wall with many gates. The caliphal residence came to resemble a small city, within which the caliph and his throne room were located, reached by a long route via gates, courtyards, gardens, antechambers and reception halls.[17] What is most distinct about this phase is the growing separation of the rulers and their subjects, because the administrative and political centres were physically separated from the Muslim urban centres.[18] By the fourth/tenth century, the caliphs had almost completed the process of isolating themselves from the general populace through architectural and ceremonial means. Eunuchs therefore became more influential due to this new style of rulership in which caliphs were private rather than public rulers, and it was thus more difficult to acquire access to them. One major consequence of the caliphs' remoteness was that potentially more power now lay in the hands of those who were mediators between the caliph and his subjects. Indeed, one could argue that eunuchs exploited the increasing secluded caliph, gaining power by controlling the distribution of favours, a consequence of their privileged proximity to the caliph. Connected with the isolation of the caliph was the use of very elaborate forms of ceremony and ritual in which eunuchs also played an important role.

An account of this role is given, for example, in the biographical encyclopaedia *Tārīkh Baghdād* (History of Baghdad) of al-Khaṭīb al-Baghdādī (d. 463/1071). Al-Khaṭīb al-Baghdādī, who was known as the "Ḥāfiẓ (memorizer) of the east" due to his knowledge of the Quran, was primarily interested in the transmission of *ḥadīth* and the reliability of its transmitters.[19] Therefore, he tended to include in his encyclopaedia the biographies of those scholars who were relevant for the science of *ḥadīth* transmission. For instance, in his description of the caliphal palace during the reign of al-Muqtadir, we read that during the visit of the Byzantine ambassadors to Baghdad in 917 "the order was given to conduct the ambassador about the palace which was staffed by eunuchs, chamberlains and black pages"[20].

One other factor that shaped the eunuch institution in Islam was the harem (*ḥarīm),* a word that derives from the root *ḥ*r*m*, meaning "scared", "inviolable", "forbidden". By implication, it was a space to which general access was forbidden or controlled.[21] The term *ḥarīm* is seldom used in the Abbasid sources, which refer instead to the caliph's *ḥuram*, his women. Thus, the reference is to a group of people rather than a particular building or physical location.[22] For example, when the sources describe the imprisonment of the vizier Ibn al-Furāt and the looting of his palace by order of the caliph al-Muqtadir, they do not use the term *ḥarīm* to refer to the women's quarters.[23] Others used different terms; for instance, the Iraqi historian and geographer al-Masʿūdī (d. 345/956) speaks of the *dār al-ḥuram*,[24] and the chronicler ʿArīb (b. Saʿd al-Qurṭubī, d. ca. 370/980), who composed the *Ṣilat ta'rīkh al-Ṭabarī*,[25] a continuation of the well-known history of al-Ṭabarī, uses the term *dūr* (plural of *dār*, dwelling). Miskawayh (d.421/1030), who worked at the Abbasid court as a secretary and a librarian and was both a philosopher and a historian, wrote in his book *Tajārib al-umam* (Experiences of the Nations) that Ibn al-Furāt's *ḥuram* were disgraced and his dwellings (*dūrahu*) pillaged.[26]

In any event, the harem signified the women's quarters in a household to which access was forbidden. The Muslim women's seclusion rendered the employment of eunuchs inevitable. Eunuchs acted as guardians of the harem but were also "neutral emissaries in a moral universe highly charged with sexual tension, a universe in which the forces of *fitna,* a word that signifies sexual temptation as well as political discord and civil strife, were seen as an omnipresent threat to the social and moral order".[27]

Connected to their roles within the harem was their appointment as leaders of the *ḥajj* (pilgrimage) caravan, because a considerable number of women, including women of the Abbasid court, performed this holy obligation. ʿArīb reports that in 312/924 the *ḥajj* caravans were attacked and that among those captured were "Māzij al-Khādim, the eunuch in charge of the imperial parasol, Fulful *al-fatā* and Naḥrīr, the *fatā* of the caliph's mother, who was the commander of the third caravan".[28]

A number of court eunuchs also held important military positions and led a number of military campaigns, but significantly, and again in contrast to the Byzantine context, we do not find in any sources the kind of rhetoric that questioned the eunuchs' military abilities.[29] Related to these military activities, eunuchs were frequently involved in exchanges of prisoners between the Byzantine and Abbasid states. Al-Masʿūdī refers to exchanges that were conducted by prominent eunuchs; for example, the exchange *(fidā')* of Mu'nis (in the month of Rabīʿ al-Thānī 305/ September 917) and the exchange of Mufliḥ (in the month of Rajab 313/September–October 925).[30]

Eunuchs thus acquired multiple roles as they managed to establish themselves in posts and positions of vital importance, allowing them to actively participate in the political life of the state. But concomitantly, their closeness to the caliphs rendered the eunuchs' position highly delicate and involved strict rules and regulations. The *Rusūm Dār al-Khilāfa* of Hilāl al-Ṣābiʾ (a secretary at the Abbasid court, d. 448/1056), a work that is mainly concerned with the protocol at the court and in official correspondence,[31] describes such formalities in advice he gave to the caliph's entourage, which would have included eunuchs:

> Beware of arguing with the sultan when he is angry or of urging him to leniency when he is obstinate .... Try to avoid him when you detect his wrath mounting. Wait to present your excuse ... until his anger is calmed ... guard against the temptation of speech. Let your answer about matters with risky consequences be more of a hint than a direct expression; more of the probable than of the definite. It is easier for you to say what you have not said than to retract what you have already uttered.[32]

The people in close proximity to the caliph had to meticulously weigh their gestures and expressions as well as each of their utterances. The precarious position in which they found themselves meant that at any moment in their "performance", something could happen to bring about their downfall.

Guarding the harem

Eunuchs were integral members of the Abbasid caliphal harem, which was populated by a very large and diverse community, including the caliph's mother, the wives of the caliph, his concubines, his children and his unmarried, widowed or divorced sisters and aunts. In addition, eunuchs also worked alongside harem stewardesses, the female servants who performed the housekeeping tasks of the harem, and female slaves. Eunuchs were placed in charge of guarding its members and taking care of some of their needs. Referring to the large numbers involved, Hilāl al-Ṣābiʾ states: "It is generally believed that in the days of al-Muqtadir bi-Allāh ... the residence contained 11,000 eunuchs (*khādim*) – 7,000 blacks and 4,000 white Slavs – 4,000 free and slave girls and thousands of chamber servants".[33]

The eunuchs' castration provided access to the harem, where they were entrusted with the task of protecting and serving the women and educating the children. They were permitted to move freely in all parts of the building or complex. Their duties embraced the whole compound of the court so that they served as intermediaries between their master and his wives, concubines and female relatives. These circumstances gave eunuchs direct access to the person of the ruler, whose living quarters were connected to the harem by an exclusive entrance used only by women and eunuchs.[34]

Al-Tanūkhī (d. 384/994), a judge and a secretary of the Abbasid empire, who worked for a while in the capital Baghdad, wrote in his compilation of anecdotes, the *Kitāb al-faraj baʿda al-shidda*, a story that highlights the roles that eunuchs played in the interior spaces of the palace of al-Muqtadir. He describes a merchant trying to sneak into the women's quarter with the aim of asking the caliph's mother for her permission to marry her stewardess (*qahramāna*). Al-Tanūkhī relates that during this perilous journey, the merchant had to pass through groups of eunuchs who guarded the doors of various apartments in the harem.[35] This unique anecdote is significant in emphasising how the court eunuchs are located at the heart of the caliphal harem, strictly monitoring access. The anecdote has a happy ending as the caliph's mother meets the merchant and accepts his marriage to her stewardess.

Access to royal women gave eunuchs further opportunities to influence men in high positions. Their association with the mother of caliph al-Muqtadir, Shaghab, was especially important due to her influence over her young son. A number of sources highlight the close relationship between the caliph and his mother. The historian Miskawayh (d. 420/1030) mentions "an apartment belonging to al-Sayyida [the caliph's mother], but frequently used by the caliph when he sat with her".[36] Mother and son seem to have visited one another regularly, and on one occasion when she appeared to ask for a special favour, his first words were "Oh Sittī [my Lady], this is the regular time for your visit".[37] Shaghab figures prominently in the chronicles of this period, likely due to her political influence and her financial contributions during her son's reign. The significant relationship between her and influential eunuchs is apparent from the outset of the young caliph's reign. During the plot aimed at replacing the untried young caliph with the older and more experienced Ibn al-Muʿtazz, she ordered that the eunuch Muʾnis, the loyal commander of the army, be brought back from Mecca. The intervention of Muʾnis on behalf of al-Muqtadir, coupled with the loyalty of the young caliph's palace retinue, would save his reign. [38]

The importance of eunuchs during the early fourth/tenth century was thus explicitly connected to the prominence of the harem and the influence of the caliph's mother and her harem stewardesses. Restricted as she was to the harem, Shaghab had to use eunuchs for all her transactions and dealings at court. One such instance concerned the education of her grandson. Abū Bakr al-Ṣūlī, appointed as the tutor of al-Muqtadir's son Abū l-ʿAbbās in 307/919–20, recalls a day when Abū l-ʿAbbās was reading the poetry of Bashār b. Burd (d. 168/783); alongside him was a number of philological and historical books. His grandmother's eunuchs arrived and interrupted his reading, upsetting him by taking away his treasured books. Al-Ṣūlī, who was also there, tried to calm the boy down by saying that his grandmother had been informed that he was reading "proscribed" books. A few hours later, however, the eunuchs returned the books. In their actions, the eunuchs were not only obeying Shaghab's directions but were also acting as her informers. Indeed, al-Ṣūlī goes on to relate that the eunuchs had reported to al-Muqtadir and his mother that he had been teaching the prince the names of the genital organs – this was in reference to a number of philological treatises, including the work entitled *Khalq al-insān*, by al-AṢmaʼī (d.213/828).[39]

Many of the roles assigned to eunuchs in the fourth/tenth century Abbasid court were deemed unmasculine tasks; these included acting as "masters of ceremonies", controlling access to the caliph, operating as doorkeepers and servants and dwelling in the company of women and children in the harem. It was precisely these unmasculine tasks, closely intertwined with their gender, that gave them precious access to the caliph, and it is their ensuing political clout that will be discussed next.

Protecting the state

The role that the eunuch Ṣāfī al-Ḥ uramī played in the early years of the reign of al-Muqtadir was pivotal. Present at the deathbed of caliph al-Muktafī, Ṣāfī was able to secretly escort al-Muqtadir to the palace and ensure his succession by obtaining for him the *bayʿa*, the oath of allegiance.[40] Ṣāfī's close proximity to the dying caliph, in his private chambers, which were restricted to eunuchs, guaranteed a significant influence in the matter of succession. This delicate and sensitive effort granted him power and influence throughout al-Muktafī's reign, and he also reappears in the sources at an important juncture in the early caliphate of al-Muqtadir.

Indeed, shortly after his accession, in 296/908, al-Muqtadir was deposed in favour of the Abbasid prince and poet Ibn al-Muʿtazz.[41] The *khawāṣṣ* of al-Muqtadir are singled out among those who refused to partake in this conspiracy. The chronicler Miskawayh (d.421/1030) states: "There were present [as part of the conspiracy] the commanders of the army, the heads of bureaux ... the judges and notables (*wujūh al-nās*), with the exception of Ibn al-Furāt and the *khawāṣṣ* of al-Muqtadir".[42] In the translation of this particular passage, David Samuel Margoliouth translates *khawāṣṣ* as "the persons attached to al-Muqtadir".[43] Such individuals like the eunuch Ṣāfī al-Ḥuramī resisted an attempt that, if successful, would have left them with no link to the caliphate. Eunuchs were personally bound to al-Muqtadir; defending him was necessary for their survival and in order to maintain their position of power. The caliph, in turn, expected from his protégés (*muṣṭanaʿ*) a lifelong commitment in return for the benefits and favour that they received.[44]

Ṣāfī showed his loyalty to al-Muqtadir repeatedly and was entrusted with a number of sensitive missions. One assignment involved him in a plot against the chamberlain Sawsan, whose power had become uncontrollable. ʿArīb relates that one day, when al-Muqtadir was entering the square together with Sawsan, Ṣāfī helped the caliph execute his plan by feigning sickness. Sawsan dismounted to assist him and at that very moment, armed men assaulted Sawsan, took him away and placed him in custody, shortly after which he died in prison.[45]

Al-Ṣūlī's obituary of Ṣāfī, who died in the year 298/910, sheds light on the power and sway that he had achieved: "Ṣāfī had been the master of the state affairs; he was responsible for the Caliph's residence". He adds that Ibn al-Furāt, the most important statesman of the reign, "never contradicted him".[46] Ṣāfī was, moreover, the governor of the Syrian frontier district (*al-thughūr al-shāmiyya*). Respect for Ṣāfī was such that the illustrious commanders of the army used to dismount for him. Concerning the wealth that Ṣāfī amassed, al-Ṣūlī reports: "I never saw as much money as in the residence of Qāsim, Ṣāfī's *ghulām* (slave boy)". After his death, "people claimed that in his possession were found precious stones, vessels, gold, silver, arms, expensive garments and furniture".[47] Ṣāfī al-Ḥuramī, therefore, was intimately linked to the protection and support of al-Muqtadir. His closeness and direct access to the caliph, and the latter's trust in him, provided Ṣāfī with opportunities to exercise influence and to accumulate wealth.

The possibilities and range of power that eunuchs attained at the court of al-Muqtadir is even more evident in the career of the black eunuch Mufliḥ, whose influence was intimately connected to his role as mediator. This role required him to carry messages to and from the caliph, and this is repeatedly stressed in the sources. One conspicuous episode concerns the vizier Ḥāmid who, following his dismissal, sought to have an audience with the caliph. The reliance on Mufliḥ was, however, inescapable, he "being the official who demanded admissions to al-Muqtadir when the latter was in his private apartments".[48] His power stemmed directly from his spatial access to the caliph in his private quarters. Indeed, Miskawayh states that "Mufliḥ was high in al-Muqtadir's favor, and constantly in attendance".[49] His meditation and intercessions were lucrative, for we know that Mufliḥ managed to accumulate much wealth, becoming the owner of vast estates.

Mu'nis, general commander of the armed forces, was also a central figure of power during this period. He restored al-Muqtadir to the throne following the failed coup by Ibn al-Muʿtazz and subsequently became all-powerful, having a say in the appointment of viziers and being increasingly in control of the government.[50] The eventful episodes in Mu'nis' military career are recounted by Hugh Kennedy in this volume, but what I would like to highlight here is an element connected to his role as an educator of the caliph's eldest son, Abū l-ʿAbbās. A common designation for eunuchs was that of *ustādh* (teacher, educator); indeed, it seems that their role as educators of the sons of rulers was a fairly common phenomenon. Al-Ṣūlī states that at some point in his education, Abū l-ʿAbbās was placed under the tutorship of Mu'nis.[51] We do not know what kind of tutorship Abū l-ʿAbbās received from Mu'nis, but the loyalty that they felt towards each other was obvious during the years to come. Upon the death of al-Muqtadir, Mu'nis came out clearly in favour of the succession of Abū l-ʿAbbās, asking that he be placed on the throne for "he is my nursling (*tarbiyatī*)".[52]

Competition among eunuchs

Eunuchs at the highest echelons of the Abbasid state were not members of a group that shared a sense of solidarity that precluded divisions and competition. The evidence, if anything, points to the contrary. Al-Ṣūlī states that Mu'nis was not present at the accession of al-Muqtadir, having been exiled to Mecca. Soon after his accession, al-Muqtadir brought him back and "delegated command to him, increased his station, and exalted his position".[53] The return of Mu'nis at this juncture was not accidental; it was tied up with the death of Ṣāfī al-Ḥuramī, who had always tried to keep Mu'nis far from the caliph. Ṣāfī used to slander him, perhaps seeing Mu'nis as a threat to his influence with al-Muqtadir. Ṣāfī, for instance, suggested that al-Muqtadir send Mu'nis to lead a *Ṣā'ifa* (a summer raid in the Byzantine frontier area) in order to keep him away from Baghdad. It was only when Ṣāfī died that Mu'nis became "master of the affair".[54]

Clearer evidence of competing interests between eunuchs, verging sometimes on the antagonistic, is found in a letter written by Mu'nis to the caliph in which he complained of the money and land wasted upon the eunuchs and women of the court and their participation in the administration. He demanded their dismissal and removal from the palace, with seizure of their possessions.[55] In his reply to Mu'nis, al-Muqtadir acknowledges the powerful eunuchs – and women – as fief-holders and points to the privileges they have. Reference is also made to their interference in the administration:

> Now what our friends propose in the matter of the eunuchs and women … so I am giving orders for the seizure of some of their fiefs, for the abolition of their privileges … and for the removal from the palace of all whom it is permissible to expel while those who remain shall not be permitted to interfere with my administration or counsels.[56]

Mufliḥ's resistance to Mu'nis is understandable in light of the latter's effort to curb the influence and wealth of the court eunuchs. The caliph's belief in Mufliḥ's loyalty and devotion was absolute. In the end, it was Mufliḥ, together with the other courtiers who hated Mu'nis, who prevailed upon the caliph to confront Mu'nis.[57] The caliph was, however, killed during this confrontation.

Conclusion

Many of the roles and functions ascribed primarily to eunuchs involved them acting as mediators, moving in the liminal, in-between spaces. The eunuchs served as go-betweens in transactions between men and women of the court and between the court and the outside world. Eunuchs were involved in brokering and transmitting messages between people who were constrained by etiquette from meeting the caliph directly. Eunuchs acted as messengers because they could enter spaces that were forbidden to other men. This access gave them considerable influence, as reflected in the evidence that we have concerning the eunuchs Ṣāfī and Mufliḥ. Ṣāfī played an important role in installing the young al-Muqtadir on the throne, while Mufliḥ carried letters, demanded admission to the caliph and used his proximity to the caliph to influence appointments and other significant political matters. Proximity to the caliph and the favour this ensured was the crucial basis of the court eunuchs' power.

With the increasing importance of ceremony and seclusion from the public, eunuchs became power brokers, a situation rendered more advantageous still by the repeated removal of successive viziers, which would in turn increase competition among bureaucrats. The eunuchs schemed for or against particular bureaucrats by bringing information to the caliph that only they could deliver. The sustained influence that court eunuchs were able to bring to bear during the reign of al-Muqtadir is demonstrated by their occupation of an increasing number of high-ranking offices. Eunuchs also played at times a primary role in the military.

It was thanks to a subtle game of alliances and clashes between pressure groups that someone like Mu'nis managed to integrate himself more fully into the political system. Mu'nis placed himself at the centre of the Abbasid government, partly due to his condition as a member of the *khuddām* (pl. of *khādim*) or servants of the Abbasid state, which provided them with a specific legal status. His unique position inside the state apparatus was largely due to institutional mechanisms that allowed such social integration, namely, a system that is closely tied up with *walāʾ*, clientship. According to Roy Mottahedeh, the "slave soldier and his patron were bound together by the tie of *walāʾ*"; the slave soldier owed his training and privileged place in society to his patron, who in return received his gratitude.[58] Mohamed Meouak has put forward the hypothesis that Mu'nis was, in some respects, the inalienable property of the Abbasid state, and that as such he was part of the Abbasid institutional "patrimoine".[59]

At once servants, guardians and officers within the military, the eunuchs had a cultural fluidity that helps explain the possibilities that were open for such liminal figures. Due to this specific position at court, eunuchs like Muʾnis, Ṣāfī and Mufliḥ could and did act in particularly flexible and often unexpected ways. Their influence could extend beyond a specific reign since, as already mentioned, they played a role in the upbringing of the sons of caliphs. Their political sway and consequent success has to be explained with reference to their distinctive gender and to the fact that they were cut off from their original environment with no family or tribe, a situation that made them safer, dependent and loyal.

One of the main conclusions of this chapter is that we should not think of eunuchs as a coherent group but rather think of the system as one of gradation, implicating not only race, that is, black versus white, but also the actual position that eunuchs found themselves in, whether military or domestic. These snapshots, incidents and moments merely provide fragmented information on eunuchs in the early fourth/tenth century Abbasid court. Studies of the eunuch institution in other periods are necessary if we are to understand the development of their roles, networks and influence and the general social and cultural placement of eunuchs in the Abbasid period.

Notes

1 Some of the material in this chapter appeared in my earlier article entitled "Servants at the Gate: Eunuchs at the Court of al-Muqtadir," *The Journal of the Social and Economic History of the Orient* 48, no. 2 (2005): 234–252.

2 David Ayalon, *Eunuchs, Caliphs and Sultans: A Study in Power Relationships* (Jerusalem: Magnes Press, Hebrew University, 1999), 104.

3 Abū 'Uthmān 'Amr b. Baḥr al-Jāḥiẓ, *Kitāb al-Ḥayawān*, ed. 'Abd al-Salām Hārūn (al-Qāhira: Muṣṭafā al-bābī al-ḥalabī, 1938–1945), 1:124. See also A. Cheikh Moussa, "Ǧāḥiẓ et les Eunuques ou la confusion du meme et de l'autre," *Arabica* 29, fasc. 2 (1982): 184–214.

4 'Abd al-Jabbār b. Aḥmad al-Hamadhānī, *Tathbīt dalā'il al-nubuwwa*, ed. 'Abd al-Karīm 'Uthmān (Beirut: Dār al-'Arabiyya, 1967), 1:168. This "polemical" attitude towards Christians and Jews is also justified by the specific source, which is a description of the proofs of Muḥammad's prophethood against those who refute it.

5 Shaun Tougher, *The Eunuch in Byzantine History and Society* (New York: Routledge, 2008), 61–67. Cristina de la Puente, "Sin linaje, sin alcurnia, sin hogar: eunucos en el Andalus en época Omeya," in *Identidades Marginales*, ed. Cristina de la Puente (Madrid: Consejo Superior de Investigaciones Cientificas, 2003), 147–193.

6 Steven Runciman, *The Emperor Romanus Lecapenus and His Reign: A Study of Tenth-Century Byzantium* (Cambridge: Cambridge University Press, 1963), 30.

7 Judith Tucker, *Women, Family and Gender in Islamic Law* (Cambridge: Cambridge University Press, 2008), 38.

8 This prophetic tradition, which is present in compilations of *ḥadīths,* was incorporated in popular *adab* anthologies such as Ibn Qutayba, *'Uyūn al-akhbār*, ed. Yūsuf 'Alī Ṭawīl (Beirut: Dār al-Kutub al-'Ilmiyya, 1985), 4:19; and Ibn 'Abd Rabbih, *al-'Iqd al-farīd*, ed. Aḥmad Amīn et al. (Cairo: Maṭba'at Lajnat al-Ta'līf wa-l-Tarjama wa-l-Nashr, 1940–1949), 6:82.

9 Nicolas Oikonomides, *Les listes de préséance byzantines des IXe et Xe siècles* (Paris: Centre de recherches de logique, 1972), 124–134.

10 Ibid., 302.

11 Ayalon, *Eunuchs, Caliphs and Sultans,* 6.

12 Ibid., 6–7; Moussa, "Ǧāḥiẓ et les eunuques"; A. Cheikh Moussa, "De la synonymie dans les sources arabes anciennes: Le cas de Ḫādim et de Ḫaṣiyy." *Arabica* 32, fasc. 3 (1985): 309–322; David Ayalon, "On the Term Khādim in the Sense of 'Eunuch' in the Early Muslim Sources," *Arabica* 32, fasc. 3 (1985): 289–308.

13 Harold Bowen, *The Life and times of 'Alī Ibn 'Īsā, "the Good Vizier"* (Cambridge: Cambridge University Press, 1928), 88.

14 Ayalon, *Eunuchs, Caliphs and Sultans,* 197, and Appendix H.

15 'Arīb b. Sa'd al- Qurṭubī, *Ṣilat ta'rīkh al-Ṭabarī,* ed. Michael Jan De Goeje (Leiden: Brill, 1897),19.

16 Richard Ettinghausen and Oleg Grabar, *The Art and Architecture of Islam: 650–1250* (Harmondsworth and New York: Penguin Books, 1987), 86.

17 Guy Le Strange, *Baghdad during the Abbasid Caliphate: From Contemporary Arabic and Persian Sources* (Oxford: Clarendon Press, 1900), 262.

18 Jere L. Bacharach, "Administrative Complexes, Palaces and Citadels: Changes in the Loci of Medieval Muslim Rule," in *The Ottoman City and Its Parts: Urban Structure and Social Order*, ed. Irene A. Bierman, Rifaat Abou-el-Haj and Donald Preziosi (New Rochelle: A. D. Caratzas, 1991), 111–128.

19 See *Encyclopaedia of Islam*, 2nd ed., s. v. "al- K̲h̲aṭīb al- Bag̲h̲dādī".

20 al-Khaṭīb al-Baghdādī, *Tārīkh Baghdād wa-dhuyūluhu*, ed. Muṣṭafā 'Abd al-Qādir 'Aṭā (Beirut: Dār al-Kutub al-'Ilmiyya, 1997), 1:116. For the role of eunuchs in Fatimid ceremonials, see Paula Sanders, *Ritual, Politics, and the City in Fatimid Cairo* (Albany, NY: State University of New York Press, 1994) and the chapter of Serena Tolino in this volume.

21 Shaun Marmon, *Eunuchs and Sacred Boundaries in Islamic Society* (New York and Oxford: Oxford University Press, 1995), 6.

22 Hugh Kennedy, *The Court of the Caliphs: The Rise and Fall of Islam's Greatest Dynasty* (London: Weidenfeld & Nicolson, 2004), 160.

23 Maaike van Berkel et al., *Crisis and Continuity in the Abbasid Court: Formal and Informal Politics in the Reign of al-Muqtadir (295–320/908–32)* (Leiden: Brill, 2013), 166.

24 'Alī b. al-Ḥusayn al-Mas'ūdī, *Murūj al-dhahab wa ma'ādin al-jawhar*, ed. Charles Pellat (Beirut: Université libanaise, 1965–1979), 4:248 and 5:215.

25 'Arīb, *Ṣilat*, 29.

26 Abū 'Alī Ahmad Miskawayh, *Tajārib al-umam,* ed. Henry Frederick Amedroz. 3 vols. Miṣr 1914–1919 (repr. Baghdad in the 1960s); ed. and trans. in English

David Samuel Margoliouth, *The Eclipse of the Abbasid Caliphate* (London: Blackwell, 1920–1921). The book consists of seven volumes; the first three volumes are the Arabic text, which has been mostly edited by H. F. Amedroz, who died in 1917, before the book was completed. The translation (vols. 4–6) was completed by D. S. Margoliouth, who also composed a preface and an index (vol. 7). For reasons of clarity, the title *Tajārib* is used when referring to the Arabic text, the title *Eclipse* when referring to the English translation.

27 Marmon, *Eunuchs and Sacred Boundaries*, 5–6. See also the collection of articles in *Harem Histories: Envisioning Places and Living Spaces*, ed. Marilyn Booth (Durham and London: Duke University Press, 2010).

28 ʿArīb, *Ṣilat*, 119. ʿArīb uses *fatā* for eunuch; the term was common in Spain, where he was from.

29 Kathryn M. Ringrose, *The Perfect Servant: Eunuchs and the Social Construction of Gender in Byzantium* (Chicago: Chicago University Press, 2003), 141.

30 ʻAlī b. al-Ḥusayn al-Masʿūdī, *al-Tanbīh wa-l-Ishrāf*, ed. Michael Jan de Goeje (Leiden: Brill, 1894), 193.

31 *Encyclopaedia of Islam*, 2nd ed., s. v. "Hilāl b. al-Muḥassin b. Ibrāhīm al- Ṣābiʾ".

32 Hilāl al-Ṣābiʾ, *Rusūm dār al-Khilāfa*, ed. Mīkhāʾīl ʻAwwād (Baghdad: Maṭbaʻat al-ʻĀnī, 1964), 87–88; trans. Elie Adib Salem, *Rusūm dār al-Khilāfa: The Rules and Regulations of the Abbasid Court* (Beirut: American University of Beirut, 1977), 70–71.

33 al-Ṣābiʾ, *Rusūm*, 8.

34 David Ayalon, "On the Eunuchs in Islam," *Jerusalem Studies in Arabic and Islam* 1 (1979): 67–124. Reprinted in David Ayalon, *Outsiders in the Lands of Islam: Mamluks, Mongols and Eunuchs* (London: Variorum Reprints, 1988).

35 al-Tanūkhī, *Kitāb al-faraj baʿda al-shidda*, ed. ʻAbbūd al-Shāljī (Beirut: Dār Ṣādir, 1978), 4:362–368.

36 Miskawayh, *Tajārib*, 1:118.

37 Abū l-Faraj b. al-Jawzī, *al-Muntaẓam fī ta'rīkh al-mulūk wa-l-umam*, ed. Muḥammad ʻAbd al-Qādir ʻAṭā and Muṣṭafá ʻAbd al-Qādir ʻAṭā (Beirut: Dār al-Kutub al-ʻIlmiyya, 1992), 13:71.

38 Nadia Maria El Cheikh, "Gender and Politics in the Harem of al-Muqtadir," in *Gender in the Early Medieval World: East and West, 300–900*, ed. Leslie Brubaker and Julia M. H. Smith (Cambridge: Cambridge University Press, 2004), 147–161.

39 Abū Bakr al-Ṣūlī, *Akhbar al-Rāḍī bi-llāh wa l-Muttaqī li-llāh*, ed. J. Heyworth Dunne (Cairo: Maṭbaʻat al-Ṣāwī, 1935), 25–26.

40 Miskawayh, *Tajārib*, 1:3–4.

41 Ibn al-Muʻtazz was the grandson of the caliph al-Mutawakkil, who was killed in 247/861; his father was deposed and Ibn al-Muʻtazz had to give up his political aspirations, like many other Abbasid princes. See *Encyclopaedia of Islam*, 2nd ed., s. v. "Ibn al-Muʻtazz".

42 Miskawayh, *Eclipse*, 4: 5; *Tajārib* 1:5.

43 Miskawayh, *Eclipse*, 4:5.

44 Roy Mottahedeh, *Loyalty and Leadership in an Early Islamic Society* (Princeton: Princeton University Press, 1980), 82–93.

45 ʿArīb, *Ṣilat*, 29–30.

46 Ibid.

47 Abū Bakr al-Ṣūlī, *Ma lam yunshar min awrāq al-Ṣūlī: akhbār al-sanawāt 295–315 H.*, ed. Hilāl Nājī (Beirut: ʻĀlam al-Kutub, 2000), 73–74.

48 Miskawayh, *Tajārib*, 1:96, *Eclipse*, 4:107–108; al-Ṣūlī, *Ma lam yunshar*, 131.

49 Miskawayh, *Tajārib*, 1:87; *Eclipse*, 4:96.

50 Van Berkel, *Crisis and Continuity in the Abbasid Court*, 111–141.

51 al-Ṣūlī, *Akhbār al-Rāḍī*, 5. For the role of eunuchs as educators, see also Hamid Haji, "A Distinguished Slav Eunuch of the Early Fatimid Period: al-Ustadh Jawdhar," in *Fortresses of the Intellect: Ismaili and Other Islamic Studies in Honour of Farhad Daftary*, ed. Omar Ali-de-Unzaga (London and New York: I. B. Tauris, 2011), 261–273.
52 Miskawayh, *Eclipse*, 1:272. For the Arabic, see Miskawayh, *Tajārib*, 1:241–242.
53 al-Ṣūlī, *Ma lam yunshar*, 30–31.
54 Ibid., 59.
55 Miskawayh, *Tajārib*, 1:189; *Eclipse,* 4: 213.
56 Miskawayh, *Eclipse*, 4:213–214. For the Arabic text, see Miskawayh, *Tajārib,* 1:189–190.
57 ʿArīb, *Ṣilat*, 165–166, 175.
58 Mottahedeh, *Loyalty and Leadership,* 84.
59 Mohamed Meouak, "De la périphérie au centre du pouvoir ʻabbaside. La carrière politique de Mu'nis al-Ḫādim al-fatā al-Muẓaffar," in *Identidades Marginales*, ed. Cristina de la Puente (Madrid: Consejo Superior de Investigaciones Cientificas, 2003), 195–214.

3 Muʾnis al-Muẓaffar

An exceptional eunuch

Hugh Kennedy

The emergence of eunuchs as a major political and social presence in Islamic courts is a development of the third/ninth century.[1] For the first two centuries of Muslim political life, they were almost unknown, and their role, if they had one, would have been marginal. Eunuchs were effectively unknown in the Hijaz at the time of the Prophet and the Rashidūn caliphs.[2] Perhaps more surprisingly, given the importance of eunuchs in the Byzantine imperial system, they do not seem to have played a significant role in the Umayyad court or in Umayyad political life from 41/661 to 132/750. Eunuchs first became an important presence in Islamic political life at the Abbasid court, especially from the beginning of the third/ninth century until the mid-fourth/tenth century; this followed the Būyids' seizure of power, which caused the Abbasid court to be much reduced in numbers and wealth and effectively restricted to a domestic role. The emergence of powerful eunuchs is closely related to two other changes in court life in the third/ninth century. The first was the gradual restriction of female members of the ruling dynasty to the caliphal palace.[3] In the first half century of Abbasid rule (132–193/750–809), the most prominent female members of the ruling dynasty had their own palaces and households, often in gardens along the banks of the Tigris, but by the third/ninth century, these had largely disappeared, and the women lived in the Dār al-Khilāfa, the high rambling palace on the east bank of the Tigris. The second change was the whole nature and design of palaces. Umayyad palaces, the ruins of a number of which survive, were modest in size, much like large Roman villas. They were sometimes exquisitely decorated but were centred on one or two courts or perhaps a bath house. The palaces of the mid-ninth century as we find them in Samarra were very much larger, enclosing vast numbers of chambers and gardens. They were like small towns in area and complexity, and there was no need for the inhabitants to emerge into the outside world.[4] Within these vast palaces, there were harem areas, strictly segregated from the rest of the complex and forbidden to male visitors. Both these developments put much more power into the hands of the gatekeepers of these new enclosed spaces, and these gatekeepers were often eunuchs because they alone could mediate between the caliphal household and the outside world.

Not all eunuchs, however, lived in this enclosed palace environment: Eunuchs might also serve in the Abbasid army. They were, however, exceptional. In this chapter, I shall examine the career of one military eunuch, Mu'nis, and show how it extends the paradigm of eunuch activity beyond the palace walls and the domestic sphere. It offers as well a very different image from the usual paradigm of the effeminate, devious, scheming and vicious eunuch that is so common in later Western stereotypes concerning eunuchs and their political influence.

This discussion of the biography and role of Mu'nis is essentially based on two sources. The first is the *Tajārib al-umam* (Experiences of the Nations) of Abū ʿAlī Miskawayh (d.421/1030),[5] whose narratives are the most important source we have for the politics of the period in general. The second is the *Ṣilat ta'rīkh al-Ṭabarī* (The Continuation of the History of al-Ṭabarī) by ʿArīb b. Saʿd (or Saʿīd) al-Qurṭubī (d. ca. 370/980),[6] who was more contemporary with the events of Mu'nis' life. ʿArīb work claims to be a continuation of al-Ṭabarī's *Ta'rīkh* and is similarly meticulous in its chronology and attention to detail. Although the author was writing in Cordoba and never seems to have visited the East, he was astonishingly well informed. These two sources give an extraordinarily rich and entertaining account of the period of Mu'nis' life.

As regards the *Tajārib al-umam*, Miskawayh was as much a philosopher as a historian, and his work is very concerned with the character of the major players and ethical issues of what makes good and bad political actors. In Miskawayh's writing, the personality of Mu'nis is developed as the perfect soldier, efficient and honest, working in partnership with that paragon of administrative virtue, the "good vizier". He also earned the respect of the mother of the caliph al-Muqtadir (d. 320/932), Shaghab, the most powerful figure in the palace and harem and a woman who exercised a huge influence over her young and ineffectual son until the day of his death. She is said to have described Mu'nis to her son as "your sword and the one you can rely on",[7] while his colleague, and occasional rival, the *ḥājib* (chamberlain) Naṣr al-Qushūrī described him as "the man who kept enemies at bay and defended the state".[8]

Mu'nis, known as Mu'nis al-Khādim (the eunuch)[9] but later, and more respectfully as al-Muẓaffar (the victorious), was the most distinguished and successful military commander during the reign of the caliph al-Muqtadir (295–320/908–932).[10] For almost the entire period of this long reign, he led the armies of the caliph against outside enemies like the Byzantines and the Fatimids, as well as threats from much closer to home, like the Shiʿi Qarāmiṭa (Carmathians) of north-east Arabia. Still more immediate, and more dangerous, was faction fighting within the Abbasid military, a problem that became increasingly acute as the financial problems of the government became more pressing and the competition for resources between different groups in the army became more violent. Mu'nis' long career in the army lasted for half a century, and he was still taking an active part in politics and military affairs at the time of his execution by the caliph al-Qāhir in 321/933.

As a military man, Mu'nis was part of the Abbasid army. At this time, the army was a large and rather unruly group, divided into factions that constantly challenged each other. The core of the army was composed of *ghilmān* (sing. *ghulām*). The Arabic word originally meant "boy", but by the late ninth and tenth centuries, the term had come to refer to boys and young men, usually of Turkish origins. Most of these were non-castrated men, and Mu'nis was one of the few eunuchs in this core. His status as a eunuch, unusual among the highest ranks of the military, may have contributed to the trust he enjoyed because, unlike other senior officers like Naṣr the chamberlain or, later, Yāqūt and Rā'iq, both of whom had demanding and unruly offspring, he had no ambitious children to look after. On the other hand, it may have been a problem for him as he grew older that he, unlike his rivals Yāqūt and Rā'iq, had no children who might offer long-term prospects to his followers.

One characteristic feature of eunuch status was that eunuchs, unlike non-castrated men, were able to visit the harem quarters where the women of the caliphal household lived. The harem was politically very important during the reign of al-Muqtadir, and the caliph's mother Shaghab was one of the most powerful, and one of the richest, figures in the state. It might be thought that Mu'nis would have used his gender status to secure privileged access to the harem areas, but in fact this never seems to have been the case. Like his non-castrated colleagues, he was restricted to the public areas and the parade ground. Jokes were made about his eunuch status. On one occasion, ʿAbd Allāh b. Ḥamdān, one of his leading subordinates, says, "We will fight for you, O Ustādh (the title given to military leaders by their *ghilmān* and others) until your beard grows" (which, of course, it never would: a clear indication that eunuchs were obviously different in appearance from Muslim non-castrated men, who always sported beards).[11] Despite these jocular references, there can be no doubt about the respect in which Mu'nis was held by his fellow commanders and his subordinates.

We have no idea about his origins but, like many of the *ghilmān* of the period, he probably came from Central Asia (modern Kazakhstan and Kirghizstan) and was of Turkic stock. If so, he would have been captured or sold and taken west via the Sāmānid capital at Samarqand. It was possibly there that he was castrated before being sold on to al-Muʿtaḍid, then building up his forces for his campaign against the Zanj rebels in southern Iraq. It is here in 267/880 that he first enters the historical record fighting in the campaign against the rebels.[12] Later, in 287/900 we find him campaigning in the caliph's army on the Byzantine frontier, where the elite of the Abbasid played their role as defenders of the Muslim state.

Not only did Mu'nis' personality and achievements dominate the military history of the caliphate of al-Muqtadir, but he also played a central role in the tangled politics of the administration. The caliph al-Muqtadir came to the throne in August 908 on the death of his elder brother al-Muktafī (caliph from 289/902 to 295/908). There was considerable resistance to this appointment because of the new caliph's youth (he was only 13 years old) and his obvious inexperience. This resistance came to a head in December of the same year when there was an attempted coup in favour of an older and more experienced member of the Abbasid family, ʿAbd Allāh, son of the caliph al-Muʿtazz. The course of events is reasonably clear.[13] ʿAbd Allāh b. al-Muʿtazz and his supporters soon gained control over the *dār al-khilāfa* (caliphal palace) and were in the process of celebrating and making new appointments to government offices. The young al-Muqtadir escaped and took refuge with Muʾnis, who refused to accept the coup and led the *ghilmān* who had remained with al-Muqtadir. They sailed by boat up the Tigris to the riverside palace where the new caliph was staying and, according to one account, started firing volleys of arrows. The supporters of Ibn al-Muʿtazz panicked and fled and dispersed; the coup collapsed. Muʾnis then restored al-Muqtadir to the throne and invited the one leading figure in the bureaucracy who had not supported the coup, Ibn al-Furāt, to serve as vizier. As a result of this, Muʾnis became the effective leader of the Baghdad military and began his close alliance with his namesake Muʾnis al-Khāzin (the treasurer), the palace *ghilmān* and the queen mother's brother, Gharīb, a coterie that was to serve as the corner-stone of al-Muqtadir's support for the first years of his reign. Mu'nis' motivation and actions were a product of his upbringing. He had been educated and promoted in the military entourage of the caliph al-Muʿtaḍid, the father of al-Muqtadir. Having no family of his own, his main loyalties lay with his master, his master's family and the *ghilmān* among whom he had grown up; they were his kin. Al-Muqtadir may have been young and inexperienced, but he was his father's son. Mu'nis was determined that power should remain in his branch of the extensive Abbasid family and among the *ghilmān* who formed their military household.

After the collapse of Ibn al-Muʿtazz's coup, the next years were comparatively peaceful, and Mu'nis' duties included leading the armies of his master, al-Muqtadir, against outside enemies. In 297/910, we hear of Muʾnis leading the traditional summer raid, the *ṣāʾifa*, against the Byzantines in the name of the Abbasid caliphate.[14] No great conquests were made and no famous victories achieved, but this was an important symbolic role. The leadership of the Muslim armies against the ancient foe was an important part of the caliph's rule, emphasising his leadership of the Muslim community. It was the only military campaign in which the Umayyad and Abbasid caliphs had participated in person. In the absence of the caliph himself, the commander he appointed was the most prestigious of his generals. He was certainly the first and probably the last eunuch to lead the armies of the Muslim *umma* in this way. He had with him a large army and a group of *quwwād* (military commanders). He based himself in Tarsus, the main Muslim base on the Byzantine frontier. According to the dispatch he sent to Baghdad, which was read out in public, he killed many Byzantines and won a notable victory. At the same time, Mu'nis was a jealous leader who did not want to share the limelight with anyone. Among the troops accompanying him was one Abū-l-Agharr Khalīfa b. Mubārak al-Sulamī, of whom everyone agreed that "there was at this time no knight (*fāris*) among the Arabs or Persians (*'ajam*) braver, stronger or more steadfast than him".[15] Mu'nis complained to the caliph about him, and he was ordered back to Baghdad and imprisoned. He may have objected to Abū-l-Agharr because he was an Arab of Bedouin stock or simply because he was so popular; can we see something of the eunuch's insecurity among his military peers and colleagues or simply a person determined to hold on to the reputation he had acquired? We can never know.

The next important campaign in Fārs (Persia) followed the next year.[16] Fārs was a very important province for the Abbasids at this time because it was one of the few areas outside southern Iraq that could be expected to send reasonable quantities of revenue to the capital. It had been ruled in the Abbasid interest by a governor named Subkarā, who paid a fixed sum of money every year, but when it fell into the hands of Layth b. 'Alī the Ṣaffārid, sworn enemy of the Abbasids, it was considered necessary to regain control. In Ramaḍān 297/early summer 910, Mu'nis, with an army of 5,000 elite troops, set out for the province. The officers in charge of collecting supplies for the military of the cities of Iṣfahān and Ahwāz were ordered to provide supplies. Even as the army was en route, problems emerged because the army had not been paid their salaries, and they sacked the camp of the financial administrator Mu'nis had brought with him. Despite these troubles, the campaign was a success: Layth was defeated and sent as a prisoner to Baghdad, entering the city on the back of an elephant so that all the citizens could witness his defeat and the power of the caliphal armies.

This, however, was not the end of the story and what followed illustrates some of the problems of enforcing government policy and the role Mu'nis played. Mu'nis seems to have believed that it would be in his interests for Subkarā to remain as governor of Fārs, and when Subkarā offered to increase the amount of money he paid, Mu'nis opened negotiations.[17] Some years before, the province had paid four million *dirham* per year to the Abbasid government, and Subkarā now offered seven million. The vizier Ibn al-Furāt, always jealous of Mu'nis' status, refused; Mu'nis raised the bid to nine million, pointing out that Subkarā needed the rest to pay the army in the province. Ibn al-Furāt refused to accept anything less than thirteen. Mu'nis advised Subkarā to agree, but he refused to offer anything more than ten. Negotiations broke down; Mu'nis was ordered back to Baghdad and a new military expedition was sent out, which eventually captured Subkarā, but the negotiations left a nasty taste in the mouth and were one of the reasons for the growing estrangement between Mu'nis and Ibn al-Furāt. Provincial government was not a systematic business, nor was it arranged by caliphal decree, but by a complex series of bargains and compromises among the various interested parties, with Muʾnis as much a diplomat and businessman as he was a soldier.

Muʾnis now became one of the young caliph's closest advisers. When, in the year 300/913, the vizier al-Khāqānī's government began to run into serious financial difficulties and there was widespread unrest in Baghdad, it was to Muʾnis that al-Muqtadir turned. He had thought of bringing back Ibn al-Furāt as vizier, but Muʾnis advised against; it would look very bad to restore to office a man who had so recently been dismissed. Instead, he recommended the appointment of ʿAlī b. ʿĪsā, and this cemented the relationship of Muʾnis with ʿAlī, which was to be one of the most important power axes in the turbulent and fissiparous court.[18]

He was soon entrusted with another important command and was sent in 304/916 with an army to impose terms on Ibn Abī al-Sāj, effective ruler of Armenia and Azerbaijan. The mission was not a success. Muʾnis suffered the only major military defeat of his long career, his army was routed and he himself was taken prisoner. But Ibn Abī al-Sāj was too clever to humiliate or injure so influential a figure and instead allowed him and 300 of his *ghilmān* to return to Baghdad.[19] He may or may not have regretted his decision when, the next year, Muʾnis returned and defeated him at Ardabīl and took him as a prisoner to the capital.[20] However, this was all part of the complex negotiation and bargaining that was typical of relations between the caliph and the provinces nominally under his rule, and there seems to have been no lasting ill feeling. His defeat did not mean that the areas came back under direct Abbasid rule, for one of his *ghilmān* stepped into Ibn Abī al-Sāj's shoes, agreeing to contribute an annual sum to Baghdad, which, in fact, he never paid. Here again we see how Mu'nis' diplomatic skills were at least as important as his military ones. He ended up with both the caliph on one hand, and Ibn Abī al-Sāj on the other, beholden to him. Again, one has to wonder whether his eunuch status and the fact that he could not pose any dynastic threat to either of them helped or enabled him to move with such apparent ease among the different parties.

Muʾnis' next important military mission was to Egypt in 302–3/915–6; the country was under threat from the Fatimids, now ruling in Ifrīqiya (Tunisia), but the latter were determined to extend their power to the East and overthrow the Abbasids as universal caliphs. Here again, he was successful, and the Fatimid forces were driven back.[21]

In 305/917, Muʾnis was back in Baghdad with a place of honour at the magnificent reception that Ibn al-Furāt (who had been reinstated as vizier) laid on for the Byzantine ambassadors. As soon as the visit was over, it was Muʾnis who went to the frontier to put into effect the prisoner swap that had been agreed upon.[22] In 309/921, he was again in Egypt, organizing the defences against another Fatimid attack,[23] and he was given some financial control over both Egypt and Syria.

When he returned to Baghdad in 310/922–3, he was in high favour with the caliph, being invited to drink with the monarch. It is not stated what was being drunk but, bearing in mind the caliph's known proclivities, it is likely to have been wine. He also secured the release of his old sparring partner, Ibn Abī al-Sāj, who returned to Armenia and Azerbaijān. However, he seems to have left some of his men behind because from this time on, we find Sājī *ghilmān* serving under Mu'nis' command.[24]

No-one's political position was secure in the snake-pit of al-Muqtadir's court. When Ibn al-Furāt became vizier for the third time in 311/923, he set out to undermine Mu'nis' position with the caliph because the general had openly criticised the cruelty and excesses of the vizier and his son al-Muḥassin. Since it was impossible to take direct action against so powerful and respected a figure, he decided to send him and his army to Raqqa on the Euphrates. He argued that there were insufficient financial resources to allow them to remain in Baghdad. If he went to Raqqa, the resources of the Jazīra and Syria would be available to pay his army. Mu'nis recognised this specious argument for what it was, a ruse to get him away from the capital and allow the vizier a free hand to act against Naṣr the chamberlain and other allies of Mu'nis.[25]

All the vizier's calculations were upset by the attack on the *ḥajj* (pilgrimage caravan) by the Qarāmiṭa as it crossed the Arabian Desert from Iraq to the Holy Cities and the outrage this provoked in Baghdad. The Qarāmiṭa were a group of Isma'ili Shi'is who had established a radical anti-Abbasid movement on North-eastern Arabia. Unlike the Byzantines or the warlords of Fārs and Azerbaijān, they formed an existential threat to the caliphate. They were later to be responsible for murderous attacks on the *ḥajj* caravan, travelling under the protection of the caliphate, and of stealing the black stone from the Ka'ba itself. Furthermore, they were poised to attack the centres of Abbasid power in Iraq and even Baghdad itself.

Despite his visceral dislike of Mu'nis, the vizier was forced to write to his rival asking him to return, and he had to show him the greatest respect when he arrived. The tables were now turned, and Mu'nis and Naṣr the chamberlain took Ibn al-Furāt and his son into custody; Ibn al-Furāt is said to have wanted to be handed over to Mu'nis "even though he is my enemy" because he trusted him not to ill-treat him. In the end, though, the execution of the veteran vizier was left to others.[26]

After the death of Ibn al-Furāt, Mu'nis became once more the key figure in the administration and once more he championed the cause of his main ally in the bureaucracy 'Alī b. Īsā. In 313/925, he secured the appointment of 'Alī as superintendent (*mushrif*) of the finances of Syria and Egypt, and in 315/927, he secured his appointment to the vizierate for the second time. Mu'nis himself was given a robe of honour when he was dispatched to the Byzantine frontier where the emperor himself had led his armies to take the city of Samsat and, to the scandal of the Muslims, celebrated church services in the mosque.[27] But the year was also marked by an unpleasant incident after which, in the words of the chronicler, "the loyalty of Mu'nis al-Muẓaffar showed signs of failing".[28] One of the caliph's eunuchs (perhaps we can see an instance of solidarity among eunuchs here?) revealed to Muʾnis that there was a plot to lure him into the palace where a pit had been prepared for him to fall into. The caliph was obliged to write in his own hand denying this, and Muʾnis in turn replied accepting his version, but was nevertheless careful not to visit the palace. Relations between the caliph and his leading general were always a bit fraught. Al-Muqtadir certainly resented the general esteem in which Muʾnis was held and his firm support for ʿAlī b.ʿĪsā in his attempt to curtail palace spending. And Muʾnis, for his part, would have been only too aware of the fate of his father al-Muʿtaḍid's chief general Badr, swiftly put to death by his brother al-Muktafī when he became caliph.

These tensions were put to one side by the other main event of the year. 315/927 saw the most serious military crisis of the reign thus far when the Qarāmiṭa seemed to be on the verge of taking Baghdad itself. Needless to say, Muʾnis, along with Naṣr the chamberlain, played a leading role in the defence, going to Anbār to prevent the Qarāmiṭa from crossing the Euphrates and then shadowing them up the river and supporting the people of Raqqa in driving the enemy off.

The retreat of the Qarāmiṭa did little to solve the internal conflicts within the administration. No sooner had they disappeared than elements of the army mutinied for more pay. There was also the issue of the choice of a new vizier to replace the incompetent al-Khaṣībī. Once again, al-Muqtadir turned to Muʾnis, and once again, Muʾnis recommended ʿAlī b. ʿĪsā, but he refused, saying that he would only take on the office if Muʾnis was to remain in the capital, whereas Muʾnis was bound for Raqqa and the Byzantine frontier. So the office was offered to the able but young and inexperienced Ibn Muqla.

Muʾnis could not afford to be away from Baghdad for long. When he was away, there were rumours that Hārūn b. Gharīb was to be appointed *amīr al-umarāʾ* (commander of commanders).[29] Hārūn was the queen mother's maternal cousin. His father, Gharīb, her brother, had established himself as a military commander in Baghdad without apparently leading any major expeditions or enjoying any widespread support among the soldiery. His rather fragile position had been inherited by his son Hārūn, who now tried to supplant Muʾnis as the leading figure in the military. The title of *amīr al-umarāʾ* seems to have been a new invention, and no one had held it thus far, but the implications of the office were generally understood. It meant that Hārūn would be the chief of the whole Abbasid army, effectively supplanting Mu'nis. But the implications of this title went beyond the conflict of personalities. The appointment of such a figure would be, in essence, a military coup subordinating the whole civil administration, including the vizier, to the dictates of the military. The precarious balance between the bureaucracy and the army commanders would be lost, probably for ever. This is indeed what happened a decade later in 324/936, when Ibn Rāʾiq formally adopted the title, but for the moment these were just ideas in the wind.[30]

The whole situation rapidly descended into farce as Hārūn's men came to blows with the troops of Nāzūk, the chief of police, over an attractive boy they both coveted. On 8 Muḥarram 317/21 February 929, Mu'nis returned from the frontier to confront the caliph in an attempt to secure his own position. Mu'nis emerged as the leading spokesman of the army, demanding administrative reform and a curb on the influence and financial privileges of the palace servants and the harem. There then began an exchange of correspondence between Mu'nis and the caliph and his advisers. Mu'nis stated the army's grievances "about the amount of money and land wasted upon the eunuchs and women of the court and their interference in the administration", and he went on to demand their removal from the palace and the seizure of their possessions. The caliph replied with a long letter, the text of which has been preserved in full in Miskawayh's chronicle and in part in ʿArīb's annals; it was obviously very well publicised. In it, he expressed his devotion to and admiration for Mu'nis in the most fulsome terms. He went to explain that while he could cut back on allowances, he could not abolish them altogether. He would strive his utmost to meet Mu'nis' demands. Finally, if this was not enough, he would accept his fate, just as the caliph ʿUthmān had accepted his, without making any effort to defend himself.[31]

It was a desperate attempt to save his position and emphasise the centrality of Mu'nis' role. He and his allies considered the reply and agreed to demand the removal of Hārūn b. Gharīb, who was accordingly ordered to the Byzantine frontier, although in the end, he did not go.[32] On 10 Muḥarram 317/23 February 929, Mu'nis and his friends and supporters entered the city but, typically, avoided the palace in case it was damaged by the troops. Two days later, however, the army occupied the whole palace ,and the now deposed caliph, his mother and his womenfolk were taken upriver to Mu'nis' house, where they were to be accommodated in safety.[33]

The next stage was to find a new caliph in the palace of Ibn Ṭāhir, where redundant members of the Abbasid family were housed. Al-Muqtadir's younger brother Muḥammad was chosen, but the man in charge of the house would not release him from his effective imprisonment without a direct order from Mu'nis, now clearly regarded as arbiter of the fate of the caliphate. The new caliph was duly installed in the palace with the title of al-Qāhir under the protection of Nāzūk, the chief of police and, at least temporarily, an ally of Mu'nis. But Mu'nis, as often, played a cautious game. He avoided the palace himself and watched the disastrous collapse of Nāzūk's attempted coup from a safe distance, telling people that he had never wanted the complete deposition of al-Muqtadir. When it was all over, and Nāzūk was dead, it was Mu'nis who arranged for the return of the caliph to the palace and the shrewd Mu'nis made his peace with the restored caliph.[34]

At first, relations between Mu'nis and al-Muqtadir seem to have been good. At his suggestion, the two sons of Rā'iq, a military follower of his, were given charge of the *shurṭa* (police) and re-established order in the city. The harmony did not last long, however. The main bone of contention was the presence of one of Mu'nis' major rivals in the army, the upcoming Yāqūt and his sons who were in the city, and the favour that the caliph had shown them. In the end, Muʾnis forced al-Muqtadir to expel them; it is reported that they and their followers left by water "with more than forty ships, laden with money, arms, saddles, swords, belts and other things". Their houses were promptly burned down.[35] Mu'nis seemed to have triumphed, but his defeated rivals were not to be gone for long.

The cause of the final breach between Muʾnis and the caliph was rivalries over power in Baghdad. Muʾnis was by this time an old man. He had had an active military role for more than 50 years. He was suffering from gout or arthritis and rarely left his house, but he still wanted to be in charge. Having secured the expulsion of Yāqūt, he had his protégés, the sons of Rāʾiq, restored to the all-important *shurṭa*, but they now enjoyed the caliph's favour and wanted to assert their own power. And they became suspicious that Muʾnis wanted to replace them with his new favourite, his *ghulām* Yalbaq.[36] And so it was that Muʾnis and his remaining followers left for Mosul while his enemies in Baghdad, including the returned Yāqūt and the Banū Rāʾiq, plotted his downfall.

It was this alienation that led to the tragic battle in which Muʾnis' soldiers killed the caliph he had served so well for 30 years. As so often, there are differing accounts of the course of battle, but it is clear that the caliph was killed during the action and that the body was left unburied on the field of battle. It is unlikely that this was the outcome that Mu'nis would have wanted, although it is clear that the caliph's deviousness had exasperated him on many occasions. Nonetheless, this was the man whom Mu'nis had supported through thick and thin since he had been a teenage monarch more than 30 years before. The chronicler ʿArīb adds a detail that gives an insight into the feelings of the old, sick general at this time. He had been brought up in the Abbasid court and had always attempted to keep the door open for reconciliation with the caliph. When he was away from Baghdad, just before the final battle, he and his followers had stayed in the deserted imperial capital at Samarra in the palace known as the Qaṣr al-Jiṣṣ. While they were there, an accidental fire destroyed one of the ceilings and "this upset Muʾnis and he made great efforts to put of the fire but it proved impossible and when he left on his way to Mosul, he was overcome with sadness about the fire".[37] It is hard not to see this as a symptom of a wider melancholy about the collapse of the caliphate. When al-Muqtadir's head was brought to him, he was apparently overwhelmed with grief, despite all the quarrels and strife they had had.[38]

The death of the caliph al-Muqtadir saw Mu'nis at the height of his power and, paradoxically, at his most vulnerable. Although he commanded the allegiance and respect of a large part of the Abbasid army, he was growing older. He had served in the military for more than 50 years and was probably in his early seventies. His political and analytical mind may have been as clear as ever, but his physical mobility was impaired and he moved slowly. Furthermore, he had, of course, no children to whom his followers could look to continue his leadership when he passed away. He had favoured protégés who he had promoted to positions of importance – notably, in his last years, the *ghulām* Yalbaq and his son ʿAlī – but this was not the same as having his own sons.

The first struggle was to find a new caliph. Mu'nis, out of loyalty to the memory of his dead master, recommended the appointment of al-Muqtadir's son, Abū l-ʿAbbās, who was eventually to become caliph with the title of al-Rāḍī but was still at this stage young and inexperienced. He was opposed by a group led by a bureaucrat called Isḥāq al-Nawbakhtī who expressed his clear opinion, saying, "After all the trouble which it has taken us to get rid of one with a mother and an aunt and eunuchs (*khudum*) are we going to have the same thing again?" So the proposal was dropped. Mu'nis then interviewed two other possible candidates, Muḥammad, son of al-Muqtadir's brother al-Muktafī; and Muḥammad, al-Muqtadir's brother, who had briefly been caliph before with the title of al-Qāhir.[39] Ibn al-Muktafī declined, saying that his uncle had a better claim, a move he must have regretted bitterly a year later when the sadistic and brutal al-Qāhir ordered that he be bricked up alive in one of the arches of the caliphal palace.

So power passed to al-Qāhir, an unstable and violent psychopath, whose cruelties went way beyond the harsh norms of the day. He personally took charge of the physical torture of the dead caliph's mother, already distraught at her son's death, in order to force her to surrender her – largely non-existent – wealth. Her treasures, mostly fabrics and perfumes, were sold and the proceeds handed over to Mu'nis, who used them to pay the customary accession gift (*ṣilat al-bayʿa)*. Relations between Mu'nis, the vizier Ibn Muqla and Yalbaq and his son, on one side, and al-Qāhir and another military leader, Muḥammad b. Yāqūt on the other, soon deteriorated. Mu'nis and his allies put the caliph under a form of house arrest and attempted to banish his allies. But, inevitably, the caliph began a counter intrigue. The details are complex and reveal the febrile and over-heated nature of the politics of Baghdad during this period. Basically, Mu'nis was persuaded by his followers and allies to arrest and depose al-Qāhir, but the caliph got wind of this and arranged for all the plotters to be arrested. The protests of Mu'nis' soldiers only made the caliph more determined to destroy him forever. ʿAlī b. Yalbaq was the first to die, and his severed head was sent to his father, who suffered the same fate. The heads were sent to Mu'nis, who cursed their slayer. Then it was his turn, an event that is recorded thus: "he was dragged by the foot to the gutter and there slaughtered like a sheep while al-Qāhir looked on". The three heads were taken in basins to be displayed to the army, leaving no doubt of their death, before being returned to the palace to be stored in the "treasury of heads, as was the custom".[40]

It was a terrible end to a long and distinguished career. Mu'nis' death symbolised the end of the army's power, which his first patron al-Muʿtaḍid had built up more than half a century before and which had formed the foundation of the Abbasid power ever since. Mu'nis' great age meant that he was the last of that generation, the only man who could command support among the rival groups in the military. With his passing, any sense of unity was lost, the different commanders were bent on destroying their rivals and the collapse of the caliphate was inevitable. Mu'nis' was a remarkable career, made more remarkable by his eunuch identity. That the exemplar of military power, of honest politics, of devoted service, should be a eunuch flies in the face of all the stereotypes and clichés of eunuchs that historians have repeated through the ages.

Notes

1 For the political history of the period, see Hugh Kennedy, *The Prophet and the Age of the Caliphates* (London: Longmans, 2004). On the court culture, see Hugh Kennedy, *The Courts of the Caliphs* (London: Weidenfeld and Nicolson, 2004).

2 The term means "Rightly Guided". They were the first four caliphs (Abū Bakr, 'Umar, 'Uthmān and 'Alī) after the death of the Prophet Muḥammad. They ruled from 11/632 to 40/661.

3 On this point, see also Nadia Maria El Cheikh's contribution in this volume.

4 Nothing of the palaces of Baghdad has survived. For the almost contemporary Abbasid palaces at Samarra, see Alastair Northedge, *The Historical Topography of Samarra* (London: British School of Archaeology in Iraq, 2007).

5 Abū 'Alī Aḥmad Miskawayh, *Tajārib al-umam,* ed. Henry Frederick Amedroz, 3 vls. Miṣr 1914–1919 (repr. Baghdad in the 1960s); ed. and trans. in English David Samuel Margoliouth, *The Eclipse of the Abbasid Caliphate* (London: Blackwell, 1920–1921). The title *Tajārib* is used when referring to the Arabic text, the title *Eclipse* when referring to the English translation.

6 ʿArīb b. Saʿd al- Qurṭubī, *Ṣilat ta'rīkh al-Ṭabarī* ed. Michael Jan De Goeje (Leiden: Brill, 1897). Unfortunately, this work has not been translated into any Western language.

7 Miskawayh, *Tajārib*, 1:117.

8 Ibid., 1:121.

9 *Khādim* (pl. *khudum)* in Arabic, both classical and modern, means simply a servant, but in the Abbasid court and later medieval Muslim courts, it almost always means a eunuch. On this topic, see also David Ayalon, "On the term 'Khādim' in the sense of 'Eunuch' in the Early Muslim Sources," *Arabica* 32, fasc. 3 (1985): 289–308 and A. Cheikh Moussa, "De la synonymie dans les sources arabes anciennes. Le cas de 'Hadim' et de 'Hasiyy," *Arabica* 3, fasc. 3 (1985): 309–322. The word *khaṣī* (pl. *khiṣyān*) is also used to describe castrated males but is seldom used to describe court eunuchs or other elite individuals.

10 Maaike van Berkel et al., *Crisis and Continuity in the Abbasid Court: Formal and informal politics in the reign of al-Muqtadir (295–320/908–32)* (Leiden: Brill, 2013); Harold Bowen, *The Life and times of ʿAlī Ibn ʿĪsā, "the Good Vizier"* (Cambridge: Cambridge University Press, 1928).

11 Miskawayh, *Tajārib*, 1:160.

12 Muḥammad b. Jarīr al-Ṭabarī, *Taʾrīkh al-rusul wa-l-mulūk,* ed. Michael Jan De Goeje et al. (Leiden: Brill, 1879–1901), 3:1953.

13 al-Ṭabarī, *Taʾrīkh,* 3:2282–2283, Miskawayh, *Tajārib*, 1:6–7, ʿArīb, *Ṣilat*, 27–29.

14 al-Ṭabarī, *Taʾrīkh,* 3:2284–2285; ʿArīb, *Ṣilat*, 31–32.

15 ʿArīb, *Ṣilat*, 31.

16 For the Fārs campaign, al-Ṭabarī, *Taʾrīkh,* 3:2285, ʿArīb, *Ṣilat*, 32–33, Miskawayh, *Tajārib*, 1:16–19.

17 The negotiations are described in Miskawayh, *Tajārib*, 1:18–19.

18 Ibid., 1:25–27.
19 Ibid., 1:46.
20 Ibid., 1:47.
21 Muḥammad b. Yūsuf al-Kindī, *The governors and judges of Egypt; or, Kitâb el 'umarâ (el wulâh) wa Kitâb el qudâh of el Kindî*, ed. Rhuvon Guest, J. W. Gibb memorial series 19 (Leiden: Brill and London: Luzac, 1912), 273.
22 Miskawayh, *Tajārib*, 1:55–56.
23 al-Kindī, *Governors*, 277–279.
24 Miskawayh, *Tajārib*, 1:116.
25 Miskawayh, *Tajārib*, 1:115–116; 'Arīb, *Ṣilat*, 112.
26 Miskawayh, *Tajārib*, 1:130.
27 Ibid., 1:159.
28 Ibid.
29 Ibid., 1:188–189.
30 For these developments, see Kennedy, *The Prophet and the Age of the Caliphates*, 194–197.
31 Miskawayh, *Tajārib*, 1:189–192; 'Arīb, *Ṣilat*, 140.
32 Miskawayh, *Tajārib*, 1:192.
33 'Arīb, *Ṣilat*, 141.
34 Ibid., 143–144.
35 Ibid., 160.
36 Ibid., 166.
37 Ibid., 168–169.
38 Ibid., 180.
39 Miskawayh, *Tajārib*,1:242.
40 Ibid., 1:267–268.

4 Harem and eunuchs

Liminality and networks of Mughal authority

Ruby Lal

Imperial eunuchs – a contradiction in terms? In fact, eunuchs were an imposing presence in the Greek and Roman empires, in imperial China and Mughal India and Ottoman Turkey. Commonly used as slaves and guards, imperial eunuchs were allowed entry to the innermost domestic spaces, on account, it is said, of their de-sexualised (castrated) condition. Yet, the liminal condition of eunuchs within various royal regimes of the pre-modern world clearly reflects other important characteristics of their status, apart from their physical condition (or ambiguous gender). Their ability to straddle the inner and the outer domains of the court and their extraordinary access to power and influence has much to do with an elevated status, a sanctity, even a magical power attached to their lives. It is this dimension of the history of eunuchs that I will explore further through a consideration of the special conditions and rhetoric that surrounded eunuchs in Mughal India during the reigns of Akbar (r. 1556–1605) and Jahāngīr (r. 1605–1627).[1]

Eunuchs are regularly mentioned in the context of the organization of imperial affairs and the administrative and military apparatus of the Mughal empire. In an early excellent piece on the trade in eunuchs in Mughal Bengal, Gavin Hambly argued that eunuchs from the eastern province of Bengal were a regular "commodity" among the polygamous societies of India, whether Hindu or Muslim. Their numbers, however, were few, hence the demand for them remained constant throughout this period and the prices paid for them high. In an essay on the question of slavery, Saleem Kidwai indirectly considered the role of eunuchs in the Delhi Sultanate, a Muslim kingdom (1206–1526), which was eventually replaced by the Mughal empire. He stressed the enslavement and commodification of eunuchs and their prized role in harem management. Indrani Chatterjee has shown that eunuch slaves were in charge of diplomatic and military undertakings and acted as confidantes and advisors, and that some held literary posts in the courts of Farrukabad, Awadh and Hyderabad. Finally, Shadab Bano, in a recent study, has detailed the rich and varied character of the roles and activities of the Mughal eunuchs, especially in the reign of Akbar (r. 1556–1605).[2] Thus, the prominent and widespread image of the Mughal eunuch as attached to the harem as a guard, and critical in the supervision of imperial domestic arrangements, is already expanded upon in these divergent studies.

Indeed, eunuchs appear as protectors of kings, influential messengers, important office-holders and persons of wealth. Their biographical sketches and the discussion of them in court histories show that they lived in liminal modes, transcending the personal, political and gender boundaries of the time. Although eunuchs were very much part of the semi-nomadic life of the courts of Central Asia, the first Mughal emperor, Bābur (r. 1526–1530), does not mention a single eunuch in his great memoir, the *Bābur-nāmah*. Nevertheless, we do learn about eunuchs in his time from other sources.[3] Gulbadan Begum, the daughter of Bābur, wrote about the peripatetic conditions of her brother, the second Mughal king, Humāyūn, as he attempted to find a foothold. She writes about the valorous acts of Nāẓir ‘Ambar, the superintendent and the royal agent (*mulk-mukhtar*), in guarding women during the time the royal retinue took refuge in the fort of Bālā Ḥiṣṣār.[4] By the time of Bābur's grandson, the third Mughal, Akbar, however, eunuchs appear prominently in the records as an integral part of the newly ordered and institutionalized court and harem.

The focus of this chapter is to explore the historical emergence, placement and engagements of eunuchs in the imperial regime of the Mughals. How – and in what terms and manner – were eunuchs integrated into the ideology of the Mughal rule? What were the terms of legitimation, forms of address, practices of honour – in a word, the rhetoric and vocabulary surrounding the eunuch? A central goal of this chapter is to demonstrate that as imperial "servants" and as an essential part of the bureaucracy of Akbar's empire, eunuchs engaged in crisscrossing networks of authority. Although mentioned in important roles in earlier documents, eunuchs appear as distinctly noteworthy officials at the time when Akbar gave orders for the creation of the first set of physically segregated harem quarters. The appearance of a highly institutionalized and eminent harem was accompanied by a well-regulated and carefully distributed bureaucracy, of which eunuchs were a central part.

Indeed, this new elevation and placement of women in grand, but confined, quarters was paralleled by a new elevation of eunuchs as Mughal officials. Both of these developments were reinforced by a new imperial philosophy, which was laid out in striking terms in the first Mughal official history, the *Akbar-nāmah* (and its accompanying voluminous compendium, the *Āʾīn-i Akbarī*), at the behest of emperor Akbar, written by his chosen historian Abū l-Fażl.

In an unexpected way, royal women and royal eunuchs came to occupy a similar liminal zone, and so the accounts of their agency, opportunities and achievements can parallel one another in many ways. We are familiar with the astute, imaginative and agential Mughal women. Notwithstanding the many prescriptions that were laid down for their residence – including the declaration (for the first time in Mughal history) that they were considered *pardagiyān*, the veiled ones, and at once, the *cupola of chastity*, the *veiled ones of the curtains of fortune*, the *chaste secluded ladies* – women challenged the limits of royal instructions. For example, under the leadership of Gulbadan Begum, the elderly aunt of Akbar, the royal women went on an all-women's ḥajj. The women of the harem were central figures in peace negotiations and often counselled men at critical moments. Nūr Jahān, the last wife of the fourth Mughal emperor Jahāngīr, became the *de facto* empress of Mughal India (r. 1611–1627).[5]

There is certainly something, therefore, about the new placement of Mughal women in Akbar's time – secluded and sacred, confined yet powerful – that might provide a clue to the status and function of royal eunuchs in this period: each can be said to have negotiated power within the "highly charged boundaries of moral and physical space".[6]

The making of the first imperial harem

In chapter 15 of the *Ā'īn-i Akbarī*, a compendium of the imperial history that includes many subjects pertaining to the Mughal empire, Abū l-Fażl, the imperial chronicler of Akbar, set down the regulations regarding the imperial harem:[7]

> His Majesty is a great friend of good order and propriety in business ... For this reason, the large number of women [*pardagiyān*] – a vexatious question even for great statesmen – furnished his Majesty with an opportunity to display his wisdom, and to rise from the low level of worldly dependence to the eminence of perfect freedom. The imperial palace and household are therefore in best order .... His Majesty has made a large enclosure with fine buildings inside, where he reposes. Though there are more than five thousand women, he has given to each a separate apartment. He has also divided them into sections, and keeps them attentive to their duties. Several chaste women have been appointed as *dārūghas*, and superintendents over each section, and one has been selected for the duties of writer. Thus, as in the imperial offices, everything is here also in proper order.[8]

Abū l-Fażl relates how, in this increasingly institutionalized and grandiose Mughal regime, Akbar had judged that it was appropriate for royal women to now live behind carefully guarded walls. In this discussion of the new sanctified space that was to be created through the seclusion of women, Abū l-Fażl refers to the arrangements for the security of the harem by what he calls "sober and active women". According to him, the most trusted women were placed in the quarters of Akbar. The eunuchs were assigned to guard the outside enclosure, and at some distance from them, the Rājpūts formed another line of watchmen.[9] Alongside the more secure enclosure of their space, other rules were promulgated concerning the surveillance of the harem quarters, including restrictions on the women's movement and instructions regarding who could visit them. Akbar, the Great Mughal, as he was called in Europe, was of course not creating an entirely new body of rules regarding royal women and the spaces in which they dwelled. His ancestors, the former nomadic kings, even as they struggled to find firmer territorial locations, had maintained strict codes of modesty and separation with regards to royal women. However, it was under Akbar that this official statute was issued on the royal household – a first for the Mughal dynasty. In this, as noted earlier, the women were officially designated *pardagiyān*, the veiled ones. In ideological terms, women's spaces were fixed through legislation more secularly than in previous periods.

The institutionalization of the harem was reflected not only in the physical topographies at Fateḥpūr-Sīkrī, the Mughal capital, but in its conceptual framework as well. In the grand city of Fateḥpūr-Sīkrī that Akbar built, the court and the harem were, for the first time, separated from each other by huge walls. A compartmentalized harem (*Shabistān-i Iqbāl*) was designed to segregate women in a space of their own – for "good order and propriety", as Abū l-Fażl stated.[10] Indeed, in the drive to coordinate all aspects of imperial life, the domestic world needed to be carefully regulated. A neatly classified women's domain was thus manifested in its physical structures, in its ritual practices and in imperial regulations. The court and the domestic world of the harem were now markedly separated from each other.

Akbar's sovereign philosophies

Akbar is known to have been motivated by a variety of Indic and non-Indic traditions in developing his wide-ranging political engagements, spiritual quests, matters of faith and questions concerning how one should live. The ideological impetus for his sovereignty, of which the demarcation of the harem was a crucial part, is manifest most strikingly in the first official Mughal history, the *Akbar-nāmah*, and in its compendium *Ā'īn-i Akbarī*, which provides details of the institutionalized nature of the harem. The sacred language deployed by Akbar's court historian, Abū l-Fażl, heralds the striking construction of a new genealogy for Akbar, and with it, the elevation of the emperor to a near-divine status. All of this was part of the pronouncement of a new imperial normative – a new sovereign ideal that tied together Akbar's establishment of a confident and secure politically powerful regime (the dream of his forefathers) with an emphasis upon consolidating and expanding territories and cementing political networks and alliances.

We can examine the impact of this new ideological discourse if we explore the terminology used to describe the domestic world of Akbar. Officially, the harem came to be designated as the *Shabistān-i Iqbāl* (literally, the fortunate place of sleep or dreams) in the *Ā'īn-i Akbarī*.[11] The etymology of the word harem is critical in understanding its various associations, certain aspects of which the Akbarī chroniclers might have drawn from. To begin with, closely linked with the idea of the holy family is the institution known in ancient Arabia as the harem (and in contemporary South Arabia as *ḥawṭa*).[12] In pre-Islamic Arabia, at the top of the social stratification were the armed tribes, ranging from camel-owning desert tribes to tribesmen living in settled villages. Customary law was central to how these tribal units governed their relationships. Since there were always times when tribal leaders needed to appeal to a greater authority than their own, they turned to a divine power, sometimes through the medium of a prophet or a saint. It was incumbent upon people to show this authority respect (*iḥtirām*), and any infringement or violation of the sanctity of its domain was likely to bring "condign punishment".[13]

Among the Bedouin, the harem was "a sacred area around a shrine; a place where the holy power manifests itself". As an adjective, the term represented "everything that is forbidden to the profane and separated from the rest of the world. The cause of this prohibition could be either impurity (temporary or intrinsic) or holiness, which is a permanent state of sublime purity".[14] The harem subsequently came to accumulate many more meanings: those behind the curtain, not to be seen *(pardagiyān*); that which is inside, internal, within, intrinsic (*andarūn, andarūnī*); a house where the wives and the household live (*ḥaramsarā*); a place of sleep (*shabistān,* used as a synonym for harem); Mecca, Medina, the area around the *Kaʿba* and the garden of the Prophet Muḥammad (*Rawżah-yi Rasūl*).[15]

The fabric of invocations for Akbar's dwellings and of its inhabitants is drawn from the model and practices of the Prophet, including the holy sites associated with him: his garden, Mecca, Medina and the *Kaʿba*. In this construction, the centrality of Akbar in the harem is presented as absolute, like that of Muḥammad in his harem. The parallel that is drawn between the Prophet and Akbar is thus significant. Such symbolism is yet another component of the claim that Akbar's empire is a hallowed and 'blessed' empire – here, premised upon domestic order. The frequent use of a vocabulary resplendent with divine invocations is therefore hardly unexpected but clearly purposeful.

Such rhetoric can be seen as well in the terminology Akbar uses in his correspondence with the Persian Shāh 'Abbās (d. 1629). In one letter, Akbar spoke about the imperial household as *ahl-i bayt. Ahl* may be understood as companion or relative, persons, people of distinction, servants and attendants. In the plural, the word means kinsmen (*kisan*), relatives (*khvīshāvand*), race or tribe (*qawm*) and friends (*payruvān, yārān, aṣḥāb*).[16] *Bayt* means a house, a temple, edifice, fabric.[17] As a compound word, *ahl-i bayt* (the equivalent of *ahl al-bayt* in Arabic) renders the sense of a household – an expression that is also found in the autobiography of Akbar's grandfather, Bābur, in the context of extended familial structures.

The term *bayt* is used 15 times in the Quran to describe God's house; aside from a simple house, it is also designated as "the first house", "the ancient house", and the "sacred house (*al-bayt al-ḥarām*)".[18] Most of these Quranic references to God's house relate to the period after Muḥammad and his followers had settled in Medina[19] – following the Prophet's revelations, when a new religio-political community (*umma*) was being formed. The phrase *ahl-i bayt* appears at only three places in the Quran. In each instance, it is connected with the household of a major prophet and involves references to female members of the household. Eduardo Juan Campo tells us that the "most important aspect of the 'people of the house' phrase is not its use in the Quran per se, however, but what Muslims later made of it". After Muḥammad's death, the term came to designate the Prophet and his family as well as his "noble" descendants.[20]

Between early Islamic history and the sixteenth century, the meaning of *ahl-i bayt* was critical to Shiʿa-Sunni dialogue. So it is no coincidence, therefore, that by claiming a common membership to the *ahl-i bayt*, Abū l-Fażl was not only pointing to a spiritual connection but was also making a strong claim against the exclusive legitimacy of the Safavid dynasty. Abū l-Fażl, the imperial chronicler, thus invoked a traditional Prophetic-familial (and Shiʿa) association for Akbar's new dynasty. Significantly, the emperor was represented as being one of a community of divine monarchs, enhancing what Abū l-Fażl refers to as the "spiritual relationship" between Akbar and the Safavid king, both of whom are described as members of the *ahl-i bayt*.[21] Once the spiritual connection with the *ahl-i bayt* was made, the virtues of such a "divine household" would become the model for Akbar's own earthly household – both in expectation and portrayal. The term *ahl-i bayt* is not used regularly in the contemporary chronicles of Akbar's time. Its spirit, however, is imbued in other parallel terms employed to represent and describe Akbar's domestic world. These terms include *dūdmān-i quddūsī* (holy family),[22] *dūdmān-i valā* (sublime family)[23] and *dūdmān-i dawlah* (illustrious family), to use a few examples.[24]

The eunuchs of the sacred harem

What was the particular place of eunuchs in this ideology? In an evocative study, Shaun Marmon brought to life the "sacred society of eunuchs" established at the tomb of Prophet Muḥammad in Medina sometime in the mid-twelfth century. The "holy eunuchs", the "eunuchs of the Prophet", "the guardians and mediators of the *baraka*, the charismatic force that infused the Prophet's tomb and the surrounding sanctuary" emerged as a powerful institution, especially under the patronage of the Mamluk Sultans of Egypt. As guardians of the Prophet's tomb, eunuchs became a symbol of authority. They were the *khuddām* or the servants of the Prophet, a status that endowed them with power. The biographers of these eunuchs described them as inspiring *mahāba*, "a respect bordering on dread". According to a fifteenth-century observer, writes Marmon, "the eunuch's right and obligation to spend the night ... inside the sanctuary after all other believers had been expelled 'was the original reason for their [the eunuchs'] creation.'"[25]

The sacred society of the Prophet's eunuchs would not go unnoticed by Akbar's chosen chronicler, who, as shown above, evoked the genealogy of the prophet's family for his patron. The institution and use of eunuch servants was well known. In fifteenth-century Medina, as well as east- and west-African eunuchs, eunuchs from the Indian subcontinent resided there. Communities of eunuchs had already appeared at the tombs of sultans of Cairo, at the Kaʿba in Mecca, at the Dome of the Rock in Jerusalem and at the tomb of Abraham in Hebron.[26]

Abū l-Fażl drew on this well-known model of "sacred" eunuchs in his elaboration of the necessary characteristics of a sanctified domain – represented thus in Akbar's imperial harem – seclusion, sacredness and inaccessibility. In the organization of Akbar's harem, however, new elements were added, drawing upon a variety of overlapping Indic and Islamic traditions; the use of warrior Rājpūts, for instance, was a feature of the Mughal pluralistic undertakings for most of the dynasty's history. Different groups held various responsibilities. The innermost section of the harem was guarded by "sober and active women", the most trustworthy of them placed about the apartments of Akbar. Outside the enclosure stood the eunuchs; at some distance from them, the Rājpūts; and beyond them, the porters of the gates. Eunuchs were placed at the boundary between women and men, royal women on one side, Rājpūt soldiers on the other, all in designated spaces, each group with their own specific function and responsibilities. The eunuchs' placement echoed the well-established institutions of other harems (women–eunuchs–non-eunuchs). However, their particular location and the rituals of protection that they were expected to perform were of particular significance, for in accomplishing this task they called forth the protection of the "divine", "veiling and secluding ... something holy".[27]

While Akbar's harem was guarded and unreachable for most people, it was not closed off from the world, nor were those enclosed within bereft of power or uninterested in public affairs. The theory of a new strong and indomitable empire, which found tangible form in the sacred harem, was never so successful as to wipe out contradictions, tensions, human volition or unexpected departures. Indeed, Mughal women responded to the new imperial ideology, and to new sovereign ideals, by participating in the formulation of monarchical ideas and practices – and at times, they did so by transgressing these very ideals. As with women, the place or the presence of the eunuchs in the Mughal courts was not restricted to prescriptive exemplars. In this following section, I will further extend the inquiry of the sacred, elevated eunuchs in Akbar's imperial ideology.

The *Āʾīn-i Akbarī* lists almost every office and institution of Akbar's empire but does not discuss eunuchs in detail or as a separate category, as in the case, for example, of the *Chelās* or faithful disciples. There are, however, numerous references to eunuchs in other documents of Akbar's time. For example, Abū l-Fażl does not mention the eunuch Ambar, but he is known to have accompanied Akbar's mother from Kabul to Delhi in the emperor's second regal year.[28] One eunuch, named Niʿamat, features in the illuminated manuscripts of the *Akbarnāma*; here, he is shown at the entrance of the harem trying to stop Akbar's foster-brother, Adham Khān, from entering. We are told in the *Akbarnāmah* that Adham Khān had killed the *vakīl* (deputy or assistant) and that after the murder he had gone to the harem where Akbar was sleeping. With the help of several attendants and servants, including Ni'amat, Adham was overpowered and then executed by the emperor, who threw him from a great height.[29]

Another prominent case of an important eunuch is that of Phul Mālik, who had initially served under Islām Shāh Sūr (1545–1553). With the end of the Sur empire, he was enrolled in Akbar's service as *khwājasarā'ī*, the chief eunuch of the harem, and renamed Iʿtimād Khān.[30] The reason for his elevation was that the emperor wished him (at the death of Shams al-Dīn Muḥammad Atkeh Khān, Akbar's foster-father) "to remodel the finances, making him a commander with a numerical rank of one thousand, and conferring upon him the title of Iʿtimād Khān".[31] Abū l-Fażl reports that in subsequent years, Iʿtimād performed his duties to Akbar's satisfaction. In 1565, for example, he conveyed the daughter of Mīrān Mubārak, the king of Khāndēsh, to Akbar's harem. He also distinguished himself in the subjugation of Bengal, and consequently in 1576 he would be appointed the governor of Bhakkar. When Akbar went to Punjab in 1578, Iʿtimād Khān is said to have wanted to join him. In order to finance himself and to equip his contingent adequately, Iʿtimād collected the rents and outstanding payments of that year "with much harshness". Ultimately, his actions resulted in political machinations against him and his murder in the same year.[32]

'Abd al-Qādir Badā'ūnī, who wrote an account of the events of Akbar's empire, makes a scathing comment on Iʿtimād's various appointments. He quotes a tradition to make his point: "A time will come on men, when none will become favourites but profligates ... and then the government shall be by the counsel of women, and the rule of boys, and the management of eunuchs".[33] At the same time, he does, however, applaud Iʿtimād's "enterprise and economy" as being quite unprecedented. Recording the events from 1562–1563, Badā'ūnī says, in that year Iʿtimād Khān "obtained the highest consideration in the harem, and even in state matters became the sovereign's confidant".[34] It is then hardly surprising that it was also Iʿtimād Khān who conveyed a new queen to the harem, fulfilling a classical eunuch's task. He also undertook many other services that earned him a central position both in the harem as well as in state matters. His participation in Akbar's attempts to subjugate Bengal was in keeping with his required service as a protector of both the emperor and the empire itself. Although Iʿtimād the *khwājasarā'ī* was a "man of sense and discretion",[35] even according to a critic such as Badā'ūnī, what the eunuch had achieved led to some consternation and disapproval from contemporaries, perhaps an indication of the unease that underlay the emerging importance of non-kin relationships (fictive kinship) in Akbar's harem. Badā'ūnī brings out this tension in his discussion of Iʿtimād Khān.[36]

Eunuchs were the "servants" of the empire. Complicated gradations of rank and their accompanying notions of honour were fundamental to the behaviour and demeanour of those employed by Akbar. Service in a court context was an intricate and complex undertaking. There were no fixed demarcations of tasks, no caste divisions whereby particular errands, jobs and responsibilities were confined to some and denied to others. A water-carrier could (and did) write a memoir, a foster nurse could serve as a diplomat and a swordsman could be a storyteller, however strict the codes of conduct that they were expected to follow. Thus, many eunuchs in the service of the sacred harem, close to the sacred person of the emperor and the Mughal women, were both "servants" and "officers" of the empire. Their function (or "office") was not strictly or narrowly defined.[37] Therefore, Mughal eunuchs could embody very different roles and also accumulate different offices.

In one incident, we see eunuchs sacrificing themselves for the empress they had to protect. The background for this story comprises the events of 1626, when emperor Jahāngīr was detained and taken prisoner during the course of a coup by the general Mahābat Khān. While Mahābat had served as a loyal general until this time, several sources suggest tensions rising between him and the empress Nūr Jahān and her influential brother, Āṣaf Khān. Some documents also explain that Mahābat had not paid his dues, and imperial orders were repeatedly sent insisting that he pay them. In retaliation, Mahābat assembled an army of Rājpūts and made his way towards the river Bahat, where the imperial camp was stationed. Upon arrival in the imperial camp, he succeeded in taking Emperor Jahāngīr into custody. However, the empress Nūr Jahān managed to escape across the river to the tent mansion of her brother and here made plans to rescue the emperor. Accompanied by the head of the palace eunuchs, Jawāhir Khān, her own eunuch Nadīm and several distinguished nobles, she commanded the Mughal forces to advance into the swiftly moving river Bahat. At the same time, Āṣaf Khān, along with a number of distinguished courtiers and soldiers next to her palanquin, secured the riverbank opposite Mahābat's troops. As it turned out, it was the worst possible crossing, for in three or four places, there were broad stretches of deep water, and so it became impossible for the troops to retain order. The sources describe how each group fell in a different direction. Following this, Mahābat's forces drove forward their war elephants. Even before they reached the middle of the stream, therefore, the empress's forces were in disarray: They dispersed into isolated and bewildered groups. Several officers rushed about in the chaos, not knowing where to move or how to direct their men. The opposite bank, lined with fearsome elephants that guarded the captive emperor, was like an impenetrable wall.

Against the odds, some of Nūr Jahān's men made it to the opposite bank but were immediately confronted by more of Mahābat's elephants. The soldiers fled from the devastation. Muʿtamad Khān, paymaster and court chronicler, along with another dignitary, crossed the river and stood on the banks of a stream contemplating the tricks of fate. Nadīm, Nūr Jahān's eunuch, approached with a reprimand: "Her Majesty wants to know why you have stopped to contemplate. Be brave, for as soon as you enter the battle, the foe will be routed".[38] They rushed into the river. Mahābat's men drove more Rājpūts soldiers into the river. As Nūr Jahān approached Mahābat's side, shelling fiery shots, her elephant received two sword wounds on its trunk. She turned back just as two spears cut wounds in the elephant's back. Her eunuchs Jawāhir and Nadīm were killed while protecting the empress. Following this battle, Nūr Jahān would reassemble her resources and eventually free the emperor.

Jawāhir and Nadīm appear in this story as intrinsic to Nūr Jahān's survival and eventual success: first in calling other dignitaries into battle, and finally giving their own lives in the fulfilment of their duty. Eunuchs, like imperial women, offered loyalty, engaged in a range of rich activities, gave "critical" reminders as they battled and guarded the "sacred" person of their empress.

In contrast to this heroic self-sacrifice, we are provided with another representation of eunuch service in the famous case of the eunuch called Shāh Qulī Khān Maḥram, that is, one who was admitted to the sanctified space of the harem. Qulī went to the lengths of castrating himself when he entered Akbar's harem. This was an act of devotion to the emperor, one that underlined a deep level of loyalty and commitment and was to generate a special intimacy with the person of the emperor. His status and occupations were nonetheless governed by the rigors of discipline and formality. Furthermore, his position was complicated by the fact that he loved a boy named Qabūl Khān. Since Akbar, according to Abū l-Fażl, "did not approve of this kind of conduct in any of his servants ... he prohibited it". Shāh Qulī, however, did not restrain his feelings. His beloved boy was then handed over to the guards (presumably to be killed, although this is not clear in the records), and Qulī retired to live the life of a hermit.[39]

There is a great deal to be said about how this poignant story can be situated within the broader contexts of Akbar's imperial ideology. Abū l-Fażl's writing emphasizes Akbar's controlled sexuality: Proper forms of bodily and sexual behaviour and the comportment (restraint) of the monarch himself were all part of the sovereign's ideal model of appropriate norms. To highlight one example, the chroniclers applaud the emperor's almost exclusive concentration upon marriage, considered primarily if not exclusively for reproduction. Imperial regulations on marriage are a striking example of how a broader sexual regime was patterned upon the model set by and reproduced by the emperor.[40]

It is useful in this context to briefly compare Bābur's discussion of marriage, love and poetry, which appear together in his memoir, along with his delineation of an ethos wherein male and female love were both permissible, with Abū l-Fażl's (or Akbar's) later emphasis on the institutionalization of marriage, and his declared abhorrence of male–male love as intrinsically base and innately depraved.[41] In the context of Bābur's 'perpetual traveling', it was relatively difficult to maintain strict control over marital and other sexual or romantic relationships. The entire tendency of Akbar's politics, on the other hand, as it developed, was one of extending control in different spheres of Mughal society in order to maximize the emperor's power. There was little place in this system of disciplined sexuality for what might be called irrationality or emotionalism – the emotionalism of poetry or, it must be said, of Qulī's love for Qabūl.

Jahāngīr's deliberations on young eunuchs

The ideology that inspired the making of Akbar's harem, the arrangements of the domestic spaces in his palace, influenced where and how the eunuchs were to be positioned – spatially and in terms of role ascription. However, in spite of the new disciplinary regime that marked Akbar's times, royal eunuchs (like women) could never be confined to these prescriptive spaces and roles. Their sanctified position and their inventiveness meant they had room for manoeuvre and opportunities for taking the initiative.

It is in the context of Akbar's new regime that we might examine another event concerning eunuchs from the reign of Jahāngīr, the son of Akbar. In 1608, Jahāngīr issued an imperial order to restrict a practice in Sylhet (Bengal) of having children castrated and sent to regional authorities, as well as to the Mughal court, in lieu of revenue payments. The trade in eunuchs posed a moral dilemma for Jahāngīr. This was not surprising, given the sacred connotations that his father had drawn upon in the making of the harem, particularly the placement of the eunuchs as guards of this sanctuary. The harem was one of the most consecrated spaces of Jahāngīr's boyhood, which would have been deeply familiar to him from that time.

Indeed, the construction of Akbar's new capital, Fateḥpūr-Sīkrī, where the first royal harem was built, was tied to the birth of Jahāngīr. Although Akbar had had several children from his many marriages, none had survived except Jahāngīr. A number of courtiers suggested that he seek the blessings of the Sufi saint Salīm Chishtī in the village of Sīkrī. When Akbar visited Salīm Chishtī, the saint blessed him and foretold that he would have three sons. On August 30, 1569, Prince Salīm (later named Jahāngīr) was born in the quarters of the Sufi master and was named after the mystic. At a thanksgiving to the Sufi saint, Akbar ordered the construction of the city of Fateḥpūr-Sīkrī. The prince came of age in the harem quarters of Sīkrī. After his circumcision, his formal education began there.

In a princely household, in which marriage and the right to share the empire's financial resources were markers of adulthood, large numbers of women and eunuchs would often accompany and serve the young prince.

Eunuchs had a number of responsibilities concerning the prince. The prince would sleep either in his own chambers or with one of his wives or concubines. If he slept with the latter, "he was likely undressed by eunuchs appointed to the harem". Eunuchs and servants would heat coals to warm the prince's bathing water, prepare his food, lay out his clothes, sharpen his swords and dagger, prime his muskets, clean his saddle and so on.[42] Jahāngīr's memoir, the *Jahāngīr-nāmah*, details his affectionate relationships with harem women, especially Akbar's older wife, Ruqayya Begum, and another wife, Salīma Sulṭān Begum, his stepmothers. Salīma interceded and asked for forgiveness on Jahāngīr's behalf when, as a prince, he had rebelled against Akbar. Along with the women of the harem, he would also be deeply favoured by his tutors (*atālīq*) and the eunuchs too. Inevitably, Jahāngīr would have had enormous respect for the people attached to the sacred institution of the harem in which he grew up as a specially treasured son and heir.

It is in this context that we might understand the unusual order that he issued in 1608. Although "all Mughal emperors from Akbar down to Awrangzēb made gestures toward forbidding the castration of young boys",[43] no one had previously issued an injunction against a practice that had enslaved young boys and turned them into eunuchs without their consent. Yet, it is important to note that in the context of Jahāngīr's injunction, there were ethical considerations that had to be taken into account when considering the practice of trading eunuchs. Such a reflection rested upon a close understanding of the imperial networks and structures that Jahāngīr inherited and carried forward, of which eunuchs were a part. Certainly, Jahāngīr's contemporary policies need to be understood in relation to the various traditions and customs that existed throughout his empire.

For example, in Sylhet in Bengal, the tribute of slave-girls or eunuchs to an overlord in the neighbouring region was an established practice. The move to send eunuchs in lieu of revenue payment from Bengal to the imperial court dates to the mid to late fourteenth century, specifically attributed to the reign of Fīrūz Shāh Tughlaq (r. 1351–1380). This practice was still in vogue in 1605, the first year of Jahāngīr's reign.[44] In fact, a number of contemporary European observers and court chroniclers noted that during the sixteenth and seventeenth centuries, Bengal enjoyed "an unenviable reputation as the principle source of eunuchs" for the entire Mughal empire.[45] In 1608, however, Jahāngīr sent orders to the governor of Bengal, Islām Khān, to put an end to the practice in Sylhet, in which castrated boys were sent to the province headquarters in lieu of revenue payments. Other subdivisions were following Sylhet and were sending eunuchs to their individual headquarters. The emperor noted the widespread nature of this practice of paying tribute in the form of young eunuchs:

> In Hindustan, especially in the province of Sylhet, which is a dependency of Bengal, it was the custom of the people of those parts to make

> eunuchs of some of their sons and give them to the governor in place of revenue (*māl-vājibī*). This custom by degrees had been adopted in other provinces, and every year some children are thus ruined and cut off from procreation. This practice had become common. At this time I issued an order that hereafter no one should follow this abominable custom, and that the traffic in young eunuchs should be completely done away with. Islām Khān and the other governors of the sūbah [administrative division] of Bengal received firmāns that whoever should commit such acts should be capitally punished and that they should seize eunuchs of tender years who might be in anyone's possession. No one of the former kings had obtained this success. Please Almighty God, in a short time this objectionable practice will be completely done away with, and the traffic in eunuchs being forbidden, no one shall venture on this unpleasant and unprofitable proceeding.[46]

The emperor decreed that the making of young eunuchs, which was "objectionable", would be henceforth treated as a capital crime. Following this order, from the region of Bihār, the governor Afżal Khān sent several people who had been found guilty of castrating children to the court. In 1610, Jahāngīr is said to have stated in reference to this, "I had repeatedly given orders that no one should make eunuchs or buy or sell them, and whoever did so would be answerable as a criminal. At this time Afżal Khān sent some of these evildoers to court for the sūbah of Bihār. I ordered these unthinking ones (*bi-'aqibatan*) to be imprisoned for life".[47]

For the next decade, the emperor did not allude to the subject again. In 1621, he mentioned that the governor of Bengal Ibrāhīm Khān Fatḥ Jang had sent two eunuchs to the court, along with 19 elephants, one slave, 41 fighting cocks, 12 bullocks and seven buffaloes. Whether these were adult or child eunuchs is not clear from the source. In 1621, the emperor received 42 eunuchs.[48] The following year, in 1622, Jahāngīr again noted that Ibrāhīm Khān had sent more eunuchs; one of these was a hermaphrodite.[49] The practice of trade in eunuchs continued. It is recorded that Sa'īd Khān Chaghatā'ī, a prominent noble at both Akbar's and Jahāngīr's court, was so taken with eunuchs that he maintained 12,000 of them. When Jahāngīr ascended the throne, Chaghatā'ī was offered the governorship of Punjab with the condition that he should prevent his eunuchs from committing oppressive acts against the weak and the poor, which Chaghatā'ī promised to do.[50]

Jahāngīr's attempt to curtail the trade in younger eunuchs was, however, unsuccessful. Hambly notes that irrespective of Jahāngīr's feelings, there was no fall in the demand for eunuchs.[51] Yet, regardless of the outcome of Jahāngīr's order, it still tells us much about his wider moral landscape. Jahāngīr reasoned openly that the practice of castrating younger eunuchs, turning them into commodities, was abhorrent; in other words, it was not in keeping with their revered status, an important construction of the Mughal imperial ideology. That Jahāngīr made no intervention in the case of adult eunuchs is also worth bearing in mind. It was not the presence or the employment of the eunuchs that was the problem. Rather, Jahāngīr sought to control the unthinking, and routine, one might say, mundane practice of converting young boys into eunuchs.

Concluding thoughts

Eunuchs exemplified a number of vital and diverse roles. Among many others, there were Jawāhir Khān and Nadīm, in the inner circle of the Mughal empress Nūr Jahān as she boldly attempted to save the emperor. Along with the nobles who formed a line of defence around the empress, Jawāhir and Nadīm remained next to Nūr Jahān in the midst of the battle – carrying her order to her forces and sacrificing their lives in the end; they were among the most valuable protectors of the empress. In fact, eunuchs continued to take on significant responsibilities in the reigns of the later Mughal emperors. No one relied on them "as heavily as the aging Awrangzēb", one scholar notes. Awrangzēb's head eunuch Khwāja Ṭālib/Khidmatgār (d. 1704) was especially prominent. One of the last surviving members of the emperor's generation, he had served as Prince Muʿaẓẓam's primary caretaker when he was under house arrest for treason. Khidmatgār had several eunuch protégés that served other princes. Awrangzēb's sons and daughters wooed this eunuch and showered him with gifts and audiences. As a prime source of communication with the emperor, he was a force to reckon with.[52]

Even the stigmatized community of *hijrās* in India today seem to carry something of the special powers, the *baraka*, of the eunuchs of the earlier times, and they invoke Mughal eunuchs as their ancestors. In other words, from the sacred eunuchs of Prophet Muḥammad to today's *hijrās* – with all the differences in the construction of their identities, their reinvention in time and in rather diverse moral and physical spaces – something of the charisma has survived.[53] To negotiate their stigmatized identity, the *hijrās* have made claims about their very personhood being a source of power – the power to bless or curse, to bring or bar prosperity and salvation. Appropriately enough, as several ethnographic accounts have noted, the *hijrās* have pointed out that "their ancestors were accorded high respect in the Mughal period".[54]

Notes

1 **Acknowledgements:** A draft of this chapter was presented at a workshop on "Eunuchs and Bishops in World History", hosted by the Department of History, University of Zurich, in August 2013. I wish to thank Almut Höfert, Matthew M. Mesley and Serena Tolino for the invitation and all the participants in the workshop for their reactions. Special thanks to my colleagues at Emory for their reading and critiques – especially to Gyan Pandey and V. Narayana Rao. My gratitude to Francis Robinson, Michael Fisher, Nadia Maria El-Cheikh, Shadab Bano and Stephen Dale for thought-provoking suggestions.

A note on transliteration and citations: For the transliteration, the *IJMES (International Journal of Middle East Studies)* system was used. All the information included in square brackets is mine. Shaun Marmon, *Eunuchs and Sacred Boundaries in Islamic Society* (New York: Oxford University Press, 1995), wrote a thought-provoking volume on the sacred eunuchs of Medina. Details from her volume appear in the following section.

2 Satish Kumar, "Eunuchs: Past and Present," *Eastern Anthropologist* 37 (1984): 381–389; R. Nath, "Mughal Institution of Khwajasara," in *Medieval Indian History and Architecture* (New Delhi: APH Publishing Corporation, 1995); Gavin Hambly, "A Note on the Trade in Eunuchs in Mughal Bengal," *Journal of the American Oriental Society* 94, no. 1 (1974): 125–130; Saleem Kidwai, "Sultans, Eunuchs and Domestics: New Forms of Bondage in Medieval India," in *Chains of Servitude: Bondage and Slavery in Medieval India*, ed. Utsa Patnaik and Manjari Dingwaney (Madras: Sangam Books, 1985); Indrani Chatterjee, "A Slave's Quest for Selfhood in Eighteenth-Century Hindustan," *Indian Economic & Social History Review* 37 (2000): 53–86; Shadab Bano, "Eunuchs in Mughal Royal and Aristocratic Establishment," *Proceedings of Indian History Congress* (Kolkata, 2009): 417–427.

3 Eunuchs, termed *ghulām-i akhta*, are discussed by a cousin of Bābur, in Mīrzā Ḥaidar Dūghlāt, *Ta'rīkh-i Rashīdī*, trans. E. Denison Ross (Patna: Academica Asiatica, 1973), 258.

4 Gulbadan Bānū Bēgum, *Aḥvāl-i Humāyūn Bāshā*, British Library MS. Or.166; Gulbadan Bānū Bēgum, *The History of Humāyūn: Humāyūn-Nāma,* trans. Annette Susannah Beveridge (1902, reprint, Delhi, 1994); Ibid., 184–185; Gulbadan, *Aḥvāl,* fo. 70a–71a.

5 Ruby Lal, *Domesticity and Power in the Early Mughal World* (New York: Cambridge University Press, 2005).

6 Marmon, *Eunuchs and Sacred Boundaries*, ix.

7 Abū l-Fażl, *The Ā'īn-i Akbarī*, trans. Heinrich Blochmann (1873; reprint, Calcutta: Asiatic Society of Bengal, 1993), 1:45.

8 Ibid., 1:45–46.

9 Ibid., 1:46–47.

10 As part of the process of the institutionalization of the imperial harem, the term itself came to be the common description of the women's sphere, signifying important changes in the Mughals' domestic life. See Ruby Lal, "Settled, Sacred and 'Incarcerated': The Imperial Haram", chap. 6 in *Domesticity and Power*, 176–213.

11 Abū l-Fażl, *The Ā'īn-i Akbarī*, 39. See also *The Ā'īn-i Akbarī*, xxi. The title *Shabistān-i Iqbāl* is rendered "The Imperial Harem" in Blochmann's translation of *The Ā'īn-i Akbarī*, 15.

12 Robert Bertram Serjeant, "Haram and Hawtah, the Sacred Enclave in Arabia," in *Melanges Taha Husain*, ed. 'Abd al-Raḥmān Badawī (Cairo: Dār al Ma'ārif, 1962), reprinted in Francis E. Peters, ed., *The Arabs and Arabia on the Eve of Islam* (Aldesrhot: Asghate, 2010), 167–184.

13 Ibid., 43–44.

14 *Encyclopaedia of Islam*, 2nd ed., Glossary and Index of Terms, s. v. "Ḥarām".

15 'Alī Akbar Dihkhudā, *Lughatnāmah-i Dihkhudā* (Tehran: Mu'assasa-i Intishārāt Chap-i Dānishgāh-i Tehrān, 1993), 6:7786–7789.

16 Ibid., 2:3149.

17 Francis Joseph Steingass, *A Comprehensive Persian-English Dictionary, including the Arabic Words and Phrases to be met with in Persian Literature* (London: Routledge & K. Paul, 1892), s. v. "bayt".

18 Juan Eduardo Campo, *The Other Side of Paradise: Explorations into the Religious Meanings of Domestic Space in Islam* (Columbia: University of South

Carolina Press, 1991), 9. The material for the discussion that follows on the religious meanings of domestic spaces is taken from Campo, unless indicated otherwise.

19 Ibid., 3.

20 Ibid., 19.

21 Abū l-Fażl, *The Akbarnama of Abu-l-Fazl*, trans. Henry Beveridge (1902; reprint, Delhi: South Asia Books, 1993), 3:1009.

22 For Persian, I use Abū l-Fażl, *Akbarnāmah*, ed. ʻAbd al-Raḥīm Mawlayī (Calcutta, The Asiatic Society, 1873–1886), along with Beveridge's English translation cited above; hereafter Mawlayī, *Akbarnāmah*, 2:217; Beveridge, *Akbarnama*, 2:335.

23 Mawlayī, *Akbarnāmah*, 2:289; Beveridge; *Akbarnama*, 2:426.

24 Mawlayī, *Akbarnāmah*, 1:6; Beveridge, *Akbarnama*, 1:16.

25 Marmon, *Eunuchs and Sacred Boundaries*, ix, x, 40, 43.

26 Ibid., 39.

27 Ibid., 33.

28 Bano, "Eunuchs in Mughal Royal and Aristocratic Establishment," 418.

29 Lal, *Domesticity and Power*, 196–202.

30 *Beveridge; Akbarnama*, 3:131, and Abū l-Fażl, *Āʼīn-i Akbarī*, 1:13, fn. 1.

31 Abū l-Fażl, *The Āʼīn-i Akbarī*, 1:13, fn. 1.

32 Ibid.

33 ʻAbd al-Qādir Badāʼūnī, *Muntakhab al-Tavārīkh*, ed. and trans. George S. A. Ranking, W. H. Lowe and Sir Wolseley Haig (1884–1925; repr. Delhi: Renaissance Publishing House, 1986), 2:63–64.

34 Ibid.

35 Ibid.

36 I have also discussed this issue in relation to the high-ranking appointments of Shams al-Dīn Muḥammad of Ghazni and his son ʻAzīz Kūkah, and of Khwāja Maqṣūd of Herat and his sons Sayf Khān and Zayn Khān Kūkah – the foster community of Akbar in my *Domesticity and Power*. See especially pages 188–196.

37 Lal, *Domesticity and Power*, especially 69–78.

38 The events of 1626–1627 are described in the following works: Farid Bhakkari, *Nobility Under the Great Mughals: Based on Dhakhīratul khawanīn of Shaikh Farīd Bhakkari*, trans. Z. A. Desai, (New Delhi: Sundeep Prakashan, 2003), 2:14–21; Muʻtamad Khān, *Iqbālnāmah-yi Jahāngīri*, (Ghāzīpur: n.p., 1863); Henry Miers Elliot and John Dowson, *The History of India as told by Its Own Historians* (Allahabad: Kitab Mahal Pvt. Ltd. 1964), 6:420–428; See also Kāmī Shīrāzī, *Fatḥnāmah-i Nūr Jahān Bēgum* (Np.: n.p., 1626) which is built around this very episode; W. H. Siddiqui, ed. and trans., *Waqa-i-uz-Zaman (Fath Nama-i-Nur Jahan Begam; A Contemporary Account of Jahangir)* (Rampur: Ramur Raza Library, 2003). The eighteenth-century account of Muḥammad Hādī advanced Muʻtamad's account, added a continuation from 1624 and brought his chronicle to the point of Jahāngīr 's death in 1627. Thackston provides an excellent, reader-friendly translation of Hādī, from which the above citation is drawn, Wheeler M. Thackston, trans., *The Jahangirnama: Memoirs of Jahangir, Emperor of India by Jahangir* (New York, Oxford University Press, 1999), 442.

39 Beveridge, *Akbarnama*, 2:21.

40 For a detailed discussion, see Lal, "Settled, Sacred, and All-Powerful: The New Regime under Akbar", chap. 6 in *Domesticity and Power*, 140–175.

41 Beveridge, *Akbarnama*, 2:104; Lal, *Domesticity and Power*, 114–115.

42 Munis D. Faruqui, *The Princes of the Mughal Empire* (Cambridge: Cambridge University Press, 2012), 117, citation on 127.

43 Faruqui, *The Princes of the Mughal Empire*, 89.

44 Kidwai, "Sultans, Eunuchs and Domestics", 84; Hambly, "A Note on the Trade in Eunuchs in Mughal Bengal," 128.

45 Hambly, "A Note on the Trade in Eunuchs in Mughal Bengal," 125.
46 Alexander Rogers, trans., Henry Beveridge ed., *Tūzuk-i-Jahāngīrī, or, Memoirs of Jahāngīr* (New Delhi: Atlantic Publishers and Distributors, 1989), 1:150–151.
47 Ibid., 1:168.
48 Ibid., 2:194–195, and note * on 2:195.
49 Ibid., 2:201.
50 Ibid., 1:12–13. See also Abū l-Fażl, *The Āʾīn-i Akbarī*, 352.
51 Hambly, "A Note on the Trade in Eunuchs in Mughal Bengal," 29.
52 Faruqui, *The Princes of the Mughal Empire*, 239–240.
53 Swapna Taparia, "Emasculated Bodies of Hijras: Sites of Imposed, Resisted and Negotiated Identities," *Indian Journal of Gender Studies* 18, no. 2 (2011): 167–184.
54 Ibid., 171.

Part II

Networks and kinships

5 Celibate, but not childless

Eunuch military dynasticism in medieval China

Michael Hoeckelmann

Throughout the history of imperial China (221 BC–AD 1911), eunuchs were notorious for meddling in political affairs, which traditionally were considered to be the domain of Confucian scholar-officials.[1] Yet eunuchs were influential in other spheres as well: Less well known in the West, even by historians of China, is the fact that eunuchs also led family lives as husbands and fathers. Even less recognized are their military functions: During certain eras, eunuchs not only strong-armed their way into civil bureaucracy but also held sway over important branches of the military. One such period was the late Tang 唐 Dynasty (618–907), when eunuchs enjoyed a monopoly on positions within the palace army and military surveillance of the provinces. In the aftermath of the disastrous Rebellion of An Lushan 安祿山 (755–763), the eunuch Yu Chao'en 魚朝恩 (722–770) took control of the Army of Divine Strategies (*shence jun* 神策軍) and played a crucial role in restoring imperial authority. After his downfall, Yu was succeeded by other eunuchs, who provided their adopted sons – often eunuchs themselves – with important positions in the bureaucracy and military. These adoptions created a unique feature of the medieval Chinese eunuch institution: *eunuch dynasticism* (*huanguan shijia* 宦官世家). This chapter describes the important role that eunuch adoptive networks played in the late Tang and contextualizes those networks within the vast array of ranks that eunuchs occupied during that time. It begins, however, with a survey of the historical sources for Chinese eunuchs, first of the traditional histories from the tenth and eleventh centuries and second of the epigraphic sources that have been excavated since the mid-twentieth century and should be employed in order to reconstruct eunuch lives, networks, and status.

Sources and resources of eunuchs in China

The presence of eunuchs at courts in China can be dated as far back as the mid-first millennium BC.[2] Evidence for castration as corporal punishment is found on the oracle bones of the Yin-Shang 殷商 Dynasty (sixteenth–eleventh c. BC), the earliest written sources from China.[3] Nevertheless, one has to be careful not to conflate the legal punishment of castration with the institution of eunuchs, as the majority of eunuchs did not come from the ranks of convicted criminals or prisoners of war. In fact, castration as a punishment was abolished on several occasions, first in the second century BC and then in the late sixth century AD, while the institution of eunuchs prevailed until the end of imperial China in 1911.[4] Previous scholars believed that the majority of eunuchs under the Tang came from slave markets in the south and southeast of China,[5] but research over the last 15 years has revealed that most eunuchs came not from the south, but in fact from the capital regions in the north, in particular around Chang'an 長安 (modern-day Xi'an 西安).[6]

Furthermore, eunuchs appeared only in military offices after their first domination in the Later Han Dynasty 後漢 (25–220), around the beginning of the fifth century, and then only in north China.[7] It remains an open question as to why the Turkic people that ruled the north at this time adopted the eunuch institution. Some have suggested it was a means of controlling their Chinese subjects; more broadly, Tani Yutaka 谷泰 suggests that ancient Middle Eastern empires extended the use of bellwethers (castrated rams) to lead their sheep by way of analogy to castrated humans as intermediaries between them and subdued populations. Yet he admits that the pastoral Turkic and Mongolian peoples of Northeast Asia do not use bellwethers.[8] Likewise, no theory has been proposed so far as to why the phenomenon of eunuchs in the military in China disappeared in the late sixth century, only to reappear after nearly two centuries in the mid-eighth.

Pre-twentieth-century Chinese historical writing granted eunuchs biographical treatment in 11 of the 24 "standard histories" (*zhengshi* 正史), works on the history of previous dynasties sponsored by the court, starting with Fan Ye's 范曄 (398–445) *History of the Later Han (Hou Hanshu* 後漢書).[9] However, the space given to them is small compared with other important figures such as emperors and scholar-officials: only one out of 150 biographies or 200 chapters altogether in the *Old Tang History* (*Jiu Tangshu* 舊唐書)[10] and two out of 150/225 in the *New Tang History* (*Xin Tangshu* 新唐書).[11] Furthermore, whereas most biographies in the standard histories deal with individuals, eunuchs are only treated as a group.[12] The *Old History* contains biographies for 15 eunuchs (two are even attached to a more illustrious figure), the *New History* for 21 (with five attached).

Studies on Tang eunuchs remain rare in the West, and scholars tend to focus on those within the Later Han and Ming 明 dynasties (1368–1644).[13] The one notable exception is J. K. Rideout, whose work was cut short by his death; he considered the history of eunuchs up to the mid-eighth century – but before their rise to power.[14] Two American dissertations from the 1970s add some new facets but largely summarise the traditional sources, of course then the only ones available.[15] Most general surveys in English show a propensity to treat eunuchs either sensationally as guileful and power-hungry or, less often, as victims of "Oriental despotism";[16] only Jennifer W. Jay offers a more balanced view of eunuchs and kinship.[17]

Table 5.1 Eunuchs who have biographies in the Two Tang dynastic histories

Old Book (ch. 184)	*New Book (ch. 207)*	*New Book (ch. 208)*
1 Yang Sixu 楊思勗 (勖)	1 Yang Sixu 楊思勗	
2 Gao Lishi 高力士	2 Gao Lishi 高力士	
3 Li Fuguo 李輔國		11 Li Fuguo 李輔國
4 Cheng Yuanzhen 程元振	3 Cheng Yuanzhen 程元振, Luo Fengxian 駱奉先	
5 Yu Chao'en 魚朝恩, Liu Xixian 劉希暹, Jia Mingguan 賈明觀	4 Yu Chao'en 魚朝恩	
6 Dou Wenchang 竇文場	5 Dou Wenchang 竇文場, Huo Xianming 霍仙鳴	
7 Huo Xianming 霍仙鳴		
	6 Liu Zhenliang 劉貞亮	
8 Ju Wenzhen 俱文珍		
9 Tutu Chengcui 吐突承璀	7 Tutu Chengcui 吐突承璀	
	8 Ma Cunliang 馬存亮, Yan Zunmei 嚴遵美	
	9 Qiu Shiliang 仇士良	
10 Wang Shoucheng 王守澄		12 Wang Shoucheng 王守澄
		13 Liu Keming 劉克明
11 Tian Lingzi 田令孜		14 Tian Lingzi 田令孜, Yang Fugong 楊復恭
12 Yang Fuguang 楊復光	10 Yang Fuguang 楊復光	
13 Yang Fugong 楊復恭		
		15 Liu Jishu 劉季述
		16 Han Quanhui 韓全誨, Zhang Yanhong 張彥弘

Tang eunuchs come to the fore occasionally in studies from China and Taiwan, but more often than not, these studies single out individual eunuchs who are represented as archetypical eunuch-villains. Mainland scholars further suffer from both Confucian and Marxist biases, in that they treat eunuchs as epitomes of feudal society that reflect the abuse of imperial power. Of course, the scarcity of transmitted sources greatly restricted the scope of studies in the past; apart from the standard histories, only texts of a handful of eulogies, originally inscribed on stone and buried with the dead, were transmitted in authorial anthologies.[18] The meticulous research by Wang Shounan 王壽南 is a case in point: Although the charts of eunuch lineages he provides are invaluable for any study of Tang eunuchs, it is based entirely on that transmitted record.[19] In comparison, the newly discovered epigraphic material described in the following paragraph has been employed by Du Wenyu[20] 杜文玉 and Zhao Pei 趙沛.[21] Apart from mainland China and Taiwan, Chiu Yu Lok 趙雨樂 from Hong Kong has investigated the role of eunuchs in the administration of the Tang and early Song 宋 Dynasty (960–1279).[22]

Over the last decade and a half, historians of the Tang in the People's Republic and Taiwan have exhibited a strong interest in what they term *huanguan shijia*, rendered here as *eunuch dynasticism*.[23] That interest has been fuelled by the excavation of thousands of tomb inscriptions (*muzhiming* 墓志) on stone slabs buried with the dead in the vicinities of Xi'an and the second capital of Luoyang 洛陽 since the mid-twentieth century. So far, about 100 of these have been identified as those of eunuchs, their spouses and their adopted children.[24] The word *dynasticism* here, of course, does not refer to eunuchs as ruling emperors – that would have been unconceivable even for the Tang, which saw China's only female emperor.[25] Instead, it refers to the practice of eunuchs handing down their property to an adopted son, usually a cousin or other agnatic relative, who was often made a eunuch himself. They did not bequeath their office in a like manner. Although medieval China had so-called great clans, unlike those of Europe, China's were not a landed aristocracy, and the state strictly prohibited the heredity of offices.[26]

Early research on *muzhiming* unearthed in the Mang Mountains 邙山 near Luoyang, a traditional burial place of the Tang elite, was conducted by Patricia Ebrey and Rainer von Franz.[27] Von Franz published a groundbreaking study of the linguistic and poetical features of this extremely allusive genre, which, overall, is less concerned with its historical, biographical or religious content. More research on structural and functional differences between interred inscriptions and spirit road epitaphs is necessary, as their concurrence cannot be explained sufficiently with prescriptions of frugality. Sumptuary regulations proscribing the erection of a spirit-road epitaph for officials below a certain rank existed in Tang times, but, as with most regulations, it is far from clear whether these were always followed.[28] The vast majority of Tang *muzhiming* are indeed dedicated to lower strata of the elite, which left no other traces in the official or unofficial, historical or literary record.

There is no exhaustive survey of epigraphic sources regarding eunuchs, but we can reach some preliminary conclusions from an initial survey. A few hundred eulogy texts have been passed down through the centuries in literary anthologies of individual Tang authors,[29] but that number pales in light of those texts that have been unearthed near the former Tang capitals since 1949. Although one can detect huge variations in length, the language and content of these epigraphic sources were highly standardized and allow them to be divided into two genres: "interred tomb inscriptions" (*muzhiming*) and "spirit-road epitaphs" (*shendaobei* 神道碑). The *muzhiming* are usually written in a more formalized language, rich with allusions and set expressions in parallel style, whereas *shendaobei* in parts appear plainer in language but are also longer and more detailed with regard to the dedicatee's life. Apart from being a reflection of individual author's predilections, this is also due to the different performative functions of *muzhiming* and *shendaobei*: Only the highest members of the elite were entitled to receive the latter, which were aimed at a living and contemporaneous public. Both types of inscriptions nonetheless share certain commonalities: Neither ever refers explicitly to the incumbent's being castrated, apart from the consistent mention of "palace attendant" (*neishi* 內侍) in his office titles, which are a clear indication that he was a eunuch.[30]

Expressions that refer to the dedicatee's simultaneous possession of civil and military virtues are frequent within the inscriptions.[31] This may bear a specific relevance for the role of eunuchs, as their position was wedged in between the traditional virtues of *wen* 文 (civility) and *wu* 武 (martiality). Underlying this is the question as to how eunuchs serving in the military were reconciled cosmologically with their traditional function as body servants of the emperor; one major dichotomy in Chinese thought is that between female Yin 陰 and masculine Yang 陽. Heaven and emperor were the epitomes of Yang, while imperial spouses and sometimes officials represented submissive Yin. Translated into the political realm, that dichotomy re-entered as that between *wen* and *wu*. Indeed, if one thinks of eunuchs as standing between Yin and Yang and *wen* and *wu*, they could be seen as an important harmonizing node in the workings of these forces in the palace and in the realm at large, especially when these forces were out of balance.[32] The Song Dynasty, arguably because of the Tang experience, went out of its way to minimise the role of the military, but in the Tang, civil and martial were on a par and were not even strictly kept separate.[33] Eunuchs occupied a neutral position and, by controlling the palace and the capital and by monitoring the military commissioners, served as mediators between an impotent civil bureaucracy and a self-aggrandizing provincial military.

Eunuchs in the Tang Dynasty

The number and status of eunuchs increased dramatically during the Tang, and although there were attempts to curtail their power, both as individuals and as a group, such measures ultimately failed to stop their rise in influence. The second Tang emperor, Li Shimin 李世民 (Taizong 太宗, 599–649, r. 626–49), ordered that eunuchs should not be allowed to hold office above the third rank (in the system of nine ranks that the Tang had inherited from earlier dynasties) and that their duties be limited to guarding gates, sweeping the courts and serving food.[34] However, by the time of the emperor Li Longji 李隆基 (Xuanzong 玄宗, 685–762, r. 712–56), the number of eunuchs who wore purple (first to third rank) and crimson (fourth to fifth) robes is said to have exceeded 1,000.[35] In 791, Li Kuo 李适 (Dezong 德宗, 741–805, r. 779–805) allowed eunuchs from the fifth rank upwards to adopt one son (from their lineage and below the age of ten) in order to continue their ancestral line.[36] That limitation did not prevent Yang Fugong 楊復恭 from adopting 600 sons at the end of the Tang, many of them being officers in the military.[37] But before that, the most dramatic increase in the number of eunuchs came after the Rebellion of An Lushan (*An Shi zhi luan* 安史之亂, 755–63).

In 755, a "military commissioner" (*jiedu shi* 節度使) of Central Asian origin began a rebellion in North China. His name was An Lushan 安祿山 (707–57), and while he barely lived into the third year of an almost ten-year rebellion, it came to be identified with his name. Although the rebellion brought the dynasty to the brink of collapse, the court eventually regained control over the capitals Chang'an and Luoyang. Nevertheless, the rebellion had a huge effect on the administration of the realm, which became divided into military circuits, its commissioners often only paying lip service to the throne while secretly seeking to entrench their positions and thus becoming *de facto* independent. This left the court almost defenceless, so that in 763, when another rebellion erupted, only a eunuch, Yu Chao'en, came to the rescue of Emperor Li Yu 李豫 (posthumously Daizong 代宗, 727–79, r. 762–79); Yu was the "surveillance commissioner" (*jianjun shi* 監軍使) over a border defense army in the northwest called the "Army of Divine Strategies" (*shence jun*).[38] While most of the military commissioners at this time were "hedging their bets" and awaiting the outcome of the rebellion, Yu took sole command of the *shence jun* and, after the Uighur allies of the Tang had once again recaptured Chang'an, escorted Li Yu back. He encamped the *shence jun* in the palace, where it became a Praetorian Guard that deposed and killed several emperors during the ninth century and maintained power by offering sinecures for spoiled sons of the capital elite.[39] The major consequence of Yu's actions was that in the long term, the court eunuchs succeeded in achieving almost total control over the capital. Faced with obstructive factionalism among the officials at court and military insurrection in the provinces, a series of particularly weak emperors turned to eunuchs as their allies. Since imperial princes spent most of their childhood secluded in the palace and surrounded by women and eunuch servants, and the advancement of a eunuch, at least in theory, relied solely on the grace of the emperor, initially this must have seemed like a natural alliance to the mutual benefit of both sides.

The most prominent posts that eunuchs held after the early ninth century were (1) the two "Protectors-in-Chief" or "Conciliatory Inspectors of the Left and Right Army of Divine Strategies" (*shence jun hujun zhongwei/guan junrong shi* 神策軍護軍中尉/觀軍容使) in Chang'an and (2) the army surveillance commissioners that were dispatched from the court to the various military circuits. In the eighth century, a palace secretariat or "Court of State Secrets" (*shumi yuan* 樞密院) had been founded to handle the communication between the outer court – that is, the departments and ministries staffed with Confucian officials – and the inner court of emperors, their kin, and the eunuchs. In the early ninth century, the secretariat came to be headed by (3) two eunuch "Commissioners for State Secrets" (*shumi shi* 樞密使) and effectively allowed the eunuchs to look at all proposals ministers made to the emperor and later even to issue their own imperial edicts.[40] Taken together, these three kinds of posts gave the eunuchs significant leverage in all civil and military affairs. As the scholar-official and contemporary

Du Mu 杜牧 (803–852) put it in a dedicatory inscription for the court of army surveillance commissioners in Huainan 淮南, the surveillance commissioners "come from the Protectors-in-Chief (of the palace army) and Commissioners for State Secrets and, upon returning, become Protectors-in-Chief and Commissioners for State Secrets".[41]

The various "palace commissionerships" (*nei zhusi shi* 内諸司使) and military posts held by eunuchs have received some attention, but rarely with a focus on epigraphic material. According to some, the Protectors-in-Chief were at the top of the eunuch hierarchy;[42] others argue that the Commissioners for State Secrets were on a par with them or perhaps more powerful, because they oversaw the promotion of the surveillance commissioners.[43]

By coming from ignoble families, by being accountable to the emperor alone, and in staffing a government body of their own – the Palace Domestic Service (*neishi sheng* 內侍省)[44] – eunuchs were spared the "thorny gates of learning" and networking associated with officialdom.[45] At the same time, they were allowed to promote their adopted sons into similar high positions behind the curtains of that confined hierarchy, making their career paths almost hereditary. Their social situation can best be compared to military officers, who likewise often came from humbler origins than most ministers; both can be said to represent the evolving meritocracy of the second millennium AD.[46]

Prior to the Rebellion of An Lushan, non-eunuch commissioners had been appointed irregularly to specific tasks or to monitor provinces (*dao* 道), which were superimposed on the system of prefectures (*jun* 郡 or *zhou* 州) and counties (*xian* 縣) that the Tang had inherited from the preceding Sui 隋 Dynasty (581/89–618). Most prominent among those were the military commissioners, "inspection commissioners" (*guancha shi* 觀察使), "commissioners for the monopoly on salt and iron" (*yantie shi* 鹽鐵使) and "commissioners for transport" (*zhuanyun shi* 轉運使).[47] Initially, these posts were filled with regular career officials *ex officio*, and their numbers pale in comparison with the eunuch commissioners that existed in the imperial household from the beginning of the dynasty. However, after the rebellion, as a consequence of the decentralized nature of the government, commissioners began to multiply and gradually supplant the former system.[48] As yet, a link between the commissionerships inside the palace and those for regional administration in terms of institutional evolution has to be established.

In the 760s, another commissionership, the "Commissioners for Cultivating Merit" (*xiu gongde shi* 修功德使), was established, which gave the eunuchs direct control over the state funds for the upkeep of monasteries in Chang'an.[49] Along with their political, military and administrative power, eunuchs were also patrons of religion, in particular Buddhism. For example, Yu Chao'en donated his mansion in the capital to be converted into a Buddhist temple in memory of a deceased empress-dowager.[50] Eunuchs were a "surrogate for imperial patronage",[51] because the emperor could not endorse one religion exclusively, unless he was willing to anger the Confucian officials.

Eunuchs, family and gender

Considering eunuchs as husbands and fathers might initially appear as a contradiction in terms, but in fact, throughout China's imperial history, eunuchs have been able to marry and also to adopt children (*yang (jia)zi* 養假子, *yang (yi)er* 養義兒, or *yang nü* 養女); their sons could be either eunuchs or non-eunuchs. Most often they and their sons and daughters came from lower strata of society, families that could not afford a Confucian education or, more common under the Tang, lacked the aristocratic pedigree that was a prerequisite for an official career. Less well-reputed families, who worked as merchants or served in the military, might try to enhance their social standing by marrying off their daughters to eunuchs or entering adoptive relationships with them.

The patterns of adoptive networks of eunuchs and military families not only shared certain characteristics, as Mao Yangguang 毛阳光 argues,[52] but also, as Wang Shounan claims,[53] intersected with and thus served as a link between military circuits and court eunuchs. The adoption of non-agnatic kin was sneered at, even legally forbidden in medieval China.[54] Nevertheless, some leeway was granted for particular exceptions, for example, when one branch of a clan had no biological heir and none of the other branches could provide a substitute.[55] The first eunuch believed to have adopted a daughter (*yang yinü* 養義女) is Zhao Gao 趙高 (d. 207), minister of the Qin 秦 Dynasty (221–206 BC).[56] Eunuch adoptions were first formalized under the Later Han: In 129 or 130 (the Chinese lunar calendar allows no more specific date), emperor Shun 順帝 (r. 125–44) permitted eunuchs to hand down titles and land to one adopted son.[57] By the 180s, when the first of three eunuch-dominations reached its peak, eunuch adoptees could make impressive careers, as is shown in the case of the famous general and first emperor of the Wei 魏 Dynasty (220–265), Cao Cao 曹操 (155–220).[58]

Consequently, even if their sexual organs (penis and testicles) were removed before puberty, eunuchs in China were anything but child- or kinless.[59] In comparison to their brethren in the Christian Orient,[60] they had not arisen from a religious context. Eunuchs were also not considered sacred in China. Their existence was justified cosmologically at times by being related to a cluster of stars in proximity to the celestial emperor or *Di* 帝, a high god or ancestor, but even that link gave them a political dimension.[61] In fact, the more eunuchs became ubiquitous in the palace, the more they created an aura of seclusion around the emperor and became a symbol of imperial despotism. In contrast, the discourse on *paṇḍakas* (Chin. *huangmen* 黃門) – often and controversially translated as "eunuchs" in English and other languages – in Buddhist India as a different gender seems to have played no role in China.[62] Indeed, the manliness or masculinity of eunuchs was not challenged before the Song Dynasty, when historians such as Ouyang Xiu 歐陽修 included denunciations of eunuchs in their work,[63] fuelled by a Neo-Confucian gender ideology that was also associated with misogyny: "Since antiquity, when eunuchs wreaked havoc on the empire of man, its roots ran deeper than the calamity of women".[64] Previously, the unmanliness of eunuchs was, if ever, only alluded to, such as in a memorial presented to the emperor in 809 by Bai Juyi 白居易 (772–846) against the appointment of a eunuch to the field command of an army:

> How can there be an Executive General and Campaign Commander, and a palace commissioner [eunuch] charged with both duties? Your servant fears when the people of the realm hear this, they certainly are going to disdain the court; when the Barbarians of the four directions [outside China] hear of this, they certainly are going to mock the Middle Kingdom [China]; when Wang Chengzong [a rebellious military commissioner] hears of this, it certainly is going to increase his vigor; and when the national histories record this, how is posterity going to regard it?[65]

What Bai is arguing against in the year 809 is the overlap of duties rather than a lack of manliness on part of the eunuch-commander Tutu Chengcui 吐突承璀; a servant of the inner palace, he should not be given a field command. Criticism of his effeminacy only becomes palpable when Bai insinuates the appointment might "increase the vigor" of a real man, here the rebellious military commissioner Wang Chengzhong 王承宗.[66]

It is nevertheless undeniable that Chinese historians were negatively inclined towards eunuchs long before the Song, usually highlighting their viciousness and reducing their biographies to sequences of treacherous behaviour. But in that, they were not necessarily different from other men. There were exceptions to that rule, notably the historian Sima Qian, who, although he was punished with castration as an adult, was not viewed as a eunuch by most Confucians.[67]

The origin of adoptive networks

Mass adoptions of subordinates in the military are believed to have originated in the era of the Sixteen Kingdoms, also known as "Sixteen Kingdoms of the Five Barbarians" (*Wuhu Shiliu guo* 五胡十六國, 304–439), and they continued throughout the Tang and Five Dynasties (Wudai 五代, 907–960).[68] The prevalent view relates these adoptions to the large-scale change or bestowal of surnames (*gai/ci xing* 改/賜姓) by non-Han-Chinese regimes in the north as part of their policies of *sinicisation* and *de-sinicisation*, most notably by the Xianbei 鮮卑 dynasties Northern Wei (北魏, 386–534), Western Wei (西魏, 535–56) and Northern Zhou 北周 (557–81).[69] Northern Wei Emperor Xiaowen 孝文帝 (471–99) changed Xianbei to Han surnames per decree in 495–96;[70] Chen Yinke believed that during Yuwen Tai's 宇文泰 (507–56) reign of the Western Wei, Xianbei superiors and their Han subordinates had the same Xianbei surnames conferred on them in an attempt to blur any ethnic distinction between them.[71]

During the Tang, adoptions of non-agnates were especially numerous in the military circuits of the north, where Chinese and barbarian peoples had mingled for centuries, the rebel leader An Lushan himself being a case in point.[72] Yu Chao'en, the eunuch who led the *shence* army into the capital, had an adopted son, Shang Kegu 尚可孤, who was of Xianbei origin. In contrast to many other adoptive sons of eunuchs, Shang never became a eunuch. Initially a follower of An Lushan and another ringleader of the rebellion, Shi Siming 史思明 (703–761), Shang later switched sides and joined the imperial cause, eventually obtaining the office of general in the Army of Divine Strategies. When Yu adopted him, Shang took on the name Yu Zhide 魚智德; later, when Yu had fallen from grace and met a violent end, the emperor bestowed the name Li Jiaxun 李嘉勳 on Zhide – Li being the imperial family name. Still later, after Jiaxun had squashed the rebellion of another man who had been conferred the imperial surname, Li Xilie 李希烈, and been awarded a small appanage, he re-changed his name back to Shang Kegu.[73]

Evidence such as this, which shows that adoptive kinship originated with the bestowal of surnames by the Xianbei, however, is scarce; such evidence is also often reduced to a discussion of the moral or ethnic inferiority of the "barbarians" vis-à-vis the "Han".[74] Recently, Jonathan K. Skaff has argued that "fictive kinship" via mass adoptions of subordinates from outside one's own lineage – explicitly forbidden by Chinese law[75] – was an essential part of the Northern Dynasties' military culture and a long-standing tradition among proto-Mongol or Turkic people in Northeast Asia.[76] It has to be borne in mind, however, that "fictive" kinship is as real to many cultures as biological kinship, and adoption is often practiced as a substitute to compensate for gaps in the biological family, that is, the lack of a biological male heir. So this practice might have at least partially originated in China as well.

Conclusion

Eunuchs were ubiquitous at the imperial courts of China from 221 BC to 1911 AD, but only the Tang witnessed a phenomenon termed *huanguan shijia* or *eunuch dynasticism*, the rise of eunuch fathers and sons in the Army of Divine Strategies and the Court for State Secrets. However, tenure in the highest offices – the Protectors-in-Chief and the Commissioners for State Secrets – shifted with each succession, as it depended on the favour each emperor granted to his own "mighty castrates" (*quanyan* 權閹),[77] whom he knew and trusted. Only a small number of eunuch sons managed to secure positions powerful enough to enter the traditional records themselves, and the lives of most sons and daughters of eunuchs have fallen into oblivion.

The traditional histories focus on factions of officials for the late Tang, however, and even a cursory reading suggests that there were at least as many factions of eunuchs. Each new emperor had formed his own networks with eunuchs and officials while he was still an imperial prince; likewise, factions of eunuchs tried to promote their favoured princes to become emperors. Unlike the case of Cao Cao in the Later Han, so far no eunuch son from the Tang has surfaced who gained recognition by, for example, taking the coveted *jinshi* 進士 exam and embarking on an official career, as did members of the imperial family by the late eighth century.[78] The reasons for this are clear: Despite their careful efforts to construct family identities around themselves, eunuchs were considered outsiders, not because they were a gender of their own but because they were incapable of continuing the biological lineage. The fact that they were allowed to marry and adopt children could not compensate for their inability to father children – a point certainly not lost on even the most tolerant ancestor-fearing Confucian.

Notes

1 For the transliteration of Chinese, I use the Hanyu Pinyin system, with the exception of titles and citations from works that use other transcriptions (most commonly Wade–Giles). The scholar-officials or *literati* were a type of state functionary distinctive to imperial China. Largely endowed with civil duties, they also played a crucial role in the state ritual. Their self-ascribed identity rested on education in the classics associated with the person of Confucius (trad. 551–479 BC). This education set them apart from other elites such as military officers, Buddhist priests, Daoist monks, and eunuchs.

2 They are mentioned repeatedly in *Zuozhuan* 左傳, a work finished in the fourth century, but covering the years 722–463 BC. See Yang Bojun 楊伯峻, *Chunqiu Zuozhuan zhu* 春秋左傳注 (Beijing: Zhonghua Shuju, 1983), 281, 305, 374, 376, 414, 436, 901, 1118, 1137, 1277–1278, 1320, and 1694.

3 See Jennifer W. Jay, "Castration and Medical Images of Eunuchs in Traditional China," in *Current Perspectives in the History of Science in East Asia,* ed. Yung Sik Kim and Francesca Bray (Seoul, National University Press, 1999), 385. *Oracle bones* is a collective term for the divination records of the Shang Dynasty. An ideal-typical oracle bone inscription consists of a pair of "charges" (e.g. "If the queen will give birth on such and such a day, it will be auspicious; if the queen will give birth on such and such a day, it will be inauspicious") inscribed on plastrons or scapulae. The answer was reached by so-called "pyromancy": a small cavity drilled into the reverse of the bone, to which a hot poker was applied in order to create cracks on the surface. These cracks were read as responses by ancestors or a divinity (Chinese language is ambiguous with regard to that). See David N. Keightley, *Sources of Shang History: The Oracle-Bone Inscriptions of Bronze Age China* (Berkeley: University of California Press, 1978).

4 See Ban Gu 班固 (32–92), *Hanshu* 漢書 (Beijing: Zhonghua Shuju, 1975), 23:1097–1098. Citations of most primary sources follow scholarly convention by giving the traditional chapter or "fascicle" (*juan* 卷) and page numbers. See also Cheng Shude 程樹德, *Jiu chao lü kao* 九朝律考 (Beijing, Zhonghua Shuju, 1963), 433.

5 See John Kennedy Rideout, "The Rise of the Eunuchs during the T'ang Dynasty: Part One (618–705)," *Asia Major, New Series* 1 (1949–1950): 54–55. The

opinion originated with Zhao Yi 趙翼 (1727–1814) in his *Nian'er shi zhaji* 廿二史劄記 (Beijing, Zhonghua Shuju, 1984), 20:429, and it was perpetuated by eminent historians such as Chen Yinke 陳寅恪 (1890–1969), *Tangdai zhengzhi shi shu lun gao* 唐代政治史述論稿 (Shanghai: Shanghai Guji, 1997), 23–25 and Tang Changru 唐長孺 (1911–1994), "Tangdai huanguan jiguan yu nankou jinxian" 唐代宦官籍貫與南口進獻, in *Tang Changru wenji* 唐長孺文集 8: *Shanju cungao xubian* 山居存稿續編 (Beijing: Zhonghua Shuju, 2011), 359–366.

6 See Chen Ruoshui 陳弱水, "Tangdai Chang'an de huanguan shequn – te lun qi yu junren de guanxi" 唐代長安的宦官社群——特論其與軍人的關係, *Tang yanjiu* 唐研究 15 (2009): 171–198 and Du Wenyu 杜文玉, "Tangdai huanguan de jiguan fenbu" 唐代宦官的籍贯分布, *Zhongguo lishi dili luncong* 中国历史地理论丛 1 (1998): 161–174.

7 Ma Zhiqiang 马志强 focuses on eunuchs of the period of division known as "Southern and Northern Dynasties" (*Nanbeichao* 南北朝, 316–589) and concludes that their role at the southern, Han Chinese, courts was negligible. He collects data for 28 high-ranking eunuchs from the north, who all served in high military capacities. See "Lüe tan Nanbeichao huanguan de junshi biaoxian" 略谈南北朝宦官的军事表现, *Shanxi Datong Daxue xuebao* 山西大同大学学报 21, no. 2 (2007): 41–42.

8 See his "Two Types of Human Interventions into Sheep Flock: Intervention into the Mother–Offspring Relationship, and Raising the Flock Leader," in *Domesticated Plants and Animals of the Southwest Eurasian Agro-Pastoral Culture Complex*, ed. Yutaka Tani and Sadao Sakamoto (Kyoto: The Research Institute for Humanistic Studies, Kyoto University, 1986), 1–42 (especially 27 and 40). Jennifer Jay assumes that the nomads adopted the eunuch institution from the Han Chinese but thereby fails to recognise the differences between its workings under Chinese and non-Chinese regimes. See her "The Eunuchs and Sinicization in the Non-Han Conquest Dynasties of China" (paper presented at the *Asian Studies on the Pacific Coast Conference*, Forest Grove, OR, June 16–18, 1995).

9 See Fan Ye, *Hou Hanshu* (Beijing: Zhonghua Shuju, 1973), 78:2507–2543.

10 See Liu Xu 劉昫 (888–947) *et al.*, *Jiu Tangshu* (Beijing: Zhonghua Shuju, 1975), 184:4753–4779.

11 See Ouyang Xiu 歐陽修 (1007–72) and Song Qi 宋祁 (996–1061), *Xin Tangshu* (Beijing: Zhonghua Shuju, 1975), 207:5855–208:5902. The Tang has two standard histories, because the *Old History*, compiled in the tenth century, was considered not to conform to stylistic standards of the eleventh.

12 We know almost nothing about the worldview of eunuchs before the Ming, since they left no traces in the record. Sima Qian's 司馬遷 (145–86 BC) "Letter to Ren Shaoqing" ("Bao Ren shaoqing shu" 報任少卿書) is the only powerfully eloquent exception. See Jennifer W. Jay, "Random Jottings on Eunuchs: Ming *Biji* Writings as Unofficial Historiography," *Hanxue yanjiu* 漢學研究 11, no. 1 (1993): 269–285.

13 See Robert B. Crawford (1926–1987), "Eunuch Power in the Ming Dynasty," *T'oung Pao* 49 (1961–1962): 115–148; Ulrike Jugel, *Politische Funktion und soziale Stellung der Eunuchen zur späten Han-Zeit (25–220 n.Chr.)* (Wiesbaden: Steiner, 1976); Shih-shan Henry Ts'ai [蔡石山], *The Eunuchs in the Ming Dynasty* (Albany: State University of New York Press, 1996); and Kenneth J. Hammond, "The Eunuch Wang Zhen [王振] and the Ming Dynasty," in *The Human Tradition in Premodern China*, ed. Kenneth J. Hammond (Wilmington: Scholarly Resources, 2002), 143–155.

14 The second part of his "The Rise of Eunuchs during the T'ang Dynasty" was published posthumously in *Asia Major*, *New Series* 3 (1952): 42–58.

15 Marianne Louis Carlson, "The Rationale of Eunuch Power in the Government of T'ang China, 618–805" (Ph.D. diss., University of Chicago, 1971); and Ming-yu Wang, "The Involvement in Recurrent Power Struggles of the Han, T'ang, and Ming Eunuchs" (Ph.D. diss., St. John's University New York, 1974).

16 An example of the former is Mary M. Anderson's *Hidden Power: The Palace Eunuchs of Imperial China* (Buffalo: Prometheus, 1990). Steven I. Levine has the following to say about Anderson's book, which is solely based on secondary literature: "Colorful and compelling, although light on analysis, her book is a vivid reminder of the role lust and power played in China's imperial past", *Library Journal* 115, no. 4 (1990): 102. For the latter, see Karl August Wittfogel (1896–1988), *Oriental Despotism: A Comparative Study of Total Power* (New Haven: Yale University Press, 1957), 354–358.

17 Jennifer W. Jay, "Another Side of Chinese Eunuch History: Castration, Marriage, Adoption, and Burial," *Canadian Journal of History/Annales canadiennes d'histoire* 28 (1993): 459–478.

18 Nicolas Tackett discusses transmitted versus excavated sources of the late Tang in *The Destruction of the Medieval Chinese Aristocracy* (Cambridge, MA: Harvard University Asia Center, 2014), 13 and 250. All transmitted sources went through often obscure editorial processes in the following centuries; see Stephen Owen, "The Manuscript Legacy of the Tang: The Case of Literature," *Harvard Journal of Asiatic Studies* 67, no. 2 (2007): 295–326.

19 See his *Tangdai huanguan quanshi zhi yanjiu* 唐代宦官權勢之研究 (Taibei: Zhengwu Shuju, 1971; repr. as *Tangdai de huanguan* 唐代的宦官 [Taibei: Taiwan Shangwu Yinshuguan, 2004]), 120–138.

20 Du has published widely on eunuchs and kinship under the Tang. Works pertinent to the present study are cited in the notes; moreover, see his "Tangdai huanguan shijia kaoshu" 唐代宦官世家考述, *Shaanxi Shifan Daxue xuebao* 陕西师范大学学报 27, no. 2 (1998): 78–85 and "Tangdai huanguan hunyin ji qi neibu jiegou" 唐代宦官婚姻及其内部结构, *Xueshu yuekan* 学术月刊 6 (2000): 88–95.

21 "Chuantong zongfa wenhua yu huanguan yangzi xijue zhi feng" 传统宗法文化与宦官养子袭爵之风, *Langfang shizhuan xuebao* 廊坊师专学报 1 (1994): 16–20 and "Han–Tang shiqi de huanguan yangzi yu huanguan shijia" 汉唐时期的宦官养子与宦官世家, *Dongyue luncong* 东岳论丛 26, no. 4 (2005): 116–119.

22 *Cong gongting dao zhanchang: Zhongguo zhonggu yu jinshi zhu kaocha* 從宮廷到戰場——中國中古與近世諸考察 (Hong Kong: Zhonghua Shuju, 2007).

23 *Shijia* is commonly translated as "hereditary houses", sometimes understood as aristocratic clans; that, however, would be misleading here as eunuchs often came from commoner families, not from the "eminent clans" described below. The term *shijia* originated as a generic title for a series of chapters in China's first universal history, the *Shiji* 史記; see *The Grand Scribe's Records, Volume 5.1: The Hereditary Houses of Pre-Han China, Part I, by Ssu-ma Ch'ien*, ed. William H. Nienhauser (Bloomington: Indiana University Press, 2006), xi–xix.

24 See Nicolas Tackett, *Tang Wudai renwu zhuanji yu shehui wangluo ziliaoku* 唐代人物傳記與社會網絡資料庫 (Prosopographic and Social Network Database of the Tang and Five Dynasties, version 1.0, tbdb010.mdb), http://history.berkeley.edu/people/nicolas-tackett, accessed July 17, 2015.

25 Wu Zetian 武則天 (624–705), reigning as "emperor" in her own right from 690 to 705 but tending to government business since the 660s, when she was empress of the ailing Li Zhi 李治 (Gaozong 高宗 [628–83, r. 649–83]).

26 See David G. Johnson, "The Last Years of a Great Clan: The Li Family of Chao Chün in Late T'ang and Early Sung," *Harvard Journal of Asiatic Studies* 37,

no. 1 (1977): 5–102. It is in fact still not understood completely how these clans, despite the obvious absence of large landholdings and hereditary offices, could maintain their social status over centuries. See Helwig Schmidt-Glintzer, "The Scholar-Official and His Community: The Character of the Aristocracy in Medieval China," trans. Thomas Jansen, *Early Medieval China* 1 (1994): 60–83.

27 Patricia Buckley Ebrey, *The Aristocratic Families of Early Imperial China: A Case Study of the Po-Ling Ts'ui Family* (Cambridge: Cambridge University Press, 1978) and Rainer von Franz, *Die chinesische Innengrabinschrift für Beamte und Privatiers des 7. Jahrhunderts* (Stuttgart: Steiner, 1996).

28 See Niida Noboru 仁井田陞 (ed.), *Tōrei shūi* 唐令拾遺 (1933; repr. Changchun: Changchun Chubanshe, 1989), 766; Changsun Wuji 長孫無忌 (?–659) *et al.*, *Tanglü shuyi jianjie* 唐律疏議箋解 (Beijing: Zhonghua Shuju, 1996), §134 (11:846–847), trans. Wallace Johnson, *The T'ang Code: Volume 2, Specific Articles* (Princeton: Princeton University Press, 1997), 102–104, Li Linfu 李林甫 (?–752) and Chen Zhongfu 陳仲夫, ed. *Tang liu dian* 唐六典 (1992, 3rd repr. Beijing: Zhonghua Shuju, 2008), 4:120, and Wang Pu 王溥 (922–982), *Tang huiyao* 唐會要 (Shanghai: Shanghai Guji, 2006), 38:809. Such regulations had been promulgated since 205 AD, see Kenneth K.S. Ch'en, "Inscribed Stelae during the Wei, Chin, and Nan-Ch'ao," in *Studia Asiatica: Essays in Asian Studies in Felicitation of the Seventy-Fifth Anniversary of Professor Ch'en Shou-yi*, ed. Lawrence G. Thompson (San Francisco: Chinese Materials Center, 1975), 77. See also von Franz, *Die chinesische Innengrabinschrift*, 37–40; Patricia Buckley Ebrey, "Later Han Stone Inscriptions," *Harvard Journal of Asiatic Studies* 40, no. 2 (1980): 333; and Angela Schottenhammer, "Einige Überlegungen zur Entstehung von Grabinschriften," in *Auf den Spuren des Jenseits: Chinesische Grabkultur in den Facetten von Wirklichkeit, Geschichte und Totenkult*, ed. Angela Schottenhammer (Frankfurt: Lang, 2003), 25.

29 Usually compiled in the Song Dynasty, see n. 18 above. Eulogies were considered high literature, and transcripts were included in the collected works of their authors.

30 The terminology for eunuchs and castration in Chinese is numerous; for the period under purview here, the most frequent expression is *huanguan* 宦官, while in later dynasties *taijian* 太監 is more common. For the earliest period, see Michael Loewe, "On the terms *baozi*, *yin gong*, *yin guan*, *huan*, and *shou*: Was Zhao Gao a Eunuch?," *T'oung Pao* 91 (2005): 301–319. Nobody except Yan Yaozhong 严耀中 has questioned that members of the Palace Domestic Service were universally eunuchs; see his "Tangdai zhonghouqi neishisheng guanyuan shenfen zhiyi" 唐代中后期内侍省官员身份质疑, *Shilin* 史林 5 (2004): 77–81.

31 For instance, *wen wu bu zhui* 文武不墜, *you wen you wu* 有文有武, *wen wu jie quan* 文武皆全, *wen wu bei ti* 文武備體 and so on. Most epitaphs included in this survey were for officers of the *shence* army. To be sure, being able in both civil and martial skills was by no means a privilege of eunuchs but was often seen as a virtue of the truly cultivated man. One finds similar expressions describing scholars almost a millennium later, see Martin W. Huang, *Negotiating Masculinities in Late Imperial China* (Honolulu: University of Hawai'i Press, 2006), 56, 156, 159, and 176.

32 In fact, Fan assumes that because their vital energy is not complete (*qi ti fei quan qi* 其體非全氣), eunuchs are docile and malleable into inner servants (i.e. for the palace women), see Fan Ye, *Hou Hanshu,* 78:2507.

33 See David L. McMullen, "The Cult of Ch'i T'ai-kung and T'ang Attitudes to the Military," *T'ang Studies* 7 (1989): 59–103. Many of the military commissioners mentioned earlier were civil officials.

34 Several sources quote the decree, for example, Liu, *Jiu Tangshu* 184:4754 and Ouyang and Song, *Xin Tangshu,* 207:5855. See also Zhang Wenbin 张文斌,

"Tangdai huanguan yangzi zhidu tan lüe" 唐代宦官养子制度探略, *Yunmeng xuekan* 云梦学刊 23 (2002): 42–43. For the system of nine ranks, see Ts'en Chung-mien, "The T'ang System of Bureaucratic Titles and Grades," trans. Penelope Ann Herbert, *T'ang Studies* 5 (1987): 25–31.

35 See Liu, *Jiu Tangshu*, 184:4754; Ouyang and Song, *Xin Tangshu*, 207:5857.

36 Du You 杜佑 (734–812) *et al.*, *Tongdian* 通典 (Beijing: Zhonghua Shuju, 1988), 27:757.

37 See Ouyang and Song, *Xin Tangshu*, 208:5890 and Liu, *Jiu Tangshu,* 184:4775 for his more powerful relations. The number 600 should not be taken at face value, as the historian probably intended to exaggerate the degree of Yang's corruption.

38 See Obata Tatsuo 小畑龍雄, "Jinsakugun no seiritsu" 神策軍の成立, *Tōyōshi kenkyū* 東洋史研究 18 (1959): 35–56, and Yat-wing Liu, "The two Shen-ts'e Armies: Their Role in the Frontier Defence System and the Pacification of Rebellious Provinces, 754–820 A.D.," *Papers on Far Eastern History* 14 (1976): 1–35. See also Wang Jilin 王吉林, "Tangdai de shuofang jun yu shence jun" 唐代的朔方軍與神策軍, *Di yi jie guoji Tangdai xueshu huiyi lunwenji* 第一屆國際唐代學術會議論文集 (1989): 914–922.

39 That is not to say that Yu Chao'en and other eunuchs did not act out of sincere loyalty to the dynasty, as Confucian historians would have it. However, while a plot to oust them failed in 835, their survival came to rest on their ability to use the emperor as a bargaining chip. See Michael T. Dalby, "Court Politics in Late T'ang Times," in *The Cambridge History of China, Volume 3: Sui and T'ang China, 589–906, Part 1*, ed. Denis C. Twitchett (Cambridge: Cambridge University Press, 1979), 654–659.

40 Yuan Gang 袁刚, "Tangdai de shumi shi" 唐代的枢密使, *Shandong Jiaoyu Xueyuan xuebao* 山东教育学院学报 3 (1994): 68–76.

41 See Du Mu, "Huainan jianjun shiyuan tingbi ji" 淮南監軍使院廳壁記, in Du, *Fanchuan wenji* 樊川文集 (Shanghai: Shanghai Guji, 1978), 10:159. Apparently, this is not meant as a critique or, if so, it is a concealed one: Du juxtaposes the surveillance commissioners, whom he praises as "worthy and diligent" (*xianliang qinlao* 賢良勤勞), with virtuous ministers who, upon return from Huainan, rise to become chancellors.

42 See Wang Shoudong 王守栋, "Tangdai shence jun zhongwei kao" 唐代神策军中尉考, *Dezhou Xueyuan xuebao* 德州学院学报 19 (2003): 65–68, "Lun Tang zhonghouqi nanya dui beisi de yifu" 论唐中后期南衙对北司的依附, *Ha'erbin Xueyuan xuebao* 哈尔滨学院学报 24.9 (2003): 102–105, and "Tangdai 'quanyan si gui' kao xi" 唐代"权阉四贵"考析, *Qiusuo* 求索 9 (2007): 204–206; Yuan, "Tangdai de shumi shi" and *Sui Tang zhongshu tizhi de fazhan yanbian* 隋唐中樞體制的發展演變 (Taibei: Wenjin Chubanshe, 1992); and Zhang Guogang 张国刚, *Tangdai fanzhen yanjiu* 唐代藩镇研究 (Changsha: Hunan Jiaoyu, 1987), 138–164 and "Tangdai de shence jun" 唐代的神策軍, in *Tangdai zhengzhi zhidu yanjiu lunji* 唐代政治制度研究論集 (Taibei: Wenjin, 1992), 113–156.

43 See Zhao Mingyi 趙明義, "Zhongguo gudai jianjun zhidu tantao" 中國古代監軍制度探討, *Fuxinggang xuebao* 復興崗學報 84 (2005): 114 and He Zhong 贺忠, "Tangdai shiren Wang Jian yu huanguan Wang Shoucheng guanxi kaolun: yi Wang Jian 'Zeng shumi' shi wei zhongxin" 唐代诗人王建与宦官王守澄关系考论—以王建《赠枢密》诗为中心, *Shenyang Gongcheng Xueyuan xuebao* 沈阳工程学院学报 5, no. 4 (2009): 531–535, the latter analysing the *Jishi beiyao* 記室備要 fragment from Dunhuang 敦煌 (P. 3723, Pelliot collection of Dunhuang Manuscripts, Bibliothèque Nationale de France, Paris).

44 In contrast to ancient Rome, the Chinese state prohibited private ownership of eunuchs. See Mathew Kuefler, *The Manly Eunuch: Masculinity, Gender Ambiguity, and Christian Ideology in Late Antiquity* (Chicago: University of Chicago Press, 2001), 61–63 and Rideout, "Rise of Eunuchs", 55.

45 I take the expression from John W. Chaffee, *The Thorny Gates of Learning in Sung China: A Social History of Examinations* (Cambridge and New York: Cambridge University Press, 1985). Research on the Palace Domestic Service and eunuch commissionerships was begun in the 1950s by Yano Chikara 矢野主税, "Tōdai kangan kensei kakutoku inyu kō" 唐代宦官権勢獲得因由考, *Shigaku zasshi* 史学雑誌 63 (1954): 920–934 and resumed by Muronaga Yoshizō 室永芳三, "Tō naishishō chi naishishō ji" 唐内侍省知内侍省事, I–III, *Nagasaki Daigaku Kyōiku Gakubu Shakai kagaku ronsō* 長崎大学教育学部社会科学論叢 38–40 (1989–90): 1–10, 1–10, and 1–7.

46 See Denis C. Twitchett, *The Birth of the Chinese Meritocracy: Bureaucrats and Examination in T'ang China* (London: The China Society, 1976).

47 For a summary of their establishment, see Denis C. Twitchett, *Financial Administration under the T'ang Dynasty*, 2nd ed. (Cambridge: Cambridge University Press, 1970), 106–120.

48 See Penelope Ann Herbert, "Perceptions of Provincial Officialdom in Early T'ang China," *Asia Major, Third Series* 2, no. 1 (1989): 25–57 and Denis C. Twitchett, "Varied Patterns of Provincial Autonomy in the T'ang Dynasty", in *Essays on T'ang Society: The Interplay of Social, Political, and Economic Forces*, ed. John Curtis Perry and Bardwell L. Smith (Leiden: Brill, 1976), 90–109.

49 This aspect is explored in more detail by Stanley Weinstein, *Buddhism under the T'ang* (Cambridge: Cambridge University Press, 1987), 85–86 *et passim* and Tang Yijie 汤一介, "Gongde shi kao – du *Zizhi tongjian* zhaji" 功德使考——读《资治通鉴》札记, *Wenxian* 文献 2 (1985): 60–65.

50 See Liu, *Jiu Tangshu*, 184:4764 and Ouyang and Song, *Xin Tangshu*, 207:5865.

51 Hammond, "The Eunuch Wang Zhen", 150; see further Jing Yali 景亚鹂, "Tangdai huanguan feng Fo sixiang tanwei – yi Xi'an beilinguan cang muzhi wei li" 唐代宦官奉佛思想探微——以西安碑林馆藏墓志为例, *Shaanxi Shifan Daxue xuebao* 陕西师范大学学报 39, no. 1 (2010): 71–75.

52 See Mao, "Tangdai fanzhen yangzi shulun" 唐代藩镇养子述论, *Shangqiu Shifan Xueyuan xuebao* 商丘师范学院学报 17, no. 5 (2011): 52–55.

53 See Wang, *Tangdai huanguan*, 120–138.

54 Jennifer W. Jay argues that the Tang was the first dynasty that legalised non-agnatic adoptions by eunuchs. See Jay, "Another Side", 468. She cites no source in support of that claim.

55 See Xing Tie 邢铁, *Tang Song fenjia zhidu* 唐宋分家制度 (Beijing: Shangwu Yinshuguan, 2010), 114–131.

56 Lang Ying 郎瑛 (1487–ca. 1566), *Qi xiu lei gao* 七修類稿 (Beijing: Zhonghua Shuju, 1959), 27:415. Whether Zhao Gao was a eunuch, is discussed by Loewe, "Was Zhao Gao a Eunuch?" 311–314.

57 See Fan, *Hou Hanshu,* 6:264 and 78:2518.

58 Cao Cao's father, Cao Song 曹嵩, had been adopted by the eunuch Cao Teng 曹騰. See Jay, "Another Side," 469–472. The three great dominations, called "eunuch maladies" (*huanguan zhi huo* 宦官之禍), are those of the Eastern Han, Tang and Ming. See Zhao, *Nian'er shi zhaji*, 20:424. Cao Cao was made first emperor of the Wei Dynasty posthumously by his son, Cao Pi 曹丕 or Emperor Wen 文帝 (187–226, r. 220–226).

59 At least as far as we can tell from evidence of the nineteenth century, see Jennifer W. Jay, "Castration and Medical Images," 389. Ulrike Jugel, who argues that in the Han, castration likewise meant removal of both penis and

testicles, lists ancient methods of castration in *Eunuchen zur späten Han-Zeit*, 14–17.

60 See Daniel F. Caner, "The Practice of Prohibition of Self-Castration in Early Christianity," *Vigiliae Christianae* 51, no. 4 (1997): 396–415.

61 See Jay, "Another Side," 461.

62 For the discourse on *paṇḍakas*, see Céline Grünhagen, *Geschlechterpluralismus im Buddhismus. Zur Tragweite westlicher Wissenschaftskonstruktionen am Beispiel frühbuddhistischer Positionen und des Wandels in Thailand* (Wiesbaden: Harrassowitz, 2013), 133–137.

63 See Jennifer W. Jay, "Song Confucian Views on Eunuchs," *Chinese Culture: A Quarterly Review* 35, no. 3 (1994): 45–51.

64 Ouyang Xiu, "Biographies of Eunuchs," in *Historical Records of the Five Dynasties*, ed. Ouyang Xiu and trans. Richard L. Davis (New York: Columbia University Press, 2004), 320.

65 Bai Juyi, "Lun Chengcui zhiming zhuang" 論承璀職名狀, in *Bai Juyi ji jianjiao* 白居易集箋校, ed. Bai Juyi and Zhu Jincheng 朱金城 (Shanghai: Shanghai Guji, 1988), 59:3357–3358. The memorial is also quoted in historical sources of the eleventh century and translated in Michael Höckelmann, "Not Man Enough to be a Soldier? Eunuchs in the Tang Military and Their Critics," in *Verflechtungen zwischen Byzanz und dem Orient/ Entanglements between Byzantium and the Orient*, ed. Michael Grünbart (Berlin: LIT, forthcoming).

66 See Charles A. Peterson, "Court and Province in Mid- and Late T'ang," in Twitchett, *Sui and T'ang China,* 527–538.

67 See Jay, "Random Jottings," 269. Qian's biography and famous letter to Ren An, in which he justified his decision to accept castration rather than execution, can be found in Ban, *Hanshu*, 62:2725–2737.

68 See Wolfram Eberhard, *Conquerors and Rulers: Social Forces in Medieval China*, 2nd ed. (Leiden: Brill, 1970), 149–150; Chen Yinke, "Lun Tangdai zhi fanjiang yu fubing" 论唐代之蕃将与府兵, *Zhongshan Daxue xuebao* 中山大学学报 1 (1967): 167; Dai Xianqun 戴显群, "Tang Wudai jiazi zhidu de lishi genyuan" 唐五代假子制度的历史根源, *Renwen zazhi* 人文杂志 6 (1989): 83–88; and "Tang–Wudai jiazi zhidu de leixing ji qi xiangguan de wenti" 唐五代假子制度的类型及其相关的问题, *Fujian Shifan Daxue xuebao* 福建师范大学学报 108 (2000): 105–110; Mao, "Tangdai fanzhen yangzi," Du Wenyu and Ma Weibin 马维斌, "Lun Wudai Shiguo shouyang jiazi fengqi de shehui huanjing yu lishi genyuan," 论五代十国收养假子风气的社会环境与历史根源, *Shaanxi Shifan Daxue xuebao* 39, no. 3. (2010): 111–116. The best documented example is that of the Korean Gao Yun 高雲 (r. 407–9), who had the ruling family's surname of the Later Yan 後燕 (384–407), Murong 慕容, conferred on himself and who ruled as its last ruler for a few months before assuming the throne of the Northern Yan 北燕 (407–436) under his original surname. See Fang Xuanling 房玄齡 (578–648), *Jinshu* 晉書 (Beijing: Zhonghua Shuju, 1974), 124:3108.

69 Albert Dien, "The Bestowal of Surnames under the Western Wei–Northern Chou: A Case of Counter-Acculturation," *T'oung Pao* 63, no. 2–3 (1977): 137–177. Ethnic origins thus became blurred, causing doubts even over the ancestry of the Tang imperial house, surnamed Li in Chinese; see Chen Yinke, *Tangdai zhengzhi*, 1–13.

70 For a list of the "barbarian" (*hu* 胡) surnames and their Chinese equivalents, see Wei Shou 魏收 (506–72), *Weishu* 魏書 (Beijing: Zhonghua Shuju, 1974), 113:3005–3015.

71 See Chen Yinke, *Sui Tang zhidu yuanyuan lüe lun gao* 隋唐制度淵源略論稿 (Beijing: Zhonghua Shuju, 1963), 131.

72 An had been adopted by Yang Yuhuan 楊玉環, better known as Emperor Xuanzong's "favoured concubine Yang" (Yang guifei 楊貴妃), see Ouyang and Song, *Xin Tangshu*, 150:6413.

73 See Liu, *Jiu Tangshu*, 144:3911; Ouyang and Song, *Xin Tangshu*, 110:4128; and Jonathan Karam Skaff, *Sui-Tang China and Its Neighbors: Culture, Power, and Connections 580–800* (Oxford: Oxford University Press, 2012), 227.

74 This state of the field in mainland China is lamented by Du and Ma "Wudai Shiguo shouyang jiazi," 113. Their conclusion differs from that outlined above: They assume the custom of adoption did not originate with the "barbarians" (*huzu* 胡族) and then spread to the Han rulers of the Sui and Tang, but vice versa, that the frowned-upon but sanctioned practice of adopting children not belonging to one's lineage originated with the Han and was thereafter adopted by the Northern conquerors. In Japan, faked father–son relationships (*kari fushi* 仮父子) have been explored by Yano Chikara 矢野主税, Hori Toshikazu 堀敏— and Kurihara Masuo 栗原益男. See Yano Chikara, "Tōdai ni okeru karikosei no hatten ni tsuite" 唐代に於ける仮子制の発展について, *Nishi Nihon shigaku* 西日本史学 6 (1951): 86–97; Hori Toshikazu, "Tōmatsu moro hanran no seikaku – Chūgoku ni okeru kizoku seiji no botsuraku ni tsuite" 唐末諸叛乱の性格一中国における貴族政治の没落について, *Tōyō bunka* 東洋文化 7 (1951): 52–94; Kurihara Masuo, "Tōmatsu–Godai no kari fushi teki ketsugō ni okeru seimei to nenrei" 唐末五代の仮父子的結合における姓名と年齢, *Tōyōgakuhō*東洋学報38(1956):430–57;andKuriharaMasuo,"Tō–Godainokarifushi teki ketsugō no seikaku – shu toshite hansochi teki shihai kenryoku to no kanren ni oite" 唐五代の仮父子的結合の性格 — 主として藩帥的支配権力との関連において, *Shigaku Zasshi* 史学雑誌 62 (1963): 514–543. For many of these references, I am indebted to Takase Natsuko 高瀬奈津子 of Sapporo University 札幌大学 (email from 26 April 2013), who also works on Tang eunuch epitaphs. See her "'Tō Ri Hosō boshi' shakudoku"「唐李輔光墓誌」釈読, *Meidai Ajia shi ronshū* 明大アジア史論集 13 (2009): 211–223.

75 See Changsun, *Tang*lü §157.2 (12:941), trans. Johnson, *T'ang Code*, 131.

76 See Skaff, *Sui-Tang China*, 224–227.

77 See Wang, "Tangdai quanyan". The four mighty castrates of the late Tang were the two Defenders-in-Chief and the Commissioners for State Secrets.

78 David L. McMullen, "Tomb text with introduction for his excellency Li of Longxi" (paper presented at the Workshop New Frontiers in the Study of Medieval China, Rutgers University, NJ, May 15–16, 2015).

6 Spiritual heirs and families

Episcopal relatives in early medieval Francia[1]

Rachel Stone

Introduction

Studies of the church reform movement of the mid-eleventh century often argue that married clergy and their sons succeeding to clerical office were commonplace across western Europe until this period.[2] Some historians have also linked reformers' campaigns against clerical marriage and simony (the selling of holy things and, specifically, the purchase of clerical office) to worries about church property. As Robert Moore puts it, "the problem of provision for the [clerical] family was acute", and he cites claims by Bishop Atto of Vercelli (d. ca. 960) that churches in mid-tenth century Italy were "despoiled" by married clerics.[3] Moore also argues that the restoration of land to churches became inextricably linked to celibacy: "they [the cathedral chapter] guaranteed that the land which was handed over to them would not at any time in the future become the basis for the founding of a new secular dynasty".[4] Celibate men, in this view, could both offer the Mass with hands "clean" from sexual contact with women and stand outside the existing medieval kinship system.[5]

Yet there are difficulties with this paradigm. Threats to church property were not a new concern in the eleventh century. Studies of clerical career patterns suggest that in some regions of early medieval Europe, uncle–nephew succession was the predominant pattern, rather than father–son.[6] Nor was the eleventh-century ideology surrounding the need for clerical celibacy particularly novel; instead it had much older roots.[7] From the fourth century onwards, there were frequent demands in the Western church that bishops, priests and deacons should all be permanently continent because of the purity required of those serving at the altar. Papal decretals, church councils and individual moralists repeated such statements for centuries.[8]

The frequent assumption, however, has been that such calls for clerical celibacy were a dead letter in the early medieval west; priestly and episcopal dynasties are seen as typical of the period.[9] This chapter questions this paradigm by exploring celibacy and family strategies concerning episcopal office in one of the largest and best documented early medieval societies, the Carolingian empire (ca. 750–900 CE). I show a disconnection between the canonical theories that still allowed married priests and bishops and the rarity of such men in most of the empire. I also explore possible reasons for this pattern, focusing on the interaction between changing forms of clerical education, the ideology of succession to office and noble strategies for family advancement.

Before discussing the Carolingian evidence, however, we need to make some conceptual distinctions; these are complicated by the fact that the term *celibacy* can be used either for the state of being unmarried (as in this discussion) or to that of being continent (abstaining from sexual activity). Sexual activity by clerics, married clerics and the existence of heirs to a cleric's office and/or property did not necessarily coincide. Clerics desiring heterosexual encounters might voluntarily seek irregular unions rather than marriage; any resulting children would not necessarily have inheritance rights.[10] Conversely, the concept of the chaste marriage, in which the spouses agreed to abstain from sexual activity, is visible from the late second century onwards.[11] Finally, a family's control over office and the property associated with it could be maintained without transmission in the direct male lineage, such as via uncle–nephew transmission of clerical office.[12]

Clerical families in the pre-Carolingian west

The framework for clerical continence established in the late antique west continued into the post-Roman kingdoms of Merovingian Francia (ca. 450–750 CE). Western church councils frequently repeated that the higher clergy could not marry after ordination. A married man could be ordained, but he must then give up sexual relations with his wife. This was coupled with regulations prohibiting clerics having "strange" women living with them, lest it give rise to scandal.[13]

This emphasis on post-marital continence reflected a compromise developed in the fourth century. Some ascetics and monks at that time attempted to use their sexual abstinence to demonstrate their superior manly virtue compared to married men of senatorial rank. Kate Cooper and Conrad Leyser describe the "shrill asceticism" of the patristic writer Jerome (d. 420) as "an attempt to participate in, while altering the rules of, the ancient game of masculinity".[14] The more restricted demand that married men who were ordained abandoned sexual activity allowed high-status men, whose previous secular lives had often been marked by the violent use of public power, to renounce one aspect of "the flesh". With this symbolic cleansing, they could become an acceptable alternative to monks as candidates for clerical office.[15]

Nevertheless, it has often been presumed that married clergy became marginalised in the Western Roman Empire with the rise of the monk-bishop. David Hunter, however, has recently argued that late antique churches often still preferred to elect married men from the municipal elite as bishops.[16] Such mature men, who had married only once while in lay life and were now either widowers or continent within marriage, were often seen as better able to deal with the responsibilities of an episcopal role than monks. Episcopal dynasties developed, such as that of Ruricius, the bishop of Limoges (ca. 485–510). One of his sons, Ommatius (d. ca. 528), later became the bishop of Tours, and a grandson was a bishop of Limoges in the mid-sixth century.[17]

Such patterns of post-marital ordination relied on laymen's ability to acquire a secular education adequate for a bishop's role. By the sixth century, this was increasingly difficult in Gaul;[18] instead, most would-be bishops entered the church as young boys, and their prospects for advancement were improved if they remained unmarried.[19] Some conciliar texts from later sixth-century Francia already imply that married priests were a relatively rare phenomenon, to be legislated about only as an afterthought.[20] Prosopographical data on married bishops and priests in France also suggests a decline in their number between the sixth and seventh centuries.[21]

In some regions of Italy, however, more opportunities for the secular education of boys remained, and an older pattern of clerical education and training may have been preserved. The *Liber Pontificalis*, a series of papal biographies, describes several eighth- and ninth-century popes as being educated by their fathers or uncles before entering the church, although their exact age of entry into major orders is not known.[22]

Married clerics in Carolingian histories

Pippin III, the first Carolingian king, usurped the Frankish throne from the Merovingians in around 750 CE. His son, Charlemagne (d. 814), expanded the kingdom into an empire that stretched from Catalonia to Hungary and also included northern and central Italy. This empire was divided between Charlemagne's grandsons in 843 but retained much cultural unity for the rest of the ninth century.

References in Carolingian sources to married clerics and bishops show an intriguing pattern: a continued theoretical acceptance of ordaining married men but little contemporary evidence for married priests, continent or not. Carolingian councils reused earlier canons on clerical continence, but their focus changed. There are repeated demands that clergy, implicitly unmarried men, should avoid keeping unrelated women in their house.[23] Such demands are sometimes specifically linked to the need for ritual purity for priests when offering Mass.[24] The normal expectation, therefore, was that priests would not be married.

In contrast, only a few Carolingian church canons discuss the continence demanded from married men who became priests.[25] Yet such post-marital ordination remained an option, even for bishops. For example, Archbishop Hincmar of Rheims, one of the most prominent churchmen of the later ninth century, wrote a letter to the people of the city of Beauvais in Picardy in 881, discussing the qualities required when electing a new bishop. He told them that they should not choose unsuitable men, including anyone who had been married twice.[26]

Some Carolingian historical texts went further, including positive images of bishops with sons. The best known of such texts connects an episcopal family to the Carolingian royal house itself. Paul the Deacon's *Gesta episcoporum mettensium* from 784 celebrates the two sons of Bishop Arnulf of Metz (d. ca. 640), who were "procreated from the bond of a legitimate marriage" when the saint was young.[27] One of Arnulf's sons, Clodulf, himself later became bishop of Metz.[28] The accuracy of the story is uncertain, but the desire of the Carolingians to attach themselves firmly to a saint led them to claim Arnulf as a direct ancestor.[29]

Several other hagiographical texts from the period offer evidence of varying degrees of reliability for father–son episcopal succession in pre-Carolingian Francia. For example, the *Actus Pontificum Cenomannis in urbe degentium* is a series of biographies of the bishops of Le Mans. This forms part of a vast complex of documents forged between 855 and 863 by the cathedral canons of Le Mans (or their close associates) in their attempt to claim property for the see. The *Actus* recounts how St Martin of Tours (d. ca. 396), going to Le Mans because the then bishop, Liborius, was dying, saw the subdeacon Victurus working in his vineyard and, by divine inspiration, recognised him as the future bishop. After Liborius' death, Martin ordained Victurus bishop, veiled Victurus' wife Maura and baptised their son Victurius. When Victurius was older, Martin took him away to educate him and Victurius subsequently succeeded his father as bishop.[30] The *Actus* draws on an earlier *Vita Victuri et Victurii*, which also shows both father and son as bishops.[31] Given the forger's ingenuity, however, it seems unlikely that concerns for accuracy would have stopped him removing the father–son succession from his own text if he had found it problematic.

The most peculiar father–son succession, however, appears in Hincmar of Rheims' *vita* of Archbishop Remigius of Rheims (d. 533), completed in around 880.[32] Hincmar made several significant changes to the depiction of the saint's family from earlier sources, including the invention of two relatives of Remigius who were successively bishops of the newly created see of Laon: St Genebaudus and his son Latro. I discuss the complexities of Genebaudus' story below, but it is worth noting here that despite Hincmar's strictness on priestly continence, he still accepts that the son of a bishop could succeed to his father's see. A bishop could lawfully have children in these and other Carolingian narratives of past times.[33]

Carolingian-era married clerics

In contrast to such historical examples of father–son episcopal succession, evidence for the same practice in eighth- and ninth-century Francia is very limited. The claim that Bishop Gewilib of Mainz (d. 758) carried out a feud against the Saxon who had killed his father, the previous bishop, first appears only in an eleventh-century text.[34] A dispute brought before

Charlemagne in the 780s over the church of Trier's control of the abbey of Mettlach included a statement by witnesses about the monastery's history:

> and they asserted that Leudwin, the former bishop, father of Milo and Wido, through documents assigned it [Mettlach] to the share of the church of St Peter ... and they said how Milo, who was the successor to bishop Leudwin, and at that time governed the bishopric of St Peter of Trier, sent abbots into the monastery from the same city.[35]

The text does not make clear whether Milo was officially consecrated as bishop of Trier but suggests his father was, and neither Leudwin nor Milo are portrayed negatively.[36] Unfortunately, although this charter is the earliest evidence that Milo was the son of a bishop, it is only transmitted in a fourteenth-century cartulary, and the mention of Leudwin may be a later interpolation, since he was venerated as a saint from the eleventh century.[37]

Indeed, we have little evidence even for married priests in most regions of the Carolingian empire.[38] Wendy Davies records examples in Brittany, and around 900 the parishioners of a priest called Angelric in Vanault complained about him marrying.[39] The most heated denunciations of Frankish clerical incontinence, however, come from the Anglo-Saxon missionary Boniface, who worked in the east (Hesse, Thuringia and Bavaria) from the early 720s onwards.

Unfortunately, only one of the letters associated with Boniface refers specifically to married priests, and most of Boniface's other discussions of clerical offences are frustratingly opaque about their details.[40] For example, Boniface denounces "bishops and priests of the Frankish race, who were the most violent adulterers and fornicators, whose sons born of fornication during their episcopacy and priesthood expose them".[41] While his use of both "adultery" and "fornication" may imply that he is distinguishing between extramarital affairs by married clerics and the sexual incontinence of unmarried clerics, Boniface, like other Carolingian authors, is often very imprecise in his use of such charged sexual terms.[42]

Boniface's over-heated rhetoric, however, is noteworthy because of its isolation. Other Carolingian reformers did not denounce married priests, either for sexual immorality or as a danger to church property. The negative evidence of Hincmar is particularly revealing, since he frequently wrote in a polemical style and was deeply concerned with protecting church property. We are also unusually well informed about his administration of the archdiocese of Rheims.[43] Hincmar complained that some of the clergy in his diocese were buying up land, building on it and then installing women (by implication textile workers) there. He was unhappy that such properties were not left to the church but sold off, sometimes to the priest's own relatives.[44] Yet Hincmar also allowed priests to use some of the income of their churches to support "a brother or some other relative, who is feeble and very poor". If the priest wanted to have other relatives living with him, however, he was to feed and clothe them from his own share of the tithes.[45] Again, there is no mention of priests' wives here, suggesting that they were not an issue in the Frankish heartlands.

The situation in Italy, however, was noticeably different. Joaquìn Martìnez Pizarro argues that Agnellus of Ravenna made an implicit attack in the mid-ninth century on the married clergy of Ravenna; a substantial number of Italian charters also refer to married priests.[46] There is also evidence for married bishops in eighth- and ninth-century Italy. Agnellus says that Sergius, archbishop of Ravenna (d. 769) was in a chaste marriage.[47] The only two ninth-century bishops shown as having children were both based in Rome. Hincmar reports how in 868, the daughter of Pope Hadrian II and his wife Stephanie was abducted and then killed by Eleutherius, son of Bishop Arsenius of Orte. This happened on the advice "it is said" of Eleutherius' brother Anastasius.[48] While Hincmar is the sole source for this story and may not be accurate about the relationship between Eleutherius, Anastasius and Arsenius, his overall account has normally been accepted.[49] There are good reasons, after all, why papal sources may have concealed the details of such a scandal.

Carolingian episcopal families

Outside Italy, there is thus little hard evidence of Carolingian bishops fathering children, let alone them becoming bishops in their turn. Nor is a pattern similar to Anglo-Saxon England visible, in which bishops who themselves were celibate were often the sons of married clerics.[50] The Carolingian priesthood also seems to have been largely unmarried, if not necessarily continent.[51]

What we do see repeatedly, however, is both uncle–nephew succession to a bishopric and cases where both uncle and nephew are bishops of different sees.[52] The best documented of these uncles and nephews are Hincmar of Rheims and Hincmar of Laon; although the younger Hincmar began as a protégé of his uncle, he later became a hated adversary.[53] Marie-Céline Isaïa has argued that Hincmar's invention of stories around St Remigius of Rheims and St Genebaudus of Laon were intended partly to emphasise that Laon was a daughter church of Rheims and hence to reinforce the need for Hincmar of Laon to submit to the authority of his own uncle.[54]

Uncle–nephew episcopal successions were therefore a present reality for Carolingian authors; father–son successions, or even bishops with children, did not generally occur (outside Italy), even though they were still theoretically permitted by Carolingian canons.[55] This disjunction reveals a church tradition that had not yet fully adapted to social realities. A number of church councils were held in Francia under Merovingian and Carolingian rulers; these councils, searching for an authoritative past, continued to promulgate late antique canons that allowed continent married priests and bishops, even as the need to acquire a suitable education gradually made post-marital ordination less feasible. This gradual change may have aroused less opposition from bishops and priests than the head-on collision of Gregory VII and his successors with married priests. By around 800 CE, as Mayke de Jong puts it, "the higher clergy no longer had legitimate wives to abstain from".[56]

Many of the Carolingian clerical elite, unlike in late antiquity, now entered the church as child oblates. There was also a shift in concepts of chastity in the monastic communities that developed in the west from the sixth century onwards. In this new form of monasticism, chastity was no longer seen as being the outcome of a battle fought by individual (male) ascetics. Instead, it was a corporate virtue shared by the whole monastic community, secured by careful surveillance and training from childhood.[57] Hincmar, for example, had been raised at St-Denis "from the beginnings of infancy".[58] As adults, such men's minds were expected to contain an internal cloister, protecting their purity instinctively wherever they went.[59] This Carolingian model of future priests carefully trained from pure boyhood onwards in monasteries was also, in theory, to be replicated on a smaller scale outside the cloister. Local priests were expected to educate their own clerics "in an environment of sincerity and chastity".[60]

Hincmar's celibate male identity, along with that of other elite Carolingian clerics, was thus formed in childhood. Demonstrating masculinity for such men focused more on steadfastness in clerical office than refraining from or indulging in sexual activity.[61] Hincmar might accept a previously married man becoming bishop of Beauvais, but any such candidate must be a man who, if a barbarian attack occurred, "would know to offer help to you [the clergy and people of the city] with prudence, would be strong with manliness, would reflect with temperance".[62]

Inheritance and succession

Why, in Francia, did the uncle–nephew pattern of inheritance take hold rather than the father–son pattern seen in England, some other northern regions of Europe and possibly also in Italy? I have already mentioned the impact of educational opportunities and changing practices of chastity, but it is also useful to look both at the shared political interests of rulers and noble families and at Carolingian ideas of family and nobility.[63] Control of clerical office was a valuable prize in the Frankish empire. As a number of studies have demonstrated, most Merovingian and Carolingian bishops were noble, and their family's support was often important to them obtaining office.[64] In turn, these men commemorated their families and also helped ensure that they kept control of property donated to the church.[65]

Yet direct inheritance of episcopal office created losers as well as winners within the elite. Ecclesiastical dynasties preserved the position of the noble family holding a particular bishopric but thereby excluded local rivals from office. Inheritance of episcopal office also restricted the ruler's ability to appoint bishops and thus limited families' opportunities to gain additional honours via royal favour. The differing inheritance patterns seen for bishops and various subgroups of clergy (such as cathedral canons) across western Europe thus probably reflected varied balances between families' contradictory wishes to keep control of existing offices and to gain new ones. The patterns were also affected by how closely rulers at various levels supervised appointments.[66]

In Francia, although bishops almost always came from the social elite, royal patronage for gaining episcopal office was already important in the later Merovingian period.[67] The early Carolingian rulers gradually eliminated the "episcopal republics" of seventh- and eighth-century Francia, where bishops held relatively independent power in one region.[68] The last known such "episcopal dynasty", the Victorids, had lost control of the bishopric of Chur by 806/807 at the latest.[69]

In contrast to such locally focused families, from the seventh century, aristocratic families developed that had extensive land holding and influence in more than one region.[70] Such supra-regional interests might be expressed via episcopal office; for example, members of the extended family of St Liudger held four different sees during the ninth century.[71] Episcopal dynasties did not disappear under the Carolingians but instead took different forms, more closely tied into the ruling centre.

Reflecting this, competition for bishoprics in the Carolingian period could be intense; Notker the Stammerer (ca. 840–912) in his biography of Charlemagne has several anecdotes about court clerics' scrambles for sees.[72] Noble families could not take dominance of a see for granted. In Freising, one family, the Huosi, were able to provide four successive bishops between 764 and 854. However, when the last of these four, Erchanbert, attempted to cede the see to his nephew Reginbert, King Louis the German instead decided in favour of an episcopal candidate from another prominent local family. Later, the see passed to the Salomonid family, who had also controlled the bishopric of Constance for a substantial period in the ninth century. The see of Freising thus shows the contradictory pressures both enabling and limiting a family's inheritance of episcopal office. Looser patterns of uncle–nephew patronage were better able to respond to such pressures than a more rigid father–son transmission of office; for example, such patterns facilitated brothers, like the Salomonids Salomo and Waldo, holding office simultaneously.[73]

Episcopal ideology

The same pressures are visible in the distinctively Carolingian ideology of nobility and episcopal office-holding that developed. To understand this, it is first useful to look at a late ninth-century comment on *secular* office. In 882, Hincmar of Rheims wrote a treatise on government called *De ordine palatii*. Advising the young king Carloman on how to restore palace institutions, Hincmar says:

> I know no-one to be now alive from those who were seen at the time of the lord emperor Louis [Louis the Pious] as palace administrators and governors of the kingdom. Yet I know that sons were born from

> their nobility to replace them, although I do not know their character and qualities .... To the extent of their merit, let them fill the places and offices of their fathers.[74]

Hincmar's vision here is not strictly of hereditary succession but instead of hereditary preference. In a society which believed that moral qualities were transmitted by blood, he considered it self-evident that the highborn relatives of previous officeholders were suitable candidates to replace them.[75] Yet at the same time, the prevalent rhetoric of virtue as a prerequisite for office meant that a simple presumption of inheritance was unacceptable. Relatives were instead to be given enhanced opportunities to demonstrate their suitability for advancement.

The same pattern is visible for clerical office; Charlemagne warned bishops and abbots that they should not request advancement for less suitable ordinands because they were relatives of theirs, while restricting the advancement of worthier unrelated candidates.[76] Steffan Patzold has shown how ecclesiastical reformers in the 820s constructed a new model of episcopal *ministerium* (ministry) and the relationship of the bishop to the ruler and the people. This model stressed the moral responsibilities of the bishop, who was answerable to God for the salvation of all his flock, including the king.[77] As Patzold shows, in accordance with this model, the numerous late ninth-century episcopal *vitae* not only often mention the nobility of the bishop concerned but also claim that he was nobler in virtue than by birth.[78] These men were rarely shown as related by blood to their predecessors, although ties of education or spiritual kinship were sometimes stressed.[79] Bishops were almost invariably noble, but in theory they were not bishops *because* they were noble.

A family's continued control of clerical office was therefore acceptable only if it could be made to appear "virtuous". Even uncle–nephew connections could occasionally be seen as problematic. Hincmar of Rheims was accused of ordaining Hincmar of Laon as a bishop because he was his nephew and hastily pointed out that Jesus had made some of his own relatives apostles.[80] One ninth-century episcopal *vita*, Herard of Tours' life of Bishop Chrodegang of Sées, includes an awful warning about promoting unsuitable relatives. Chrodegang appointed his nephew Chrodebert to administer the bishopric while he made a pilgrimage to Rome. Chrodebert then had himself elected bishop and murdered Chrodegang on his return.[81]

Some of the texts I have already mentioned include what one might call "firebreaks", indications that family succession was not automatic and implicitly should not be. The *Gesta* of the bishops of Auxerre, for example, describes how three successive relatives became bishop. Heribald, who succeeded his uncle Angelelm in 824, is described as having been educated at the palace from a young age before being made bishop by "solemn election of the clergy and people", an election overseen by the archbishop of Sens.[82] Heribald's successor, his brother Abbo, abbot of St-Germain of Auxerre, was elected "at the order of King Charles".[83]

Similar patterns are seen when sources record pre-Carolingian father–son successions. Paul the Deacon shows Arnulf as the 29th bishop of Metz; his son Clodulf is the 32nd. Between them are two bishops, Goericus and Godo, for whom Paul gives only names, as with the majority of bishops in his text.[84] The *actus* of the bishops of Le Mans does show Victurius succeeding directly to his father Victurus, but the emphasis in the account is on Victurius being raised, educated and ordained by St Martin of Tours.[85]

Finally, there is Hincmar's treatment of sons in the *Vita Remigii.*[86] Remigius was archbishop of Rheims, while his brother Principius was bishop of Soissons. Principius' successor was Lupus, whom Remigius' own will calls "son of my brother" and whom Remigius made the chief heir to his property after the church of Rheims. The most likely hypothesis is that Lupus was the son of Principius; Hincmar claims, however, that Lupus was the son of an otherwise unknown third brother and thus the nephew of both Principius and Remigius.[87]

In contrast to this "removal" of a son, Hincmar also adds both a nephew and a son to the story. He states that Remigius created the see of Laon and made Genebaudus, the husband of Remigius' niece, the first bishop.[88] Hincmar then tells an extraordinary story about Genebaudus. Although he had left his wife in order to lead a religious life, after he became bishop, he over-confidently allowed her to visit him frequently and ended up conceiving two children with her. Genebaudus gave these children symbolic names: a son called Latro (Robber) and a daughter called Vulpecula (Little Fox).[89] He subsequently confessed his sin to Remigius and did penance for seven years, after which Remigius restored him to the see. Genebaudus' successor as bishop of Laon was his son Latro.[90]

Why did Hincmar make one episcopal son as successor appear (Latro) and one disappear (Lupus)? I would suggest that recording Lupus as both Remigus' legal heir and the successor to his own father in a bishopric made the themes of inheritance a little too prominent for Hincmar's taste. In contrast, Latro's entire purpose, from his name onwards, is as a vehicle for moral instruction, displaying not only Genebaudus' fall from grace (and from marital continence) but also his redemption. Hincmar ends his account of the bishop by recounting how "Genebaudus died in peace, numbered among the saints of God while he was living in the bishopric, so that Latro, his son, a bishop and himself holy, succeeded to him".[91] Latro's succession is made the ultimate prize for Genebaudus' sincere penance, not any kind of role model for an episcopal dynasty. Such a bishop's son was safe enough for Carolingian reformers to cope with.

The Frankish empire and beyond

Carolingian rulers developed appointment practices that continued to provide noble families with their traditional privileged access to both secular and religious office, while still allowing kings the opportunity to influence local aristocratic societies.[92] Rulers who permitted uncle–nephew succession in sees accommodated deeply held beliefs in virtue as hereditary, while preventing bishoprics being formally inherited and also maintaining adherence to the canonical rules on clerical celibacy.

In turn, the new episcopal ideology developed from the 820s reflected such inheritance patterns. The stress was predominantly on the generic nobility of a virtuous bishop rather than on the specific claims of a family to a particular see.[93] Some bishoprics might in practice be monopolised by one family, but there was an ideological presumption against this; Carolingian bishops did not have heirs to their office. Reflecting this, it is often not possible to reconstruct genealogies for bishops, even when several of them are clearly related to one another.[94]

The Carolingian evidence also suggests that noble families adopted varied strategies for advancement in response to this situation. Geneviève Bührer-Thierry has argued for the ninth-century development of "ecclesiastical lineages". These were families who are repeatedly visible holding high ecclesiastical office but rarely secular office; one example is the Salomonids.[95] The Fulda Annals record how in 890, after Bishop Salomo of Constance died, "he was succeeded by his namesake, the younger Salomo, who was the third of that name to hold the episcopal see".[96] Salomo was a nephew rather than a son of the previous bishop, but the shared name suggests a planned succession. Salomo's brother Waldo became bishop of Freising, and a letter from their former teacher at the monastery of St Gall refers to them as a *sacerdotale genus*, a priestly race.[97]

These indirectly transmitted episcopal dynasties relied on favour from a powerful ruler but allowed the possibility of further expansion; a bishop's brother or nephews might gain sees elsewhere in the kingdom. Tenth-century Germany shows the continued existence of the Carolingian balance; neither kings, dukes nor local families had a monopoly in choosing bishops.[98]

In contrast, when western Francia began to fragment into smaller political units and kings lost power, families might act more directly to ensure continued control of a see. Less than 50 years after Hincmar's death, in 925, an archbishop of Rheims was installed who was five years old.[99] Hugh of Vermandois was elected on the "counsel" of his father, Heribert, Count of Rheims, to avoid the division of the bishopric by "outside people".[100] Such control of bishoprics by laymen may have been partly a reaction to a more difficult political climate, focusing on the defence of existing power rather than expansion into a wider sphere.[101] The married bishops and clerics of northwest France in the tenth and eleventh century may similarly reflect societies with narrower horizons for family advancement.[102] Certainly the Anglo-Norman defenders of clerical marriage particularly stressed the loss of honour for themselves and their wives that reform threatened.[103] Father–son inheritance allowed the maintenance of existing status but fewer opportunities for advancement at the expense of rival clerical dynasties.

Conclusion

I want to finish by returning to Robert Moore, who comments: "the campaign for clerical celibacy in the eleventh century must be regarded in part, like so many other aspects of the reform ... as an attempt to subordinate local hierarchies to central authority".[104] As has been shown, however, the wish by a central authority to control local church hierarchies was not new in the eleventh century, even if the identity of the would-be subordinator – the papacy – was.

Efforts to ensure clerical continence were also a recurring theme from late antiquity, but the approaches taken varied, reflecting both changing methods of clerical recruitment and the identity of the would-be reformers. In the Carolingian empire, a relatively consensual approach is visible, combining increasing central authority and adherence to clerical celibacy together with frequent family control of priestly and episcopal offices over several generations. Both Carolingian kings and reforming clerics such as Hincmar saw such family strategies as largely acceptable and not intrinsically threatening to church property.

The Frankish evidence also suggests that we should not overestimate the prevalence of married bishops and priests across the Western church before the eleventh century. Some early medieval societies developed patterns of inherited clerical office that did not involve father–son succession. We may also need to be more sceptical as to the genuineness of tenth- and eleventh-century reformers' concerns about married priests as a threat to church property.

As a parallel, it is useful to note another key concern of eleventh-century reformers: simony. A Carolingian synod at Attigny in 822 saw the "simoniacal heresy" as involving not only preferment for the sake of money but also that due to consanguinity or friendship.[105] In contrast, as Timothy Reuter has shown, eleventh-century reformers eventually came to a relatively narrow interpretation of simony, limited solely to the sale and purchase of office.[106] Similarly, attacks on priests' wives as a threat to church property were probably less about actual abuses than about using such women as a symbol of the corrupt ties between the "church" and the "world". Married clerics and their wives were probably a convenient target for such symbolic attacks, since relatively few bishops were themselves married.[107] As with the fourth-century requirement of clerical continence, the prohibition of marriage for priests was intended as a stand-in for their wider detachment from secular influence.

However, this demand for permanent continence was being addressed neither to the mature candidates for clerical office of late antiquity nor to a Carolingian priesthood who had theoretically been trained from early boyhood for a celibate life. Instead, the requirement to avoid marriage was now addressed to adolescents and young men on the border between minor and major orders. These young men were liable to influence by their secular peers, whose youthful masculinity allowed them considerable sexual licence. Developing a distinctively clerical masculine identity was probably more difficult than in previous centuries, and problems in enforcing the church's rules were perhaps not surprising.[108]

Nevertheless, the reforms of the central Middle Ages eventually delegitimized (quite literally) the children of clerics. Despite what some historians have suggested, however, these reforms did not remove the ties between clerics and their families; throughout the Middle Ages and beyond, bishops continued to ensure the advancement within the church of their close kin. The strategies used for such advancement may have changed, but desires to ensure the success of episcopal relatives were constant.

Notes

1 My thanks to Charles West, Fraser McNair, Norman G. Owen, Julia Barrow and the editors for their comments and advice on this chapter. Many of the quoted sources have been edited in various series of the Monumenta Germaniae Historica (abbreviated as MGH). Further abbreviations of the MGH-series can be found online at www.dmgh.de, together with the digitalised editions (open access).

2 See, for example, Jennifer D. Thibodeaux, "Introduction: Rethinking the Medieval Clergy and Masculinity," in *Negotiating Clerical Identities: Priests, Monks and Masculinity in the Middle Ages*, ed. Jennifer D. Thibodeaux, (Basingstoke: Palgrave Macmillan, 2010), 5; Helen L. Parish, *Clerical Celibacy in the West, c. 1100–1700* (Farnham: Ashgate, 2010), 90. The Carolingian practices of priestly celibacy discussed by Mayke de Jong, "*Imitatio morum*: the cloister and clerical purity in the Carolingian world," in *Medieval Purity and Piety: Essays on Medieval Clerical Celibacy and Religious Reform*, ed. Michael Frassetto (New York: Garland, 1998), 49–80, are overlooked by the authors of several other chapters in that book.

3 Robert I. Moore, "Family, Community and Cult on the Eve of the Gregorian Reform," *Transactions of the Royal Historical Society* 5th ser., 30 (1980): 62, citing Atto of Vercelli, *Epistola* 9, in *Patrologia Latina* 139, ed. J.-P. Migne (Paris, 1841–64), col. 116–19. Cf. Dyan Elliott, "The Priest's Wife: Female Erasure and the Gregorian Reform," in *Medieval Religion: New Approaches*, ed. Constance Hoffman Berman (New York: Routledge, 2005), 125; Ruth Mazo Karras, *Unmarriages: Women, Men, and Sexual Unions in the Middle Ages* (Philadelphia: University of Pennsylvania Press, 2012), 119.

4 Robert I. Moore, *The First European Revolution, c. 970–1215* (Oxford: Blackwell, 2000), 88.

5 "The reason for popular hostility in the eleventh century to the marriage of priests and to the sale or gift of benefices in the church was ... because they represented ties which bound the priest to his lord and family." (Moore, *The First European Revolution*, 61–62).

6 See Julia Barrow, *The Clergy in the Medieval World: Secular Clerics, Their Families and Careers in North-Western Europe, c.800–c.1200* (Cambridge: Cambridge University Press, 2015), 115–157.

7 Megan McLaughlin, *Sex, Gender, and Episcopal Authority in an Age of Reform, 1000–1122* (Cambridge: Cambridge University Press, 2010) demonstrates, however, that some of the uses of familial language by eleventh-century reformers were new.

8 Christian Cochini, *Origines apostoliques du célibat sacerdotal* (Paris: Lethielleux, 1981). The Eastern church developed a different practice, in which married priests were expected to abstain only temporarily from their wives, but bishops were expected to be either unmarried or to separate from their wives on their elevation to the episcopacy. Cochini, *Origines apostoliques*, 431–46; Parish, *Clerical Celibacy in the West*, 59–86.

9 See for example, Paul Beaudette, "'In the World but not of It': Clerical Celibacy as a Symbol of the Medieval Church," in *Medieval Purity and Piety,* ed. Frassetto, 36; Moore, *The First European Revolution*, 62. Eugen Ewig, "Milo et eiusmodi similes," in *Spätantikes und fränkisches Gallien: Gesammelte Schriften (1952–1973)* (Munich: Artemis, 1979), 212–13 talks of "episcopal republics" as existing in seventh-century Francia.

10 James A. Brundage, *Law, Sex and Christian Society in Medieval Europe* (Chicago: University of Chicago Press, 1987), 300; Karras, *Unmarriages*, 26–7.

11 Peter Brown, *The Body and Society: Men, Women, and Sexual Renunciation in Early Christianity* (New York: Columbia University Press, 1988), 96; Dyan Elliott, *Spiritual Marriage: Sexual Abstinence in Medieval Wedlock* (Princeton: Princeton University Press, 1993).

12 See Julia Barrow's chapter in this volume.

13 Michel Dortel-Claudot, "Le prêtre et le mariage: Évolution de la législation canonique des origines au XII siècle," *L'année canonique* 17 (1973): 319–44; Cochini, *Origines apostoliques*, 283–446. On Merovingian rules and attitudes, see Robert Godding, *Prêtres en Gaule mérovingienne* (Brussels: Société des Bollandistes, 2001), 111–54; Brian Brennan, "'Episcopae': Bishops' Wives Viewed in Sixth-Century Gaul," *Church History* 54 (1985): 311–23.

14 Kate Cooper and Conrad Leyser, "The Gender of Grace: Impotence, Servitude and Manliness in the Fifth-Century West," *Gender and History* 12 (2000): 539.

15 Brown, *The Body and Society*, 356–62.

16 David G. Hunter, "Clerical Marriage and Episcopal Elections in the Latin West: from Siricius to Leo I," in *Episcopal Elections in Late Antiquity*, ed. Johan Leemans et al. (Berlin: De Gruyter, 2011), 183–202.

17 Ralph W. Mathisen, "Ruricius' Family, Friends and Historical Context," in Ralph W. Mathisen (transl.) *Ruricius of Limoges and Friends: A Collection of Letters from Visigothic Gaul* (Liverpool: Liverpool University Press, 1999), 19–27.

18 Pierre Riché, *Education and Culture in the Barbarian West: From the Sixth through the Eighth Century*, trans. John J. Contreni (Columbia, SC: University of South Carolina Press, 1976), 79–99.

19 Barrow, *The Clergy in the Medieval World*, 118–120. On oblates (children offered to the church), see Mayke de Jong, *In Samuel's Image: Child Oblation in the Early Medieval West* (Leiden: Brill, 1996).

20 Godding, *Prêtres en Gaule mérovingienne*, 131–4.

21 Ibid., 448–449, 467–527 provides a partial prosopography of priests in Merovingian Gaul, which lists 16 married priests for the sixth century (out of 266 priests probably to be dated from that period) and 2 from the seventh century (out of 76); Cochini, *Origines apostoliques*, 134–143 cites 19 married bishops and 6 married priests for sixth-century France, compared to 8 bishops and 1 priest for France in the seventh century.

22 Louis Duchesne, ed., *Le Liber Pontificalis: texte, introduction et commentaire*, 2 vols (Paris: Thorin, 1886–92). See, for example, the lives of Hadrian I, s. 2–3 (1:486); Sergius II, s. 1–2 (2:86), where Sergius is sent to the *schola cantorum* (a school to train youths to chant the papal liturgy) at the age of around 12, after he has been left an orphan; Benedict III, s. 1 (2:140); Nicholas I, s. 1–2 (2:151).

23 Godding, *Prêtres en Gaule mérovingienne*, 133–34. As he points out (138), the Merovingian councils' statements on this topic never mention the priest's wife among the relatives that the priest may keep in his house. For Carolingian capitularies (royal decrees) and councils discussing women in priest's houses, see for example, *Pippini principis capitulare Suessionense* 744, no. 12, cap. 8, in *Capitularia regum Francorum*, ed. Alfred Boretius and Victor Krause, 2 vols, MGH Capit., (Hanover: Hahn, 1883–97) (1:30): only mother, sister or niece allowed; *Admonitio generalis* 789, no. 22, cap. 4 (1:54): only mother, sister, or someone non-suspicious; *Concilium Aquisgranense* 816, no. 39, cap. 39, in *Concilia aevi Karolini*, ed. Albert Werminghoff, 2 vols, MGH Conc. 2, 1 (Hanover: Hahn, 1906–08) (2.1:360): only mother, sister, aunt or someone non-suspicious.

24 See, for example, Theodulf of Orléans, Second capitulary, cap. 4, in *Capitula episcoporum*, ed. Peter. Brommer *et al.*, 4 vols, MGH Capit. episc. (Hanover: Hahn, 1984–2005) (1:170); Hincmar, Second capitulary, cap. 21, in *Capitula episcoporum*, ed. Brommer (2:52–59); Hincmar, *De cavendis vitiis et virtutibus exercendis,* ed. Doris Nachtmann, MGH QQ zur Geistesgeschichte 16 (Munich: MGH, 1998), 2, 6, pp. 210–12.

25 See, for example, Council of Worms 868, no. 25, cap. 9, in *Die Konzilien der karolingischen Teilreiche 843–859*, ed. Wilfried Hartmann, MGH Conc. 3 (Hannover: Hahn, 1984) (3:267); *Codex Carolinus* in *Epistolae Merowingici et Karolini aevi,* ed. W. Gundlach, MGH Epp. 3 (Berlin: Weidmann, 1892), *Epistola* 3, cap. 11, 483.

26 Hincmar of Rheims, *Epistola* XXXIX, in *Patrologia Latina* 126, ed. J.-P. Migne, (Paris, 1841–64), col. 260. On Hincmar, see Jean Devisse, *Hincmar, Archevêque de Reims 845–882*, 3 vols. (Geneva: Droz, 1975–76); Rachel Stone and Charles West, eds, *Hincmar of Rheims: Life and Work* (Manchester: Manchester University Press, 2015). Cf. *Episcoporum ad imperatorem de rebus ecclesiasticis relatio*, 821, no. 179, cap. 1 in *Capitularia regum Francorum,* ed. Boretius and Krause, MGH Capit. 1 (1:368).

27 Paul the Deacon, *Gesta episcoporum mettensium*, ed. George Henry Pertz, MGH Scriptores 2 (Hanover: Hahn, 1829), 264. On the text, see Damien Kempf, "Paul the Deacon's *Liber de episcopis Mettensibus* and the Role of Metz in the Carolingian Realm," *Journal of Medieval History* 30 (2004): 279–99; Janet L. Nelson, "Charlemagne the Man," in *Charlemagne: Empire and Society*, ed. Joanna Story (Manchester: Manchester University Press, 2005), 32–4.

28 Paul the Deacon, *Gesta episcoporum mettensium*, 267.

29 Paul Fouracre and Richard A. Gerberding, eds, *Late Merovingian France: History and Hagiography, 640–720*, (Manchester: Manchester University Press, 1996), 308–9, 311, 339 suggest that the genealogical connections are a later development.

30 Margarete Weidemann, ed., *Geschichte des Bistums Le Mans von der Spätantike bis zur Karolingerzeit: Actus pontificum Cenomannis in urbe degentium und Gesta Aldrici*, 3 vols. (Mainz: Verlag des Römisch-Germanischen Zentralmuseums, 2002), capitula 5–6 (1:42–3).

31 *Vita Victuri et Victurii*, in *Acta Sanctorum*, ed. Societas Bollandiensi, August V, 145–147. Walter A. Goffart, *The Le Mans Forgeries: A Chapter from the History of Church Property in the Ninth Century* (Cambridge, MA: Harvard University Press, 1966), 55–57, 157 argues for a seventh or eighth-century dating on stylistic grounds.

32 Hincmar, *Vita Remigii episcopi Remensis auctore Hincmaro*, in *Passiones vitaeque sanctorum aevi Merovingici*, ed. Bruno Krusch and Wilhelm Levison, 5 vols, MGH SS rer. Merov 3 (Hanover: Hahn, 1896–1920) (3:250–341); on the dating, see Marie-Céline Isaïa, *Remi de Reims: Mémoire d'un saint, histoire d'une église* (Paris: Editions du Cerf, 2010), 528–529.

33 Another ninth-century *vita* connected to Rheims, Altmann of Hautvilliers, *Vita Nivard episcopi Remensis auctore Almanno monacho Altivillarensi*, cap. 1 in *Passiones vitaeque sanctorum aevi Merovingici*, ed. Krusch and Levison MGH SS rer. Merov 5 (5:160), says that the seventh-century archbishop of Rheims Reolus married Nivard's niece while still a count. On ninth-century discussions of St Severus, bishop of Ravenna, see Elliott, "The Priest's Wife," 127–31; Steffen Patzold, *Episcopus: Wissen über Bischöfe im Frankenreich des späten 8. bis frühen 10. Jahrhunderts* (Ostfildern: Jan Thorbecke, 2008), 501–3.

34 Ewig, "Milo et eiusmodi similes," 199–200; Boniface, *Epistolae, Die Briefe des heiligen Bonifatius und Lullus*, ed. Michael Tangl., MGH Epp. sel. 1 (Berlin: Weidmann, 1916), *Epistola* 60, 124 complains about Gewilib but does not mention him being the son of a bishop, arguing against the story.

35 Engelbert Mühlbacher, ed., *Die Urkunden der Karolinger, 1:Urkunden Pippins, Karlmanns and Karl der Grossen*, MGH DD Kar. 1 (Hannover: Hahn, 1906), no. 148, 201: "et adseruerunt, ut Leodonius quondam episcopus genitor Miloni et Widoni partibus ecclesie sancti Petri ... per sua strumenta delegasset; et dixerunt, qualiter Milo, qui fuit successor ipsius Leodoni episcopi et eo tempore episcopio sancti Petri Treverice urbis regebat, abbates in ipso monasterio de ipsa civitate misisset."

36 Olaf Schneider, *Erzbischof Hinkmar und die Folgen: der vierhundertjährige Weg historischer Erinnerungsbilder von Reims nach Trier* (Berlin: De Gruyter, 2010), 66–108 shows how Ewig, "Milo et eiusmodi similes," 190–199 produces his account of Milo's career by combining sources from several centuries apart.

37 Schneider, *Erzbischof Hinkmar*, 250–251.

38 Henry C. Lea, *History of Sacerdotal Celibacy in the Christian Church*, 3rd ed. (London: Williams and Norgate, 1907), 1:141–63 provides an overwrought account but fails to find many specific examples. There are also some references to married clerics, but it is difficult to be sure if these men were in major orders.

39 Wendy Davies, "Priests and Rural Communities in East Brittany in the Ninth Century," in *Brittany in the Early Middle Ages: Texts and Societies* (Farnham: Ashgate, 2009), 191; Charles West, *Reframing the Feudal Revolution: Political and Social Transformation Between Marne and Moselle, c. 800–c. 1100* (Cambridge: Cambridge University Press, 2013), 38, citing Mantio, Bishop of Chalons, *Epistola* in *Patrologia Latina* 131, ed. J.-P. Migne (Paris, 1841–64), col. 23.

40 Boniface, *Epistola* 51, 87–89 has Pope Zacharias in 743 stating that adulterous clerics or those with more than one wife are not to be allowed and complains that some are marrying after ordination. He also reassures Boniface that proven adulterers or fornicators have not received indulgence from him.

41 Boniface, *Epistola* 50, 85: "Episcopi quoque et presbiteri generis Francorum, qui fuerunt adulteri vel fornicatores acerrimi, quos in gradu episcopatus vel presbiterii fornicationum filii nati arguunt". Compare *Epistola* 59, 112: "Synodalia iura spernens proprio sensu [Clemens] adfirmat se post duos filios sibi in adulterio natos sub nomine episcopi esse posse legis christianę episcopum".

42 Rachel Stone, *Morality and Masculinity in the Carolingian Empire* (Cambridge: Cambridge University Press, 2011), 281–282.

43 On his administration, see Martina Stratmann, *Hinkmar von Reims als Verwalter von Bistum und Kirchenprovinz* (Sigmaringen: Thorbecke, 1991); on his episcopal statues, see Carine van Rhijn, *Shepherds of the Lord: Priests and Episcopal Statutes in the Carolingian Period* (Turnhout: Brepols, 2007).

44 Hincmar, Fourth capitulary, cap. 4 in *Capitula episcoporum*, ed. Brommer (2:84).

45 Hincmar, Second capitulary, cap. 17 in *Capitula episcoporum*, ed. Brommer (2:50).

46 Joaquìn Martìnez Pizarro, *Writing Ravenna: The Liber pontificalis of Andreas Agnellus* (Ann Arbor: University of Michigan Press, 1995), 137–141 on Agnellus

of Ravenna, *Liber pontificalis ecclesiae Ravannentis*, in *Scriptores rerum Langgobardicarum et Italiacum saec. VI-IX,* ed. O. Holder-Egger, MGH SS rer. Lang (Hanover: Hahn, 1878), cap. 96–97, 339–341; Gabriella Rossetti, "Il matrimonio del clero nella società altomedievale," in *Il Matrimonio nella società altomedievale, 22–28 Apr 1976*, Settimane di studi sull'alto medioevo 24, 2 vols (Spoleto, Centro Italiano di Studi sull'Alto Medioevo, 1977), 1:533–537. I discuss Italian patterns further in Rachel Stone, "Exploring Minor Clerics in early Medieval Tuscany", to appear in *Reti Medievali Rivista.*

47 Elliott, "The Priest's Wife," 127–128, citing Agnellus, *Liber pontificalis*, capitula 154 and 157, pp. 377–379. See also Duschesne, ed., *Liber pontificalis,* Stephen III, s. 19 (1:475).

48 Hincmar, *Annales Bertiniani*, ed. G. Waitz, MGH SS rer. Germ. 5 (Hanover: Hahn, 1883), s.a. 868, 92. For discussion, see Council of Rome 868, no. 27, *Die Konzilien der karolingischen Teilreiche 860–874*, ed. Wilfried Hartmann, MGH Conc. 4 (Hannover: Hahn, 1998) (4:316); Raymond Davis, trans., *The Lives of the Ninth-Century Popes (Liber pontificalis): The Ancient Biographies of Ten Popes from A.D. 817–891* (Liverpool: Liverpool University Press, 1995), 249–52.

49 See Ibid., 169, n. 9.

50 See Barrow, *The Clergy in the Medieval World*, 139–142.

51 Mayke de Jong, "*Imitatio morum*," 51–53, 59.

52 See Barrow, *The Clergy in the Medieval World*, 122–128; Patzold, *Episcopus*, 506, n. 282. See also *Actus pontificum Cenomannis* cap. 18, p. 111 on Franco I and II of Le Mans; Regino of Prüm, *Chronicon*, ed. Friederich Kurze, MGH SS Rer. Germ. 50 (Hanover: Hahn, 1890), s.a. 869, 98 on Bishop Adventius of Metz obtaining the bishopric of Trier for his nephew Bertulf; West, *Reframing*, 53 on Bernhard, Dado and Barnuin, late ninth and early tenth-century bishops of Verdun.

53 On Hincmar of Laon, see Peter R. McKeon, *Hincmar of Laon and Carolingian Politics* (Urbana: University of Illinois Press, 1978); Charles West, "Lordship in Ninth-Century Francia: The Case of Bishop Hincmar of Laon and his Followers," *Past and Present* 226 (2015): 3–40.

54 Isaïa, *Remi de Reims*, 154–155. On the story, see below, 184–85.

55 It is unlikely that these clerical "nephews" were, in fact, illegitimate sons; given the fierce rivalries between many of the ninth-century bishops mentioned and the voluminous surviving material discussing them, we would expect to find traces of such allegations.

56 de Jong, "*Imitatio morum*," 51.

57 Albrecht Diem, "The Gender of the Religious: Wo/men and the Invention of Monasticism," in *The Oxford Handbook of Women and Gender in Medieval Europe*, ed. Judith M. Bennett and Ruth Mazo Karras (New York: Oxford University Press, 2013), 437–40.

58 Hincmar, *Epistolae* ed. E. Perels, MGH Epp. 8 (Berlin: Weidmann, 1939), *Epistola* 198, 210.

59 de Jong, "*Imitatio morum*," 61–63.

60 Ibid., 64, citing Walter of Orléans, Episcopal capitulary, cap. 6, in *Capitula episcoporum*, ed. Brommer, MGH Capit. episc. 1 (1:189).

61 Stone, *Morality*, 317–321.

62 See also Rachel Stone, "Gender and Hierarchy: Archbishop Hincmar of Rheims (845–882) as a Religious Man," in *Religious Men and Masculine Identity in the Middle Ages*, ed. P. H. Cullum and Katherine J. Lewis (Woodbridge: Boydell and Brewer, 2013), 29, citing Hincmar of Rheims, *Epistola* XXIX, in Patrologia Latina 126, ed. J.-P. Migne, (Paris, 1841–64), col. 260. Christopher Fletcher, "The

Whig Interpretation of Masculinity? Honour and Sexuality in Late Medieval Manhood," in *What is Masculinity? Historical Dynamics from Antiquity to the Contemporary World*, ed. John H. Arnold and Sean Brady (Basingstoke: Palgrave Macmillan, 2011), 57–75 similarly argues that ideas of late medieval "manhood" (both clerical and lay) focused on strength and vigour more than sexual activity.

63 Régine Le Jan, *Famille et pouvoir dans le monde franc (VIIe–Xe siècle): Essai d'anthropologie sociale* (Paris: Publications de la Sorbonne, 1995) provides a wide-ranging overview.

64 See for example, Wilhelm Störmer, *Früher Adel: Studien zur politischen Führungsschicht im fränkischen-deutschen Reich vom 8. bis 11. Jahrhundert* (Stuttgart: Hiersemann, 1973), 2:311–57; Ian Wood, *The Merovingian Kingdoms, 450–751* (London: Longman, 1994), 77–87; Patzold, *Episcopus*, 27–30.

65 Geneviève Bührer-Thierry, "Des évêques, des clercs et leurs families dans la Bavière des VIIIe-IXe siècles," in *Sauver son âme et se perpétuer: Transmission du patrimoine et mémoire au haut Moyen Âge*, ed. François Bougard, Cristina La Rocca and Régine Le Jan (Rome: École française de Rome, 2005), 239–64.

66 Geneviève Bührer-Thierry, *Évêques et pouvoir dans le royaume de Germanie: Les Églises de Bavière et de Souabe, 876–973* (Paris: Picard, 1997), 151–205.

67 Wood, *Merovingian Kingdoms*, 78–79.

68 Paul Fouracre, *The Age of Charles Martel* (Harlow: Longman, 2000), 71–74, 90–93.

69 On the Victorids, see Reinhold Kaiser, *Churrätien im frühen Mittelalter: Ende 5. bis Mitte 10. Jahrhundert* (Basel: Schwabe, 1998), 45–55. His reconstruction of the family tree (p. 49) includes an "episcopa" (a bishop's wife) in the later seventh century but uncle–nephew succession subsequently.

70 Matthew Innes, *State and Society in the Early Middle Ages: The Middle Rhine Valley, 400–1000* (Cambridge: Cambridge University Press, 2000), 174–80.

71 Karl Hauck, "Apostolischer Geist im genus *sacerdotale* der Liudgeriden. Die 'Kanonisation' Liudgers und Altfrids gleichzeitige Bischofsgrablege in Essen-Werden," in *Sprache und Recht: Beiträge zur Kulturgeschichte des Mittelalters: Festschrift für Ruth Schmidt-Wiegand zum 60. Geburtstag*, ed. Karl Hauck (New York: de Gruyter, 1986), 208.

72 Notker Balbulus, *Gesta Karoli Magni imperatoris*, ed. Hans F. Haefele, MGH SS rer. Ger. N.S. 12 (Berlin: Widemann, 1959), I, cap. 4–6, pp. 5–9.

73 Bührer-Thierry, "Évêques," 241–242; On the Salomonids, see below, note 96.

74 Hincmar of Rheims, *De ordine palatii*, ed. Thomas Gross and Rudolf Schieffer, MGH Font. iur. Germ. 3 (Hanover: Hahn, 1980) cap. 37, p. 96: "quoniam de his, quos tempore domni Hludovici imperatoris vidi palatii procuratores et regni praefectos, ne minem scio esse superstitem; scio tamen de illorum nobilitate natos pro patribus filios, licet illorum mores ac qualitates ignorem. Ipsi vero procurent ... quatenus merito patrum loca et officia suppleant."

75 On Carolingian ideas of nobility, see Janet L. Nelson, "Nobility in the Ninth Century," in *Nobles and Nobility in Medieval Europe: Concepts, Origins, Transformations*, ed. Anne J. Duggan (Woodbridge: Boydell, 2000), 43–51; Stone, *Morality*, 126–133.

76 *Capitulare missorum generale*, 802, no. 33, cap. 16 in *Capitularia regum Francorum*, ed. Boretius and Krause (1:94). Enhanced opportunities for priest's relatives could also be offered: Theodulf of Orléans, First capitulary, cap. 19, in *Capitularia episcoporum*, ed. Brommer (1:115–116) allowed the priests of his diocese to send their nephew or another relative to one of the cathedral or monastic schools under his control, offering considerable opportunities for advancement.

77 Patzold, *Episcopus*.
78 Ibid., 499–501.
79 Ibid., 503–505.
80 Hincmar, *Opusculum in LV capitulis*, in *Die Streitschriften Hinkmars von Reims und Hinkmars von Laon 869–871*, ed. Rudolf Schieffer, MGH Conc. 4, Supplement 2 (Hanover: Hahn, 2003), cap. 42, p. 306. My thanks to Charles West for this reference.
81 Patzold, *Episcopus*, 506–507, discussing Herard of Tours, *Vita Chrodegangi*, *Acta Sanctorum*, ed. Societas Bollandiensi, September I, 768–773.
82 *Gesta pontificum Autissiodorensium, Les gestes des évêques d'Auxerre*, 3 vols., eds. Michel Sot, Monique Goullet and Guy Lobrichon (Paris: Belles lettres, 2002–09) cap. 36, pp. 148–149.
83 Ibid., cap. 37, pp. 154–155.
84 Paul the Deacon, *Gesta episcoporum mettensium*, 267.
85 *Actus pontificum Cenomannis*, cap. 6, p. 43.
86 See also Rachel Stone, "Gender and Hierarchy," 42–44.
87 *Hincmar, Vita Remigii*, cap. 32, p. 336. On the text and the family of Remigius, see Isaïa, *Remi de Reims*, 52–60.
88 *Hincmar, Vita Remigii*, cap. 16, pp. 300–301. A bishop of Laon called Genebaudus is known from other sources, but it is unlikely that he was a relative of Remigius: see Isaia, *Remi de Reims*, pp. 151–156, 437–440.
89 Hincmar, *Vita Remigii*, cap. 16, p. 301.
90 Hincmar, *Vita Remigii*, cap. 16, p. 306.
91 Hincmar, *Vita Remigii*, cap. 16, p. 305.
92 Innes, *State and Society in the Early Middle Ages*, 188–193.
93 Patzold, *Episcopus*, 501 notes an exception: Hildegar of Meaux, *Vita Faronis episcopi Meldensis*, cap. 102, in *Passiones vitaeque sanctorum aevi Merovingici*, ed. Krusch and Levison, MGH SS rer. Merov 5 (5:194) talks about Faro's hereditary claims on the bishopric of Meaux "lege consanguinitatis quasi iure haereditatis".
94 See for example, Hauck, "Apostolischer Geist," 208–209.
95 Bührer-Thierry, *Évêques et pouvoir*, 171–172.
96 *Annales Fuldenses*, ed. Friedrich Kurze, MGH SS rer. Germ. 7 (Hanover: Hahn, 1891), s. a. 890, p. 119.
97 *Collectio Sangellensis*, in *Formulae Merowingici et Karolini aevi*, ed. Karl Zeumer, MGH Formulae (Hanover: Hahn, 1886) no. 43, p. 426. On the letter and its author, see Alice Rio, *Legal Practice and the Written Word in the Early Middle Ages: Frankish Formulae, c. 500–1000* (Cambridge: Cambridge University Press, 2009), 156–157.
98 Bührer-Thierry, *Évêques et pouvoir*, 151–152.
99 Godding, *Prêtres en Gaule mérovingienne*, 91–94: Merovingian councils allowed a man to become a deacon at 25 and a priest at 30. The prohibition on becoming a priest before 30 was repeated in *Admonitio generalis*, 789, no. 22, cap. 50, in *Capitularia regum Francorum,* ed. Boretius and Krause, MGH Capit. 1 (1:57).
100 Flodoard of Rheims, *Historia Remensis ecclesiae*, ed. Martina Stratmann, MGH Scriptores 36 (Hanover: Hahn, 1998), IV, cap. 20, p. 411. Edward Roberts, "Flodoard of Rheims and the Tenth Century," (PhD diss., University of St Andrews, 2013), 25–40 discusses Flodoard's reactions to the conflicts over the archbishopric.
101 For other French examples, see Jean Dunbabin, *France in the Making, 843–1180*, 2nd ed. (Oxford: Oxford University Press, 2000), 121–123.
102 See Jacques Boussard, "Les évêques en Neustrie avant la Réforme grégorienne (950–1050 environ)", *Journal des savants* 3, no. 1 (1970): 174–176, 181–182,

186–187; Jean Gaudemet, "Le célibat ecclésiastique. Le droit et la pratique du XIe au XIIIe siècle," *Zeitschrift der Savigny-Stiftung für Rechtsgeschichte, Kanonistische Abteilung* 68 (1982): 5; David Bates, *Normandy before 1066* (London: Longman, 1982), 209. My thanks to Fraser McNair for his advice on the topic.

103 Parish, *Clerical Celibacy in the West*, 91; Jennifer D. Thibodeaux, "The Defence of Clerical Marriage: Religious Identity and Masculinity in the Writings of Anglo-Norman Clerics," in *Religious Men and Masculine Identity in the Middle Ages*, ed. Cullum and Lewis, 57–59.

104 Moore, *The First European Revolution*, 62.

105 *Capitula ab episcopis Attiniaci data*, 822, no. 174, cap. 6 in *Capitularia regum Francorum*, ed. Boretius and Krause, MGH Capit. 1 (1:358): "Ut heresis simoniaca ita caveatur, ut non solum propter munerum acceptionem, sed neque consanguinitate familiaritatis aut cuiuslibet amicitiae aut obsequii causa deinceps ullus prebeat." The implication is presumably that of advancing *unworthy* candidates because of a relationship, as with Charlemagne's concerns.

106 Timothy Reuter, "Gifts and Simony," in *Medieval Transformations: Texts, Power, and Gifts in Context*, ed. Esther Cohen and Mayke de Jong (Leiden: Brill, 2001), 157–168.

107 Barrow, *The Clergy in the Medieval World*, 128–129.

108 Jennifer D. Thibodeaux, "From Boys to Priests: Adolescence, Masculinity and the Parish Clergy in Medieval Normandy," in *Negotiating Clerical Identities: Priests, Monks and Masculinity in the Middle Ages*, ed. Jennifer D. Thibodeaux (Basingstoke: Palgrave Macmillan, 2010), 136–158.

7 Eunuchs and the East India Company in north India[1]

Jessica Hinchy

From the middle of the eighteenth century, as the British East India Company expanded its territories and brought Indian polities under indirect colonial rule, various Indian scribal and administrative communities sought to accommodate or negotiate with this expanding colonial power. Among these communities of officials were *khwāja-sarā'ī*, eunuch slaves who were central to the courtly culture and governance of many Indian states. High-ranking *khwāja-sarā'ī* could wield significant political authority on their master's or mistress's behalf and could become powerful military magnates, revenue farmers and administrators. This chapter explores how *khwāja-sarā'ī* responded to the Company's deepening involvement in the administration and court politics of Indian states through a case study of eighteenth and nineteenth-century Awadh, a state in north India. This study seeks to highlight both the long-term impacts of colonial modernity upon *khwāja-sarā'ī* slave-nobles as well as to provide an investigation of the significance of family, slavery and discourses of masculinity to the politics of indirect colonial rule in Awadh.

Early eighteenth-century Awadh was a province of the Mughal empire (beginning ca. 1580). In the 1720s, the Ṣūbadār (governor) of the province of Awadh, the Persian noble Sa'ādat 'Alī Khān, turned the Mughal province into an autonomous state, which nevertheless recognised Mughal sovereignty, and henceforth the rule of this state was hereditary.[2] The Awadh rulers were known as "Nawwāb-Wazīr", the deputy or first minister to a sovereign. As a Mughal "successor state",[3] the Indo-Persian culture of the Mughals remained the key link between the Persianate Shi'i Nawwābs and the largely Brāhmaṇ and Rājpūt rural landholders, who recognised Mughal sovereignty.[4] In part, the early Nawwābs entrenched their power by utilising networks of *chelā* or disciples, which included eunuch slaves or *khwāja-sarā'ī*.[5] By the 1760s, Awadh was an important power in north India. Yet the third Nawwāb, Shujā' al-Dawla, became embroiled in military conflict with the Company and was forced to surrender in 1764.[6] The Company restored Shujā' to the throne but annexed part of his territories. It also secured duty-free trade in Awadh and large, ongoing payments from the Nawwāb for the defence of his territories.[7] In 1775, the fourth Nawwāb, Āṣaf al-Dawla, shifted the capital of Awadh from Faizābād to Lucknow, which became a cultural centre that rivalled the Mughal capital, Delhi. In the late 1770s, a Company "Resident" or representative was posted in Lucknow to provide "advice", facilitating Company interventions in the Awadh administration.[8] By the early nineteenth century, the Awadh Nawwābs had largely withdrawn from involvement in day-to-day administration, though they were still important cultural patrons.[9] Meanwhile, *khwāja-sarā'ī* were still prominent in the Awadh court and acted as officials in the truncated Awadh administration and military.[10] In the late 1840s, the Company resolved to annex Awadh when the opportunity arose.[11] To justify annexation, Company officials compiled a case for the maladministration of the Awadh state in which eunuchs featured prominently as mere "menial" servants who were apparently unacceptable and "corrupt" officials.[12] The eventual British annexation of Awadh in 1856 resulted in the complete dismantling of the structures of patronage upon which eunuchs had depended.

Why could some *khwāja-sarā'ī* aspire to prominent positions in the Awadh court and administration? Historians have often explained the eunuch's social role as a result of their 'androgynous' gender, which, in societies that practiced female seclusion, allowed eunuchs to move between social and domestic spaces designated masculine and feminine. Moreover, eunuchs' inability to reproduce is a commonly cited motivation for their employment, because their lack of heirs apparently ensured their loyalty to their employer.[13] To some extent, both of these factors played a role in the employment of eunuchs in Awadh; *khwāja-sarā'ī* could move between masculine and feminine spaces of households and were deployed by rulers who wished to concentrate power within the state administration on their person.[14] However, this case study suggests that neither gender androgyny nor an inability to reproduce are wholly satisfactory explanations.

A wider range of factors was important to eunuchs' political and social roles in Awadh, such as master–slave proximity, networks of adopted kin and disciples and adherence to hegemonic codes of masculinity. First, local structures of slavery in which slaves could achieve social mobility through increasing their proximity to, and intimacy with, their master facilitated the political influence of *khwāja-sarā'ī*. Master–*khwāja-sarā'ī* relations often changed over the course of *khwāja-sarā'ī*'s lives and frequently became asymmetrical but reciprocal patron–client ties. Yet *khwāja-sarā'ī*'s continued dependence on their master or mistress meant that their political power could be extremely tenuous – a situation that the Company occasionally sought to exploit. Second, *khwāja-sarā'ī* in Awadh sought to extend their political influence and entrench their control over multiple administrative posts by forming large networks of adopted kin, disciples and dependents, which included other slaves as well as non-slaves. Indeed, by the mid-nineteenth century, networks of kin and disciples were central to *khwāja-sarā'ī*'s attempts to challenge Company interventions into Awadh. In this context, eunuchs' social role cannot be explained solely in terms of kinlessness.

My study of *khwāja-sarā'ī* kinship builds on the work of historians such as Indrani Chatterjee and Sumit Guha, who have shown that the Indian modern/nationalist conjugal family ideal of the late nineteenth and early twentieth century has obscured the complexities of domestic forms and varieties of kinship making in the early modern period.[15] Finally, *khwāja-sarā'ī* in Awadh displayed aspects of dominant forms of elite masculinity in order to secure the loyalty of followers, suggesting that androgyny was not the only interpretation of eunuch gender in Awadh. This chapter suggests that further research into Indian representations of eunuchs is necessary to determine how eunuch gender was constructed within different contexts.[16]

In this chapter, I explore the ways that eunuchs reacted to the new political circumstances of indirect colonial rule through three controversies involving eunuchs and the East India Company that took place during the eighteenth and nineteenth centuries. These three case studies illustrate the vulnerabilities of slave status, which were only exacerbated by Company interventions. At the same time, these three episodes show the significance of master–slave intimacy, kinship and discipleship to the political strategies of *khwāja-sarā'ī* under indirect colonial rule. I conclude by examining the repercussions of the British annexation of Awadh in 1856. As a result of annexation, Awadhi *khwāja-sarā'ī* lost their status as slave-nobles, were marginalised by colonial bureaucratic culture and were effectively depoliticised, as their role was thereafter limited to domestic service.

Unfortunately, I am not aware of any text written by an Awadhi *khwāja-sarā'ī*, aside from a handful of mid–late-nineteenth-century petitions to the British government.[17] As such, this chapter primarily draws on two sets of primary sources: first, Muḥammad Fā'iz Bakhsh's *Ta'rīkh-i Faraḥbakhsh*, which was written around 1818; and second, East India Company records. Fā'iz Bakhsh's *ta'rīkh* (history) of Faizābād focused on the lives of his two *khwāja-sarā'ī* patrons, Jawāhir 'Alī Khān and Dārāb 'Alī Khān; and their mistress, the dowager Bahū Begam, the mother of Nawwāb Āṣaf al-Dawla.[18] The purpose of history in the Mughal tradition was to "record [the] collective memory" of the elites as part of a "commemorative enterprise".[19] Indo-Islamic histories represented the ideologies and values of scholar bureaucrats like Fā'iz Bakhsh.[20] In particular, *adab* – "the embodiment of ethical norms through intellectual knowledge, spiritual cultivation, and correct behavior"[21] – was central to the self-definition of the bureaucratic class who wrote histories.[22]

Fā'iz Bakhsh's patronage by *khwāja-sarā'ī* slave nobles was another significant factor that shaped his account. The *khwāja-sarā'ī* Dārāb 'Alī Khān was Fā'iz Bakhsh's employer in the late 1810s and "favoured the undertaking" of the *ta'rīkh*.[23] Although Dārāb 'Alī's death prior to the completion of the manuscript appears to have provided Fā'iz Bakhsh with slightly greater latitude to criticise his patron, there was a good dose of hagiography in Fā'iz Bakhsh's representation of powerful *khwāja-sarā'ī*.[24] Another factor in Fā'iz Bakhsh's decision to write a history of Faizābād was the Company's demand for Indian-authored histories as part of its information gathering efforts.[25] Fāʾiz Bakhsh was not commissioned by the Company, as were several other Indian historians of this period. Nevertheless, he was indirectly communicating Awadh's past to "an alien political regime, while at the same time seeking to represent the ideology and values which characterised the [Mughal] social and political order".[26]

In addition to Fāʾiz Bakhsh's *taʾrīkh*, this chapter also draws upon eighteenth and nineteenth-century East India Company records. These records include correspondence between British Residents and their superiors in the Company, as well as English-language translations of Persian correspondence between the Residents, the Awadh rulers and Awadhi elites (like the eunuch Almās ʿAlī Khān), which are archived in the National Archives of India in Delhi (hereafter NAI).[27] The perspectives of colonial officials and processes of translation obviously shaped such records, requiring us to analyse what was included and what was excluded from the colonial archives.

Eunuchs in eighteenth-century Awadh: Slavery, kinship, discipleship and masculinity

From the reign of Saʿādat ʿAlī Khān, the Nawwābs of Awadh sought to consolidate their power by relying on family members, dependents and slaves, including *khwāja-sarāʾī*.[28] The eunuchs of the Awadh Nawwābs were either transported across the Indian Ocean from Africa, principally Ethiopia, or had been enslaved within the subcontinent following their capture in war, kidnapping or sale by relatives in circumstances of poverty or famine.[29] Fāʾiz Bakhsh's *taʾrīkh* narrates how child eunuchs were required to convert to Shiʿi Islam, to acquire Persian, to read Urdu, to become proficient in the norms of courtly culture[30] and to cultivate *adab*, a combination of "intellectual knowledge, spiritual cultivation, and correct behaviour".[31] In Awadh, it appears that Indian eunuchs and African, or *ḥabshī*, eunuchs were generally employed alongside each other.[32] Eunuchs worked as guards, attendants and administrators of the *zanāna* (feminine quarters of homes). *Khwāja-sarāʾī*'s association with the households of rulers and nobles could be a source of their power. In the Mughal world, power radiated outwards from the body of the ruler and onto his household and, then, kingdom.[33] The household was a politically significant space, and servants and slaves typically traversed the "inner" and "outer" spheres in their duties.[34] Successful *khwāja-sarāʾī* had multiple responsibilities, not only in household administration but also in the management of their master's businesses, the collection of land revenue and, in the case of the Nawwāb's eunuchs, in the state administration.[35] Eunuchs were particularly prominent as intelligencers, due to their ability to move between the *zanāna* and masculine spaces, as well as their intimacy with their owner's family. Masters and mistresses also deployed their eunuchs as negotiators and diplomats. Meanwhile, *khwāja-sarāʾī* were prominent commanders of the Nawwābs' and nobles' military forces.[36]

One eunuch named Basant 'Alī Khān reportedly commanded 14,000 of the Nawwāb's troops in the 1770s.[37] *Khwāja-sarā'ī* could aspire to become significant figures of authority but generally remained dependent on their master or mistress, illustrating the limits to their political power.

In order to explore the ways that *khwāja-sarā'ī* operated in Awadhi politics, it is necessary to understand four aspects of *khwāja-sarā'ī*'s lives: bonds of slavery, kinship-making, discipleship networks and gender. Turning first to slavery, in the Indian Ocean region, slavery was the condition of being wholly dependent upon an institution or individual.[38] Generally speaking, there was not a strict or impermeable boundary between master and slave, as in the Atlantic plantation model. Master–slave relationships were asymmetrical but also intimate, and the success of a slave depended on increasing their proximity to their master.[39] An indication of *khwāja-sarā'ī*'s close proximity to their master or mistress is the posting of eunuchs in the innermost spaces of the *zanāna*.[40] Whereas child and low-ranking eunuchs were wholly dependent on their master, some *khwāja-sarā'ī*'s ties to their master could transform into patron–client relationships. Fā'iz Bakhsh depicted high-ranking *khwāja-sarā'ī* exercising considerable day-to-day autonomy in their administrative responsibilities.[41] Yet cultivating an intimate relationship to their master was essential to *khwāja-sarā'ī*'s accumulation of administrative offices and political influence. As such, eunuchs' interests generally lay with their master or mistress, and *khwāja-sarā'ī* did not band together to form political factions.[42]

Second, *khwāja-sarā'ī* in Awadh formed kinship networks with adopted relatives, even though part of the rationale for the employment of eunuchs was that, as kinless persons, they would be loyal only to their master. If we are to believe Fā'iz Bakhsh, at least one *khwāja-sarā'ī*, Dārāb 'Alī Khān, was in contact with his natal family in adulthood.[43] However, in most cases, *khwāja-sarā'ī* kin were adopted. In Awadh, child *khwāja-sarā'ī* became the brothers of fellow boy eunuchs. Meanwhile, adult *khwāja-sarā'ī* adopted relatives, in particular sons, who were sometimes first purchased as slaves. Kinship-making was also sometimes a political strategy to reconcile former political enemies, though such kinship ties were often fragile.[44] Fā'iz Bakhsh recounted an instance of the establishment of brotherhood between a *khwāja-sarā'ī*, Dārāb 'Alī Khān, and a rival noble in Faizābād. The brotherhood was apparently formalised through a ceremony that involved Dārāb 'Alī's mistress, Bahū Begam, but the brothers soon fell out. This instance suggests not only that politically motivated kinship relationships were susceptible to tensions and fracturing but also that owners of eunuchs sometimes condoned their kinship relationships.[45]

These instances of kinship-making appear to conflict with classical Islamic law, which "generally does [not] recognise as valid any mode of filiation where the parentage of the person adopted is known to belong to a person other than the adopting father".[46] However, several historians of the Mughal empire and its successor states have demonstrated the political and social significance of forms of adoption in Indian Islamic polities. Ruby Lal noted adoption within sixteenth-century Mughal royal households, in particular, women's adoption of the children of other women within the haram.[47] Because "the biological and the guardian mothers were members of the same domestic community", Ruby Lal argued "taking charge" may be a more appropriate term than "adoption".[48] However, it is evident that in the eighteenth and nineteenth centuries in the successor state of Murshidābād in Bengal, forms of "adoption" incorporated into the royal household both male and female children, often slaves, whose birth mothers were located outside the household.[49] While motherhood allowed women of both slave and non-slave backgrounds to achieve high status in the ruler's household, women who failed to produce a son or failed to attract the ruler were "compensated for this by purchasing and rearing children whom they then ceremonially 'adopted' as their own". Thus, "it was not birth but 'public acknowledgement as mother' which was the effective determinant of the privileges of the women".[50] Indian rulers also adopted sons when they lacked male offspring. For instance, the Awadh Nawwāb Āṣaf al-Dawla's chosen heir was Wazīr 'Alī, a boy whom he had purchased from a Muslim family of carpet-sellers and subsequently adopted.[51] In sum, notwithstanding textual abrogation of adoption, forms of "adoption" or "taking charge" of children were practiced in several Islamic polities in India. In this context, *khwāja-sarā'ī* kinship-making does not appear so anomalous. Yet despite the social acknowledgement of *khwāja-sarā'ī*'s kinship-making noted above, owners of eunuchs often resisted eunuchs' efforts to provide for heirs following their death. In the context of Murshidābād (another "successor state" of the Mughal empire), Indrani Chatterjee has argued that "the genealogical heirlessness of slave-eunuchs was obvious – and social heirship from them was disputed among the free heirs of a master".[52] Nevertheless, during *khwāja-sarā'ī*' lifetimes, kinship relationships were not only important to their social and emotional lives but also to their political strategies.

Third, to understand *khwāja-sarā'ī*'s efforts to expand their political authority, the importance of teacher–disciple ties in early-modern Indian governance is key. Indrani Chatterjee recently characterised early-modern Indian states as a specific form of governmentality she called "monastic governmentality", in which "student-disciples" submitted to the "legal-moral and disciplinary practices" of "teachers-governors".[53] *Khwāja-sarā'ī* often exercised political influence through discipleship networks. Discipleship relationships between *khwāja-sarā'ī* teachers (*guru*) and *khwāja-sarā'ī* disciples (or *chelā*) structured the eunuch corps of nobles and rulers.[54] *Khwāja-sarā'ī guru* were responsible for ensuring their *chelā's* acquisition of scholarly knowledge, administrative skills, cultural proficiency and *adab* (the combination of learning, spirituality and ethical conduct).[55] Often, *chelā* inherited the administrative appointments of their *guru*. A young eunuch's ties to his *khwāja-sarā'ī* teacher were thus essential to his political and occupational success. Additionally, *khwāja-sarā'ī* formed hierarchical discipleship relationships with non-eunuchs, including slaves and non-slaves.[56] The maintenance of a large establishment of disciples demonstrated the prestige of *khwāja-sarā'ī*, while people who wished to increase their political influence sought discipleship to high-ranking eunuchs.[57] The greater the disciple's permitted physical proximity to the *khwāja-sarā'ī*, the higher their rank.[58] *Khwāja-sarā'ī*'s amassing of disciples was vital to the expansion of their political influence and, often, their control of numerous administrative posts. This use of kinship and discipleship networks to entrench one's power in the administration was a typical approach of Awadh administrators.[59]

Finally, demonstrations of elite codes of masculinity were important to *khwāja-sarā'ī*'s "conspicuous consumption of followers".[60] Existing studies of eunuchs in India and the Middle East have generally stressed the androgynous gender of eunuchs in explaining their power.[61] A degree of gender ambiguity was important to eunuchs' ability to move between differently gendered spaces.[62] More broadly, in north India, rulers like the Nawwābs of Farrukhābād and other elites thought that too much association with the *zanāna* made a man womanly.[63] However, *khwāja-sarā'ī* sought to extend their political influence and form alliances through exhibitions of elite masculinity. Rosalind O'Hanlon has shown how elite men in eighteenth-century north India performed a "plain soldierly style" of manliness through the following: their "prestige as ... skillful and fearless fighter[s]"; contests of martial skills; the exhibition of the "splendor" of their physique; and the adoption of an "austerely plain" mode of dress and entertainment. Elite men balanced this martial manliness with proficiency in courtly culture.[64]

Fā'iz Bakhsh described his since-deceased former patron, Jawāhir 'Alī Khān, in the terms of this martial, but cultured, masculinity. Fā'iz Bakhsh valorised the austere dress of Jawāhir 'Alī, as well as his physique; he reportedly was a "shapely, well-made, and well-proportioned man, erect, but of middle height". Jawāhir 'Alī apparently excelled in martial and sporting skills, particularly horse riding, and galloped so "violently" that "[n]ot one of his escort could keep up with him".[65] Meanwhile, Jawāhir 'Alī eschewed what were considered effete entertainments like dancing, while patronising "men of learning and art".[66] In light of Jawāhir 'Alī's past patronage of Fā'iz Bakhsh, we can assume this depiction reflects the desired self-image of powerful *khwāja-sarā'ī*. Elite men who did not depend on eunuch patronage may have had a more sceptical view of eunuch masculinity. However, it is notable that another Awadhi from a prominent family of officials, 'Abdul Ḥalīm Sharar, did not describe eunuchs in negative terms in the early twentieth century.[67] Moreover, it is evident that elite *khwāja-sarā'ī* like Jawāhir 'Alī successfully expanded their political influence and grew their retinues partly through demonstrations of elite masculinity, suggesting their claims to manliness had some purchase in Awadhi courtly culture.

Under indirect colonial rule, slave–master proximity, kinship, discipleship and masculine codes continued to be significant to *khwāja-sarā'ī*'s political strategies. From 1775 until the close of the eighteenth century, during the reign of the fourth Nawwāb, Āṣaf al-Dawla, *khwāja-sarā'ī* had varying success in negotiating the solidification of the Company's indirect colonial rule. The structures of the slave-based Awadh polity[68] still provided opportunities for *khwāja-sarā'ī* slaves to assume significant administrative roles and amass wealth. But non-slaves, including the Awadh Nawwāb and the Company, could exploit the dependency of eunuch slaves to their advantage.

Power "too great for a subject": The family of Almās 'Alī Khān in the politics of indirect colonial rule

The last quarter of the eighteenth century saw the rapid rise of the eunuch Almās 'Alī Khān, who was a commercial magnate, the head of a military force that was larger than the Nawwāb's and the *de facto* ruler of approximately a third of Awadh territory. Almās 'Alī managed to turn both his proximity to his mistress and the new political and economic circumstances of indirect colonial rule to his advantage so successfully that the Company feared he would secede from Awadh.[69] While he was no doubt exceptional, Almās 'Alī's story highlights the possible extent of *khwāja-sarā'ī* political, military and economic power in the late eighteenth century. Throughout the last quarter of the eighteenth century, the Nawwāb and the Company both attempted to contain Almās 'Alī's power. Almās 'Alī's family were crucial to the Nawwāb's and the Company's political schemes, highlighting the significance of *khwāja-sarā'ī* kinship in Company and Nawwābī politics. Almās 'Alī never rebelled, but he remained a major player in north Indian politics until his death in 1808.

While it is evident that Almās 'Alī was the son of a Jat cultivator,[70] the circumstances in which he was sold into slavery are obscure.[71] Almās 'Alī was part of the dowry of Bahū Begam – the wife of the third Nawwāb, Shujā' – and was initially employed as a cupbearer and attendant.[72] Shujā''s and Bahū Begam's son Āṣaf, the future Nawwāb, called Almās 'Alī *mamu*, or maternal uncle. Almās 'Alī was thus symbolically incorporated into his mistress's family, highlighting the use of kinship terms to describe bonds of enslavement and suggesting that slavery could be a mode of symbolic incorporation into the family. When Bahū Begam was granted a *jāgīr* (rent-free land grant) in Goṇḍa and Faizābād districts, she appointed Almās 'Alī as the manager of her estates.[73] Unlike Bahū Begam's other powerful eunuchs (see below), Almās 'Alī was eventually able to operate independently, and his political fortunes were not tied to that of his mistress.[74] Almās 'Alī was a rare example of a eunuch whose fate amidst the changes in Awadhi politics was not dependent on that of his mistress. Nevertheless, his early intimacy with his mistress and her son, Āṣaf, were vital to his subsequent accumulation of administrative responsibilities and revenue farms.

By 1771, Almās 'Alī had accrued sufficient wealth to establish his own town named Mian Ganj in Unnāo district. Such town-building was typical of the late eighteenth century, when "military and service gentry" established towns that they used as "headquarters from which they could penetrate the land-revenue system".[75] Meanwhile, town-building was also driven by the establishment of fixed rural markets or *ganj*, particularly for the sale of cash crops.[76] According to one British traveller, in the early 1800s, Mian Ganj was "populous, and in a thriving condition" with strong fortifications and wide, tree-lined streets.[77] Mian Ganj was also a significant market centre, the headquarters of Almās 'Alī's commercial operations and the location of his indigo factories.[78] When Āṣaf (Almās 'Alī's "nephew") assumed the throne in 1775, Almās 'Alī became the Amil (revenue farmer) of Kora and thus the single largest revenue farmer in Awadh, in control of almost a quarter of the total revenue collected in the state.[79] By 1783, Almās 'Alī was also the revenue farmer of Sharah, Jagdīshpur and Etawa.[80] On two occasions, Āṣaf proposed that Almās 'Alī be made his chief minister. The Company blocked these moves citing concerns about Almās 'Alī's character, though it is likely the further expansion of his sizeable economic and military power was a key consideration.[81] Notwithstanding Company apprehensions about Almās 'Alī, a significant factor in his rise was his successful manipulation of the political and economic circumstances of indirect colonial rule. Almās 'Alī lent significant sums to British officials and private individuals.[82] He also secured an arrangement through which he paid revenue collected from his districts directly to the East India Company rather than to the Nawwāb, in repayment of the Nawwāb's "debt" to the Company.[83] As such, the financial fortunes of both individual Britons and the Company depended upon Almās 'Alī.

In the 1780s, the Company became anxious that Almās 'Alī's power was "too great for a subject" and that he might secede from Awadh and establish his own state, upsetting the balance of power in north India and alienating a huge proportion of the Awadh land revenue.[84] As a consequence, the Nawwāb and the Company's Resident at Lucknow sought to limit Almās 'Alī's power by reducing his revenue farms and his military. Although the mid-nineteenth century would see colonial interventions aimed to regulate eunuchs' work and reduce their political influence, the late eighteenth-century Company merely aimed to prevent powerful eunuchs from compromising British dominance in Awadh.

In 1782, Almās 'Alī left Awadh with his family and considerable wealth, which the Company interpreted as an act of "rebellion".[85] I explore Almās 'Alī's family in more detail below, but for now it will suffice to say that Almās 'Alī, like some other powerful eunuchs, appears to have had a network of adopted relatives and a large household establishment of kin, slaves and dependents. Considering that in 1782, Almās 'Alī also became involved in Mughal court politics and drew up treaties pledging support to other regional powers (including the Maratha Mahadaji Shinde and the Raja of Benares), leaving Awadh with his family appears to have been a political strategy, possibly to leverage the Nawwāb or, as the British believed, to form an autonomous state out of the territories he revenue-farmed and effectively ruled.[86] The Company construed Almās 'Alī's correspondence with "foreign" powers as "illegal", because Awadh's foreign policy was conducted through the Company. On several occasions, Almās 'Alī also failed to follow the Nawwāb's orders.[87] These acts of disobedience only increased Almās 'Alī's power relative to the Nawwāb. In 1782, the Nawwāb and Almās 'Alī entered into a series of written agreements outlining the conditions of Almās 'Alī's return to the Nawwāb's territories.[88] The governor-general, William Hastings, was enraged that the agreements "resemble[d] more a Treaty between equal States, than a Transaction between a Sovereign, and his Vakal [*vakil*, official or agent]".[89] Another concern of the Company was that it was unable to acquire accurate intelligence from the districts Almās 'Alī controlled.[90] Meanwhile, Almās 'Alī's significant networks of intelligencers had infiltrated the Company's military forces, and the British found it impossible to identify and expel his spies.[91]

The Company henceforth took an interventionist policy. Hastings instructed the new British Resident, John Bristow, that Almās 'Alī's revenue farms should be immediately reduced.[92] However, Bristow's efforts did not succeed. Both the Resident and the Awadh Minister believed that Almās 'Alī would resist militarily if his revenue farms were reduced. Moreover, the odds were apparently in Almās 'Alī's favour.[93] As Bristow later explained:

> Almass had an army of above twelve thousand horse & foot as allowed to him by the Vizier [Nawwāb] ... [and] ... irregulars entertained by his own authority, of at least an equal number. ... He had treasure, stores, and ammunition, with the fort of Codar Cote. ... On the other hand, I received charge of my office with an empty treasury, and the burden of a heavy debt. ... [T]he principal resource in my hands was from Almass Ally Cawn [,] the assignment[94] on [whom] is for twenty seven Lacs of rupees, the very man against whom I was to engage.[95]

The Company's capacity to defeat Almās 'Alī in battle thus relied on funds from Almās 'Alī himself! The British Resident, Bristow, not only failed to limit Almās 'Alī's power; his attempts to take the Awadh administration into his own hands backfired in 1784, forcing the Company to retreat from heavy-handed interference in Awadh. Almās 'Alī secured an agreement with the Company that established his and the other Amils' right to withdraw if any Company agent interfered in their revenue farms.[96] As such, Almās 'Alī's revenue farms were only reduced in his old age, when he desired to go into semi-retirement,[97] though he held significant territories "either in his own name, or that of some of his followers, till his death in 1808".[98]

Almās 'Alī's family was important to the Nawwāb's and the Company's strategies to restrict his power in the 1780s and 1790s. The individual identities of only a few of Almās 'Alī's family members are known. William Sleeman reported that Almās 'Alī "had a brother, named Rahmut, after whom the town of Rahmutgunge [near Mian Ganj] ... took its name".[99] Almās 'Alī's "brother-in-law" and deputy was Rājā Bhagmul, a revenue farmer or Amil with several sons and grandsons.[100] According to the Company archives, Almās 'Alī also had at least one "adopted son", though the nature of this adoption is not clear in the records. Almās 'Alī's son reportedly had a family of his own, perhaps making Almās 'Alī a grandfather by adoption.[101]

The Company and the Nawwāb considered the presence in Lucknow of Almās 'Alī, his adopted relatives and his dependants essential to ensuring his loyalty to the Nawwāb.[102] The Nawwāb recognised Almās 'Alī's adopted relatives and dependents as his "family", suggesting the social recognition of *khwāja-sarā'ī* kin in Awadh. After Almās 'Alī left Awadh in 1782, he would not return to the Nawwāb's territories without assurances of personal security for his family. The Nawwāb officially proclaimed his duty to protect Almās 'Alī's kin and dependents. In one treaty, the Nawwāb and his Minister "engage[d] ... to consider ourselves as Guardians of his [Almās 'Alī's] Honour and that of his Family, Friends, and Dependents".[103]

What was more, the British also referred to Almās 'Alī's kin and other household members as his "family". Prior to the late eighteenth century, British definitions of "family" had referred to either ancestral lineages or *all* the members of a household, including non-kin. However, increasingly, the term *family* was applied to close relatives by birth and marriage only.[104] Yet on the peripheries of the late eighteenth-century British empire, British men appear to have applied a wider definition of family that incorporated kinship-making practices and relationships of dependency beyond affinal and biological kinship. This was partly due to European men's knowledge of local domestic arrangements through their relationships with Indian wives and concubines.[105] Claude Martin – a major general in the East India Company army and subsequently a superintendent of the arsenal for the Nawwāb of Awadh, Āṣaf al-Dawla – apparently even employed eunuchs in his *zanāna*.[106]

Throughout the 1780s and 1790s, Company officials monitored and repeatedly discussed the whereabouts of Almās 'Alī's "family". "[A]pprehensions of the fidelity of Almas Ally Khan" arose in 1785 when the Company learned he had "withdrawn his family from [the] Capital [Lucknow]".[107] Almās 'Alī subsequently assured the governor-general that reports "that I had taken some Alarm & was sending my Family away from Lucknow" had no basis.[108] In 1789, when the Nawwāb's Minister again became concerned that Almās 'Alī was secretly leaving Awadh, the Resident reported that "as Almauss's family as well as that of an adopted son, remains at Lucknow the minister is in hopes that there is no great apprehension of his withdrawing himself for the present from his Excellency's Dominions".[109] In sum, the Company attempted to negotiate and manipulate the balance of power in north India by keeping Almās 'Alī's familial relations under surveillance. Even under the indirect rule of the Company, the kinship networks of *khwāja-sarā'ī* were politically significant.

As Almās 'Alī's death appeared imminent, his domestic relations only increased in consequence. Whereas both the Company and the Nawwāb recognised Almās 'Alī's adopted kin and dependents as a "family" during his life, neither acknowledged his heirs upon his death. In this period, whether the Company recognised the claims of eunuchs' heirs depended on its political interests in the particular case.[110] Bahū Begam claimed Almās 'Alī's property as his mistress, but the Company supported the Nawwāb's claim to Almās 'Alī's wealth acquired in government service because he had no "legitimate" heirs.[111] However, Almās 'Alī had taken measures to ensure that his adopted family and *chelā* would inherit his wealth. A colonial official, Charles Alfred Elliot, claimed that when the Nawwāb's agents came to Mian Ganj and "opened the treasure chests, [they] found nothing in them but a large quantity of old shoes".[112] In the following half century, Almās 'Alī's heirs retained an identity as his kin and disciples. Some remained socially prominent at the local level, through donations of public buildings or their status as landholders.[113] It is difficult to see Almās 'Alī's slave status as one of 'social death', either during his lifetime or after, when not only his family but also the popular social memory of him lived on. Almās 'Alī had successfully exploited his early intimacy and proximity to his mistress's family, as well as the growing power of the Company, to his advantage. As such, his kinship and discipleship networks were an important factor in the Company's attempts to manipulate the balance of power in north India.

The vulnerability of eunuchs in Awadh politics: The imprisonment of Jawāhir 'Alī Khān and Bahār 'Alī Khān

The story of Almās 'Alī Khān shows that eunuchs could aspire to become entrepreneurs, military commanders, powerful revenue farmers and even *de facto* rulers. Nevertheless, Almās 'Alī was a rarity. It is striking that Almās 'Alī was not entangled in one of the major political controversies of the period, an ongoing dispute between his mistress Bahū Begam and her son, the Nawwāb Āṣaf al-Dawla, in contrast to two of her other high-ranking eunuchs named Jawāhir 'Alī Khān and Bahār 'Alī Khān. These two eunuchs' embroilment in their mistress's conflict with her son illustrates that even elite *khwāja-sarā'ī* could become pawns in the political machinations of their masters and other non-slaves. Jawāhir 'Alī, for instance, was a *khwāja-sarā'ī* success story. During the reign of the previous Nawwāb, Shujā' al-Dawla, Jawāhir 'Alī held numerous appointments within the Nawwāb's household and the Awadh administration. Jawāhir 'Alī supervised the *zanāna* (female quarters); new appointments and palace procurements; "eight maháls in the south" of Awadh; the payment of pensions to the aristocracy; a regiment of foot soldiers and cavalry; the stables and cattle-breeding; and various tolls.[114] After Shujā''s death in 1775, Jawāhir 'Alī continued to have wide-ranging responsibilities as Bahū Begam's general agent and the manager of several of her *jāgīrs* (rent-free lands).[115] Bahū Begam's other high-ranking *khwāja-sarā'ī*, Bahār 'Alī Khān, also wielded significant authority as her treasurer. According to Fā'iz Bakhsh, both men interacted with the Nawwāb's courtiers as equals, though Fā'iz Bakhsh's former status as a client of Jawāhir 'Alī may have influenced the emphasis he placed on this point.[116] In any case, when the *khwāja-sarā'ī*'s mistress was locked in a dispute with the Nawwāb, both eunuchs became vulnerable due to their dependency on their mistress.

In the 1770s, Āṣaf – with the backing of the Company – exerted intense pressure on his mother, Bahū Begam, and his grandmother, Nawwāb Begam, to surrender their substantial treasure, which he laid claim to as his father's heir. Āṣaf also moved to restrict the income and landholdings of his mother.[117] Bahū Begam deployed her *khwāja-sarā'ī* as negotiators to try to resolve the dispute, demonstrating that they functioned as important agents. In 1780, Bahū Begam sent Bahār 'Alī to Calcutta for a series of interviews with the governor-general, Warren Hastings. The negotiations broke down when a political rival, the Nawwāb's minister Hyder Beg Khān, offered the Company a sizeable sum to reject Bahār 'Alī's proposals. On his departure, Bahār 'Alī objected to the ritual exchange of robes on the basis that it would only be appropriate if he had succeeded in his mission. Hastings was much offended by the audacity of "this eunuch, who is only a slave".[118] Fā'iz Bakhsh wrote that Bahār 'Alī "had been accustomed to lord it over the chief citizens of Faizábad ... and [he] had no knowledge of the ceremonies ... of the courts of other kings and foreign powers, [and] his head was filled with old notions".[119] At this stage, the attitude of the Company towards eunuchs was uncertain: The governor-general initially accepted a *khwāja-sarā'ī* as an appropriate envoy but evoked Bahār 'Alī's slave status when offended by the way he conducted negotiations. The disjuncture between the Persian- and Mughal-influenced political culture of the Awadh *khwāja-sarā'ī* and that of the Company would only grow in the nineteenth century. Unlike Almās 'Alī, Bahār 'Alī did not successfully negotiate the new norms of diplomacy that emerged as a result of the indirect colonial rule of Awadh.

Following the failure of Bahār 'Alī's diplomatic overtures, in 1781, Bahū Begam and Nawwāb Begam took advantage of a revolt in Benares and ordered Jawāhir 'Alī and Bahār 'Alī to recruit a rebel force to rout the Company from Benares. This force was referred to as the *gaonwālā* (villagers), reflecting their recruitment from rural areas. In 1781, Jawāhir 'Alī and Bahār 'Alī successfully stopped the Company *dāk* (postal service) and intercepted Company communications.[120] The rebellion lasted only a few months but demonstrated the military and intelligence effectiveness of *khwāja-sarā'ī*.

After the Company suppressed the Benares rebellion, Bahū Begam's *khwāja-sarā'ī* became the Nawwāb's and the Company's primary bargaining chip in their dispute with the Begam. The Nawwāb and the Company considered Jawāhir 'Alī and Bahār 'Alī crucial to securing Shujā''s treasure, since they had trusteeship over Bahū Begam's wealth. In 1782, the Nawwāb and the Company arrived in Faizābād, where Bahū Begam's palace and court were located, with a significant military force. For several days of tense military stalemate, Bahū Begam refused to hand over either her *khwāja-sarā'ī* or the treasure to the Nawwāb. Eventually, Bahū Begam sacrificed her two highest-ranking eunuchs to end the military standoff with her son.

Bahū Begam reprimanded her *khwāja-sarā'ī* for exacerbating tensions with the Nawwāb and ordered Jawāhir 'Alī and Bahār 'Alī to hand themselves over to the Nawwāb. The two *khwāja-sarā'ī* spent over a year under arrest until payment of substantial sums by Bahū Begam, Nawwāb Begam and the *khwāja-sarā'ī* secured their release. Jawāhir 'Alī continued on as Bahū Begam's chief agent and Bahār 'Alī as her treasurer, notwithstanding their estrangement the previous year. While Jawāhir 'Alī and Bahār 'Alī had been in control of Bahū Begam's significant financial resources and had amassed considerable fortunes of their own, their dependency upon their mistress as slaves meant that they were susceptible to becoming pawns in the political schemes of non-slave nobles.

In this incident, both non-slaves and *khwāja-sarā'ī* themselves deployed the language of slavery for various political purposes. In Fā'iz Bakhsh's account, the Nawwāb's minister, Hyder Beg Khān, repeatedly reminded the Nawwāb of the unfree status of Jawāhir 'Alī and Bahār 'Alī to legitimise his attempts to obtain money from Bahū Begam and her eunuchs.[121] When Bahū Begam became dissatisfied with her *khwāja-sarā'ī* and ordered them to surrender to the Nawwāb in 1872, she reportedly told her *khwāja-sarā'ī*, "If you can, go [surrender] to him [the Nawwāb]. You are his father's slaves. If he will punish you, submit to it, for it is no disgrace to you".[122] Fā'iz Bakhsh recounts,

> As it was an affair between mother and son, *and they had no other status but that of slaves and servants* ... the moment they got this clear expression of her will, they were astounded, but dared not make any reply.[123]

A mistress's allusion to slave status literally silenced her *khwāja-sarā'ī*, though they were both wealthy and politically influential. When Jawāhir 'Alī and Bahār 'Alī decided to surrender to the Nawwāb, Bahār 'Alī reportedly referred to his slave status: "I will go first and present myself. He is my lord and master. Whatever is his will, I submit to it".[124] In India, non-slaves often used metaphors of slavery and masterhood to express subordination, while slaves were usually referred to through euphemisms. Thus, actual bonds of slavery were cloaked in silence, whereas slavery was rhetorically used to describe other types of dependency.[125] Non-slaves' explicit references to *khwāja-sarā'ī*'s slave status harshly stated what was usually indirectly described. There was real threat behind allusions to slave status by masters and other non-slaves, highlighting the dependency of *khwāja-sarā'ī*, despite their considerable social and economic capital and political influence.

Contesting Company interventions in the mid-nineteenth century

Following Āṣaf al-Dawla's death in 1798, it would be another 50 years until *khwāja-sarā'ī* were at the centre of the politics of indirect colonial rule. Throughout the first half of the nineteenth century, *khwāja-sarā'ī* nevertheless remained evident among the favourites and courtiers of Awadh rulers, in the administration of the palaces, as military commanders and as intelligencers. For example, as late as 1849, several *khwāja-sarā'ī* remained prominent as commanders of regiments, although the number of troops *khwāja-sarā'ī* commanded had declined significantly since the late eighteenth century as a result of the restrictions the Company placed on the size of the Nawwāb's army. Ḥājī 'Alī Sharīf commanded the "Khasromee Corps of Cavalry", consisting of 394 men; and the "Futteh Mobaruk Regiment" of 855 men. A *khwāja-sarā'ī* named Bashīr al-Dawla commanded the 971 men of the "Hydree Regiment of Najeeb", while another eunuch named Fīrūz al-Dawla commanded the "Hydree Corps of African Cavalry", consisting of 314 men; and the "Hoseynee Corps of African [Cavalry]", with 112 men.[126] Eunuch commanders still received high incomes – for instance, Fīrūz's daily income was reportedly Rs. 500, or Rs. 182 500 per annum (the equivalent of approximately £18 250 at the time).[127] Yet no nineteenth-century *khwāja-sarā'ī* would match Almās 'Alī's political, military and economic power.

The early nineteenth century saw a tightening of Company control over the Awadh administration. British Residents established the Residency as a court that vied with the Awadh ruler's court in political prominence. The Company encouraged the crowning of the Awadh ruler as Bāshā (Emperor) in 1819. However, this formal repudiation of Mughal sovereignty over Awadh did not increase the power of the Awadh ruler or stop the trend towards a more intrusive Company policy.[128] By 1847, when Wājid 'Alī Shāh became Bāshā, the Company had determined upon the annexation of Awadh when the opportunity arose.[129] In 1848, the new governor-general, Dalhousie, determined to expand British territory throughout India through his "doctrine of lapse", which allowed the Company to annex the territory of any ruler who did not have a biological heir.[130] In the following years, the British compiled a case for the "mismanagement" of Awadh affairs, which would serve to justify annexation in 1856.

In the 1840s and 1850s, in building their case for annexation, the Company repeatedly criticised *khwāja-sarā'ī* as being politically corrupt. The Company also denounced eunuchs as unmanly, excessively violent and tyrannical. William Sleeman, a British Resident, criticised the "insolent" actions of eunuch commanders like Fīrūz al-Dawla, "one of the most despicable and mischievous of these wretched Eunuchs", who apparently "render[ed] life and property insecure in every part of [Wājid 'Alī Shāh's] dominions".[131] British officials also claimed that eunuchs' kinship and discipleship networks were mere avenues for political corruption and no longer called *khwāja-sarā'ī*'s kin and dependents their family.[132] In 1848, under pressure from the Company, the Pasha signed an agreement banning eunuchs from all "official" functions – including in the military, intelligence and the collection of tolls – but protecting their employment in the politically significant space of the household.[133] Elsewhere, I have explored in detail the equation of misgovernment with gender and sexual disorder in the Company's criticism of eunuchs.[134] Here, I foreground the strategies that *khwāja-sarā'ī* employed to evade colonial interventions, particularly highlighting the role of discipleship networks and proximity to their master (the Bāshā).

Discipleship ties remained channels for *khwāja-sarā'ī*'s political influence and became a means to contest and limit colonial interventions. For instance, *khwāja-sarā'ī*'s networks of disciples helped them to control intelligence networks, despite their prohibition from employment in the Intelligence Department. According to successive Residents, the intelligence reports from the districts were inaccurate or fabricated since the *akhbār nawīs* (news writers) were the *chelā* of *khwāja-sarā'ī* and other courtiers, upon whom their positions depended.[135] *Khwāja-sarā'ī* dominated intelligence networks within the Bāshā's palaces in Lucknow. In 1849, Bāshā Wājid 'Alī requested his minister "to let him know all that was done and said in the palace", but was informed by the minister "that the Eunuchs had charge of all the intelligence department about the palace, and never condescended to mention to him what took place, and that he was therefore more ignorant on the subject than His Majesty himself".[136] Although Bayly has suggested that the importance of eunuchs as "carriers of information and intrigue" declined significantly from the beginning of the nineteenth century, in Awadh, *khwāja-sarā'ī* maintained their position as "knowledgeable" persons.[137] Their command of information within the Bāshā's palaces, as well as the *akhbār nawīs* networks in rural Awadh, was largely due to their use of discipleship networks.

Through discipleship networks, *khwāja-sarā'ī* were also able to entrench their power in the military and acquire substantial wealth. In 1850, Sleeman claimed that three-quarters of the Awadh military was commanded by either eunuchs, musicians or "their creatures". Some of the eunuch commanders "never saw their Regiments", according to Sleeman, instead placing dependents and *chelā* in charge of regiments. This was apparently a highly lucrative arrangement for *khwāja-sarā'ī*.[138] On the eve of British annexation, in 1855, *khwāja-sarā'ī* only directly controlled those regiments designated as the Bāshā's personal bodyguard.[139] However, their control over other regiments continued through nominal appointees who were their disciples or dependents.

"Private attendance" on the Bāshā or ruler, Wājid 'Alī Shāh, also cemented *khwāja-sarā'ī*'s positions as key figures in his court. The basis of eunuchs' powerful position in court politics was their close physical proximity to the ruler. Several of the prominent eunuchs in the Bāshā's inner circle had served him prior to his ascension to the throne.[140] *Khwāja-sarā'ī* reinforced their intimacy with and dependence upon the Bāshā through *nazr* (gift-giving to a superior) and by providing for his entertainment. For instance, on February 15, 1855, the Residency diary mentions that the "eunuch Basheer made a present of a pair of Camel-leopards to the King", while on March 30, "the King received some pigeons from the Eunuchs Bushier and Dianut".[141]

As late as the 1850s, *khwāja-sarā'ī* were prominent in political factions of the Awadh court. Elites and nobles paid *khwāja-sarā'ī* to exert influence with the Awadh ruler on their behalf, and court eunuchs were sometimes seen as an alternative and competing locus of power to the Company's representative, the Resident.[142] The still-important position of *khwāja-sarā'ī* in Awadh court politics is evidenced by a property dispute in 1853 between four brothers of the wealthy Lal family. The family had enlisted the assistance of Sleeman, the British Resident, in distributing their father's inheritance to his heirs. However, the youngest brother, Kundun, came to the conclusion that the Awadh ruler's eunuchs could secure an outcome more favourable to his interests than could the Resident. Kundun consequently "purchased" the influence of the ruler's eunuchs "at a high price",[143] and the *khwāja-sarā'ī* managed to sway the outcome of the dispute in several ways.[144]

The power of *khwāja-sarā'ī* within the administration and the court threatened the position of the Awadh chief minister, 'Alī Nakhī Khān.[145] The minister could not risk offending or alienating *khwāja-sarā'ī* who had the ear of the Awadh ruler, Wājid 'Alī.[146] Meanwhile, *khwāja-sarā'ī* and musicians controlled and restricted the minister's access to the ruler.[147] British Residents also perceived the power of *khwāja-sarā'ī* as a threat to the integrity of the Company in Awadh. Historian Michael Fisher notes that one of the few strategies open to the Awadh ruler and administration was to "seduc[e] the Resident and the members of his staff into the world of the Awadh court" by offering honours and financial rewards.[148] One British Resident, Sleeman, believed that *khwāja-sarā'ī* were attempting to corrupt Company officials, for instance, by "ingratiat[ing] themselves" with officials through horseracing and gambling in Lucknow.[149] In sum, when the Company sought to regulate the employments of eunuchs in the late 1840s and 1850s, *khwāja-sarā'ī* used their networks of kin and disciples to control aspects of the administration from which they were banned. Eunuchs also maintained their influence in court politics through their intimate relationship with their master, the Bāshā. Yet the failure of the Company to restrict the power of *khwāja-sarā'ī* in Wājid 'Alī Shāh's reign justified annexation in 1856.[150]

Conclusion

The social status, political authority and employment opportunities of *khwāja-sarā'ī* in north India declined markedly from the late 1850s. The fall of both the Awadh and Mughal states in 1856–7 resulted in a sharp contraction in eunuchs' prospects for patronage. Although the Awadh Bāshā, Wājid 'Alī Shāh, continued to employ eunuchs in his court-in-exile in Bengal,[151] the vast majority of the Bāshā's *khwāja-sarā'ī* and other slaves were deprived of income, patronage and protection.[152] The Company provided for some of Wājid 'Alī's former slaves and dependents, but *khwāja-sarā'ī*, as well as courtesans, were associated with the apparently immoral and decadent culture of the Awadh court and were generally denied support.[153] British annexation of Awadh resulted in the impoverishment of Awadhi *khwāja-sarāʾī*, as well as their effective domestication. *Khwāja-sarāʾī*'s role was increasingly restricted to service within the *zanāna* or female quarters of elite homes.

In the 1860s and 1870s, by which time *khwāja-sarāʾī*'s political importance had largely collapsed in north India, the colonial government in this region ironically defined *khwāja-sarāʾī* as "respectable eunuchs" in contrast to the "suspect eunuchs" of the *hijṛā* community.[154] *Hijṛā* were generally male-embodied people who were castrated or "impotent", identified as feminine and had a role as performers and alms-collectors, particularly in contexts associated with fertility and childbirth. In 1871, Part II of the Criminal Tribes Act of 1871 provided for the registration of eunuchs who were "reasonably suspected" of kidnapping, castration and sodomy – crimes to which the colonisers claimed *hijṛā* were "addicted" – as well as the prohibition of *hijṛā* practices like cross-dressing and performing.[155] *Khwāja-sarāʾī*, however, were largely exempted from this law.

By 1870, the withdrawal of political patronage had largely limited *khwāja-sarāʾī* in north India to domestic functions. They could be labelled "respectable", even if associations of immorality lingered. The most prominent Muslim intellectual of the period, Sayyid Aḥmad Khān, argued that *khwāja-sarāʾī* should not be policed: "As this class are exclusively confined to the domicile of their masters, they have consequently no opportunity of outraging public decency by any immoralities".[156] Yet in the following decades, even the role of eunuchs in domestic service would gradually disappear. Elite Muslim men – who had been important employers of *khwāja-sarāʾī* – increasingly defined slavery as contrary to modern family and social life in the late nineteenth and early twentieth century.[157] Whereas the *hijṛā* endured as a socio-cultural category and a gender role – notwithstanding British attempts to cause the community to "die out" – in contrast, the early twentieth century saw the gradual disappearance of eunuch slaves in Indian courts and households. These slave nobles, who had exerted political power through the intimacy of slave-master ties, the formation of extensive kinship and discipleship networks and the performance of masculinity, did not survive the historical transformations of colonial modernity in South Asia.

Notes

1 For archival sources, I use the following abbreviations: UPSA stands for Uttar Pradesh State Archives; NAI/FD/PC stands for National Archives of India, Foreign Department, Political Consultations; BL/IOR stands for British Library, India Office Records. As regards transliteration, I follow the guidelines of the *International Journal of Middle East Studies* for Persian, and the system ISO 15919 as regards Hindu/Urdu. Foreign terms have not been pluralized with a final "s" even when plural is used grammatically.

2 Richard B. Barnett, *North India Between Empires: Awadh, the Mughals and the British, 1720–1801* (New Delhi: Manohar, 1987), 33.
3 "Successor states" were provinces of the Mughal empire that broke away to form autonomous states.
4 Michael H. Fisher, *A Clash of Cultures: Awadh, the British and the Mughals* (New Delhi: Manohar, 1987), 42–43.
5 This point is evident in the historical memory of Awadh elites. ʿAbdul Ḥalim Sharar, whose father was a member of the court of the last Awadh ruler, wrote in his history of Awadh (published ca. 1915) that the ruler of Farrukhābād, Aḥmad Khān Bangash, had advised Shujāʿ al-Dawla, the third Nawwāb, to "put no trust in the Mughals but work with your other subordinates and khwaja-saras," advice that Shujāʿ apparently heeded. Abdul Halim Sharar, *Lucknow: The Last Phase of an Oriental Culture*, ed. and trans. E. S. Harcourt and Fakhir Hussain (New Delhi: Oxford University Press, 2001), 30–31.
6 Shujāʿ aimed to force the Company to restore Mīr Qāsim, the nominal Mughal Ṣūbadār of Bengal, whom the British had deposed.
7 Barnett, *North India*, 49–64; Fisher, *Clash of Cultures*, 38; P. D. Reeves, "Introduction," in *Sleeman in Oudh: An Abridgement of W. H. Sleeman's A Journey Through the Kingdom of Oude in 1849–50*, ed. P. D. Reeves (Cambridge: Cambridge University Press, 1971), 4.
8 Fisher, *Clash of Cultures*, 40.
9 Ibid., 71–79.
10 William Henry Sleeman, Resident at Lucknow, to Secretary, Government of India, 30 October 1849, NAI/FD/PC 24/11/1849, 165.
11 Fisher, *Clash of Cultures*, 166–169.
12 For example, see Dalhousie, "Minute by the Governor-General of India on Oude," 18 June 1855, NAI/FD/PP 28/12/1855 319.
13 In an Indian context, Chatterjee described *khwāja-sarāʾī* as "androgynous anti-kin," while in the context of Mecca, Marmon similarly foregrounded eunuchs' androgyny. Shaun Marmon, *Eunuchs and Sacred Boundaries in Islamic Society* (New York: Oxford University Press, 1995); Indrani Chatterjee, *Gender, Slavery and Law in Colonial India* (New Delhi: Oxford University Press, 1999).
14 On the latter point, see Fisher, *Clash of Cultures*, 53.
15 Indrani Chatterjee, "Introduction," in *Unfamiliar Relations: Family & History in South Asia*, ed. Indrani Chatterjee (Delhi: Permanent Black, 2004), 13–14; Chatterjee, *Gender, Slavery and Law*, particularly chap. 3; Chatterjee, "Slave's Quest," 53–86; Indrani Chatterjee and Sumit Guha, "Slave-Queen, Waif-Prince: Slavery and Social Capital in Eighteenth-Century India," *Indian Economic and Social History Review* 36, no. 2 (1999): 165–182; Sumit Guha, "The Family Feud as Political Resource in Eighteenth-Century India," in *Unfamiliar Relations: Family & History in South Asia*, ed. Indrani Chatterjee (Delhi: Permanent Black, 2004), 73–94; Michael H. Fisher, "Becoming and Making 'Family' in Hindustan," in *Unfamiliar Relations*, ed. Chatterjee, 95–121.
16 The observations about eunuchs' gender I make in this chapter are limited to the particular case study of Awadh, and the question warrants further research.
17 For example, a eunuch named Nāẓir al-Dawla, a mid-ranking eunuch of the last ruler, Wājid ʿAlī Shāh, wrote at least eight petitions to the colonial government of Oudh (formerly Awadh) following annexation, from the late 1850s to 1870s. His 1874 petition was the lengthiest and most detailed: Nāẓir al-Dawla, "Petition to Chief Commissioner of Oudh," 4 January 1874, UPSA/L/BR/LD 1140. For an analysis of this petition, see Jessica Hinchy, "The Sexual Politics of Imperial Expansion: Eunuchs and Indirect Colonial Rule in Mid-Nineteenth-Century North India," *Gender & History* 26, no. 3 (2014): 429–430. One of the Mughal

Emperor Awrangzīb's eunuchs, Bakhtāwar Khān, wrote a history titled *Mir'āt al-'ālam* ("The Mirror of the World") in 1667–1668. See Henry Miers Elliott, *The History of India as Told by its Own Historians* (London: Trubner Company, 1871), 7:145–166.

18 Fā'iz Bakhsh's career began in the service of Jawāhir 'Alī Khān, who would become Bahū Begam's chief eunuch, and Fā'iz Bakhsh eventually became the eunuch's treasurer. Fā'iz Bakhsh was also the tutor of the *khwāja-sarā'ī* Dārāb 'Alī Khān in the 1780s. Upon Jawāhir 'Alī's death in 1799, Dārāb 'Alī became Bahū Begam's chief eunuch and Fā'iz Bakhsh's patron. Muḥammad Fā'iz Bakhsh, *Memoirs of Delhi and Faizábád, Being a Translation of the Ta'rīkh-i Faraḥbakhsh of Muhammad Faiz-Bakhsh*, ed. and trans. William Hoey (Allahabad: Government Press, 1888), 1:iii; 2:192–193, 195–196. For a detailed analysis of Fā'iz Bakhsh's history, see Jessica Hinchy, "Enslaved Childhoods in Eighteenth Century Awadh," *South Asian History and Culture* 6, no. 3 (2015): 380–400.

19 Nile Green, "The Uses of Books in a Late Mughal Takiyya: Persianate Knowledge Between Person and Paper," *Modern Asian Studies* 44, no. 2 (2010): 246.

20 Kumkum Chatterjee, "History as Self-Representation: The Recasting of a Political Tradition in Late Eighteenth-Century Eastern India," *Modern Asian Studies* 32, no. 4 (1998): 920.

21 Barbara Daly Metcalf, "Introduction," in *Moral Conduct and Authority: The Place of Adab in South Asian Islam*, ed. Barbara Daly Metcalf (Berkeley: University of California Press, 1984), 15.

22 Chatterjee, "History as Self-Representation," 920.

23 Fā'iz Bakhsh, *Ta'rīkh-i Faraḥbakhsh*, 1:v–vi.

24 Eaton has noted in the context of the Deccan region that accounts of historical figures' lives exist on a "continuum" between biography and hagiography. When constructing a narrative of an individual life, "one is to some extent also reconstructing the culture of the community that had preserved his or her memory." Richard M. Eaton, *A Social History of the Deccan, 1300–1761: Eight Indian Lives* (Cambridge: Cambridge University Press, 2005), 4–5.

25 I have not found any evidence that Fā'iz Bakhsh was subsequently employed by the East India Company. However, the context of indirect colonial rule of Awadh also shaped William Hoey's late nineteenth-century translation of Fā'iz Bakhsh's *ta'rīkh*, which I draw upon in this chapter. Hoey saw Fā'iz Bakhsh's account as a "picture of Oriental life ... untouched" by colonialism. He was also interested in the "political significance" of Fā'iz Bakhsh's narrative of the political crisis in the 1770s examined below, which pitted the dowager Bahū Begam against her son, the Awadh Nawwāb, and the Company. In line with his perspective on the value of the *ta'rīkh*, Hoey excluded a handful of passages that he did not regard as relevant to history, including some poetic and metaphorical sections and "moral platitudes." William Hoey, "Translator's Preface," in Fā'iz Bakhsh, *Ta'rīkh-i Faraḥbakhsh*, 1:iii–vi.

26 Chatterjee, "History as Self-Representation," 916–917.

27 Generally, only the English translations are archived in the National Archives of India (NAI).

28 Fisher, *Clash of Cultures*, 53.

29 Gavin Hambly, "A Note on the Trade in Eunuchs in Mughal Bengal," *Journal of the American Oriental Society* 94, no. 1 (1974): 125–127; Abū l-Fażl 'Allāmī, *Ā'īn-i Akbarī*, trans. Heinrich Blochmann (Calcutta: Asiatic Society Bengal, 1873), 1:389–390; Fā'iz Bakhsh, *Ta'rīkh-i Faraḥbakhsh*, 2:46–9, 218–219. On broader processes of enslavement in India, see Richard M. Eaton, "Introduction," in *Slavery & South Asian History*, ed. Indrani Chatterjee and Richard M. Eaton (Bloomington: Indiana University Press, 2006), 1–16.

30 Fā'iz Bakhsh, *Ta'rīkh-i Faraḥbakhsh*, 2:48, 195.
31 Metcalf, "Introduction," 15. The prominence of the concept of *adab* in Fā'iz Bakhsh's portrayal of eunuchs is also a symptom of its importance to the ethos of the Mughal administrative class of which he was a member.
32 However, some Awadh rulers, including the final ruler Wājid 'Alī Shāh, did organise *ḥabshī* slaves into African military corps. Sleeman to Secretary GoI, 30 Oct 1849, NAI/FD/PC 24/11/1849 165.
33 Ruby Lal, *Domesticity and Power in the Early Mughal World* (New Delhi: Cambridge University Press, 2005), 142, 152; Chatterjee, *Gender, Slavery and Law*, 36–37; Rosalind O'Hanlon, "Kingdom, Household and Body: History, Gender and Imperial Service under Akbar," *Modern Asian Studies* 41, no. 5 (2007): 889–923.
34 Lal, *Domesticity and Power*, 166, 194–196.
35 Fā'iz Bakhsh, *Ta'rīkh-i Faraḥbakhsh*, 2:49–50.
36 On the intelligence, diplomatic and military roles of eunuchs: Fā'iz Bakhsh, *Ta'rīkh-i Faraḥbakhsh*, 2:7, 25–26, 48–49, 129–130, 138–139, 192–193; Barnett, *North India*, 130, 200–201; Christopher Alan Bayly, *Empire and Information: Intelligence Gathering and Social Communication in India, 1780–1870* (New York: Cambridge University Press, 1996), 94.
37 Fā'iz Bakhsh, *Ta'rīkh-i Faraḥbakhsh*, 2:7.
38 Eaton, "Introduction," 2; Gwyn Campbell, "Introduction: Slavery and other forms of Unfree Labour in the Indian Ocean World," in *Structure of Slavery in Indian Ocean Africa and Asia*, ed. Gwyn Campbell (London: Frank Cass, 2004), xxii–xxiii.
39 Campbell, "Introduction," xvii–xviii; Ramya Sreenivasan, "Drudges, Dancing Girls, Concubines: Female Slaves in Rajput Polity, 1500–1850," in Chatterjee and Eaton, *Slavery & South Asian History*, 136–161; Eaton, *A Social History of the Deccan*, 111–112.
40 Fā'iz Bakhsh, *Ta'rīkh-i Faraḥbakhsh*, 2:176.
41 Ibid., 2:113–114, 163, 304.
42 Ibid., 2:76, 110–111, 123–124, 161, 215–216. This was typical of slaves' identities in the Indian Ocean region. See Capmbell, "Introduction," xx–xxii.
43 Fā'iz Bakhsh, *Ta'rīkh-i Faraḥbakhsh*, 2:306.
44 For examples, ibid., 2:139, 289, 297–298, 306, 312–314.
45 Ibid., 2:289.
46 Ali Raza Naqvi, "Adoption in Muslim Law," *Islamic Studies* 19, no. 4 (1980): 288.
47 Lal, *Domesticity and Power*, 120–123.
48 Ibid., 123.
49 Chatterjee, *Gender, Slavery and Law*, 106.
50 Ibid., 105.
51 Barnett, *North India*, 233.
52 Shi'i law did not categorically bar slaves from passing on property insofar as the *walā'* principle provided that a *manumitted* slave's blood relatives (regardless of proximity of the relation) had prior claims to inherit the property of the deceased former slave over the master or mistress of the slave. However, masters and their kin claimed rights to the property of eunuch slaves who were considered heirless. Chatterjee, *Gender, Slavery and Law*, 151 and also 140–141, 169–170. In Awadh, some *khwāja-sarā'ī* attempted to dispose of property to heirs, although it appears that most were unable to. Mrs Meer Hassan Ali, *Observations on the Mussulmauns of India* (London: Parbury, Allen and Co., 1832), 1:72; Charles Alfred Elliott, *The Chronicles of Oonao, a District in Oudh* (Allahabad: Allahabad Mission Press, 1862), 131.

53 Chatterjee reworks Michael Foucault's concept of "governmentality" in the early-modern Indian context. Indrani Chatterjee, "Monastic Governmentality, Colonial Misogyny, and Postcolonial Amnesia in South Asia," *History of the Present* 3, no. 1 (2013): 60.
54 Fā'iz Bakhsh, *Ta'rīkh-i Faraḥbakhsh*, 2:186.
55 Ibid., 2:193–196.
56 Ibid., 2:225–226, 229.
57 Ibid., 2:50–52, 225–226.
58 Ibid., 2:171.
59 Fisher, *Clash of Cultures*, 67.
60 Christopher A. Bayly, *Rulers, Townsmen and Bazaars: North Indian Society in the Age of British Expansion, 1770–1870* (Cambridge: Cambridge University Press, 1988), 60.
61 Marmon, *Eunuchs and Sacred Boundaries*; Chatterjee, *Gender, Slavery and Law*, 44–57.
62 Chatterjee, *Gender, Slavery and Law*, 44–57.
63 Rosalind O'Hanlon, "Issues of Masculinity in North Indian History: The Bangash Nawabs of Farrukhabad," *Indian Journal of Gender Studies* 4, no. 1 (1997): 9.
64 Ibid., 7–9.
65 Fā'iz Bakhsh, *Ta'rīkh-i Faraḥbakhsh*, 2:59.
66 Ibid., 2:229–231.
67 Sharar wrote that Shujā' al-Dawla improved his army through the appointment of several *khwāja-sarā'ī*. Whereas *khwāja-sarā'ī*'s prominence in the military was a focus of colonial criticism in the 1840s and 1850s, Sharar wrote that Wājid 'Alī Shāh, the last Awadh ruler, rewarded "deserving soldiers." He did not characterise eunuchs' official and court roles as evidence of Wājid 'Alī's moral corruption, as did the Company, and instead pointed to the role of "dissolute women, singers and dancers." Sharar, *Lucknow*, 32, 62.
68 Chatterjee uses the term "slave-based polity" to describe another successor state, Murshidābād. Chatterjee, *Gender, Slavery and Law*, 35.
69 C. Cornwallis, Governor-General, India, to Resident at Lucknow, 1 October 1787, NAI/FD/SC 08/11/1787 7.
70 Baden Henry Powell, *The Land Systems of British India* (New Delhi: Low Price Publications, 1990 [1892]), 2:12.
71 In the 1860s, a British official, Charles Alfred Elliott, reported, "Ilmas Ali was the son of a Jat cultivator near Hoshyarpoor [Hoshiarpur], a Eunuch from his birth." Elliott, *Chronicles of Oonao*, 124.
72 Barnett, *North India*, 182; Hamid Afaq Qureshi, *The Mughals, the English and the Rulers of Awadh From 1722 A.D. to 1856 A.D.* (Lucknow: New Royal Book Co., 2003), 157.
73 Elliott, *Chronicles of Oonao*, 124–125.
74 Ibid., 125.
75 Indeed, some of Almās 'Alī's followers also established "attenuated urban centres" for this purpose. Christopher A. Bayly, "Town Building in North India, 1790–1830," *Modern Asian Studies* 9, no. 4 (1975): 486–487.
76 Bayly, "Town Building in North India," 492–494. Bayly notes elsewhere that 42 such *ganj* were established between 1750 and 1819. Bayly, *Rulers, Townsmen and Bazaars*, 98.
77 George Viscount Valentia, *Voyages and Travels to India, Ceylon, the Red Sea, Abyssinia, and Egypt, in the Years 1802, 1803, 1804, 1805, and 1806* (London: F. C., and J. Rivington, 1811), 1:142–3. *Mian* was Almās 'Alī's popular title and a common address for *khwāja-sarā'ī*. Chatterjee, *Gender, Slavery and Law*, 48.

78 Bayly, *Rulers, Townsmen and Bazaars*, 98–99.

79 Revenue farmers paid a fixed annual sum to the Awadh treasury, pocketing any revenue extracted above this amount. Barnett, *North India*, 168–169, 182; Fisher, *Clash of Cultures*, 204–207.

80 C. R. Crommeling to J. Morgan, 27 April 1781, NAI/FD/SC 27/04/1781 18; J. Bristow, Resident at Lucknow, to Governor-General and Council, India, 4 November 1782, NAI/FD/SC 22/11/1782 2; Appendix: J. Bristow, Resident at Lucknow, to Hyder Beg Khan, Minister of Nawwāb, 5 August 178, NAI/FD/SC 17/02/1784.

81 As Fisher notes, Almās 'Alī had "a long and generally respected record of service". Fisher, *Clash of Cultures*, 64. In 1777, Almās 'Alī turned down an offer of the position of chief minister, stating that he would rather go on revenue farming his territory of the Doab, with its ten million rupees in revenue, than have to contend with the Company, the Nawwāb's debt and the politics of the court. Barnett, *North India*, 133–134.

82 On private European merchants in Awadh and their connections to Almās 'Alī Khān, see Peter James Marshall, "Economic and Political Expansion: The Case of Oudh," *Modern Asian Studies* 9, no. 4 (1975): 465–482, especially 479.

83 Under treaties between the Company and Awadh, the Nawwābs had to pay significant sums to the Company in return for the military protection of the Company's troops, hence creating a significant debt. Appendix: J. Bristow, Statement of the Etaya (Etawa) and Kora provinces during Almās 'Alī Khān's administration, ca. 1782, NAI/FD/SP 17/02/1784.

84 C. Cornwallis to Resident at Lucknow, 1 Oct 1787, NAI/FD/SC 08/11/1787 7.

85 W. Hastings, Governor-General, India, to Resident at Lucknow, 10 August 1782, NAI/FD/SC 15/08/1782 6. See also W. Hastings, Governor-General, India, to Minister of Nawwāb, circa August 1782, NAI/FD/SC 15/08/1782 9.

86 H. Lloyd, Acting Persian Interpreter, Intelligence Reports, 17 November 1782, NAI/FD/SC 15/01/1783 2; J. Bristow, Resident at Lucknow, to Governor-General, India, 5 November 1782, NAI/FD/SP 17/02/1784 Appendix; J. Bristow, Resident at Lucknow, to Governor-General and Council, India, 13 December 1783, NAI/FD/SP 27/12/1783 21; Almās 'Alī Khān to Mahadaji Shinde, circa 1872–1873, NAI/FD/SP 17/02/1784 Appendix.

87 J. Bristow, Resident at Lucknow, to Governor-General and Council, India, 14 April 1783, NAI/FD/SP 23/06/1783 34A.

88 "Engagement entered into with Ilmass Ally Khan to which were Affixed the Seals of the Nabob and his Ministers Hussin Zexa Cawn and Hyder Beg Khawn and the Signature of Mr. Johnson," ca. 1872, NAI/FD/SC 17/02/1784 Appendix. See also "Translation of Hyder Beg Cawn's Narrative on Almass Ally Cawn's Succession," circa 1782–3, NAI/FD/SC 17/02/1784 Appendix.

89 W. Hastings, Governor-General, India, to Resident at Lucknow, 23 October 1782, NAI/FD/SC 21/04/1783 14.

90 Hyder Beg Khan, Minister to Nawwāb, to Resident at Lucknow, ca. April 1783, NAI/FD/SP 17/02/1784 Appendix; J. Bristow, Resident at Lucknow, to Minister to Nawwāb, 20 April 1783, NAI/FD/SP 17/02/1784 Appendix.

91 J. Ironside to Commander in Chief, 25 February 1785, NAI/FD/SC 19/02/1785 1–4.

92 Ibid.

93 J. Bristow, Resident at Lucknow, to Governor-General and Council, India, 4 October 1783; J. Bristow, Statement of the Etawa and Kora provinces during Almās 'Alī Khān's administration, ca. 1782, NAI/FD/SP 17/02/1784 Appendix; J. Bristow, Resident at Lucknow, Statement of Almās 'Alī Khān's troops, 27 August 1783, NAI/FD/SP 29/09/1783 7 Enclosure.

94 This referred to the fixed annual amount Almās 'Alī paid to the Company, instead of the Nawwāb, in repayment of the Nawwāb's debt to the Company.

95 J. Bristow, Resident at Lucknow, to Governor-General, India, 20 December 1783, NAI/FD/SP 12/05/1783 17.

96 Almās 'Alī Khān and the other Amils to the Government of the Nawwāb, circa August 1784, NAI/FD/SC 08/10/1784 5: See also W. Hastings, Governor-General, India, to Edward Wheler and Council, 20 September 1784, NAI/FD/SC 08/10/1784 1; Āṣaf al-Dawla, Nawwāb of Awadh, to Governor-General, India, 25 August 1784, NAI/FD/SC 08/10/1784 4.

97 Extract of Political Letter to Bengal, 15 March 1799, in Lawrence D. Campbell and E. Samuel, *Asiatic Annual Register, or View of the History of Hindustan, and of the Politics, Commerce and Literature of Asia, For the Year 1799* (London: J. Debrett, 1801), 40; Letter from W. Scott, Resident at Lucknow, Memorial to the Nawwāb, 16 March 1801, in East India Company, *A Collection of Facts and Documents Relative to Batta* (Calcutta: S. Smith & Co., 1829), 117–118.

98 Elliott, *Chronicles of Oonao*, 131.

99 William Henry Sleeman, *A Journey Through the Kingdom of Oude, in 1849–1850* (London: Richard Bentley, 1858), 1:130.

100 Elliott, *Chronicles of Oonao*, 125.

101 Edward Otto Ives, Resident at Lucknow, to Governor-General, India, 29 March 1789, NAI/FD/SPC 08/04/1789 22.

102 See, for example, Hastings to Res. Lucknow, 10 Aug 1782, NAI/FD/SC 15/08/1782 6; Hastings to Hyder Beg, circa Aug 1782, NAI/FD/SC 15/08/1782 9; J. Morgan, Commander of 2nd Brigade, to Commander in Chief, 1 October 1782, NAI/FD/SC 14/10/1782 10; Bristow to Governor General and Council, 4 Nov 1782, NAI/FD/SC 22/11/1782 2.

103 "Engagement entered into with Ilmass Ally Khan," ca. 1872, NAI/FD/SC 17/02/1784 Appendix.

104 John Tosh, *Manliness and Masculinities in Nineteenth-Century Britain: Essays on Gender, Family and Empire* (London: Pearson Longman, 2005), 21.

105 However, from the end of the eighteenth century, colonial attitudes towards both British men's relationships with Indian women and diverse Indian domestic arrangements were increasingly negative. Durba Ghosh, *Sex and the Family in Colonial India: The Making of Empire* (Cambridge: Cambridge University Press, 2006), 74–76. In the nineteenth century, colonial ideas about domesticity and colonial law shaped elite Indian family arrangements in important ways. For example, see Mytheli Sreenivas, *Wives, Widows, and Concubines: The Conjugal Family Ideal in Colonial India* (Bloomington: Indiana University Press, 2008).

106 Rosie Llewellyn-Jones, *A Man of the Enlightenment in Eighteenth Century India: The Letters of Claude Martin, 1766–1800* (New Delhi: Permanent Black, 2003), 391.

107 J. Ironside to Commander in Chief, 25 January 1785, NAI/FD/SC 19/02/1785 2.

108 Almās 'Alī Khān to Governor-General, India, 19 April 1785, NAI/FD/SC 26/04/1785 24.

109 Ives to Governor General, 29 Mar 1789, NAI/FD/SPC 08/04/1789 22.

110 In contrast to its policy in relation to Almās 'Alī, in the early nineteenth century, the Company encouraged the Nawwāb to protect and provide for the kin of the *khwāja-sarā'ī* Tashin Ali Khan. Pandit Bishun Narayan Das, Petition of Janki Parshad, Birj Nath and Murli Dhar to Governor-General, India, 29 April 1896, UPSA/L/FD/P/121/1; J.O. Miller, Secretary, North-Western Provinces and Oudh, to Secretary, Government of India, 19 June 1897, UPSA/L/FD/P/121/2; H. Daly, Deputy Secretary, Government of India, to Secretary, North-Western

Provinces and Oudh, 21 July 1897, UPSA/L/FD/P/121/3; S.F. Bayley, Assistant Secretary, Government of India, to Secretary, North-Western Provinces and Oudh, 11 January 1898, UPSA/L/PD/P/11/332A.

111 Walter Hamilton, *The East-India Gazetteer* (London: W.M.H. Allen and Co., 1828), 2:350.

112 Elliott, *Chronicles of Oonao*, 131.

113 Ibid., 125–128; Bayly, *Rulers, Townsmen and Bazaars*, 166; Sleeman, *Journey*, 1:247, 273, 322; Reginald Heber, *Narrative of a Journey Through the Upper Provinces of India, From Calcutta to Bombay, 1824–1825* (Philadelphia: Carey, Lea and Carey, 1828), 1:302; Ali, *Observations*, 1:72.

114 *Mahal* could refer to either a district or a palace, and it is not clear from the text which is intended. Fā'iz Bakhsh, *Ta'rīkh-i Faraḥbakhsh*, 2:49–50.

115 Ibid., 2:2, 61, 189, 220, 292, 300.

116 Ibid., 2:50.

117 Unless otherwise stated, the account below is based upon Fā'iz Bakhsh, *Ta'rīkh-i Faraḥbakhsh*, 2:113–158, 179–212; Barnett, *North India*, 205–212.

118 Fā'iz Bakhsh, *Ta'rīkh-i Faraḥbakhsh*, 2:86–87, 90–94.

119 Ibid., 2:48–49, 192–193.

120 Barnett, *North India*, 200–201.

121 Fā'iz Bakhsh, *Ta'rīkh-i Faraḥbakhsh*, 2:123.

122 Ibid., 2:144–145.

123 Italics mine. Ibid., 2:145.

124 Ibid., 2:148.

125 Indrani Chatterjee, "Slavery, Semantics, and the Sound of Silence," in Chatterjee and Eaton, *Slavery & South Asian History*, 287–315.

126 Sleeman to Secretary, GoI, 30 Oct 1849, NAI/FD/PC 24/11/1849 165.

127 Ibid.

128 Fisher, *Clash of Cultures*, 120–141.

129 Ibid., 166–169.

130 Ibid., 234.

131 W. H. Sleeman, Resident at Lucknow, to Secretary to the Government of India, 30 October 1849, NAI/FD/PC 24/11/1849 165. For further examples, see Hinchy, "The Sexual Politics of Imperial Expansion," 421–427.

132 For example, W. H. Sleeman, Resident at Lucknow, to Secretary, Government of India, 6 April 1850, NAI/FD/PC 23/05/1850 161; Dalhousie, "Minute by the Governor-General of India on Oude," 18 June 1855, NAI/FD/PP 28/12/1855 319.

133 Wājid 'Alī Shāh, Bāshā of Awadh, Agreement, 22 June 1848, NAI/FD/PC 08/07/1848 65.

134 Hinchy, "Sexual Politics".

135 Dalhousie, "Minute," 18 June 1855, NAI/FD/PP 28/12/1855 319. See also W. H. Sleeman, Resident at Lucknow, to Bāshā of Awadh, 17 August 1853, NAI/FD/PP 18/11/1853 127.

136 Sleeman to Secretary, GoI, 30 October 1849, NAI/FD/PC 24/11/1849 165.

137 Bayly, *Empire and Information*, 94–96.

138 Sleeman claimed that *khwāja-sarā'ī* and other courtiers would pocket the amount allocated for the feeding of the troops and bullocks and force the regiment to forage for supplies. Sleeman to Secretary, GoI, 6 Apr 1850, NAI/FD/PC 23/05/1850 161.

139 J. Outram, Resident at Lucknow, to Secretary, Government of India, 21 June 1855, NAI/FD/PC 28/12/1855 335.

140 Wājid 'Alī Shāh, Bāshā of Awadh, to Resident at Lucknow, 25 June 1847, NAI/FD/PP 11/12/1847 162.

141 Extracts from the diaries of the Resident at Lucknow, Appendix to J. A. Dorin, Member, Council of the Governor-General, Minute, 11 July 1855, NAI/FD/PP 28/12/1855 324.
142 W. H. Sleeman, Resident at Lucknow, to Secretary, Government of India, 10 October 1851, NAI/PF/PC 16/01/1852 94; W. H. Sleeman, Resident at Lucknow, to Secretary, Government of India, 28 October 1849, NAI/FD/PC 24/11/1849 156.
143 W. H. Sleeman, Resident at Lucknow, to Under Secretary, Government of India, 20 October 1853, NAI/FD/PP 18/11/1853 125.
144 W. H. Sleeman, Resident at Lucknow, to the Civil and Sessions Judges and Collectors of Patna, Agra, Chhapra, Kanpur, Farrukhābād and Budaun, 9 November 1852, NAI/FD/PP 18/11/1853 129; Sleeman to Secretary, GoI, 20 Oct 1853, NAI/FD/PP 18/11/1853 125.
145 Fisher, *Clash of Cultures*, 203.
146 Richmond to Sec, GoI, 24 Nov 1848, NAI/FD/PC 30/12/1848 99.
147 W. H. Sleeman, Resident at Lucknow, to Secretary, Government of India, 26 October 1849, NAI/FD/PC 24/11/1849 163; Richmond to Sec, GoI, 24 Nov 1848, NAI/FD/PC 30/12/1848 99.
148 Fisher, *Clash of Cultures*, 178–179.
149 W. H. Sleeman, Resident at Lucknow, to Secretary, Government of India, 24 March 1851, NAI/FD/PC 19/04/1851 163; H. Elliot, Secretary, Government of India, to Resident at Lucknow, 8 April 1851, NAI/FD/PC 19/04/1851 165.
150 Hinchy, "Sexual Politics of Imperial Expansion," 428.
151 G. F. Edmonstone, Secretary, Government of India, Note, 15 June 1857, NAI/FD/SP 26/06/1857 131.
152 Rosie Llewellyn-Jones, "The Colonial Response to African Slaves in British India – Two Contrasting Cases," *African and Asian Studies* 10, no. 1 (2011): 59–70; Veena Talwar Oldenburg, *The Making of Colonial Lucknow: 1856–1877* (Princeton: Princeton University Press, 1984), 200–204.
153 Nāẓir al-Dawla, Petition to Chief Commissioner of Oudh, 4 January 1874, UPSA/L/BR/LD 1140.
154 W. Roberts, Judge, and R. Spankie, Officiating Judge, Nizamut Adawlut, North-Western Provinces, "Draft Act," 24 March 1866, BL/IOR/P/438/62; J.F. Stephen quoted in BL/IOR/V/9/11: W. Stokes, Secretary, Government of India, Abstract of the proceedings of the Council of the Governor-General of India, 3 October 1870.
155 "An Act for the Registration of Criminal Tribes and Eunuchs," Act No. 27 of 1871 Passed by the Governor-General of India in Council, BL/IOR/V/8/42.
156 Sayyid Aḥmad Khān to John Strachey, 14 April 1870, NAI/HD/JB 30/07/1870 53–54.
157 Avril A. Powell, "Indian Muslim Modernists and the Issue of Slavery in Islam," in Chatterjee and Eaton, *Slavery & South Asian History*, 279–280.

Part III

Religious authority and sacredness

8 Physical and symbolic castration and the Holy Eunuch in late antiquity, third to sixth centuries CE[1]

Mathew Kuefler

The Mediterranean in late antiquity fairly teemed with eunuchs. At least, that is the impression left by our sources. They existed in large numbers in the administration of the later Roman empire, probably from the early third century on, and increasingly in the following centuries. The presence of eunuchs in royal households in the eastern Mediterranean has a much older history, and it was likely their usefulness in a variety of servile functions – and eunuchs were almost always slaves – that prompted their adoption by the later Roman emperors. They were outsiders – not only slaves but also often from ethnic peoples on the borders of the Roman empire – and this status meant that they depended for their lives and their careers entirely upon the goodwill of the emperor. As such, they often functioned as go-betweens, liaisons between the emperor, his family, the other members of his court and the many functionaries of the growing imperial bureaucracy.[2] The position often called *grand chamberlain* in English (*praepositus sacri cubiculi* in Latin) was the highest administrative post and seems to have been reserved for eunuchs.[3] One eunuch, Eutropius, who lived in the second half of the fourth century, achieved the honour of consul (an appointment only for one year, but the highest in the empire) in 399 because of his service to the emperor Arcadius (r. 395–408). The honour was all the greater since Eutropius had been a slave, as were most eunuchs in the later empire, albeit by the time of his appointment, he had been freed and was a powerful and wealthy individual.[4]

Eunuchs also regularly served women. Eunuchs in the imperial household attended empresses. Since empresses were not permitted to be in public unless chaperoned, eunuchs served as their link to the public world of men, both escorting them when they did travel out of their homes and also serving as their messengers. The famous mid-sixth-century historian Procopius wrote of the palace eunuchs who surrounded Theodora, consort to the emperor Justinian (ruled 527–565), as always being ready to assist her in accomplishing her wicked plans.[5] Yet eunuchs could be found outside the imperial palaces, too, for much the same reasons, in the homes of many of the wealthy, since no respectable Roman woman could be seen outside of her home unescorted. The late fourth-century Christian priest and writer

Jerome mentioned "crowds" and "armies" of eunuchs who accompanied rich women in public, who guarded them on the streets in the cities, carried them in litters and even ushered them to church or attended them in the baths that were so much a part of Roman life.[6] Eunuchs also guarded a woman's safety and her reputation in her home, and that is also doubtless why they proliferated in the later imperial period. (What women and eunuchs could get up to behind closed doors is another matter – and one about which some Roman men worried – but at least there could be no risk of pregnancy or illegitimate children.)[7]

In the countryside, too, late-ancient eunuchs wandered about as itinerant devotees of a popular fertility goddess, Cybele. By the fourth and fifth centuries, devotion to the Phrygian goddess Cybele, a deity perhaps of Hittite origins who was often called simply the Great Mother (*Magna Mater*) or the Mother of the Gods (*Mater Deum*), existed throughout the Mediterranean region. She was assimilated in part to other goddesses in late antiquity, including the Egyptian Isis, the Greek Rhea and the Roman Aphrodite. Legends gave Cybele a consort named Attis, who was castrated and died of his wounds but was then restored to life; different versions say only the last or all of these actions were done by the Mother herself. For this reason her cult was staffed by eunuch priests. Most ancient religions relied on sacrifice of the part for the sake of the whole, so castration in a fertility cult should not be all that surprising. Unlike the slave eunuchs who lived in the imperial household or homes of the wealthy, eunuch priests of the Mother, called *galli* in Latin and *galloi* in Greek, were probably free men who chose their own fate, according to some, castrating themselves in public rituals of frenzied bloodletting.[8]

In late Roman antiquity, worship of the Great Mother and of the other ancient gods and goddesses was gradually replaced by the cult of Christ. Christian churchmen of the era (the so-called Fathers of the Church or patristic writers) vehemently denounced all of the principles behind devotion to Cybele and Attis: the veneration of the wrong god, of course, but also the emasculation of men in divine service, as well as the sacred or ritual prostitution that most critics claimed formed part of this service. The nature and extent of sacred prostitution – ritual sex between priests or priestesses and male followers of a fertility religion – is much debated by modern scholars. It was veiled in enough secrecy that outsiders never seem to understand the details and give confused accounts, but not enough, it seems to me, to dismiss the whole of the rite as imagined.[9] The gendered and sexual distinctions that marked these men – their castration, certainly, but also their ritual crossdressing, their effeminate appearance and their "feminine" sexual appetites – all seemed equally disturbing to Christian writers and a threat to their understanding of proper norms.[10]

In their denunciations, Christian churchmen were relying on like-minded biblical discussions of eunuch priests. Again, scholars have debated the presence of the fertility cult among the ancient Hebrews and of eunuch priests who were also sacred prostitutes. The existence of sacred female prostitutes – called *qədēshōth*, "sacred ones" in the feminine in Hebrew and likened to secular prostitutes – is generally accepted, but the role played by their associates – called *qədēshōm*, "sacred ones" in the masculine and compared to dogs – is often called into question. I see no reason why they could not have both been sacred prostitutes. The priests of Yahweh repeatedly "cleansed" the religion of the ancient Hebrews of the presence of both *qədēshōm* and *qədēshōth* and of the so-called abominations they committed even from the precinct of the Temple.[11] They also forbade eunuchs from serving as priests of Yahweh, possibly to discourage *qədēshīm* within this cult.[12] Writers of the New Testament held similar attitudes: Paul condemned what he perceived to be the gender and sexual violations of the fertility cult, and the anonymous author of the book of Revelation also decried the eunuch priests as dogs, insisting that they would not be saved.[13]

Little room for any sacred eunuchs in the Christian mind, one might think. Even so, there are a number of interesting parallels between the cult of the Great Mother and Christianity as it developed in late antiquity. Both worshipped an incarnated divine being who had been killed but raised back to life. Also important to both was the role of the blood sacrifice of individual followers, in martyrdom and in self-castration – a parallel noticed by late ancient Christians, though the late-fourth-century poet Prudentius insisted that the difference was immense: Christians shed their blood only unwillingly because of persecution, while eunuchs did so voluntarily, and so the result was salvific for Christians but profitless for eunuchs.[14] (The enthusiasm for martyrdom among some early Christians belies at least in part this distinction.) Both insisted that the sacrifice of one's fertility, whether seen as the renunciation of sexual desire, marriage or family life, was pleasing to God, especially among his priests. Tertullian, writing in the early third century, was alone in referring to Christ as a eunuch, but the similarities remained.[15]

What I am suggesting is that there is another way of thinking about eunuchs in the early Christian tradition that is distinct from their denunciation by biblical and patristic writers, a space where eunuchs might not be despised but rehabilitated and even celebrated. There are hints of such a reclamation even in the bible. The author of the book of Isaiah offered the opinion that eunuchs who keep the commandments of God will enjoy "a monument and a name better than sons and daughters".[16] The book of Acts in the Christian bible described an encounter between the apostle Philip and a eunuch, attendant to the Ethiopian queen, that ended in the eunuch's baptism – a scene that seems to have embodied the entirety of Paul's dictum that "in Christ there is neither Jew nor Greek, neither free nor slave, neither male nor female".[17]

Among the varied groups that claimed the name of Christian in the first centuries of the Common Era were many that renounced sex and marriage and often abandoned alongside them most practical distinctions between men's and women's roles. Other groups exhorted followers to shed all gender differences so as to accomplish Paul's words above or for other theological purposes. Both the sexless and genderless ideals among early Christians are well known to scholars, and the encouragement of sexual renunciation even within mainstream Christianity by the fourth and fifth centuries is also a familiar theme.[18] There were, it seems, a few groups who took these ideals one step further, enjoining on male followers the obligation of self-castration or at least encouraging the practice. Two second-century Gnostic teachers in Alexandria, Basilides and Julius Cassian, were apparently both advocates, insofar as their teachings can be reconstructed from those of their opponents.[19] Epiphanius of Salamis, who catalogued many heretical Christian sects in the late fourth century, included in his list the Valesians, who he said practiced self-castration.[20] We know little more than their name and this single fact about them, but there is little reason to doubt their existence.

Self-castration among Christians was not limited to a few isolated groups. Throughout the writings of the era, there are hints at a more widespread practice, although the precise extent can never be known. Perhaps the most famous self-made eunuch was the Christian philosopher Origen of Alexandria, who was said to have castrated himself in the early third century so as to preclude any concerns about his teaching of women. Eusebius, the fourth-century Christian historian who first described the deed, referred to him as "immature" in doing so but also as offering thereby "the highest proof of faith and continence".[21] Even before that, in the early second century, the Christian writer called Justin Martyr mentioned with apparent approval a man who had wished to castrate himself, believing he would be able to lead a better Christian life.[22] The first decree of the Christian bishops assembled from across the Roman empire at the first universal church council held in Nicaea in 325 was to remove self-made eunuchs from the clergy, a decree that demonstrates their hostility to the idea of self-castration but also admits to the presence of such men within these ranks.[23]

It is possible to read between the lines of the extant denunciations of Christian self-castration among patristic writers so as to imagine how self-made Christian eunuchs justified their actions as holy. Foremost would have been their appeal to the Gospel of Matthew, where Jesus commands those of his followers who are willing to "castrate themselves" or "make themselves eunuchs" for the sake of the kingdom of heaven.[24] Patristic writers repeatedly metaphorised this command and enjoined Christian men not to take this passage literally, but their opinions may well have been shaped by those who felt otherwise.[25] Odd patristic commentaries on the biblical heroes who "girded their loins" and the insistence that the phrase did not refer to self-castration may have been prompted by similar concerns.[26]

It is even possible to envision the ways in which Christian eunuchs may have seen themselves as joining an imagined cosmological past, present and future through their actions. If sexual desire came into the world as the result of human sin, as many Christian writers of late antiquity insisted, then men who attempted to remove from themselves the possibility of sex through self-castration may have seen themselves as restoring an original innocence to humanity. (Moreover, if one thinks of the legend of Adam and Eve as the splitting of an original androgynous person into the two sexes, the removal of the external markers of maleness may have also been prompted by a desire to return to a primordial humanity.[27]) Jesus had declared that in heaven there would be no more marrying or being given in marriage (neither the male nor female role in marriage, in other words), but that those in heaven would live like the angels. Self-made eunuchs may well have seen themselves as participating in such a paradisal and angelic life, beginning already on earth a life of sexlessness – and, since angels were considered as beings without maleness or femaleness, a life also of genderlessness.[28] (It should be noted that a rationale such as this for castration, that is, for the sake of a genderless ideal, is fundamentally different than the sacrifice of fertility apparently at the heart of castration in the cult of Cybele or the practical justifications used for eunuch slaves who were bureaucrats or guardians of women.)

Patristic writers used quite different reasoning to reject self-castration. To be sure, they could not criticize the ideal of sexual renunciation that Christian eunuchs represented: that was also dear to their hearts. But they latched onto the gender renunciation, condemning the abandonment of maleness by eunuchs as the greatest sign of its error. Ambrose, the late fourth-century bishop of Milan, condemned self-made eunuchs. "There are some who regard it as a state of holiness [or manliness, *virtus*] to restrain guilt with a knife", by castrating themselves, he wrote, but he himself thought of it as "a declaration of weakness [*ad professionem infirmitatis*]" rather than "an emblem of strength [*ad firmitatis gloriam*]", since, as he insisted, it was the will (*voluntas*) rather than necessity (*necessitas*) that made it happen. He continued: "How can someone with a virtuous character [or a manly one, *virtute animae*] castrate himself?"[29]

Once again, it would be easy to stop with such condemnations and consider the opinions of these churchmen as reflecting broader opinion. A much more positive perspective is provided by the several eunuchs revered as saints in late antiquity. Here I will consider three pairs of eunuch saints venerated in late antiquity in similar legends. The first pair are Nereus and Achilleus, said to have been eunuch slaves belonging to the niece of the first-century emperor Domitian. After she and her household became Christians, they were banished and eventually executed. The second pair, Protus and Hyacinthus, brothers and eunuchs, were supposed to have been slaves of Eugenia, the daughter of a Roman governor of Egypt, baptized together with her and later beheaded with her by order of a third-century emperor. The third pair, Calocerus and Parthenius, were said to have belonged to Typhenia, wife of the third-century emperor Decius, and were once again martyred for their faith. None of these legends is all that reliable, and little was known about these individuals even in antiquity, though their relics were venerated at Rome and their feast days commemorated even then.[30] A fourth-century church in Rome holds the remains of Saints Nereus and Achilleus and took their name from at least the end of the sixth century.[31]

It is hard to determine the full meaning of these cults of eunuch saints with so little to go on as evidence, but a few points of comparison may be made. The fact of their having been remembered as pairs and through such parallel stories probably suggests that they should be considered as representing broader types of sanctity. They perhaps represent the notion that even the lowliest slave (a lowliness intensified by the prominence of the households in which they were said to serve) can achieve the glory of sanctity. Their loyalty to their mistresses is mirrored in their adherence to their faith, so that their martyrdoms reinforce both human virtue and the certainty of their salvation. The accompaniment of their mistresses even in death hints not only at the sexual purity of their charges but also at their own. They were "perfect servants", as all Christians were enjoined to be.[32] Their names – most taken from Greek mythology, if invented – probably also points to the heroism and bravery of their sacrifice. Whether or not these individuals ever existed, the legends of their deaths offered the possibility of sanctity even to eunuchs.[33]

The martyrdom of these eunuchs lent them a sort of manliness. Many patristic writers likened the martyrs to soldiers, especially in their bravery in the fight against persecution and in their willingness to die for the cause for which they fought.[34] The stories of martyr eunuchs juxtaposed manliness and unmanliness in an ironic manner. That one of these pairs should be linked to Saint Eugenia, whose legend had her dress as a man, enter a male monastery and become its abbot before being accused unjustly of the seduction of a local woman, is subtly reinforced in the gender ambiguity of her eunuch slaves.[35]

There is another type of eunuch remembered for his holiness in late antiquity: the symbolic eunuch. I know of three such individuals, all of whom were also monks. The oldest seems to be Pachon of Scetis in Egypt, mentioned by the fifth-century Christian writer Palladius. So troubled was he by sexual thoughts, even as an old man, that, as he wandered naked into the desert, he tried to get an asp to bite his penis, when he suddenly heard a voice announce to him that he had at last conquered his desires and would no longer be bothered by them.[36] Both Serenus, an Egyptian monk discussed by the fifth-century monastic writer John Cassian, and Equitius, abbot of Valeria in sixth-century Italy described by the bishop of Rome Gregory the Great, were said to have been castrated by angels sent from God, after which they had no further sexual thoughts.[37] These stories share the same final outcome: The individual loses his sexual desire without actually being castrated. All of these stories are late ones, fifth century and beyond, when the Christian ideal of sexual renunciation was widely established but also after physical self-castration by Christians had been repeatedly rejected by ecclesiastical authorities. By this point, too, the category of Christian sainthood had been expanded beyond the martyrs to encompass ascetics. So the timing of these legends suggests that they may represent a "second wave" of castration saints. It is worth pointing out that these men do not castrate themselves, nor do they actually lose their genitals. Instead, God achieves for them what they might have done themselves. There is thus clearly a didactic nature to them.

The space opened for a positive assessment of Christian eunuchs stands in contrast to the contemporary Jewish tradition. In the first century, Philo of Alexandria, commenting on the story of the biblical patriarch Joseph in Egypt, described his Egyptian master Potiphar as

> a eunuch gelded of the soul's generating organs, a vagrant from the men's quarters, an exile from the women's, a thing neither male nor female, unable either to shed or receive seed, twofold yet neuter, base counterfeit of the human coin.[38]

According to the Mishnah (compiled in the early third century from earlier Rabbinic opinions), eunuchs could not participate as men in Jewish congregations.[39] The Talmud (compiled in perhaps the fifth or sixth century) extended this discussion to the different possibilities for castration – whether accidental or congenital, for example, or done to a slave – and how they affected this incapacity and also the right to marry, and it mostly denied eunuchs the privileges of other men.[40]

The reception of eunuchs in the Christian tradition also stands in sharp contrast to other contemporary Roman depictions by pagan authors. In their writings, eunuchs demonstrate only the worst of human actions. Ammianus Marcellinus, a fourth-century historian, in the midst of his glowing account of the emperor Julian, found himself having to paint a positive portrait of the eunuch Eutherius, Julian's grand chamberlain; his distaste is palpable.[41] The anonymous author of the fourth-century *Historia Augusta* displayed similar antipathy whenever eunuchs are mentioned.[42] The negative tone can also be seen in Roman laws against castration. Roman legal tradition, for example, had outlawed castration within the empire from the third century on – even if these laws were obviously commonly ignored.[43] This opposition remained in post-Roman law. The laws of the Franks, for example, punished with a fine anyone who castrated a slave.[44]

The hostility towards eunuchs did not disappear entirely from Christian discourse. Perhaps the most vicious of commentators was Basil the Great, fourth-century bishop of Kayseri in Anatolia, who wrote to a noblewoman, insulting her eunuchs as:

> a disgraceful and detestable set ... neither woman nor man, lustful, envious, ill-bribed, passion-filled, effeminate, slaves of the belly, mad for gold, ruthless, grumbling about their dinner, inconstant, stingy, greedy, insatiable, savage, jealous. What more need I say? At their very birth they were condemned to the knife. How can their mind[s] be right ...? They are lecherous to no purpose, of their own natural vileness.[45]

Yet many other Christian writers harboured no similar ill-will. In the early fifth century, the historian Sozomen wrote of the eunuch Tigrius, living in Constantinople, that

> he was originally a slave in the house of a man in power, and on account of his faithful services had obtained his freedom. He was afterwards ordained as presbyter, and was distinguished by his moderation and meekness of disposition, and by his charity towards strangers and the poor.[46]

This praise makes sense; in important ways, eunuchs lived the ideal life for Christians. Foremost was their abandonment of sex, marriage and family life. The low status of eunuchs also reminded Christians of the need for humility, and as slaves to the great, eunuchs might symbolise the need for all Christians to think of themselves as slaves to God. I have suggested elsewhere that the ideal life for monks came to share much of what had been imagined for eunuchs, but with the imposition of clerical celibacy in the west, even imperfectly, other groups of Christian men, especially bishops, also adopted what might be considered a "eunuch lifestyle".[47]

There remained certain tensions between eunuchs and the perfect Christian life. The young age of most castrations both preserved in eunuchs a boyish appearance (without facial or body hair) and even created for them a sort of feminized appearance (especially in a higher pitched voice and in the enlargement of breasts and hips).[48] Either aspect might have provided a sexual distraction for men. Legends of women who disguised themselves as eunuchs so as to enter male monasteries, it has been suggested, might betray the temptations of a gender-ambiguous sexual desire.[49] Jerome inadvertently admitted that eunuchs might be good looking in a letter in which he cautioned a wealthy Christian virgin to avoid the temptation of purchasing attractive ones, advising her that "they should be selected for their morals more than for a graceful appearance", and that all slaves' "sense of sexual modesty [*pudicitia*] should be considered, even for those whose bodies have been violently maimed [through castration; *truncatorum corporum uiolentia*]".[50]

The recuperative possibilities for eunuchs within a Christian context might help to explain a unique episode from the sixth-century history of Gregory, bishop of Tours, in post-Roman Gaul. Gregory himself was called to the female monastery of Poitiers to adjudicate a bitter division between the nuns. One nun had accused the abbess of living like an empress, attended by a eunuch servant. The individual was called forward and explained that he was a man who had had a serious illness and had been castrated by a physician to be healed. Afterward he had decided to dress as a woman, though he insisted that he was living a virtuous life. Gregory recounted the story without any apparent surprise or disdain, and when he found out that the man was not actually living in the monastery, he declined to pass judgment.[51]

The story of the eunuch in late Roman antiquity forms a curious counterpoint to the otherwise straightforward narrative told about late ancient Christianity: of solidifying conservative and patriarchal attitudes among Christians, and especially of the growing inflexibility toward gender variance. These restrictions had the biggest impact on women, whose ritual and leadership roles in the Christian churches were increasingly removed from them.[52] Perhaps even here is an instance of historical male privilege, since eunuchs seem still to have been able to renounce traditional gender roles and identities when women could no longer do so.[53] In late Roman antiquity, some eunuchs exercised authority as bureaucratic participants in a growing imperial administration. Others found a semblance of power as attendants to wealthy aristocratic women. Still others found a spiritual sort of dominion as embodiments of Christian ideals of sexual and gender renunciation. Some were outsiders as slaves and foreigners; others stood outside the bounds of the traditional gendered identities of Romans. Not entirely welcome even within the Christian challenge to the rules of Roman society, eunuchs still managed to earn respect, even occasional veneration, for their conformity to the principles of their faith. Indeed, it was perhaps because they were found at the margins of conventional society that they might approach the centre of a new dispensation. It was likely in their simultaneous defiance of and conformity to convention that they found the greatest potential for spiritual authority, and in that regard, they are not unlike the bishops and monks of later Christian centuries. The lives of most ancient eunuchs could not have been easy ones. Yet between the third and sixth centuries, the enmity that otherwise universally marks the place of the eunuch in the Mediterranean gradually gave way to acceptance, even approval, if still somewhat less than wholehearted. Indeed, it was possibly only in the figure of the eunuch that the early Christian genderless ideal survived, and the dictum "no more male or female" remained more than words spoken.[54]

Notes

1 I am very grateful to Almut Höfert, Matthew M. Mesley, and Serena Tolino, the organizers of the conference "The Gender of Authority: Celibate and Childless Men in Power: Ruling Bishops and Ruling Eunuchs, c. 400–1800," for their invitation to participate in the conference as well as for their help in improving this chapter, and to all of the other participants and attendees for a stimulating and fruitful event. All dates given are CE unless otherwise specified. All translations are my own unless otherwise specified.

2 Numbers of eunuchs are difficult to determine; a later (tenth-century) Arab observer estimated that there were 5000 eunuchs in the imperial palace of Constantinople – a number that seems difficult to believe. See Georges Sidéris, "Une société de ville capitale: Les eunuques dans la Constantinople byzantine (IVe-XIIe siècle)," in *Les villes capitales au moyen âge*, ed. Société des historiens médiévistes de l'enseignement public (Paris: Publications de la Sorbonne, 2006), 258. On the political role of eunuchs in the later Roman Empire, see Keith Hopkins, "The Political Power of Eunuchs," chap. 4 in *Conquerors and Slaves*

(Cambridge: Cambridge University Press, 1978); Peter Guyot, *Eunuchen als Sklaven und Freigelassene in der griechisch-römischen Antike* (Stuttgart: Klett-Cotta, 1980), esp. chap. 7; Dirk Schlinkert, "Der Hofeunuch in der Spätantike: Ein gefährlicher Aussenseiter?" *Hermes: Zeitschrift für klassische Philologie* 122 (1994): 342–59; Susan Tuchel, *Kastration im Mittelalter* (Düsseldorf: Droste Verlag, 1998), 35–44; and Shaun Tougher, "The Court Eunuchs of the Later Roman Empire," chap. 4 in *The Eunuch in Byzantine History and Society* (London: Routledge, 2008). On the dating of the use of eunuchs in the imperial administration to the third century, see Mathew Kuefler, *The Manly Eunuch: Masculinity, Gender Ambiguity, and Christian Ideology in Late Antiquity* (Chicago: University of Chicago Press, 2001), 63–65.

3 On this position, see esp. Helga Scholten, *Der Eunuch in Kaisernähe: Zur politischen und sozialen Bedeutung des praepositus sacri cubiculi im 4. und 5. Jahrhundert n. Chr.* (Frankfurt am Main: Peter Lang, 1995) – including a prosopographical list of all office holders (205–242). In 384, grand chamberlains were raised from the rank of *clarissimus* (held by all senators) to *illustris* (held only by prefects); in 422, their rank was raised again to *eminentissimus* (held only by the *magistri militum*, supreme commanders of the armies, and the praetorian prefects); *Codex Theodosianus*, ed. Theodor Mommsen and Paulus Meyer (Berlin: Weidmann, 1905) 7.8.3 and 6.8.1.

4 On Eutropius, our most detailed source, though hostile and not reliable, is the poem *In Eutropium* by the poet Claudian, ed. John Hall (Leipzig: B. G. Teubner, 1985). See also Jacqueline Long, *Claudian's In Eutropium: Or, How, When, and Why to Slander a Eunuch* (Chapel Hill: University of North Carolina Press, 1996); and Helga Schweckendick, *Claudians Invektive gegen Eutrop (In Eutropium): Ein Kommentar* (Hildesheim: Olms-Weidmann, 1992). Claudian's service included his leadership of a successful military campaign against the Huns in 398, in addition to his work as grand chamberlain. But within a year of his elevation to the consulship, he was disgraced, exiled and then executed. For the example of another eunuch who achieved real influence in the eastern Roman Empire in the early fifth century, see Geoffrey Greatrex and Jonathan Bardill, "Antiochus the 'Praepositus': A Persian Eunuch at the Court of Theodosius II," *Dumbarton Oak Papers* 50 (1996): 171–197.

5 Procopius, *The Anecdota or Secret History*, ed. and trans. Henry Bronson Dewing, Loeb Classical Library 290 (Cambridge, MA: Harvard University Press, 1935), 15.24–35, for one example. On the reliability of this author, see Anthony Kaldellis, *Procopius of Caesarea: Tyranny, History, and Philosophy at the End of Antiquity* (Philadelphia: University of Pennsylvania Press, 2004).

6 Jerome, *Epistula*, ed. Jérôme Labourt (Paris: Belles Lettres, 1949–63), 22.16 (a group of eunuchs called "a crowd" [*greges*]), 54.13 (a group of eunuchs called "an army" [*exercitus*]), 66.13 and 108.7 (on women borne by eunuchs on litters in the streets), 22.32 (on a woman who brought her eunuchs to church), 107.11 (on women bathing with eunuchs).

7 A variety of methods of castration apparently existed in late antiquity: tying up the scrotum in order to sever the *vas deferens*, crushing or removing the testicles and amputating the penis. Some eunuchs continued to experience sexual desire after castration, and those with penises intact might still become erect. John Cassian, for example, said in the fifth century that eunuchs woke with erections and might still be experiencing sexual desire (*Collationes*, ed. Étienne Pichery, Sources chrétiennes 54, [Paris: du Cerf, 1958], 12.9–10), and Basil the Great quipped that even a dehorned bull will still attempt to butt with its head (*De virginitate*, Patrologia Graeca 30 [Paris: J.-P. Migne, 1857], 63). The clearest medical writer on the subject is the seventh-century Paulus

Aegineta, *Compendium medici*, ed. Johann Ludwig Heiberg (Leipzig: B.G. Teubner, 1921), 6.65. To be sure, castration in any form did not preclude other forms of sexual activity between women and eunuchs, including cunnilinctus. See also Kuefler, *The Manly Eunuch*, 33, 96–99; or Tougher, *The Eunuch in Byzantine History*, 32–34. Tertullian, for example, complained of some women having mutilated men "for purposes of lust [*ad licentiam scetis*]". *Ad uxorem*, eds. Dom E. Dekkers et al., Corpus Christianorum Series Latina 1 (Turnhout: Brepols, 1954), 2.8.4.

8 The most detailed discussion of these cults in late antiquity remains Henri Graillot, *Le culte de Cybèle: Mère des dieux, à Rome et dans l'empire romain* (Paris: Fontemoing, 1912), but see also Gabriel Sanders, "Kybele und Attis," in *Die orientalischen Religionen im Römerreich*, ed. Maarten Vermaseren (Leiden: Brill, 1981), 267–297; Jane L. Lightfoot, "Sacred Eunuchism in the Cult of the Syrian Goddess," in *Eunuchs in Antiquity and Beyond*, ed. Shaun Tougher (London: Duckworth, 2002), 71–86; and Kuefler, *The Manly Eunuch*, 246–254. There is an extensive scholarly literature for these cults in earlier historical periods, but a good overview of the Roman evidence is by Jacob Latham, "'Fabulous Clap-Trap': Roman Masculinity, the Cult of Magna Mater, the Literary Constructions of the *Galli* at Rome from the Late Republic to Late Antiquity," *Journal of Religion* 92, no. 1 (2012): 84–122.

9 See Mary Beard and John Henderson, "With This Body I Thee Wed: Sacred Prostitution in Antiquity," in *Gender and the Body in the Ancient Mediterranean*, ed. Maria Wyke (Oxford: Blackwell, 1998), 56–79; or Stephanie L. Budin, *The Myth of Sacred Prostitution in Antiquity* (Cambridge: Cambridge University Press, 2010). Early Christian writers repeatedly denounce the *galli* for participating in sexual ritual – and it would be odd for them to have invented this invective out of nothing; see, for example, Firmicus Maternus, *De errore profanarum religionum*, Patrologia Latina 12 (Paris: J.-P. Migne, 1845), 4.2; Lactantius, *Divinae institutiones*, Patrologia Latina 6 (Paris: J.-P. Migne, 1844), 1.17; or Augustine, *De civitate Dei*, eds. Bernhard Dombart, Alfons Kalb, Corpus Christianorum Series Latina 47 (Turnhout: Brepols, 1955), 7.27.

10 Augustine, for example, described the eunuch priest as "neither changed into a woman nor left as a man" (*De civitate Dei* 7.24). For other examples, see Kuefler, *The Manly Eunuch*, 249.

11 The Hebrew terms in the singular are קדש and קדשה. Recent contributions to this ongoing scholarly debate include Joan Westenholz, "Tamar, *Qĕdēšā, Qadištu*, and Sacred Prostitution in Mesopotamia," *Harvard Theological Review* 82 (1989): 245–266; Karen van der Toorn, "Female Prostitution in Payment of Vows in Ancient Israel," *Journal of Biblical Literature* 108 (1989): 193–205; and Phyllis Bird, "'To Play the Harlot': An Inquiry into an Old Testament Metaphor," in *Gender and Difference in Ancient Israel*, ed. Peggy Day (Minneapolis: Fortress, 1989), 75–94. Arguing for the existence of male sacred prostitution in antiquity, see Will Roscoe, "Priests of the Goddess: Gender Transgression in Ancient Religion," *History of Religions* 35 (1996): 195–230; arguing against it, see Phyllis Bird, "The End of the Male Cult Prostitute: A Literary-Historical and Sociological Analysis of Hebrew *qādēš-qĕdēšīm*," *Supplements to Vetus Testamentum* 66 (1997): 37–80. See also the discussion in Kuefler, *The Manly Eunuch*, 255–258 (where I note that, regardless of the ancient meaning of the term, Jerome believed the *qədēshīm* to be equivalent to the *galli* of his day in translating the bible into Latin in late antiquity. *Commentarius in Ose*, ed. G. Morin, B. Capelle and J. Fraipont, Corpus Christianorum Series Latina 78 (Turnhout: Brepols, 1958), 1.4.14.

12 Deut. 23:1.

13 For Paul on eunuchs, see Rom. 1:23–29 (and see also Kuefler, *The Manly Eunuch*, 256–257, for my justification of this interpretation to the passage, not one generally recognised by scholars) and Gal. 5:12 (and the analysis of this passage in relation to the *galli* by James R. Edwards, "Circumcision, the Mother Goddess, and the Scandal of the Cross," *Novum Testamentum* 53 [2011]: 319–37). For eunuchs as dogs who will not be saved, see Apoc. 22:15 (and further examples and analysis in Kuefler, *The Manly Eunuch*, 257–258).

14 Prudentius, *Peristephanon*, ed. and trans. Henry John Thomson, Loeb Classical Library 398 (Cambridge, MA: Harvard University Press, 1953), 10, lines 1059–93.

15 Tertullian, *De monogamia,* Corpus Christianorum Series Latina 13 (using the word *spado*); cf. *ibid.* 5 (also referring to Jesus as a *spado*). For more examples of Tertullian's frequent positive discussion of eunuchs, see Kuefler, *The Manly Eunuch*, 265–267. Hippolytus of Rome described a group he called Naassenes, who worshipped Attis alongside Christ. *Refutatio omnium haeresium*, ed. Miroslav Marcovich (Berlin: de Gruyter, 1986), 5.1–6. For more on these similarities, see Andrew T. Fear, "Cybele and Christ," in *Cybele, Attis, and Related Cults: Essays in Memory of M. J. Vermaaseren*, ed. Eugene N. Lane (Leiden: Brill, 1996), 37–50.

16 Isa. 56:3–5. For further discussion of this passage and other mentions of eunuchs in the bible, see also Pascal Boulhol and Isabelle Cochelin, "La réhabilitation de l'eunuque dans l'hagiographie antique (IVe-VIe siècles)," in *Memoriam sanctorum venerantes: Miscellanea in onore di Monsignor Victor Saxer* (Vatican City: Pontificio Istituto di archeologia cristiana, 1992), 59–62.

17 Acts 8:26–39.

18 The recent scholarly literature on discouragement of sexual activity among early Christians is vast, but the best overview is Peter Brown, *The Body and Society: Men, Women, and Sexual Renunciation in Early Christianity* (New York: Columbia University Press, 1988).

19 Both Irenaeus of Lyon and Hippolytus of Rome wrote to oppose Basilides' ideas, and Clement of Alexandria, those of Julius Cassian. See the discussion in Walter Stevenson, "Eunuchs and Early Christianity," in Tougher, *Eunuchs in Antiquity and Beyond*, 128–29.

20 Epiphanius, *Adversus octaginta haereses*, Patrologia Graeca 41 (Paris: J.-P. Migne, 1863), 58. Cf. Augustine of Hippo, *De haeresibus*, ed. Michael Petrus Josephus van den Hout et al., Corpus Christianorum Series Latina 46 (Turnhout: Brepols, 1969), who also described the Valesian Christians as advocating self-castration.

21 Eusebius, *Historia ecclesiastica,* Patrologia Graeca 21 (Paris: J.-P. Migne, 1857), ed. and trans. Philip Schaff and Henry Wace, *Eusebius Pamphilius: Church History, Life of Constantine, Oration in Praise of Constantine*, Nicene and Post-Nicene Fathers, 2nd. ser., vol. 1 (Edinburgh: T. and T. Clark, 1885), 6.8. Jerome also referred to Origen's self-castration in a similar way as showing "zeal for God" but not "proper understanding" (*Epistula* 84.8). See also Stevenson, "Eunuchs and Early Christianity," 123–142; and John Dechow, *Dogma and Mysticism in Early Christianity: Epiphanius of Salamis and the Legacy of Origen* (Macon, GA: Mercer University Press, 1988), 128–135, for detailed discussions of whether Origen physically castrated himself or not.

22 Justin Martyr, *Apologia prima pro Christianis,* Patrologia Graeca 6 (Paris: J.-P. Migne, 1857), 29.2–3.

23 "Concilium Niceaenum," in *Conciliorum oecumenicorum decreta,* ed. Giuseppe Alberigo et al. (Bologna: Edizioni Dehoniane, 1991), canon 1. Cf. a similar decree in the early third-century regulations titled *Traditio apostolica* (ed. B. Botte, Sources chrétiennes 11, [Paris: du Cerf, 1968]), 16, and one in the decrees of the

Iberian regional church council held at Braga in 572 (ed. José Vives, *Concilios visigóticos e hispano-romanos* [Madrid: Consejo superior de investigaciones científicas, 1963], 92), 21. Eusebius of Caesarea praised a second-century eunuch bishop, Melito of Sardis in Anatolia, but did not provide details as to whether his castration was voluntary or involuntary. *Ecclesiastical History*, trans. Kirsopp Lake, Loeb Classical Library 153 (Cambridge, MA: Harvard University Press, 1926), 5.24.

24 Matt. 19.12. The Greek phrase for "they castrate themselves" is ευνούχισαν εαυτούς. See also the discussion of this passage in Kuefler, *The Manly Eunuch*, 258–260; for patristic and early medieval commentaries on the passage, see Tuchel, *Kastration im Mittelalter*, 120–126.

25 See Kuefler, *The Manly Eunuch*, 267–268, for examples; and Stevenson, "Eunuchs and Early Christianity"; and especially Daniel F. Caner, "The Practice and Prohibition of Self-Castration in Early Christianity," *Vigiliae Christianae* 51, no. 4 (1997): 396–415, for further discussion of the extent of self-castration among early Christians.

26 See, for example, Jerome, *De Exodo in vigilia Paschae*, Corpus Christianorum Series Latina 78; *Epistula* 22.11; Paulinus of Nola, *Epistula*, Corpus scriptorum ecclesiasticorum latinorum 29, ed. Wilhelm Hartel (Vienna: Academia litterarum caesareae, 1894), 24.14.

27 For this interpretation, see Wayne Meeks, "The Image of the Androgyne: Some Uses of a Symbol in Earliest Christianity," *History of Religions* 13 (1974): 165–208.

28 The separation of Adam and Eve is found in Gen. 2:21–24; angelic life in paradise, in Matt. 22:30. On the androgyny of angels according to patristic writers, see, for example, Jerome, *Epistula* 108.23 (where he contrasted the sexual differentiation of human beings from its lack among angels). On the frequent association between angels and eunuchs in later Byzantine history, see especially Kathryn M. Ringrose, *The Perfect Servant: Eunuchs and the Social Construction of Gender in Byzantium* (Chicago: University of Chicago Press, 2003), chap. 7.

29 Ambrose, *De viduis*, Patrologia Latina 16 (Paris: J.-P. Migne, 1845), 13.75–77. Jerome also contrasted will and necessity as distinguishing the chastity of metaphorical and physical eunuchs (*Epistula* 22.19).

30 For the sources for the legend of Nereus and Achilleus, see *Acta Sanctorum* (Antwerp and Brussels: Société des Bollandistes, 1643–1940), 12 Maii; for Protus and Hyacinthus, see *Acta Sanctorum*, 11 Septembris; for Calocerus and Parthenius, see *Acta Sanctorum*, 19 Maii. Other eunuch saints include Indes, Tigrius, the pair Bocthazat and Azat, and the group of three Dorotheus, Gorgonius and Peter. On eunuch saints, see Baudouin de Gaiffier, "Palatins et eunuques dans quelques documents hagiographiques," *Analecta Bollandiana* 75 (1957): 17–46; now updated by Boulhol and Cochelin, "La réhabilitation de l'eunuque," esp. 62–63; and, mostly for later periods of Byzantine history, Shaun Tougher, "Holy Eunuchs! Masculinity and Eunuch Saints in Byzantium," in *Holiness and Masculinity in the Middle Ages*, ed. P. H. Cullum and Katherine J. Lewis (Cardiff: University of Wales Press, 2004), 93–108; and Georges Sidéris, ""Eunuchs of Light": Power, Imperial Ceremonial and Positive Representations of Eunuchs in Byzantium (4th–12th Centuries AD)," in Tougher, *Eunuchs in Antiquity and Beyond*, 161–175.

31 See Umberto Fasola, *La basilica dei SS. Nereo ed Achilleo e la catacomba di Domitilla* (Rome: Marietti, 1960).

32 The phrase is Ringrose's, from her *The Perfect Servant*.

33 Boulhol and Cochelin, "La réhabilitation de l'eunuque," 70, remind us that many of the hagiographical accounts of these eunuch saints are unreliable and better treated as legends.

34 For examples, see Kuefler, *The Manly Eunuch*, 110–117. There is a definite distance between being a soldier who preferred to be killed rather than to kill, and that difference was recognized by ancient Christian writers: see, for example, Tertullian, *Apologeticus*, Corpus Christianorum Series Latina 1, 37.5; or Prudentius, *Peristephanon* 1 (on the martyred soldiers Emeterius and Chelidonius).

35 *Vita sanctae Eugeniae*, Patrologia Latina 73 (Paris: J.-P. Migne, 1849). There is also a vast scholarly literature on the cross-dressing female saint legends of late antiquity, an excellent example of which is Elizabeth Castelli, "'I Will Make Mary Male': Pieties of the Body and Gender Transformation of Christian Women in Late Antiquity," in *Body Guards: The Cultural Politics of Gender Ambiguity*, ed. Julia Epstein and Kristina Straub (New York: Routledge, 1991), 29–49.

36 Palladius, *Historia Lausiaca*, Patrologia Graeca 34 (Paris: J.-P. Migne, 1860), 29.

37 John Cassian, *Conlationes*, Patrologia Latina 49 (Paris: J.-P. Migne, 1846), 7.2; Gregory, *Dialogi,* Patrologia Latina 77 (Paris: J.-P. Migne, 1862), 1.4.

38 Philo (*De somniis* 2.184), quoted and translated by Ra'anan Abusch, "Eunuchs and Gender Transformation: Philo's Exegesis of the Joseph Narrative," in Tougher, *Eunuchs in Antiquity and Beyond*, 109. It is interesting that the Talmud includes the comment that Potiphar had been castrated by the angel Gabriel, a parallel with the Christian stories mentioned above (*Babylonian Talmud, Seder Nashim, Sotah* 13b).

39 *Mishnah, Seder Nashim, Jebamot* 8:1 and 8:2 (a commentary on Deut. 23.1).

40 *Babylonian Talmud, Seder Nashim, Yebamoth* 75a–76b, 79b–81a, *Seder Nezikim, Baba Bathra* 155b; *Seder Tohoroth, Niddah* 32a and 47b. The Hebrew term is *saris* (סירם), and while in biblical texts it is also often used to mean an "official," in later texts it clearly means a castrated male, though it might also refer to a male whose genitals did not develop at puberty.

41 Ammianus Marcellinus, *Res gestae*, ed. Wolfgang Seyfarth (Leipzig: Teubner, 1978) 16.7.4,8. It seems clear that even if Ammianus Marcellinus had wanted to depict Julian's grand chamberlain in a negative way, he could not without diminishing his otherwise idealized depiction of Julian. See also Shaun Tougher, "Ammianus and the Eunuchs," in *The Late Roman World and Its Historian*, ed. Jan Willem Drijvers and David Hunt (London: Routledge, 1999), 64–73.

42 *Historia Augusta*, ed. and trans. David Magie, Loeb Classical Library 140 (Cambridge, MA: Harvard University Press, 1924), *Alexander Severus* 23.4–6, 66.3–4. On this text, see Alan Cameron, "Eunuchs in the 'Historia Augusta,'" *Société d'Études latines de Bruxelles* 24, no. 1 (1965): 155–58. For other examples, see Kuefler, *The Manly Eunuch*, 36. Shaun Tougher sees both these negative assessments as continuing into the Byzantine period: see *The Eunuch in Byzantine History*, chap. 7.

43 See Tuchel, *Kastration im Mittelalter*, 25–35, for these laws. How enforced they were is unclear, though many of the known eunuchs of the later Roman Empire seem to have come from beyond the eastern borders of the empire. See also Jane F. Gardner, "Sexing a Roman: Imperfect Men in Roman Law," in *When Men Were Men: Masculinity, Power and Identity in Classical Antiquity*, ed. Lin Foxhall and John Salmon (London: Routledge, 1998), 136–152, for more on the legal incapacities of eunuchs.

44 Franz Beyerle and Rudolph Buchner, eds, *Lex ribuaria*, Monumenta Germaniae Historica Leges nationum Germanicarum (hereafter abbreviated as MGH, LL nat. Germ) 3. 2 (Hannover and Leipzig: Hahn, 1954), ch. 28 (27), p. 84. The fine was 36 *solidi*, as compared to a fine of 200 *solidi* for anyone who castrated a free man (*ibid.*, ch. 6, p. 76). This law code, although compiled in the early seventh century, likely relies on older legal customs. The roughly contemporary law of the Salian Franks fined only someone who castrated a free man (Karl August Eckhardt, ed., *Pactus leges salicae*, MGH, LL nat. Germ 4.1 (Hannover

and Leipzig: Hahn, 1961), ch. 29.17, p. 117. For other early medieval laws on castration, see Mathew Kuefler, "Castration and Eunuchism in the Middle Ages," in *Handbook of Medieval Sexuality*, ed. Vern L. Bullough and James A. Brundage (New York: Garland, 1996), 288; or Tuchel, *Kastration im Mittelalter*, 64–73.

45 Basil, *Epist.*, Patrologia Graeca 32 (Paris: J.-P. Migne, 1857), ed. and trans. Philip Schaff and Henry Wace, *Basil: Letters and Select Works,* Nicene and Post-Nicene Fathers, 2nd. ser., vol. 8 (Edinburgh: T. and T. Clark, 1885), 191.115. On Christian antipathy towards eunuchs, see also Boulhol and Cochelin, "La réhabilitation de l'eunuque," 55–59.

46 Sozomen, *Historia ecclesiastica*, Patrologia Graeca 67 (Paris: J.-P. Migne, 1864), ed. and trans. Philip Schaff and Henry Wace, *Socrates, Sozomenus: Church Histories*, Nicene and Post-Nicene Fathers, 2nd. ser., vol. 2 (Edinburgh: T. and T. Clark, 1885), 8.24. For other examples of late ancient and early medieval holy eunuchs, see Tuchel, *Kastration im Mittelalter*, 131–41.

47 On monks as symbolic eunuchs, see Kuefler, *The Manly Eunuch*, 273–282. Shaun Tougher finds evidence for eunuchs as patrons and benefactors of church-building projects in the eastern Roman Empire from the fifth century on and eunuch monasteries from the sixth century. See *The Eunuch in Byzantine History*, 72–73 (on eunuch monasteries), 80–81 (on eunuch benefactors); see also Sidéris, "Une société de ville capitale," 254–257. The imposition of celibacy on bishops happened much earlier than on priests and other lower clergy. See William E. Phipps, *Clerical Celibacy: The Heritage* (New York: Continuum, 2004), esp. chap. 5.

48 On the appearance of eunuchs, see Long, *Claudian's In Eutropium*, 108–109. From modern evidence, she suggests that eunuchs may have had unusually long limbs, a susceptibility to curvature of the spine and osteoporosis, sallow skin prone to wrinkles and increased fat deposits in the abdomen, breasts and buttocks. Some ancient writers commented on the appearance of eunuchs. Sidonius Apollinaris, for example, wrote in the fifth century of the pendulous breasts of a eunuch (*Letters: Books 3–9*, ed. and trans. William B. Anderson, Loeb Classical Library 420 [Cambridge, MA: Harvard University Press, 1965], 3.13). On ancient pederasty and its connection to the castration of boys, see Guyot, *Eunuchen als Sklaven*, 59–66; Kuefler, *The Manly Eunuch*, 99–102; or Mathew Kuefler, "Sex with Eunuchs, Sex with Boys, and the Implications of Sexual Difference," in *Comportamenti e immaginario della sessualità nell'alto medioevo,* Settimane di studi sull'alto medioevo 53 (Spoleto: Centro italiano di studi sull'alto medioevo, 2006), 139–172.

49 John Anson, "The Female Transvestite in Early Monasticism: The Origin and Development of a Motif," *Viator* 5 (1974): 1–32. See also the comments of Tougher, *The Eunuch in Byzantine History*, 74–79, on this subject.

50 Jerome, *Epistula* 130.13.

51 Gregory of Tours, *Historia Francorum*, Patrologia Latina 71 (Paris: J.-P. Migne, 1849) 10.15. See also the discussion of this story in Nancy Partner, "No Sex, No Gender," *Speculum* 68 (1993): 419–43.

52 The scholarly literature is substantial. For an overview, see Francine Cardman, "Women, Ministry, and Church Order in Early Christianity," in *Women and Christian Origins*, ed. Mary Rose d'Angelo and Ross Shepard Kramer (Oxford: Oxford University Press, 1999), 300–29.

53 See Mathew Kuefler, "Clothes (Un)Make the (Wo)Man: Dress and Gender Crossings in Late Antiquity," in *Il genere nella ricerca storica: Atti del VI Congresso della Società Italiana delle Storiche*, ed. Saveria Chemotti and Maria Cristina La Rocca, vol. 1 (Padua: Il Poligrafo, 2015), 128–136.

54 Again, there has been much written on the genderless ideal. For an overview, see Mathew Kuefler, "Desire and the Body in the Patristic Period," in *Oxford Handbook of Theology, Sexuality, and Gender*, ed. Adrian Thatcher (Oxford: Oxford University Press, 2015), 241–254.

9 Monastic superiority, episcopal authority and masculinity in Caesarius of Heisterbach's *Dialogus Miraculorum*

Matthew M. Mesley

Introduction: Episcopal authority

Religious authority was an essential feature of the medieval episcopal office. Yet, although they had power, bishops were held accountable for those whom they governed, and to be effective leaders, they were expected to administer the *cura animarum* for all within their diocese. Indeed, on a diocesan level, their duties included, but were not limited to, an obligation to educate and maintain clerical and monastic standards of learning and behaviour; the former in order to ensure that the laity received reliable and appropriate pastoral care.[1] More broadly, medieval bishops legitimised their role within society by using religious sanctions as a mechanism for maintaining their status and of enforcing political and social order. The eleventh-century Peace of God movement, originally a southern-French phenomenon, is a case in point; through synods, bishops proposed spiritual sanctions for members of the aristocracy who used violence against non-combatants.[2] In seeking such measures, bishops attempted to police what was deemed to be acceptable elite lay behaviour, acting, as it were, as the peacekeepers of medieval society.[3] The understanding of the bishop as a mediator or arbitrator was also reinforced in narratives and images of episcopal sanctity; the function of these sources was often to validate the episcopal office and the religious authority bishops held by illustrating how these men served to engender a united Christian community.[4] Indeed, authors of biographies or saints' lives applied traditional episcopal motifs or *topoi* of sanctity – for example, the reluctant bishop, the protector of orphans and widows, the king's counsellor – in ways that facilitated a model of ideal episcopal behaviour.[5] Writers often did so, however, in response to the specific local and institutional needs of the community for which they wrote.[6] These texts were not necessarily about the bishop *per se* so much as a reflection of how a community envisaged their bishop. By associating depictions of authority with the holy and sacred, such texts highlighted the ways in which contemporaries conceptualised religious power and how they believed it was expected to function. Initially, such ideas were often used to express the charisma and personal authority of individual bishops; from the central Middle

Ages, expectations of how bishops should act increasingly became more prescriptive and routinised. In emphasising the universality of the church, even in the face of specific regional challenges, these models emphasised a shared understanding of the bishop's role, and contributed to what Ian Forrest has labelled the high and late medieval "culture of episcopacy".[7]

This chapter offers an analysis of a thirteenth-century Latin text entitled *Dialogus miraculorum – The Dialogues of Miracles* (hereafter the *DM*), which was written by the Cistercian monk Caesarius of Heisterbach in the diocese of Cologne, Germany.[8] In so doing, it will examine how broader ideals about the religious vocation, subject themselves to variation and reform, are positioned within specific textual contexts. It thus explores a significant aspect of episcopal authority, often neglected in previous studies, and characterized by Bjorn Weiler as the "framework of moral expectations and norms, [or] the cultural and religious horizons of episcopal power".[9] Through an analysis of medieval narratives, we can interrogate the ways in which patterns of episcopal and clerical authority and leadership are conceptualised. We can also consider how religious authority was construed in gendered ways, as male clerical behaviour was often perceived and presented in relation to societal ideals and hierarchical and familial relationships.[10] Gender has been discussed previously in reference to the *DM*, although more often in regards to anxieties about chastity or virginity and the fragility of clerical or monastic masculinity vis-à-vis lay masculinities.[11] Conceptions of religious masculinities were never homogenous, however, and narratives often conveyed arguments or disputes between the religious.[12] This diversity of perspectives highlights how religious men responded in different ways to cultural and social change.

Furthermore, one focus of this chapter is to consider how intra-religious disagreements, while a significant indicator of the polylithic nature of medieval attitudes to authority, were also, in and of themselves, a way of consolidating particular religious identities. It does so primarily by exploring the ways in which Caesarius depicts the thirteenth-century secular church and its personnel. Caesarius used the vocabulary and related imagery of religious authority in order to present particular claims about the monastic life, the role of religion in the public sphere and the relationship between the religious, the clergy and the laity. Narratives such as the *DM* can reveal the ways in which cultural tensions about authority, status and gender were articulated and negotiated; and how religious or social identities were constructed and expressed in didactic texts.

Caesarius of Heisterbach: Themes

In Caesarius's *DM*, members of the church hierarchy are criticised primarily for behaving like their secular peers. Just as religious men were expected to be distinguished visually from the laity, their performance as political actors (and men) also needed to be differentiated. In his criticisms, Caesarius mirrored other thirteenth-century monastic writers who alleged that medieval bishops often used their office, and the authority it imbued, inappropriately in order to amass personal wealth and power.[13] This was not, of course, a new departure; as Julia Barrow has rightly commented, "throughout the entire period of existence of the Church, monastic authors have proclaimed their superior spiritual qualities vis-à-vis those of the clergy".[14] Nevertheless, episcopal misuse of authority and power was a live issue in thirteenth-century Europe; both in England and Germany, archbishops such as Hubert Walter (d. 1205) and Adolf of Altena (at Cologne from 1193 to 1205) were repeatedly censured by both the regular and secular clergy for acting like tyrants or opportunists.[15] Caesarius himself commented that "after the death of Emperor Henry, [Adolf] offered the Empire up for sale, degraded himself with the poison of avarice, and thereby brought many to ruin".[16] The *DM* thus reflects broader misgivings about the behaviour of prominent religious men and particularly the consequences their actions had upon the Universal Church.

An example in the *DM* in which Caesarius highlights existing anxieties about the behaviour of men who held the episcopal office is found in a chapter entitled "Of a clerk who said that German bishops could not be saved" (*De clerico, qui dixit Episcopos Alemanniae non posse salvari*). Here, Caesarius recounts some contemporary gossip that had been voiced against bishops by an anonymous clerk from Paris. The cleric had exclaimed: "I can believe a great deal, but there is one thing I can never believe, namely, that any bishop in Germany can ever be saved!"[17] The apparent reason for his strong assertion is explained in the text:

> Because all the bishops in Germany have both swords committed to them; I mean the temporal power as well as the spiritual; and since they hold the power of life and death, and make wars, they are compelled to be more anxious about the pay of their soldiers than the welfare of the souls committed to their charge.[18]

The statement above, which is also repeated in one of Caesarius's homilies, highlights the doubts that contemporaries felt about bishops who had fallen short of the standards of their office, in part because they acted like territorial lords with temporal powers.[19] In many ways, such criticisms reflected the practice of episcopal lordship. The same ideology promoted by Gregorian reformers of the eleventh century, which had on the one hand promoted the pastoral and spiritual qualities of religious leaders, had also, on the other, tended to stress the participation of the clerical hierarchy in secular affairs and to reiterate their authority vis-à-vis laymen in the temporal as well as spiritual spheres.[20] To take thirteenth-century Germany as an example, (arch)bishops were considered to be comparable to secular princes; entitled princes of the empire (*principes imperii*), they were landowners and vassals of the crown and ruled their own semi-autonomous territories, administering both the legal and economic aspects of their jurisdiction.[21]

They also frequently commanded armies, and as such they had considerable military power.[22] The nature of their office is summed up amply by J. Jeffrey Tyler:

> the medieval German bishop had a vast arsenal of powers, privileges and pontifical functions: he was lord of the city, prince of the empire, and shepherd of the church. His rule could extend from the individual to the corporate, from the local to the national, from the confessional to the marriage bed, from the neighbourhood parish to the market place, the election of town councillors, the formulation of civic foreign policy, and the negotiations of the imperial diet.[23]

It is precisely this "hybrid identity", which in fact tolerated and indeed provided validation to those bishops who identified or were distinguished by the "worldly" aristocratic features of their social milieu, that was problematic for Caesarius. Indeed, in his *vita* of Engelbert, the martyred Archbishop of Cologne, Caesarius sought to resolve this problem by suggesting that the gruesome nature of Engelbert's murder was the principal reason for his claims to sanctity, and that his death made up for his spiritual failings during his lifetime. In many respects, the *vita* is an exposé of Engelbert's lordship and patronage rather than a portrait of his saintliness or religious piety. As such, even as his biographer, Caesarius levelled a number of criticisms at the saint; one passage is particularly revealing of his attitude to Engelbert:

> Being a bishop and a duke, he [Engelbert] paid little attention to the former and was too preoccupied with the latter. Therefore one of our monks said to him: 'My Lord, you are a good duke, but not a good bishop'.[24]

If we return to the "two-sword" example in the *DM*, his thinking is elucidated. Holding both secular and spiritual offices did not necessarily make one an inferior bishop; Caesarius points out that the Cologne Church has had many incumbents who were both bishops and dukes, yet they were still remembered as men of great sanctity. [25] Like many reform-minded writers, Caesarius implies that what had been common in a "Golden-age past" was now sadly a rare phenomenon.

Indeed, although reformers had attempted since the eleventh century to reify the distinctions in lifestyle and behaviour of the clergy and the laity, Caesarius's *DM* reflects an ongoing critique – one of many – of the limitations of reform efforts, yet it simultaneously reveals how contemporaries sought to build upon earlier attempts to revitalise the religious life. Members of the episcopate were a particular concern as they normally came from the same class and lineage as secular magnates, and their actions often tended to blur the line between secular and ecclesiastical politics and between patronage and nepotism.[26] Monastic critics focussed on the coercive power bishops had within a temporal context, but their opinions had a broader traction within medieval society, and criticism came too from those of non-monastic backgrounds – and also from prelates themselves.[27] Indeed, religious self-criticism could itself be vital for institutional renewal, yet such critiques also acted like *apologia* that justified the continuing use of episcopal authority within society. As John H. Mundy astutely points out: "By blaming individuals for falling short, churchmen allayed anxiety about the inherent impossibility of attaining the ideal".[28] At this point it would be fruitful to contextualise Caesarius and the *DM* and to set out the circumstances in which the latter was composed, its function and its intended audience.

Contextualising Caesarius's *Dialogus Miraculorum*

Born around 1180 in Cologne or in its surrounding environs, Caesarius entered the Priory of Heisterbach at around the age of 19. Due to his theological abilities and learning, he was later made master of novices by Abbot Henry (1208–44); a charter dated to around 1219–22 endowed him with this title.[29] Caesarius's worldview was not limited to that of his own monastery, for he often accompanied Abbot Henry during his journeys to other religious houses and to cities and towns within the diocese. Further, both his background and education ensured that he had considerable knowledge of Cologne's history – both of the city and the diocese. His literary fame and reputation as an author ensured a steady stream of patrons; he would be asked to compose a *vita* of Engelbert, Archbishop of Cologne, following his death in 1225; and that of the Hungarian princess Elisabeth of Thüringen (d. 1231), who was canonised shortly after her death in 1235.[30] Caesarius wrote for both internal and external audiences over the course of his life, yet the *DM* is a text that was primarily directed at a Cistercian audience.

The *DM* was a sizeable work and was written over a number of years. The text was divided into two volumes, each of which had six sections, thus 12 distinctions. Each distinction was centred on a particular theme; the first two, for example, were concerned with inner and outer spiritual conversion. The work consisted in total of 746 chapters. We lack specific evidence to know for certain when Caesarius composed the *DM*, but earlier scholars such as Karl Langosch and Fritz Wagner, drawing upon internal evidence from the text, have estimated that Caesarius completed the text in the third decade of the thirteenth century – that is, in the early 1220s.[31] More recent authors, however, have suggested that a lengthier timeframe is more likely.[32]

What was Caesarius's purpose in writing the *Dialogues*? Primarily, it had a hortatory function and was written, in the first instance, for an internal audience of monastic novices. Instead of using complex and sometimes abstract theological arguments, Caesarius was able to illustrate by way of stories and *exempla* the moral precepts and way of life for which a trainee monk should strive.[33] Such *exempla* were used to reiterate what behaviour was deemed to be appropriate, in order that community cohesion and social harmony could be maintained. Caesarius thus also provided examples, both within the cloister and outside, that highlighted specific models of male behaviour that could be imitated or striven for, thus enabling a process that one scholar has termed "monastic socialization".[34] To further this aim, the entire narrative was also constructed as a dialogue between a novice and a more senior monk. This was a traditional didactic tool that had been employed by earlier patristic writers and was a useful way of introducing novices to questions of faith, doctrine and appropriate conduct. In particular, Caesarius patterned the form of his work upon Gregory the Great's widely read *Dialogues* (written ca. 593).[35] However, he also drew inspiration from a wide range of written and oral sources, relying heavily on Cistercian models that had evolved from the twelfth century.[36] Thus, Caesarius employed traditional authorities but combined them with a vocabulary that channelled contemporary monastic ideals in a way that made his material germane for his audience.

Caesarius himself has been used as a reference point for medieval scholars. Certainly, his vivid and detailed stories act as a useful entree into the cultural and religious beliefs of the period. As the *DM*'s editors recently put it, his text provides "ein kaleidoskopartiges Bild der zeitgenössischen Welt".[37] Historical events and figures contemporaneous to Caesarius feature in the *DM*, yet the main focus is upon the interaction between the daily everyday life and challenges of the religious, and the spiritual wonders and the miraculous – visions, confrontations with demons, the sanctity of holy men and women – all of which demonstrate God's intervention in the world. Furthermore, the text's depiction of early thirteenth-century religious life and the values underpinning its *exempla* are necessarily related, although not exclusively, to monastic (if not Cistercian) concerns and interests.[38]

Indeed, at the heart of the *DM* is an oppositional understanding of medieval society, in which the ascetic monastic environment is contrasted to the dangers of the secular world, populated by non-monks (*saecularis*). Thus, of chief importance for those who entered a monastery was the process of *conversio*, in which monks rejected worldly wealth and relationships and at the same time developed their spiritual abilities, coming closer to God and holiness. Yet, as Caesarius amply demonstrates throughout his text, a tension remains; the monastic world was not sealed off from the profane or worldly. This tension can be explored by analysing how Caesarius depicts men who navigated their way from the secular world to a monastic environment. Moreover, it is also emphasised in the criticisms of bishops and the secular clergy, whom in the *DM* are often found wanting when it comes to their responsibilities and duties.[39] Such examples might be dismissed as simply anecdotes, but this ignores the importance of *exempla* to medieval monastic culture and their capacity for conveying contemporary concerns.[40] McGuire has put it rather well: "Caesarius is a handy treasury of stories that reflect the monastic reaction to the situation of the church and the challenges of the secular world of the early thirteenth century".[41] However, these responses did not echo only within monastic circles, as *exempla* "were intended not only to reflect social realities but were also active in shaping those realities".[42] Increasingly from the thirteenth century, in relation to developments in pastoral care, *exempla* were incorporated into sermons and homilies and disseminated to broader audiences – in this way, *exempla* often acted as a bridge between the religious orders and the laity.[43] Cistercians were very much at the vanguard of this new development.[44]

Caesarius of Heisterbach: Conversion and the secular church in the *DM*

While the stories in the *DM* are recounted primarily for a Cistercian audience, they demonstrate that Caesarius also was, in part, sympathetic to non-monastic lifestyles. Before conversion, men came from a number of backgrounds, and Cistercian houses often had entrants from noble or knightly families.[45] In part, such men were attracted to the Cistercian religious culture; indeed, its emphasis upon military imagery and symbols would have appealed to members of the knightly class.[46] While Caesarius is careful to contrast the behaviour and moral standards of the secular and cloistered worlds, he also demonstrates how "knightly values" could be redirected in positive ways within a monastic environment. One device Caesarius uses is gendered "imagery". In other words, his examples highlight how the monastic life was suitable for men from diverse backgrounds, including those who had previously fathered children or had been married.

This was not to say that Caesarius did not emphasise cultural oppositions. In the first distinction, he relates how, when his own abbot Henry had entered Heisterbach (*De conversione Henrici Abbatis*), his brothers had tried to capture him en route in order to prevent his admittance into the monastery. Caesarius states that they did this "because as worldly men they loved the flesh more than spiritual things, the temporal more than the Eternal".[47] Attempts to hinder conversion appear in a number of stories; when Henri de France (1121/1123–1175), the brother of King Louis VII (king from 1137–1180) decided to become a monk shortly after visiting Clairvaux, one of his servants is said to have flown into a rage (*insanum mentisque impotem vociferabatur*) and tried to persuade him against converting.[48] In reading against the grain, we see in these *exempla* how some secular men might have thought that entering into the monastic life was a way of squandering one's opportunities or prospects in life.

Caesarius had to tread a fine line, and one way to do so was to satirise the reasons people had for not converting. For instance, in one story he suggests that living within the monastery was a courageous act in itself. The *exemplum* begins with a conversation between a monk and a knight; the latter is considering entering the monastic orders but admits that he is put off by the monastic dress: "It is the lice that infest your robes: the woollen cloth harbours so much vermin".[49] His friend, a monk, wittily replied "Alas! What a valiant soldier! You whom swords could terrify when fighting for the devil, are you to be frightened by lice now that you are going to be a soldier of Christ".[50]

The reader was meant of course to draw a comparison between this "valiant soldier" and the life within the monastery serving as "a soldier of Christ".[51] Such an anecdote acted to remind those from knightly backgrounds how their lives could be still envisioned as a spiritual battle, and perhaps it also demonstrated, in a light-hearted way, the frivolous concerns of those who remained in the world. It also reiterated the idea that once you entered the monastery, you were supposed to leave behind previous symbols of secular masculinity. Caesarius, for instance, recounts how when one knight decided to convert, he came to the monastery in full armour and undressed in front of the brothers before putting on the habit: "It seemed to him fitting and proper that he should lay down the warlike trappings of the world there where he proposed to assume the garments of a soldier of Christ".[52]

Such a ritual made it clear that while the knight's external appearance might change, his manliness was now contingent on spiritual warfare (*militiam spiritualem*). If these anecdotes were meant to edify and entertain, they nonetheless had a serious point, drawing the attention of the *DM*'s audience to the distinctions and priorities between secular and monastic men: the carnal and temporal temptations of the former, and the spiritual happiness and salvation found within the monastery. The example of one monk, called Theobald, acted as a useful warning: "before his conversion", Theobald had "been reckless and wild, given over to wine and dice, and notorious throughout Cologne for his ridiculous behaviour".[53] Caesarius had even been eyewitness to such events: "often did I myself see him walking along the streets of that city stark naked".[54] Theobald's behaviour, however, changed entirely within the cloister. Nonetheless, as soon as he left to visit his relatives in France, he returned again to his old ways and behaviour. Conversion to the religious life was an on-going process – and, as this *exemplum* suggested, sin was something that one could fall back into without supervision and a like-minded community.[55]

The cloister was intended to be a safe environment where the likelihood of salvation was more assured for its members. Consequently, when describing the secular world, Caesarius is usually more ambiguous; to some extent, the secular clergy or the laity were viewed as tainted by their association and contact with their environment, its trapping and temptations. Caesarius's comments about bishops are enlightening in this respect. As has been mentioned, bishops were expected to act as exemplars of religious behaviour within the world, yet they had responsibilities and obligations in non-religious spheres, which might include commanding armies or providing hospitality for members of the aristocracy. What they prioritised might often seem to be as much influenced by secular concerns as by the traditional ideals of their office. This is why monastic critics often felt that bishops used their authority irresponsibly.[56]

In the *DM*, Caesarius recounts how for one fellow Cistercian, the very thought of being made a bishop was to him unthinkable. We are told that although this monk was elected to a bishopric, he refused to accept the office and died shortly after. In a vision following his death, he spoke to another monk and stated "If I had obeyed and accepted the bishopric, I would have been eternally dammed".[57] He added that "The condition of the Church, has come to this, that it is no longer worthy of being ruled by any but reprobate bishops".[58] In the *DM*, in response to this anecdote, the novice suggests that there exists holy and saintly bishops, but his teacher counters with the argument that poor bishops are far more common, and that good bishops were a rarity. The lack of virtuous episcopal authority, the monk argues, has the effect of inspiring more wickedness (*malitia*) among the laity. Caesarius here adds a verse from the book of Job to reiterate the dangers of worldly bishops: "That the hypocrite reign not, lest the people be ensnared".[59] In this regard, an episcopal tyrant could be thought of as even more dangerous than a secular tyrant, because with the former, people's souls were at stake. A tyrannous bishop, or one who was too involved in politics or the secular world, would naturally fail in his pastoral and sacramental duties; ideally, bishops were, in contrast, expected to act like shepherds who took excellent care of their flock. Indeed, as representatives of divine power on earth, bishops were expected to resist the tyranny or unjust actions of kings and nobles; ecclesiastical tyranny was thus antithetical. In critiquing contemporary bishops, Caesarius appears to be aware that his comments needed to be justified. In his final remark, he states that it is because the episcopate hardly fulfil their pastoral duties – his examples include healing the contrite of heart, hearing their confessions and imposing penances – that it is sometimes fair that their subjects and the sick (*subiectis et infirmis*) judge them to be deficient.[60]

Because the episcopal office was so important, Caesarius shows how any negligence or immoral actions on the part of a bishop had broader consequences for the whole of society. The theme of episcopal tyranny resurfaces on a number of occasions within the *DM*. His description of Leopold (or Lupold), bishop of Worms (1196–1217), is a case in point. Caesarius describes him as "a bishop only in name, in all his actions a tyrant" (*solo quidem nomine Episcopus, opere autem, tyrannus*). He adds that he was a man of extreme vanity, who had no piety, care or reverence for religion.[61] In this way, Caesarius depicts Leopold's character as if it was an inversion of the right order, for even his brother, a member of the nobility, suggested that his behaviour scandalised the laity, and that he acted only in his self-interest. He was so devilish (*diabolicus*) that during the Civil War between the rival claimants to the German throne Otto IV (1175– 19 May 1218) and Philipp of Swabia (1177– 21 June 1208) (respectively of the Welf and Hohenstaufen houses), Leopold laid waste to Mainz without sparing churches or cemeteries. When his soldiers asked him if it was not forbidden to steal from cemeteries, he replied "if you take the bones, first rob the cemeteries".[62] Even after Pope Innocent III sought to remove Leopold's office for the crimes he had committed, he resisted, and under Philip of Swabia's instructions, he marched into Italy with an army in an attempt to re-establish German control.[63] Because of his actions during his lifetime, Caesarius questioned whether Leopold finally found repentance. In this *exemplum*, Caesarius demonstrated the effects of episcopal tyranny and the need for bishops to follow spiritual goals rather than involve themselves in secular affairs or seek secular gains. Leopold's behaviour was no different here from a secular oppressor; the fact that it was the lay people surrounding him who questioned his actions reiterated the inversion of moral and social hierarchies.

It has been noted previously how Caesarius was not only concerned with the monastic orders. McGuire, for instance, convincingly argues that the *DM* "reveal[s] a genuine interest on Caesarius's part in the condition of the laity and the priests who are supposed to be looking after its spiritual needs".[64] Indeed, it is the secular church and its personnel, rather than the laity, that are more often than not the object of Caesarius's criticisms. In part, this again touched upon the behaviour of those who held religious authority and revolved around two interrelated themes: sexual temptations and pastoral care, although the latter was primarily in respect of religious leaders. For the former, Caesarius describes in a few stories how secular priests took mistresses. Sometimes this is simply a supplementary detail – where he mentions as an aside that a priest had a mistress or concubine; on other occasions, he links this to the moral of the story.[65] Yet Caesarius is primarily concerned with how sexual relationships could have serious repercussions for priests who were expected to provide pastoral care to their parishioners. Caesarius's *exempla* suggest that the imposition of clerical celibacy by church reformers was not without its problems.[66]

Yet Caesarius's criticisms of priests also provide an insight into their social worlds, particularly how they were integrated amongst kinship networks and lay communities. Caesarius's story about a priest named Adolphus highlights the complications that arose when the secular clergy did not mark themselves as distinct from the laity and shows that this was particularly evident in respect to pastoral care. Adolphus, we are told, was obsessed with dicing and, during one game, was interrupted a number of times by a parishioner who asked that he give confession to his sick mother. Adolphus refused and complained to a fellow kinsmen and player that the man was disrupting the game. The consequences of his actions were tragic: The sick relative died without absolution or final communion; further, the kinsman crossed the son's path three days later and murdered him after remembering Adolphus's complaint.[67] Although an extreme example, it reiterated two consistent and connected themes of Caesarius's stories: first, a need in respect of behaviour for a separation between the clergy and the laity; and second, how such a distinction in lifestyle was indispensable if pastoral care was to be undertaken appropriately. In terms of religious leaders, this was considered even more desirable due to the number of people in their charge. For example, Caesarius tells the case of an unnamed Bishop of Lombardy who asked the Bishop of Mainz whether he knew all the parishioners in his diocese. When the latter did not provide a satisfactory answer, the former produced a piece of paper that listed all the names of his flock. Even in casting a German bishop once more in a poor light, Caesarius still emphasises the importance of episcopal accountability. His point is made explicit by the "Novice" who, after hearing this story, exclaims "How can one man rule over so many souls without danger?"[68]

Concluding thoughts: Clerical masculinities, gender and authority

How can we use Caesarius's *Dialogus* to think about the question of gender? Discussions of religious masculinities have often focussed upon the relationship between gender and sex rather than on the links between gender, authority and power.[69] Of course, such categories overlap, but a number of recent studies demonstrate how religious authority (and indeed authority in other spheres) could be gendered as much in terms of status, vocation and kinship than its relation to sexual behaviour. It is worth interrogating why scholars of medieval gender and women are less hesitant in exploring these connections. Indeed, as the *exempla* about German bishops highlights, contemporaries were concerned with categorising men and clarifying what their office or status entailed in respect of behaviour and conduct. Throughout the Middle Ages, there was much debate about what was appropriate for religious leaders, whether this concerned their role in warfare, for example, or the extent to which men in positions of religious authority could juggle their spiritual duties at the same time as their secular affairs.[70] In this respect, attitudes towards how certain men performed in office, or judgements related to whether bishops lived according to the ideals of their vocation, were still relevant to the construction of gendered expectations.

Perhaps one problem for those considering the relationship between clerical masculinities, gender and authority is that much of the earlier historiography often considered religious men in the context of their inability to attain a secular ideal of manhood.[71] In a still influential article, written in 1994, Jo Ann McNamara argued that the Western church reforms of the eleventh and twelfth century brought about a crisis in clerical understandings of their own masculinity and place in society. No longer allowed to associate themselves with the symbols of "normative" masculinity (their ability to have offspring or bear arms), they instead sought to fashion a gender ideal that emphasised their sexual self-control and detachment from women.[72] Such ideas remain influential, as even a work published in 2015 appears to articulate changes in understandings of religious men's masculinity as reactive or a response to a biological view of masculinity that was apparently universal.[73] Yet to assume that lay markers of masculinity were always deemed normative components of manhood in every context does not recognise how clerics (celibate or otherwise) always had been significant figures of authority who used equally potent (and gendered) symbols and images to emphasise their power.[74] Sometimes such imagery shared commonalities with what scholars have pinpointed as components of lay masculinity. For example, a cleric or bishop did not need to have children in order to fulfil a fatherly role; neither did he have to bear arms to be considered, as Caesarius demonstrates, as an active soldier in Christ's army.[75] The argument, therefore, that clergy were somehow "failed men"[76] or in "crisis"[77] assumes that there was only a single culturally approved form of masculinity.[78]

Recent scholars stress not only the multiplicity of masculinities, but also, as Steckel and Kluge demonstrate, how cultural understandings of appropriate religious behaviour were subject to ongoing debate and dialogue; much of this dialogue was also not necessarily between secular and religious men but instead reflected competing ideals between different groups of religious men.[79]

Returning to Caesarius's narrative, clearly on one level he is concerned with the superiority of one class of men – monks – over another – the secular clergy. But we see that the more significant dichotomy is not that of the religious versus the laity. Nevertheless, his criticisms of the secular church and bishops do draw attention to the ways in which religious authority was problematised. Authors such as Caesarius used the behaviour of priests and bishops in an oppositional way, as a didactic method; the failure of these men to live up to their vocation was a useful tool for monastic socialization and could be juxtaposed with the benefits accrued by following the prescriptions of monastic male behaviour. The *DM* certainly addresses Heisterbach's own community's concerns and needs, and in this respect, audience and genre is important to reflect upon. Caesarius was directing his *exempla* to a group that would have included men from different ages and backgrounds. Such stories had to be able to speak to different kinds of men; for novices, they reinforced their choice of vocation, but for more mature men, they might act to reassure them of the advantages and compensations of this new life – a way of life in which they could still perform their roles as "knight", "warrior" or "father". Conversion narratives, however, should not be viewed as simply a consequence of an "anxious masculinity" that encouraged monks to counter secular norms. Instead, these texts reflect and play a part in broader cultural dialogues about the relationship between different gradations of power and what was deemed acceptable behaviour.

Narrative representations shine a significant light upon societal expectations and ideals; they demonstrate how contemporaries believed relationships between men should be regulated and measured – whether between subordinates and their superiors, between the laity and the religious or between different groups within the religious. As I have written elsewhere, "cultural understandings of gender are not simply about attributes, but also to do with how symbols work within texts to demarcate and normalise power".[80] The appropriate uses of authority and power were intrinsically tied to contemporary ideas about religious leadership. The themes of accountability and obligation in the *DM* were linked to ideals in which gender played a part; by critiquing how bishops and priests behaved and carried out their duties, contemporaries were able to articulate how and in what manner religious men should rule.

Notes

1 The historiography is vast, but recent works on this topic include Sarah Hamilton, "Bishops, Education, and Discipline", in *The Oxford Handbook of Medieval Christianity*, ed. John H. Arnold (Oxford: Oxford University Press, 2014), 531–549; and John Sabapathy, *Officers and Accountability in Medieval England 1170-1300* (Oxford: Oxford University Press, 2014), 135–158.

2 *The Peace of God: Social Violence and Religious Response in France around the Year 1000,* ed. Thomas Head and Richard Landes (Ithaca, NY, and London: Cornell University Press, 1992); Jehangir Yezdi Malegam, *The Sleep of Behemoth: Disputing Peace and Violence in Medieval Europe, 1000–1200* (Ithaca, NY, and London: Cornell University Press, 2013).

3 For some of the tools they used, excommunication and penance, see Sarah Hamilton, *Church and People in the Medieval West, 900–1200* (London: Routledge, 2013), 322–327.

4 See Sean Gilsdorf, "Preface," in *The Bishop: Power and Piety at the First Millennium*, ed. Sean Gilsdorf (Münster: LIT, 2004), xiii–xvii; John S. Ott, "'Both Mary and Martha': Bishop Lietbert of Cambrai and the Construction of Episcopal Sanctity in a Border Diocese around 1000", in *The Bishop Reformed: Studies of Episcopal Power and Culture in the Central Middle Ages*, ed. John S. Ott and Anna Trumbore Jones (Aldershot and Burlington: Ashgate, 2007), 137–160; and Evan A. Gatti, "Building the Body of Church: A Bishop's Blessing in the Benedictional of Engilmar of Parenzo," in Ott and Trumbore, *The Bishop Reformed*, 92–121.

5 The *topos* of the reluctant bishop is discussed in relation to its impact on understandings of kingship in Björn Weiler, "The *Rex renitens* and the Medieval Idea of Kingship, ca. 900–ca. 1250," *Viator* 31 (2000): 1–42. Gratian's important twelfth-century *Decretum* would enshrine the idea of bishops as protectors of the poor and weak, but this image was already well established: Miri Rubin, *Charity and Community in Medieval Cambridge* (Cambridge: Cambridge University Press, 1987), 238. For the bishop as king's counsellor, see n. 9.

6 See Matthew M. Mesley, *The Construction of Episcopal Identity: The Meaning and Function of Episcopal Depictions within Latin Saints' Lives of the Long Twelfth Century*. (PhD diss., University of Exeter, 2010).

7 Ian Forrest, "Continuity and Change in the Institutional Church," in *The Oxford Handbook of Medieval Christianity*, ed. John H. Arnold (Oxford: Oxford University Press, 2014), 192.

8 The text was initially edited in *Caesarii Heisterbacensis monachi ordinis Cisterciensis Dialogus miraculorum*, ed. Joseph Strange, 2 vols. (Cologne, Bonn and Brussels: H. Lempertz and Co, 1851). An English translation has been provided in *The Dialogue on Miracles*, trans. H. von E. Scott and C. C. Swinton Bland, 2 vols. (London: Routledge, 1929). There are, however, some omissions in the latter. The latest edition is Caesarius of Heisterbach, *Dialogus Miraculorum*, ed. and German trans. Nikolaus Nösges and Horst Schneider, 5 vols. (Turnhout: Brepols, 2009).

9 Björn Weiler, "Bishops and Kings in England, c. 1066–c. 1215," in *Religion und Politik im Mittelalter / Religion and Politics in the Middle Ages*, ed. Ludger Körntgen and Dominik Waßenhoven (Berlin and Boston: de Gruyter, 2013), 162.

10 See, in particular, Megan McLaughlin, *Sex, Gender, and Episcopal Authority in an Age of Reform, 1000–1122* (New York and Cambridge: Cambridge

University Press, 2010) and Christopher Fletcher, "Manhood, Kingship and the Public in Late Medieval England," *Edad Media. Revista De Historia* 13 (2012): 123–142.

11 Eva Niklesová, "Frauen und Männer im Dialogus miraculorum des Caesarius von Heisterbach," *Graeco-Latina Brunensia* 15, no. 1 (2010): 65–85; and Jacqueline Murray, "Masculinizing Religious Life: Sexual Prowess, The Battle for Chastity and Monastic Identity," in *Holiness and Masculinity in the Middle Ages*, ed. P. H. Cullum and Katherine J. Lewis (Cardiff: Cardiff University Press, 2004), 24–42. The latter uses Caesarius and a number of other twelfth and thirteenth-century writers in an article that explores internal monastic masculinities.

12 Derek Neal, "What can Historians do with Clerical Masculinity? Lessons from Medieval Europe," in *Negotiating Clerical Identities: Priests, Monks and Masculinity in the Middle Ages*, ed. Jennifer D. Thibodeaux (Basingstoke and New York: Palgrave Macmillan, 2010), 16–36; Matthew M. Mesley, "Episcopal Authority and Gender in the Narratives of the First Crusade," in *Religious Men and Masculine Identity in the Middle Ages*, ed. P. H. Cullum and Katherine J. Lewis (Woodbridge: Boydell and Brewer, 2013), 94–111. Further literature is cited throughout the essay.

13 Paul B. Pixton, *The German Episcopacy and the Implementation of the Decrees of the Fourth Lateran Council, 1216–1245: Watchmen on the Tower* (Leiden, New York and Cologne: Brill, 1995), 90–183. The misuse of tithes was a particular complaint that bishops faced: John Eldevik, *Episcopal Power and Ecclesiastical Reform in the German Empire: Tithes, Lordship and Community, 950–1150* (Cambridge: Cambridge University Press, 2012), 62–102. For early medieval precedent, see J. J. Contreni, "'By Lions, Bishops are Meant; By Wolves, Priests': History, Exegesis, and the Carolingian Church in Haimo of Auxerre's Commentary on Ezechiel," *Francia: Forschungen zur westeuropäischen Geschichte* 29 (2002): 29–52.

14 Julia Barrow, *The Clergy in the Medieval World: Secular Clerics, Their Families and Careers in North-Western Europe, c. 800–c. 1200* (Cambridge: Cambridge University Press, 2015), 4.

15 For the English context, see Hugh M. Thomas, *The Secular Clergy in England, 1066–1216* (Oxford: Oxford University Press, 2014), 81–86, 114–116 and 139–153; and for Adolf, see Hugo Stehkämper, "Über das Motiv der Thronstreit-Entscheidungen des Kölner Erzbischofs Adolf von Altena 1198–1205: Freiheit der fürstlichen Königswahl oder Aneignung des Mainzer Erstkurrechts?" *Rheinische Vierteljahrsblätter* 67 (2003): 1–20.

16 Cited from Pixton, *The German Episcopacy*, 99.

17 Nösges and Schneider, *Dialogus Miraculorum*, 1:466–467: "Omnia credere possum, sed non possum credere, quod unquam aliquis Episcopus Alemanniae possit salvari".

18 Ibid. "Quid pene omnes Episcopi Alemanniae utrumque habent gladium, spiritualem videlicet et materialem: et quia de sanguine iudicant et bella exercent magis eos sollicitos esse oportet de stipendiis militum, quam de salute animarum sibi commissarum". The "Two Swords Doctrine" was originally used by Pope Gelasian I in a letter he wrote to Emperor Anastasius I in 494, in which he stated that the world was governed by royal authority and sacred authority. From the eleventh century, church reformers increasingly interpreted Gelasian's ideas in order to promote the superiority of papal power over secular authority. It was also used, as here, to describe the often overlapping duties of medieval bishops. See I. S. Robinson, *The Papacy, 1073–1198: Continuity and Innovation* (Cambridge: Cambridge University Press, 1990), 295–321. The image appears also in Caesarius' *Vita Engelberti*: see *Vita et Miracula Engelberti*, ed. Fritz Zschaeck, in *Die Wundergeschichten des Caesarius von Heisterbach*, ed. Alfons Hilka (Bonn: Hanstein, 1937), 3:242.

19 Caesarius of Heisterbach "Dominica secunda post pascha," in *Homiliae Festivae*, ed. Joannes A. Coppenstein (Cologne: P. Henningius, 1615), 2, 99.
20 Maureen C. Miller, "Religion Makes a Difference: Clerical and Lay Cultures in the Courts of Northern Italy, 1000–1300," *American Historical Review* 105 (2000): 1095–1130.
21 The historiography is vast, but for the German background, see Timothy Reuter, "A Europe of Bishops: The Age of Wulfstan of York and Burchard of Worms," in *Patterns of Episcopal Power: Bishops in 10th and 11th Century Western Europe/ Strukturen bischöflicher Herrschaft im westlichen Europa des 10. und 11. Jahrhunderts*, ed. Ludger Körntgen and Dominik Waßenhoven (Berlin and Boston: de Gruyter, 2011), 17–38; Benjamin Arnold, "Episcopal Authority Authenticated and Fabricated: Form and Function in Medieval German Bishops' Catalogues", in *Warriors and Churchmen in the High Middle Ages: Essays Presented to Karl Leyser*, ed. Timothy Reuter (London and Rio-Grande: Hambledon Press, 1992), 63–78; Benjamin Arnold, *Count and Bishop in Medieval Germany: A Study in Regional Power 1100–1350* (Philadelphia: University of Pennsylvania Press, 1991); Benjamin Arnold, *Princes and Territories in Medieval Germany* (Cambridge: Cambridge University Press, 1991); and Eldevik, *Episcopal Power and Ecclesiastical Reform.* Also useful as a comparative study is Björn Weiler, *Kingship, Rebellion and Political Culture: England and Germany, c. 1215–c. 1250* (New York: Palgrave MacMillan, 2011).
22 Timothy Reuter, "Episcopi cum sua militia: The Prelate as Warrior in the Early Staufer Era," in Reuter, *Warriors and Churchmen in the High Middle Ages*, 79–94; Benjamin Arnold, "German Bishops and their Military Retinues in the Medieval Empire," *German History* 7 (1989): 161–183. This was not specific to Germany however; Craig M. Nakashian, "The Political and Military Agency of Ecclesiastical Leaders in Anglo-Norman England," *Journal of Medieval Military History* 12 (Woodbridge, 2014): 51–80.
23 J. Jeffrey Tyler, *Lord of the Sacred City: The Episcopus Exclusus in Late Medieval and Early Modern Germany* (Leiden, Boston and Cologne: Brill, 1999), 21.
24 "Cum episcopus esset ex dux, minus illus intendebat et ad ista nimis descendebat, ita ut quidam monachorum nostrorum illi diceret: Domine vos estis bonus dux, sed non bonus episcopus", *Vita et Miracula Engelberti*, ed. Zschaeck, 3:90–91. A useful study of Engelbert's death as depicted in the *vita* is Jacqueline E. Jung, "From Jericho to Jerusalem: The Violent Transformation of Archbishop Engelbert of Cologne," in *Last Things: Death and the Apocalypse in the Middle Ages*, ed. Caroline Walker Bynum and Paul H. Freedman (Philadelphia: University of Pennsylvania Press, 2000), 60–82. Michael Goodich suggests that Caesarius' preface to the *vita* has a somewhat "grudging tone"; Michael Goodich, *Vita Perfecta: The Ideal of Sainthood in the Thirteenth-Century* (Stuttgart: Hiersemann, 1981), 63.
25 Nösges and Schneider, *Dialogus Miraculorum*, 1:466–467: "Invenimus tamen ex Episcopis Coloniensibus, qui Pontifices simul fuerunt et Duces, aliquos fuisse sanctos, beatum videlicet Brunonem, sanctum Heribertum et sanctum Annonem".
26 For an earlier perspective on this hybrid position, see C. Stephen Jaeger, "The Courtier Bishop in *Vitae* from the Tenth to the Twelfth Century," *Speculum* 58 (1983): 291–325; C. Stephen Jaeger, *The Origins of Courtliness: Civilizing Trends and the Formation of Courtly Ideals, 939–1210* (Philadelphia: University of Pennsylvania Press, 1985).
27 See John D. Cotts, *The Clerical Dilemma: Peter of Blois and Literate Culture in the Twelfth Century* (Washington, DC: The Catholic University of America Press, 2009), *passim.*
28 John H. Mundy, *Europe in the High Middle Ages 1150–1300*, 3rd edition (New York and Abingdon: Routledge, 2000), 335.

29 Nösges and Schneider, *Dialogus miraculorum*, 47. McGuire, however, suggests that although he may have been master of novices earlier in the thirteenth century, he was unlikely to have occupied the office at the time of writing the *Dialogus miraculorum*: Brian Patrick McGuire, "Friends and Tales in the Cloister: Oral Sources in Caesairus of Heisterbach's *Dialogus Miraculorum,*" *Analecta Cisterciensia* 36 (1980): 172. For the office, see Mirko Breitenstein, "The Novice Master in the Cistercian Order," in *Generations in the Cloister: Youth and Age in Medieval Religious Life/Generationen im Kloster. Jugend und Alter in der mittelalterlichen vita religiosa*, ed. Sabine von Heusinger and Annette Kehnel (Zürich and Münster: LIT, 2008), 145–155.

30 Both works are found in Hilka's edition *Die Wundergeschichten des Caesarius von Heisterbach*, ed. Alfons Hilka (Bonn: Hanstein, 1937), vol. 3.

31 Nösges and Schneider, *Dialogus miraculorum*, 59–60; see Karl Langosch, "Caesarius von Heisterbach," in *Die Deutsche Literatur des Mittelalters: Verfasserlexikon*, ed. Wolfgang Stammler and Karl Langosch, 2nd rev. ed. (Berlin: de Gruyter, 1978), 1:1152–1168; and Fritz Wagner, "Studien zu Caesarius von Heisterbach," *Analecta Cisterciensia* 29 (1973): 79–95.

32 McGuire, "Friends and Tales in the Cloister," 198. Brian Patrick McGuire provides a credible hypothesis, suggesting the following schema: Distinction 1 was written in 1219; Distinctions 2–5 in 1220; Distinctions 6–9 in 1221; and Distinctions 10–12 in 1222, with the final editing and completion in 1223. Nösges and Schneider are generally in agreement with McGuire but suggest that the text may have evolved from an earlier starting date, with Caesarius beginning to collect *exempla* from as early as 1214; Nösges and Schneider, *Dialogus miraculorum*, 64–65.

33 He also followed a Cistercian tradition in this respect: Brian Patrick McGuire, "Written Sources and Cistercian Inspiration in Caesarius of Heisterbach," *Analecta Cisterciensia* 35 (1979): 227–282. See also, for the importance of remembering, Victoria Smirnova, "'And Nothing will be wasted': Actualization of the Past in Caesarius of Hesiterbach's *Dialogus Miraculorum*," in *The Making of Memory in the Middle Ages*, ed. Lucie Doležalová (Leiden and Boston: Brill, 2010), 253–265.

34 McGuire, "Friends and Tales in the Cloister," 191. Furthermore, through *exempla*, Caesarius was able to demonstrate God's active intervention in the world and how one's actions inevitably affected both one's life and life after death.

35 For Latin examples of this period, including Caesarius' *Dialogus miraculorum*, see Carmen Cardelle de Hartmann, *Lateinische Dialoge, 1200–1400: Literaturhistorische Studie und Repertorium* (Leiden and Boston: Brill, 2007). For how dialogues were used within monastic houses at the time, see Mirko Breitenstein, "'Ins Gespräch gebracht': der Dialog als Prinzip monastischer Unterweisung," in *Understanding Monastic Practices of Oral Communication*, ed. Steven Vanderputten (Turnhout: Brepols, 2011), 205–229.

36 Discussed thoroughly by McGuire, "Written Sources and Cistercian Inspiration in Caesarius of Heisterbach".

37 Nösges and Schneider, *Dialogus miraculorum*, 1:59.

38 For a few examples of scholars looking at particular themes within the *Dialogus miraculorum*, see William J. Purkis, "Crusading and Crusade Memory in Caesarius of Heisterbach's *Dialogus miraculorum*," *Journal of Medieval History* 39 (2013): 100–127; Steven Justice, "Eucharistic Miracles and Eucharistic Doubt," *Journal of Medieval and Early Modern Studies* 42 (2012): 307–322; Hans Peter Broedel, "Gratuitous Examples and the Grateful Dead: Appropriation and Negotiation of Traditional Narratives in Medieval Exemplary Ghost Stories," in *Translatio, Or the Transmission of Culture in*

the Middle Ages and the Renaissance: Modes and Messages, ed. Laura H. Hollengreen (Turnhout: Brepols, 2008), 97–122; and Barbara Bombi, "The Authority of Miracles: Caesarius of Heisterbach and the Livonian Crusade," in *Aspects of Power and Authority in the Middle Ages*, ed. Brenda M. Bolton and Christine E. Meek (Turnhout: Brepols, 2007), 305–325.

39 Such criticisms perhaps reflect the limitations of earlier efforts to reform the secular clergy in the light of the eleventh-century reform movements.

40 For a survey on this genre, see Nigel F. Palmer, "Exempla," in *Medieval Latin: An Introduction and Bibliographical Guide*, ed. Frank. A. C. Mantello and A. G. Rigg (Washington, DC: Catholic University of America Press, 1996), 583–588. As he states, "Collections of exempla were useful treasure houses of tales that could be extracted for use in preaching and religious instruction" (584).

41 For the wider Cistercian *exempla* genre, see Brian Patrick McGuire, "Cistercian Storytelling – A Living Tradition: Surprises in the World of Research," *Cistercian Studies Quarterly* 39 (2004): 281–309.

42 Spencer E. Young, "More Blessed to Give *and* Receive: Charitable Giving in Thirteenth- and Early Fourteenth-Century *Exempla*," in *Experiences of Charity, 1250–1650*, ed. Anne M. Scott (Farnham: Ashgate, 2015), 71.

43 Leonard E. Boyle, "The Fourth Lateran Council and Manuals of Popular Theology," in *The Popular Literature of Medieval England*, ed. Thomas J. Heffernan (Knoxville: University of Tennessee Press, 1985), 30–43. Increasingly, however, scholars have shown that these developments were occurring prior to 1215 (Lateran IV).

44 Brian Patrick McGuire, "The Cistercians and the Rise of the 'Exemplum' in Early Thirteenth-Century France: A Reevaluation of *Paris BN MS lat. 15912*," *Classica et Mediaevalia* 34 (1983): 211–267.

45 Constance H. Berman, *The Cistercian Evolution: The Invention of a Religious Order in Twelfth-Century Europe* (Philadelphia, University of Pennsylvania Press, 2000).

46 For background, see Martha G. Newman, *The Boundaries of Charity: Cistercian Culture and Ecclesiastical Reform 1098–1180* (Stanford: Stanford University Press, 1996), 24–37.

47 Nösges and Schneider, *Dialogus miraculorum*, 1:244–245: "et sicut homines saeculares carnalia spiritualibus et temporalia aeternis praeponentes".

48 Ibid., 1:260–265.

49 Ibid., 2:788–789: "Vermiculi vestimentorum. Pannus enim laneus multos vermiculos nutrit".

50 Ibid. "Och fortem militem! Qui in bello diaboli non timuit gladios, in militia Christi timere debet pediculos?".

51 For the interaction between monastic and knightly culture, see Katherine Allen Smith, *War and the Making Medieval Monastic Culture* (Woodbridge: Boydell and Brewer, 2011); and Richard W. Kaeuper, *Holy Warrior: The Religious Ideology of Chivalry* (Philadelphia: University of Pennsylvania Press, 2009).

52 Nösges and Schneider, *Dialogus miraculorum*, 1:314–315: "Visum est ei congruum, ibi militiam deponere saecularem, ubi assumere proponebat militiam spiritualem".

53 Ibid., 4:682–685: "ante conversionem leccator opere, vino et tesseribus deditus totus, et propter suam scurrilitatem in tota civitate Coloniensi notissimus".

54 Ibid., "Saepe illum nudum per plateas eiusdum civitatis incedere vidi".

55 Newman, *The Boundaries of Charity*, 16–19. G. R. Evans, *Bernard of Clairvaux* (Oxford and New York: Oxford University Press, 2000), 23–27.

56 For the German context for these criticisms, see Pixton, *The German Episcopacy*, 93–100.

57 Nösges and Schneider, *Dialogus miraculorum*, 2:468–469: "Si obediens fuissem, et Episcopatum illum suscepissem, damnatus essem aeternaliter".

58 Ibid. "Ad hoc ... iam devenit status Ecclesiae, ut non sit digna regi, nisi a reprobis Episcopis".

59 Ibid., 470–471: "Qui regnare facit hypocritam propter peccata populi".

60 Ibid., 468–469: "Unde quia pauci nostri temporis Episcopi in tali physica student, et practicam eius minus exercent, iuste aliquando a subiectis et infirmis iudicantur".

61 Ibid., 392–393: "Hic cum esset vanissimus nil in se habens pietatis, nil religiositatis". For Lupold, see Friedrich Knöpp, "Lupold, Bischof von Worms 1196–1217," in *Die Reichsabtei Lorsch. Festschrift zum Gedenken an ihre Stiftung 764*, ed. Friedrich Knöpp (Darmstadt: Hessische Historische Kommission, 1973), 1:361–366.

62 The full quotation is given. Ibid., pp. 394–395: "Et cum ei milites sui dicerent: 'Domine, non licet nobis spoliare cimiteria'; respondit: 'Si ossa mortuorum tollitis, tunc primum cimiteria spoliatis'".

63 David Abulafia, *Frederick II: A Medieval Emperor* (New York and Oxford: Oxford University Press, 1988), 105.

64 McGuire, "Friends and Tales in the Cloister", 231.

65 Such stories have been examined by Dyan Elliott, *Fallen Bodies: Pollution, Sexuality, and Demonology in the Middle Ages* (Philadelphia: University of Pennsylvania Press, 1999), 107–126.

66 Ibid., 81–126. Also, for example, Christopher Nugent Lawrence Brooke, "Gregorian Reform in Action: Clerical Marriage in England, 1050–1200", in *Medieval Church and Society: Collected Essays* (London: Sidgwick and Jackson Limited, 1971), 69–99; and Monique Vleeschouwers-Van Melkebeek, "Mandatory Celibacy and Priestly Ministry in the Diocese of Tournai at the End of the Middle Ages," in *Peasants and Townsmen in Medieval Europe: Studia in Honorem Adriaan Verhulst,* ed. Jean-Marie Duvosquel and Erik Thoen (Ghent: Snoeck-Ducaju and Zoon, 1995), 681–692.

67 Nösges and Schneider, *Dialogus miraculorum*, 4:1635–1637.

68 Ibid., 472–473: "Quomodo ergo unus homo tot animas regere posset sine periculo?".

69 Clearly sex, gender and power could also interact. See Joyce E. Salisbury, "Gendered Sexuality," in *Handbook of Medieval Sexuality*, ed. Vern L. Bullough and James A. Brundage (New York and London: Garland Publishing, 1996), 81–102. See also McLaughlin, *Sex, Gender, and Episcopal Authority*.

70 Much has been written from a gendered perspective on the relationship between religious authority and women – see the following excellent collections: *Gendering the Master Narrative: Women and Power in the Middle Ages*, ed. Mary C. Erler and Maryanne Kowaleski (Ithaca, New York: Cornell University Press, 2003); and *Negotiating Community and Difference in Medieval Europe: Gender, Power, Patronage and the Authority of Religion in Latin Christendom*, ed. Katherine Allen Smith and Scott Wells (Leiden: Brill, 2009). Similar studies for men remain few, but an excellent exception is *Negotiating Clerical Identities: Priests, Monks and Masculinity in the Middle Ages*, ed. Jennifer D. Thibodeaux (Basingstoke and New York: Palgrave Macmillan, 2010). As I hope to have made clear, although in the *Dialogus Miraculorum* the sexual behaviour of bishops might not be highlighted, this did not mean that the stories or images used have no gendered connotations.

71 Recent trends against this include Derek G. Neal, *The Masculine Self in late Medieval England* (Chicago: Chicago University Press, 2008). See also Jennifer

D. Thibodeaux, "Man of the Church or Man of the Village? Gender and the Parish Clergy in Medieval Normandy," *Gender and History* 18 (2006): 380–399.

72 Jo Ann McNamara, "The Herrenfrage: The Restructuring of the Gender System, 1050–1150," in *Medieval Masculinities: Regarding Men in the Middle Ages*, ed. Claire A. Lees (Minneapolis: University of Minnesota Press, 1994), 3–29. See also Dyan Elliott, "Pollution, Illusion, Masculine Disarray: Nocturnal Emissions and the Sexuality of the Clergy," in *Constructing Medieval Sexuality*, ed. Karma Lochrie, Peggy McCraken and James A. Schultz (Minneapolis: University of Minnesota Press, 1998), 1–23. See, for instance, the criticisms of Simon Yarrow, "Prince Bohemond, Princess Melaz, and the Gendering of Religious Difference in the *Ecclesiastical History* of Orderic Vitalis," in *Intersections of Gender, Religion and Ethnicity in the Middle Ages*, ed. Cordelia Beattie and Kirsten A. Fenton (London: Palgrave MacMillan, 2010), 140–157.

73 Michelle M. Sauer, *Gender in Medieval Culture* (London and New York: Bloomsbury, 2015).

74 See Thibodeaux, "Introduction: Rethinking the Medieval Clergy and Masculinity," *Negotiating Clerical Identities*, 1–15; and McLaughlin, *Sex, Gender, and Episcopal Authority, passim.* At the same time, writers could also use female symbols to represent male authority and holiness. See Caroline Walker Bynum, *Holy Feast and Holy Fast: The Religious Significance of Food to Medieval Women* (Berkeley and Los Angeles: University of California Press, 1987), 282–288.

75 For example, see Megan McLaughlin, "The Bishop as Bridegroom: Marital Imagery and Clerical Celibacy in the Eleventh and Early Twelfth Centuries," in *Medieval Purity and Piety: Essays on Medieval Clerical Celibacy and Religious Reform*, ed. M. Frassetto (New York: Garland Publishing, 1998), 209–229; and Matthew M. Mesley, "Episcopal Authority and Gender in the Narratives of the First Crusade," in Cullum and Lewis, *Religious Men and Masculine Identity*, 94–113.

76 This is not to say that there were not marginalized forms of masculinity within the medieval period but that being a member of the religious classes did not automatically entail such marginalization.

77 As Ruth Mazo Karras states, "Scholars tend to identify the period of their own focus as the important turning point, the period of crisis and resolution, of revolutionary change". Ruth Mazo Karras, *From Boys to Men: Formations of Masculinity in Late Medieval Europe* (Philadelphia, University of Pennsylvania, 2003), 8.

78 Fenton argues for "a common language of masculinity being used by both lay and clerical men". Kirsten A. Fenton, "The Question of Masculinity in William of Malmesbury's Presentation of Wulfstan of Worcester," *Anglo-Norman Studies* 28 (2006): 136.

79 See, for instance, Jennifer D. Thibodeaux, "The Defence of Clerical Marriage: Religious Identity and Masculinity in the Writings of Anglo-Norman Clerics," in Cullum and Lewis, *Religious Men and Masculine Identity*, 46–63.

80 Mesley, "Episcopal Authority and Gender", 97.

10 The chief harem eunuch of the Ottoman empire

Servant of the sultan, servant of the Prophet

Jane Hathaway

This chapter focuses on the chief harem eunuch of the Ottoman empire, an office that existed from 1588 through to 1909 and exercised a vast degree of political and economic influence. Here, in particular, I consider the often-overlooked spiritual and sacral components of the chief eunuch's functions. Following a brief overview of the employment of eunuchs in pre-modern empires, both Islamic and otherwise, I examine the increasing centrality of the harem, and thus the chief harem eunuch, to the functioning of the Ottoman imperial palace and the continuation of the Ottoman dynasty. This service to the dynasty was mirrored in the chief eunuch's service to the Prophet Muḥammad. The office of chief harem eunuch was, from its inception, linked to the supervision of the imperial pious foundations for the Muslim holy cities of Mecca and Medina. Beginning in the late eleventh/seventeenth century, moreover, former chief eunuchs routinely led the corps of eunuchs who guarded the Prophet Muḥammad's tomb in Medina; this posting typically capped decades of establishing religious schools and other pious endowments that underlined the chief eunuch's role in the dissemination of state-sponsored Sunni Islam. At the end of his life, the chief eunuch might well be buried in Istanbul's ancient Eyüp Cemetery, named for the Prophet Muḥammad's standard-bearer, around whose tomb the cemetery was built. Thus, the chief eunuch's entire career, and indeed his office, embodied a life-long devotion to the Ottoman sultan, to the continuing prosperity of the dynasty he represented, to the Prophet Muḥammad and to the cultivation and regeneration of the Muslim community.

Eunuchs in global perspective

As many of the other contributions to this volume will have demonstrated, eunuchs, or castrated men, were employed at the courts of most pre-modern Asian and Mediterranean empires as well as in many African kingdoms. Their use dates at least to the first millennium BC. Smooth-cheeked eunuchs appear alongside heavily bearded monarchs and warriors in the famous stone friezes carved by the masons of the Neo-Assyrian empire, which ruled much of what are now Iraq and Syria from the tenth through the seventh century

BC, to commemorate royal battle victories and hunts.[1] Both the biblical book of Esther and the ancient Greek historian Herodotus (ca. 484–425 BC) describe eunuchs at the court of the Persian Achaemenid empire.[2] Roman and Byzantine eunuchs are familiar from both imperial chronicles and physical depictions on sarcophagi and in mosaics.[3] In China, meanwhile, eunuchs date to the Zhou dynasty (ca. 1045–221 BC).[4] The great exceptions to this global use of eunuchs were the various kingdoms of western Europe, on the one hand, and Pharaonic Egypt, on the other – although eunuchs would have been introduced to Egypt during the rule of the Ptolemaic dynasty, which took control of the region in the wake of Alexander the Great's death in 323 BC.[5]

So far as sub-Saharan Africa is concerned, the earliest mention of eunuchs appears in the New Testament book of Acts, which describes "a man of Ethiopia, an eunuch of great authority under Candace queen of the Ethiopians, who had the charge of all her treasure" (Acts 8:27). This man, apparently a Jew, was converted to Christianity by St Philip the Evangelist while on the way back from a pilgrimage to Jerusalem. Although the verse portrays the eunuch as Ethiopian, he would more logically have come from the kingdom of Kush in what is now Sudan. Candace, or Kandake, was the title of Kush's queen, and indeed, 11 Kandakes ruled Kush between the fourth century BC and the fourth century AD.[6]

In Ethiopia itself, which converted to Christianity in the fourth century AD, church law prohibited castration. As a result, the only eunuchs employed at the Ethiopian court were apparently prisoners of war who had been castrated in enemy territory, while uncastrated males held offices that entailed close proximity to the ruler.[7] In contrast, both Muslim and non-Muslim kingdoms and empires in other parts of sub-Saharan Africa during the medieval and early modern eras employed eunuchs, whom they usually acquired from the marginal regions of their own domains or from neighbouring polities, whether in warfare or through trade.[8]

Eunuchs in Islamic empires

Following the pattern of ancient Near Eastern and Mediterranean empires, early Islamic dynasties, beginning with the Umayyads (41–132/661–750), employed eunuchs at their courts. Unfortunately, records of the Umayyad court are so meagre as to preclude reliable conclusions about the dynasty's use of eunuchs. The Abbasid empire (132–656/750–1258), however, clearly established lasting patterns in terms of the provenances of the eunuchs it employed and the roles they fulfilled; many of these, in turn, derived from the usages of earlier, pre-Islamic empires, above all those of the Byzantines and the Sasanians. As with virtually all pre-modern empires in the eastern hemisphere (excluding western Europe), the Abbasids acquired eunuchs, as well as uncastrated slaves, from the peripheries of the territories that they ruled or from outside their domains entirely. Central Asia, Iran, East

Africa, and India were key pools of Abbasid eunuchs, as was the apparently Slavic population known as Ṣaqāliba in south-eastern Europe.[9] Abbasid court eunuchs served as companions to the caliph, military commanders, educators of princes and guardians of the imperial harem. Eunuchs of all the above-mentioned provenances could serve as caliphs' companions or as keepers of the royal treasury, a duty assigned to eunuchs since remote antiquity, presumably because of their reputation for unwavering loyalty to the dynasties that employed them. On the other hand, eunuchs of Central Asian or Iranian origin were more likely to serve as military commanders, while those of African, Indian, or Ṣaqāliba origin tended to serve as princes' tutors, harem guardians, and supervisors of young, uncastrated male slaves. All eunuchs, regardless of provenance or function, were apparently radically castrated; that is, their genitalia were removed in their entirety, in contrast to Byzantine practice, which allowed eunuchs to retain their penises.[10]

Semi-autonomous regional powers under the Abbasids' aegis followed the Abbasids' lead in employing eunuchs in the roles just mentioned, with similar ethno-regional occupational distinctions. Thus, for the most notable examples, we find East African, and occasionally Indian and Ṣaqāliba, harem eunuchs at the courts of the Būyids, who ruled Iran and Iraq from 334–447/945–1055; the Great Seljuqs, who displaced them in these regions in 447/1055 and dominated through the end of the sixth/twelfth century; the Sāmānids, who governed Transoxiana during the third/ninth and fourth/tenth centuries; and the Ghaznavids, who dominated north-eastern Iran, Afghanistan and northern India during the fifth/eleventh and sixth/twelfth centuries.[11] Meanwhile, the Abbasids' arch-enemies, the Isma'ili Shi'i Fatimid caliphs, who carved out a rival empire in North Africa in the early fourth/tenth century, eventually conquering Egypt, Syria and the Muslim holy cities of Mecca and Medina in the Arabian peninsula, employed corps of both East African and Ṣaqāliba eunuchs that numbered in the thousands.[12]

The Mamluk sultans, a Sunni regime that ruled Egypt, Syria, south-eastern Anatolia, and the Muslim holy cities from 648/1250 until their conquest by the Ottomans in 922/1516–17, followed this template as well. However, they also began to acquire eunuchs from new locales and introduced new duties to their repertory of functions. Taking advantage of their proximity to East African slave-trade routes, the early Mamluks appear to have acquired unprecedentedly large numbers of Ethiopian eunuchs, in particular from the Muslim kingdom of Hadiya in what is now south-western Ethiopia; castration was carried out at the town of Washilu within Hadiya's territory.[13] (Production of eunuchs at this location ceased when the kingdom of Ethiopia conquered Hadiya in 732/1332.) They likewise acquired eunuchs from India, although exactly what part is unclear; and, like so many empires before them, from the Greek-speaking population of Anatolia.

As part of their distinctive military infrastructure, the Mamluks introduced a new eunuch office, that of *muqaddam al-mamālik al-sulṭāniyya* ("chief of the sultan's mamluks [military slaves]"), who supervised the training of new mamluk recruits and, in the process, prevented sexual abuse of new recruits by older mamluks.[14] Though an innovative office, it was clearly a variation on the traditional eunuch role of educator of princes or supervisor of male pages. On the other hand, eunuchs generally did not serve as military commanders under the Mamluk Sultanate.

Ottoman court eunuchs

Well before the Ottomans absorbed the territories of the Mamluk Sultanate in 922/1516–17, they had been influenced by Mamluk court culture, including some of the Mamluks' methods of employing eunuchs. However, what we might call Ottoman "eunuch culture" was also affected by other traditions that did not influence the Mamluks, above all those of the Byzantine empire, with which the Ottomans were in constant contact (and conflict) during the first two centuries of their empire's existence. The first eunuchs to serve at the Ottoman court, as at the courts of other Turkish emirates in western Anatolia, were almost certainly Byzantine, acquired either in warfare or through purchase. The second Ottoman sultan, Orhan (r. 726–63/1326–62), famously bequeathed the Anatolian village of Mekece, including a sufi lodge, to a manumitted eunuch named Muqbil, who was almost certainly of Byzantine origin.[15] During this early period, Ottoman envoys occasionally presented Rūmī, or Anatolian Greek, slaves, presumably acquired from the Byzantines, to the Mamluk sultan as gifts;[16] these may have included eunuchs. The introduction in the late eighth/fourteenth or early ninth/fifteenth century of the *devşirme* – the distinctive Ottoman system of "collecting" Christian boys from villages in the Balkans and Anatolia, converting them to Islam and training them for military or administrative service – guaranteed a steady supply of eunuchs for service as the sultan's companions and military commanders. A number of the boys chosen for the palace were castrated, although how the selection was made is unclear. As in earlier Muslim empires, palace eunuchs supervised the training of uncastrated pages; in contrast to the eunuchs of the Mamluk sultanate, however, they did not oversee the training of the soldiery.

The tradition of employing African eunuchs as harem guardians was apparently well-established among the Ottomans before Mehmed II's conquest of Constantinople from the Byzantines in 857/1453. Numerous Ottoman and European observers insisted that even radical castration did not prevent the occasional harem eunuch from seeking sexual gratification of some sort with the aid of one or another harem resident.[17] Even if such sexual contact occasionally occurred, it appears to have been the exception that proved the rule. For the most part, the Ottoman harem eunuchs, like the Mamluks' *muqaddam al-mamālik al-sulṭāniyya*, were expected to control, rather than facilitate, the sexuality of the population they oversaw.[18] Gülru Necipoğlu's exhaustive study of the evolution of Topkapi Palace, constructed shortly after the conquest, demonstrates that the original palace harem, a small suite of rooms for the sultan's slave concubines at the back of the Third Court, was overseen by 25 eunuchs, most of them African.[19] Once the Ottomans had conquered the Mamluk sultanate in 922/1516–17, followed by Yemen in 945/1538 and the Red Sea coast of Africa in the late 950s/1550s, they began to import annually hundreds of Ethiopian and other East African eunuchs, as well as far larger numbers of female and uncastrated male slaves from the same region.

Under these circumstances, a fairly rigid division took shape between harem eunuchs, who were largely, although not, at first, exclusively, African; and white eunuchs who served as the sultan's companions. This was in marked contrast to what David Ayalon calls the "fluid movement between service in harem and barracks" that was practiced in Mamluk Cairo.[20] In Topkapi Palace, this dichotomy in the eunuchs' roles played out spatially. A corps of white eunuchs, drawn primarily from the *devşirme* and prisoners of war and, by the seventeenth century, purchased slaves from the Caucasus, guarded the Babűsaade ("Gate of Felicity"). This was the threshold separating the semi-public space of the palace's Second Court from the Third Court, which was the private abode of the sultan and his pages – a veritable "male harem", as Leslie Peirce has pointed out.[21] The head of these threshold eunuchs was known as the Kapı Ağası ("Āghā [Commander] of the Gate") or occasionally as Babűsaade Ağası. This official enjoyed overall supervision of the sultan's household, including the pages of the Third Court and the imperial harem; this meant that the head of the harem eunuchs was his subordinate.[22] In addition, the Kapı Ağası supervised the imperial pious foundations for Mecca and Medina (Awqāf al-Ḥaramayn), which the Ottomans had inherited on conquering the Mamluk sultanate and attaining the holy cities in 922/1517; under the Ottomans, however, the Awqāf evolved into an elaborate hierarchy of imperial foundations, including new foundations by Hürrem Sultan, wife of Süleyman I (r. 926–74/1520–66); Murad III (r. 982–1003/1574–95); and Mehmed IV (r. 1058–99/1648–87), to which lands and properties throughout the empire were endowed.[23]

Between the ninth/fifteenth and the early eleventh/seventeenth century, the highest-ranking eunuchs of the Third Court could follow the non-eunuch *devşirme* career path and become military commanders, provincial governors and even grand viziers. Thus, the admiral Khādim Süleyman Pāşā, a Hungarian eunuch, conquered Yemen for Sultan Süleyman I in 945/1538 and served as grand vizier from 948–60/1541–53.[24] By the mid-eleventh/seventeenth century, however, eunuch military commanders and administrators had virtually disappeared. Ottoman abandonment of the *devşirme* surely played some role, although some military eunuchs, particularly in the late sixteenth and early seventeenth centuries, were not *devşirme* recruits but elite slaves from the Caucasus.

A more serious blow to the Third Court eunuchs was the transfer of the women of the imperial family to Topkapi from the so-called Old Palace, which Meḥmed II had built immediately after conquering Constantinople on the current site of Istanbul University. This relocation, which occurred towards the middle of the tenth/sixteenth century, enhanced the harem eunuchs' influence dramatically. Around 939/1534, Hürrem Sultan, the wife of Süleyman I, moved to Topkapi, accompanied by an entourage of both African and white eunuchs.[25] From this point until the mid-nineteenth century, all female members of the reigning sultan's household resided in the Topkapi harem, which consequently increased exponentially in size, as did the corps of almost entirely African eunuchs who guarded it, peaking at some 600–800 by the end of the tenth/sixteenth century (as opposed to some 30 Third Court eunuchs). The Kapı Ağası retained nominal control of the harem until 996/1588, when Murad III, in recognition of the harem eunuchs' predominance, transferred supervision of the Awqāf al-Ḥaramayn from the powerful Kapı Ağası Gazanfer Ağa, a Venetian renegade (who is pictured on this volume's cover), to Habeşi ("Abyssinian" or Ethiopian) Mehmed Ağa, the chief of the harem eunuchs, who likewise received the title Darűsaade Ağası, or Āghā of the Abode of Felicity, referring to the harem.[26] Hereafter, the Kapı Ağası oversaw only one pious foundation founded by Hürrem Sulṭan.

Murad III's reign represented a turning point for the harem eunuchs in other ways as well. While his father, Selim II, had apparently begun to sleep in the harem, Murad spent most of his waking hours there, at least when he was not leading military campaigns, holding audiences, observing parades and the like. To accommodate his near-constant presence, he had residential quarters built for himself in the harem and oversaw a massive physical expansion of the overall harem precinct, so that it began to resemble the "independent city" on the western side of the palace that tourists visit today.[27] It was during his reign that the corps of harem eunuchs, now overwhelmingly East African, grew to the numbers noted above. In these new circumstances, the chief eunuch and lower-ranking harem eunuchs had unprecedented access to the sultan. In fact, harem eunuchs began to take the place in the sultan's routine that had formerly been occupied by palace pages. In illuminated court chronicles produced during Murad III's reign, not surprisingly, Habeşi Mehmed Ağa is pictured at the sultan's side on numerous occasions.[28]

Changes in the pattern of dynastic succession at the end of the tenth/sixteenth century, followed by a dynastic crisis, further increased the chief eunuch's influence. Beginning in the reign of Murād III's son, Meḥmed III (r. 1003–12/1595–1603), Ottoman princes were no longer sent out to govern provinces in Anatolia in order to learn statecraft. Furthermore, the death of a sultan no longer precipitated a race to the capital by his sons, followed by the successful candidate's execution of his brothers. Instead, all princes were raised in the harem, and succession was decided largely by seniority. Under the new order, the chief harem eunuch, along with the sultan's mother, was a key influence upon the shaping of a future sultan's character. The chief eunuch oversaw a prince's early education, which took place in the harem, just outside the chief eunuch's apartments. Once the prince had been circumcised, at the age of between eight and twelve, he began to acquire what amounted to a household staff. On reaching maturity, he moved to an apartment at the rear of the harem complex, appropriately known as the *ḳafes* or cage, along with a lower-ranking harem eunuch who served as a sort of household manager.[29]

Beginning with Ahmed I (r.1012–26/1603–17), a series of sultans died young, leaving no heirs or only young children. The resulting power vacuum allowed the sultan's mother and favourite concubine (and grandmother, in the case of Mehmed IV) to become key players in court politics.[30] The chief eunuch was often the ally of one or more of these influential women and, as such, played a critical role in the accession and deposition of sultans, grand viziers and other key palace personnel; and in the shaping of imperial policy. In perhaps the most famous example of such an alliance, the chief harem eunuch Uzun ("Tall") Süleyman Ağa and the lower-ranking harem eunuchs joined with Turhān Sultan, the mother of Mehmed IV, who took the throne in 1058/1648 at the age of seven, to oppose the sultan's powerful grandmother, Kösem Sultan, who was allied with the Janissaries (the Ottoman elite infantry) and the pages of the Third Court. In a scene worthy of a television soap opera, the harem eunuchs chased the 62-year-old Kösem through the harem and, according to some accounts, strangled her with her own braids. Several chroniclers accuse Uzun Süleyman himself of carrying out the murder.[31]

Over and above all these alliances and counter-alliances, the chief harem eunuch's role in policing the imperial harem contributed to the harem's key function: dynastic reproduction. The chief eunuch, in concert with the sultan's favourite concubine and, from the end of the sixteenth century onwards, the sultan's mother, upheld the hierarchy of age and status that prevailed in the Ottoman harem. This meant ensuring that each concubine produced only one son and mediating the competition among concubines for their sons' accession to the throne.[32] At the same time, through his role in overseeing the princes' education, the chief eunuch contributed to a form of dynastic reproduction, in the sense of transmitting knowledge and traditions to a new generation of the imperial family.

The chief harem eunuch's devotion to the Prophet Muḥammad

The chief harem eunuch's devotion to the Ottoman dynasty was mirrored by his devotion to the Prophet Muḥammad and the Muslim holy cities of Mecca and Medina. In the late seventeenth century, it became common for a deposed chief eunuch to serve as head of the corps of eunuchs who guarded the Prophet Muḥammad's tomb in Medina. As Shaun Marmon has explained, the tradition of a eunuch guard at the Prophet's tomb, as well as a smaller contingent at the Kaʿba in Mecca, purportedly originated with either the sixth/twelfth-century Crusader fighter Nūr al-Dīn ibn Zangī or with his client, the great Kurdish general Ṣalāḥ al-Dīn (Saladin).[33] The Mamluk sultanate codified this practice as part of a strategy of reinforcing Sunni Islam in the Muslim holy cities. At the time, a majority of Medina's population were Zaydī or Isma'ili Shi'is who objected to Sunni preachers in the Prophet's mosque and to the presence in the tomb precinct of the graves of Abū Bakr and 'Umar; these men were recognized by Sunnis as the first two caliphs but were regarded by Shi'is as usurpers of the caliphate from 'Alī ibn Abī Ṭālib.

The eunuchs prevented occasional indignant Shi'is from heckling the mosque preachers and from throwing rubbish or worse into the tombs of Abū Bakr and 'Umar; more generally, they enforced orderly behaviour among all visitors to the mosque and tomb.[34] By the late ninth/fifteenth century, according to the Egyptian biographer al-Sakhāwī (d. 902/1497), cited by Marmon, the guard at the Prophet's tomb consisted of roughly forty eunuchs of East and West African, Indian, and Greek origin.[35] This number remained stable throughout the first 250 years of Ottoman rule over the holy cities, to judge from the report of the German surveyor Carsten Niebuhr, who visited the Hijaz in the early 1760s. By the time Sir Richard Francis Burton visited the holy cities in the 1850s, disguised as an Anatolian pilgrim, however, the "Tomb Eunuchs" numbered 120, all of them East African.[36] In a move that was perhaps related to their reinforcement of the eunuch tomb guard, the Mamluks also appointed palace eunuchs to oversee royal pious foundations endowed to Mecca and Medina (the germ of what would become, under the Ottomans, the Awqāf al-Ḥaramayn).

Intriguingly, the Mamluk sultanate extended the institution of eunuch tomb guardians to Cairo, where eunuchs were stationed at the tombs of the sultans.[37] This custom seems to have been unknown in other parts of the Muslim world, either before or after the Mamluks adopted the practice. The only parallel of which I am aware is in Ming-dynasty China (1368–1644), where it became customary for eunuchs to guard the imperial tombs.[38] On the one hand, we can regard this development as an extension of the eunuch as the ruler's companion: Eunuchs controlled access to the deceased ruler just as they had during his lifetime. On the other hand, it accords with the notion of the ruler's tomb, rather like the Prophet's, as a sacred space whose boundaries must be protected. In this sense, tomb eunuchs belong to the same category as the stone and ceramic statues of men and mythical beasts that guarded the tombs of the rulers of medieval China and Korea or the gates of Buddhist temples in the same regions. Apart from protecting the site in question, they mark the transition from mundane to sacred, or taboo, space.

Similar to Medina's "tomb eunuchs" was a party of eunuchs whom the well-known Moroccan traveller Ibn Baṭṭūṭa (703–79/1304–77) encountered patrolling the tomb complex of 'Alī ibn Abī Ṭālib in the city of Najaf in southern Iraq. These eunuchs, however, were only one part of an elaborate "royal retinue" that included chamberlains and "deputies" (*nuqabā'*).[39] Southern Iraq at the time of Ibn Baṭṭūṭa's visit was under the rule of the Jalāyirids, a Mongol offshoot who adhered to Sunnism. This tomb entourage, like its counterparts in Medina and even in Cairo, accords with the conception of the tomb as the private sanctum in the "household" of the deceased. When southern Iraq was under Sunni rule, moreover, this retinue no doubt served to protect the tomb from particularly zealous Sunnis who objected to the fervour of Shiʿi reverence for ʿAlī. What sets this tomb entourage apart from other instances of eunuch tomb guardians is, first, that eunuchs were not the only group who served as guards; and, second, that the presence of such an elaborate retinue suggests an attempt to mark ʿAlī off as a parallel, or alternative, ruler.

Under the Ottomans, the head of the tomb eunuchs held the title Shaykh al-Ḥaram al-Nabawī, literally "head of the Prophetic sanctuary", reflecting the fact that Mecca and Medina are known in Islamic tradition as sacred or taboo spaces or sanctuaries (Arabic singular *ḥaram*). There was also a Shaykh al-Ḥaram of Mecca, who was usually a military commander with the rank of *pāşā*. Until the mid-seventeenth century, it appears, both the Shaykh al-Ḥaram of Medina and his counterpart in Mecca were Muslim scholar officials or *ʿulamāʾ*. In 1644, however, one Muṣāḥib Beşir, a harem eunuch who had held the post of companion (*muṣāḥib*) to Sultan Murad IV (r. 1032–49/1623–40) as well as supervisor in Egypt of one of the holy cities' pious foundations, became head of Medina's eunuchs.[40] Thereafter, the Shaykh al-Ḥaram was almost always a former palace harem eunuch, and he would appoint the subordinate tomb eunuchs, most of whom were also former palace harem eunuchs.

In 1102/1691, Yusuf Ağa, who had served as chief harem eunuch from 1082–98/1671–1687, arrived in Medina from Cairo to take up the post of Shaykh al-Ḥaram; he was the first former chief eunuch to hold the office. The circumstances of his transfer were unique in that he had been stripped of his property and banished to Cairo in connection with the military revolt that deposed Sultan Mehmed IV. Since the early eleventh/seventeenth century, deposed harem eunuchs had customarily relocated to Cairo for a period of what might be called honourable exile, often resembling retirement, during which they collected a pension, inhabited palatial residences and even purchased slaves.[41] Yusuf, in contrast, had arrived in Cairo disgraced and penniless. The posting to Medina resulted from a sultanic pardon and represented a fresh start for him.[42] Nonetheless, it set a definite precedent. Some 25 years later, Ḥācı Beşir Ağa served as Shaykh al-Ḥaram for roughly a year (1127–28/1715–16) after an equally brief sojourn in Cairo and immediately *before* being recalled to Istanbul to take up the office of chief harem eunuch.[43] By the end of the twelfth/eighteenth century, a career trajectory that had once been an aberration had become the norm: The Shaykh al-Ḥaram was customarily a former chief harem eunuch who had spent several years in exile in Egypt. This development contributed to a three-way link among the eunuchs of Istanbul, Cairo and Medina, which in turn enhanced palace control, at least in theory, over the transmission of money and grain from Egypt to the holy cities with the annual *ḥajj* caravan. Ottoman eunuchs did not, on the other hand, guard the tomb of any member of the Ottoman imperial family.

In general terms, the use of eunuchs, in preference to uncastrated males, as guardians of tombs, whether those of sultans or those of the Prophet Muḥammad and his companions, speaks to the eunuch's distinctive status as an intermediary between the mundane space and linear time of the everyday world and the sacred space and suspended time of the tomb. As Marmon has pointed out, eunuchs, castrated before puberty and thus unable to mature to physical adulthood, were like perpetual children and, as such, were "intermediate being[s], safe in both worlds and belonging to neither".[44] The mediating role of the tomb eunuchs was similar to that of the harem eunuchs, who policed the boundary separating the taboo space of the sultan's family from the semi-public space of Topkapi Second Court. Expanding on the theme of eunuch mediation, the scholar of comparative slavery Orlando Patterson has argued that the eunuch was "the closest approximation in the human species to an androgynous being ... both male and female, both weak and strong, both dirty and pure" and thus uniquely equipped to navigate the boundary separating the "sacred" absolute ruler from his mortal subjects.[45] Whether they were guarding the Prophet's tomb or the sultan's inner sanctum, the defining marginality of eunuchs rendered them uniquely suitable for service in liminal, and therefore ritually dangerous, spaces such as tomb precincts and the sacral space surrounding absolute rulers.

Chief eunuch religious/educational endowments

Supervising the imperial endowments to the holy cities and serving as Shaykh al-Ḥaram in Medina were not the only ways in which an acting or former chief harem eunuch could demonstrate his devotion to the Prophet Muḥammad. A number of chief eunuchs made public displays of their reverence by endowing charitable and educational foundations that provided young Muslim boys and other members of the Muslim community with a basic religious education; a more advanced education would have included access to collections of the Prophet's sayings (*ḥadīth*) and seminal works of Sunni jurisprudence of the Ḥanafī legal rite, the official rite of the Ottoman state.[46] Haci Beşir Ağa (term 1129–59/1717–46), the most powerful chief harem eunuch in Ottoman history, endowed a wide range of such institutions across the empire's territory. In 1151/1738, he endowed a school for the study of *ḥadīth* in Medina, where he had briefly served 20 years previously as chief of the eunuchs who guarded the Prophet's tomb. The endowment deed for this school stipulates that it is to serve twenty Rūmī orphan boys – that is, Turcophone boys from the Ottoman central lands, particularly Istanbul and nearby parts of Anatolia. Indeed, the document goes on to specify that the students must not be married, Maghrebian, Persian (*ʿAcem*), Indian (*Hindī*), peasant (*fellāḥ*), Shiʿi (*revāfıż*, implying "heretic") or of any other ethno-regional origin.[47] Since virtually all Rūmī Muslims belonged to the Ḥanafī legal rite, the *hadith* school helped to reinforce the Ḥanafī presence in a part of the Ottoman empire in which Shi'is and Sunnis of other legal rites were probably still more numerous among the mass of the population. A similar purpose was served by Beşir Ağa's endowment of books, most of them surely works of Ḥanafī law and theology, to the residential college (*riwāq*) of the Turks at Cairo's famous al-Azhar mosque/university in 1129/1717 and to the mosque–tomb complex of Abū Ḥanīfa, the eponymous founder of the Ḥanafī rite, in Baghdad in 1146/1734.[48]

Beşir Ağa's charitable endowments culminated in a religious–educational complex (*külliye* in Ottoman Turkish) near Topkapi Palace, established in 1158/1745, the year before the eunuch's death at the age of 90. The complex housed a mosque; a *madrasa*, or theological seminary; a lodge for the Naqshbandī sufi (mystical) order; a Quran school; and a library of 1007 volumes, comprising seminal works of *ḥadīth*, Quranic exegesis, Ḥanafī law and theology and Ottoman history and literature.[49] (The collection is now housed in Istanbul's Süleymaniye Library.) It thus brought together the religious and educational missions of so many chief eunuch endowments: providing young boys with knowledge of the Quran and *hadith* and, at the same time, with a basic Ḥanafī interpretation of Islamic practice; training future Ḥanafī scholar-officials; providing access to seminal works of Ḥanafī law and exegesis; and giving a home to a widespread sufi order that counted members of the Ottoman court among its followers.

Like Beşīr Ağa's earlier endowments, this one exemplifies the chief eunuch's devotion to the Prophet Muḥammad and to Sunni Islam as a whole, while emphasizing his educational mission. In many respects, it also mirrors his role as educator of Ottoman princes. More generally, the chief eunuch's charitable foundations reflect the effects of his service in the imperial harem: He contributed to a new generation of Muslims, much as he contributed to the reproduction of the Ottoman dynasty, by providing the raw materials and the infrastructure for their religious education. Charity and education became, in this context, the medium of figurative reproduction.

Chief harem eunuchs in Eyüp cemetery in Istanbul

A fair number of chief harem eunuchs, particularly in the later Ottoman period, died in Medina and were buried there. However, for chief eunuchs who died in Istanbul, whether in office or after deposition, burial in the famous old cemetery at Eyüp, at the western end of the Golden Horn, provided a different sort of opportunity to demonstrate devotion to the Prophet. The cemetery and neighbourhood are named after Abū Ayyūb al-Anṣārī, the standard-bearer of the Prophet Muḥammad, who converted to Islam on the Prophet's arrival in Medina from Mecca in 622 CE. According to Muslim tradition, Abū Ayyūb died during one of the early Muslim sieges of Constantinople in 52/672 and, at his own request, was buried under the Byzantine land walls. After the Ottomans conquered Constantinople in 857/1453, Abū Ayyūb's tomb was allegedly rediscovered, and a mosque and tomb complex was erected on the site. Abū Ayyūb's tomb is still visited by Turkish Muslims, and numerous luminaries of Ottoman and modern Turkish history are interred in the vast cemetery that surrounds the mosque. These include several imperial women (though no sultans) and no fewer than ten chief harem eunuchs, most of them from the late Ottoman period. All but two of the chief eunuchs interred at Eyüp are buried in graves marked by stones carved in the shape of the chief harem eunuch's headgear; headgear tombstones of this type were standard for Ottoman officials of all kinds. Before the westernizing Tanzimat reforms of the mid- to late nineteenth century introduced the fez for all Ottoman officials, regardless of rank, the chief harem eunuch wore a very distinctive high sugar-loaf hat; thus, the grave of a pre-Tanzimat chief eunuch is easy to recognize.

Two of the most powerful chief eunuchs in Ottoman history, Ḥācı Mustafa Ağa (terms 1014–29/1605–20 and 1033/1624) and the aforementioned Haci Beşir Ağa, are buried in tombs on either side of Abū Ayyūb's own tomb. Access to Mustafa Ağa's tomb is, in fact, through the tomb of Abū Ayyūb. Beşir Ağa's tomb is on the opposite side of Abū Ayyūb, abutting the public courtyard. The epitaph for Beşir, which is inscribed on the courtyard side of the tomb, describes his death as a journey in which he "halts" at Abū Ayyūb's tomb:

> For when he realized that the happiness of the world was not everlasting,
> See the sincerity with which he set out on his final journey.
> A halting place was made for him in the vicinity of Khālid [i.e., Abū Ayyūb al- Anṣārī] ….

It seems clear that Mustafa and Beşir Ağa identified with Abū Ayyūb al-Anṣārī; like him, they were converts to Islam who served the Prophet. Beşir Ağa, in addition, mimicked Abū Ayyūb by serving him in Medina, then journeying from Medina all the way to Constantinople in his service. Medina and the neighbourhood of Eyüp are linked as sacred sites through the mediation of Abū Ayyūb al-Anṣārī and, a millennium later, through the mediation of these two chief eunuchs. And in the same way that Abū Ayyūb's tomb is a distant reflection of the Prophet's tomb in Medina, so the harems of Topkapi – both the female harem and the "male harem" of the Third Court – are distant likenesses of the *ḥaram* in Medina, that is, the Prophet's mosque and tomb. In this sense, serving the sultan and serving the Prophet were intertwined and mutually reinforcing – indeed, mirror-image – components of the chief harem eunuch's office.

Even after his death, then, the duality, or paradox, of the chief eunuch's identity and function was on display: an emasculated East African convert to Islam, of slave origin, who was instrumental to the regeneration, both literal and figurative, of the Ottoman dynasty and to the propagation of Muslim tradition within that dynasty and in Ottoman society at large. The tombs of Haci Mustafa and Haci Beşir Ağa, furthermore, underline the chief eunuch's role in mediating between the two *ḥarams* in Istanbul and in Medina. Proximity to and identification with the Prophet's standard-bearer constituted one more bond connecting the chief eunuch to the Muslim holy cities, in addition to his many charitable endowments and his supervision of the Awqāf al-Ḥaramayn. These bonds in turn helped to legitimize the Ottoman sultan's status as custodian of the holy cities (*khādim al-ḥaramayn*). In death, the chief eunuch continued to do what he had done throughout his career: bring the Ottoman sultan and the Prophet of Islam together.

Notes

1 See, for example, Austen Henry Layard, *Discoveries in the Ruins of Nineveh and Babylon, with Travels in Armenia, Kurdistan and the Desert* (London: John Murray, 1853), 451–458.

2 Esther 2:3, 8, 14, 15; 4:4, 5, 9, 10; 6:2, 14; 7:9; Herodotus, *The Persian Wars*, trans. George Rawlinson (New York: The Modern Library, 1942), 250, 258, 275, 307, 572–573, 636–637.

3 On Byzantine eunuchs, see, for example, Kathryn M. Ringrose, *The Perfect Servant: Eunuchs and the Social Construction of Gender in Byzantium* (Chicago: University of Chicago Press, 2003); Shaun Tougher, *The Eunuch in Byzantine History and Society* (London: Routledge, 2008).

4 Mary M. Anderson, *Hidden Power: The Palace Eunuchs of Imperial China* (Buffalo, NY: Prometheus Books, 1990), chap. 1–2.

5 On the debate over whether eunuchs existed in Pharaonic Egypt, see Frans Jonckheere, "L'Eunuque dans l'Égypte pharaonique," *Revue d'Histoire des Sciences* 7, no. 2 (1954): 139–155. See also Gerald E. Kadish, "Eunuchs in Ancient Egypt?," in *Studies in Honor of John A. Wilson*, ed. E. B. Hauser, Studies in Ancient Oriental Civilization 35 (Chicago: University of Chicago Press, 1969), 55–62. A notable example of a Ptolemaic eunuch is Ganymedes, tutor to Cleopatra's half-sister Arsinoë. See Cassius Dio Cocceianus, *Dio's Roman History, with an English Translation by Earnest Cary, on the Basis of the Version of Herbert Baldwin Foster* (London: Heinemann, New York: Putnams, 1916), 4:174–177 (42.39.1–2, 42.40.1).

6 László Török, *The Kingdom of Kush: Handbook of the Napatan-Meroitic Civilization* (Leiden: Brill, 1997), 443, 452, 455, 456, 459, 484. On the eunuch, see Frank M. Snowden Jr., *Blacks in Antiquity: Ethiopians in the Greco-Roman Experience* (Cambridge, MA: The Belknap Press of Harvard University Press, 1970), 206–207.

7 Harold G. Marcus, *A History of Ethiopia* (Berkeley: University of California Press, 1994), 55; James Bruce, *Travels to Discover the Source of the Nile in the Years 1768, 1769, 1770, 1771, 1772, and 1773* (Dublin: William Sleater, 1790–1791), 3:273, 518, 596.

8 Humphrey Fisher, *Slavery in the History of Muslim Black Africa* (New York: New York University Press, 2001), 281–293; J. S. Eades, *The Yoruba Today* (Cambridge: Cambridge University Press, 1980), 20–21; J. S. Boston, *The Igala Kingdom* (Ibadan: Oxford University Press, 1968), 21, 54, 93, 105, 163–175, 197–199, 209–213.

9 On the Ṣaqāliba, see David Ayalon, "On the Eunuchs in Islam," *Jerusalem Studies in Arabic and Islam* 1 (1979): 92–124; Ayalon, *Eunuchs, Caliphs, and Sultans:*

A Study in Power Relationships (Jerusalem: The Magnes Press, The Hebrew University, 1999), 349–352.

10 On this point, see Ayalon, *Eunuchs, Caliphs, and Sultans*, 307–314.

11 *Encyclopaedia Iranica*, s. v. "Eunuchs: The Early Islamic Period;" Milton Gold, trans., *The Tārīkh-e Sīstān* (Rome: Istituto Italiano per il Medio ed Estremo Oriente, 1976), 282; Clifford Edmund Bosworth, *The History of the Ṣaffārids of Sīstān and the Maliks of Nīmrūz (247/861 to 949/1542–3)* (Costa Mesa, CA: Mazda Publishers, 1994), 349; ed. and trans. D. S. Richards *The Annals of the Saljuq Turks: Selections from al-Kāmil fī'l-Ta'rīkh of ʿIzz al-Dīn ibn al-Athīr* (London: Routledge, 2002), 284.

12 Ayalon, *Eunuchs, Caliphs, and Sultans*, 21, 49–54, 139, 141–143, 340–342.

13 Richard Francis Burton, *First Footsteps in East Africa, or, An Exploration of Harār* (London: Tylston and Edwards, 1894), 2:2–3. See also J. Spencer Trimingham, *Islam in Ethiopia* (London: Frank Cass, 1965), 66–67, 182; Taddesse Tamrat, *Church and State in Ethiopia, 1270–1527* (Oxford: Clarendon Press, 1972), 86–87, 135–137, 155, 173; Ayalon, *Eunuchs, Caliphs, and Sultans*, 305–306; Fisher, *Slavery in the History of Muslim Black Africa*, 280.

14 Ayalon, *Eunuchs, Caliphs, and Sultans*, 41–42, 54–57, 309; Shaun Marmon, *Eunuchs and Sacred Boundaries in Islamic Society* (Oxford and New York: Oxford University Press, 1995), 11–12.

15 Heath W. Lowry, *The Nature of the Early Ottoman State* (Albany, NY: State University of New York Press, 2003), 75–77, translated from the Turkish edition of İsmail Hakkı Uzunçarşılı, "Gāzī Orhan Bey Vaḳfīyesi," *Belleten* 5 (1941): 277–288.

16 Cihan Yüksel Muslu, *The Ottomans and the Mamluks: Imperial Diplomacy and Warfare in the Islamic World* (London: I.B. Tauris, 2014), 88, 98.

17 Dervīş ʿAbdullāh Efendi, *Risāle-i Teberdārīye fī aḥvāl-i āgā-yı dāru's-saʿāde*, Istanbul, Köprülü Library, MS 233, fols. 91b-92b; N. M. Penzer, *The Harem: An Account of the Institution as It Existed in the Palace of the Turkish Sultans, with a History of the Grand Seraglio from Its Foundations to Modern Times* (Philadelphia: J.B. Lippincott, 1936; 2nd ed. London: Spring Books, 1965; repr. New York: Dover Press, 1993), 145–150.

18 Jane Hathaway, *Beshir Agha, Chief Eunuch of the Ottoman Imperial Harem* (Oxford: Oneworld, 2005), 14–16.

19 Gülru Necipoğlu, *Architecture, Ceremonial, and Power: The Topkapı Palace in the Fifteenth and Sixteenth Centuries* (New York: Architectural History Foundation; Cambridge, MA: MIT Press, 1991), 91–92, 159–162.

20 David Ayalon, "Eunuchs in the Mamluk Sultanate," in *Studies in Memory of Gaston Wiet*, ed. Myriam Rosen-Ayalon (Jerusalem: Institute of Asian and African Studies, Hebrew University of Jerusalem, 1977), 269.

21 Leslie Peirce, *The Imperial Harem: Women and Sovereignty in the Ottoman Empire* (Oxford: Oxford University Press, 1993), 11.

22 Necipoğlu, *Architecture, Ceremonial, and Power*, 160–161.

23 Jane Hathaway, "The Role of the Ḳızlar Ağası in 17th–18th Century Ottoman Egypt," *Studia Islamica* 75 (1992): 141–142.

24 Jane Hathaway, *A Tale of Two Factions: Myth, Memory, and Identity in Ottoman Egypt and Yemen* (Albany, NY: State University of New York Press, 2003), 82.

25 Necipoğlu, *Architecture, Ceremonial, and Power*, 163; Peirce, *The Imperial Harem*, 62.

26 Gülru Necipoğlu, *The Age of Sinan: Architectural Culture in the Ottoman Empire* (London: Reaktion Books, 2005), 498. See also Mustafa Güler, *Osmanlı Devlet'inde Ḥaremeyn Vaḳıfları (16. ve 17. Yüzyıllar)* (Istanbul: Tarih ve Tabiat Vakfı, 2002), 213–215, which reproduces a sultanic order to the governor-general

of Anatolia naming Mehmed Ağa as supervisor: Ottoman Prime Ministry Archives, Mühimme Defteri 62, no. 563, p. 249, Istanbul, 2 Rajab 996/27 May 1588.

27 Necipoğlu, *Architecture, Ceremony, and Power*, 164–175.

28 On this point, see Emine Fetvacı, *Picturing History at the Ottoman Court* (Bloomington, IN: Indiana University Press, 2013), 155–161; Zeren Tanındı, "Topkapı Sarayı'nın Ağaları ve Kitaplar," *Uludağ Üniversitesi Fen-Edebiyat Fakültesi Sosyal Bilimler Dergisi* 3, no. 3 (2002): 44–46; Jane Hathaway, "Ḥabeşī Meḥmed Agha: The First Chief Harem Eunuch (Darüssaade Ağası) of the Ottoman Empire," in *The Islamic Scholarly Tradition: Studies in History, Law, and Thought in Honor of Professor Michael Allan Cook*, ed. Asad Q. Ahmed, Behnam Sadeghi, and Michael Bonner (Leiden: Brill, 2011), 184–186.

29 Penzer, *The Harem*, 24, 25, 128, citing the report of the Venetian ambassador Ottaviano Bon.

30 Peirce, *The Imperial Harem*, 97–112.

31 Dervīş ʿAbdullāh Efendi, *Risāle-i Teberdārīye*, fols. 61a-62b, 79b; Muṣṭafā Nāʿīmā, *Tārīh-i Nāʿīmā* (*Ravżatü'l-Ḥüseyn fī hulāṣati ahbāri'l-ḫāfiḳayn*), ed. Mehmet İpşirli (Ankara: Türk Tarih Kurumu, 2007), 3:1325–1333, 1338.

32 Peirce, *The Imperial Harem*, 42–45 and chap. 4.

33 Marmon, *Eunuchs and Sacred Boundaries*, 31–45.

34 Richard Francis Burton, *Personal Narrative of a Pilgrimage to al-Madinah and Meccah* (London: Tylston and Edwards, 1893; repr. New York: Dover Publications, 1964), 1: 315–316, 322 n.2, 333, 337.

35 Marmon, *Eunuchs and Sacred Boundaries*, 39. According to Ayalon, the number was increased from 24 in 742/1342, right after the death of Sultan al-Nāṣir Muḥammad b. Qalāwūn; see "Eunuchs in the Mamluk Sultanate," 270.

36 Niebuhr, cited in Marmon, *Eunuchs and Sacred Boundaries*, 97; Burton, *Personal Narrative*, 1:308, n. 4, 371–372. It is possible that Niebuhr, who did not actually visit the tomb, is simply echoing al-Sakhāwī or other Muslim sources.

37 Marmon, *Eunuchs and Sacred Boundaries*, 15–26; Ayalon, "Eunuchs in the Mamlūk Sultanate," 269–270.

38 Shih-shan Henry Tsai, *The Eunuchs in the Ming Dynasty* (Albany, NY: State University of New York Press, 1996), 57.

39 Marmon, *Eunuchs and Sacred Boundaries*, 26–28.

40 Nāʿīmā, *Tārīh-i Nāʿīmā*, 3:997, 2:825.

41 Hathaway, "The Role of the Ḳızlar Āğāsı," 142.

42 Defterdār Ṣarı Meḥmed Pāşā, *Zübde-i Veḳāyīʿāt: Taḥlīl ve Metin, 1066–1116/1656–1704*, ed. Abdülkadir Özcan (Ankara: Türk Tarih Kurumu, 1995), 240–241, 249; Silāḥdār Fındıḳlılı Meḥmed Āğā, *Silāḥdār Tārīhi* (Istanbul: Orhaniye Matbaası, 1928), 2:277–280, 288–291, 296–298, 305–308, 368.

43 Hathaway, *Beshir Agha*, 40–59.

44 Marmon, *Eunuchs and Sacred Boundaries*, 88–92, quotation at 90.

45 Orlando Patterson, *Slavery and Social Death: A Comparative Study* (Cambridge, MA: Harvard University Press, 1982), 322–331, quotation at 326.

46 Sunni Islam recognizes four schools of law (Arabic singular *madhhab*): the Ḥanafī, the Mālikī, the Shāfiʿī, and the Ḥanbalī. They emerged in the early centuries of Islam, mainly in response to regional differences in practice. They differ in interpretations of personal status law, legal methodology and some religious rituals.

47 Istanbul, Süleymaniye Library, MS Hacı Beşir 682, fols. 24a–30b.

48 Daniel Crecelius and Ḥamza ʿAbd al-ʿAzīz Badr, "The *Awqāf* of al-Ḥājj Bashīr Āghā in Cairo," *Annales Islamologiques* 27 (1993): 301; Istanbul, Süleymaniye Library, MS Yazma Bağışlar 2524.

49 Hathaway, *Beshir Agha*, 87–93.

Part IV

Gender and masculinities

11 Byzantine court eunuchs and the Macedonian dynasty (867–1056)

Family, power and gender

Shaun Tougher

Introduction

This chapter is concerned with the court eunuchs of the Byzantine empire. Despite its name – a modern invention – this empire was the successor of the Roman empire in the east, centred on the city of Constantinople, as the ancient Greek city of Byzantium was renamed by Constantine the Great in AD 324. For the span of its existence, from the fourth to the fifteenth centuries AD, the Byzantine court was distinguished by its use of eunuchs, inheriting this tradition from the Roman empire, which in turn was indebted to Hellenistic and near-Eastern practices.[1] For the majority of this time, the Byzantine empire witnessed a sequence of powerful court eunuchs, as well as a more general eunuch presence at court. In this chapter, I will focus on these powerful eunuchs as members of the ruling elite, considering in particular the family connections of such eunuchs, specific cases of powerful court eunuchs (see table 11.2 for a list of key eunuchs) and, especially, the perception of the gender of these eunuchs. I will concentrate on a defined period, when the empire was ruled by the Macedonian dynasty (867–1056).[2] This dynasty was founded by Basil I and expired with the empress–nun Theodora, his great-great-great-granddaughter (see table 11.1 for the list of rulers in this period). The period marked by the rule of this family can be thought to denote the Golden Age of the Byzantine empire and thus is a vital one to consider. The chapter concludes with an analysis of the place of powerful court eunuchs within Byzantium and the perceptions of them by contemporaries. It argues that to properly understand eunuchs' identity – of which gender is only a part – eunuchs need to be studied together with Byzantine men as a whole. Indeed, the study of Byzantine men is a major lacuna in the field of Byzantine studies and requires urgent attention.

Family

As noted, the presence of court eunuchs in the Byzantine empire was owed to its predecessor, the Roman empire. While the Roman empire had witnessed the use of eunuchs from at least the early first century AD, it was in the third century AD that eunuchs became an institutional feature of the

Table 11.1 List of Byzantine Rulers, 867–1056

Basil I (867–886)
Leo VI (886–912)
Alexander (912–913)
Constantine VII (913–959)
Romanos I Lekapenos (920–944)
Romanos II (959–963)
Nikephoros II Phokas (963–969)
John I Tzimiskes (969–976)
Basil II (976–1025)
Constantine VIII (1025–1028)
Zoe and Theodora (1028–1056) (Zoe died 1050)
Romanos III Argyros (1028–1034)
Michael IV (1034–1041)
Michael V (1041–1042)
Constantine IX Monomachos (1042–1055)

Table 11.2 List of Prominent Court Eunuchs in Byzantium

Eusebius (fourth century)
Eutropius (fourth century)
Narses (sixth century)
Samonas (Leo VI)
Constantine the Paphlagonian (Leo VI, Constantine VII)
Theophanes (Romanos I Lekapenos)
Joseph Bringas (Romanos II)
Peter "Phokas" (Nikephoros Phokas, John Tzimiskes, Basil II)
Basil Lekapenos (especially Nikephoros Phokas, John Tzimiskes, Basil II)
John the *Orphanotrophos* (Romanos III Argyros, Michael IV, Michael V)

court.[3] This development is often associated with the emperor Diocletian (284–305) and his supposed "persianisation" of the imperial office. Eunuchs became a regular presence at the court, especially in the role of chamberlains (*cubicularii*), headed by the grand chamberlain (*praepositus sacri cubiculi*).[4] However, it is important to emphasise and appreciate that the Byzantine and later Roman systems were not identical. The system of eunuch offices and honours had evolved, as can be seen in a comparison of the fourth–fifth-century *Notitia Dignitatum* and the ninth-century *Kletorologion* of Philotheos, court texts that provided information about the hierarchy of civil and military officials.[5] Yet the differences were not only apparent in the names of offices and honours and the organisation of the system. The later Roman empire largely used eunuchs who were foreigners, imported as part of the slave trade. For instance, in the sixth century, the historian Procopius observed that most of the eunuchs at the court in Constantinople were from Abasgia, on the eastern shore of the Black Sea.[6]

In the Byzantine empire, however, it seems that eunuchs were largely drawn from native families, presumably created at the wishes of each family in order to supply demand in Constantinople and in the hope of good economic return.[7] This is well illustrated by the figure of Constantine the Paphlagonian, a eunuch who at the court of Leo VI (886–912) rose to become *parakoimomenos* (effectively grand chamberlain) and who played a key part in the regency of Zoe Karbonopsina for her young son Constantine VII in the 910s, after the death of her husband Leo VI in 912.[8] Several eunuchs in the middle Byzantine period (eighth–twelfth centuries AD) are known to have hailed from Paphlagonia (on the south coast of the Black Sea), and one of the texts related to the eunuch Constantine – an entry in the *Synaxarion of Constantinople* – details how his father Metrios, a farmer in Paphlagonia, imitated the practice of his neighbours by castrating his son and sending him to Constantinople to work at the court.[9] The prominence of the families of eunuchs in Byzantium is also revealed by another text related to Constantine, a consolation written to him by the patriarch of Constantinople Nicholas on the death of the eunuch's sister (ca. 916).[10] This consolation refers also to the mother of Constantine, his deceased father, his widowed brother-in-law and his family and friends in general. This serves as a complete contrast with the later Roman system and the medieval Middle East, where one of the advantages of eunuchs is thought to have been that since foreign slaves were kinless, they had no other ties in society. Such eunuchs would then devote themselves to the service of the rulers on whom they were utterly dependent, creating a vital counterbalance to the power of the aristocratic elite.[11]

This difference obviously has implications for the power wielded by eunuchs in Byzantium. If eunuchs had family ties in Byzantine society, they also could have alternative agendas to the concerns of the emperors. In the case of Constantine the Paphlagonian, his brother-in-law was Leo Phokas, one of the leading generals of the day and a contender for imperial power during the minority of Constantine VII (although he eventually lost out to Romanos Lekapenos).[12] Clearly both Leo and Constantine might have benefitted from this family connection. Another good example is John the *Orphanotrophos*, who was prominent during the reign of Romanos III Argyros (1028–1034) (the first husband of Zoe the Macedonian). John worked for the advantage of his own family and succeeded in securing its imperial status. His brother would become Emperor Michael IV and second husband of Zoe after the death of Romanos; his nephew, another Michael, became Emperor Michael V and was adopted by Zoe after the death of his uncle. Other brothers of John the *Orphanotrophos* – Niketas and the eunuchs Constantine and George – also benefitted from his political importance.[13] John's great predecessor, the eunuch Basil Lekapenos, held imperial status by his own family connections, his father having become Emperor Romanos I Lekapenos in 920 (though his mother, a "Scythian" woman, was not the legitimate wife of Romanos). Basil was also brother-in-law of Constantine VII, uncle of Romanos II and great-uncle of Basil II and Constantine VIII.[14] Basil Lekapenos' devotion to Basil II is likened by the eleventh-century courtier and author Michael Psellos to that of some kindly foster parent (τροφεύς).[15] In relation to family connections of eunuchs, it is also worth remarking that Leo VI issued *Novels* (new laws) that allowed eunuchs to adopt since they could not have children of their own *(Novel* 26) but upheld the ban on eunuchs taking wives since marriage was for the purpose of procreation (*Novel* 98).[16] Leo's own concern to become a father may have made him sympathetic to the childlessness of eunuchs – he was generally well disposed towards them, having several eunuch favourites as well as building a monastery for eunuchs, the monastery of St Lazarus.

However, it is important to acknowledge that not all eunuchs in Byzantium were from native families.[17] An interesting case is that of Samonas, a leading figure at the court of Leo VI.[18] From Melitene in eastern Anatolia on the Abbasid frontier with Byzantium, Samonas entered the emperor's service after winning his favour for reporting a plot. Since he was an Arab, it is likely that Samonas was a slave or a prisoner of war, but this did not prevent him from forging close ties with Leo and his family. He rose to the position of *parakoimomenos*, chief eunuch, and stood as sponsor to Leo's son Constantine VII at his baptism in 906. Further, he even came into contact with his own father when the latter visited Constantinople as part of an embassy from the Abbasid Caliphate.

Fundamentally, slaves and servants were part of the household (*oikos*) in Byzantine society so were considered part of the family (the Byzantines had no word for the nuclear family).[19] A good example is that of Peter, one of the eunuch servants or slaves of the emperor Nikephoros II Phokas, for whom Phokas created the military position of *stratopedarches* (chief general) and who rendered good service to the Macedonians until his death in the reign of Basil II, when opposing the usurper Bardas Skleros in battle.[20] Sometimes Peter is even referred to as Peter Phokas.

It is clear that in the Byzantine empire, court eunuchs could be native Byzantines themselves and maintain and foster relationships with family members. Further, while the example of Constantine the Paphlagonian suggests that eunuchs tended to hail from less socially distinguished families, court eunuchs could achieve social prominence and wealth for themselves and for their families and could be members of the imperial family, as the cases of Basil Lekapenos and John the *Orphanotrophos* demonstrate. These features of Byzantine court eunuchs mark them out sharply from their Roman predecessors.

Power

However, although distinctions can be made between late Roman and Byzantine court eunuchs in terms of origin and of family connections, both groups were united in being perceived as powerful political figures, as having influence with the ruler (both emperors and empresses) and, at times, being *de facto* rulers themselves. Such power was usually wielded by the grand chamberlain or chief eunuch. Famous examples of powerful late-Roman court eunuchs include Eusebius (under Constantius II), Eutropius (under Arcadius especially) and Narses, a military commander as well as *praepositus sacri cubiculi* (primarily under Justinian I in the sixth century).[21] In Byzantium under the Macedonian dynasty, a series of court eunuchs had political influence or held sway, most notably Samonas, Constantine the Paphlagonian, Theophanes, Joseph Bringas, Basil Lekapenos and John the *Orphanotrophos*. Byzantine sources tend to be quite matter of fact about eunuchs wielding power. Nevertheless, they can take contrasting views about the exercise of power by eunuchs (as will be discussed below in relation to gender).

To explore the nature and extent of the power of court eunuchs under the Macedonian dynasty, it is useful to focus first on the specific case of Basil Lekapenos, as he is one of the most powerful court eunuchs in the entire history of the Byzantine empire and also one of the best documented. Basil was the illegitimate son of emperor Romanos Lekapenos, and his career and rule lasted for several decades. Although prominent under Constantine VII (he was *protovestiarios* then *parakoimomenos* and played a military role too, e.g. at Samosata in 958), Basil achieved particular distinction when he supported Nikephoros Phokas's seizure of imperial power in 963, in opposition to a rival eunuch Joseph Bringas, *parakoimomenos* under Romanos II.[22] Raising men and supplies for Nikephoros Phokas in Constantinople, Basil ensured Nikephoros' success.[23] Such was Nikephoros Phokas' gratitude to Basil that he created a new title for him, that of *proedros* (translated as "president of the senate"), which other eunuchs would use in the future.[24] In 969, Basil retained his position and office under John Tzimiskes, Nikephoros' nephew, murderer and successor. When John Tzimiskes himself died in 976, Basil in effect acted as regent for the young emperors Basil II and Constantine VIII, until he was pushed out of power and exiled by his eponymous great-nephew Basil II in 985. The eunuch Basil's power and status was reflected in his role as a prominent patron.[25] Best known is his hand in the creation of the Limburg reliquary, which contained relics of the true cross and other relics and was constructed to house a cross–reliquary commissioned by Constantine VII and Romanos II. He was also responsible for a "monastery ... manuscripts, chalices, patens and rings".[26] Tellingly, when Basil II ousted his great-uncle, he moved against the eunuch's major monastic foundation dedicated to his namesake St Basil (Basil the Great, one of the 'Cappadocian Fathers'), effectively destroying it. This was clearly a very visible sign of the fall of the eunuch.[27]

Basil was not unique in exerting great political influence, even direct power. The story of Nikephoros Phokas' accession to power focuses much on the figure of another eunuch, the already mentioned Joseph Bringas, the *parakoimomenos* of Romanos II, who sought to protect the interests of Romanos' widow Theophano and her children Basil and Constantine. Bringas, like Basil, is presented in a number of Byzantine sources – most notably the chronicle of Theophanes Continuatus and a version of the Logothete chronicle, as well as the history of Leo the Deacon – as in effect running the empire, making the key political and strategic decisions. Further, to use another example, John the *Orphanotrophos*' position after the death of Romanos III Argyros is nicely symbolised by the fact that at the funeral of the emperor, the eunuch preceded the bier, as witnessed by Michael Psellos.[28]

It is evident that eunuchs could wield power and flourish in particular contexts: in the time of regencies, female rulers, youthful emperors and sick emperors (e.g. Constantine the Paphlagonian's prominence in the regency of Zoe for Constantine VII; Joseph Bringas' role in the regency for Basil II and Constantine VIII; Basil Lekapenos ruling for the young emperors Basil and Constantine; and John the *Orphanotrophos* governing for his brother Michael IV). However, such specific contexts do not represent the whole explanation for the power of court eunuchs. In the Byzantine empire, there was a persistent acceptance of eunuchs as traditionally important and effective ministers, not only in civil administration and finance but also in the military. Indeed, one of the most striking aspects of the role of court eunuchs in Byzantium is that they could also become military commanders, with some being very successful and celebrated.[29] The most famous example is that of Narses, who in the sixth century defeated the Ostrogoths in Italy, having been appointed to the Supreme Command in 551.[30] From the Macedonian period there is Peter, the eunuch of Nikephoros Phokas, who was made stratopedarch and who went on to serve under John I Tzimiskes as well as Basil II and Constantine VIII.

Thus it was accepted in Byzantium that eunuchs could and did play major administrative, political and military roles. On the other hand, there were still limitations to the power of eunuchs. As castrated men, they were barred from becoming emperors themselves, as Psellos remarks in relation to the specific case of Basil Lekapenos (*Chronographia* 1.3); an emperor was to be physically intact. Eunuchs could also suffer from the vicissitudes of fortune that affected all court personnel and officials generally: They could be outplayed by other eunuchs or officials in the competition for power (e.g. the cases of Samonas and Constantine the Paphlagonian, Bringas and Basil Lekapenos, and Basil Lekapenos and Nikephoros Ouranos); they could become associated with particular regimes and thus fall when a new one was established (e.g. Constantine the Paphlagonian, Bringas); and they could outstay their welcome and suffer from tensions within regimes (e.g. Basil Lekapenos and both John Tzimiskes and Basil II; and John the *Orphanotrophos* and his own nephew and brothers).

It is worth speculating whether Byzantine eunuchs studied the careers of their predecessors to learn how to succeed or what pitfalls to avoid, seeking to learn lessons from the past and from the fates of contemporaries. It is certainly instructive to note what Michael Psellos says about the interrelationship between Basil Lekapenos and his great-nephew Emperor Basil II; he remarks that Basil Lekapenos governed the empire but that Basil II had to confirm his great-uncle's measures orally and in writing.[31] Thus ultimately it was the emperor who had real authority, as Basil II was to make clear in his later dealings with Basil the eunuch, which led to the latter's downfall. Not only was the eunuch exiled and his monastery destroyed, but in 996 Basil II annulled the chrysobulls issued by his great-uncle. One is put very much in mind of recent political history in North Korea, when the Supreme Leader of the Democratic People's Republic, Kim Jong-un (who had succeeded his father Kin Jong-il in 2011), had his uncle Jang Sung-taek executed in 2013. The limitations upon the power of court eunuchs are not to be ignored.

Gender

Discussion of the power of court eunuchs in Byzantium brings us to the final aspect of eunuch identity to be addressed: gender. To what extent was gender identity a concern for Byzantines when writing about the exercise of power by castrated men? Was it a matter for controversy or accepted without comment? What do comments, if they exist, tell us about Byzantine perceptions of eunuch gender identity? While chronicles exist covering the span of the history of the Macedonian dynasty – for example, the chronicles of Symeon the Logothete, Theophanes Continuatus, Skylitzes and Kedrenos – such is the abbreviated nature of chronicles that they do not necessarily dwell in detail on such issues. Also, at times, such sources can utilise earlier material so may repeat the views of other sources, for example, the use of the *History* of Leo the Deacon by Skylitzes. But there are historical texts that offer more meat, such as the *History* of Leo the Deacon and the *Chronographia* of Michael Psellos.[32] Leo's history was written in the late tenth century and recorded the reigns of Nikephoros II Phokas and John I Tzimiskes. Psellos' *Chronographia* was written in the late eleventh century and provides biographical accounts of the reigns of Byzantine rulers, beginning with Basil II – where Leo the Deacon left off – and including the last Macedonian Theodora. The eye-witness aspects of these texts are significant; Leo was a contemporary of the emperors Nikephoros Phokas and John Tzimiskes and thus knew the eunuchs Basil Lekapenos, Joseph Bringas and Peter the stratopedarch, and Psellos was already at court at the time of the eunuch John the *Orphanotrophos*, though he had no direct knowledge of Basil Lekapenos. Leo and Psellos thus serve as important case studies of narrative responses to powerful court eunuchs.

One of the leading eunuch characters in the history of Leo the Deacon is the famous Basil Lekapenos. Strikingly, Leo presents Basil in a largely positive manner, praising his boldness, energy and gift for forethought at the time of his assistance of Nikephoros Phokas' coup in 961 (3.7: "παῤῥηςίαν … δραςτήριος … προμηθέςτατος").[33] Leo can contrast the positive qualities of Basil with the fact that he was a eunuch. In his account of the beginning of John I Tzimiskes' reign, he says, "although he happened to be a eunuch, he was still an exceptionally energetic and shrewd [δραςτήριός τε καὶ ἀγχίνους] man, able to adapt himself cleverly to the circumstances at times of crisis" (6.1).[34] As Alice-Mary Talbot and Denis F. Sullivan note, the phrase "energetic and shrewd" is also used by Leo of his hero Nikephoros Phokas himself (1.5) and is ultimately drawn from Procopius' *Wars* in relation to the Persian shah Kabades.[35] However, more appositely, Procopius says of the famous eunuch general Narses that he was "keen [ὀξὺς] and more energetic [δραςτήριος] than would be expected of a eunuch".[36] This perhaps takes on further significance in relation to the fact that Basil Lekapenos did go on campaign with John Tzimiskes, taking charge of the siege machinery while on campaign against the Rus in 971 (8.4) (and, as has been mentioned, Basil had previous military experience too). The one negative note in Leo's presentation of Basil is shown in John Tzimiskes' annoyance about the eunuch's greed (πλεονεκτικὴν) when he discovers that Basil has taken over recently recovered estates (Longinias and Drize) in Cilicia and Cappadocia (10.11) (foreshadowing the tensions that arose between Basil II and Basil Lekapenos). It was this that led to their falling out and, it seems, John Tzimiskes' death. Although Leo does not specifically link Basil's greed to his identity as a eunuch, it was a long-standing rhetorical complaint about eunuchs.[37] Otherwise Leo's presentation of Basil is remarkably positive and does not dwell significantly on the fact that he was a eunuch. Indeed, he indicates that Basil achieved what he did despite being a eunuch (6.1); there is the sense that he transcended Byzantine expectations of eunuchs.[38]

This sense is reinforced when one examines Leo's account of the eunuch Joseph Bringas. In contrast to Theophanes Continuatus' glowing account, Leo presents Joseph as a villain who sought to neutralise the emperor Nikephoros Phokas (2.11). While Leo himself does not directly deploy anti-eunuch rhetoric against Bringas, he has characters express such sentiments within the text, especially John Tzimiskes. Attempting to rouse his uncle Nikephoros against Bringas, John directly comments on the fact that Bringas is a eunuch (3.3), contrasting his effeminate nature with the martial and heroic Nikephoros Phokas:

> [To think of] your labors and battles and prowess, while the [dastardly deed] is planned by an effeminate fellow [παῤ ἀνδραρίου], whose very sex is doubtful, an artificial woman who knows nothing except what goes on in the women's quarters [ἀμφιβόλου τε καὶ ἀνάνδρου, καὶ γυναίου τεχνητοῦ]!' ... Let us rather act gallantly and courageously, so that Joseph [Bringas], and anyone else who thinks like him, may realize that they are not contending with delicate and sheltered women, but with men possessed of invincible strength, who are feared and admired by barbarians. ... I think it is wrong, nay intolerable, for Roman generals to be led and to be dragged by the nose, hither and thither, like slaves, by a wretched eunuch [τομίου οἰκτροῦ] from the wastes of Paphlagonia, who has insinuated himself into political power.[39]

Such rhetoric echoes Leo's direct verdict on another eunuch, Constantine Gongylios, whose Cretan expedition in 949 failed "on account of the cowardice [ἀνανδρίᾳ] and lack of experience of the commander, who was a eunuch of the bedchamber, an effeminate fellow [ἀνδραρίου ςκιατραφοῦς] from Paphlagonia ... the entire ... army ... was cut to pieces by the barbarians".[40] The contrast between masculine warriors and effeminate palace staff is all too clear. But it is important to grasp that in the case of Joseph Bringas, Leo is putting words in John Tzimiskes' mouth and that there is evidently a literary model at play again, for a sixth-century historian, Agathias, discusses reaction to the eunuch Narses in similar terms. When Agathias remarks upon Narses' good qualities,[41] he observes that "these ... were all the more remarkable in a eunuch [τομίας] and in one who had been brought up in the soft and comfortable atmosphere of the imperial court".[42] Agathias also has the Alamanni leaders Leutharis and Butilinus comment on Narses:

> they were surprised at the Goths being so terrified of a puny little man, a eunuch of the bedchamber [ἀνδράριόν τι θαλαμηπόλον ςκιατραφές], used to a soft and sedentary existence, and with nothing masculine about him.[43]

The point being made is that the barbarians are wrong footed, that a eunuch can be a successful general, as Leo himself shows in his presentation of Peter, the eunuch who was made stratopedarch by emperor Nikephoros Phokas. In relation to Peter's role in the capture of Antioch in 969, Leo remarks that "the *patrikios* and *stratopedarches* Peter [was] a eunuch, but still extremely active and robust [ῥέκτην δὲ τὴν ἄλλως καὶ ῥωμαλεώτατον]" (5.4).[44] He also relates that Peter was one of the generals sent against the Rus by the emperor John Tzimiskes in 970 (6.11)[45] and records a previous episode to demonstrate Peter's military ability: Peter had been made stratopedarch by Nikephoros Phokas "because of his inherent valour and heroic feats in battle [τὰ κατὰ τοὺς πολέμους ἀνδραγαθήματα], for it is said that once, when the Scythians were raiding Thrace, it came about that Peter, although a eunuch [καίτοι τομίαν ὄντα], met them in pitched battle with the corps that was following him". Peter then faced the Rus commander in one-to-one combat, each on horseback: "Peter, filled with inconceivable valour and spirit [ἀλκῆς καὶ μένους], impetuously urged his horse on with his spurs, and, after brandishing his spear mightily, thrust it with both hands at the Scythian's chest". The spear went right through the enemy commander, killing him, so that "the Scythians turned to flight, amazed at this novel and strange sight". Once again, there is encountered the view that eunuchs can be both successful administrators and generals; despite being eunuchs, they could overcome their perceived limitations and in time prove themselves to be worthy of such positions.[46]

Turning to Psellos' treatment of Basil Lekapenos and John the *Orphanotrophos*, one is struck by how different his approach to eunuchs is;

he assesses them in a matter-of-fact way, generally praising them but also criticising aspects of their behaviour and disposition, but in none of this does he engage with the notion of them as eunuchs. Recounting how the emperor Basil II had to depend on Basil Lekapenos at the beginning of his reign, he describes the eunuch as "the most remarkable person in the Roman empire, outstanding in intellect, bodily stature, and regal appearance", and he compares the eunuch to an athlete competing in the games while the young Basil II observed in order to learn from him.[47] Michael Psellos also appears sympathetic to Basil Lekapenos on his fall from power, noting that the eunuch had done and suffered much for his great-nephew, who treated him with ingratitude.[48] Overall, Psellos seems far more interested in Basil Lekapenos' family ties with the Macedonian dynasty and in the fate of the eunuch as an example of the fickleness of fortune. He was not concerned with the fact that he was a eunuch.

His treatment of the eunuch John *Orphanotrophos*, of whom he had direct knowledge,[49] is similarly pitched, though he does include some negative aspects. However, Psellos appears more interested in the low social origin of John rather than his being a eunuch. He dwells on the obscure and lowly background of the eunuch's family. He notes the humble origins of John's brother Michael.[50] Discussing John's nephew Michael, he says his father came from a remote country place but was not engaged in agriculture, instead applying pitch to new-assembled ships, and he asserts that his mother's branch of the family were of similar ilk (Michael's mother Maria was John's sister).[51] As with his treatment of the eunuch Basil Lekapenos, Psellos also draws attention to the family issues of the eunuch's imperial family: "the eldest brother, John, administered [the] affairs [of his wicked brothers] with great dexterity. It was he who assuaged the emperor's wrath and he who won for his brothers' permission to do what they liked. And he did this, not because he exactly approved of their attitude, but because, despite it, he cared for his family".[52] Psellos records that after the death of Michael IV, Michael V knew that his uncle John "was still in the position of a father to the whole family".[53] One has the sense that Psellos is treating John as an individual rather than as a stereotype.[54] He notes that he had "many sides to his character": he had wit, he was shrewd, showed "meticulous care to his duties", was industrious, had particular skill in finance, was not malicious, could be fierce in expression, was a real brother for Michael and was supportive, vigilant, zealous, observant and honest with the emperor. However, he could also be changeable, greedy and indecent, and he liked a drink. He was observant even when drunk, and people came to fear him more when he was drunk. He was a monk in dress but not in sentiment.[55] In general, though, Psellos presents John as a serious administrator who took his job seriously and presented himself as fierce, perhaps as a method of commanding authority.

Thus there are differences in how Leo the Deacon and Michael Psellos present court eunuchs. The significance of these differences needs to be considered. One might be tempted to conclude that there had been a change in social attitudes between the ninth and eleventh century towards eunuchs, in that they became treated as individuals in their own right rather than being moulded to stereotypical perceptions as a group. However, there are grounds for hesitation in accepting this conclusion. Although Psellos does not explicitly engage with stereotypes about eunuchs in his presentation of John, it is clearly informed by some of them – the able administrator, the greedy official – even though the overall effect is rather different. In contrast, in the chronicle by his contemporary Skylitzes, the stereotypical rhetoric dominates. He follows Leo the Deacon directly in some verdicts: he describes the eunuch Constantine Gongylios (in relation to his failed Cretan campaign) as "an effeminate, sedentary fellow [θηλυδρίαν ἄνθρωπον καὶ ϛκιατραφῆ] with no experience of war, one of the eunuchs of the bedchamber at the palace";[56] while of Peter the eunuch of Nikephoros Phokas, he observes "he was a eunuch but very dynamic [τομίαν μὲν ἄνθρωπον, δραϛτήριον δὲ ἄλλως] and highly experienced in military matters".[57] However, Skylitzes can also add different material and present different versions of events. In his account of emperor John Tzimiskes falling out with Basil Lekapenos, he has the emperor make a disparaging remark about Basil as a eunuch.[58] In his account of a rebellion against the emperor Basil II, he has the leader of the rebellion (Bardas Skleros) reflect on his military rival Bardas Phokas, whom the emperor had appointed in order to suppress his rebellion: "he [Bardas Skleros] thought that now for the first time the fight would be against a true soldier [Bardas Phokas], one who well knew how to conduct military operations with courage and skill; not, as formerly, against pitiful fellows, eunuchs, fostered in chambers and raised in the shade [ἀνδράρια ἐκτετμημένα θαλαμευόμενα καὶ ϛκιατραφῆ]".[59] Commenting on Constantine VIII employing eunuchs as his ministers and generals, Skylitzes describes them as "wine-sodden, servile eunuchs, bloated with every kind of disgusting abomination".[60] On the eunuch Orestes, the *protospatharios* sent by Basil II to Sicily, he notes that he was "inexperienced in war and had no administrative ability".[61] Skylitzes' comments on eunuchs then are more stereotypical and more negative. Perhaps he was reflecting the supposed aristocratic reservation of the Komnenian dynasty (1081–1185) about the use of court eunuchs, since he attained distinction under the emperor Alexios I Komnenos (1081–1118), during whose reign he wrote his history.[62] However, perhaps Skylitzes' simpler historiographical project made for less nuanced images of court eunuchs, or perhaps he had personal reasons for disliking eunuchs. The example of the last great court eunuch, Nikephoritzes, who was a key agent of the emperor Michael VII Doukas (1071–1078) and died under torture after his master's abdication, may have tainted the reputation of court eunuchs.[63] Whatever the explanation for his attitudes, they serve to underscore how the views of Psellos on eunuchs are more unusual and more interesting. One should be cautious in identifying a single Byzantine position on eunuchs.

Conclusion

To conclude, it is clear that in Byzantium, court eunuchs are a recurring part of the political landscape. They are regularly found as civil ministers but can also serve in military roles. By the middle Byzantine period, court eunuchs tend to be drawn from Byzantine families themselves, which distinguishes them from the foreign slave eunuchs of the later Roman and early Byzantine empires and brings a different dimension to the issue of power. Certain powerful eunuchs tend to dominate narratives of politics and court affairs, but this does not mean that they were exceptional. During the Macedonian period, there were several of them, and they tend to follow in succession. Such court eunuchs are not just a feature of the regimes of court-based sedentary emperors and empresses but also distinguish the reigns of macho military men, such as Nikephoros II Phokas and John I Tzimiskes.

Regarding Byzantine perceptions of eunuchs, those who worked at court tend to be assessed by their performance, but this is not necessarily objective. Byzantine authors and texts can have specific agendas and can be deliberately negative or positive in their assessments. This can affect the presentation of the identity of eunuchs, including the gender aspect. One modern view of Byzantine eunuchs – that of Kathryn Ringrose (2003) – is that they were constructed positively as a third gender, as the perfect servant, and then judged against this; this view seems too fixed, however, as I have argued elsewhere.[64] Byzantium inherited diverse perceptions of eunuchs, and Byzantines can assess eunuchs as it suited them. One can get the sense that Byzantine contemporaries generally held a low opinion of eunuchs and that eunuchs had to prove themselves worthy of acceptance but could also earn admiration. However, some authors, such as Psellos, seem to distance themselves from the negative stereotypes and consider eunuchs on an individual basis.

With the subject of eunuchs – castrated men – gender inevitably raises its head, and it is clearly a relevant and significant issue. However, it is not the only issue important for identity; for instance, class, age and ethnicity all need to be considered too. Further, and more fundamentally, there is a danger that eunuchs are being removed from the company of other men. It is easy to draw a contrast between effeminate eunuchs and masculine warriors, but where does this leave, for example, non-eunuch civil servants, of which there were many in Byzantium? What is their gender identity? In Byzantine studies certainly, before we can truly understand the identity of Byzantine eunuchs, we need to establish a holistic view of the identity of Byzantine men.[65]

Notes

1 For Byzantine eunuchs, see in particular Rodolphe Guilland, "Les eunuques dans l'empire byzantine. Étude de titulaire et de prosopographie byzantines," *Revue*

des études byzantines 1 (1943): 197–238; Kathryn M. Ringrose, *The Perfect Servant: Eunuchs and the Social Construction of Gender* (Chicago and London: University of Chicago Press, 2003); Shaun Tougher, *The Eunuch in Byzantine History and Society* (London and New York: Routledge, 2008); and the chapters by Niels Gaul, Margaret Mullett, George Sidéis and Shaun Tougher in *Eunuchs in Antiquity and Beyond*, ed. Shaun Tougher (London: Duckworth and The Classical Press of Wales, 2002). See now also Charis Messis, *Les eunuques à Byzance, entre réalité et imaginaire* (Paris: Centre d'études byzantines, néo-helleniques et sud-est européennes, 2014), which was published after the writing of this chapter.

2 For the Macedonian dynasty, see for instance Albert Vogt, *Basile Ier, Empereur de Byzance (867–886) et la civilisation byzantine à la fin du IXe siècle* (Paris: A. Picard et fils, 1908); Norman Tobias, *Basil I, Founder of the Macedonian Dynasty: A Study of the Political and Military History of the Byzantine Empire in the Ninth Century* (Lampeter: The Edwin Mellen Press, 2007); Shaun Tougher, *The Reign of Leo VI (886–912): Politics and People* (Leiden: Brill, 1997); Steven Runciman, *The Emperor Romanus Lecapenus and His Reign: A Study of Tenth-Century Byzantium* (Cambridge: Cambridge University Press, 1929); Arnold Toynbee, *Constantine Porphyrogenitus and His World* (London, New York and Toronto: Oxford University Press, 1973); Gustave Léon Schlumberger, *Un empereur byzantine au dixième siècle, Nicéphore Phocas* (Paris: Firmin-Didot, 1890); and Catherine Holmes, *Basil II and the Governance of Empire (976–1025)* (Oxford: Oxford University Press, 2005). For family relationships within the dynasty, see also Shaun Tougher, "Imperial Families: The Case of the Macedonians (867–1056)," in *Approaches to the Byzantine Family*, ed. Leslie Brubaker and Shaun Tougher (Farnham and Burlingtion VT: Ashgate, 2013), 303–326.

3 See for instance Keith Hopkins, "Eunuchs in Politics in the Later Roman Empire," *Proceedings of the Cambridge Philological Society* 189 (1963): 62–80, and Hopkins, *Conquerors and Slaves* (Cambridge: Cambridge University Press, 1978), 172–96; Peter Guyot, *Eunuchen als Sklaven und Freigelassene in der griechisch-römischen Antike* (Stuttgart: Klett-Cotta, 1980), 130–76; Tougher, *The Eunuch in Byzantine History and Society*, 36–53.

4 For the grand chamberlain, see for instance James E. Dunlap, "The Office of the Grand Chamberlain in the Later Roman and Byzantine Empires," in *Two Studies in Later Roman and Byzantine Administration* ed. Arthur E. R. Boak and James E. Dunlap (New York and London: The Macmillan Company, 1924), 161–324; Helga Scholten, *Der Eunuch in Kaisernähe: Zur politischen und sozialen Bedeutung des* praepositus sacri cubiculi *im 4. und 5. Jahrhundert n. Chr.* (Frankfurt am Main: Peter Lang, 1995).

5 *Notitia Dignitatum*, ed. Otto Seeck, *Notitia dignitatum, accedunt Notitia urbis Constantinopolitanae et latercula provinciarum* (Berlin: Weidmann, 1876); Nicolas Oikonomidès, ed., *Kletorologion*, in *Les listes de préséance byzantines des IXe et Xe siècles* (Paris: Editions du Centre National de la Recherche Scientifique, 1972), 81–235. For comparison of the two texts, see for instance Shaun Tougher, "Social Transformation, Gender Transformation? The Court Eunuch, 300–900," in *Gender in the Early Medieval World: East and West, 300–900*, ed. Leslie Brubaker and Julia M. H. Smith (Cambridge: Cambridge University Press, 2004), 70–82.

6 Procopius, *History of the Wars*, trans. H. B. Dewing, Loeb Classical Library 217 (1928; repr. Cambridge, MA: Harvard University Press, 1992), 5:78–80, par. 8.3.12–21.

7 See for instance Shaun Tougher, "Byzantine Eunuchs: An Overview, with Special Reference to Their Creation and Origin," in *Women, Men and Eunuchs: Gender in Byzantium*, ed. Liz James (London and New York: Routledge, 1997), 168–184, esp. 177–180, "In or Out? Origins of Court Eunuchs," in Tougher, *Eunuchs in Antiquity and Beyond*, 143–161, esp. 148–149, and Tougher, *The Eunuch in Byzantine History and Society*, 60–67.

8 For Constantine, see for instance Romilly J. H. Jenkins, "A 'Consolatio' of the Patriarch Nicholas Mysticus," *Byzantion* 35 (1965): 159–166, repr. in his *Studies on Byzantine History of the 9th and 10th Centuries* (London: Variorum Reprints, 1970); Tougher, *The Reign of Leo VI*, 200–201. For the office of *parakoimomenos*, see for instance Rodolphe Guilland, "Le parakimomène," *Revue des études byzantines* 2 (1944): 191–201. For Zoe Karbonopsina, see for instance Lynda Garland, *Byzantine Empresses: Women and Power in Byzantium AD 527–1204* (London and New York: Routledge, 1999), 114–125.

9 On eunuchs hailing from Paphlagonia, see Paul Magdalino, "Paphlagonians in Byzantine High Society," in *Η Βυζαντινή Μικρά Αςία (6ος-12ος αι.)*, ed. Stelios Lampakis (Athens: Institute for Byzantine Research, 1998), 141–50; Tougher, "Byzantine Eunuchs," 178–9. *Synaxarion of Constantinople*: *Acta Sanctorum*, Propylaeum Novembris, 721–4.

10 Romilly J. H. Jenkins and L. G. Westerink, ed. and trans., *Nicholas I Patriarch of Constantinople, Letters* (Washington DC: Dumbarton Oaks, 1973), letter 47, 266–74. See also Jenkins, "A 'Consolatio'".

11 On this idea, see for instance Hopkins "Eunuchs in Politics," and *Conquerors and Slaves*, 172–196; Tougher, "In or Out?" esp. 144, 150–152.

12 For Leo Phokas, see for instance J.-C. Cheynet, "Les Phocas," in *Le traité sur la guerrilla* (De velitatione) *de l'empereur Nicéphore Phocas (963–969)*, ed. Gilbert Dagron and Haralambie Mihăescu (Paris: Éditions du Centre National de la Recherche Scientifique, 1986), 296–297; Runciman, *The Emperor Romanus Lecapenus*, 54–61.

13 For John the *Orphanotrophos*, see for instance Raymond Janin, "Un ministre byzantine: Jean l'orphanotrophe (XIe siècle)," *Echos d'Orient* 30 (1931): 431–43.

14 For Basil Lekapenos, see W. G. Brokkaar, "Basil Lacapenus: Byzantium in the Tenth Century," *Studia Byzantina et Neohellenica Neerlandica* 3 (1972): 199–234.

15 Michel Psellos, *Chronographie ou Histoire d'un siècle de Byzance (976–1077)*, ed. and trans. Émile Renauld, 2 vols (Paris: Les Belles Lettres, 1926), 1:3.16.

16 For Leo's *Novels*, see Pierre Noailles and Alphonse Dain, *Les Novelles de Léon VI le Sage* (Paris: Les Belles Lettres, 1944), "Novel 26", 100–105, and "Novel 98", 320–327. For more recent discussion of the *Novels*, see for instance Juan Signes Codoñer, "The Corpus of Leo's Novels. Some Suggestions Concerning Their Date and Promulgation," *Subseciva Groningana* 8 (2009): 1–33, and "Las Novelas de León el Sabio," in *Introduzione al diritto bizantino. Da Giustiniano ai Basilici,* ed. Jan H. A. Lokin and Bernard H. Stolte (Pavia: IUSS Press, 2011), 267–321. For Leo's relationships with, and interest in, eunuchs, see Tougher, *The Reign of Leo VI*, esp. 196–203.

17 See for example Tougher, *The Eunuch in Byzantine History and Society*, 60–61.

18 For Samonas, see for instance Raymond Janin, "Un arabe ministre à Byzance: Samonas (IXe-Xe)," *Echos d'Orient* 34 (1935): 307–318; Romilly J. H. Jenkins, "The Flight of Samonas," *Speculum* 23 (1948): 217–235, repr. in *Studies on Byzantine History*; Lennart Rydén, "The Portrait of the Arab Samonas in Byzantine Literature," *Graeco-Arabica* 3 (1984): 101–8; Tougher, *The Reign of Leo VI*, esp. 197–199.

19 For the Byzantine family and concepts of it, see for instance Leslie Brubaker and Shaun Tougher, eds., *Approaches to the Byzantine Family* (Farnham and Burlington, VT: Ashgate, 2013).
20 For Peter, see for example Cheynet, "Les Phocas," 306; Ralph-Johannes Lilie, Claudia Ludwig, Thomas Pratsch and Beate Zielke, *Prosopographie der mittelbyzantinischen Zeit, Zweite Abteilung (867–1025)* (Berlin: de Gruyter, 2013), Petros #26496, 5:395–398.
21 See for instance Dunlap, "Grand Chamberlain," esp. 260–299; Shaun Tougher, *The Roman Castrati: Eunuchs of the Roman Empire* (forthcoming).
22 For Joseph Bringas, see for instance Athanasios Markopoulos, "Joseph Bringas: Prosopographical Problems and Ideological Trends," chap. 4 in his *History and Literature of Byzantium in the 9th–10th Centuries* (Aldershot and Burlington, VT: Ashgate Variorum, 2004).
23 An account of Nikephoros' "usurpation" and that of Basil's role is preserved in Constantine VII's *Book of Ceremonies*, Book 1, chapter 96. The edition by J. J. Reiske (published in 1829 in the Bonn Corpus) is reprinted in Ann Moffatt and Maxeme Tall, *Constantine Porphyrogennetos, The Book of Ceremonies* (Canberra: Australian Association of Byzantine Studies, 2012), 1:433–40. Significantly, the main surviving manuscript of the *Book of Ceremonies* may have been produced at the direction of Basil Lekapenos himself; see Michael Featherstone, "Further Remarks on the *De Cerimoniis*," *Byzantinische Zeitschrift* 97 (2004): 113–121.
24 Leo the Deacon, *History* 3.8, ed. C. B. Hase (Bonn, 1828), 49.8–10. The appointment of the *proedros* is described in the *Book of Ceremonies* 1.97 and seems to be a description of the ceremony for Basil; see for instance Featherstone, "Further Remarks."
25 See for instance Bissera V. Pentcheva, "Containers of Power: Eunuchs and Reliquaries in Byzantium," *Res* 51 (2007): 109–120.
26 Pentcheva, "Containers of Power," 114, n. 20.
27 Psellos, *Chronographia* 1.20.
28 Psellos, *Chronographia* 4.3–4.
29 See the chapters of Nadia Maria El-Cheikh, Hugh Kennedy and Michael Hoeckelmann in this volume, which discuss military eunuchs for the Middle East and China.
30 See for example Shaun Tougher, "Byzantine Eunuchs as Generals: The Case of Narses" (forthcoming).
31 Psellos, *Chronographia* 1.3.
32 For Leo the Deacon, see for instance Alice-Mary Talbot and Denis F. Sullivan, *The History of Leo the Deacon: Byzantine Military Expansion in the Tenth Century* (Washington DC: Dumbarton Oaks, 2005), esp. 9–51. For reflections on Leo's treatment of gender, see also Athanasios Markopoulos, "Gender Issues in Leo the Deacon," chap. 23 of his *History and Literature*. For Michael Psellos, see Stratis Papaioannou, *Michael Psellos: Rhetoric and Authorship in Byzantium* (Cambridge: Cambridge University Press, 2013).
33 It is interesting that Leo associates these positive qualities with Basil's mixed racial origins (as half "Scythian").
34 Translation in Talbot and Sullivan, *The History of Leo the Deacon*, 143.
35 Ibid., 143 n. 8.
36 Procopius, *History of the Wars*, trans. H. B. Dewing, Loeb Classical Library 107 (1916; repr. Cambridge, MA: Harvard University Press, 1993), 3:403, par. 6.13.16.
37 See for instance Tougher, *The Eunuch in Byzantine History and Society*, esp. 96–97, 103.

38 Which also matches the comments of Procopius – and his contemporary Agathias – concerning Narses: see further below.
39 Translation in Talbot and Sullivan, *The History of Leo the Deacon*, 90. See also the comments of Talbot and Sullivan on Leo the Deacon on eunuchs at ibid., 30.
40 Leo the Deacon 1.2, translation in Talbot and Sullivan, *The History of Leo the Deacon*, 59–60.
41 When he speaks to his troops after the death of the Herul Fulcaris.
42 Agathias 1.16.1–2. For the Greek text, see Rudolf Keydell, ed., *Agathiae Myrinaei,* Historiarum Libri Quinque (Berlin: de Gruyter, 1967), 30. For the English translation see Joseph D. Frendo, *Agathias, The Histories* (Berlin and New York: de Gruyter, 1975), 24. Agathias continues, "The fact is that the nobility of soul cannot fail to make its mark, no matter what obstacles are put in its path".
43 *Agathias* 1.7.8, trans. Frendo, *Agathias*, 16.
44 Translation in Talbot and Sullivan, *The History of Leo the Deacon,* 132.
45 Ibid., 158.
46 Markopoulos, "Gender Issues in Leo the Deacon," 14–16, emphasises Leo's negative attitude towards eunuchs at the expense of the more positive views expressed in the history, arguing that the "exceptions…merely serve to underline the negative rule" (16).
47 Michael Psellus, *Chronographia* 1.3. For the English translation, see Edgar Robert Ashton Sewter, *Michael Psellus, Fourteen Byzantine Rulers* (Harmondsworth: Penguin, 1966), 28.
48 *Chronographia* 1.19–22, trans. Sewter, *Psellus*, 37–39.
49 *Chronographia* 4.12, trans. Sewter, *Psellus*, 92, "when I was starting to grow a beard, I saw the man (τὸν ἄνδρα) himself and I heard him speak and witnessed his actions".
50 *Chronographia* 4.10.
51 *Chronographia* 4.26–28.
52 *Chronographia* 4.11, trans. Sewter, *Psellus*, 92.
53 *Chronographia* 5.9, trans. Sewter, *Psellus*, 126. Psellos does seem very interested in the subject of eunuchs and their families.
54 For Psellos' assessment of John, see especially *Chronographia* 4.12–14, trans. Sewter, *Psellus*, 92–94.
55 For eunuchs in religious roles in Byzantium, as bishops, clergy, monks and saints, see for instance Ringrose, *The Perfect Servant*, esp. 111–127; and Tougher, *The Eunuch in Byzantine History and Society*, esp. 68–82.
56 Skylitzes, Constantine VII 15, ed. Ioannes Thurn, *Ioannis Scylitzae Synopsis Historiarum* (Berlin and New York: de Gruyter, 1973), 245.4. For the English translation, see John Wortley, *John Skylitzes, A Synopsis of Byzantine History 811–1057* (Cambridge: Cambridge University Press, 2010), 237.
57 Skylitzes, Basil II and Constantine VIII 1, ed. Thurn, *Scylitzae*, 315.79, trans. Wortley, *Skylitzes*, 299.
58 Skylitzes, John I Tzimiskes 22, ed. Thurn, *Scylitzae*, 312.13, trans. Wortley, *Skylitzes*, 296.
59 Skylitzes, Basil II and Constantine VIII 8, ed. Thurn, *Scylitzae*, 324.51, trans. Wortley, *Skylitzes*, 308.
60 Skylitzes, Constantine VIII 1, ed. Thurn, *Scylitzae*, 370.27–28, trans. Wortley, *Skylitzes*, 349.
61 Skylitzes, Romanos III Argyros 8, ed. Thurn, *Scylitzae*, 383.98–99, trans. Wortley, *Skylitzes*, 362.
62 See Tougher, *The Eunuch in Byzantine History and Society*, esp. 119–122.

63 For Nikephoritzes, see Tougher, *The Eunuch in Byzantine History and Society*, esp. 56.
64 Tougher, *The Eunuch in Byzantine History and Society*, esp. 96–111.
65 For some preliminary work on Byzantine men, see for example Charles Barber, "Homo Byzantinus?", in James, *Gender in Byzantium*, 185–199; Myrto Hatzaki, *Beauty and the Male Body in Byzantium: Perceptions and Representations in Art and Text* (Basingstoke and New York: Palgrave Macmillan, 2009); Shaun Tougher, "Cherchez l'homme! Byzantine Men: A Eunuch Perspective," in *The Byzantine World*, ed. Paul Stephenson (London and New York: Routledge, 2010), 83–91.

12 Eunuchs in the Fatimid empire

Ambiguities, gender and sacredness

Serena Tolino

Introduction

This chapter examines the roles that eunuchs had in the Fatimid empire, a shiʿi dynasty that reigned in North Africa and Yemen from 297/909 until 567/1171. The historical context in which the Fatimid empire emerged makes this investigation particularly compelling. The Fatimids emerged as a clandestine ʿAlid movement, which competed for legitimacy with the official ruling dynasty of that time, the Abbasids. Due to its secretiveness, it was crucial that the early Fatimids could count on the absolute loyalty of their supporters and servants, which is why they probably relied greatly upon eunuchs.

Eunuchs were first and foremost slaves; even if many of them were able to secure their freedom later in life, they still remained in a subaltern status, having been removed from their place of origin. Moreover, eunuchs, unlike other slaves, could not procreate. This might help us to make sense of their perceived loyalty: Having lost their families and social ties before their arrival in Islamic territories, they were isolated and had only their patron and the advantages that their attachment to him could guarantee. In the case of the early Fatimids, the eunuch's master was the head of a clandestine organization, and thus their perceived loyalty assumed an even greater importance.

The chapter focuses on two themes: first, there is an analysis of the eunuchs' gender; and second, an examination of the links eunuchs had with sacredness. There is an extensive theoretical debate in reference to the concepts of gender and sacredness, which cannot be addressed fully in this chapter; here the preliminary results of a still on-going investigation will be presented. When referring to these two concepts, I build upon two significant works on this topic: Shaun Marmon's research on the "society of eunuchs" guarding the tomb of the Prophet Muḥammad in Medina,[1] and Kathryn Ringrose's investigation of eunuchs in Byzantium.[2]

According to Marmon, the "society of eunuchs" that guarded the Prophet's tomb in Medina was founded sometime in the twelfth century. In the different accounts of the foundation of this society, three elements remain consistent:

1 the role of a "strong Sunni" sultan in its establishment, either Ṣalāḥ al-Dīn (d. 589/1193) or Nūr al-Dīn (d. 511/1174), who are represented as strongly connected to the Prophet Muḥammad;
2 the description of the eunuchs as guards and servants of the Prophet;
3 the prestige and power which was attached to them.[3]

Marmon argues that "the struggles between Shi'i and Sunni factions in Medina during the Mamluk[4] period inform the enduring image of the holy eunuch constructed by Sunni authors in the fourteenth and fifteenth centuries".[5] It is certainly likely that conflicts between Shi'i and Sunni Muslims had an impact upon the construction and development of the "holy eunuch". However, it could be argued that this understanding of the eunuch began to be formed before the society of eunuchs was founded in Medina and that it was already a recognized interpretation during the late phase of the Fatimid empire (from ca. 1060). It is not accidental that Ṣalāḥ al-Dīn, one of the two rulers to which the foundation of the society is attributed, was also the commander who ousted the Fatimids, bringing Egypt back into the Sunni orbit of influence.

Marmon focuses on the eunuchs of Medina, but she also includes an analysis of the eunuchs who guarded the sultans' tombs in Cairo and convincingly establishes a link between these two groups. This was based on the "*baraka*" (divine charisma) emanating from both tombs; in her words, the tombs were "a kind of sanctuary, and the eunuchs who surrounded him [the imam-caliph] not only controlled access to his person and his family, but also served to emphasize the sacred power of rulership".[6] As we shall see, this applies more so in respect to the Fatimid imams. The link between eunuchs and sacredness was a product of a gradual "sanctification" of the imam/caliph, which was to become increasingly "sacred", isolated and inaccessible. *Baraka*, "charisma", as Shaun Marmon and Heinz Halm translated it, literally means "blessing". It indicates a force coming from God, which can be imbued within his prophets and saints. Muḥammad and his family, the *ahl al-bayt*, are considered to be the bearers of this *baraka,* as are his descendants – which the Fatimid imams claimed to be.

The gradual sanctification of the Fatimid imam can be contextualized within what Garth Fowden described as "imperial monotheism".[7] As Almut Höfert has argued, if we apply the concept of imperial monotheism to pre-modern societies, we can suggest that the Roman–Byzantine empire, the Umayyad and Abbasid caliphates, the Carolingian empire and the papacy are specific variants of the same imperial monotheism, which built upon either Islam or Christianity. The figure of Christ provided contemporaries with a way of establishing a direct link between the emperor and God: The emperor, as Christ, became God's deputy on the earth.[8] This sanctioned the idea that the divine could be concentrated in a single person: sacredness was not pervasive, as it was in antiquity, but became in the Middle Ages a specific prerogative of the emperor on the one hand and the caliph on the other.[9] If we include the Fatimid imam within the latter context, the eunuchs' closeness to him can be understood as an affinity with sacredness.

Marmon also argues that the institutionalization of eunuchs as guardians of tombs and their relation with the sacred was a consequence of their representation as "a category of non-gendered individuals who both defined and crossed highly charged boundaries of moral and physical space in the world of the living and in the world of the dead".[10] According to Marmon, eunuchs crossed not only spatial (both real and metaphorical) boundaries, but also temporal boundaries; being sterile, and as a consequence of their castration, eunuchs were removed from the normal cycle of life and the normal flow of time. This provided them with a means to adapt in different situations. Marmon's suggestion that there is a relationship between eunuchs, sacredness and "time" is well made and convincing. However, her definition of eunuchs as "non-gendered individuals" could be argued to be problematic.

Kathryn Ringrose, in her investigation of eunuchs in Byzantium, also analysed the relationship between eunuchs and sacredness and used gender in her analysis; indeed, she stated that "Byzantine society was constructed to accommodate a third gender category".[11] According to her analysis, this third gender was created for and by eunuchs, whose "a-sexual nature" comprised "a very important and positive part of their role as servants".[12] Ringrose's use of gender as an analytical category in looking at eunuchs is certainly appreciable but, as argued also by Shaun Tougher in this volume, it often appears too fixed.

In this chapter, it is argued that eunuchs were not understood as a "third gender" but were instead gendered according to the different contexts in which they acted or were represented. What we know about eunuch gender identities is what the sources tell us. Authors who had diverse aims and audiences compiled these sources, and consequently eunuchs are represented in different ways. To make this point clear, various kinds of sources are examined within the chapter: the literary genre of *adab*,[13] chronicles, medical, legal and religious sources.

Eunuchs in classical *adab*: The case of al-Jāḥiẓ

One prominent Arabic source that extensively describes eunuchs is the first chapter of al-Jāḥiẓ's (d. 255/868) work *Kitāb al-Ḥayawān*,[14] which is devoted to the subject of castration. This encyclopaedic work, which is often translated as "The Book of Animals", should instead be understood as "The book of living beings", as the word *ḥayawān* is a term used to refer to all living creatures.[15] Although al-Jāḥiẓ lived at the Abbasid Court in Baghdad, and not in the Fatimid empire, his description of eunuchs merits investigation for two reasons: first, al-Jāḥiẓ was one of the most influential intellectuals of the Islamic Middle Ages, who dedicated his life and career to prose writing; second, his work, which deals with castration, provides a number of insights into contemporary attitudes towards eunuchs.

According to al-Jāḥiẓ, castration has both physical and psychological consequences, which make eunuchs different from non-castrated men (*fuḥūl*); the author not only analyses "gender", but also brings race into focus. Indeed, according to him, there are five groups of eunuchs: *ṣaqāliba*,[16] eunuchs coming from the Sind,[17] black eunuchs (from Ethiopia, Nubia and Sudan), *rūmī* (from Byzantium) and Sabaeans.[18] This classification is slightly different from that used by the famous Arabic geographer al-Muqaddasī (d. 380/991), who divided eunuchs into black and white eunuchs. Black eunuchs are then divided into three sub-groups according to their provenance (Egypt, Yemen and Abyssinia), and white eunuchs into two (*ṣaqāliba* and *rūmī*).[19]

Al-Jāḥiẓ believed that certain effects of castration characterised all eunuchs, no matter where they had originated: these included a terrible stink,[20] longer bones and feet, curved fingers and skin that became dry and wrinkled with age.[21] Moreover, when eunuchs walked, they moved with heavy steps, as if they could not control their legs and muscles; the reason given was because "the penis was stretching the nerves, the articulations and the muscles".[22] Another common characteristic was the voice, which became different from both the feminine and masculine voice.[23] As for their hair, al-Jāḥiẓ argues that if a man is castrated before puberty, he lost his hair entirely, except his pubic hair. Nevertheless, for him eunuchs did not experience real baldness (a symbol of wisdom) but a form of receding hairline, such as women suffered from.[24] Castration also was said to affect the longevity of eunuchs, who were assumed to live longer than non-castrated men; al-Jāḥiẓ attributed this to "the lack of coupling, because the shortage of ejaculation does not weaken the dorsal spine".[25] Regarding the psychological effects, al-Jāḥiẓ stresses the importance of race: In the case of the *ṣaqāliba,* castration apparently had a positive influence on intelligence and eloquence,[26] yet it was deemed to have a negative impact on black eunuchs, who, because of castration, became "lower compared to their equivalents".[27]

According to al-Jāḥiẓ, eunuchs could manifest "masculine characteristics", such as being particularly gifted with skills like archery and cavalry.[28] Nevertheless, in general, al-Jāḥiẓ highlights how castration positioned eunuchs closer to the world of women and children. Their gender ambiguity is, for al-Jāḥiẓ, the main problem; as a consequence of castration, the eunuch

> becomes like the mule that is neither a donkey nor a horse, and his nature is divided between the one of the male and the one of the female. His behavior will be neither pure nor clear, not that of a man or a woman, but mixed.[29]

The focus on the behaviour of eunuchs is repeated a number of times. For example, al-Jāḥiẓ argues that "the eunuch becomes interested in frivolity, like playing with the birds and other things that are typical of the behavior of women and children". Eunuchs are also said to have "a greed for food, a behavior of children (and women)", and to "become quick in changing from anger to happiness and incapable of keeping secrets", again a characteristic attributed to women and children.[30] Eunuchs also were considered talented with sweeping, cleaning and all domestic activities, "like it happens to women".[31]

The above-mentioned descriptions of eunuchs seem to echo the stereotypical criticisms of eunuchs that Ringrose found in Byzantine sources.[32] As she stated, "Eunuchs are regularly accused of being unable to curb their acquisitiveness, whether for power or for treasure". Certainly, a number of Byzantine figures made this connection: In the fourth century, St Basil described eunuchs as "mad for gold", whereas in the sixth century, John of Antioch said that they were "grasping". Moreover, "like women, eunuchs cannot control their emotions. They are quick to anger and fly into rages. They can become depressed and weep into their food. Their voices are high and shrill, like those of women".[33]

Al-Jāḥiẓ's description of the eunuch as an ambiguous figure, and their stereotypical representation, could be thought a little suspicious, especially as we know he was convinced that Byzantium was "the origin of every castration in the world".[34] Indeed, al-Jāḥiẓ must have been familiar with Greek and Byzantine sources; in the Abbasid court of the ninth century, these sources were widely translated into Arabic and were accessible by the cultural elite. Al-Jāḥiẓ himself also translated works by Greek scientists and philosophers into Arabic. Moreover, it is also important to point out that al-Jāḥiẓ's explicit representation of the eunuch as an ambiguous figure stands as quite exceptional, as an analysis of chronicles, legal, medical and religious sources will demonstrate.

Going beyond the "third gender" model

Although I do not consider eunuchs to be a "third gender", it can be argued that some aspects of their gender were conceptualised in a way that we could define as "ambiguous". This gender "ambiguity" was not explicitly conceptualized (with the standing exception of al-Jāḥiẓ) but can be inferred from the way the sources talk about them and from the duties that were assigned to them. For example, if eunuchs were considered "complete" men, they could not have acted as harem guardians, which was in fact one of their basic functions. However, in other situations, they were considered as other men and were well established in the administrative, political and military elite as commanders, admirals, heads of police, provincial governors and so on.

When looking at specific historical sources – chronicles, for example – it is often very difficult to distinguish a eunuch from a non-castrated man within the text. In Arabic, there are specific terms to identify a castrated man: *khāṣī*, a man whose testicles have been cut; *majbūb*, a man whose penis has been cut; and *mamsūḥ,* a man whose testicles and penis have been cut. These terms, however, are mostly used in legal texts and not in historical narratives; in the latter, more ambiguous words are used, the most common being *khādim*, which means "servant". David Ayalon has argued that the term is only used to refer to eunuchs, yet other scholars have disagreed and suggested that it has a broader meaning.[35] Moreover, eunuchs, like every individual, also had a *kunya*, which is a name given to an adult, usually derived from his/her eldest child. Although, generally speaking, the *kunya* refers to the bearer's first-born, it may also be used in a hypothetical or metaphorical sense.[36] It is difficult, of course, to then know whether a man actually had a child or not.

Regarding Islamic law, although castration constitutes a change in God's creation, which is strictly forbidden,[37] the Prophet Muḥammad was said to have accepted a eunuch as a gift.[38] Moreover, eunuchs were usually castrated outside the Islamic world, where Islamic law did not apply. Therefore, jurists took them for granted and never discussed or debated whether they should be "categorized" as men or women. This appears to be a particularly egregious absence if we acknowledge that in Islamic law, what was considered appropriate for men and women regarding their duties, rights, dress codes and so on was strictly prescribed; ambiguity was hardly tolerated, at least in legal theory. While Muslim jurists spent much time discussing the gender of a hermaphrodite,[39] they did not do so in regards to eunuchs.

Nevertheless, it is still possible to infer what jurists' thought about the gender of eunuchs, particularly if we examine those fields of law where being either a man or a woman determined what was legislated, such as marriage, divorce and attributing paternity/maternity. For example, Muslim jurists discussed the issue of a eunuch's marriage and unanimously agreed on its validity. At the same time, they also tried to protect the right of a married woman to obtain sexual satisfaction, and they agreed that a woman whose husband was not "able to penetrate her" had the right to dissolve their marriage. In this specific case, the man was granted an *ajl* (postponement); he had one year to consummate the marriage, and if he could not, then the marriage was nullified. But this was not specifically aimed at men who had been castrated, as we find the same discussion with regards to impotent men.

A similar reasoning was followed for divorce. In Islamic law, there are many different ways of ending a marriage, the most important of which is the *ṭalāq*, which is initiated by the husband; and the *khulʿ*, which is initiated by the wife. Strictly speaking, the *ṭalāq* is a form of unilateral repudiation, with the husband saying to his wife: "I divorce you". The *khulʿ* is also a form of repudiation, but in this case the woman asks the husband to divorce her in exchange for financial compensation, or she may petition a judge, but in this case she usually renounces all her rights. Eunuchs, like non-castrated men, had a right to *ṭalāq*.

Attributing the paternity of a child to a eunuch was also discussed; if a castrated man still had his testicles, then the paternity could be assigned to him without any doubt. If he had a penis, but not his testicles, according to the great majority of jurists, paternity could not be attributed, while for others the case should be referred to a doctor/s. If he had neither his penis nor testicles, the majority of jurists believed that the paternity could not be attributed.[40]

In short, jurists clearly did not debate the eunuchs' gender identity *per se* but simply took for granted that eunuchs were men, even if they were "mutilated" men. There is a *ḥadīth*, which is attributed to ʿĀʾisha, Muḥammad's wife, that corroborates this understanding of eunuchs as being men. Apparently she stated that castrated men should be forbidden to look at women, exactly as non-castrated men were, because "castration is a mutilation, and does not make licit what was forbidden before it".[41]

Regarding medical thought, as Dor Ze'evi argues in his book on sexuality in the Ottoman empire, the pre-modern Islamic medical discourse did not properly define a gender binary. Instead, a man and a woman were understood "as part of a continuum of perfection, leading from the basest creatures to the celestial. Man in this scheme of things was the crowning achievement of terrestrial creatures, whereas woman was regarded as a less-developed version of man, physically and mentally".[42] Moreover, as the ninth-century Persian physician al-Rāzī wrote, "not every male is masculine in the extreme and not every female is feminine in the extreme and there exist masculine women and feminine men".[43] One such authoritative supporter of this "continuum of perfection" idea was the Prophet Muḥammad himself, who said that women would be the majority of those who suffered Hell-fire, as they were *imperfect* (*nāqiṣāt*, literally "missing") in intellect and religion.[44]

Although many scholars have debated the authenticity of the *corpus* of the Prophetic sayings,[45] it is not relevant here whether Muḥammad and ʿĀʾisha in fact pronounced these sentences; what matters is that someone thought of attributing these ideas to Muḥammad and ʿĀʾisha as a way of legitimising what some contemporaries within society must have believed in.

Therefore, if we follow Dor Ze'evi and consider men and women as being two poles of a "continuum of perfection", then eunuchs should also be considered part of this continuum. Medical, legal and religious sources all point to how eunuchs were considered closer to the masculine pole than the feminine one; even if not as perfect as non-castrated men, still eunuchs were "closer to perfection" than women were.

Struggling for legitimation: The (proto)Sunni and (proto)Shiʿi fracture

The Fatimid case is a good example of a context in which eunuchs can be viewed as "perfect servants", to use Ringrose's expression. The Fatimids started their rise to power as a clandestine ʿAlid movement and became the first ruling Shiʿi dynasty of the Islamic world. Their rule explicitly challenged the Abbasids claim of a universal caliphate centred in Baghdad. The establishment of this counter-caliphate can be understood as the moment in which the fracture between Shi'i and Sunni Islam was conceptualised; beforehand, there were only different groups which aimed for power.[46] It is important to understand how the Fatimid caliphs constructed their sacredness as rulers and religious leaders in order to consider the special relationship between caliphs and eunuchs. As such, below I briefly sketch this background.

The division between Shi'i and Sunni Islam did not originate with Muḥammad, nor was it based on theological differences; it was instead founded on a power struggle following the death of the Prophet Muḥammad, in particular concerning who had the right to guide the Islamic community. The main medieval concept for both the Fatimid and the Abbasid caliphate was not in fact the Arabic word for "caliphate" (*khilāfa*) but rather the term *imamate*. The word imam refers literally to a person that stands "ahead"; the term can identify the person who leads the prayer or also a renowned religious scholar. In the ninth century, imam also became the official title of the Abbasid caliph.[47] As al-Mawardī (d. 450/1058) stated in his classic work on the caliphate: "Allah, may his power be radiant, has delegated a leader to the *umma* [the Islamic community] who stands in as a successor to Prophethood, and has encompassed the affair of the nation by him".[48] This "leader" is the imam (which here means "the caliph"). According to al-Māwardī, the "imamate is thus a principle on which the foundations of the nation are established and by which the public interest of the *umma* is maintained". Moreover, the "imamate is prescribed to succeed prophethood as a means of protecting the *dīn* [religion] and of managing the affairs of the world" [in Arabic *siyāsat al-dunyā*].[49] Therefore, the imam has a double role, in charge of and protecting both religious and mundane affairs.

The clash between what we could define as "proto-Sunni" and "proto-shi'i" was not based on how each group understood and conceptualized the imamate but rather on who was entitled to become the imam, as well as the different levels of importance ascribed to those who descended from the *ahl al-bayt*, the Prophetic family. Considering that Muḥammad did not have heirs, the genealogy had to pass through 'Alī (that is why they became known as *shi'at 'Alī*, the party of 'Alī, later simply "Shi'a") and his wife Fāṭima, the daughter of the Prophet Muḥammad (for whom the Fatimids are named).

When Muḥammad died in 11/632, Abū Bakr, a senior Companion and father-in-law of Muḥammad became caliph (in Arabic *khalīfa,* literally "deputy"). After his death two more Companions (but not blood-relatives) of the Prophet, 'Umar ibn al-Khaṭṭāb (d. 23/644) and 'Uthmān ibn 'Affān (d. 47/656) took upon this office, and it was only following the latter's death that 'Alī, Muḥammad's cousin, finally attained the caliphship. One group of Muslims had always supported the idea that only 'Alī (and later his descendants) had the right to become Muḥammad's successor[50] and had thus refused to acknowledge the first three caliphs. Later, the 'Alids would quarrel over the legitimate line of succession; after the death of the fourth imam ‘Alī b. al-Ḥusayn (d. 95/713), the majority of ‘Alids supported his first son, Muḥammad al-Bāqir (d. 114/731–2) as his successor, while a minority supported another son, Zayd ibn ‘Alī (d. 122/740).[51] Those who supported Muḥammad al-Bāqir continued to follow the genealogy of the imamate from his progeny until the death of the sixth imam, Jaʿfar al-Ṣādiq (d. 148/765). At this point another fracture occurred: Before dying, Jaʿfar al-Ṣādiq designated as his successor his son Ismā‘īl, who died before his father. While the majority of the ‘Alids recognized another son of Jaʿfar al-Ṣādiq as imam, Mūsā al-Kāẓim (d. 182/798), and followed his progeny until Muḥammad al-Mahdī, the twelfth imam (this is why they are called Twelvers),[52] others instead chose his first son Ismā‘īl. They believed either that Ismā‘īl's death was not actually real or that he had passed the imamate to his son, Muḥammad ibn Ismā‘īl (d. 197/813). They identify seven imams; for this reason they are called "Seveners" or, from the name of Ismā‘īl, "Isma‘ilis". The Fatimids belonged to this group.[53]

Within the Isma‘ilis, the imamate acquired a stronger and esoteric meaning. According to them, the Quran has an outer (*ẓāhir*) and an inner meaning (*bāṭin*). While the *ẓāhir* consists of the obligatory acts and the *sharīʿa* (Islamic law) can be known by every Muslim, the *bāṭin*, the hidden and truer meaning of the Quran, is known in its entirety only to the imam. The imam is able to gradually reveal its meaning to initiates who undergo special training.[54] Because it was believed other humans were not able to comprehend the *bāṭin* (inner meaning), God provided humanity with the so-called speaker (*nāṭiq*) prophets. Six of these speaker prophets have already appeared: Adam, Noah, Abraham, Moses, Jesus and Muḥammad. Each of them brought the exoteric message of God, which was embedded into various rites, ceremonies, and laws. The protection of the *bāṭin* meaning of the divine message was in contrast assigned to a "plenipotentiary" (a *waṣī* or *asās*) which, in the case of Muḥammad, was ʿAlī. According to Isma‘ilis, when both the speaker and the plenipotentiary died, God sent seven imams who were responsible for preserving the hidden meaning of the divine message and for gradually revealing it to initiates. Muḥammad was considered to be the speaker Prophet of the sixth era, while ʿAlī the *waṣī* and his descendants are the seven imams; this explains the importance that was given to ʿAlī's progeny. The Isma‘ilis believed that the last imam, Muḥammad b. Ismā‘īl, went on *occultation*, (hidden from view); that is, that he disappeared and will one day return and come back as a messianic figure, the awaited Mahdi (the "truly guided one") or also the Qā'im (the one who appears), who would gather again all Muslims and bring peace and justice to the world.

When the Fatimids rose to power, they were forced to provide a genealogy that legitimised their claims to lead the *umma* (the Islamic community). With regards to the genealogy, they claimed to descend from the Prophet Muḥammad, but this claim has been heavily contested and even ridiculed.[55]

The early Fatimids: From secrecy to power

When the Isma'ilis started to expand their network of supporters, the Islamic world was ruled by the Abbasid dynasty, who claimed their legitimacy from the Prophet Muḥammad through an uncle of his.[56] Isma'ilis were, to begin with, nothing more than a clandestine and rebel group. Notwithstanding this, the Isma'ili system of propaganda, the *da'wat al-Ḥaqq* (the call to the truth) or *al-da'wa al-Hadiya* (the rightly guided mission)[57] or simply *al-da'wa*, was an articulate and organized movement that recruited supporters and collected funds in support of Muḥammad b. Ismā'īl, the awaited Mahdī, who was believed to be in occultation.

While he was concealed, the Mahdī required a deputy who could communicate with his supporters, which were spread far and wide throughout the Islamic world; in the middle of the third/ninth century, a man named 'Abd Allāh, who was based in Salamiyya (Syria), claimed to be in contact with the Mahdī, and it was he who would become the head of the secret *da'wa*. A few years later, a nephew of this man, Abū 'Alī Muḥammad Abū al-Shalaghlagh, announced he was the anticipated imam, while his nephew, Sa'īd ibn al-Ḥusayn 'Abd Allāh, was declared to be the Mahdī.

This foundational moment in Fatimid history is recounted through the voice of a eunuch, Ja'far; his secretary, who was also a eunuch, composed his biography.[58] Ja'far had grown up together with the "supposed" Mahdī, who had been his milk-brother and was a few months older, thus born around 260/873. Both men lived through the period in which the Fatimids rose to become a ruling dynasty. Ja'far's biography is an invaluable source, for it offers a window into the first phase of Fatimid history. It demonstrates that even in its early foundation, a significant connection existed between the Fatimid imam-caliphs and eunuchs; furthermore, eunuchs were not only political actors but were also engaged in recording Fatimid history and influenced the construction of dynastical memory.

In declaring himself to be the Mahdī, Sa'īd ibn al-Ḥusayn 'Abd Allāh undertook a dangerous move, considering the Abbasids' supremacy in the Islamic world at the time. The situation in Salamiyya indeed became dangerous, and al-Mahdī escaped to North Africa, where the local *dā'ī* had organized a powerful network of supporters. During this unsafe journey, Ja'far was a companion of al-Mahdī but, once they arrived in Sijilmāsa, al-Mahdī was confined in his house by order of the Abbasids. Ja'far was imprisoned and tortured, and he proved his loyalty by not revealing the intent of al-Mahdi's mission.[59] When Ja'far was released, al-Mahdī sent him to Salamiyya to retrieve the treasures he had left there and to return them by concealing the cache in a cargo of cotton.[60]

In the meantime, Isma'ilis conquered Raqqāda (today in Tunisia) and then later Sijilmāsa, following which they freed al-Mahdī, who would became the first imam–caliph of the Fatimid dynasty in 296/909. For his previous service, Ja'far was awarded the office of *ḥājib* (chamberlain), which involved greeting those people who came to honour the new imam–caliph and instructing them on how to address al-Mahdī and how to pray for him.[61] Ja'far, a eunuch, became the "door" to the imam–caliph, a role that was a particular honour if we consider the function the imam had for the Fatimids and the *baraka* (divine charisma) that was supposed to emanate from him.

The previous discussion demonstrates that Ja'far was considered to be a loyal (perhaps "perfect") servant of the dynasty. It is important to note that no explicit mention of Ja'far's gender is recorded in his biography, nor do we find any stereotypes that relate to eunuchs. There is only one allusion to Ja'far's gender. When al-Mahdī married, Ja'far sat in front of his bedroom together with some women until al-Mahdī came out of the room and threw a veil at him, probably a bloody sheet. Ja'far put it on his head and danced with the women, who were playing with him and congratulating him, as he was the milk-brother of the new-married imam–caliph. We can assume that Jaʿfar was allowed to spend the wedding night in front of al-Mahdī's room, surrounded by women, because he was a eunuch. Nevertheless, in the source, the focus seems to be more on the intimacy of the scene than on Ja'far's gender; it seems to me that the author of the biography, a eunuch himself, and Ja'far's secretary, was not interested in Ja'far's gender but only in Ja'far's political role and importance for the dynasty.

The eunuch Jawdhar and the early imperial phase: A "perfect servant"?

After the Fatimids conquered Raqqāda, a *ṣaqlabī* eunuch, Jawdhar, who was already a prominent court eunuch of the former dynasty, became one of the closest advisors to the early imams. As with the case of Ja'far, we are fortunate in that we have Jawdhar's biography, composed by his secretary al-Manṣūr.[62] This source gives us another perspective into how eunuchs perceived their role in the service of the Fatimid dynasty and demonstrates again the importance that eunuchs held as recorders of the Fatimid past.

In this biography, one anecdote shows how enthusiastically al-Jawdhar appeared to have embraced the new Isma'ili faith. In the account, we are told there were some tensions at court, so al-Mahdi decided to send one of his servants, a *ṣaqlabī*, to investigate the matter. He returned with information, so al-Mahdi was able to settle the dispute, and he rewarded the *ṣaqlabī* with his *baraka*. However, the *ṣaqlabī* was disappointed, because he would have preferred a "material" reward. While he was leaving, he met Jawdhar, who sensed his disappointment and asked him what the matter was. The *ṣaqlabī* explained the situation and Jawdhar, surprised that he would have preferred a "material" reward to the *baraka* of the imam, paid him 20 dinārs to "buy" this *baraka*. When al-Mahdi heard about this, he summoned Jawdhar and asked him to confirm the account. Once Jawdhar did so, al-Mahdi granted his *baraka* to the eunuch and, because of his devotion, asked God to bless his servant until his last day.[63]

His commitment to the imperial family was well appreciated, as a long list of Jawdhar's appointments demonstrates. He was nominated director of the public treasure[64] and of the magazine of textiles and, most importantly, he became the personal intermediary of the second, third and fourth imam–caliphs, al-Qā'im (d. 334/946); al-Manṣūr (d. 341/953), who granted him freedom; and finally al-Mu'izz (d. 365/975). When the imam al-Manṣūr left the capital to fight against rebels, Jawdhar was declared governor of the entire province of Ifrīqiya.[65] Furthermore, after the imam–caliph al-Manṣūr moved to the new capital, al-Manṣūrīya, Jawdhar was appointed as administrator of the old capital, al-Mahdiya.

Jawdhar, like Ja'far, appears in his biography as a "perfect" and loyal servant, one who enjoyed the complete confidence of the imperial family. For example, during al-Mahdi's burial, his successor, al-Qā'im, reportedly told Jawdhar that he was not permitted to bury "an imam until he has appointed his own *ḥujja*" (proof). Yet later, al-Qā'im asked Jawhdar to come nearer and give him his hand. Then, while Jawdhar was filled with "fear and awe because of the reverence for him", he informed him that the new *ḥujja* was his son Ismā'īl, who would become the imam–caliph al-Manṣūr.[66] According to his biography, Jawdhar kept this secret for seven years, a period that was useful to al-Qā'im, who was able to strengthen the caliphate and Ismā'īl's position. Nevertheless, in reality, there are suggestions that Ismā'īl (al-Manṣūr) became the successor due to an intrigue masterminded by Jawdhar and Ismā'īl's mother and wet-nurse; all three had influence with him and would have benefited from his caliphate.[67]

According to Jawdhar's biography, as the imam–caliph al-Qā'im was dying, he assembled his son and successor al-Manṣūr and told him that he wanted to entrust in him "a trust which I would like you not to lose after me", and then added: "The trust I want to confide to you is poor Jawdhar. Protect him. May he not be humiliated after me". At that point, al-Manṣūr reassured his father and said: "Oh my Lord, is not Jawdhar one of us?"[68]

Jawdhar's close association, almost kinship, with the imperial family, as depicted in his biography, is worth interrogating further. Indeed, the Fatimid family was not only the imperial family but were considered to be descendants of the *ahl al-bayt*. Al-Manṣūr trusted Jawdhar so much that he bequeathed him with the care of the books of previous imams, which contained the secret doctrine of the Isma'ilis. In this way, Jawdhar became the protector of the dynasty's history, but also acted as a guardian of the religious message of the Isma'ilis. Moreover, when al-Manṣūr freed Jawdhar, he was allowed to put on the *ṭirāz*, imperial textiles embroidered with gold and silver brands and inscribed with the imam–caliph's name and the following sentence: "Manufactured through Jawdhar, Client of the Commander of the Faithful, at al-Mahdiyya the Pleasing (to God)".[69] This was clearly considered a great honour, as his name was placed beside that of the imam. If, at the beginning of his story, Jawdhar had purchased the imperial *baraka* for 20 dinārs, he subsequently earned this with his loyalty, acting as the most "perfect" of servants.

Once again, in his biography there is no reference to his gender, but we might infer that this did not matter, either to himself or to the Fatimid rulers.

The decline of the Empire: The isolation of the imam

During the following years of Fatimid rule, the dynasty was able to conquer all of North Africa and Sicily. Their most important military success was in 358/969, when the general Jawhar al-Ṣiqillī (d. 381/992) conquered Fuṣṭāṭ in Egypt. He remained here for four years as the deputy of the fourth imam-caliph al-Mu'izz (d. 365/975) and began building what would become the new capital, "the Victorious of al-Mu'izz", *al-Qāhira al-Mu'izzīya*, Cairo, where the Fatimid court moved in 362/973.

In this phase of the Fatimid empire, the sources mention several eunuchs who, as with Ja'far and Jawdhar, were close to the imam–caliphs, for example, Barjawān, who was appointed by the caliph al-ʿAzīz (d. 386/996) as guardian of his son, al-Ḥākim (d. 411/1021), the sixth imam-caliph, who would ascend to the throne at the age of 11. Barjawān was the latter's regent for four years before al-Ḥākim killed him in 390/1000, probably to rid himself of any unwelcome interference. As with the early history of the empire, eunuchs still appear as well positioned and powerful *individuals*. Later, when the dynasty faced a deep crisis, eunuchs as a *group* became instead the mark of the sacredness of the imam.

The crisis became particularly intense during the 1060s, when Egypt suffered a serious famine that triggered a civil war between different factions of the army, among them Turks, Black Africans and Kutāma Berbers. The imam–caliph of the time, al-Mustanṣir bi-llāh (d. 487/1094), asked for the assistance of general al-Badr al-Jamālī (d. 487/1094), who was at the time governor of Acre (in Palestine). He was able to quell the rebellion and was subsequently acclaimed as the saviour of Egypt and appointed as its vizier. This marked the beginning of the last phase of the Fatimid empire, when the role of the imam–caliph was gradually reduced to being that of a figurehead, while the real power-holders were the military viziers.

Chronicles make no reference to any exceptionally powerful eunuchs during this phase. It is likely that the military viziers, who wielded increasing power, would not tolerate eunuchs who challenged their position. Nevertheless, the eunuchs' role became further institutionalised, as can be seen when examining the administrative structure of the empire. Such a structure is described by al-Qalqashandī (d. 821/1418), who composed one of the most important works of Arabic administrative literature.[70] Al-Qalqashandī's main source was a lost chronicle of Ibn al-Ṭuwayr, who was a high-ranking official of the later Fatimids and early Ayyūbids; therefore, his description must date to the late phase of the Fatimid empire. According to al-Qalqashandī, one group of people had a particular prominence within the dynasty, the so-called "*muḥannakūn*" eunuchs, "who wrap their head turban to cover their mouths as the Bedouins and the Maghrebines do now. They are the closest to the caliph and his favourite and they are more than one thousand".[71]

The fact that the *muḥannakūn* eunuchs covered their mouths is significant. Indeed, covering and veiling one's person was a marker of sacredness for the Fatimids; for example, before the ritual Friday prayer, when the imam recited his sermon, a group of 12 people ascended the *minbar* (the pulpit) where the imam was sitting. Each of them took a piece of curtain and covered the imam, who could not be viewed while speaking.[72]

Al-Qalqashandī states that the *muḥannakūn* eunuchs had nine functions that were strictly reserved for them: the *shādd al-tāj*, the one who was responsible for wrapping the crown of the caliph in a specific way; the *ṣāḥib al-majlis*, who had the function of a chamberlain; the *ṣāḥib al-risāla*, who was responsible for delivering the caliph's messages; the *zimam al-quṣūr*, the chief steward or major-domo; the *ṣāḥib bayt al-māl*, the director of the treasury; the *ṣāḥib al-daftar*, who was in charge of recording what happened during audiences with the caliph; the *ṣāḥib al-dawāh*, in charge of the inkwell (an imperial insignia); the *zamm al-aqārib*, in charge of the caliphal family; and the *zamm al-rijāl*, in charge of the caliphal's food and banquets.[73] To carry out these functions, proximity to the imam–caliph (and his *baraka*) was necessary. This implied a relationship between eunuchs and sacredness that was already evident, on the individual level, with eunuchs such as Ja'far and Jawdhar, but which was now more greatly institutionalised and was particularly evident in the ceremonial of the court.

Philippe Buc has raised several doubts about rituals as object of historical analysis.[74] Moreover, one should be particularly cautious with the Fatimid case; as Paula Sanders noted, "most of what we know about Fatimid ceremonial has come to us from Mamluk texts that decontextualize and depoliticize the ceremonies".[75] Indeed, the descriptions we have of Fatimid rituals were compiled by three Mamluk authors: al-Qalqashandī (d. 821/1418), al-Maqrīzī (d. 845–6/1442) and Ibn Taghrī Birdī (d. 874–5/1470), all of whom wrote subsequent to the fall of the Fatimid empire. Nevertheless, these three authors each refer to the same source, the lost chronicle of Ibn al-Ṭuwayr; therefore, although we do not know to what extent we can take those authors' description as realistic, we still can learn much from them.

What is certain, as Sanders demonstrated, is that for the Fatimids, ceremonial was particularly important, even more so because they remained a Shi'i minority ruling over an area that was basically Sunni. Rituals, and especially parades that began in the palace but continued throughout the city, acted to legitimise the Fatimid imam–caliph's sovereignty in Cairo – which could be conceived of as a "ritual city".[76] The construction of this "ritual city" was a process that took several generations, but it became particularly important when, paradoxically, the imam–caliph was increasingly inaccessible. In this period, rituals became a way of balancing the interests of different actors and factions, who claimed their positions of power through their proximity to the imam–caliph.

A useful example is al-Qalqashandī's description of the procession that took place during the first day of the month of Ramadan. Preparations for this parade began 10 days prior, when insignia, arms, clothing and horses were brought out from the palace storehouses and were appraised by the caliph.[77] On the day of the procession, before dawn, the masters "of the sword and the pen" assembled in the area between the two imperial palaces (*bayna al-qaṣrayn*).[78] After the *umarā'* (princes) and the vizier reached the palace, the caliph's horse was brought and his entourage was prepared. The caliph mounted his horse from a chair, which was covered by a curtain (again, what is "sacred" was covered), and the three main insignia (the parasol, the sword and the inkstand) were given to their respective porters.[79] The vizier was situated close to the caliph and the *ṣāḥib al-majlis*, a eunuch who was responsible for raising the curtain, in this way revealing the "sacred" to the public. The caliph, led by his *muḥannakūn* eunuchs, rode towards the palace gates. As soon as he left the palace, his guards took the place of the caliph's eunuchs.[80] A eunuch remained, however, close to him with a parasol – an imperial insignia – and two other eunuchs were situated ahead of the caliph's horse with the flyswatters, another imperial insignia.[81]

The order of the procession was as follows: the *umarā'* (princes), their sons together with groups of soldiers, then the low-ranking *umarā'*, the *umarā'* of the silver staff and the *umarā'* of the collar.[82] Then, in close proximity to the caliph, there followed the *muḥannakūn* eunuchs. Next came the porters of the imperial insignia (who were also eunuchs), each of whom was surrounded by 10–20 people, and then finally the caliph with his horsemen. In front of the caliph was a large empty space.[83] Behind the caliph and his entourage followed the vizier with his own entourage of around 500 men.[84] They were succeeded by musicians playing the drums, cymbals and flutes, and after them came several thousand archers, soldiers and cavalry.[85] When the procession arrived at the mosque al-Aqmar, it divided so as to allow the vizier to move to the front of the procession, so that he could escort the caliph back to the palace. When the caliph reached the palace door, the *muḥannakūn* eunuchs dismounted and surrounded the caliph once more,[86] shielding him from the sight of the others.

This parade had the power to create what was perceived as a "sacred space" and a "sacred time". Mircea Eliade described "sacred time" as that in which the ordinary temporal duration is believed to be interrupted.[87] Rituals allow us to a-historicise a specific historical moment, which is then made eternal; in this case, the revelation of the Quran to Muḥammad, which is said to have occurred first during the month of Ramadan, is removed from that historical moment and is made eternal. Moreover, the space through which the parade travelled was also believed to become sacred. This has been explained by Eliade as a "hierophany", an irruption of the sacred (in this instance, the imam–caliph himself and his *baraka*) into the profane.[88] As Sanders has pointed out:

> the procession cortege was composed of several blocks, each organized internally according to the ranks of the troops relative to one another,

> but positioned as a *whole* in terms of proximity to the caliph … . What mattered in the procession was rank relative to the caliph, and this was expressed by proximity to the caliph more than absolute position in the cortege.[89]

Although at this point the real power-holder was the vizier and not the imam–caliph, it was still the latter, as a descendant of the *ahl al-bayt,* who legitimised, at least nominally, the vizier. In other words, the extreme sanctification of the imam was a political act and served to endorse the vizier's power and, more broadly, the entire imperial structure.

The significance of the *muḥannakūn* eunuchs marking the imam's sacredness also can be appreciated in a report of the imam's sermon at the Festival of the Fast Breaking, which occurs at the end of the month of Ramadan. On this important festival, a procession is taken from the palace to the mosque. When the imam–caliph ascends the pulpit for the sermon, he is situated above a number of notable figures: the vizier, the chief judge, the chief of the army, the director of the treasury, the porter of the lance, the *ṣāḥib al-bāb* (the majordomo), the *ṣāḥib al-sayf* (the one in charge of the imperial sword), the *ṣāḥib al-risāla* (the one who was responsible for delivering the caliph's messages), the *ṣāḥib daftar al-majlis* (the one who was in charge of recording what happened during audiences with the caliph), the *ṣāḥib al-miẓalla* (the porter of the parasol), the *zimam al-ashrāf al-aqārib* (the one in charge of the caliph's family) and the *naqīb al-ashrāf al-ṭālibīn* (the one responsible for the descendants of the Prophet Muḥammad).

However, the vizier is next to ascend the pulpit, kisses the imam–caliph's hands and then stands at his right-hand side. When the imam–caliph makes a sign, the chief judge follows up to the seventh step, waits for another sign and then reads from a piece of paper that was written by the chancery. After a number of ritual blessings, he calls – one by one – for those who remain at the base of the pulpit to ascend. Each of them takes a piece of a curtain and covers the caliph so that he would be hidden during his sermon. Once he finishes, they uncover him and then descend from the pulpit.[90] The great majority (excepting the vizier, the chief judge, the army commander and the porter of the lance and the porter of the sword) of those in charge of covering and then uncovering the imam–caliph, thus revealing what is sacred to the profane world, were eunuchs: This includes the porter of the parasol and the *ṣāḥib al-bāb*, the *ṣāḥib al-risāla*, the *ṣāḥib daftar al-majlis*, the *zimam al-ashrāf al-aqārib*, the director of the treasury and the *naqīb al-ashrāf al-ṭālibīn.* Twelve people were given this important responsibility, and a majority of them were eunuchs.

Conclusions

This chapter has explored eunuchs in the Fatimid dynasty, focusing particularly on gender and sacredness. It has been argued that eunuchs were not represented in a stable or fixed way but were gendered (or not gendered) by different kinds of authors in various ways, and that the context in which eunuchs were acting played a crucial role. Regarding *adab*, in analysing al-Jāḥiẓ's chapter on castration, we see that eunuchs could move between the world of men and the world of women. Indeed, he attributes to eunuchs characteristics that were usually considered feminine and that can also be found in Byzantine sources, such as greediness, bad temperedness and the inability to keep secrets. Nevertheless, eunuchs also maintained some masculine characteristics, such as being skillful in cavalry and archery; this ambiguity, which made al-Jāḥiẓ compare eunuchs with mules, is what appeared to disturb him most.

With regards to chronicles and biographies, like those of Ja'far and Jawdhar, the eunuchs' gender is usually not addressed, and it is very difficult to ascertain if a servant was in fact castrated or not. While we can be sure that a man who had the duty of guarding the harem was a eunuch, the fact that some eunuchs had roles that were considered masculine and acted as governors or army commanders means it is not always possible to identify who was a eunuch.

When considering Islamic law, jurists did not explicitly discuss the eunuchs' gender as they did with regards to the hermaphrodite; they simply took for granted that they were men. For example, they considered their marriage to a woman as perfectly valid, and it was only if the wife complained about her husband's ability to penetrate her that a judge was called for. Muslim jurists also agreed that eunuchs could repudiate their wives just as non-castrated men did, and in some cases, even their paternity could be attributed. All in all, Muslim jurists seemed to understand eunuchs not as a "third gender" but as men, even if they were "imperfect" men. This is in line with the ideas of medical authors of the time, who recognised different degrees of masculinity (and femininity). They represented this as a continuum of perfection, ranging from two poles: The man and the woman denoted each pole, and eunuchs were considered closer to the masculine rather than the feminine pole.

In examining the Fatimid dynasty, we see that eunuchs enjoyed a special closeness to the imam–caliph. In the early and central phases of the Fatimid empire, this intimacy was a characteristic of *individual* eunuchs, like Ja'far or Jawdhar, but in the last phase, this was a characteristic of eunuchs as a *group* and, especially, of the *muḥannakūn* eunuchs. The latter had important functions at the caliph's court, enjoyed intimate access to him and were in charge of all his personal needs. The imam–caliph held a special role for the Fatimids, the custodian of God's real message and of the divine *baraka*. In this respect, eunuchs were not simply his "guardians" but also "guardians of the sacred". This was particularly evident in rituals, with eunuchs being the closest group to the imam during processions, and the fact they had the privilege of covering and uncovering the imam during the ritual prayer; they were responsible for displaying (or concealing) his "sacredness" to the profane world. This connection with sacredness was a consequence of the gradual sanctification of the imamate, which was a way to legitimise the imperial structure and the viziers' power, but which, at the same time, isolated the imam from his subjects. As he became more sacred, he became inaccessible and separated from society. A defensive "wall" of anonymous eunuchs would stand between him and his people.

Acknowledgements

I would like to thank Almut Höfert, Matthew M. Mesley and Claudio Lo Jacono for their comments and suggestions on this chapter; and Ashraf Hassan for his support with the Arabic sources. My research on eunuchs in Islamic law, which is discussed in the third paragraph of this chapter, has been made possible thanks to a generous fellowship of the Islamic Legal Studies Program, Faculty of Law, University of Harvard, which allowed me to spend a semester doing research at the Islamic Law Section of the Library of the Faculty of Law.

Notes

1 Shaun Marmon, *Eunuchs and Sacred Boundaries in Islamic Societies* (New York: Oxford University Press, 1995).
2 Kathryn M. Ringrose, *The Perfect Servant. Eunuchs and the Social Construction of Gender in Byzantium* (Chicago: The University of Chicago Press, 2003).
3 Marmon, *Eunuchs and Sacred Boundaries,* 32.
4 The term, literally meaning "possessed", "slave", here refers to the Mamluk sultanate of Egypt and Syria (648/1250 to 922/1517).
5 Marmon, *Eunuchs and Sacred Boundaries*, X.
6 Ibid., 12–13.
7 Garth Fowden, *Empire to Commonwealth: Consequences of Monotheism in Late Antiquity* (Princeton: Princeton University Press, 1993).
8 Almut Höfert, *Kaisertum und Kalifat. Der imperiale Monotheismus im Früh- und Hochmittelalter* (Frankfurt: Campus Verlag, 2015).
9 This caused tensions and various struggles for power and led to different groups of men wanting to be in charge of interpreting God's will, like bishops in the West and *'ulamā'* in the Islamic world. See Höfert, *Kaisertum und Kalifat.*
10 Marmon, *Eunuchs and Sacred Boundaries*, IX.
11 Ringrose, *The Perfect Servant*, 34.
12 Ibid., 40.
13 The concept of *adab* included different kinds of "profane" culture in opposition to religious culture, like poetry, oratory, history and linguistics.
14 Abū 'Uthmān 'Amr b. Baḥr al-Jāḥiẓ, *Kitāb al-Ḥayawān* (Cairo: Muṣṭafā al-bābī al-ḥalabī, 1965–1969). A detailed analysis of this chapter on eunuchs has been written by A. Cheikh Moussa, "Ǧāḥiẓ et les Eunuques ou la confusion du meme et de l'autre," *Arabica* 29, fasc. 2 (1982): 184–214 and Hans-Peter Pökel, *Der unmännliche Mann. Zur Figuration des Eunuchen im Werk von al-Ǧaḥiẓ (gest. 869)* (Würzburg: Ergon Verlag, 2014), especially 98–107; 200–285.

15 Pökel, *Der unmännliche Mann*, 42.
16 There is much debate on the meaning of the term *ṣaqāliba*, but it is used roughly in medieval Islamic sources to refer to Slavs and other peoples from eastern Europe.
17 This name was given to the region around the lower course of the Indus (Pakistan today), the easternmost province of the Umayyad Caliphate.
18 The term refers to a culture that flourished over a millennium before Islam, whose main centre was at Maryab in Yemen.
19 Abū ʿAbd Allāh Muḥammad al-Muqaddasī, *Aḥsan al-Taqāsīm fī maʿrifat al-aqālīm* (Leiden: Brill, 1906), 242 (trans. Basil Collins, *The Best Divisions for Knowledge of the Regions* [Reading: Garnet, 2001]).
20 al-Jāḥiẓ, *Kitāb al-Ḥayawān*, 1:106. For his description of eunuchs, see also Pökel, *Der unmännliche Mann*, 185 ff.
21 al-Jāḥiẓ, *Kitāb al-Ḥayawān*, 1:107.
22 Ibid., 1:116.
23 Ibid., 1:113.
24 Ibid., 1:113–114.
25 Ibid., 1:137.
26 Ibid., 1:117.
27 Ibid., 1:119.
28 Ibid., 1:136.
29 Ibid., 1:108.
30 Ibid., 1:135.
31 Ibid.
32 Ringrose, *The Perfect Servant*, 20.
33 See Ringrose, *The Perfect Servant*, 36, quoting St Basil and Leo the Deacon.
34 al-Jāḥiẓ , *Kitāb al-Ḥayawān*, 1:124–125.
35 David Ayalon, "On the term *Khādim* in the sense of 'Eunuch' in the Early Muslim Sources," *Arabica* 32, fasc. 3 (1985): 289–308 and A. Cheikh Moussa, "De la synonymie dans les sources arabes anciennes: Le cas de Ḫādim et de Ḫaṣiyy," *Arabica* 32, fasc. 3 (1985): 309–322.
36 For example, the Palestinian leader Yasser Arafat was known as Abū 'Ammār, even though he never had a son. I would like to thank Regula Forster for her input on this topic.
37 This is explicitly forbidden by the verse 30:30 of the Quran, which states: "So direct your face toward the religion, inclining to truth. [Adhere to] the fiṭra of Allah upon which He has created [all] people. No change should there be in the creation of Allah. That is the correct religion, but most of the people do not know".
38 According to the sources, the eunuch, whose name was Mābūr, was offered to him together with Maria the Copt (who gave birth to Ibrāhīm, the Prophet's only son, who died in his infancy), her sister and other gifts by al-Muqawqis, usually identified with the Melkite Patriarch of Alexandria. Muḥammad b. Saʿd, *Kitāb al-Ṭabaqāt al-Kabīr* (Cairo: Maktabat al-Khānjī, 2001), 10:201.
39 See for example Agostino Cilardo, "Historical Development of the Legal Doctrine Relative to the Position of the Hermaphrodite in the Islamic Law", *The Search: Journal for Arab and Islamic Studies* 7 (1986): 128–170; and Paula Sanders, "Gendering the Ungendered Body: Hermaphrodites in Medieval Islamic Law," in *Women in Middle Eastern History: Shifting Boundaries in Sex and Gender*, ed. Nikki R. Keddie and Beth Baron (New Haven: Yale University Press, 1991), 74–95.
40 For example, Muḥammad b. Muḥammad al-Ghazālī, *Al-Wasīṭ fī-l-madhhab*, ed. Aḥmad Maḥmūd Ibrāhīm. 7 vols. (Cairo: Dār al-Salām, 1997), 6:109.

41 This is reported in Burhān al-Dīn al-Marghīnānī, *al-Hidāya, Sharḥ Bidāyat al-Mubtadī* (Cairo: Dār al-Salām, 2000), 4:1494.

42 Dror Ze'evi, *Producing Desire: Changing Sexual Discourse in the Ottoman Middle East, 1500–1900* (Berkeley, Los Angeles: University of California Press, 2006), 22. This is in line with Thomas Laqueur's theory, according to which in pre-modern societies only one sex was conceptualised, with the woman being considered to be an imperfect version of the man. See Thomas Laqueur, *Making Sex: Body and Gender from the Greeks to Freud* (Cambridge, MA: Harvard University Press, 1990).

43 Franz Rosenthal, "Ar-Rāzī on the hidden illness," *Bullettin of the History of Medicine* 52, no. 1 (1978): 54.

44 This *ḥadīth* is reported by both al-Bukhārī and Muslim, authors of the two most important and authoritative collection of *ḥādīths*.

45 For this debate, see for example Ignaz Goldziher, "Kämpfe um die Stellung des Ḥadīth im Islam," *Zeitschrift der Deutschen Morgenländischen Gesellschaft* 61 (1907): 860–872; Gautier A. H. Juynboll, *Muslim Tradition: Studies in Chronology, Provenance and Authorship of Early Ḥadīth* (New York: Cambridge University Press, 1983); Harald Motzki, *The Origins of Islamic Jurisprudence: Meccan Fiqh before the Classical Schools* (Leiden: Brill, 2002); Joseph Schacht, *An Introduction to Islamic Law* (Oxford: Clarendon Press, 1964).

46 The Fatimid empire should not be considered an exception, as in the same period other (proto)-Shi'i dynasties emerged, like the 'Uqaylids, the Būyids and the Ṣulayḥids. This period has been defined by Marshall Hodgson as the "Shi'i century" and by Louis Massignon as the "Isma'ili" century. Marshall G. S. Hodgson, *Conscience and History in a World Civilization*, vol. 2 of *The Venture of Islam* (Chicago, London: The University of Chicago Press, 1977), 36–39; Louis Massignon, "Mutanabbi, Devant Le Siècle Ismaelien De l'islam," in *Al Mutanabbî. Recueil publié a l'occasion de son millénaire*, ed. Régis Blachère, Marius Canard and Maurice Gaudefroy-Demombynes (Beirut: Institut français de Damas, 1936), 1.

47 For a complete analysis of the different titles of emperors in Europe and caliphs in the Islamic world, see Almut Höfert, *Kaisertum und Kalifat.*

48 Abū al-Ḥasan al-Māwardī, *al-Aḥkām al-Ṣulṭāniyya wa-l-wilāyāt al-dīniyya* (Kuwait City: Maktabat Dār Ibn Qutayba, 1989), 1–2, translated in English as al-Māwardī, *Al-Ahkam As-Sultaniyyah. Laws of Islamic Governance*, trans. Asadullah Yate (London: Ta-Ha Publishers, 1996), 8.

49 al-Mawardı, *al-Aḥkam* ar.: p. 3, en.: p. 10.

50 They believed that Muḥammad himself appointed 'Alī as his successor in 10/632, when, returning from the Pilgrimage, he stopped at the Ghadīr Khumm, the Pond of Khumm and, taking ʿAlī's hand, said: "He of whom I am the *mawlā*, of him ʿAlī is also the *mawlā*". The term could mean here both "Lord" and "helper". *Encyclopedia of Islam Online,* 2nd ed., s. v. "G̲h̲adīr K̲h̲umm," accessed October 13, 2015, http://referenceworks.brillonline.com/entries/encyclopaedia-of-islam-2/ghadir-khumm-SIM_2439?s.num=0&s.f.s2_parent=s.f.book.encyclopaedia-of-islam-2&s.q=ghadir+khumm.

51 Which is why they would be known as Zaydīs. They are also called Fivers, because they recognize five imams. Today they are mostly based in Yemen, where they constitute about 35–40% of the Muslim population.

52 Today, they are mostly spread between Iran (where they represent the official religion), Iraq, Azerbaijan and Bahrain, with important minorities in Lebanon and Kuwait.

53 Nowadays, there are several groups within Isma'ilism, the most consistent of which are the Nizārīs, who recognize the Aga Khan IV as the legitimate 49th

imām. Under his leadership, the Aga Khan Foundation and the Aga Khan Trust for Culture have been founded, under which aegis there are, for example, the Aga Khan Program for Islamic Architecture at Harvard University and the Institute of Isma'ili Studies in London.

54 See *Encyclopedia of Islam Online,* 2nd ed., s. v. "al-Ẓāhir wa'l-Bāṭin," accessed October 13, 2015, http://referenceworks.brillonline.com/entries/encyclopaedia-of-islam-2/al-z-a-hir-wa-l-ba-t-in-SIM_8078.

55 See for example Shainool Jiwa: "The Baghdad Manifesto: A Lineage Exposed or an Exposé on Lineage?" a paper presented at the panel "One Empire, Many Religions: Religion and Society under Fatimid Rule", 4th World Congress for Middle Eastern Studies (WOCMES), Ankara, 18–22 August 2014.

56 Namely al-ʿAbbās b. ʿAbd al-Muṭṭalib b. Hāshim. This dynasty ruled, at least nominally, from 132/750 to 656/1258. For what regards the first phase of the Fatimid empire, there are several reference works: Heinz Halm, *Das Reich des Mahdi. Der Aufstieg der Fatimiden* (Munich: Beck, 1991), translated into English as Halm, *The Empire of the Mahdi: The Rise of the Fatimids* (Leiden: Brill, 1997); Vladimir Ivanow, *Ismaili Tradition concerning the Rise of the Fatimids* (London: Oxford University Press, 1942); Yacov Lev, *State and Society in Fatimid Egypt* (Leiden: Brill, 1991); Farhad Daftary, *The Ismāʿīlīs: Their History and Doctrines* (New York: Cambridge University Press, 1990); Daftary, *A Short History of the Ismailis: Traditions of a Muslim Community* (Edinburgh: Edinburgh University Press, 1998); Michael Brett, *Fatimids: The World of the Mediterranean and the Middle East in the Fourth Century of the Hijra, Tenth Century CE* (Leiden: Brill, 2001); and Paul P. Walker, *Exploring an Islamic Empire: Fatimid History and Its Sources* (London, New York: I. B. Tauris, 2002).

57 On the concept of *daʿwa* and the characteristics of a good *dāʿī* (propagandist), see Vladimir Ivanow, "The Organization of the Fatimid Propaganda," *Journal of the Bombay Branch of the Royal Asiatic Society* 15 (1939): 1–35, which analyses al-Naysābūrī's *al-Risāla al-mujāza al-kāfiya fī adab al-duʿāt.*

58 Vladimir Ivanow has compiled both an edition and a translation of Jaʿfar's biography. For the edition, see Muḥammad b. Muḥammad al-Yamānī: "Sīrat Jaʿfar al-ḥājib," ed. Vladimir Ivanow, *Bullettin of the Faculty of Arts of the University of Egypt* 4 (1936): 89–133; for the English translation, see Vladimir Ivanow, *Ismaili Tradition concerning the rise of the Fatimids* (London: Oxford University Press, 1942), 184–223.

59 al-Yamānī, "Sīrat Jaʿfar", 123.

60 Ibid., 114.

61 Ibid., 130–131.

62 There are two editions of Jawdhar's biography: Hamid Haji, *Inside the Immaculate Portal: A History from Early Fatimid Archives* (London: I.B. Tauris, 2012), which also includes an English translation; and Abū ʿAlī Manṣūr al-ʿAzīzī al-Jawdharī, *Sīrat al-Ustādh Jawdhar*, ed. Muḥammad Kāmil Ḥusayn and Muḥammad ʿAbd al-Hādī (Cairo: Dār al-Fikr al-ʿArabī, 1954). In this article, I make reference to the 2012 edition. For an account of Jawdhar's life, see also Hamid Haji, "A Distinguished Slav Eunuch of the Early Fatimid Period: al-Ustadh Jawdhar," in *Fortresses of the Intellect - Ismaili and other Islamic Studies in Honour of Farhad Daftary,* ed. Omar Ali-de-Unzaga (London: I. B. Tauris, 2011), 261–274.

63 Haji, *Inside the Immaculate Portal*, 24–26.

64 Ibid, 27.

65 Ibid., 33–34.

66 Ibid., 27–28.

67 Halm, *The Empire of the Mahdi,* 311.

68 Haji, *Inside the Immaculate Portal*, 33.

69 Ibid., 43.
70 Al-Qalqashandī was a legal scholar and secretary in the Mamluk chancery. His work *Ṣubḥ al-aʿshā fī ṣināʿat al-inshāʾ* (Cairo: Dār al-Kutub al-Miṣriyya, 1922), is considered the most important book of Arabic chancery.
71 al-Qalqashandī, *Ṣubḥ al-aʿshā*, 3:481.
72 Ibid., 3:513.
73 Ibid., 3:485–486. See also Heinz Halm, *Kalifen und Assassinen. Aegypten und der Vordere Orient zur Zeit der ersten Kreuzzüge 1074–1171* (Munich: Beck, 2014), 147–152.
74 Philippe Buc, *The Dangers of Ritual: Between Early Medieval Texts and Social Scientific Theory* (Princeton: Princeton University Press, 2002). For a critique of Buc's approach, see Geoffrey Koziol, "Review article: The dangers of polemic: Is ritual still an interesting topic of historical study?," *Early Medieval Europe* 11, no. 4 (2002): 367–388. See also Buc's reply to Koziol and his other critics, Philipp Buc: "The Monster and the Critics: A Ritual Reply," *Early Medieval Europe* 15, no. 3 (2007): 441–452.
75 Paula Sanders, *Ritual, Politics, and the City in Fatimid Cairo* (New York: Suny Press, 1994), 10.
76 Ibid., 9.
77 For a complete description of the New Year procession, which was also the model for other processions, see Sanders, *Ritual, Politics, and the City*, 87–98 and al-Qalqashandī, *Ṣubḥ al-aʿshā*, 3:504 ff.
78 The men of the sword were those men that had military functions, while the men of the pen were those who had administrative functions; see al-Qalqashandī, *Ṣubḥ al-aʿshā*, 3:481 ff.
79 The porter of the parasol had a very important military function, the fourth one in the army, after the *vizier*, the *ṣāḥib al-bāb* and the commander of the army. He was often a eunuch, like the *ṣāḥib al-bāb*. Ibid., pp. 482–484.
80 Ibid., 3:506–507; Sanders, *Ritual, Politics, and the City,* 87–98.
81 al-Qalqashandī, *Ṣubḥ al-aʿshā*, 3:474.
82 Respectively *umarāʾ* commanding between 5 and 10 men, *umarāʾ* that received as an honour from the caliph a silver staff and *umarāʾ* who received from the caliph collars of gold and commanded 1000 men or more.
83 al-Qalqashandī, *Ṣubḥ al-aʿshā*, 3:507; Sanders, *Ritual, Politics, and the City*, 87–98.
84 al-Qalqashandī, *Ṣubḥ al-aʿshā*, 3:507.
85 Ibid., 3:508.
86 Ibid., 3:508–509.
87 Mircea Eliade, *The Sacred and the Profane. The Nature of Religion*, trans. Williard R. Trask (New York: Harcourt, 1987), 71 ff.
88 Ibid., 26.
89 Sanders, *Ritual, Politics, and the City*, 94.
90 al-Qalqashandī , *Ṣubḥ al-aʿshā*, 3:513.

13 Under pressure

Secular–mendicant polemics and the construction of chaste masculinity within the thirteenth-century Latin church

Sita Steckel and Stephanie Kluge

Linking gender and authority in thirteenth-century polemics

How are celibate or chaste masculinities transformed and how do social, religious or political contexts and developments impact them? Typically, research has linked specific forms of gendered identity to certain social or religious groups and their milieu-specific values and practices – for example, bishops in Latin Europe or eunuchs in the Fatimid empire, subject of the present volume; or, to choose another example, medieval Christian monks, for whom chastity held a high religious value.[1] But it has also been observed that the tension between competing masculinities seems to be responsible for certain dynamics – mainly, frictions between clerical and lay concepts of masculinity, which have been studied fairly intensively for medieval Europe.[2] In the following contribution, we would like to draw attention to a more specific pressure exerted on the cultural construction of masculinities – competition between different groups of chaste men rather than between chaste and sexually active men. With the emergence of a great number of new religious orders and of heterodox religious movements within the high and late-medieval Latin church, several types of chaste, celibate men increasingly competed with each other. In the thirteenth century, in particular, growing intra-Christian religious diversity led to conflicts about the respective religious authority of different elites. Such confrontations seem to have had a marked impact on the cultural formation of masculinities.[3]

A thirteenth-century example can illustrate the background: In his *Cronica*, a work finished in the 1280s and ranging in tone from acute political observations to colourful anecdotes and edifying *exempla*, the Franciscan friar Salimbene of Parma (d. after 1288) includes an interesting little scene that seems to describe his ideals of masculine behaviour. As Salimbene reports, he once made the acquaintance of a well-spoken and noble nun, who asked him to become her particular friend and confessor.[4] But the modern reader's hope of encountering a medieval example of mixed-gender friendship or male–female spiritual and intellectual cooperation are immediately dashed: Salimbene replied to the nun in a negative if not harsh manner. As he put it, he did not wish for a friend with whom he was not even supposed to speak – as she, a cloistered nun, was supposed to stay within her monastery's walls. The nun, defeated by this hostile reproach, suggested that they should at least wish each other well in charity and mutual prayer, as the bible suggested. Yet Salimbene took care to rebuff even this simple request, dramatically stating, in the words of Saint Arsenius, that he would "pray to God that he will erase your memory from my heart".[5]

Unsurprisingly, Salimbene's violent rebuttal of the nun's suggestions rested on fears about his celibacy and purity: He saw the nun's request as an amorous advance and explained this to his readers.[6] This explicitly stated fear marks this episode of Salimbene's *Cronica* off from other stories and anecdotes – where Salimbene, in clear contrast, argued not against but for close pastoral relationships with women and generally showed respect and compassion towards them; as it happened, he later also mitigated his harsh stance towards the friendly nun.[7] The story about the nun's wish for spiritual friendship should thus obviously not be taken as a direct or comprehensive indicator for Salimbene's – or thirteenth-century Franciscans' – ideals of chaste masculinity.

Rather, the anecdote illuminates a specific link between gendered masculine identity and authority. Salimbene's intense reaction should be read against a particular horizon of conflict, as the Franciscans were engaged in the so-called secular–mendicant controversy in the second half of the thirteenth century.[8] This was a series of acrid conflicts within the Latin church, and especially in France and Italy, in which the established or "secular" clergy, that is, bishops, parish priests and other clerical personnel, were confronted with the growing role of a new type of religious order. The mendicant orders, such as the Franciscans (*Ordo Fratrum Minorum*, Friars Minor) and Dominicans (*Ordo Fratrum Praedicatorum*, Order of Preachers), who had only emerged onto the increasingly diverse religious scene in the early thirteenth century, advocated radical asceticism and embraced forms of absolute poverty.[9] But in contrast to older monastic orders such as the Benedictines and Cistercians, whose monks and nuns also led ascetic lives and renounced individually owned property, the mendicants did not aim to leave the world. They wished to serve it, and they built their convents in well-populated cities instead of desert-like remoteness. Instead of devoting themselves to prayer and a life of individual sanctification inside a monastery's walls, they engaged in pastoral care in urban centres, most importantly through preaching, hearing confessions and offering burial in their cemeteries.

The latter task especially quickly generated large amounts of revenue – revenue that had been hitherto allocated to the local clergy. Although the new orders' pastoral efforts were supported by the papacy and by many members of the episcopate, their unaccustomed role eventually caused an increasing number of conflicts with the local clergy, visible from the 1240s onwards. The mendicants were meant to help the local priests – but they also turned out to constitute genuine competition for them, and not only in financial terms. Combining the lofty goal of absolute poverty with superior learning acquired at the emerging European universities, the friars' lifestyle inspired the most devout and wealthy members of the urban elites to favour their churches. This greatly lessened the prestige of local priests, on occasion apparently reducing the local parish churches to second-class places of worship.[10]

Legal conflicts and theological debates ensued, and from 1253 onwards, a local quarrel at one of the most important hubs of communication within Latin Christianity, the University of Paris, caused the controversy to escalate into a highly publicised polemical battle of European dimensions.[11] The years 1253 to 1257 witnessed a series of practical and theoretical confrontations between the most learned and well-connected proponents of the new orders and of their opponents, an alliance of theologians from the secular clergy and some bishops. Both sides alerted their respective political networks and issued statements and refutations. With an urban public sphere linking the discourse arenas of political conflict management, theological and juridical university disputations and popular opinion, the conflict encouraged a multi-layered, pluri-medial public debate about the respective merits and legitimacy of the established clergy and the new elites.[12]

As it happens, several accusations uttered against the mendicants in the wake of the heated escalation at Paris fit exactly with Salimbene's worries about illicit friendships. After legal suits attempting to limit the new friars' privileges had failed in 1255 and the university party supporting the secular clergy was defeated, the Paris conflicts devolved into bitter polemics[13] aiming to discredit the foundations of the mendicants' privileged legal status – their high ascetic goals. In particular, the main spokesperson of the secular clergy at the university, the Burgundian theologian and canonist William of Saint Amour (d. 1272), published polemical writings accusing the Franciscan and Dominican friars of prideful, greedy and power-hungry behaviour. Taking up a tradition of eschatological thought that allowed him to attack "pseudo-preachers" without having to name his opponents, he even associated them with the antichrist and the dangers of the end times.[14]

Altogether, this escalation and its decades-long aftermath generated a multi-sided exchange that, intriguingly, debated the religious meaning and merit of various religious, social, economic and, eventually, sexual practices. Besides ecclesiological aspects, William of St Amour mainly disputed the claim that the mendicants' practice of begging constituted a laudable form of ascesis. Citing the biblical passages stating that even Jesus and his disciples had had a common purse, William emphasised the importance of the established, time-honoured lifestyles of the clergy and the older monastic orders, based on tithes and commonly held possessions respectively.[15] At the same time, he sowed doubt about the friars' radical poverty. In his view, their lifestyle of begging led to a preoccupation with money, dependence upon charitable patrons and resulting flattery.[16] Rather than being a mark of the *vita apostolica* and adding a sacred quality to their life, William suggested, their specific kind of poverty threatened to undermine their religious goal.

Other voices in the protests made parallel arguments concerning chastity and purity, for example the poet Rutebeuf (d. ca. 1285), who authored a number of *Dits* against the mendicant orders in the vernacular French and thus spoke to a rather broader audience than the theologian William.[17] As Rutebeuf put it in a poem usually dated to 1259, one could not help but wonder about the friars' close relationships with women; they kept being seen with women who affected piety and admired their sanctity, and they did nothing to avoid this female company. Yet even St Bernard of Clairvaux had cautioned that superhuman strength was necessary to avoid giving in to nature if women and men freely spent time with each other.[18] As Rutebeuf put it: "I don't know what to make of it – I see them sitting close to each other so that one hood seems to cover both heads. And they are neither angels nor beasts".[19] He thus implied that the friars were human, too, and must eventually be tempted and incur guilt in the process. Where William cast doubt on the religious merit of the friars' poverty, Rutebeuf cast doubt on the religious merit of their spiritual ties to women.

Rutebeuf's reference to the Cistercian abbot Bernard of Clairvaux (d. 1153), the leading figure of the great reform order of the previous century, underlined the advice given to monks of the older monastic orders in this respect; Bernard was repeating older warnings that the close company of and intimate familiarity with women was to be avoided for men in the religious life. Generally, monks and nuns were cloistered and kept separate to avoid the emotions and bodily temptations that must invariably spring up where the sexes spent time together.[20] As Bernard put it, only the apostles, who had been of confirmed sanctity, had the supernatural power to resist temptation – but they also had the power to raise the dead, which his opponents had not:

> Who would suspect anything evil of those who raised the dead? Do you likewise, and I will believe in man and woman sleeping together! Otherwise, you are boldly usurping for yourselves the prerogative of those whose sanctity you have not. ... Daily you sit beside a maiden at the table, your bed is next to hers in the chamber, your eyes meet hers in conversation, your hands touch hers in work – and do you wish to be thought continent? Perhaps you are, but I doubt it.[21]

That this twelfth-century warning popped up in a vernacular polemical poem against the friars was no accident – Rutebeuf was probably armed with this citation (and others) by the highly literate circle of university clerics around William of Saint Amour.[22] William himself does not seem to have attacked the friars' chastity in the 1250s, but he certainly did so later; although royal and papal measures forced him to leave Paris in disgrace in 1256/7 and to move back to his native Burgundy, he did not stop producing polemics.[23] In the middle of the 1260s, William finished his *Collectiones catholicae et canonicae scripturae*, a massive intellectual armoury that compiled all sorts of authorities, arguments and accusations designed to support the ongoing fight against the mendicants' privileges.[24] Besides citing St Bernard's warnings against unsupervised interaction among the sexes verbatim, William also called to mind that St Francis, the founder of the Franciscans himself, had commanded his brothers in their officially confirmed rule, the *Regula bullata*, that they were not to enter nuns' convents unless under papal orders to do so.[25]

It seems to be these warnings that the Franciscan Salimbene of Parma was demonstratively heeding in his defence against the amicable nun. Salimbene's remarks on the nun's cloistered status seem to answer William of Saint Amour's and Rutebeuf's accusations that Franciscan friars were trespassing against their own sainted founder's orders in becoming too friendly with female religious. Salimbene's rather astonishing initial refusal to pray for the nun and his wish to forget all about her, moreover, show his awareness of contemporary theories about the growth of carnal desire:[26] Impurity was not only thought to be the result of illicit sexual acts but was seen to begin in the mind. Carnal thoughts were imagined to be nourished and fostered within the body and soul by the mere presence of a desirable person as well as thoughts about him or her. Desire and lustful thinking turned the ascetic's mind away from God – and thus already constituted a form of pollution that diminished his or her religious virtue. To keep mind and body pure enough to turn towards God, meetings and the cultivation of illicit memories and emotions were to be avoided. Monks and clerics were typically encouraged to prove their masculinity in a mental battle against temptation.

Masculinizing religious life

Salimbene of Parma's words about the friendly nun may thus have rather less to do with women than we think at first glance – even though the events may have happened as he described. His words seem to be addressed to other men challenging his masculine virtue while also giving an example of good behaviour to brothers of his own order. Far from being universally harsh to women or disposed completely against pastoral care for female parishioners (as shall be discussed below), Salimbene seems to be using the anecdote of the nun to engage in an ongoing polemical exchange.

Salimbene could, in fact, be just as suggestive and polemical as Rutebeuf – or even more so. So could other mendicant friars. Already in the 1250s, the young Dominican theologian Thomas Aquinas (d. 1274), who began his career in the thick of the university conflict, had made hints about the secular clergy's lack of chastity. Thomas countered William of Saint-Amour's veiled attacks on the Dominicans, namely that some unnamed "learned preachers" might in fact be harbingers of the Antichrist because of their greed and hypocrisy, with a brief but suggestive remark: To him, it seemed more likely that "those might be learned preachers of the Antichrist who induced the people to lascivity with their secular lifestyle".[27] In his *Cronica*, Salimbene spelled out in drastic words what this short accusation only implied; recounting a large-scale debate between secular clerics and mendicant friars about their respective rights and privileges during an Italian synod, Salimbene had the leading pro-mendicant speaker, Archbishop Philipp of Ravenna, end the debate with a dramatic statement. The archbishop "grew irate" and supposedly upbraided the garrulous clerics:

> You miserable madmen, to whom shall I give the task of confessing the laypeople, if not the Friars Minor and the Preachers? I cannot give it to you with a clear conscience, for when the laypeople come to you for confession seeking medicine for their souls, you give them poison instead. For you take the women behind the altar on the pretext of confessing them, and there you know them carnally ... which is an evil to speak of and worse to do. Thus the Lord complains of you through his prophet Hosea [6.10]: "I have seen a horrible thing in the house of Israel: the fornication of Ephraim there". Therefore, you are complaining that the Brothers hear confession because you do not want them to know of your evil deeds.[28]

This counter-accusation, formulated in rather harsher terms than Rutebeuf's sly suggestions, makes even clearer that ideals of male chastity were being instrumentalised in an ongoing struggle between different religious elites. And as was the case with the quotation taken from St Bernard, the accusation that priests lacked chastity had a pre-history, which can be traced back to the reforms of the IV Lateran council in 1215 and further back to the eleventh-century church reforms and beyond.[29] As the mutual accusations of unchaste behaviour and even of abuse were deeply embedded in broader attacks on the religious authority of competitors, however, they appear as largely "tactical" utterances.[30]

The polemical attacks in fact illustrate the close entanglement of gender and religious authority in the high and late medieval Latin church. As chastity was seen as a prerequisite for the purity and sanctification which allowed humans to communicate with the divine, it formed an important basis for religious authority. This established a latent link between gender and authority that could easily be instrumentalised in power struggles. Whereas masculine identities may also have been negotiated without respect to specifically religious concepts and values in the Middle Ages, the religious authority of Christian elites frequently led to contestations of gendered behaviour.

Put in general sociological terms, such contestations – like the manoeuvring exhibited by Salimbene and his opponents – could be described as a battle for hegemony within a social field in the sense of Pierre Bourdieu:[31] The conflictual relations and polemical exchanges between different religious elites – among others clerics, established monastic orders and new mendicant orders[32] – can be read as attempts to gain a central position on the contested field of religion. References to the actors' masculinity – specifically the sanctification of their own bodies and minds, which they sought to attain by adhering to a celibate and chaste lifestyle – were instrumentalised to establish, defend or challenge a hegemonial position within this field. Salimbene of Parma, for example, stressed the chastity that set him apart from other men. He thus aimed to set up a distinct, superior form of masculinity,[33] supporting the argument that he and his Franciscan brothers were better suited to a position of authority than the unchaste clergy. Rutebeuf, in contrast, challenged this claim by publicly voicing his doubts and pointing to suspicious exchanges between friars and pious women; his strategy seems to have been to deny the mendicants' claims to a superior form of chaste masculinity.

As we would argue, this specific framework of conflict-based polemical utterances linking gender and authority needs to be taken into account, especially if we attempt to map the relationship between male gender and sacralised authority in the late medieval Latin church. Of course, this is not to deny that negotiations of male identity were mainly based on membership in specific groups determined by status, age or profession. But ongoing contests over religious authority and political influence among different groups of chaste men also seem to have exerted a strong influence.

However, so far, surprisingly little work has been done on practices and concepts of masculine identity formulated by the mendicant orders or belonging to the context of their conflict with the secular clergy.[34] One reason is clearly that the highly important eleventh and twelfth centuries, or the well-documented fourteenth and fifteenth centuries, have drawn the attention of most research dealing with concepts of male chastity and purity. But generally, the strain between different types of chaste masculinities appears to have been studied less than the tensions and transfers between diverging concepts of lay and clerical masculinities. An explanation for this may lie in the fact that researchers interested in gender tend to look for instances of practice – of "doing gender". Whether the polemical texts discussed here relate directly to gendered behaviour would at first glance seem questionable – after all, polemicists on all sides seem to instrumentalise rather than to actively regulate and shape male chastity, and they frequently take recourse to established accusations, which might even be said to be *topoi*. On the other hand, we recognise today that *topoi* and other cultural constructions have a strong formative impact on social realities. As the framework of polemical accusations and counter-accusations seems to have been known and consciously spread among various audiences, it would have had its own impact on the shaping of gendered behaviour among the competing groups. It therefore seems promising to attempt an explorative overview of relevant strategies in sources illustrating Franciscan and Dominican identity-making, followed by brief observations about the impact of polemics on clerical masculinities.

Competitive chastities: Franciscans and Dominicans guarding their virtue

The followers of St Francis and St Dominic saw the provision of pastoral care, spiritual admonishment and guidance as central aspects of their form of apostolic life within the world. Women were often among the friars' strongest supporters and sought out their spiritual counsel. Both groups dealt with mixed-gender urban lay populations and with pastoral care for female religious communities; such interactions forced the mendicant orders to grapple with the problem of sexuality. Whereas older monastic orders had sought to solve the issue of purity by insisting on claustration, separation of the sexes and a retreat from the world,[35] the mendicants' pastoral role closed this avenue to them. They had to engage with extant understandings of chastity and masculinity, triggering an intensive if heterogeneous process of identity-building within their orders. As it seems, the Franciscans and Dominicans adapted older monastic and clerical concepts while also engaging in direct or indirect confrontation with these competing elites of the Latin Church.

In the case of the Friars Minor, this can be illustrated by a brief survey of St Francis' (d. 1226) attitude towards women and its later representations within the order. In the 1221 rule text, the *Regula non bullata*, St Francis exhorted his brothers strictly to keep their chastity and to show all necessary caution and distance when dealing with women:

> All brothers, wherever they are or go, shall beware of bad glances and familiarity with women. And no-one shall take counsel with them alone or go on a road, or share a dish at table. When the priests give them penitences or some spiritual counsel, they shall speak with them in all honesty. And no woman at all shall be taken into obedience by any brother, but shall be free to do her penance wherever she wants after she has received spiritual counsel. And we shall all watch ourselves and keep all our members clean, for the Lord says: "whosoever shall look on a woman to lust after her, hath already committed adultery with her in his heart".[36]

If a brother gave in and engaged in fornication, this transgression was to be punished harshly and to result in his exclusion from the order.[37]

In his *Vita secunda S. Francisci* (1246–7), Francis' biographer Thomas of Celano (d. ca. 1260) also reported that the order's founder uttered a clear warning against interaction with women. According to Thomas, St. Francis

> enjoined the absolute avoidance of that honeyed poison, familiarity with women, which leads even holy men astray .... Except in the case of the most approved man he judged it to be as easy for any one associating with women to escape their contagion as [in Scriptural phrase] to walk in the fire without burning the soles of one's feet [Prov, 6,17].[38]

Notably, this passage takes up the traditional view that a man could only resist the temptation represented by women if he possessed a literally supernatural virtue or holiness.[39]

Yet the orders were under heavy pressure to provide pastoral care for women – not least to engage in the spiritual supervision of religious women, the *cura monialium*.[40] Like the Dominicans, the Franciscans had also encouraged and included activities of female religious groups in the earliest stage of their formation and had a female branch in the followers of St Clare. But during the first decades of institutionalization, repeated attempts were made to extricate the male branch of the orders from the task of *cura monialium*,[41] even though the papacy frequently entrusted it to the mendicant orders. In the Franciscan *Regula bullata*, confirmed by Honorius III in 1223, the long passage cautioning the brothers against interaction with women, for example, appears in a shortened and less strict version:

> I firmly precept each and every friar not to have suspicious company or conversation with women, and not to enter the monasteries of nuns, except those to whom special permission has been conceded by the Apostolic See; neither are they to be godfathers of men or women [so that] scandal may not arise on this account among the friars nor concerning them.[42]

That the issue caused intense concern is clearly documented in internal discussions about pastoral care for religious women and about the relationship with female communities. Again, St Francis is credited with criticism of this task. According to Thomas of Pavia (d. 1280), Francis commented that "until now, the fistula was in our flesh, and there was hope of healing it. But now it has taken root in the bone and will be practically incurable".[43]

The situation thus forced a fissure between mendicant ideals and social realities. In practice, it was difficult to attain a compromise bridging the extremes of avoidance and familiar contact. While a comprehensive survey of Franciscan strategies in this respect remains to be done, Salimbene of Parma's *Cronica* can be used to exemplify both the strong pressure on the Franciscan brothers and the tentative solutions they seem to have found.

As the story of the friendship-seeking nun illustrated, Salimbene himself at times preferred to avoid close contact with women – and brought this attitude to the attention of his readers. But he also took the topic up in other parts of his chronicle, for example by entering warnings against the seductive presence of women that were drawn from the so-called misogynist tradition[44] – most probably, from monastic sources, background to many of the admonitions ascribed to St Francis. Salimbene's descriptions of female wiles, ascribed to church fathers, are rather colourful:

> Woman to define? That will take but two lines: A poison sweet, a fetid rose, a stinking treat/A creature always prone to what she's supposed to leave alone .... Moreover, Augustine says, "Just as oil is fuel to the fire, so women kindle the fire of lechery". Also Isidore: "Lust in the presence of women grows like green grass near the water". ... And Augustine:

> "Woman was evil from the beginning, the gate of death, the serpent's disciple, the devil's friend, the fountain of deception".[45]

Salimbene thus seems to have put great emphasis on disciplining the male Franciscan mind to shy away from women, and he recommended recourse to misogynist *topoi* to counteract any stirrings of desire.

Yet his drastic words are largely balanced out by a completely different attitude, which again derives from the highly competitive relationship between thirteenth-century clerics and Franciscans where pastoral care and the apostolic life were concerned. Salimbene not only incriminated the clergy's lack of chastity in his report of the Italian synod discussed above; he also followed up on this report with a highly emotional, accusatory story about a multiple rape. In this *narratio dolorosa*, Salimbene reports that the Franciscan friar Humilis of Milan once heard the confession of a woman who told him that she had been raped outside of the city. But when she went to her priest to confess this, he did not absolve her but rather led her behind the altar and raped her in turn, unmoved by the sanctity of the space and her own bitter tears. Two other priests, whom she sought out in her misery, did the same, raping her next to the body of the Lord. Friar Humilis granted her the desired absolution but then remarked that she seemed to have brought a knife to confession, and he wondered what it was for. Disappointing the modern readers' expectations that she had finally decided to defend herself against further abuse, the woman confessed that she had planned to kill herself if the friar, too, were to molest her. The episode ends with the friar assuring her that he would never do that and promising that paradise would still be hers if she continued to repent her sins and love God.[46]

This episode, which uses a highly emotional topic to move and influence the reader, probably with considerable success, constitutes a second answer to the Franciscans' critics: Countering their challenges, Salimbene not only insisted on chastity as a virtue but in turn created a negative image of the violence of cruel and lustful priests. The priests he describes are "perverted" in the literal sense: Their focus on the woman's body rather than her soul drives her to despair and death rather than guiding her to salvation and eternal life. At the same time, Salimbene's story not only challenges the religious authority of priests by maligning their unchaste and cruel masculinity. It also gives a positive portrayal of the Franciscan friar: He is the one authority figure who is free from temptation and never loses sight of his ultimate goal of providing spiritual counsel to the victimised woman, whom he treats with empathy and respect.

The few examples discussed so far indicate that the Franciscans drew strongly on established concepts of chastity and purity – typically transferred from monastic sources – and applied this ideal of chaste masculinity to their own situation. Both the normative sources and the relevant passages in Salimbene's *Cronica* document a pronounced awareness of the threats and dangers chaste men had to withstand in pastoral care. Yet tension remained, as the necessity of daily interaction with women in pastoral contexts was difficult to reconcile with the strategies of avoidance suggested by tradition. In their battle for religious authority, Franciscans generally claimed hegemony by conceptualising a superior masculinity that was disciplined, chaste and pious. Responding in kind to the topical innuendo questioning the friars' chastity, moreover, Salimbene also attacked and devalued the clergy, painting a negative image of undisciplined, carnal and ultimately irreligious men.

The discussion of chastity among the thirteenth-century Dominicans makes for an interesting comparison. Generally speaking, the Dominican tradition shows a reserve towards contact with women similar to the Franciscan one. Examples can be taken from normative sources, beginning with the Dominican Constitutions.[47] In his rendering of the order's beginnings, the *Libellus de principiis*, Master General Jordan of Saxony (d. 1237) wrote that Dominicus himself, on his deathbed, cautioned the community against contact with young women.[48] But more importantly, the themes of purity, chastity and positive masculine behaviour were also treated in the corpora of didactic literature produced for the order's internal use in the mid-thirteenth century. During this important episode of Dominican identity-formation – the period when the order was attacked harshly in the quarrels at the University of Paris, but also underwent a first marked generational renewal – chastity seems to have received much attention.

During the thick of the university conflicts, Humbert of Romans (d. 1277), master general of the Dominicans from 1254 to 1263, had encouraged the members of the order to document all memorable events and qualities found in the order. This initiative stood behind the compilation of large-scale hagiographical and *exempla* collections intended to sharpen and consolidate Dominican norms and identity.[49]

A text that was written in response to Humbert's directive is Gerard of Frachet's *Vitae fratrum Ordinis Praedicatorum.*[50] As the prologue states, this collection was meant exclusively for the edification of other Dominicans and thus for internal use within the order.[51] It features a chapter "About the virtue of chastity"[52], which contains, among others, the following example: As Gerard reports, an intrigue was spun at the royal court against the Dominican Friar Dominic Hispanus.[53] His enemies hired a courtesan, who was ordered to seduce the friar under the cover of wanting to confess her sins to him. But the friar quickly saw through her and, promising that he was going to prepare the scene for their amorous adventure, put her off until the next day. He then kindled a great fire and lay down in the middle of it, remaining completely untouched by the flames, and invited the woman to join him. Overwhelmed by this visible demonstration of his holiness and virtue – which recalls the bible quotation of Proverbs 6,17 ascribed to St Francis above – the woman grew quite ashamed. Her cries of remorse quickly called many others to witness the miracle.

It is hardly surprising that this exemplary story, which again highlights the supernatural *virtus* necessary to resist women, is another import from monastic sources, in this case adapting an example contained in the *Dialogus miraculorum* by the Cistercian Caesarius of Heisterbach (d. ca. 1240).[54] But the Dominicans went beyond such borrowing in their identity-formation, as emerges from another text tracing its origins to Humbert of Romans' initiative, the 1258 *Bonum universale de apibus* by Thomas of Cantimpré (d. 1272).[55] This work uses the metaphor of the beehive to discuss the life practiced by religious communities. It is a compendious and somewhat heterogeneous collection encompassing *exempla* and miracle stories treating many different themes.[56] In several chapters *De virtute castitatis*, *De fuga peccati contra naturam* and *De virtute innocentiae & simplicitatis*, Thomas deals with relevant issues.[57] Two anecdotes can be discussed to highlight aspects of new Dominican constructions of superior masculinity.

The first is a story about a Benedictine novice from the great and famous monastery of Cluny, who accompanied his abbot on a journey.[58] The abbot's retinue had to make a stop at a smithy. In his simplicity, the boy monk, who had never seen a smithy, grew fascinated with the red-hot burning of the iron. When he impulsively picked it up with his naked, unprotected hand, he did not suffer any burn. Astonished greatly, the abbot and other bystanders ascribed this to the boy's venerable innocence. While the abbot was engaged in some business, however, the boy monk then went into the smithy, where the smith's wife was playing with her child. Never having seen a baby either, the novice began to play with the child. Led by malice and provoked by the boy's lack of experience, the child's mother asked him whether he would like to have such a baby, too. When he naively assented, she seduced him, promising that this was how children were made. When the novice returned to the smithy afterwards and tried to touch the red-hot iron again, he burned himself terribly. The abbot was greatly disturbed, realizing that the boy's outer wound rested on an interior lesion that had stripped away the protection of his innocence. [59]

As the introduction to this episode clearly documents, Thomas of Cantimpré intended it as a critique of the Benedictine practice of accepting child novices and rearing them within the order.[60] Raised within the monastery's walls, these children had no experience of the world and did not know what awaited them on the outside. As Thomas advocated, novices should only be admitted as adults, at a point where they had the experience necessary to make informed decisions. Implicitly, the example also shows that Thomas thought it insufficient to establish bodily chastity through naive innocence. He highlighted the role of knowledge about dangers and of learning processes, as simplicity and innocence did not arm novices against the loss of chastity.

A second example puts a slightly different accent on this argument. It concerns the case of a scholarly cleric, who had lived chastely for many years and done much excellent and pious work in his community. Yet one day, this older man found himself alone in his bedroom with his housekeeper, a virgin of 60 years. The inescapable happened, with fatal results:

Whereas the woman killed herself in her grief about her sin, the formerly exemplary cleric, having once experienced fleshly pleasures, continued to live in a carnal and shameful manner.[61] This example teaches the recipient that the battle for chastity is a life-long process. Neither age nor a long, meritorious life in the service of God can protect a man against temptation and bodily desire.

As it seems, examples like these were part of a Dominican strategy to shape an extraordinarily self-reflexive, intellectualised ideal of chaste masculinity. The examples referring to the older orders and the clergy serve as negative foils, but as they appear in didactic texts meant for internal use only, they do not only underline the opponents' deviant behaviour but also provide lessons to the Dominican friars: Members of the order were not only to master their own desires[62] but were also to be made aware of specific dangers and temptations tied to concrete situations, in order to be able to withstand and counter them. The main strategy for maintaining chastity seems to have shifted – it is no longer one of avoiding women but of acquiring preventative knowledge about the dangers they represent. Even more than Salimbene's misogynistic *topoi* and individual anecdotes, the Dominican *exempla* were designed to create and dramatise awareness of the constant threats to male chastity. The shifts from abstract value to specific lesson and from individual experience to systematically distributed knowledge are important ones. They also manage to formulate a recipe for male chastity that relies on teaching further lessons to unchaste women – as Friar Dominic did to the courtesan – rather than on avoiding them completely to safeguard one's own virtue, as Salimbene did with the friendly nun.

If we compare the constructions of masculinity employed by the Franciscan Salimbene and the Dominican Thomas of Cantimpré further, Salimbene's vision of saintly Franciscan chastity is presented as superior to the lustful cruelty of carnal priests in a rather harsh contrast that casts his opponents as devilish "other". The historical impetus of a reform of decayed morals, which stands behind high medieval monastic concepts of purity and chastity, can still be discerned rather clearly. Thomas' comparison instead offers a gradation of different forms of chastity existing side by side in a situation of diversity. This is both more exclusive and subtler; he does not devalue the masculinity of his competitors as quasi-inhuman but presents them as examples of normal human weakness – which the Dominican elite must nevertheless rise above to become a better type of man.

Beyond, with or against nature: Polemics and the dynamic of chaste and sexualised masculinities

As will have become evident in the discussion of various texts authored within the Franciscan and Dominican orders, specific concepts of chastity and superior masculinity seem to have been formulated and used for didactic purposes. But the heterogeneous nature and diverging audiences of the examples discussed here – normative texts, a chronicle and didactic *exempla*, meant partly for internal reading within the orders, partly for outside audiences – also show that we have to tread carefully. Not only do some anecdotes, like Salimbene's wrenching story of the raped woman, appear to be designed primarily for polemical purposes; as far as this survey can tell, the diverging characteristics of the materials also suggest that the communication of ideals of male chastity was organised in a different way among the Franciscans and the Dominicans, as the latter seem to have invested more systematic efforts into providing and distributing foundational didactic texts. Further research will have to follow up on this issue, but the heterogeneity of male identity-making should be kept in mind generally. We mostly ignore where and how the extant texts were actually read, and how much emphasis may have been put on chastity by different groups within the orders or within different mendicant convents.

This applies even more strongly to clerics and their concepts of masculinity – as, in contrast to the mendicants or other religious orders, we should not assume a homogeneous identity of "the clergy". Besides divergences based on regional profiles or the agenda individual bishops may have followed for their dioceses, there were quite diverse social strata within the clergy, and specific contexts and social circles – at princely or royal courts, in schools and universities, urban centres or villages of specific types – all played a role.[63]

If we briefly ask how the controversy between secular clergy and mendicants impacted clerical concepts of chaste masculinity, this background needs to be considered. The alliance of secular clerics and laymen around William of Saint-Amour and Rutebeuf almost exclusively produced polemical texts. They were intended for different audiences at different stages of the escalating conflict of the 1250s or of later conflict episodes. Although any polemical text implicitly seeks to posit or confirm an identity by attacking the opponent's stance, William's texts in particular argue against the friars rather than for the clergy and do not realise didactic intentions to the degree visible in the mendicant texts.[64]

Still, William's polemical construction of masculinity makes for an interesting comparison to the mendicant concepts discussed so far: Salimbene of Parma and Thomas of Cantimpré in particular attempted to set the masculinity of their own in-group apart. They portrayed their superior forms of masculinity within a gendered order using three poles: Salimbene's story juxtaposed the raped woman with the chaste masculinity of Friar Humilis of Milan and its counterfoil, the perverted and unchaste raping priests; Thomas of Cantimpré's *exempla* juxtaposed women both with "standard issue", unaware and thus failure-prone monastic and clerical celibates, and, implicitly, with an elite of well-informed and chaste friars; and, put very briefly, William of Saint-Amour challenged this double construction of chaste masculinities to argue instead that all men were more or less equal where desire was concerned. To assume otherwise was hypocrisy, especially if one went so far as to actually claim the supernatural virtue necessary to become immune to the temptations of the flesh.

A long passage devoted to problems of chastity in William's mid-1260s *Collectiones catholicae et canonicae scripturae* in fact not only cited the words of St Bernard discussed above. To underline that one could not escape human nature, William collected several pages' worth of relevant biblical and patristic passages, among others the one about walking barefoot across fire (Prov 6,17), also ascribed to St Francis by Thomas of Celano.[65] An excellent polemicist, William simply bypassed the much-exploited weak point of clerics – their task of meeting women alone to hear their confessions. Instead, he went on the offensive and made much of the mendicants' pastoral care for female religious communities, especially for beguines – an open flank, as this issue was quite controversial within the mendicant orders themselves.[66]

The argument William constructed in this respect ran as follows: Scriptural and patristic authorities overwhelmingly confirmed that familiar intercourse with women brought temptation, which drew men away from God. Neither men belonging to religious orders nor clerics could clearly claim to possess confirmed divine grace, which had made the apostles rise above such temptation and even given them the power to raise the dead.[67] This made avoidance the best strategy – unless one was forced to engage in pastoral care for women by virtue of office, a duty William associated with the clergy and bishops.

For the clergy, especially bishops who had to visit female communities, William advocated safety measures that lay in constant social control rather than individual mental fortitude:[68] Where a bishop or priest visited religious women, he was to take *socii* who bore witness to his good behaviour, and if necessary, slept in the same room to document this.[69] William also cited authorities against a possible counter-argument, which bears resemblance to Thomas of Cantimpré's ideal: Some argued that good men meeting with women for the sake of preaching did well, and that this even gave these men the opportunity to "battle against their temptation and in defeating it, to merit a more glorious crown".[70] To William, this was nonsense. Citing St Paul and Ambrose, he argued that some things could be fought, but others should be fled – and according to the authorities, carnal desire should definitely be fled.[71]

William of Saint-Amour thus drew a dividing line between different chaste lifestyles: Men could reach chastity by avoiding temptation in the solitude of the monastery or by trusting in strict control and supervision if they took on temptation within the confines of their ecclesiastical office. But, as he implied, it was hubris to reach beyond nature and to want to rise above desire completely. William's continuous focus on offensive rather than defensive arguments may hint that he knew quite well that there was no perfect formula for chastity among the clergy. His claim to hegemony rather lay in his insistence on the intrinsic value of clerical office – and his repeated accusations that attempts to fulfil this office better by rising above human nature were doomed to fail and thus hypocritical. In the battle for hegemony on the thirteenth-century religious field, William thus only used the theme of absolute chastity to exclude and marginalise others and avoided a claim of superior chastity for his own group. On the one hand, this may simply be due to the lack of an independent ideal of chastity among the clergy, as most clerical ideals were closely related to or imported from monastic literature and thus identical to the ones used and adapted by the mendicants. On the other hand, we see at least faint outlines of an identity built on a different form of masculine self-discipline; altogether, William sought to trump the superlative ascetical efforts of his opponents by emphasising humility and a clear consciousness of human nature and its limitations.

A last contrasting example can help to clarify the underlying issues. If we were to look at competing masculinities rather than conflicts about superior religious authority, William's insistence on sexuality as a force of nature would have lent itself readily to further adaptations and identity-building among different clerical groups. There were related types of clerical masculinity that were constructed as superior – if not exactly as chaste. While the various and heterogeneous trends of the thirteenth century cannot be surveyed here, one particular text can at least give an impression of further dynamics – and at the same time hints at possible further inferences between the concepts of celibate and non-celibate masculinities.

In the years around 1280, the cleric Jean de Meun wrote the second part of the *Roman de la Rose*, a long didactic allegorical poem in Old French, which discusses a male lover's quest for his object of desire.[72] Consisting of two parts of considerable complexity, this famous and much-read work straddles the divide of lay and clerical audiences[73] and hence of sexualised and celibate masculinities. A first part by Guillaume de Lorris dates to c. 1230 and sets a dream-frame in which the lover, "Amant", falls in love with the unnamed "Rose", in the tradition of courtly literature. Jean de Meun's second part includes themes and styles of various genres; while some passages are openly erotic and many have a coarse and comical bent typical for vernacular stories, the long disquisitions of the various allegorical figures also reflect the author's education in the ambit of the University of Paris. Jean in fact had a keen interest in the controversy between the mendicants and the secular clergy at Paris: His part of the *Roman* openly championed William of Saint-Amour and, moreover, introduced a personification of hypocrisy, "Faus Semblant", whose description took up many aspersions William had cast on the mendicants. But Jean's lover manages to make use of this character: In the course of the story, it is (among other qualities) the personified false seeming of "Faus Semblant" which helps "Amant" win the "Rose".

While the poem does not address itself clearly to a group of either celibate or non-celibate readers, it has been argued that its treatment of love and sexual desire may have been especially pertinent for young clerics.[74] Jean de

Meun's text informed its readers about all aspects of love and sexuality and could thus also be seen as an identity-building tool to provide clerical readers with knowledge helping them to avoid and master desire. Among other things, it contains substantial passages offering misogynist thought and criticisms of marriage. More importantly, however, the lover is shown to evolve from a hapless and helpless victim of love, which dominates his whole being. Knowledge enables him to master his emotions and use a range of qualities – reason and prudence, but also dissimulation and flattery – to stage a highly strategic allegorical conquest, allowing him to attain his desire. Accompanying this strategy is the deconstruction of a morally charged, all-encompassing form of love as the goal of desire, as the *Roman de la Rose* instead recommends attaining sexual satisfaction.

As Jean de Meun does not revolve around clerical celibacy, male sexual desire is not problematised in the way discussed above. Not only does his poem end with a detailed and graphic description of the defloration of the Rose, prefaced by a jovial exhortation to the male audience to watch and learn how these things are done;[75] the speeches of "Faus Semblant" also make clear that lust and sexuality were often experienced by religious men and women, in spite of all prohibitions. Among other things, the topic of unchaste religious women is re-introduced in an image evoking Rutebeuf.[76] Other voices, notably those of "Genius" and "Natura", emphatically celebrate male sexuality as a force of nature that must be obeyed, revered and even cultivated by frequent and forceful use of one's "plow".[77]

Notably, this latter, literally earthy, concept of a highly sexualised masculinity also has a negative counter-image and thus positions itself against other masculinities. But the contrast is not one of sexual activity and chastity but of natural and "unnatural" sex, the latter primarily denoting same-sex activities between men, which are demeaned in a lengthy invective and marked as sinful and dirty.[78] As the *Roman de la Rose* does not clearly target clerical readers but takes courtly love as its point of departure, we cannot quite class this as a clerical strategy of identity-building, advocating a superior masculinity based on a heteronormative interpretation of sexuality as a force of nature. But if we were allowed to speculate for a moment, the attitude pervading the text may well have confirmed some clerical readers in a defiant attitude of "we may not be chaste, but at least we are real men" – or, on the note William of Saint-Amour emphasised in other respects, "we may be human and sinners, but at least we do not pretend to be saints".[79]

This latter juxtaposition of different ways of handling desire is not only interesting because it returns to a strategy of contrasting superior and inferior masculinities, again re-applying "othering" strategies and older *topoi* – the accusation of same-sex acts was a polemical staple used since the eleventh century, among other groups against monks.[80] More importantly, the dichotomy natural/unnatural here also contrasts diverging ideals of religiosity and personal sanctification. The classical approach, derived from monastic traditions, was to seek sanctification by battling natural desires and aiming for an angel-like purity in mind, soul and body. The counter-ideal hinted at in the writings of William of Saint-Amour instead seeks a sanctification integrating the natural, desiring male body into a higher religious duty on the basis of inward humility. As William put it in a sermon contrasting the pharisees and publicans, "it can be argued that it is better to be a humble sinner than a just man with pride – that is, a man who thinks himself just".[81] Though his brief remarks do not allow for a more elaborate interpretation, William seems to suggest that the true *locus* of purity was not the chaste body but the humble, self-aware mind.

Conclusion: Conflicts as catalysts

In conclusion, it seems legitimate to say that in regard to chaste masculinity, the tensions arising from the conflict between secular clergy, new mendicant and old monastic orders in the thirteenth century set up a framework of pressures that could not be ignored. While religious men had certainly been made to feel increased social and political pressure to preserve their chastity since the IV Lateran Council, the competition between old and new elites increased these pressures. With the escalation of conflicts, the relation between gendered behaviour and religious authority was reinforced, establishing a framework of tensions and tactical utterances. At least in part, the sheer impact of polemical encounters – or if one wants, the clever use of *topoi* – would have forced all sides to rethink and sometimes re-formulate their ideas of chaste masculinity. As orders and clergy attempted to regulate their self-image, behaviour and appearance, this discourse must have impacted everyday practices as well.

Given this catalytic impact of conflicts, it appears problematic to study the masculinities of thirteenth-century clerics or mendicant friars separately. To contribute to an understanding of the shifting historical impacts of group-related polemics and everyday local practices on masculine identities, future research should extend its strategy of studying tensions between different masculinities, especially to explore the role of conflict-based polemics. Moreover, the thirteenth century, with its sustained competition between clergy and mendicant orders, emerges as a highly transformational period as far as concepts of masculinity were concerned. As Tanya Miller Stabler aptly puts it, the secular–mendicant controversy brought a fresh wave of the "monasticization" of the clergy that began with the Gregorian reforms and was revisited with the IV Lateran council – and the mendicants "represented the ultimate monasticization of the clergy because they lived according to a rule, like monks, but served the laity like secular clerics".[82]

Although it is by no means a period of "origins", the few sources discussed here show the second half of the thirteenth century to be a time of intense intellectual work, conceptual entanglement and, eventually, of a certain re-stabilisation of extant discourses. The conflict not only revisited the traditional themes of purity and chastity but also earlier texts – as documented by the secular cleric William and the lay poet Rutebeuf quoting a warning penned by Bernard of Clairvaux (concerning, as it happened, the masculinity of "Cathar" heretics); or by the friar Salimbene of Parma radicalising the negative stereotype of non-celibate priests. These were taken from earlier clashes also caused by competing elites, such as the confrontation between married and celibate priests since the eleventh-century church reform or between new monastic orders and heretical religious reform movements in the twelfth century. Using and adapting older polemical arguments, thirteenth-century conflicts thus encouraged conceptual transfer and revision of textual traditions.

This resulted not only in new variations of older themes, but also in a new configuration of diversity where masculinities were concerned. The intellectual competition between several groups of chaste men produced several variations of superlative ideals of male chastity, but the ongoing contestations also generated concepts of masculinity linked to the pure mind rather than the pure body – or more precisely, new ways of linking the purity of mind and body. Finally, competition with the highly disciplined mendicants may also have reinforced trends among clerics – especially younger clerics – to defiantly base their male superiority on a full realisation of their natural potential for sexuality. This would have made specific sense for clerics from noble backgrounds, whose lay kinsmen would have emphasised male sexuality as well.[83]

The controversy between mendicants and secular clerics – and thus the concepts of masculinity produced in it – also had a comparatively long-lived impact: Although compromises concerning pastoral rights were reached around 1300, several topics that had been hotly debated during the controversy remained present in the increasingly dense sphere of public debate of the later medieval Latin church. After all, topics like chastity had been discussed in several political arenas, at schools and universities and in urban public space for almost half a century, generating a massive amount of documentation. The topic of chastity remained part of an evolving polemical discourse concerning the role of the mendicants.[84] But besides these "anti-fraternal" polemics, the thirteenth century witnessed intense efforts at universities and mendicant *studia* to collect and systematise extant scholarly and religious knowledge and to make it easily accessible in large compilations like *summae*, confessor's handbooks, sermon collections and encyclopaedias. These scholarly books, which often contained positions on the relation of gender and authority, were among the first to make it into print in the fifteenth century, so that we can speak of a veritable knowledge archive being shaped during this period. As it seems, thirteenth-century concepts of masculinity may thus have impacted later traditions through their sheer material presence. In the following periods, they would have oscillated in nature between *topoi* or stereotypes and actively reworked issues, but nevertheless they acted as points of crystallisation for the ongoing discussion of gender and authority.

Notes

1 Cf. Albrecht Diem, *Das monastische Experiment. Die Rolle der Keuschheit bei der Entstehung des westlichen Klosterwesens*, Vita Regularis. Ordnungen und Deutungen religiosen Lebens im Mittelalter 24 (Münster: LIT, 2005); several contributions in Jennifer D. Thibodeaux, ed., *Negotiating Clerical Identities: Priests, Monks and Masculinity in the Middle Ages* (Basingstoke and New York: Palgrave Macmillan, 2010); and for the late antique foundations, Peter Brown, *The Body and Society: 20th Anniversary Edition with a new Introduction* (New York: Columbia University Press, 2008).

2 Cf. Jo Ann McNamara, "The Herrenfrage. The Restructuring of the Gender System, 1050–1150," in *Medieval Masculinities: Regarding Men in the Middle Ages*, ed. Clare A. Lees, Thelma S. Fenster and Jo Ann McNamara, (Minneapolis: University of Minnesota Press, 1994), 3–29; Jacqueline Murray, ed., *Conflicted Identities and Multiple Masculinities: Men in the Medieval West*, Garland Medieval Casebooks (New York: Garland, 1999); Maureen C. Miller, "Masculinity, Reform, and Clerical Culture: Narratives of Episcopal Holiness in the Gregorian Era," *Church History* 72, no. 1 (2003): 25–52; John H. Arnold, "The Labour of Continence: Masculinity and Clerical Virginity," in *Medieval Virginities*, ed. Anke Bernau, Ruth Evans and Sarah Salih (Cardiff: University of Wales Press, 2003), 102–118. On medieval masculinities generally, cf. Lees, Fenster and McNamara, *Medieval Masculinities*; Dawn M. Hadley, ed., *Masculinity in Medieval Europe* (London and New York: Longman, 1999); Ruth Mazo Karras, *From Boys to Men: Formations of Masculinity in Late Medieval Europe* (Philadelphia: University of Pennsylvania Press, 2003). On concepts of celibacy and clerical masculinity, especially in the high-medieval reform period, see Anne Llewellyn Barstow, *Married Priests and the Reforming Papacy: The Eleventh-Century Debates* (Lewiston, NY: Edward Mellen Press, 1982); Robert N. Swanson, "Angels Incarnate. Clergy and Masculinity from Gregorian Reform to Reformation," in *Masculinity in Medieval Europe*, ed. Hadley, 160–177; Michael Frassetto, ed., *Medieval Purity and Piety: Essays on Medieval Clerical Celibacy and Religious Reform* (New York: Garland, 1998); Jennifer D. Thibodeaux, "Man of the Church, or Man of the Village? Gender and the Parish Clergy in Medieval Normandy," *Gender & History* 18, no. 2 (2006): 380–399; Helen Parish, *Clerical Celibacy in the West: C.1100–1700* (Farnham: Ashgate, 2010), esp. 87–122.

3 This contribution explores the link between gendered identity, polemics and religious diversity in the context of the research project "Diversitas religionum. Thirteenth-Century Foundations of European Discourses of Religious Diversity", sponsored by a Dilthey Fellowship granted by the Volkswagen Foundation to Sita Steckel. A doctoral dissertation by Stephanie Kluge on polemics concerning purity, chastity and masculinity among Dominicans and Franciscans at the Westfälische Wilhelms-Universität Münster is in preparation.

4 Salimbene de Adam, *Cronica*, ed. Giuseppe Scalia, Corpus Christianorum Continuatio Medievalis 125 (Turnhout: Brepols, 1994), 582–583. On Salimbene and his work, see *Salimbeniana. Atti del convegno per il VII centenario di Fra Salimbene, Parma 1987–1989* (Bologna: Radio Tau, 1991); Oliver Guyotjeannin, *Salimbene de Adam: Un chroniqueur franciscain*, Témoins de notre histoire (Turnhout: Brepols, 1995).

5 Salimbene de Adam, *Cronica*, 583: "Et dixi sibi:... 'Oro Deum ut deleat memoriam tuam de corde meo'." Translation from *The Chronicle of Salimbene de Adam*, trans. Joseph L. Baird, Guiseppe Baglivi and John Robert Kane, Medieval & Renaissance Texts & Studies 40 (Binghampton, New York: Medieval & Renaissance Text & Studies, 1986), 387.

6 Ibid.

7 Ibid. (the nun later learns through the local bishop that Salimbene could not acquiesce to her request because it was improper, but he does in fact pray for her) and cf. below, n. 46.

8 On this conflict, see Guy Geltner, *The Making of Medieval Antifraternalism: Polemic, Violence, Deviance, and Remembrance* (Oxford: Oxford University Press, 2012); Ramona Sickert, *Wenn Klosterbrüder zu Jahrmarktsbrüdern werden: Studien zur Wahrnehmung der Franziskaner und Dominikaner im 13. Jahrhundert.* Vita Regularis. Ordnungen und Deutungen religiosen Lebens im Mittelalter 28 (Berlin: LIT, 2006). For the ecclesiological implications and later ramifications, see also Yves M.-J. Congar, "Aspects ecclésiologiques de la querelle entre mendiants et séculiers dans la seconde moitié du XIIIe siècle et le début du XIVe," *Archives d'histoire doctrinale et littéraire du Moyen Age* 36 (1961): 35–151; Penn R. Szittya, *The Antifraternal Tradition in Medieval Literature* (Princeton, NJ: Princeton University Press, 1986).

9 On the mendicant orders, see (with further references) Donald S. Prudlo, ed., *The Origin, Development, and Refinement of Medieval Religious Mendicancies* (Leiden; Boston: Brill, 2012); Gert Melville, *Die Welt der mittelalterlichen Klöster. Geschichte und Lebensformen (*München: Beck, 2012), esp. 176–214.

10 See for example the remarks made by the monastic observer Matthew Paris (d. 1259): Matthew Paris, and Roger (of Wendover), *Chronica Majora*, ed. Henry R. Luard, Rerum Britannicarum medii aevi scriptores (London: Longman, 182), 4:11–17.

11 Beside the titles mentioned in n. 8, see the study Michel-Marie Dufeil, *Guillaume de Saint-Amour et la polémique universitaire parisienne, 1250–1259* (Paris: A. et J. Picard, 1972) – by now superseded and corrected in many points by *The Opuscula of William of Saint-Amour: The Minor Works of 1255–1256*, ed. Andrew Traver, Beiträge zur Geschichte der Philosophie und Theologie des Mittelalters N.F. 63 (Münster: Aschendorff, 2003); Andrew G. Traver, "The Forging of an Intellectual Defense of Mendicancy in the Medieval University," in *The Origin, Development, and Refinement of Medieval Religious Mendicancies*, ed. Prudlo, 157–196; id., "Rewriting History? The Parisian Secular Masters' Apologia of 1254," *History of Universities* 15 (1999): 9–45; Jacques Verger, "Coacta ac periculosa societas. La difficile intégration des réguliers à l'Université de Paris au XIIIe siècle," in *Vivre en société au Moyen Âge: Occident Chrétien VIe–XVe siècle*, ed. Claude Carozzi, Daniel Le Blévec and Huguette Taviani-Carozzi (Aix-en-Provence: Publications de l'Université de Provence, 2008), 261–280.

12 Cf. Sita Steckel, "Professoren in Weltuntergangsstimmung. Religiöse Debatte und städtische Öffentlichkeit im Pariser Bettelordensstreit, 1252–1257," in *Pluralität – Konkurrenz – Konflikt: Religiöse Spannungen im städtischen Raum der Vormoderne*, ed. Jörg Oberste, Forum Mittelalter Studien 8 (Regensburg: Schnell & Steiner, 2013), 51–74.

13 Concerning the concept of polemics, which we take in its broad sense as a text attacking an opponent (regardless of the tone or aptness of the argument), cf. Hermann Stauffer, "Art. Polemik," in *Historisches Wörterbuch der Rhetorik* (Tübingen: Max Niemeyer, 2003), 6: col. 1403–1415. Religious polemics are discussed in Theo L. Hettema and Arie van der Kooij, eds., *Religious Polemics in Context: Papers Presented to the Second International Conference of the Leiden Institute for the Study of Religions (LISOR) Held at Leiden, 27–28 April, 2000*, Studies in Theology and Religion 11 (Assen: Van Gorcum, 2004); important observations of medieval polemics on gender and the body are made by Alexandra Cuffel, *Gendering Disgust in Medieval Religious Polemic* (Notre Dame, IN: University of Notre Dame Press, 2007).

14 See the information in William of Saint-Amour, *De periculis novissimorum temporum*, ed. and trans. Guy Geltner, Dallas Medieval Texts and Translations 8 (Paris, Leuven, Dudley, MA: Peeters, 2008); William of Saint-Amour, *The Opuscula,* ed. Traver; Sita Steckel, "Ein brennendes Feuer in meiner Brust. Prophetische Autorschaft und polemische Autorisierungsstrategien Guillaumes de Saint-Amour im Pariser Bettelordensstreit (1256)," in *Prophetie und Autorschaft: Charisma, Heilsversprechen und Gefährdung*, ed. Christel Meier and Martina Wagner-Egelhaaf (Berlin: de Gruyter, 2014), 129–168.
15 Cf. Andrew G. Traver, "William of Saint-Amour's Two Disputed Questions De Quantitate Eleemosynae and De Valido Mendicante," *Archives d'histoire Doctrinale et Littéraire Du Moyen Âge* 62 (1995): 295–342.
16 Cf. William of Saint-Amour, *The Opuscula*, ed. Traver, 7–8.
17 On Rutebeuf, see *Œuvres complètes de Rutebeuf*, ed. Michel Zink, 2 vols, Classiques Garnier (Paris: Garnier, 1989–1990) and *Rutebeuf et les frères mendiants: poèmes satiriques*, ed. Jean Dufournet (Paris: H. Champion, 1991).
18 Cf. *Œuvres complètes de Rutebeuf*, ed. Edmond Faral and Julia Bastin, 2 vols (Paris: Éditions A. et J. Picard, 1959–60), 1:275–276, lines 163–170: "Je ne di pas que plus en facent, /Més il samble que pas nes hacent,/ Et sains Bernars dist, ce me samble: "Converser homme et fame ensamble/ Sanz plus ouvrer selonc nature,/ C'est vertu si nete et si pure,/ Ce tesmoingne bien li escriz,/ Com de Ladre fist Jhesuschriz".
19 *Œuvres complètes de Rutebeuf*, ed. Faral and Bastin, 1:276, line 171: "Or ne sai je ci sus qu'entendre:/ Je voi si l'un vers l'autre tendre/ Qu'en un chaperon a deus testes,/ Et il ne sont angles ne bestes."
20 For perceptions of desire and lust in monastic literature, see (with further references) Diem, *Das monastische Experiment*, esp. 33–130.
21 Bernard of Clairvaux, "Sermon 65," in *Heresies of the High Middle Ages*, ed. Walter L. Wakefield and Austin P. Evans (New York: Columbia University Press, 1991), 135.
22 Cf. Arié Serper, "L'influence de Guillaume de Saint-Amour sur Rutebeuf," *Romance Philology* 17 (1963): 391–402.
23 A different chronology is suggested in Tanya Stabler Miller, "Mirror of the Scholarly (Masculine) Soul: Scholastics, Beguines and Gendered Spirituality in Medieval Paris," in *Negotiating Clerical Identities,* ed. Thibodeaux, 240; 248–249 (and similarly in her monograph, Tanya Stabler Miller, *The Beguines of Medieval Paris: Gender, Patronage, and Spiritual Authority* [Philadelphia: University of Pennsylvania Press, 2014], esp. pp. 17–9, which appeared just after this chapter was submitted). Miller's otherwise quite convincing and insightful analysis dates William of Saint-Amour's attacks against the friars' chastity, especially concerning beguines, to the 1250s. But William's writings quoted in favour of this either treat beguines generally without reference to sexuality ("Responsiones ad obiecta," in *Guillelmi de Sancto Amore Opera Omnia*, Constantiae: Apud Alitophilos, 1632, 92–93) or date from the 1260s ("Collectiones catholicae et canonicae scripturae," in *Guillelmi de Sancto Amore Opera Omnia,* 196, 266). Miller's dating thus seems to conflate several levels of conflict escalation as well as the different voices of William as theologian and Rutebeuf as poet.
24 On the *Collectiones*, which still await a critical edition (currently in *Guillelmi de Sancto Amore Opera Omnia* (as previous note), 111–487, cited henceforth as William of Saint-Amour, *Collectiones*), see the analysis in Szittya, *The Antifraternal Tradition*, 11–61.
25 William of Saint-Amour, *Collectiones*, 269.
26 For the following, cf. Diem, *Das monastische Experiment*, esp. 91–94, with further references; Jacqueline Murray, "Masculinizing Religious Life: Sexual

Prowess, the Battle for Chastity and Monastic Identity," in *Religious Men and Masculine Identity in the Middle Ages*, ed. P. H. Cullum and Katherine J. Lewis (Woodbridge: Boydell and Brewer, 2013), 24–42.

27 Thomas Aquinas, "Contra Impugnantes Dei Cultum et Religionem," in *Opera Omnia*, ed. H.-F. Dondaine. Editio Leonina 41 A (Rome: Apud S. Sabinae, 1970), cap. 25, A163: "Illi ergo litterati sunt praedicatores Antichristi qui saeculariter viventes, populos ad lascivias mundi inducunt".

28 Salimbene de Adam, *Cronica*, 607–608: "provocatus ad iram ... dixit: "Miseri et insani, cui committam confessiones secularium personarum, si fratres Minores et Predicatores non audiunt eas? Vobis secura conscientia eas committere non possum, quia, si veniunt ad vos et petunt tiriacam volentes confiteri, venenum eis datis. Ducitis enim mulieres post altare causa confitendi et ibi eas cognoscitis: quod nefas est dicere et peius operari. Ideo Dominus de vobis conqueritur per prophetam Osee: In domo Israel vidi orrendum, ibi fornicationes Effraym. Ideo enim doletis, si fratres Minores et Predicatores confessiones audiunt, quia non vultis quod cognoscant opera vestra mala ...." Translation from *The Chronicle of Salimbene de Adam*, 405, with slight adaptions.

29 See the literature above, n. 2, and cf. Brown, *The Body and Society*; Arnold Angenendt, "'Mit reinen Händen'. Das Motiv der kultischen Reinheit in der abendländischen Askese," in *Liturgie im Mittelalter: Ausgewählte Aufsätze zum 70. Geburtstag*, ed. Thomas Flammer and Daniel Meyer, 2nd ed., Ästhetik – Theologie – Liturgik 35 (Münster: LIT, 2005), 245–267.

30 We use the idea of a "tactical" use of gender concepts on the religious field in an adaption of the sense proposed by Linda Woodhead, "Gender Differences in Religious Practice and Significance," in *The Sage Handbook of the Sociology of Religion*, ed. James A. Beckford and N. Jay Demerath (Los Angeles: SAGE, 2007), 570–575.

31 Cf. Pierre Bourdieu, "Genèse et structure du champ religieux," *Revue Française de Sociologie* 12, no 3 (1971): 295–334. For the operationalization of Bourdieu's religious field theory, we follow Astrid Reuter, *Religion in der verrechtlichten Gesellschaft: Rechtskonflikte und öffentliche Kontroversen um Religion als Grenzarbeiten am religiösen Feld*, Critical Studies in Religion 5 (Göttingen: Vandenhoeck & Ruprecht, 2014), 43–59; see also Astrid Reuter, "Charting the Boundaries of the Religious Field: Legal Conflicts over Religion as Struggles over Blurring Borders," *Journal of Religion in Europe* 2, no. 1 (2009): 1–20.

32 If the arguments were developed, other groups would need to be included – besides princes involved in church government, especially members of other religions such as Judaism and Islam.

33 In the context of this explorative contribution, recent discussions on celibate or chaste masculinities as representing a "third gender" cannot be engaged in any detail. Rather than seeing chaste masculinity as a unified "third gender", we assume that various chaste masculinities were developed by celibate or chaste religious; this develops the argument made by Ruth Mazo Karras, "Thomas Aquinas' Chastity Belt: Clerical Masculinity in Medieval Europe," in *Gender & Christianity in Medieval Europe: New Perspectives*, ed. Lisa M. Bitel and Felice Lifshitz (Philadelphia: University of Pennsylvania Press, 2008), 52–68. For further positions, see Jacqueline Murray, "One Flesh, Two Sexes, Three Genders?", ibid., 34–51; Thibodeaux, "Man of the Church"; Swanson, "Angels Incarnate". See also the observations made on sexual difference in the Middle Ages by Christof Rolker, "The Two Laws and the Three Sexes: Ambiguous Bodies in Canon Law and Roman Law (12th to 16th Centuries)," *Zeitschrift der Savigny-Stiftung für Rechtsgeschichte. Kanonistische Abteilung* 100 (2014): 178–222.

34 The extant research seems to be outweighed by far by studies on high medieval monastic and clerical masculinities or late medieval clerical masculinities,

but there are some exceptions. On anti-mendicant polemics ascribing a lack of chastity, see Ramona Sickert, "Qui toz art dou feu de luxure... Zur Tradition der Keuschheitsvorstellungen und zum Vorwurf der Unkeuschheit gegenüber Franziskanern und Dominikanern in der Dichtung des 13. Jahrhunderts," in *Studia Monastica: Beiträge zum Klösterlichen Leben im Christlichen Abendland während des Mittelalters*, ed. Reinhardt Butz and Jörg Oberste, Vita Regularis. Ordnungen und Deutungen religiosen Lebens im Mittelalter 22 (Münster: LIT, 2004), 303–323. For problems of sexual discipline and avoidance of scandal among the mendicants, see Geltner, *Making of Medieval Antifraternalism*, 96–100; on the mendicants' relationship with women, John Coakley, "Gender and the Authority of Friars: The Significance of Holy Women for Thirteenth-Century Franciscans and Dominicans," *Church History* 60 (1991): 445–460; id., "Friars, Sanctity, and Gender: Mendicant Encounters with Saints, 1250–1325," in *Medieval Masculinities: Regarding Men in the Middle Ages*, ed. Lees, Fenster, McNamara, 91–110. Also directly relevant is Miller, "Mirror of the Scholarly (Masculine) Soul".

35 See Diem, *Das monastische Experiment*, 312–324.

36 "Regula non bullata," in *Die Opuscula des Hl. Franziskus von Assisi*, ed. Kajetan Esser (Grottaferrata: Editiones Collegii S. Bonaventurae ad Claras Aquas, 1989), 388–389: "Cap. XII: De malo visu et frequentia mulierum. Omnes fratres, ubicumque sunt vel vadunt, caveant sibi a malo visu et frequentia mulierum. Et nullus cum eis consilietur aut per viam vadat solus aut ad mensam in una paropside comedat. Sacerdotes honeste loquantur cum eis dando poenitentiam vel aliud spirituale consilium. Et nulla penitus mulier ab aliquo fratre recipiatur ad obedientiam, sed dato sibi consilio spirituali, ubi voluerit agat poenitentiam. Et multum omnes nos custodiamus et omnia membra nostra munda teneamus, quia dicit Dominus: "Qui viderit mulierem ad concupiscendam eam, iam moechatus est eam in corde suo (Mt. 5,28)." Translation by Sita Steckel except for Douay-Rheims Bible.

37 "Regula non bullata," 389 (Cap. XIII: *De vitanda fornicatione)*.

38 Thomas de Celano, *Vita Secunda S. Francisci*, in *Analecta Franciscana* 10 (Florence: Ad Claras Aquas 1941), 196–197: "Cap. LXXVIII: De fugienda familiaritate mulierum, et qualiter cum eis loquebatur. Mellita toxica familiaritatis videlicet mulierum, quae in errorem inducunt etiam viros sanctos, iubebat penitus evitari. Timebat enim ex hoc tenerum cito frangi, et fortem saepe spiritum infirmari. Harum contagionem evadere conversantem cum eis, nisi probatissimum virum, tam facile dixit quam, iuxta Scripturam, in igne ambulare nec comburere plantas." Translation from *The Lives of S. Francis of Assisi by Brother Thomas of Celano*, trans. Alan G. Ferrers Howell (London: Methuen & Co., 1908), 250.

39 See above n. 21.

40 On *cura monialium* generally, see (with further references) Eva Schlotheuber, "'Nullum Regimen Difficilius et Periculosius Est Regimine Feminarum': Die Begegnung des Beichtvaters Frederik van Heilo mit den Nonnen in der Devotio Moderna," in *Spätmittelalterliche Frömmigkeit zwischen Ideal und Praxis*, ed. Berndt Hamm and Thomas Lentes (Tübingen: Mohr Siebeck, 2001), 45–84.

41 Concerning pastoral care for female religious in the mendicant context, cf. Joan Mueller "Female Mendicancy: A Failed Experiment? The Case of Clare of Assisi," in *The Origin, Development, and Refinement of Medieval Religious Mendicancies*, ed. Prudlo, 59–81; Carsten Blauth, "Dominikaner und Dominikanerinnen in Metz: Ein Beitrag zur Entstehungsgeschichte der Konvente und zur Frauenseelsorge im 13. Jahrhundert," in *Liber amicorum necnon et amicarum für Alfred Heit. Beiträge zur mittelalterlichen Geschichte*

und geschichtlichen Landeskunde, ed. Friedhelm Burgard, Christoph Cluse and Alfred Haverkamp, Trierer Historische Forschungen 28 (Trier: THF, 1996), 171–187; Andrea Löther, "Grenzen und Möglichkeiten weiblichen Handelns im 13. Jahrhundert: Die Auseinandersetzung um die Nonnenseelsorge der Bettelorden," *Rottenburger Jahrbuch Für Kirchengeschichte* 11 (1992): 223–240; Isabel Grübel, *Bettelorden und Frauenfrömmigkeit im 13. Jahrhundert: Das Verhältnis der Mendikanten zu Nonnenklöstern und Beginen am Beispiel Straßburg und Basel*, Kulturgeschichtliche Forschungen 9 (München: Tuduv-Verlagsgesellschaft, 1987); Brigitte Degler-Spengler, "'Zahlreich wie die Sterne des Himmels': Zisterzienser, Dominikaner und Franziskaner vor dem Problem der Inkorporation von Frauenklöstern," *Rottenburger Jahrbuch Für Kirchengeschichte* 4 (1985): 37–50; John B. Freed, "Urban Development and the 'Cura Monialium' in Thirteenth-Century Germany," *Viator* 3 (1972): 311–327; Herbert Grundmann, *Religiöse Bewegungen im Mittelalter: Untersuchungen über die geschichtlichen Zusammenhänge zwischen der Ketzerei, den Bettelorden und der religiösen Frauenbewegung im 12. und 13. Jahrhundert und über die geschichtlichen Grundlagen der deutschen Mystik: Anhang, neue Beiträge zur Geschichte der religiösen Bewegungen im Mittelalter*, 4th ed. (Darmstadt: Wissenschaftliche Buchgesellschaft, 1977), esp. 199–355.

42 "Regula bullata," in *Die Opuscula des Hl. Franziskus von Assisi*, ed. Kajetan Esser, 370–371: "Cap. XI: Quod fratres non ingrediantur monasteria monacharum. Praecipio firmiter fratribus universis, ne habeant suspecta consortia vel consilia mulierum, et ne ingrediantur monasteria monacharum praeter illos, quibus a sede apostolica concessa est licentia specialis; nec fiant compatres virorum vel mulierum nec hac occasione inter fratres vel de fratribus scandalum oriatur". English translation available at https://franciscan-archive.org/bullarium/TheRegulaBullataLSz.pdf, accessed April 20, 2015.

43 Thomas of Pavia, "Codex S. Antonii de Urbe, membr. Saec. XIV," in *De origine regularum ordinis S. Clarae*, ed. Livarius Oliger, Archivum Franciscanum Historicum 5 (Florence: Ad Claras Aquas, 1912), 419: "Huc usque fistula fuit in carne, spesque curationis erat; ex nunc autem in ossibus radicata incurabilis prorsus erit."

44 See Howard R. Bloch, *Medieval Misogyny and the Invention of Western Romantic Love* (Chicago: University of Chicago Press, 2009); Paul Gerhard Schmidt, "Die misogyne Tradition von der Antike bis ins Frühmittelalter." in *Comportamenti e immaginario della sessualità nell'alto medioevo*, Settimane di studi sull'alto medioevo 53 (Spoleto: Centro Italiano di Studi sull'Alto Medioevo, 2006), 419–432.

45 Salimbene de Adam, *Cronica*, 199: "Vis diffinire aut quid sit femina scire? Est fetidum cenum, rosa fetens, dulce venenum, semper prona rei, que prohibetur ei.... Augustinus: 'Oleum enutrit flammam lucerne, et ignem luxurie accendit collocutio mulierum'. Ysidorus: 'Sicut herba viridis iuxta aquas, ita concupiscentia in mulierum consideration'. ... Agustinus: 'Mala ab initio fuit mulier, porta mortis, discipula serpentis, diaboli consiliaria, fons deceptionis'." Translation from *The Chronicle of Salimbene de Adam*, 119.

46 Salimbene de Adam, *Cronica*, 620–621.

47 *De oudste constituties van den dominicanen: Voorgeschiedenis, tekst, bronnen, ontstaan en ontwikkeling (1215–1237)*, ed. A. H. Thomas, Bibliothèque de la Revue d'histoire ecclésiastique 42 (Leuven: Bureel van de R.H.E. 1965), for example 339, 360.

48 "Libellus de principiis ord. Praedicatorum auctore Jordano de Saxonia," in *Monumenta ordinis fratrum Praedicatorum Historica* 16 (Rome: Ad S. Sabinæ, 1935), cap. 92, p. 69.

49 For medieval *exempla* in general, see Claude Bremond, Jaques LeGoff and Jean-Claude Schmitt, *L'exemplum*, Typologie des Sources du Moyen Âge 40 (Turnout: Brepols, 1982). Concerning thirteenth-century mendicant *exempla* collections, see Markus Schürer, *Das Exemplum oder die erzählte Institution. Studien zum Beispielgebrauch bei den Franziskanern und Dominikanern des 13. Jahrhunderts*, Vita Regularis. Ordnungen und Deutungen religiosen Lebens im Mittelalter 23 (Berlin: LIT, 2005); Thomas Füser, "Vom *exemplum Christi* über das *exemplum sanctorum* zum 'Jedermannsbeispiel'. Überlegungen zur Normativität exemplarischer Verhaltensmuster im institutionellen Gefüge der Bettelorden des 13. Jahrhunderts," in *Die Bettelorden im Aufbau. Beiträge zu Institutionalisierungsprozessen im mittelalterlichen Religionsentum*, ed. Gert Melville and Jörg Oberste, Vita Regularis. Ordnungen und Deutungen religiosen Lebens im Mittelalter 11 (Münster: LIT, 1999), 27–105.

50 Fratris Gerardi de Fracheto O.P., *Vitae fratrum Ordinis Praedicatorum necnon cronica ordinis ab anno 1203 usque ad 1254*, ed. Benedikt M. Reichert, Monumenta ordinis fratrum praedicatorum historica 1 (Lovaniis: Typis E. Charpentier & J. Schoonjans, 1896 – henceforth cited as *Vitae fratrum Ordinis Praedicatorum*); *Lives of the Brethren of the Order of Preachers 1206–1259*, trans. Placid Conway O.P. and ed. with notes and introduction by Bede Jarrett O.P. (London: Blackfriars Publications, 1955). On the text, cf. Schürer, *Das Exemplum oder die erzählte Institution*, esp. 179–224.

51 *Vitae fratrum Ordinis Praedicatorum*, Prologus, 5: "Nolumus tamen quod extra Ordinem tradatur sine nostra licencia speciali." ("It is not our wish, however, that this should be shown outside the Order without our special leave." Translation from *Lives of the Brethren of the Order of Preachers*, xvi).

52 *Vitae fratrum Ordinis Praedicatorum*, lib. 4, cap. 4, *De virtute continencie*, 158–160.

53 Ibid., 159–160.0

54 Caesarii Heisterbacensis monachi ordinis Cisterciensis, *Dialogus miraculorum*, ed. Joseph Strange (Köln, Berlin and Brüssel: Sumptibus J. M. Heberle (H. Lempertz & Cop.), 1851), 2: 241–242, lib. 10, cap. 34. See also the version of this *exemplum* in *Thomae Cantimpratensis... Bonum universale de apibus,* ed. G. Colvener (Colvener: Douai, 1627), lib. 2, cap. 30.45, 349–351 (henceforth cited as *Bonum universale de apibus).*

55 A new edition of the *Bonum universale de apibus* text is being prepared by Julia Burkhardt (Heidelberg). Besides the older edition mentioned in the previous note, see Thomas de Cantimpré, *Les exemples du Livre des abeilles.* Présentation, traduction et commentaire par Henri Platelle (Turnhout: Brepols, 1997); Jacques Berlioz et al. "La face cachée de Thomas de Cantimpré. Complétements à une traduction française récente du Bonum universale de apibus," *Archives d'histoire doctrinale et littéraire du Moyen Âge* 68 (2001): 73–94.

56 On the text and its content, see Schürer, *Das Exemplum oder die erzählte Institution,* esp. 123–177; Lioba Geis, "'Modus vivendi claustralium': Der Bienenstaat als Vorbild klösterlichen Zusammenlebens. Zum Bonum universale de apibus des Thomas von Cantimpré," in *Ille operum custos: Kulturgeschichtliche Beiträge zur antiken Bienensymbolik und ihrer Rezeption,* ed. David Engels and Carla Nicolaye, Spudasmata 118 (Hildesheim: Olms, 2008), 185–203. Laurence Dejonckere, *Les exempla du Bonum universale de apibus de Thomas de Cantimpré. Traduction partielle et analyse thématique et critique. Apport à l'étude de la représentation médiévale de la femme et de la sexualité* (M.A. Thesis, University of Louvain, 2006).

57 *Bonum universale de apibus*, lib. 2, capitula 29, 30 and 36.

58 The following interpretation is indebted to Christian Chandon and Daniel Dorsch, "Thomas von Cantimpré. Kritik an der Kirche?" in *Innovation in Klöstern und*

Orden des Hohen Mittelalters. Aspekte und Pragmatik eines Begriffs, ed. Mirko Breitenstein, Stefan Burkhardt and Julia Dücker, Vita Regularis. Ordnungen und Deutungen religiosen Lebens im Mittelalter 48 (Berlin: LIT, 2012), 173–196.

59 *Bonum universale de apibus*, lib. 2, cap. 36.2, 384–385.

60 Ibid.: "Antiquissimo more servatum est in ordine S. Benedicti a cunabulis fere pueros indui et sic eos ibidem per vitae innocentiam educari; quod contra tamen saepius actum audivimus, nec approbamus per Omnia, puerum rationis expertum vovere, quod nescit, sed potius adultum quemlibet, qui possit discretive reprobare quod displicet, et electione digne approbare quod placet." ("In the Order of St. Benedict, the very old custom is kept that the boys are clothed with the habit almost out of the cradle and are educated there in a life of innocence. Even if we have heard that this is not always done, we cannot approve it at all that a boy without experience vows something that he doesn't know – but rather, that an adult should knowingly reject what he doesn't like and in a true choice elect what he wants)."

61 *Bonum universale de apibus*, lib. 2, cap. 30.47, 353.

62 Cf. Karras, "Thomas Aquinas' Chastity Belt."

63 For different contexts, see the literature in n. 2. The thirteenth century is treated, for example, by Thibodeaux, "Men of the Church".

64 It might be argued that William of Saint-Amour shows rudimentary efforts of identity construction for the clergy, for example in the concluding passages of his sermon *De pharisaeo et publicano*, cited partly below, n. 81 (in *The Opuscula of William of Saint-Amour*, ed. Traver, 203–205). More importantly, a more in-depth study should take into account the various initiatives to reform the clergy and ensure celibacy after the IV. Lateran Council, cf. the literature in n. 2.

65 William of Saint-Amour, *Collectiones*, 267, and more generally, 265–275.

66 See n. 41 above.

67 See esp. William of Saint-Amour, *Collectiones*, 268: "quia tamen non constat eos ad instar Apostolorum Christi virtute ex alto esse indutos, siue in gratia confirmatos, sicut nec Saeculares Clericos, idcirco, si Beguinae illae iuniores fuerint, & formosae, periculosa est illis earum frequentia corporalis". ("As it is not proven that they – or the secular clerics – have been given special virtue from above, like the Apostles of Christ, or that they are in a confirmed state of grace, frequent meetings with beguines, especially if they are young and beautiful, are dangerous for them".)

68 Cf. the different interpretation in Miller, "Mirror of the Scholarly (Masculine) Soul," 248.

69 William of Saint-Amour, *Collectiones*, 270–271.

70 Ibid., 271: "pugnant contra tentationes, quas vincendo gloriosius coronantur".

71 Ibid., 272–273.

72 Guillaume de Lorris et Jean de Meun, *Le Roman de la Rose*, ed. Félix Lecoy, 3 vols (Paris: Champion, 1965–1970), henceforth cited as *Roman de la Rose*. On the text, see Alastair Minnis, *Magister Amoris: The Roman de La Rose and Vernacular Hermeneutics* (Oxford: Oxford University Press, 2001); Geltner, *Making of Medieval Antifraternalism*, 29–37 and the literature cited below.

73 On the audiences of the Roman de la Rose, cf. Sylvia Huot, *The Romance of the Rose and Its Medieval Readers: Interpretation, Reception, Manuscript Transmission* (Cambridge: Cambridge University Press, 1993), esp. 18–26.

74 Cf. (with further references) Tracy Adams, "Faus Semblant and the Psychology of Clerical Masculinity," *Exemplaria* 23, no. 2 (2011): 171–193; Adams, "'Make Me Chaste and Continent, but Not Yet': A Model for Clerical Masculinity?" in *Masculinities and Femininities in the Middle Ages and Renaissance*, ed. Frederick Kiefer, Arizona Studies in the Middle Ages and the Renaissance 23 (Turnhout: Brepols, 2009), 1–29.

75 See *Roman de la Rose*, ed. Lecoy, esp. lines 21673ff. (exhortation to learn), lines 21696ff. (defloration).
76 Ibid., lines 12059–12064.
77 See the passage ibid., lines 19689–19735.
78 See the passage ibid., lines. 19637–19688. For the altogether complex treatment of same-sex love and sexuality in the Roman de la Rose, cf. Ellen L. Friedrich, "When a Rose Is Not a Rose: Homoerotic Emblems in the Roman de la Rose," in *Gender Transgression: Crossing the Normative Barrier in Old French Literature*, ed. Karen J. Taylor (New York: Garland, 1998), 21–44; Simon Gaunt, "Bel Acueil and the Improper Allegory of the Romance of the Rose," *New Medieval Literatures* 2 (1998): 65–93.
79 For this opposition (though without reference to sexuality at all), see William of Saint-Amour's sermon *De pharisaeo et publicano*.
80 There is no room here to explore the eleventh- and twelfth-century backgrounds; see the detailed references in Glenn Warren Olsen, *Of Sodomites, Effeminates, Hermaphrodites, and Androgynes: Sodomy in the Age of Peter Damian* (Toronto: Pontifical Institute of Mediaeval Studies, 2011).
81 *The Opuscula of William of Saint-Amour*, ed. Traver, 204: "potest argui quod melior est peccator humilis quam iustus superbus, id est, qui se reputat iustum."
82 Miller, "Mirror of the Scholarly (Masculine) Soul," 241–243, quotation at 243.
83 See esp. Thibodeaux, "Men of the Church".
84 On the formation of an "anti-mendicant" tradition, see the critical re-evaluation presented by Geltner, *Making of Medieval Antifraternalism*.

Bibliography

1. Primary sources

1.1 Archival sources

British Library, India Office Records (BL/IOR)

- North-Western Provinces Proceedings (/P/438/62: "Draft Act 24 March 1866)
- India Acts, 1870–1871 (/V/8/42: "An Act for the Registration of Criminal Tribes and Eunuchs")

National Archives of India (NAI), New Delhi

Foreign Department (FD)

- Judicial Branch (JB)
- Political Consultations (PC)
- Political Proceedings (PP)
- Secret and Political Consultations (SPC)
- Secret Consultations (SC)
- Secret Proceedings (SP)

Home Department Records (HD)

- Judicial Branch (JB)
- Public Branch (PB)

Uttar Pradesh State Archives, Lucknow Branch (UPSA/L)

- Board of Revenue, Lucknow District files (BR/LD)
- North-Western Provinces and Oudh Financial Department Proceedings (FD/P)
- North-Western Provinces and Oudh Political Department Proceedings (PD/P)

1.2 *Manuscripts*

British Library MS Or. 166: Gulbadan Bānū Bēgum, *Aḥvāl-i Humāyūn Bāshā.*
Istanbul, Körpülü Library, MS 233: Dervīş ʿAbdullāh Efendi. *Risāle-i Teberdārīye fī aḥvāl-i āgā-yı dāru's-saʿād.* Istanbul, Köprülü Library, MS 233.
Istanbul, Süleymaniye Library, MS Hacı Beşir 682.

1.3 *Edited and translated sources*

(MGH = Monumenta Germaniae Historica, for abbreviations within the MGH cf. www.dmgh.de)
Abū ʿAlī Manṣūr al-ʿAzīzī al-Jawdharī. *Sīrat al-Ustādh Jawdhar.* Edited by Muḥammad Kāmil Ḥusayn and Muḥammad ʿAbd al-Hādī. Cairo: Dār al-Fikr al-ʿArabī, 1954.
Abū l-Faraj b. al-Jawzī. *al-Muntaẓam fī ta'rīkh al-mulūk wa-l-umam.* Edited by Muḥammad ʿAbd al-Qādir ʿAṭā and Muṣṭafā ʿAbd al-Qādir ʿAṭā. Beirut: Dār al-Kutub al-ʿIlmiyya, 1992.
Abū l-Fażl ʿAllāmī. *The Ā'īn-i Akbarī*, translated by Heinrich Blochmann 1873; repr. Calcutta: Asiatic Society of Bengal, 1993.
Abū l-Fażl. *The Akbarnama of Abu-l-Fazl*, translated by Henry Beveridge. 3 vols. 1902; repr. Delhi: South Asia Books, 1993.
Abū l-Fażl. *Akbarnāmah*, ed. ʿAbd al-Raḥīm Mawlayī. Calcutta: The Asiatic Society, 1873–1886.
Aegineta, Paulus. *Compendium medici.* Edited by Johann Ludwig Heiberg. Leipzig: B.G. Teubner, 1921.
Alberigo, Giuseppe et al., eds. *Conciliorum oecumenicorum decreta.* Bologna: Edizioni Dehoniane, 1991.
Alberigo, Giuseppe, ed. *Conciliorum oecumenicorum generalium decreta.* Turnhout: Brepols, 2006.
Ali, Meer Hassan. *Observations on the Mussulmauns of India.* London: Parbury, Allen and Co., 1832.
al-Ghazālī, Muḥammad b. Muḥammad. *Al-Wasīṭ fī-l-madhhab.* Edited by Aḥmad Maḥmūd Ibrāhīm. 7 vols. Cairo: Dār al-Salām, 1997.
al-Hamadhānī, Abd al-Jabbār b. Aḥmad. *Tathbīt dalā'il al-nubuwwa.* Edited by ʿAbd al-Karīm ʿUthmān. 2 vols. Beirut: Dār al-ʿArabiyya, 1967.
al-Jāḥiẓ, Abū ʿUthmān ʿAmr b. Baḥr. *Kitāb al-Ḥayawān.* Edited by ʿAbd al-Salām Hārūn. 8 vols. 2nd ed. Cairo: Muṣṭafā al-bābī al-ḥalabī, 1965–1969.
al-Khaṭīb al-Baghdādī. *Tārīkh Baghdād wa-dhuyūluhu.* Edited by Muṣṭafā ʿAbd al-Qādir ʿAṭā. 24 vols. Beirut: Dār al-Kutub al-ʿIlmiyya, 1997.
al-Kindī, Muḥammad b. Yūsuf. *The Governors and Judges of Egypt; or, Kitâb el ʿumarâ (el wulâh) wa Kitâb el qudâh of el Kind.* Edited by Rhuvon Guest. J. W. Gibb Memorial Series 19. Leiden: Brill and London: Luzac, 1912.
al-Marghīnānī, Burhān al-Dīn. *Al-Hidāya, Sharḥ Bidāyat al-Mubtadī.* Edited by Muḥammad Muḥammad Tāmir and Ḥāfiẓ ʿĀshūr Ḥāfiẓ. 4 Vols. Cairo: Dār al-Salām, 2000.
al-Masʿūdī, ʿAlī b. al-Ḥusayn. *al-Tanbīh wa-l-Ishrāf.* Edited by Michael Jan de Goeje. Bibliotheca geographorum Arabicorum 8 a. Leiden: Brill, 1894
al-Masʿūdī, ʿAlī b. al-Ḥusayn. *Murūj al-dhahab wa maʿādin al-jawhar.* Edited by Charles Pellat. 7 vols. Beirut: Université Libanaise, 1965–1979.
al-Māwardī, Abū al-Ḥasan. *al-Aḥkām al-Ṣulṭāniyya wa-l-wilāyāt al-dīniyya.* Kuwait City: Maktabat Dār Ibn Qutayba, 1989. Translated into English as al-Mawardī,

Al-Ahkam As-Sultaniyyah. Laws of Islamic Governance by Asadullah Yate. London: Ta-Ha Publishers, 1996.

al-Muqaddasī, Abū ʿAbd Allāh Muḥammad. *Aḥsan al-Taqāsīm fī maʿrifat al-aqālīm*. Leiden: Brill, 1906. Translated by Basil Collins as *The Best Divisions for Knowledge of the Regions*. Reading: Garnet, 2001.

al-Qalqashandī, Aḥmad ibn ʿAlī ibn Aḥmad. *Ṣubḥ al-aʿshā fī ṣināʿat al-inshāʾ*. 14 vols. Cairo: Dār al-Kutub al-Miṣriyya, 1922.

al-Qurṭubī, ʿArīb b. Saʿd. *Ṣilat taʾrīkh al-Ṭabarī*. Edited by Michael Jan De Goeje. Leiden: Brill, 1897.

al-Ṣābiʾ, Hilāl. *Rusūm dār al-Khilāfa*. Edited by Mīkhāʾīl ʿAwwād. Baghdad: Maṭbaʿat al-ʿĀnī, 1964. Translated by Elie Adib Salem as *Rusūm dār al-Khilāfa: The Rules and Regulations of the Abbasid Court*. Beirut: American University of Beirut, 1977.

al-Ṣūlī, Abū Bakr. *Akhbār al-Rāḍī bi-llāh wa l-Muttaqī li-llāh*. Edited by J. Heyworth Dunne. Cairo: Maṭbaʿat al-Ṣāwī, 1935.

al-Ṣūlī, Abū Bakr. *Ma lam yunshar min awrāq al-Ṣūlī: akhbār al-sanawāt 295–315 H*. Edited by Hilāl Nājī. Beirut: ʿĀlam al-Kutub, 2000.

al-Subkī, Tāj al-Dīn ʿAbd al-Wahhāb Ibn ʿAlī. *Muʿīd al-niʿam wa mubīd al-niqam*. Edited by David W. Myhrman. London: Luzac, 1908; repr. New York: AMS Press, 1978.

al-Ṭabarī, Muḥammad b. Jarīr. *Taʾrīkh al-rusul wa-l-mulūk*. Edited by Michael Jan De Goeje et al. 15 Vols. Leiden: Brill, 1879–1901.

al-Tanūkhī. *Kitāb al-faraj baʿda al-shidda*. Edited by ʿAbbūd al-Shāljī. 5 vols. Beirut: Dār Ṣādir, 1978.

al-Yamānī, Muḥammad b. Muḥammad. "Sīrat Jaʿfar al-ḥājib." Edited by Vladimir Ivanow, *Bullettin of the Faculty of Arts of the University of Egypt* 4 (1936): 89–133.

Ambrose of Milan. *De viduis*. Patrologia Latina 16. Paris: J.-P. Migne, 1845.

Ambrose of Milan. *Verginità e vedovanza*. Edited by Franco Gori. Milan: Biblioteca Ambrosiana, 1989.

Ammianus Marcellinus. *Res gestae*. Edited by Wolfgang Seyfarth. Leipzig: Teubner, 1978.

Anonymus. "Vita venerabilis Halinardi." In *Opera omnia*, 1337–1348. Patrologia Latina 142. Paris: J.-P. Migne, 1880.

Anselm of Havelberg. *Vita Adelberti Maguntini Archiepiscopi*, in *Monumenta Moguntina*. Edited by Philipp Jaffé. Bibliotheca Rerum Germanicarum 3. Berlin: Weidmann, 1866.

Arn of Würzburg. *The Annals of Fulda*. Translated and edited by Timothy Reuter. Manchester: Manchester University Press, 1992.

Arnold, Thomas, ed. *Symeonis Monachi Opera Omnia*. 2 vols. Cambridge: Cambridge University Press, 1882–1885.

Augustine of Hippo. *De civitate Dei*. Edited by Bernhard Dombart and Alfons Kalb. Corpus Christianorum Series Latina 47. Turnhout: Brepols, 1955.

Augustine of Hippo. *De haeresibus*. Edited by Michael Petrus Josephus van den Hout et al. Corpus Christianorum Series Latina 46. Turnhout: Brepols, 1969.

Badāʾūnī, Abd al-Qādir. *Muntakhab al-Tavārīkh*. Translated and edited by George S. A. Ranking, W. H. Lowe and Sir Wolseley Haig. 1884–1925. 3 vols; repr. Delhi: Renaissance Publishing House, 1986.

Bai Juyi and Zhu Jincheng, eds. Bai Juyi *ji jianjiao*. Shanghai: Shanghai Guji, 1988.

Ban Gu. *Hanshu*. 12 vols. Beijing: Zhonghua Shuju, 1975.

Basil of Caesarea. *De virginitate*. Patrologia Graeca 30. Paris: J.-P. Migne, 1857.

Basil of Caesarea. *Epistula*. Patrologia Graeca 32. Paris: J.-P. Migne, 1857.

Basil of Caesarea. *Letters and Select Works*. Translated and edited by Philip Schaff and Henry Wace. Nicene and Post-Nicene Fathers, 2nd. ser., vol. 8. Edinburgh: T. and T. Clark, 1885.

Bede. *Ecclesiastical History of the English People*. Translated and edited by Bertram Colgrave and R. A. M. Mynors. Oxford: Clarendon Press, 1969.

Bernard of Clairvaux. "Sermon 65." In *Heresies of the High Middle Ages*, edited by Walter L. Wakefield and Austin P. Evans., 135. New York: Columbia University Press, 1991.

Bethmann, Ludwig Konrad, ed. *Chronica et gesta aevi Salici*. MGH SS 7. Hanover: Hahn, 1846.

Beyerle, Franz, and Rudolph Buchner, eds. *Lex ribuaria*, MGH Leges 1, Leges nationum Germanicarum. Hanover and Leipzig: Hahn, 1954.

Bhakkari, Farid. *Nobility under the Great Mughals: Based on Dhakhīratul khawanīn of Shaikh Farīd Bhakkari*. Translated by Z. A. Desai. 2 vols. New Delhi: Sundeep Prakashan, 2003.

Bolland, Jean and Societas Bollandiensi, eds. *Acta Sanctorum*. Antwerp and Bruxelles: Société des Bollandistes, 1643–1940.

Boniface. *Epistolae. Die Briefe des heiligen Bonifatius und Lullus*. Edited by Michael Tangl. MGH Epp. sel. 1. Berlin: Weidmann, 1916.

Boretius, Alfred, and Victor Krause, eds. *Capitularia regum Francorum*. 2 vols. MGH Capit. Hanover: Hahn, 1883–97.

Botte, Bernard, ed. *Traditio apostolica*. Sources chrétiennes 11. Paris: du Cerf, 1968.

Brommer, Peter et al., eds. *Capitula episcoporum*. 4 vols. MGH Capit. episc. Hanover: Hahn, 1984–2005.

Brown, Philippa, ed. *Domesday Book 33, Norfolk*. 2 vols. Chichester: Phillimore, 1984.

Bruce, James. *Travels to Discover the Source of the Nile in the Years 1768, 1769, 1770, 1771, 1772, and 1773*. Dublin: William Sleater, 1790–1791.

Burton, Richard Francis. *First Footsteps in East Africa, or, An Exploration of Harār*. London: Tylston and Edwards, 1894.

Burton, Richard Francis. *Personal Narrative of a Pilgrimage to al-Madinah and Meccah*. London: Tylston and Edwards, 1893; repr. New York: Dover Publications, 1964.

Byrhtferth of Ramsey. *The Lives of St Oswald and St Ecgwine*. Translated and edited by Michael Lapidge. Oxford: Oxford University Press, 2009.

Caesarius of Heisterbach. *Caesarii Heisterbacensis monachi ordinis Cisterciensis Dialogus miraculorum*. Edited by Joseph Strange. 2 vols. Cologne, Bonn and Brussels: H. Lempertz and Co, 1851.

Caesarius of Heisterbach. *The Dialogue on Miracles*. Translated and edited by H. von E. Scott and C. C. Swinton Bland. 2 vols. London: Routledge, 1929.

Caesarius of Heisterbach. *Dialogus Miraculorum*. Translated and edited by Nikolaus Nösges and Horst Schneider. 5 vols. Turnhout: Brepols, 2009.

Caesarius of Heisterbach. *Vita et Miracula Engelberti*. Edited by Fritz Zschaeck, in *Die Wundergeschichten des Caesarius von Heisterbach*, edited by Alfons Hilka. Bonn: Hanstein,1937.

Caesarius of Heisterbach. "Dominica secunda post pascha." In *Homiliae Festivae*, edited by Joannes A. Coppenstein. Cologne: P. Henningius, 1615.

Campbell, Lawrence D. and E. Samuel. *Asiatic Annual Register, or View of the History of Hindustan, and of the Politics, Commerce and Literature of Asia, For the Year 1799*. London: J. Debrett, 1801.

Cassian, John. *Collationes*. Edited by Étienne Pichery. Sources chrétiennes 54. Paris: du Cerf, 1958.

Changsun Wuji et al. *Tanglü shuyi jianjie*. 2 vols. Beijing: Zhonghua Shuju, 1996.

Cheng Shude. *Jiu chao lü kao*. Beijing: Zhonghua Shuju, 1963.

Clement of Alexandria. *Stromata I-IV*. Edited by Ursula Treu. Berlin: Akademie Verlag, 1985.

Cocceianus, Cassius Dio. *Dio's Roman History, with an English Translation by Earnest Cary, on the Basis of the Version of Herbert Baldwin Foster*. London: Heinemann; New York: Putnams, 1916.

Colgrave, Bertram, ed. and trans. *Felix's Life of Saint Guthlac*. Cambridge: Cambridge University Press, 1956.

Constantine VII Porphygenitus. *Le livre des cérémonies*. Edited by Albert Vogt. Paris: Les Belles Lettres, 1935–1940.

Damiani, Petrus. *Letters 61–90*. Translated by Owen J. Blum. Washington: The Catholic University of America Press, 1992.

Darlington, Reginald R. and Patrick McGurk, ed. and trans. *The Chronicle of John of Worcester*. 2 vols. Oxford: Clarendon Press, 1995.

Davis, Raymond, trans. *The Lives of the Ninth-Century Popes (Liber pontificalis): The Ancient Biographies of Ten Popes from A.D. 817–891*. Liverpool: Liverpool University Press, 1995.

de Lorris, Guillaume and Jean de Meun. *Le Roman de la Rose*. Edited by Félix Lecoy. 3 vols. Paris: Champion, 1965–1970.

Diekamp, Wilhelm, ed. *Vita Sancti Liudgeri auctore Altfrido*. Münster: Theissing, 1881.

Dihkhudā, Alī Akbar. *Lughatnāmah-i Dihkhudā*. 16 vols. Teheran: Mu'assasa-i Intishārāt Chap-i Dānishgāh-i Tehrān, 1993.

Duchesne, Louis, ed. *Le Liber Pontificalis: Texte, introduction et commentaire*. 2 vols. Paris: Thorin, 1886–1892.

Dufournet, Jean, ed. *Rutebeuf et les frères mendiants: Poèmes satiriques*. Paris: H. Champion, 1991.

Du Mu. *Fanchuan wenji*. Shanghai: Shanghai Guji, 1978.

Du You et al. *Tongdian*. 5 vols. Beijing: Zhonghua Shuju, 1988.

East India Company. *A Collection of Facts and Documents Relative to Batta*. Calcutta: S. Smith & Co., 1829.

Eckhardt Karl August, ed. *Pactus leges salicae*, MGH Leges nationum Germanicarum 4.1. Hanover and Leipzig: Hahn, 1961.

Elliott, Charles Alfred. *The Chronicles of Oonao, a District in Oudh*. Allahabad: Allahabad Mission Press, 1862.

Epiphanius of Salamis. *Adversus octaginta haereses*. Patrologia Graeca 41. Paris: J.-P. Migne, 1863.

Esser, Kajetan, ed. *Die Opuscula des Hl. Franziskus von Assisi*. Grottaferrata: Editiones Collegii S. Bonaventurae ad Claras Aquas, 1989.

Eusebius of Caesarea. *Historia ecclesiastica*. Patrologia Graeca 21. Paris: J.-P. Migne, 1857.

Eusebius of Caesarea. *Ecclesiastical History*. Translated by Kirsopp Lake. Loeb Classical Library 153. Cambridge, MA: Harvard University Press, 1926.

Fan Ye. *Hou Hanshu*. 12 vols. Beijing: Zhonghua Shuju, 1973.

Fang Xuanling. *Jinshu*. 10 vols. Beijing: Zhonghua Shuju, 1974.

Firmicus Maternus. *De errore profanarum religionum*. Patrologia Latina 12. Paris: J.-P. Migne, 1845.

Flodoard of Rheims. *Historia Remensis ecclesiae*. Edited by Martina Stratmann. MGH Scriptores 36. Hanover: Hahn, 1998.

Gerard de Frachet. *Vitae fratrum Ordinis Praedicatorum necnon cronica ordinis ab anno 1203 usque ad 1254*. Edited by Benedikt M. Reichert. Monumenta ordinis fratrum praedicatorum historica 1. Leuven: Typis E. Charpentier & J. Schoonjans, 1896.

Gerard de Frachet. *Lives of the Brethren of the Order of Preachers 1206–1259*. Translated by Placid Conway O.P., edited by Bede Jarrett O.P. London: Blackfriars Publications, 1955.

Frendo, Joseph D, trans. *Agathias, The Histories*. Berlin and New York: de Gruyter, 1975.

Gelasius. "Letter to emperor Anastasius in 494," in *Epistolae Romanorum pontificum genuinae et quae ad eos scriptae sunt a S. Hilaro usque ad Pelagium II*, Edited by Andreas Thiel, 350–51. Braunsberg, 1867.

Gerhard von Augsburg. *Vita Sancti Uodalrici: Die älteste Lebensbeschreibung des heiligen Ulrich*, Translated and edited by Walter Berschin and Angelika Häse. Heidelberg: Winter, 1993.

Gold, Milton, trans. *The Tārīkh-e Sīstān*. Rome: Istituto Italiano per il Medio ed Estremo Oriente, 1976.

Gregory of Nanzianz. *Discours 32–37*. Edited by Claudio Moreschini, translated into French by Paul Gallay. Paris: Les Éditions du cerf, 1985.

Gregory of Tours. *Historia Francorum*. Patrologia Latina 71. Paris: J.-P. Migne, 1849.

Gregory the Great. *Dialogi*. Patrologia Latina 77. Paris: J.-P. Migne, 1862.

Gulbadan Bānū Begum. *The History of Humāyūn: Humāyūn-Nāma*. Translated by Annette Susannah Beveridge. 1902; repr. Delhi, 1994.

Gundlach, Wilhelm. *Codex Carolinus* in *Epistolae Merowingici et Karolini aevi*. MGH Epp. 3. Berlin: Weidmann, 1892.

Hall, John B. *Claudii Claudiani carmina*. Leipzig: B. G. Teubner, 1985.

Hamilton, Walter. *The East-India Gazetteer*. 2 vols. London: W.M.H. Allen and Co., 1828.

Hartmann, Wilfried. *Die Konzilien der karolingischen Teilreiche 843–859*. MGH Conc. 3. Hanover: Hahn, 1984.

Heber, Reginald. *Narrative of a Journey Through the Upper Provinces of India, From Calcutta to Bombay, 1824–1825*. 3 vols. Philadelphia: Carey, Lea and Carey, 1828.

Hieroymus. *Epistulae*. Edited by Joseph Jabourt. 8 vols. Paris: Belles Lettres, 1949–1963.

Hincmar of Reims. *Hincmari Rhemensis Archiepiscopi opera omnia*. Patrologia Latina 126. Paris: J.-P. Migne, 1852.

Hincmar of Reims. *Annales Bertiniani*. Edited by G. Waitz. MGH SS rer. Germ. 5. Hanover: Hahn, 1883.

Hincmar of Reims. *Epistolae*. Edited by Ernst Perels. MGH Epp. 8. Berlin: Weidmann, 1939.

Hincmar of Reims. *De ordine palatii*. Edited by Thomas Gross and Rudolf Schieffer. MGH Font. iur. Germ. 3. Hanover: Hahn, 1980.

Hincmar of Reims. *De cavendis vitiis et virtutibus exercendis*. Edited by Doris Nachtmann. MGH QQ zur Geistesgeschichte 16. Munich: MGH, 1998.

Hincmar of Reims. *Opusculum in LV capitulis*, in *Die Streitschriften Hinkmars von Reims und Hinkmars von Laon 869–871*. Edited by Rudolf Schieffer. MGH Conc. 4, Supplement 2. Hanover: Hahn, 2003.

Holder-Egger, Oswald, ed. *Liber pontificalis ecclesiae Ravannentis*. MGH Scriptores rer. Lang. saec. VI–IX. Hanover: Hahn, 1878.

Holtzmann, Robert, ed. *Die Chronik des Bischofs Thietmar von Merseburg*. MGH SS rer. Germ. N.S. 9. Berlin: Weidmann, 1935.

Ibn ʿAbd Rabbih. *Al-ʿIqd al-farīd*. Edited by Aḥmad Amīn et al. 4 vols. Cairo: Maṭbaʿat Lajnat al-Taʾlīf wa-l-Tarjama wa-l-Nashr, 1940–1949.

Ibn Qutayba. *ʿUyūn al-akhbār*. Edited by Yūsuf ʿAlī Ṭawīl and Mufīd Muḥammad Qumayḥa. 4 vols. Beirut: Dār al-Kutub al-ʿIlmiyya, 1985.

Ibn Saʿd, Muḥammad. *Kitāb al-Ṭabaqāt al-Kabīr*. Cairo: Maktabat al-Khānjī, 2001.

Jenkins, Romilly J. H. and L. G. Westerink, ed. and trans. *Nicholas I Patriarch of Constantinople, Letters*. Washington DC: Dumbarton Oaks, 1973.

Jerome. *Epistula*. Edited by Jérôme Labourt. Paris: Belles Lettres, 1949–1963.

Jerome. *Tractatus sive homiliae in psalmos. In Marci evangelium. Alia varia argumenta*. Edited by G. Morin, B. Capelle and J. Fraipont. Corpus Christianorum Series Latina 78. Turnhout: Brepols, 1958.

John Cassian. *Conlationes*. Patrologia Latina 49. Paris: J.-P. Migne, 1846.

Justin Martyr. *Apologia prima pro Christianis*. Patrologia Graeca 6. Paris: J.-P. Migne, 1857.

Keydell, Rudolf, ed. *Agathiae Myrinaei*. Historiarum Libri Quinque. Berlin: de Gruyter, 1967.

Krusch, Bruno, and Wilhelm Levison. *Passiones vitaeque sanctorum aevi Merovingici*. 5 vols. MGH SS rer. Merov 3. Hanover: Hahn, 1896–1920.

Kurze, Friedrich. *Annales Fuldenses*. MGH SS rer. Germ. 7. Hanover: Hahn, 1891.

Kurze, Friedrich, ed. *Reginonis abbatis Prumiensis chronicon cum continuatione Treverensi*. MGH SS rer. Germ 50. Hanover: Hahn, 1890.

Lactantius. *Divinae institutiones*. Patrologia Latina 6. Paris: J.-P. Migne, 1844.

Lang Ying. *Qi xiu lei gao*. 2 vols. Beijing: Zhonghua Shuju, 1959.

Laurence of Liège. *Gesta episcoporum virdunensium*, in *Annales et chronica aevi Salici. Vitae aevi Carolini et Saxonici*, edited by Georg Waitz. MGH SS 10. Hanover: Hahn, 1852.

Leo the Deacon. *History*. Edited by C. B. Hase. Bonn, 1828.

Li Linfu and Chen Zhongfu, ed. *Tang liu dian*.1992. 3rd repr. Beijing: Zhonghua Shuju, 2008.

MacLean, Simon, trans. *History and Politics in Late Carolingian and Ottonian Europe: The Chronicle of Regino of Prüm and Adalbert of Magdeburg*. Manchester: Manchester University Press, 2009.

Liu Xu, et al. *Jiu Tangshu*. 16 vols. Bejing: Zhonghua Shuju, 1975.

Magie, David, ed. and trans. *Historia Augusta*. Loeb Classical Library 140. Cambridge, MA: Harvard University Press, 1924.

Mathisen, Ralph W., ed. and trans. *Ruricius of Limoges and Friends: a Collection of Letters from Visigothic Gaul*. Liverpool: Liverpool University Press, 1999.

Matthew Paris, and Roger (of Wendover). *Chronica Majora*. Edited by Henry R. Luard. Rerum Britannicarum medii aevi scriptores. London: Longman, 1872.

Meḥmed Pāşā, Defterdār Ṣarı. *Zübde-i Veḳāyiʿāt: Taḥlīl ve Metin, 1066–1116/1656–1704*. Edited by Abdülkadir Özcan. Ankara: Türk Tarih Kurumu, 1995.

Mīrzā Ḥaidar Dūghlāt. *Taʾrīkh-i Rashīdī*. Translated by E. Denison Ross. Patna: Academica Asiatica, 1973.

Miskawayh, Abū ʻAlī Ahmad. *Tajārib al-umam*, 7 vls. Vol. 1–3 edited by Henry Frederick Amedroz. Miṣr 1914–1919 (repr. Baghdad in the 1960s). Vol. 4–7: *The Eclipse of the Abbasid Caliphate*. Edited and translated by David Samuel Margoliouth. London: Blackwell, 1920–1921.

Moffatt, Ann and Maxeme Tall. *Constantine Porphyrogennetos, The Book of Ceremonies*. Canberra: Australian Association of Byzantine Studies, 2012.

Mommsen, Theodor and Paulus Meyer, eds. *Codex Theodosianus*. Berlin: Weidmann, 1905.

Mommsen, Theodor and Paul Krueger, eds. *Digesta Iustiniani Augusti*. Berlin: Weidmann, 1870.

Monumenta ordinis fratrum Praedicatorum Historica 16. Rome: Ad S. Sabinæ, 1935.

Muḥammad Fā'iz Bakhsh. *Memoirs of Delhi and Faizâbâd, Being a Translation of the Ta'rīkh-i Faraḥbakhsh of Muhammad Faiz-Bakhsh*. Edited and translated by William Hoey. 2 vols. Allahabad: Government Press, 1888–1889.

Mühlbacher, Engelbert, ed. *Die Urkunden der Karolinger 1: Urkunden Pippins, Karlmanns and Karl des Grossen*. MGH DD Kar. 1. Hanover: Hahn, 1906.

Muʻtamad Khān. *Iqbālnāmah-yi Jahāngīri*. Ghāzīpur: n. p., 1863.

Nāʻīmā, Muṣṭafā. *Tārīh-i Nāʻīmā (Ravżatü'l-Ḥüseyn fī hulāṣati ahbāri'l-ḫāfiḳayn)*. Edited by Mehmet İpşirli. Ankara: Türk Tarih Kurumu, 2007.

Niida Noboru, ed. *Tōrei shūi*. 1933. Repr. Changchun: Changchun Chubanshe, 1989.

Notker Balbulus. *Gesta Karoli Magni imperatoris*. Edited by Hans F. Haefele. MGH SS rer. Ger. N.S. 12. Berlin: Widemann, 1959.

Ouyang Xiu and Song Qi. *Xin Tangshu*. 20 vols. Beijing: Zhonghua Shuju, 1975.

Palladius. *Historia Lausiaca*. Patrologia Graeca 34. Paris: J.-P. Migne, 1860.

Paul the Deacon. *Gesta episcoporum mettensium*. Edited by George Henry Pertz. MGH Scriptores 2. Hanover: Hahn, 1829.

Paulinus of Nola. *Epistula*. Edited by Wilhelm Hartel. Corpus scriptorum ecclesiasticorum latinorum 29. Vienna: Academia litterarum caesareae, 1894.

Pertz, Georg, ed. *Annales et chronica aevi Salici*. MGH SS 5. Hanover: Hahn, 1844.

Powell, Baden Henry. *The Land Systems of British India*. 1892; repr. New Delhi: Low Price Publications, 1990.

Procopius. *The Anecdota or Secret History*. Translated by Henry Bronson Dewing. Loeb Classical Library 290. Cambridge, MA: Harvard University Press, 1935.

Procopius. *History of the Wars*. Translated by Henry Bronson Dewing. Loeb Classical Library 107. 1916; repr. Cambridge, MA: Harvard University Press, 1993.

Prudentius, *Peristephanon*. Edited and translated by Henry John Thomson. Loeb Classical Library 398. Cambridge, MA: Harvard University Press, 1953.

Psellos, Michel. *Chronographie ou Histoire d'un siècle de Byzance (976–1077)*. Edited and translated by Émile Renauld. 2 vols. Paris: Les Belles Lettres, 1926.

Rather of Verona. *Praeloquia*. Edited by Peter L. D. Reid. Corpus Christianorum: Continuatio mediaevalis 46 A. Turnhout: Brepols, 1984.

Reeves, P. D., ed. *Sleeman in Oudh: An Abridgement of W. H. Sleeman's A Journey Through the Kingdom of Oude in 1849–50*. Cambridge: Cambridge University Press, 1971.

Regino of Prüm. *Chronicon*. Edited by Friederich Kurze. MGH SS Rer. Germ. 50. Hanover: Hahn, 1890.

Rogers, Alexander, trans. and Beveridge, Henry, ed. *Tūzuk-i-Jahāngīrī, or, Memoirs of Jahāngīr*. 2 vols. New Delhi: Atlantic Publishers and Distributors, 1989.

Rutebeuf. *Œuvres complètes de Rutebeuf*. Edited by Michel Zink. 2 vols, Classiques Garnier. Paris: Garnier, 1989–1990.

Rutebeuf. *Œuvres complètes de Rutebeuf*. Edited by Edmond Faral and Julia Bastin. 2 vols. Paris: Éditions A. et J. Picard, 1959–1960.

Richards, D. S., ed. and trans. *The Annals of the Saljuq Turks: Selections from al-Kāmil fī'l-Ta'rīkh of 'Izz al-Dīn ibn al-Athīr*. London: Routledge, 2002.

Rossetti, Gabriella. "Il matrimonio del clero nella società altomedievale." In *Il Matrimonio nella società altomedievale, 22–28 Apr 1976*. Settimane di studi sull'alto medioevo 24. 2 vols. Spoleto, Centro Italiano di Studi sull'Alto Medioevo, 1977, 1:533–537.

Salimbene de Adam. *The Chronicle of Salimbene de Adam*. Translated by Joseph L. Baird, Guiseppe Baglivi and John Robert Kane. Medieval & Renaissance Texts & Studies 40. Binghampton, New York: Medieval & Renaissance Text & Studies, 1986.

Salimbene de Adam. *Cronica*. Edited by Giuseppe Scalia. Corpus Christianorum Continuatio Medievalis 125. Turnhout: Brepols, 1994.

Schieffer, Rudolf, ed. *Die Streitschriften Hinkmars von Reims und Hinkmars von Laon 869–871*. MGH Concilia 4, Suppl. 2. Hanover: Hahn, 2003.

Schmeidler, Bernhard, ed. *Magistri Adam Bremensis Gesta Hammaburgensis Ecclesiae Pontificum*. MGH SS Rer. Germ. 2. 3rd ed. Hanover and Leipzig: Hahn, 1917.

Sharar, Abdul Halim. *Lucknow: The Last Phase of an Oriental Culture*. Edited and translated by E. S. Harcourt and Fakhir Hussain. New Delhi: Oxford University Press, 2001.

Seeck, Otto, ed. *Notitia dignitatum, accedunt Notitia urbis Constantinopolitanae et latercula provinciarum*. Berlin: Weidmann, 1876.

Sewter, Edgar Robert Ashton, trans. *Michael Psellus, Fourteen Byzantine Rulers*. Harmondsworth: Penguin, 1966.

Shīrāzī, Kāmī. *Fatḥnāmah-i Nūr Jahān Bēgum*. N p., 1626.

Siddiqui, W. H., ed. and trans. *Waqa-i-uz-Zaman: (Fath Nama-i-Nur Jahan Begam); A Contemporary Account of Jahangir*. Rampur: Ramur Raza Library, 2003.

Sidonius Apollinaris, *Letters*. Edited and translated by William B. Anderson. Loeb Classical Library 420. Cambridge, MA: Harvard University Press, 1965.

Sigebert of Gembloux. *Vita Deoderici episcopi Mettensis*, in *Annales, chronica et historiae aevi Carolini et Saxonici*. Edited by Georg Heinrich Pertz. MGH SS 4. Hanover: Hahn, 1841.

Skylitzes, John. *Ioannis Scylitzae Synopsis Historiarum*. Edited by Ioannes Thurn. Berlin and New York: de Gruyter, 1973.

Sleeman, William Henry. *A Journey Through the Kingdom of Oude, in 1849–1850*. London: Richard Bentley, 1858.

Socrates. *Historia ecclesiastica*. Patrologia Graeca 67. Paris: J.-P. Migne, 1864. Edited and translated by Philip Schaff and Henry Wace as *Socrates, Sozomenus: Church Histories*. Nicene and Post-Nicene Fathers, 2nd. ser., vol. 2. Edinburgh: T. and T. Clark, 1885.

Sot, Michel, Monique Goullet, and Guy Lobrich, eds. *Gesta pontificum Autissiodorensium. Les gestes des évêques d'Auxerre*. 3 vols. Paris: Belles lettres, 2002–2009.

Sozomenus. *Historia ecclesiastica*. Patrologia Graeca 67. Paris: J.-P. Migne, 1864. Edited and translated by Philip Schaff and Henry Wace as *Socrates, Sozomenus: Church Histories*. Nicene and Post-Nicene Fathers, 2nd. ser., vol. 2. Edinburgh: T. and T. Clark, 1885.

Synaxarion of Constantinople. Propylaeum ad Acta sanctorum Novembris. Edited by Hippolyte Delehaye. Brussels: Apud Socios Bollandianos, 1902.
Tenckhoff, Franz, ed. *Vita Meinwerci episcopi Patherbrunnensis*. MGH SS rer. Germ. 59. Hanover: Hahn, 1921.
Tertullian. *Opera I*. Edited by Dom E. Dekkers et al. Corpus Christianorum Series Latina 1. Turnhout: Brepols, 1954.
Thackston, Wheeler M., trans. *The Jahangirnama: Memoirs of Jahangir, Emperor of India by Jahangir*. New York, Oxford University Press, 1999.
Thomas Aquinas. *Opera Omnia*. Edited by H.-F. Dondaine. Editio Leonina 41 A. Rome: Apud S. Sabinae, 1970.
Thomas de Cantimpré. *Les exemples du Livre des abeilles. Présentation, traduction et commentaire par Henri Platelle*. Turnhout: Brepols, 1997.
Thomas de Cantimpré. *Bonum universale de apibus*. Edited by G. Colvener. Colvener: Douai, 1627.
Thomas de Celano, *Vita Secunda S. Francisci*. In *Analecta Franciscana* 10. Florence: Ad Claras Aquas 1941.
Thomas of Celano. *The Lives of S. Francis of Assisi by Brother Thomas of Celano*. Translated by Alan G. Ferrers Howell. London: Methuen & Co., 1908.
Thomas of Pavia. "Codex S. Antonii de Urbe, membr. Saec. XIV." In *De origine regularum ordinis S. Clarae*, edited by Livarius Oliger. Archivum Franciscanum Historicum 5. Florence: Ad Claras Aquas, 1912.
Valentia, George Viscount. *Voyages and Travels to India, Ceylon, the Red Sea, Abyssinia, and Egypt, in the Years 1802, 1803, 1804, 1805, and 1806*. 3 vols. London: F. C. and J. Rivington, 1811.
Vives, José, ed. *Concilios visigóticos e hispano-romanos*. Madrid: Consejo superior de investigaciones científicas, 1963.
Waitz, Georg, ed. *Chronica et gesta aevi Salici*. MGH SS 8. Hanover: Hahn, 1848.
Waitz, Georg. ed. *Gesta episcoporum Virdunensium, Annales, chronica et historiae aevi Carolini et Saxonici*. MGH SS 4. Hanover: Hahn, 1841.
Wang Pu. *Tang huiyao*. 2 vols. Shanghai: Shanghai Guji, 2006.
Warner, David A., transl. and ed. *Ottonian Germany: The Chronicon of Thietmar of Merseburg*. Manchester: Manchester University Press, 2001.
Wei Shou. *Weishu*. 8 vols. Beijing: Zhonghua Shuju, 1974.
Weidemann, Margaret. *Geschichte des Bistums Le Mans von der Spätantike bis zur Karolingerzeit: Actus Pontificum Cenomannis in urbe degentium und Gesta Aldrici*. 3 vols. Römisch-Germanisches Zentralmuseum Monographien 56. Mainz and Bonn: Römisch-Germanisches Zentralmuseum, 2002.
Weinrich, Lorenz, ed. *Quellen zur deutschen Verfassungs-, Wirtschafts- und Sozialgeschichte bis 1250*. Darmstadt: Wissenschaftliche Buchgesellschaft, 1977.
Werminghoff, Albert, ed. *Concilia aevi Karolini*. 2 vols. MGH Conc. 2, 1. Hanover: Hahn, 1906–08.
Whitelock, Dorothy, ed. and trans. *Anglo-Saxon Wills*. Cambridge: Cambridge University Press, 1930.
William of Saint-Amour. *De periculis novissimorum temporum*. Edited and translated by Guy Geltner. Dallas Medieval Texts and Translations 8. Paris, Leuven, Dudley, MA: Peeters, 2008.
William of Saint-Amour. *Opera Omnia*. Konstanz: Apud Alitophilos, 1632.

Winterbottom, Michael, and Michael Lapidge, ed. and trans. *The Early Lives of St Dunstan*. Oxford: Oxford University Press, 2012.
Wulfstan of Winchester. *The Life of St Æthelwold*. Edited by Michael Lapidge and Michael Winterbottom. Oxford: Oxford University Press, 1991.
Yang Bojun. *Chunqiu Zuozhuan zhu*. 4 vols. Beijing: Zhonghua Shuju, 1983.
Zeumer, Karl, ed. *Formulae Merowingici et Karolini aevi*. MGH Formulae. Hanover: Hahn, 1886.
Zhao Yi. *Nian'er shi zhaji*. 2 vols. Beijing: Zhonghua Shuju, 1984.

2 Secondary sources

Abulafia, David. *Frederick II: A Medieval Emperor*. New York and Oxford: Oxford University Press, 1988.
Abusch, Ra'anan. "Eunuchs and Gender Transformation: Philo's Exegesis of the Joseph Narrative." In *Eunuchs in Antiquity and Beyond*, edited by Shaun Tougher, 103–121. London: Classical Press of Wales and Duckworth, 2002.
Acht, Peter. "Adalbert I., Erzbischof von Mainz." In *Neue Deutsche Biographie*, 1:44. 26 vols. Berlin: Duncker & Humblot, 1953–2016.
Adams, Tracy. "'Make Me Chaste and Continent, but Not Yet': A Model for Clerical Masculinity?" In *Masculinities and Femininities in the Middle Ages and Renaissance*, edited by Frederick Kiefer, 1–29. Arizona Studies in the Middle Ages and the Renaissance 23. Turnhout: Brepols, 2009.
Algazi, Gadi. "Habitus, familia and forma vitae: Die Lebensweisen mittelalterlicher Gelehrter in muslimischen, jüdischen und christlichen Gemeinden – vergleichend betrachtet." In *Beiträge zur Kulturgeschichte der Gelehrten im späten Mittelalter*, edited by Frank Rexroth, 185–217. Ostfildern: Thorbecke, 2010.
Ambos, Claus. "Eunuchen als Thronprätendenten und Herrscher im alten Orient." In *Of God(s), Trees, Kings, and Scholars: Neo-Assyrian and Related Studies in Honour of Simo Parpola*, edited by Mikko Luukko, Saana Svärd and Raija Mattila, 1–7. Helsinki: The Finnish Oriental Society, 2009.
Anderson, Mary M. *Hidden Power: The Palace Eunuchs of Imperial China*. Buffalo, NY: Prometheus Books, 1990.
Angenendt, Arnold. "'Mit reinen Händen'. Das Motiv der kultischen Reinheit in der abendländischen Askese." In *Liturgie im Mittelalter. Ausgewählte Aufsatze zum 70. Geburtstag*, edited by Thomas Flammer and Daniel Meyer, 245–267. 2nd ed. Ästhetik – Theologie – Liturgik 35. Münster: LIT, 2005.
Anson, John. "The Female Transvestite in Early Monasticism: The Origin and Development of a Motif." *Viator* 5 (1974): 1–32.
Arnold, Benjamin. *Count and Bishop in Medieval Germany: A Study in Regional Power 1100–1350*. Philadelphia: University of Pennsylvania Press, 1991.
Arnold, Benjamin. *Princes and Territories in Medieval Germany*. Cambridge: Cambridge University Press, 1991.
Arnold, Benjamin. "Episcopal Authority Authenticated and Fabricated: Form and Function in Medieval German Bishops' Catalogues." In *Warriors and Churchmen in the High Middle Ages: Essays Presented to Karl Leyser*, edited by Timothy Reuter, 63–78. London and Rio-Grande: Hambledon Press, 1992.
Arnold, Benjamin. "German Bishops and their Military Retinues in the Medieval Empire." *German History* 7 (1989): 161–183.

Arnold, John H. "The Labour of Continence: Masculinity and Clerical Virginity." In *Medieval Virginities*, edited by Anke Bernau, Ruth Evans, and Sarah Salih, 102–118. Cardiff: University of Wales Press, 2003.

Ash, Karina Marie, ed. *Conflicting Femininities in Medieval German Literature.* Farnham: Ashgate, 2012.

Austin, Gareth. "Reciprocal Comparison and African History: Tackling Conceptual Eurocentrism in the Study of Africa's Economic Past." *African Studies Review* 50, no. 3 (2007): 1–28.

Ayalon, David. "Eunuchs in the Mamluk Sultanate." In *Studies in Memory of Gaston Wiet*, edited by Myriam Rosen-Ayalon, 267–295. Jerusalem: Institute of Asian and African Studies, Hebrew University of Jerusalem, 1977.

Ayalon, David. "On the Term Khādim in the Sense of 'Eunuch' in the Early Muslim Sources." *Arabica* 32, no. 3 (1985): 289–308.

Ayalon, David. "On the Eunuchs in Islam." *Jerusalem Studies in Arabic and Islam* 1 (1979): 92–124. Reprinted in David Ayalon, *Outsiders in the Lands of Islam: Mamluks, Mongols and Eunuchs.* London: Variorum Reprints, 1988.

Ayalon, David. *Eunuchs, Caliphs, and Sultans: A Study in Power Relationships.* Jerusalem: The Magnes Press, The Hebrew University, 1999.

Bacharach, Jere L. "Administrative Complexes, Palaces and Citadels: Changes in the Loci of Medieval Muslim Rule." In *The Ottoman City and Its Parts: Urban Structure and Social Order*, edited by Irene A. Bierman, Rifaat Abou-el-Haj, and Donald Preziosi, 111–128. New Rochelle: A. D. Caratzas, 1991.

Bagnell Bury, John. *The Imperial Administrative System in the Ninth Century.* London: Franklin, 1911.

Bano, Shadab. "Eunuchs in Mughal Royal and Aristocratic Establishment." *Proceedings of Indian History Congress* (2009): 417–427.

Barber, Charles. "Homo Byzantinus?" In *Women, Men and Eunuchs: Gender in Byzantium*, edited by Liz James, 185–199. London and New York: Routledge, 1997.

Barlow, Frank. *The English Church 1000–1066.* 2nd ed. London and New York: Longman, 1979.

Barnett, Richard B. *North India between Empires: Awadh, the Mughals and the British, 1720–1801.* New Delhi: Manohar, 1987.

Barnish, Sam J. "Transformation and Survival in the Western Senatorial Aristocracy, c. A.D. 400–700." *Papers of the British School at Rome* 66 (1988): 120–155.

Barrow, Julia, and Nicholas P. Brooks, eds. *St Wulfstan and his World.* Aldershot: Asghate, 2005.

Barrow, Julia. "Wulfstan and Worcester: Bishop and Clergy in the Early Eleventh Century." In *Wulfstan, Archbishop of York*, edited by Matthew Townend, 141–159. Turnhout: Brepols, 2004.

Barrow, Julia. "The Clergy in English Dioceses c.90–c.1066." In *Pastoral Care in Late Anglo-Saxon England*, edited by Francesca Tinti, 17–26. Woodbridge: Boydell & Brewer, 2005.

Barrow, Julia. "Grades of Ordination and Clerical Careers, c. 900-c. 1200." In *Anglo-Norman Studies XXX, Proceedings of the Battle Conference 2007*, edited by Christopher P. Lewis, 41–61. Woodbridge: Boydell Press, 2008.

Barrow, Julia. *Who served the Altar at Brixworth? Clergy in English Minsters c.800-c.1200*, 28th Brixworth Lecture. Leicester, 2013.

Barrow, Julia. *The Clergy in the Medieval World: Secular Clerics, Their Families and Careers in North-Western Europe, c.800-c.1200.* Cambridge: Cambridge University Press, 2015.

Barstow, Anne Llewellyn. *Married Priests and the Reforming Papacy: The Eleventh-Century Debates*. Lewiston, NY: Edward Mellen Press, 1982.

Bartlett, Robert. *Why Can the Dead Do Such Great Things? Saints and Worshippers from the Martyrs to the Reformation*. Princeton: Princeton University Press, 2013.

Bates, David. *Normandy before 1066*. London: Longman, 1982.

Bayly, Christopher A. "Town Building in North India, 1790–1830." *Modern Asian Studies* 9, no. 4 (1975): 483–504.

Bayly, Christopher A. *Rulers, Townsmen and Bazaars: North Indian Society in the Age of British Expansion, 1770–1870*. Cambridge: Cambridge University Press, 1988.

Bayly, Christopher A. *Empire and Information: Intelligence Gathering and Social Communication in India, 1780–1870*. New York: Cambridge University Press, 1996.

Bayly, Christopher A. *The Birth of the Modern World 1780–1914*. Oxford: Blackwell, 2004.

Beard, Mary, and John Henderson. "With This Body I Thee Wed: Sacred Prostitution in Antiquity." In *Gender and the Body in the Ancient Mediterranean*, edited by Maria Wyke, 56–79. Oxford: Blackwell, 1998.

Beattie, Cordelia. "Introduction: Gender, Power, and Difference." In *Intersections of Gender, Religions and Ethnicity in the Middle Ages*, edited by Cordelia Beattie and Kirsten A. Fenton, 1–11. New York: Palgrave, 2010.

Beaudette, Paul. "'In the World but not of It': Clerical Celibacy as a Symbol of the Medieval Church." In *Medieval Purity and Piety: Essays on Medieval Clerical Celibacy and Religious Reform*, edited by Michael Frassetto, 23–46. New York: Garland, 1998.

Beled, Ilan. "Eunuchs in Hatti and Assyria: A Reassessment." In *Time and History in the Ancient Near East: Proceedings of the 56th Rencontre Assyriologique Internationale at Barcelona*, edited by Lluis Feliu et al., 785–797. Winona Lake: Eisenbrauns, 2013.

van Beneden, Pierre. *Aux origines d'une terminologie sacramentelle: Ordo, ordinare, ordinatio dans la littérature chrétienne avant 313*. Spicilegium Sacrum Lovaniens, Études et Documents 38. Leuven: Spicilegium Sacrum Lovaniense, 1974.

van Berkel, Maaike, Nadia Maria El Cheikh, Hugh Kennedy, and Letizia Osti, *Crisis and Continuity in the Abbasid Court: Formal and Informal Politics in the Reign of al-Muqtadır (295–320/908–32)*. Leiden: Brill, 2013.

Berlioz, Jacques, Pascal Collomb, and Marie Anne Polo de Beaulieu. "La face cachée de Thomas de Cantimpré. Complétements à une traduction française récente du Bonum universale de apibus." *Archives d'histoire doctrinale et littéraire du Moyen Âge* 68 (2001): 73–94.

Berman, Constance H. *The Cistercian Evolution: The Invention of a Religious Order in Twelfth-Century Europe*. Philadelphia, University of Pennsylvania Press, 2000.

Bird, Phyllis. "'To Play the Harlot': An Inquiry into an Old Testament Metaphor." In *Gender and Difference in Ancient Israel*, edited by Peggy Day, 75–94. Minneapolis: Fortress, 1989.

Bird, Phyllis. "The End of the Male Cult Prostitute: A Literary–Historical and Sociological Analysis of Hebrew *qādēš-qĕdēšīm*." *Supplements to Vetus Testamentum* 66 (1997): 37–80.

Bitel, Lisa M., and Felice Lifshitz, eds. *Gender and Christianity in Medieval Europe: New Perspectives*. Philadelphia: University of Pennsylvania Press, 2008.

Blauth, Carsten."Dominikaner und Dominikanerinnen in Metz: Ein Beitrag zur Entstehungsgeschichte der Konvente und zur Frauenseelsorge im 13. Jahrhundert."

In *Liber amicorum necnon et amicarum für Alfred Heit. Beiträge zur mittelalterlichen Geschichte und geschichtlichen Landeskunde*, edited by Friedhelm Burgard, Christoph Cluse and Alfred Haverkamp, 171–187. Trierer Historische Forschungen 28. Trier: THF, 1996.

Bloch, Howard R. *Medieval Misogyny and the Invention of Western Romantic Love*. Chicago: University of Chicago Press, 2009.

Bombi, Barbara. "The Authority of Miracles: Caesarius of Heisterbach and the Livonian Crusade." In *Aspects of Power and Authority in the Middle Ages*, edited by Brenda M. Bolton and Christine E. Meek, 305–325. Turnhout: Brepols, 2007.

Boot, Marilyn, ed. *Harem Histories: Envisioning Places and Living Spaces*. Durham and London: Duke University Press, 2010.

Boston, J. S. *The Igala Kingdom*. Ibadan: Oxford University Press, 1968.

Bosworth, Clifford Edmund. *The History of the Ṣaffārids of Sīstān and the Maliks of Nīmrūz (247/861 to 949/1542–3)*. Costa Mesa, CA: Mazda Publishers, 1994.

Bosworth, Clifford Edmund. "Eunuchs: The Early Islamic Period." In *Encyclopaedia Iranica online*. Article originally published December 15, 1998. Accessed February 1, 2016, http://www.iranicaonline.org/articles/eunuchs#iii.

Bouchard, Constance B. *Sword, Miter, and Cloister: Nobility and the Church in Burgundy, 980–1198*. Ithaca, NY: Cornell University Press, 1987.

Boulhol, Pascal, and Isabelle Cochelin. "La réhabilitation de l'eunuque dans l'hagiographie antique (Ive–VIe siècles)." In *Memoriam sanctorum venerantes: Miscellanea in onore di Monsignor Victor Saxer*, 49–76. Vatican: Pontificio Istituto di archeologia cristiana, 1992.

Bourdieu, Pierre. "Genèse et structure du champ religieux." *Revue Française de Sociologie* 12, no. 3 (1971): 295–334.

Boussard, Jacques. "Les évêques en Neustrie avant la Réforme grégorienne (950–1050 environ)." *Journal des savants* 3, no. 1 (1970): 161–196.

Bowen, Harold. *The Life and Times of ʿAlī Ibn ʿĪsā, "The Good Vizier"*. Cambridge: Cambridge University Press, 1928.

Boyle, Leonard E. "The Fourth Lateran Council and Manuals of Popular Theology." In *The Popular Literature of Medieval England*, edited by Thomas J. Heffernan, 30–43. Knoxville: University of Tennessee Press, 1985.

Brandt, Michael, and Arne Eggebrecht, eds. *Bernward von Hildesheim und das Zeitalter der Ottonen: Katalog der Ausstellung*. 2 vols. Hildesheim: Bernward, 1993.

Breitenstein, Mirko. "The Novice Master in the Cistercian Order." In *Generations in the Cloister: Youth and Age in Medieval Religious Life/Generationen im Kloster. Jugend und Alter in der mittelalterlichen vita religiosa*, edited by Sabine von Heusinger and Annette Kehnel, 145–155. Zürich and Münster: LIT, 2008.

Breitenstein, Mirko. "'Ins Gespräch gebracht': der Dialog als Prinzip monastischer Unterweisung." In *Understanding Monastic Practices of Oral Communication*, edited by Steven Vanderputten, 205–229. Turnhout: Brepols, 2011.

Bremond, Claude, Jaques LeGoff, and Jean-Claude Schmitt. *L'exemplum*. Typologie des Sources du Moyen Âge 40. Turnhout: Brepols, 1982.

Brennan, Brian. "'Episcopae': Bishops' Wives Viewed in Sixth-Century Gaul." *Church History* 54 (1985): 311–323.

Brett, Micheal. *The Rise of the Fatimids: The World of the Mediterranean and the Middle East in the Fourth Century of the Hijra, Tenth Century CE*. Leiden: Brill, 2001.

Broedel, Hans Peter. "Gratuitous Examples and the Grateful Dead: Appropriation and Negotiation of Traditional Narratives in Medieval Exemplary Ghost Stories." In *Translatio, Or the Transmission of Culture in the Middle Ages and the Renaissance: Modes and Messages*, edited by Laura H. Hollengreen, 97–122. Turnhout: Brepols, 2008.

Brokkaar, W. G. "Basil Lacapenus: Byzantium in the Tenth Century." *Studia Byzantina et Neohellenica Neerlandica* 3 (1972): 199–234.

Brooke, Christopher Nugent Lawrence. *The Medieval Idea of Marriage.* Oxford: Clarendon Press, 1989.

Brooke, Christopher Nugent Lawrence. "Gregorian Reform in Action: Clerical Marriage in England, 1050–1200." In *Medieval Church and Society: Collected Essays*, 69–99. London: Sidgwick and Jackson Limited, 1971.

Brooks, Nicholas. *The Early History of the Church of Canterbury.* Leicester: Leicester University Press, 1984.

Brown, Peter. *The Body and Society: Men, Women, and Sexual Renunciation in Early Christianity.* New York: Columbia University Press, 1988, rev. ed. 2008.

Brubaker, Leslie, and Julia M. H. Smith, eds. *Gender in the Early Medieval World: East and West, 300–900.* Cambridge: Cambridge University Press, 2004.

Brubaker, Leslie, and Shaun Tougher, eds. *Approaches to the Byzantine Family.* Farnham and Burlington, VT: Ashgate, 2013.

Brundage, James A. *Law, Sex and Christian Society in Medieval Europe.* Chicago: University of Chicago Press, 1987.

Buc, Philippe. *The Dangers of Ritual: Between Early Medieval Texts and Social Scientific Theory.* Princeton: Princeton University Press, 2002.

Buc, Philipp. "The Monster and the Critics: a Ritual Reply." *Early Medieval Europe* 15, no. 3 (2007): 441–452.

Budin, Stephanie L. *The Myth of Sacred Prostitution in Antiquity.* Cambridge: Cambridge University Press, 2010.

Bührer-Thierry, Geneviève. "Des évêques, des clercs et leurs families dans la Bavière des VIIIe-IXe siècles." In *Sauver son âme et se perpétuer: Transmission du patrimoine et mémoire au haut Moyen Âge*, edited by François Bougard, Cristina La Rocca, and Régine Le Jan, 239–264. Rome: École française de Rome, 2005.

Buhrer-Thierry, Geneviève. *Évêques et pouvoir dans le royaume de Germanie: Les Églises de Bavière et de Souabe, 876–973.* Paris: Picard, 1997.

Bynum, Caroline Walker. *Holy Feast and Holy Fast: The Religious Significance of Food to Medieval Women.* Berkeley and Los Angeles: University of California Press, 1987.

Cameron, Alan. "Eunuchs in the 'Historia Augusta.'" *Société d'Études latines de Bruxelles* 24, no. 1 (1965); 155–158.

Campbell, Gwyn, ed. *Structure of Slavery in Indian Ocean Africa and Asia.* London: Frank Cass, 2004.

Campo, Juan Eduardo. *The Other Side of Paradise: Explorations into the Religious Meanings of Domestic Space in Islam.* Columbia: University of South Carolina Press, 1991.

Caner, Daniel F. "The Practice and Prohibition of Self-Castration in Early Christianity." *Vigiliae Christianae* 51, no. 4 (1997): 396–415.

Cardelle de Hartmann, Carmen. *Lateinische Dialoge, 1200–1400: Literaturhistorische Studie und Repertorium.* Leiden and Boston: Brill, 2007.

Cardman, Francine. "Women, Ministry, and Church Order in Early Christianity." In *Women and Christian Origins*, edited by Mary Rose d'Angelo and Ross Shepard Kramer, 300–329. Oxford: Oxford University Press, 1999.

Carlson, Marianne Louis. "The Rationale of Eunuch Power in the Government of T'ang China, 618–805." Ph.D. diss., University of Chicago, 1971.

Castelli, Elizabeth. "'I Will Make Mary Male': Pieties of the Body and Gender Transformation of Christian Women in Late Antiquity." In *Body Guards: The Cultural Politics of Gender Ambiguity*, edited by Julia Epstein and Kristina Straub, 29–49. New York: Routledge, 1991.

Chaffee, John W. *The Thorny Gates of Learning in Sung China: A Social History of Examinations*. Cambridge and New York: Cambridge University Press, 1985.

Chakrabarty, Dipesh. *Provincializing Europe: Postcolonial Thought and Historical Difference*. Princeton: Princeton University Press, 2000, repr. 2008.

Chandon, Christian, and Daniel Dorsch. "Thomas von Cantimpré. Kritik an der Kirche?" In *Innovation in Klöstern und Orden des Hohen Mittelalters. Aspekte und Pragmatik eines Begriffs*, edited by Mirko Breitenstein, Stefan Burkhardt, and Julia Dücker, 173–196. Vita Regularis. Ordnungen und Deutungen religiosen Lebens im Mittelalter 48. Berlin: LIT, 2012.

Chatterjee, Indrani. *Gender, Slavery and Law in Colonial India*. New Delhi: Oxford University Press, 1999.

Chatterjee, Indrani, and Sumit Guha. "Slave–Queen, Waif–Prince: Slavery and Social Capital in Eighteenth-Century India." *Indian Economic and Social History Review* 36, no. 2 (1999): 165–182.

Chatterjee, Indrani. "A Slave's Quest for Selfhood in Eighteenth-Century Hindustan." *Indian Economic & Social History Review* 37 (2000): 53–86.

Chatterjee, Indrani, ed. *Unfamiliar Relations: Family & History in South Asia*. Delhi: Permanent Black, 2004.

Chatterjee, Indrani, "Slavery, Semantics, and the Sound of Silence." In *Slavery & South Asian History*, edited by Indrani Chatterjee and Richard M. Eaton, 287–315. Bloomington: Indiana University Press, 2006.

Chatterjee, Indrani, "Monastic Governmentality, Colonial Misogyny, and Postcolonial Amnesia in South Asia." *History of the Present* 3 (2013): 57–98.

Chatterjee, Kumkum. "History as Self-Representation: The Recasting of a Political Tradition in Late Eighteenth-Century Eastern India." *Modern Asian Studies* 32, no. 4 (1998): 913–948.

El-Cheikh, Nadia Maria. "Servants at the Gate: Eunuchs at the Court of al-Muqtadir." *The Journal of the Social and Economic History of the Orient* 48, no. 2 (2005): 234–252.

El-Cheikh, Nadia Maria. "Gender and Politics in the Harem of al-Muqtadir." In *Gender in the Early Medieval World: East and West, 300–900*, edited by Leslie Brubaker and Julia M. H. Smith, 147–161. Cambridge: Cambridge University Press, 2004.

Cheikh-Moussa, Abdallah. "Ǧāḥiẓ et les Eunuques ou la confusion du meme et de l'autre." *Arabica* 29, no. 2 (1982): 184–214.

Cheikh-Moussa, Abdallah. "De la synonymie dans les sources arabes anciennes: Le cas de Ḫādim et de Ḫaṣiyy." *Arabica* 32, no. 3 (1985): 309–322.

Ch'en, Kenneth K. S. "Inscribed Stelae during the Wei, Chin, and Nan-Ch'ao." In *Studia Asiatica: Essays in Asian Studies in Felicitation of the Seventy-Fifth Anniversary of Professor Ch'en Shou-yi*, edited by Lawrence G. Thompson, 75–84. San Francisco: Chinese Materials Center, 1975.

Chen Ruoshui. "Tangdai Chang'an de huanguan shequn – te lun qi yu junren de guanxi." *Tang yanjiu* 15 (2009): 171–198.

Chen Yinke. "Lun Tangdai zhi fanjiang yu fubing." *Zhongshan Daxue xuebao* 1 (1967): 163–170.

Chen Yinke. *Sui Tang zhidu yuanyuan lüe lun gao*. Beijing: Zhonghua Shuju, 1963.

Chen Yinke, *Tangdai zhengzhi shishu lungao*. Shanghai: Shanghai Guji, 1997.

Cheynet, J.-C. "Les Phocas." In *Le traité sur la guerrilla* (De velitatione) *de l'empereur Nicéphore Phocas (963–969)*, edited by Gilbert Dagron and Haralambie Mihăescu, 296–297. Paris: Éditions du Centre National de la Recherche Scientifique, 1986.

Chiu Yu Lok. *Cong gongting dao zhanchang: Zhongguo zhonggu yu jinshi zhu kaocha*. Hong Kong: Zhonghua Shuju, 2007.

Cilardo, Agostino. "Historical Development of the Legal Doctrine Relative to the Position of the Hermaphrodite in the Islamic Law." *The Search. Journal for Arab and Islamic Studies* 7 (1986): 128–170.

Claussen, Martin A. *The Reform of the Frankish Church: Chrodegang of Metz and the Regula Canonicorum in the Eighth Century*. Cambridge: Cambridge University Press, 2004.

Coakley, John. "Gender and the Authority of Friars: The Significance of Holy Women for Thirteenth-Century Franciscans and Dominicans." *Church History* 60 (1991): 445–460.

Coakley, John. "Friars, Sanctity, and Gender. Mendicant Encounters with Saints, 1250–1325." In *Medieval Masculinities: Regarding Men in the Middle Ages*, edited by Clare A. Lees, Thelma S. Fenster, and Jo Ann McNamara, 91–110. Minneapolis: University of Minnesota Press, 1994.

Cochini, Christian. *Origines apostoliques du célibat sacerdotal*. Paris: Lethielleux, 1981.

Cohen, Deborah. "Comparative History: Buyer Beware." *Bulletin of the German Historical Institute* 29 (2001): 23–33.

Cohen, Deborah, and Maura O'Connor, eds. *Comparison and History: Europe in Cross-National Perspective*. New York, London: Routledge, 2004.

Cohen, Jeffrey, and Bonnie Wheeler, eds. *Becoming Male in the Middle Ages*. New York, London: Garland Publishing, 1997.

Congar, Yves M.-J. "Aspects ecclésiologiques de la querelle entre mendiants et séculiers dans la seconde moitié du XIIIe siècle et le début du XIVe." *Archives d'histoire doctrinale et littéraire du Moyen Age* 36 (1961): 35–151.

Conrad, Sebastian, and Andreas Eckert. "Globalgeschichte, Globalisierung, multiple Modernitäten: Zur Geschichtsschreibung in der modernen Welt." In *Globalgeschichte*, edited by Sebastian Conrad, Andreas Eckert, and Ulrike Freitag, 7–49. Frankfurt: Campus, 2007.

Conrad, Sebastian. *Globalgeschichte: Eine Einführung*. Munich: C. H. Beck, 2013.

Conrad, Sebastian, Shalini Randeria, and Regina Römhild, eds. *Jenseits des Eurozentrismus: Postkoloniale Perspektiven in den Geschichts- und Kulturwissenschaften*. 2nd ed. Frankfurt: Campus, 2013.

Constable, Giles. *Reformation of the Twelfth Century*. Cambridge: Cambridge University Press, 1996.

Contreni, John J. "'By Lions, Bishops are Meant; By Wolves, Priests': History, Exegesis, and the Carolingian Church in Haimo of Auxerre's Commentary on Ezechiel." *Francia: Forschungen zur westeuropäischen Geschichte* 29 (2002): 29–52.

Cooper, Kate, and Conrad Leyser. "The Gender of Grace: Impotence, Servitude and Manliness in the Fifth-Century West." *Gender and History* 12, no. 3 (2000): 536–551.

Cortese, Delia, and Simonetta Calderini. *Women and the Fatimids in the World of Islam*. Edinburgh: Edinburgh University Press, 2006.

Cotts, John D. *The Clerical Dilemma: Peter of Blois and Literate Culture in the Twelfth Century*. Washington, DC: The Catholic University of America Press, 2009.

Crawford, Robert B. "Eunuch Power in the Ming Dynasty." *T'oung Pao* 49 (1961–1962): 115–148.

Crecelius, Daniel, and Ḥamza ʿAbd al-ʿAzīz Badr. "The *Awqāf* of al-Ḥājj Bashīr Āghā in Cairo." *Annales Islamologiques* 27 (1993): 291–311.

Crosby, Everett U. *The King's Bishops: The Politics of Patronage in England and Normandy 1066–1216*. New York and Basingstoke: Palgrave Macmillan, 2013.

Cubitt, Catherine. *Anglo-Saxon Church Councils c. 650–c. 850*. London: Leicester University Press, 1995.

Cubitt, Catherine. "Bishops and succession crises in tenth- and eleventh-century England." In *Patterns of Episcopal Power: Bishops in Tenth and Eleventh Century Western Europe*, edited by Ludger Körntgen and Dominik Waßenhoven, 111–126. Prinz-Albert-Forschungen 6. Berlin: De Gruyter, 2011.

Cuffel, Alexandra. *Gendering Disgust in Medieval Religious Polemic*. Notre Dame, IN: University of Notre Dame Press, 2007.

Cullum, Patricia H. and Katherine J. Lewis, eds. *Holiness and Masculinity in the Middle Ages*. Cardiff: University of Wales Press, 2004.

Cullum, Patricia H. and Katherine J. Lewis, eds. *Religious Men and Masculine Identity in the Middle Ages*. Woodbridge: Boydell and Brewer, 2013.

Daftary, Farhad. *The Ismāʿīlīs: Their History and Doctrines*. New York: Cambridge University Press, 1990.

Daftary, Farhad. *A Short History of the Ismailis: Traditions of a Muslim Community*. Edinburgh: Edinburgh University Press, 1998.

Dagron, Gilbert. *Emperor and Priest: The Imperial Office in Byzantium*. Cambridge: Cambridge University Press 2003.

Dai Xianqun. "Tang Wudai jiazi zhidu de lishi genyuan." *Renwen zazhi* 6 (1989): 83–88.

Dai Xianqun. "Tang–Wudai jiazi zhidu de leixing ji qi xiangguan de wenti." *Fujian Shifan Daxue xuebao* 108 (2000): 105–110.

Dalby, Michael T. "Court Politics in Late T'ang Times." In *The Cambridge History of China, Volume 3: Sui and T'ang China, 589–906, Part 1*, edited by Denis C. Twitchett, 561–681. Cambridge: Cambridge University Press, 1979.

Davies, Wendy. *Brittany in the Early Middle Ages: Texts and Societies*. Farnham: Ashgate, 2009.

Dechow, John. *Dogma and Mysticism in Early Christianity: Epiphanius of Salamis and the Legacy of Origen*. Macon, GA: Mercer University Press, 1988.

De Gaiffier, Baudouin. "Palatins et eunuques dans quelques documents hagiographiques." *Analecta Bollandiana* 75 (1957): 17–46.

Dejonckere, Laurence. *Les exempla du Bonum universale de apibus de Thomas de Cantimpré. Traduction partielle et analyse thématique et critique. Apport à l'étude de la représentation médiévale de la femme et de la sexualité*. M.A. thesis, University of Louvain, 2006.

Degler-Spengler, Brigitte. "'Zahlreich wie die Sterne des Himmels'. Zisterzienser, Dominikaner und Franziskaner vor dem Problem der Inkorporation von Frauenklöstern." *Rottenburger Jahrbuch Für Kirchengeschichte* 4 (1985): 37–50.

De la Puente, Cristina. "Sin linaje, sin alcurnia, sin hogar: eunucos en el Andalus en época Omeya." In *Identidades Marginales*, edited by Cristina de la Puente, 147–193. Madrid: Consejo Superior de Investigaciones Cientificas, 2003.

Devisse, Jean. *Hincmar, Archevêque de Reims 845–882*. 3 vols. Geneva: Droz, 1975–1976.

Diem, Albrecht. *Das monastische Experiment. Die Rolle der Keuschheit bei der Entstehung des westlichen Klosterwesens*. Vita Regularis. Ordnungen und Deutungen religiosen Lebens im Mittelalter 24. Münster: LIT, 2005.

Diem, Albrecht. "The Gender of the Religious: Wo/men and the Invention of Monasticism." In *Oxford Handbook of Women and Gender in Medieval Europe*, edited by Judith M. Bennett and Ruth Mazo Karras, 437–440. New York: Oxford University Press, 2013.

Dien, Albert. "The Bestowal of Surnames under the Western Wei–Northern Chou: A Case of Counter-Acculturation." *T'oung Pao* 63, no. 2–3 (1977): 137–177.

Dikici, Ezgi. "The making of Ottoman Court Eunuchs: Origins, Recruitment Paths, Family Ties and Domestic Production," *Archivium Ottomanicum* 30 (2013): 105–136.

Dortel-Claudot, Michel. "Le prêtre et le mariage: Évolution de la législation canonique des origines au XII siècle." *L'année canonique* 17 (1973): 319–344.

Drews, Wolfram, Antje Flüchter et al. *Monarchische Herrschaftsformen der Vormoderne in transkultureller Perspektive*. Berlin: De Gruyter, 2015.

Dufeil, Michel-Marie. *Guillaume de Saint-Amour et la polémique universitaire parisienne, 1250–1259*. Paris: A. et J. Picard, 1972.

Dunbabin, Jean. *France in the Making, 843–1180*. 2nd ed. Oxford: Oxford University Press, 2000.

Dunlap, James E. "The Office of the Grand Chamberlain in the Later Roman and Byzantine Empires." In *Two Studies in Later Roman and Byzantine Administration*, edited by Arthur E. R. Boak and James E. Dunlap, 161–324. New York and London: The Macmillan Company, 1924.

Du Wenyu. "Tangdai huanguan hunyin ji qi neibu jiegou." *Xueshu yuekan* 6 (2000): 88–95.

Du Wenyu. "Tangdai huanguan de jiguan fenbu." *Zhongguo lishi dili luncong* 1 (1998): 161–174.

Du Wenyu. "Tangdai huanguan shijia kaoshu." *Shaanxi Shifan Daxue xuebao* 27, no. 2 (1998): 78–85.

Du Wenyu, and Ma Weibin. "Lun Wudai Shiguo shouyang jiazi fengqi de shehui huanjing yu lishi genyuan." *Shaanxi Shifan Daxue xuebao* 39, no. 3. (2010): 111–116.

Eades, Jeremy Seymour. *The Yoruba Today*. Cambridge: Cambridge University Press, 1980.

Eaton, Richard M. *A Social History of the Deccan, 1300–1761: Eight Indian Lives*. Cambridge: Cambridge University Press, 2005.

Eberhard, Wolfram. *Conquerors and Rulers: Social Forces in Medieval China*, 2nd ed. Leiden: Brill, 1970.

Ebrey, Patricia B. *The Aristocratic Families of Early Imperial China: A Case Study of the Po-Ling Ts'ui Family*. Cambridge: Cambridge University Press, 1978.

Ebrey, Patricia B. "Later Han Stone Inscriptions." *Harvard Journal of Asiatic Studies* 40, no. 2 (1980): 325–353.

Edwards, James R. "Circumcision, the Mother Goddess, and the Scandal of the Cross." *Novum Testamentum* 53 (2011): 319–337.

Edwards, Mark. "Synods and Councils." In *Origins to Constantine*, vol. 1 of *The Cambridge History of Christianity*, edited by Margaret M. Mitchell and Frances M. Young. 367–385. Cambridge: Cambridge University Press, 2006.

Eisenstadt, Shmuel N., ed. *The Origins and Diversity of Axial Age Civilizations*. Albany: State University of New York Press, 1986.

Eldevik, John. *Episcopal Power and Ecclesiastical Reform in the German Empire: Tithes, Lordship and Community, 950–1150*. Cambridge: Cambridge University Press, 2012.

Eliade, Mircea. *The Sacred and the Profane. The Nature of Religion*. Translated by Williard R. Trask. New York: Harcourt, 1987.

Elliott, Dyan. *Spiritual Marriage: Sexual Abstinence in Medieval Wedlock*. Princeton: Princeton University Press, 1993.

Elliott, Dyan. "Pollution, Illusion, Masculine Disarray: Nocturnal Emissions and the Sexuality of the Clergy." In *Constructing Medieval Sexuality*, edited by Karma Lochrie, Peggy McCraken, and James A. Schultz, 1–23. Minneapolis: University of Minnesota Press, 1998.

Elliott, Dyan. *Fallen Bodies: Pollution, Sexuality and Demonology in the Middle Ages*. Philadelphia: University of Pennsylvania Press, 1999.

Elliott, Dyan. "The Priest's Wife: Female Erasure and the Gregorian Reform." In *Medieval Religion: New Approaches*, edited by Constance Hoffman Berman, 123–155. New York: Routledge, 2005.

Elliot, Henry Miers and John Dowson. *The History of India as Told by Its Own Historians*. 8 vols. Allahabad: Kitab Mahal Pvt. Ltd., 1963–1970.

Erler, Mary C., and Maryanne Kowaleski, eds. *Gendering the Master Narrative: Women and Power in the Middle Ages*. Ithaca, NY: Cornell University Press, 2003.

Ettinghausen, Richard, and Oleg Grabar. *The Art and Architecture of Islam, 650–1250*. Harmondsworth: Penguin Books, 1987.

Evans, Gillian R. *Bernard of Clairvaux*. Oxford: Oxford University Press, 2000.

Ewig, Eugen. "Milo et eiusmodi similes." In *Spätantikes und fränkisches Gallien: Gesammelte Schriften (1952–1973)*, edited by Eugen Ewig and Hartmut Atsma, 189–219. Munich: Artemis, 1979.

Faruqui, Munis D. *The Princes of the Mughal Empire*. Cambridge: Cambridge University Press, 2012.

Fasola, Umberto. *La basilica dei SS. Nereo ed Achilleo e la catacomba di Domitilla*. Rome: Marietti, 1960.

Fear, A. T. "Cybele and Christ." In *Cybele, Attis, and Related Cults: Essays in Memory of M. J. Vermaaseren*, edited by Eugene Lane, 37–50. Leiden: Brill, 1996.

Featherstone, Michael. "Further Remarks on the *De Cerimoniis*." *Byzantinische Zeitschrift* 97 (2004): 113–121.

Fenton, Kirsten A. "The Question of Masculinity in William of Malmesbury's Presentation of Wulfstan of Worcester." *Anglo-Norman Studies* 28 (2006): 124–137.

Fetvacı, Emine. *Picturing History at the Ottoman Court*. Bloomington, IN: Indiana University Press, 2013.

Fisher, Humphrey. *Slavery in the History of Muslim Black Africa*. New York: New York University Press, 2001.

Fisher, Michael H. *A Clash of Cultures: Awadh, the British and the Mughals*. New Delhi: Manohar, 1987.

Fisher, Michael H. "Becoming and Making 'Family' in Hindustan." In *Unfamiliar Relations: Family & History in South Asia*, edited by Indrani Chatterjee, 95–121. Delhi: Permanent Black, 2004.

Fleckenstein, Joseph. *Die Hofkapelle der deutschen Könige. Vol. 1: Die karolingische Hofkapelle. Vol. 2: Die Hofkapelle im Rahmen der ottonisch-salischen Reichskirche*. Schriften der MGH 16. Stuttgart: Hiersemann, 1959–1966.

Fletcher, Christopher. "The Whig Interpretation of Masculinity? Honour and Sexuality in Late Medieval Manhood." In *What is Masculinity? Historical Dynamics from Antiquity to the Contemporary World*, edited by John H. Arnold and Sean Brady, 57–75. Basingstoke: Palgrave Macmillan, 2011.

Fletcher, Christopher. "Manhood, Kingship and the Public in Late Medieval England." *Edad Media. Revista De Historia* 13 (2012): 123–142.

Fletcher, Richard. "An *epistola formata* from León," *Bulletin of the Institute of Historical Research* 45 (1972): 122–128.

Flüchter, Antje. *Der Zölibat zwischen Devianz und Norm: Kirchenpolitik und Gemeindealltag in den Herzogtümern Jülich und Berg im 16. und 17. Jahrhundert*. Cologne: Böhlau, 2006.

Forrest, Ian. "Continuity and Change in the Institutional Church." In *The Oxford Handbook of Medieval Christianity*, edited by John H. Arnold, 185–200. Oxford: Oxford University Press, 2014.

Fouracre, Paul, and Richard A. Gerberding, eds. *Late Merovingian France: History and Hagiography, 640–720*. Manchester: Manchester University Press, 1996.

Fouracre, Paul. *The Age of Charles Martel*. Harlow: Longman, 2000.

Fouracre, Paul. "Francia in the Seventh Century." In *The New Cambridge Medieval History 1: c.500-c.700*, edited by Paul Fouracre, 371–396. Cambridge: Cambridge University Press, 2005.

Fourneret, Pierre. "Diocèse." In *Dictionnaire de théologie catholique*, edited by Alfred Vacant, Joseph-Eugène Mangenot, and Émile Amann, 4:1362–1363. 15 vols. Paris: Letouzey et Ané, 1930–1950.

Fowden, Garth. *Empire to Commonwealth: Consequences of Monotheism in Late Antiquity*. Princeton: Princeton University Press, 1993.

Frankopan, Peter. *The Silk Roads: A New History of the World*. New York: Bloomsbury, 2015.

Frassetto, Michael, ed. *Medieval Purity and Piety: Essays on Medieval Clerical Celibacy and Religious Reform*. New York, London: Garland, 1998.

Freed, John B. "Urban Development and the 'Cura Monialium' in Thirteenth-Century Germany." *Viator* 3 (1972): 311–327.

Frend, William Hugh Clifford. *The Rise of Christianity*. London: Fortress Press, 1984.

Friedrich, Ellen L. "When a Rose Is Not a Rose: Homoerotic Emblems in the Roman de la Rose." In *Gender Transgression: Crossing the Normative Barrier in Old French Literature*, edited by Karen J. Taylor, 21–44. New York: Garland, 1998.

Füser, Thomas. "Vom *exemplum Christi* über das *exemplum sanctorum* zum 'Jedermannsbeispiel'. Überlegungen zur Normativität exemplarischer Verhaltensmuster im institutionellen Gefüge der Bettelorden des 13. Jahrhunderts." In *Die Bettelorden im Aufbau. Beiträge zu Institutionalisierungsprozessen im mittelalterlichen Religionsentum*, edited by Gert Melville and Jörg Oberste, 27–105

Vita Regularis. Ordnungen und Deutungen religiosen Lebens im Mittelalter 11. Münster: LIT, 1999.

Gardner, Jane F. "Sexing a Roman: Imperfect Men in Roman Law." In *When Men Were Men: Masculinity, Power and Identity in Classical Antiquity*, edited by Lin Foxhall and John Salmon, 136–152. London: Routledge, 1998.

Garland, Lynda. *Byzantine Empresses: Women and Power in Byzantium AD 527–1204*. London, New York: Routledge, 1999.

Gatti, Evan A. "Building the Body of Church: A Bishop's Blessing in the Benedictional of Engilmar of Parenzo." In *The Bishop Reformed: Studies in Episcopal Power and Culture in the Central Middle Ages*, edited by John S. Ott and Anna Trumbore Jones, 92–121. Aldershot: Ashgate, 2007.

Gaudemet, Jean. "Le célibat ecclésiastique. Le droit et la pratique du XIe au XIIIe siècle." *Zeitschrift der Savigny-Stiftung für Rechtsgeschichte, Kanonistische Abteilung* 68 (1982): 1–31.

Gaunt, Simon. "Bel Acueil and the Improper Allegory of the Romance of the Rose." *New Medieval Literatures* 2 (1998): 65–93.

Geevers, Liesbeth, and Mirella Marini. "Introduction: Aristocracy, Dynasty and Identity in Early Modern Europe, 1520–1700." In *Dynastic Identity in Early Modern Europe. Rulers, Aristocrats and the Formation of Identities*, edited by Liesbeth Geevers and Mirella Marini, 1–24. Farnham: Ashgate, 2014.

Geis, Lioba. "'Modus vivendi claustralium'. Der Bienenstaat als Vorbild klösterlichen Zusammenlebens. Zum Bonum universale de apibus des Thomas von Cantimpré." In *Ille operum custos. Kulturgeschichtliche Beiträge zur antiken Bienensymbolik und ihrer Rezeption*, edited by David Engels and Carla Nicolaye, 185–203. Spudasmata 118. Hildesheim: Olms, 2008.

Geltner, Guy. *The Making of Medieval Antifraternalism: Polemic, Violence, Deviance, and Remembrance*. Oxford: Oxford University Press, 2012.

Ghosh, Durba. *Sex and the Family in Colonial India: The Making of Empire*. Cambridge: Cambridge University Press, 2006.

Gibaut, John St. H. *The Cursus Honorum: A Study of the Origins and Evolution of Sequential Ordination*. Bern: Peter Lang, 2000.

Gilsdorf, Sean, ed. *The Bishop: Power and Piety at the First Millennium*. Münster: LIT, 2004.

Godding, Robert. *Prêtres en Gaule mérovingienne*. Brussels: Société des Bollandistes, 2001.

Goffart, Walter A. *The Le Mans Forgeries: A Chapter from the History of Church Property in the Ninth Century*. Cambridge, MA: Harvard University Press, 1966.

Goldziher, Ignaz. "Kämpfe um die Stellung des Ḥadīth im Islam." *Zeitschrift der Deutschen Morgenländischen Gesellschaft* 61 (1907): 860–872.

Goodich, Michael. *Vita Perfecta: The Ideal of Sainthood in the Thirteenth Century*. Stuttgart: Hiersemann, 1981.

Graillot, Henri. *Le culte de Cybèle: Mère des dieux, à rome et dans l'empire romain*. Paris: Fontemoing, 1912.

Grayson, Albert Kirk. "Eunuchs in Power: Their Role in the Assyrian Bureaucracy." In *Vom Alten Orient zum Alten Testament: Festschrift Wolfram von Soden zum 85. Geburtstag*, edited by Oswald Loretz and Manfried Dietrich, 85–98. Neukirchen-Vluyn: Neunkirchener Verlag, 1995.

Greatrex, Geoffrey, and Jonathan Bardill. "Antiochus the 'Praepositus': A Persian Eunuch at the Court of Theodosius II." *Dumbarton Oak Papers* 50 (1996): 171–197.

Green, Nile. "The Uses of Books in a Late Mughal Takiyya: Persianate Knowledge Between Person and Paper." *Modern Asian Studies* 44, no. 2 (2010): 241–265.

Griesebner, Andrea. "Geschlecht als mehrfach relationale Kategorie: Methodologische Anmerkungen aus der Perspektive der Frühen Neuzeit." In *Geschlecht hat Methode: Ansätze und Perspektiven in der Frauen- und Geschlechtergeschichte*, edited by Veronika Aegerter, 129–137. Zürich: Chronos, 1999.

Grignard, François. "Conjectures sur la famille d'Halinard, abbé de Saint-Bénigne." *Bulletin d'histoire et d'archéologie religieuses du diocèse de Dijon* 2 (1884): 202–206.

Grosse, Rolf. "Hinkmar, Bischof von Laon." In *Lexikon des Mittelalters*, 5:29. Munich: Artemis, 1991.

Grübel, Isabel. *Bettelorden und Frauenfrömmigkeit im 13. Jahrhundert: Das Verhältnis der Mendikanten zu Nonnenklöstern und Beginen am Beispiel Straßburg und Basel*. Kulturgeschichtliche Forschungen 9. München: Tuduv-Verlagsgesellschaft, 1987.

Grundmann, Herbert. *Religiöse Bewegungen im Mittelalter: Untersuchungen über die geschichtlichen Zusammenhänge zwischen der Ketzerei, den Bettelorden und der religiösen Frauenbewegung im 12. und 13. Jahrhundert und über die geschichtlichen Grundlagen der deutschen Mystik: Anhang, neue Beiträge zur Geschichte der religiösen Bewegungen im Mittelalter*. 4th ed. Darmstadt: Wissenschaftliche Buchgesellschaft, 1977.

Grünhagen, Céline. *Geschlechterpluralismus im Buddhismus. Zur Tragweite westlicher Wissenschaftskonstruktionen am Beispiel frühbuddhistischer Positionen und des Wandels in Thailand*. Wiesbaden: Harrassowitz, 2013.

Guha, Sumit. "The Family Feud as Political Resource in Eighteenth-Century India." In *Unfamiliar Relations: Family & History in South Asia*, edited by Indrani Chatterjee, 73–94. Delhi: Permanent Black, 2004.

Guilland, Rodolphe. "Les eunuques dans l'empire byzantine. Étude de titulaire et de prosopographie byzantines." *Revue des études byzantines* 1 (1943): 197–238.

Guilland, Rodolphe. "Le parakimomène." *Revue des études byzantines* 2 (1944): 191–201.

Guillemain, Bernard. "Les origines des évêques en France aux XIe et XIIe siècles." In *Le istituzioni ecclesiastiche della "Societas Christiana" dei secoli XI-XII: Papato, cardinalato ed episcopato*, 374–402. Miscellanea del Centro di studi medioevali 7. Milano: Pubblicazioni dell'Università Cattolica del Sacro Cuore, 1974.

Güler, Mustafa. *Osmanlı Devlet'inde Ḥaremeyn Vakıfları (16. ve 17. Yüzyıllar)*. Istanbul: Tarih ve Tabiat Vakfı, 2002.

Guyot, Peter. *Eunuchen als Sklaven und Freigelassene in der griechisch-römischen Antike*. Stuttgart: Klett-Cotta, 1980.

Guyotjeannin, Olivier. *Episcopus et comes: Affirmation et déclin de la seigneurie épiscopale au nord du royaume de France (Beauvais-Noyon, Xe–début XIIIe siècle)*. Geneva and Paris: Librairie Droz, 1987.

Guyotjeannin, Oliver. *Salimbene de Adam: Un chroniqueur franciscain*. Témoins de notre histoire. Turnhout: Brepols, 1995.

Gwynn, David. "Episcopal Leadership." In *The Oxford Handbook of Late Antiquity*, edited by Scott Fitzgerald Johnson, 876–915. Oxford: Oxford University Press, 2012.

Hadley, Dawn M., ed. *Masculinity in Medieval Europe*. London and New York: Longman, 1999.

Haji, Hamid. "A Distinguished Slav Eunuch of the Early Fatimid Period: al-Ustadh Jawdhar." In *Fortresses of the Intellect: Ismaili and Other Islamic Studies in Honour of Farhad Daftary*, edited by Omar Ali-de-Unzaga, 261–273. London: I. B. Tauris, 2011.

Haji, Hamid. *Inside the Immaculate Portal: A History from Early Fatimid Archives*. London: I. B. Tauris, 2012.

Hall, Stuart George. "Institutions in the pre-Constantinian *ecclesia*." In *Origins to Constantine*, vol. 1 of *The Cambridge History of Christianity*, edited by Margaret M. Mitchell and Frances M. Young, 415–433. Cambridge: Cambridge University Press, 2006.

Halm, Heinz. *Das Reich des Mahdi. Der Aufstieg der Fatimiden*. Munich: Beck, 1991. Translated into English by M. Bonner, *The Empire of the Mahdi: The Rise of the Fatimids*. Leiden: Brill, 1997.

Halm, Heinz. *Kalifen und Assassinen. Aegypten und der Vordere Orient zur Zeit der ersten Kreuzzüge 1074–1171*. München: Beck, 2014.

Hambly, Gavin. "A Note on the Trade in Eunuchs in Mughal Bengal." *Journal of the American Oriental Society* 94, no. 1 (1974): 125–130.

Hamilton, Sarah. *Church and People in the Medieval West, 900–1200*. London: Routledge, 2013.

Hamilton, Sarah. "Bishops, Education, and Discipline." In *The Oxford Handbook of Medieval Christianity*, edited by John H. Arnold, 531–549. Oxford: Oxford University Press, 2014.

Hammond, Kenneth J. "The Eunuch Wang Zhen [王振] and the Ming Dynasty." In *The Human Tradition in Premodern China*, edited by Kenneth J. Hammond, 143–155. Wilmington: Scholarly Resources, 2002.

Hanß, Stefan, and Juliane Schiel, eds. *Mediterranean Slavery Revisited (500–1800)*. Zurich: Chronos 2014.

Harries, Jill. *Sidonius Apollinaris and the Fall of Rome, AD 407–485*. Oxford: Clarendon Press, 1994.

Hartmann, Wilfried. *Die Synoden der Karolingerzeit im Frankenreich und Italien*. Paderborn: Ferdinand Schöningh, 1989.

Hartmann, Wilfried. *Kirche und Kirchenrecht um 900: Die Bedeutung der spätkarolingischen Zeit für Tradition und Innovation im kirchlichen Recht*. Hanover: MGH, 2008.

Hathaway, Jane. "The Role of the Ḳızlar Ağası in 17th–18th Century Ottoman Egypt." *Studia Islamica* 75 (1992): 141–158.

Hathaway, Jane. *A Tale of Two Factions: Myth, Memory, and Identity in Ottoman Egypt and Yemen*. Albany, NY: State University of New York Press, 2003.

Hathaway, Jane. *Beshir Agha, Chief Eunuch of the Ottoman Imperial Harem*. Oxford: Oneworld, 2005.

Hathaway, Jane. "Ḥabeşī Meḥmed Agha: The First Chief Harem Eunuch (Darüssaade Ağası) of the Ottoman Empire." In *The Islamic Scholarly Tradition: Studies in History, Law, and Thought in Honor of Professor Michael Allan Cook*, edited by Asad Q. Ahmed, Behnam Sadeghi, and Michael Bonner, 179–196. Leiden: Brill, 2011.

Hatzaki, Myrto. *Beauty and the Male Body in Byzantium: Perceptions and Representations in Art and Text*. Basingstoke and New York: Palgrave Macmillan, 2009.

Hauck, Karl. "Apostolischer Geist im genus *sacerdotale* der Liudgeriden. Die 'Kanonisation' Liudgers und Altfrids gleichzeitige Bischofsgrablege in

Essen-Werden." In *Sprache und Recht: Beiträge zur Kulturgeschichte des Mittelalters: Festschrift für Ruth Schmidt-Wiegand zum 60. Geburtstag*, edited by Karl Hauck, 191–219. New York: de Gruyter, 1986.

Haupt, Heinz-Gerhard, and Jürgen Kocka, eds. *Geschichte und Vergleich: Ansätze und Ergebnisse international vergleichender Geschichtsschreibung*. Frankfurt: Campus, 1996.

Hawkins, J. David. "Eunuchs among the Hittites." In *Sex and Gender in the Ancient Near East: Proceedings of the 47*th *Rencontre Assyriologique Internationale, Helsinki, July 2–6, 2001*, edited by Simo Parpola and Robert M. Whiting, 217–233. Helsinki: The Neo-Assyrian Text Corpus Project, 2002.

Head, Thomas and Richard Landes, eds. *The Peace of God: Social Violence and Religious Response in France around the Year 1000*. Ithaca: Cornell University Press, 1992.

Heale, Martin, ed. *The Prelate in England and Europe*. York: Boydell & Brewer, 2015.

Heinzelmann, Martin. "Bischof und Herrschaft vom spätantiken Gallien bis zu den karolingischen Hausmeiern. Die institutionellen Grundlagen." In *Herrschaft und Kirche: Beiträge zur Entstehung und Wirkungsweise episkopaler und monastischer Organisationsformen*, edited by Friedrich Prinz, 23–82. Stuttgart: Hiersemann, 1988.

Heinzelmann, Martin. Gregor von Tours (538–594): *Zehn Bücher Geschichte. Historiographie und Gesellschaftskonzept im 6. Jahrhundert*. Darmstadt: Wissenschaftliche Buchgesellschaft, 1994. Translated by Christopher Carroll as Gregory of Tours: *History and Society in the Sixth Century*. Cambridge: Cambridge University Press, 2001.

Herbert, Penelope Ann. "Perceptions of Provincial Officialdom in Early T'ang China." *Asia Major,* Third Series 2, no. 1 (1989): 25–57.

Hermann, Hans-Werner. "Saarbrücken, Grafen v.," In *Neue Deutsche Biographie*, 22:318. 26 vols. Berlin: Duncker & Humblot, 1953–2016.

Herrin, Judith. *The Formation of Christendom*. Oxford: Princeton University Press, 1987.

Hettema, Theo L., and Arie van der Kooij, eds. *Religious Polemics in Context: Papers Presented to the Second International Conference of the Leiden Institute for the Study of Religions (LISOR) Held at Leiden, 27–28 April, 2000*. Studies in Theology and Religion 11. Assen: Van Gorcum, 2004.

He Zhong. "Tangdai shiren Wang Jian yu huanguan Wang Shoucheng guanxi kaolun: yi Wang Jian 'Zeng shumi' shi wei zhongxin." *Shenyang Gongcheng Xueyuan xuebao* 5, no. 4 (2009): 531–535.

Hilka, Alfons, ed. *Die Wundergeschichten des Caesarius von Heisterbach*, 3 vols. Bonn: Peter Hanstein Verlagsbuchhandlung, 1937.

Hinchy, Jessica. "The Sexual Politics of Imperial Expansion: Eunuchs and Indirect Colonial Rule in Mid-Nineteenth-Century North India." *Gender & History* 26, no. 3 (2014): 414–437.

Hinchy, Jessica. "Enslaved Childhoods in Eighteenth-Century Awadh." *South Asian History and Culture* 6, no. 3 (2015): 380–400.

Höckelmann, Michael. "Not Man Enough to be a Soldier? Eunuchs in the Tang Military and Their Critics." In *Verflechtungen zwischen Byzanz und dem Orient/ Entanglements between Byzantium and the Orient*, edited by Michael Grünbart. Berlin: LIT, forthcoming.

Hodgson, Marshall G.S. *The Venture of Islam*. 3 vols. Chicago: The University of Chicago Press, 1974.

Hödl, Ludwig, and Johannes Neumann. "Firmung." In *Lexikon des Mittelalters*, 4:490–493. Munich: Artemis, 1989.

Höfert, Almut. "Europa und der Nahe Osten: Der transkulturelle Vergleich in der Vormoderne und die Meistererzählungen über den Islam." *Historische Zeitschrift* 287 (2008): 561–597.

Höfert, Almut. "Grenzüberschreitungen für das Mittelalter. Transkulturelles Forschen mit einer aussereuropäischen Quellensprache zwischen Geschichtswissenschaft und den Area Studies." *Schweizerische Zeitschrift für Geschichte* 64 (2014): 210–223.

Höfert, Almut. *Kaisertum und Kalifat. Der imperiale Monotheismus im Früh- und Hochmittelalter*. Frankfurt: Campus, 2015.

Holmes, Catherine. *Basil II and the Governance of Empire (976–1025)*. Oxford: Oxford University Press, 2005.

Hopkins, Keith. *Conquerors and Slaves*. Cambridge: Cambridge University Press, 1978.

Hopkins, Keith. "Eunuchs in Politics in the Later Roman Empire." *Proceedings of the Cambridge Philological Society* 189 (1963): 62–80.

Hori Toshikazu. "Tōmatsu moro hanran no seikaku – Chūgoku ni okeru kizoku seiji no botsuraku ni tsuite." *Tōyō bunka* 7 (1951): 52–94.

Huang, Martin W. *Negotiating Masculinities in Late Imperial China*. Honolulu: University of Hawai'i Press, 2006.

Hunt, Lynn. *Writing History in the Global Era*. New York, London: Norton & Company, 2015.

Hunter, David G. "Clerical Marriage and Episcopal Elections in the Latin West: From Siricius to Leo I." In *Episcopal Elections in Late Antiquity*, edited by Johan Leemans et al., 183–202. Berlin: De Gruyter, 2011.

Huot, Sylvia. *The Romance of the Rose and Its Medieval Readers: Interpretation, Reception, Manuscript Transmission*. Cambridge: Cambridge University Press, 1993.

Innes, Matthew. *State and Society in the Early Middle Ages: The Middle Rhine Valley, 400–1000*. Cambridge: Cambridge University Press, 2000.

Innes, Matthew. "'A Place of Discipline': Carolingian Courts and Aristocratic Youth." In *Court Culture in the Early Middle Ages*, edited by Catherine Cubitt, 59–76. Turnhout: Brepols, 2003.

Isaïa, Marie-Céline. *Remi de Reims: Mémoire d'un saint, histoire d'une église*. Paris: Editions du Cerf, 2010.

Ivanow, Vladimir. *Ismaili Tradition concerning the Rise of the Fatimids*. London: Oxford University Press, 1942.

Ivanow, Vladimir. "The Organization of the Fatimid Propaganda." *Journal of the Bombay Branch of the Royal Asiatic Society* 15 (1939): 1–35.

Jaeger, C. Stephen. "The Courtier Bishop in *Vitae* from the Tenth to the Twelfth Century." *Speculum* 58 (1983): 291–325.

Jaeger, C. Stephen. *The Origins of Courtliness: Civilizing Trends and the Formation of Courtly Ideals, 939–1210*. Philadelphia: University of Pennsylvania Press, 1985.

Jaeger, C. Stephen. *The Envy of Angels: Cathedral Schools and Social Ideals in Medieval Europe, 950–1200*. Philadelphia: University of Pennsylvania Press, 1994.

Janin, Raymond. "Un ministre byzantine: Jean l'orphanotrophe (XIe siècle)." *Echos d'Orient* 30 (1931): 431–443.

Janin, Raymond. "Un arabe ministre à Byzance: Samonas (IXe–Xe)." *Echos d'Orient* 34 (1935): 307–318.

Jay, Jennifer W. "Random Jottings on Eunuchs: Ming *Biji* Writings as Unofficial Historiography." *Hanxue yanjiu* 11, no. 1 (1993): 269–285.

Jay, Jennifer W. "Another Side of Chinese Eunuch History: Castration, Marriage, Adoption, and Burial." *Canadian Journal of History/Annales canadiennes d'histoire* 28 (1993): 459–478.

Jay, Jennifer W. "Song Confucian Views on Eunuchs." *Chinese Culture: A Quarterly Review* 35, no. 3 (1994): 45–51.

Jay, Jennifer W. "The Eunuchs and Sinicization in the Non-Han Conquest Dynasties of China." Paper presented at the Asian Studies on the Pacific Coast Conference. Forest Grove, OR, June 16–18, 1995.

Jay, Jennifer W. "Castration and Medical Images of Eunuchs in Traditional China." In *Current Perspectives in the History of Science in East Asia*, edited by Yung Sik Kim and Francesca Bray, 385–394. Seoul, National University Press, 1999.

Jayakumar, Shashi. "Eadwig and Edgar: Politics, Propaganda, Faction." In *Edgar, King of the English 959–975: New Interpretations*, edited by Donald Scragg, 83–103. Woodbridge: Boydell Press, 2008.

Jenkins, Romilly J. H. "The Flight of Samonas." *Speculum* 23 (1948): 217–235.

Jenkins, Romilly J. H. "A 'Consolatio' of the Patriarch Nicholas Mysticus." *Byzantion* 35 (1965): 159–166, repr. in Romilly J. H Jenkins. *Studies on Byzantine History of the* 9th *and 10*th *Centuries*. London: Variorum Reprints, 1970.

Jing Yali. "Tangdai huanguan feng Fo sixiang tanwei – yi Xi'an beilinguan cang muzhi wei li." *Shaanxi Shifan Daxue xuebao* 39, no. 1 (2010): 71–75.

Jiwa, Shainool. "The Baghdad Manifesto: A Lineage Exposed or an Exposé on Lineage?" Paper presented at the panel "One Empire, Many Religions: Religion and Society under Fatimid Rule", 4th World Congress for Middle Eastern Studies (WOCMES). Ankara, 18–22 August, 2014.

Johnson, David G. "The Last Years of a Great Clan: The Li Family of Chao Chün in Late T'ang and Early Sung." *Harvard Journal of Asiatic Studies* 37, no. 1 (1977): 5–102.

Johnson, Wallace, trans. *The T'ang Code: Volume 2, Specific Articles*. Princeton: Princeton University Press, 1997.

Jonckheere, Frans. "L'Eunuque dans l'Égypte pharaonique." *Revue d'Histoire des Sciences* 7, no. 2 (1954): 139–155.

Jong, Mayke de. *In Samuel's Image: Child Oblation in the Early Medieval West*. Leiden: Brill, 1996.

Jong, Mayke de. "*Imitatio morum*: The Cloister and Clerical Purity in the Carolingian world." *Medieval Purity and Piety: Essays on Medieval Clerical Celibacy and Religious Reform*, edited by Michael Frassetto, 49–80. New York: Garland, 1998.

Jugel, Ulrike. *Politische Funktion und soziale Stellung der Eunuchen zur späten Han-Zeit (25–220 n.Chr.)*. Wiesbaden: Steiner, 1976.

Jung, Jacqueline E. "From Jericho to Jerusalem: The Violent Transformation of Archbishop Engelbert of Cologne." In *Last Things: Death and the Apocalypse in the Middle Ages*, edited by Caroline Walker Bynum and Paul H. Freedman, 60–82. Philadelphia: University of Pennsylvania Press, 2000.

Jursa, Michael. "'Höflinge' (*ša rēši, ša rēš šarri, ustarbaru*) in babylonischen Quellen des ersten Jahrtausends." In *Die Welt des Ktesias*, edited by Josef Wiesehöfer, Robert Rollinger, and Giovanni B. Lanfranchi, 159–174. Wiesbaden: Harrassowitz, 2011.

Justice, Steven. "Eucharistic Miracles and Eucharistic Doubt." *Journal of Medieval and Early Modern Studies* 42 (2012): 307–322.

Juynboll, Gautier A. H. *Muslim Tradition. Studies in Chronology, Provenance and Authorship of Early Ḥadīth*. New York: Cambridge University Press, 1983.

Kadish, Gerald E. "Eunuchs in Ancient Egypt?" In *Studies in Honor of John A. Wilson*, edited by E. B. Hauser, 55–62. Studies in Ancient Oriental Civilization 35. Chicago: University of Chicago Press, 1969.

Kaelble, Hartmut. *Der historische Vergleich: Eine Einführung zum 19. und 20. Jahrhundert*. Frankfurt: Campus, 1999.

Kaeuper, Richard W. *Holy Warrior: The Religious Ideology of Chivalry*. Philadelphia: University of Pennsylvania Press, 2009.

Kaiser, Reinhold. *Bischofsherrschaft zwischen Königtum und Fürstenmacht: Studien zur bischöflichen Stadtherrschaft im westfränkisch-französischen Reich im frühen und hohen Mittelalter*. Pariser Historische Studien 17. Bonn: Röhrscheid, 1981.

Kaiser, Reinhold. *Churrätien im frühen Mittelalter: Ende 5. bis Mitte 10. Jahrhundert*. Basel: Schwabe, 1998.

Kaldellis, Anthony. *Procopius of Caesarea: Tyranny, History, and Philosophy at the End of Antiquity*. Philadelphia: University of Pennsylvania Press, 2004.

Karras, Ruth Mazo. *From Boys to Men. Formations of Masculinity in Late Medieval Europe*. Philadelphia: University of Pennsylvania Press, 2003.

Karras, Ruth Mazo. "Thomas Aquinas' Chastity Belt: Clerical Masculinity in Medieval Europe." In *Gender & Christianity in Medieval Europe: New Perspectives*, edited by Lisa M. Bitel and Felice Lifshitz, 52–68. Philadelphia: University of Pennsylvania Press, 2008.

Karras, Ruth Mazo. *Unmarriages: Women, Men, and Sexual Unions in the Middle Ages*. Philadelphia: University of Pennsylvania Press, 2012.

Kedar, Benjamin Z. "Outlines for Comparative History Proposed by Practicing Historians." In *Explorations in Comparative History*, edited by Benjamin Z. Kedar, 1–28. Jerusalem: The Hebrew University Press, 2009.

Keightley, David N. *Sources of Shang History: The Oracle-Bone Inscriptions of Bronze Age China*. Berkeley: University of California Press, 1978.

Kempf, Damien. "Paul the Deacon's Liber de episcopis Mettensibus and the Role of Metz in the Carolingian Realm." *Journal of Medieval History* 30 (2004): 279–299.

Kennedy, Hugh. *The Court of the Caliphs: The Rise and Fall of Islam's Greatest Dynasty*. London: Weidenfeld & Nicolson, 2004.

Kennedy, Hugh. *The Prophet and the Age of the Caliphates*. London: Longmans, 2004.

Keynes, Simon. "Cnut's Earls." In *The Reign of Cnut: King of England, Denmark and Norway*, edited by Alexander R. Rumble, 43–88. London: Cassell, 1994.

Kidwai, Saleem. "Sultans, Eunuchs and Domestics: New Forms of Bondage in Medieval India." In *Chains of Servitude: Bondage and Slavery in Medieval India*, edited by Utsa Patnaik and Manjari Dingwaney, 76–96. Madras: Sangam Books, 1985.

Kiefer, Frederick, ed. *Masculinities and Femininities in the Middle Ages and Renaissance*. Turnhout: Brepols, 2009.

Kleinheyer, Bruno. *Die Priesterweihe im römischen Ritus: Eine liturgiehistorische Studie*. Trierer Theologische Studien 12. Trier: Paulinus, 1962.

Knöpp, Friedrich. "Lupold, Bischof von Worms 1196–1217." In *Die Reichsabtei Lorsch. Festschrift zum Gedenken an ihre Stiftung 764*, edited by Friedrich Knöpp, 1:361–366. 2 vols. Darmstadt: Hessische Historische Kommission, 1973.

Kottje, Raymund. "Das Aufkommen der täglichen Eucharistiefeier in der Westkirche und die Zölibatsforderung." *Zeitschrift für Kirchengeschichte* 82 (1971): 218–228.

Koziol, Geoffrey. "Review article: The Dangers of Polemic: Is Ritual Still an Interesting Topic of Historical Study?" *Early Medieval Europe* 11, no. 4 (2002): 367–388.

Kuefler, Mathew. "Castration and Eunuchism in the Middle Ages." In *Handbook of Medieval Sexuality*, edited by Vern L. Bullough and James A. Brundage, 279–306. New York: Garland, 1996.

Kuefler, Mathew. *The Manly Eunuch: Masculinity, Gender Ambiguity, and Christian Ideology in Late Antiquity*. Chicago: University of Chicago Press, 2001.

Kuefler, Mathew. "Sex with Eunuchs, Sex with Boys, and the Implications of Sexual Difference." In *Atti del 53 Congresso Internazionale di Studi sull'alto Medioevo: Comportamenti e immaginario della sessualità nell'alto medioevo*, 139–172. Spoleto: Centro italiano di studi sull'alto medioevo, 2006.

Kuefler, Mathew. "Clothes (Un)Make the (Wo)Man: Dress and Gender Crossings in Late Antiquity." In *Il genere nella ricerca storica: Atti del VI Congresso della Società Italiana delle Storiche*, edited by Saveria Chemotti and Maria Cristina La Rocca, 1: 128–136. Padua: Il Poligrafo, 2015.

Kuefler, Mathew. "Desire and the Body in the Patristic Period." In *Oxford Handbook of Theology, Sexuality, and Gender*, edited by Adrian Thatcher, 241–254. Oxford: Oxford University Press, 2015.

Kugle, Scott. *Living Out Islam: Voices of Gay, Lesbian, and Transgender Muslims*. New York: New York University Press, 2014.

Kumar, Satish. "Eunuchs: Past and Present." *Eastern Anthropologist* 37 (1984): 381–389.

Kurihara Masuo. "Tōmatsu–Godai no kari fushi teki ketsugō ni okeru seimei to nenrei." *Tōyō gakuhō* 38 (1956): 430–457.

Kurihara Masuo. "Tō–Godai no kari fushi teki ketsugō no seikaku – shu toshite hansochi teki shihai kenryoku to no kanren ni oite." *Shigaku Zasshi* 62 (1963): 514–543.

Kurth, Godefroid. *Notger de Liège et la civilisation au Xe siècle*. 2 vols. Paris: Picard, 1905.

Lal, Ruby. *Domesticity and Power in the Early Mughal World*. New York: Cambridge University Press, 2005.

Langosch, Karl. "Caesarius von Heisterbach." In *Die Deutsche Literatur des Mittelalters: Verfasserlexikon*, edited by Wolfgang Stammler and Karl Langosch, 2nd rev. ed., 1: 1152–1168. Berlin: de Gruyter, 1978.

Lapidge, Michael. "A Frankish Scholar in Tenth-Century England: Frithegod of Canterbury/Fredegaud of Brioude." *Anglo-Saxon England* 17 (1988): 46–65.

Laqueur, Thomas. *Making Sex: Body and Gender from the Greeks to Freud*. Cambridge: Harvard University Press, 1990.

Latham, Jacob. "'Fabulous Clap-Trap': Roman Masculinity, the Cult of Magna Mater, and Literary Constructions of the *Galli* at Rome from the Late Republic to Late Antiquity." *Journal of Religion* 92, no. 1 (2012): 84–122.

Layard, Austen Henry. *Discoveries in the Ruins of Nineveh and Babylon, with Travels in Armenia, Kurdistan and the Desert.* London: John Murray, 1853.

Lea, Henry C. *History of Sacerdotal Celibacy in the Christian Church.* 3rd ed. London: Williams and Norgate, 1907.

L'Estrange, Elizabeth, and Alison More, eds. *Representing Medieval Genders and Sexualities in Europe: Construction Transformation and Subversion, 600–1530.* Farnham: Ashgate, 2011.

Le Strange, Guy. *Baghdad during the Abbasid Caliphate: From Contemporary Arabic and Persian Sources.* Oxford: Clarendon Press, 1900.

Le Jan, Régine. *Famille et pouvoir dans le monde franc (VIIe–Xe siècle): Essai d'anthropologie sociale.* Paris: Publications de la Sorbonne, 1995.

Lees, Clare A., Thelma S. Fenster and Jo Ann McNamara, eds. *Medieval Masculinities: Regarding Men in the Middle Ages.* Minneapolis: University of Minnesota Press, 1994.

Lev, Yacov. *State and Society in Fatimid Egypt.* Leiden: Brill, 1991.

Levine, Steven I. "Review of Anderson, Mary M., *Hidden Power: The Palace Eunuchs of Imperial China.* " *Library Journal* 115, no. 4 (1990): 102.

Lewin, B. "Ibn al-Muʿtazz." In *Encyclopaedia of Islam*, 2nd ed., online version. Accessed December 2, 2016, http://referenceworks.brillonline.com/entries/encyclopaedia-of-islam-2/ibn-al-mutazz-SIM_3312 (print version: vol. 3, Leiden: Brill, 1971).

Leyser, Henrietta. "Clerical Purity and the Re-ordered World." In *Christianity in Western Europe c. 1100–c. 1500*, vol. 4 of *The Cambridge History of Christianity*, edited by Miri Rubin and Walter Simons, 11–21. Cambridge: Cambridge University Press, 2009.

Lightfoot, Jane L. "Sacred Eunuchism in the Cult of the Syrian Goddess." In *Eunuchs in Antiquity and Beyond*, edited by Shaun Tougher, 71–86. London: Classical Press of Wales and Duckworth, 2002.

Lilie, Ralph-Johannes, Claudia Ludwig, Thomas Pratsch and Beate Zielke. *Prosopographie der mittelbyzantinischen Zeit, Zweite Abteilung (867–1025).* Berlin: de Gruyter, 2013.

Liu, Yat-wing. "The Two Shen-ts'e Armies: Their Role in the Frontier Defence System and the Pacification of Rebellious Provinces, 754–820 A.D." *Papers on Far Eastern History* 14 (1976): 1–35.

Llewellyn-Jones, Rosie. *A Man of the Enlightenment in Eighteenth Century India: The Letters of* Claude Martin, *1766–1800.* New Delhi: Permanent Black, 2003.

Llewellyn-Jones, Rosie. The Colonial Response to African Slaves in British India – Two Contrasting Cases." *African and Asian Studies* 10, no. 1 (2011): 59–70.

Loewe, Michael. "On the Terms *baozi, yin gong, yin guan, huan*, and *shou*: Was Zhao Gao a Eunuch?" *T'oung Pao* 91 (2005): 301–319.

Long, Jacqueline. *Claudian's In Eutropium: Or, How, When, and Why to Slander a Eunuch.* Chapel Hill: University of North Carolina Press, 1996.

Löther, Andrea. "Grenzen und Möglichkeiten weiblichen Handelns im 13. Jahrhundert: Die Auseinandersetzung um die Nonnenseelsorge der Bettelorden." *Rottenburger Jahrbuch Für Kirchengeschichte* 11 (1992): 223–240.

Lowry, Heath W. *The Nature of the Early Ottoman State.* Albany: State University of New York Press, 2003.

Magdalino, Paul. "Paphlagonians in Byzantine High Society." In *Η Βυζαντινή Μικρά Ασία (6ος-12ος αι.)*, edited by Stelios Lampakis, 141–150. Athens: Institute for Byzantine Research, 1998.

Malegam, Jehangir Yezdi. *The Sleep of Behemoth: Disputing Peace and Violence in Medieval Europe, 1000–1200*. Ithaca: Cornell University Press, 2013.

Mao Yangguang. "Tangdai fanzhen yangzi shulun." *Shangqiu Shifan Xueyuan xuebao* 17, no. 5 (2011): 52–55.

Marcus, Harold G. *A History of Ethiopia*. Berkeley: University of California Press, 1994.

Markopoulos, Athanasios. *History and Literature of Byzantium in the 9th–10th Centuries*. Aldershot and Burlington: Ashgate Variorum, 2004.

Marmon, Shaun. *Eunuchs and Sacred Boundaries in Islamic Society*. Oxford and New York: Oxford University Press, 1995.

Marshall, Peter James. "Economic and Political Expansion: The Case of Oudh." *Modern Asian Studies* 9, no. 4 (1975): 465–482.

Martìnez Pizarro, Joaquìn. *Writing Ravenna: The Liber pontificalis of Andreas Agnellus*. Ann Arbor: University of Michigan Press, 1995.

Massignon, Louis. "Mutanabbi, devant le siècle ismaelien de l'islam." In *Al Mutanabbî. Recueil publié a l'occasion de son millénaire*, edited by Régis Blachère, Marius Canard, and Maurice Gaudefroy-Demombynes, 1–17. Beirut: Institut français de Damas, 1936.

Mathisen, Ralph. *Roman Aristocrats in Barbarian Gaul: Strategies for Survival in an Age of Transition*. Austin: University of Texas Press, 1993.

Mattila, Raija. *The King's Magnates: A Study of the Highest Officials of the Neo-Assyrian Empire*. Helsinki: The Neo-Assyrian Text Corpus Project, 2000.

Maurer, Helmut. *Das Bistum Konstanz 2: Die Konstanzer Bischöfe vom Ende des 6. Jahrhunderts bis 1206*. Germania Sacra, Neue Folge 42, 1. Berlin: De Gruyter, 2003.

Mayr-Harting, Henry. *Church and Cosmos in Early Ottonian Germany: The View from Cologne*. Oxford: Oxford University Press, 2007.

Mazel, Florian. *L'espace du diocèse: Genèse d'un territoire dans l'Occident médiéval (Ve–XIIIe siècle)*. Rennes: Presses universitaires de Rennes, 2008.

Ma Zhiqiang. "Lüe tan Nanbeichao huanguan de junshi biaoxian." *Shanxi Datong Daxue xuebao* 21, no. 2 (2007): 41–42.

McGuire, Brian Patrick. "Written Sources and Cistercian Inspiration in Caesarius of Heisterbach." *Analecta Cisterciensia* 35 (1979): 227–282.

McGuire, Brian Patrick. "Friends and Tales in the Cloister: Oral Sources in Caesairus of Heisterbach's *Dialogus Miraculorum*." *Analecta Cisterciensia* 36 (1980): 177–247.

McGuire, Brian Patrick. "The Cistercians and the Rise of the 'Exemplum' in Early Thirteenth-Century France: A Reevaluation of *Paris BN MS lat. 15912*." *Classica et Mediaevalia* 34 (1983): 211–267.

McGuire, Brian Patrick. "Cistercian Storytelling – A Living Tradition: Surprises in the World of Research." *Cistercian Studies Quarterly* 39 (2004): 281–309.

McKeon, Peter R. *Hincmar of Laon and Carolingian Politics*. Urbana: University of Illinois Press, 1978.

McKitterick, Rosamond. *Charlemagne: The Formation of a European Identity*. Cambridge: Cambridge University Press, 2008.

McLaughlin, Megan. "The Bishop as Bridegroom: Marital Imagery and Clerical Celibacy in the Eleventh and Early Twelfth Centuries." In *Medieval Purity and*

Piety: Essays on Medieval Clerical Celibacy and Religious Reform, edited by Michael Frassetto, 209–229. New York: Garland Publishing, 1998.

McLaughlin, Megan. *Sex, Gender, and Episcopal Authority in an Age of Reform, 1000–1122*. Cambridge: Cambridge University Press, 2010.

McMullen, David L. "The Cult of Ch'i T'ai-kung and T'ang Attitudes to the Military." *T'ang Studies* 7 (1989): 59–103.

McMullen, David L. "Tomb Text with Introduction for His Excellency Li of Longxi." Paper presented at the Workshop New Frontiers in the Study of Medieval China. Rutgers University, NJ, May 15–16, 2015.

McNamara, Jo Ann. "The *Herrenfrage*. The Restructuring of the Gender System, 1050–1150." In *Medieval Masculinities: Regarding Men in the Middle Ages*, edited by Clare A. Lees, Thelma S. Fenster, and Jo Ann McNamara, 3–29. Minneapolis: University of Minnesota Press, 1994.

Meeks, Wayne A. "Social and Ecclesial Life of the Earliest Christians." In *Origins to Constantine*, vol. 1 of *The Cambridge History of Christianity*, edited by Margaret M. Mitchell and Frances M. Young, 145–173. Cambridge: Cambridge University Press, 2006.

Meier, Gabriele. *Die Bischöfe von Paderborn und ihr Bistum im Mittelalter*. Paderborner theologische Studien 17. Paderborn: F. Schöningh, 1987.

Melville, Gert. *Die Welt der mittelalterlichen Klöster. Geschichte und Lebensformen*. München: Beck, 2012.

Meouak, Mohamed. "De la périphérie au centre du pouvoir 'abbaside. La carrière politique de Mu'nis al-Ḫādim al-fatā al-Muẓaffar." In *Identidades Marginales*, edited by Cristina de la Puente, 195–214. Madrid: Consejo Superior de Investigaciones Cientificas, 2003.

Meouak, Mohamed. *Ṣaqāliba, eunuques et esclaves à la conquête du pouvoir: Géographie et histoires des élites politiques "marginales" dans l'Espagne umayyade*. Helsinki: Academia Scientiarum Fennica, 2004.

Mesley, Matthew M. *The Construction of Episcopal Identity: The Meaning and Function of Episcopal Depictions within Latin Saints' Lives of the Long Twelfth Century*. PhD dissertation. University of Exeter, 2010.

Mesley, Matthew M. "Episcopal Authority and Gender in the Narratives of the First Crusade." In *Religious Men and Masculine Identity in the Middle Ages*, edited by Patricia H. Cullum and Katherine J. Lewis, 94–111. Woodbridge: Boydell and Brewer, 2013.

Messis, Charis. *Les eunuques à Byzance, entre réalité et imaginaire*. Paris: Centre d'études byzantines, néo-helleniques et sud-est européennes, 2014.

Metcalf, Barbara Daly, ed. *Moral Conduct and Authority: The Place of Adab in South Asian Islam*. Berkeley: University of California Press, 1984.

Midell, Matthias. "Kulturtransfer und Historische Komparatistik." *Comparativ* 10 (2000): 7–41.

Millant, Richard. *Les eunuches à travers les âges*. Paris: Vigot Frères, 1908.

Miller, Maureen C. "Religion Makes a Difference: Clerical and Lay Cultures in the Courts of Northern Italy, 1000–1300." *American Historical Review* 105 (2000): 1095–1130.

Miller, Maureen C. "Masculinity, Reform, and Clerical Culture: Narratives of Episcopal Holiness in the Gregorian Era." *Church History* 72, no. 1 (2003): 25–52.

Miller, Maureen C. *Clothing the Clergy: Virtue and Power in Medieval Europe, c. 800–1200*. Ithaca: Cornell University Press, 2014.

Miller, Tanya Stabler. "Mirror of the Scholarly (Masculine) Soul: Scholastics, Beguines and Gendered Spirituality in Medieval Paris." In *Negotiating Clerical Identities: Priests, Monks and Masculinity in the Middle Ages*, edited by Jennifer D. Thibodeaux, 238–264. Basingstoke and New York: Palgrave Macmillan, 2010.

Miller, Tanya Stabler. *The Beguines of Medieval Paris: Gender, Patronage, and Spiritual Authority*. Philadelphia: University of Pennsylvania Press, 2014.

Mills, Robert. *Seeing Sodomy in the Middle Ages*. Chicago: The University of Chicago Press, 2015.

Minnis, Alastair. *Magister Amoris: The Roman de La Rose and Vernacular Hermeneutics*. Oxford: Oxford University Press, 2001.

Mommertz, Monika. "Theoriepotentiale 'ferner Vergangenheiten': Geschlecht als Markierung / Ressource /Tracer." In *L'homme: Europäische Zeitschrift für feministische Geschichtswissenschaft* 26, no. 1 (2015): 79–97.

Moore, Robert I. "Family, Community and Cult on the Eve of the Gregorian Reform." *Transactions of the Royal Historical Society* 5th ser., 30 (1980): 49–69.

Moore, Robert I. *The First European Revolution, c. 970–1215*. Oxford: Blackwell, 2000.

Mottahedeh, Roy. *Loyalty and Leadership in an Early Islamic Society*. Princeton: Princeton University Press, 1980.

Motzki, Harald. *The Origins of Islamic Jurisprudence. Meccan Fiqh before the Classical Schools*. Leiden: Brill, 2002.

Mueller, Joan. "Female Mendicancy: A Failed Experiment? The Case of Clare of Assisi." In *The Origin, Development, and Refinement of Medieval Religious Mendicancies*, edited by Donald S. Prudlo, 59–81. Leiden and Boston: Brill, 2012.

Mundy, John H. *Europe in the High Middle Ages 1150–1300*. 3rd edition. New York: Routledge, 2000.

Muronaga Yoshizō. "Tō naishishō chi naishishō ji." *Nagasaki Daigaku Kyōiku Gakubu Shakai kagaku ronsō* 38–40 (1989–1990): 1–10, 1–10, 1–7.

Murray, Jacqueline, ed. *Conflicted Identities and Multiple Masculinities: Men in the Medieval West*. New York: Garland, 1999.

Murray, Jacqueline. "Masculinizing Religious Life: Sexual Prowess, the Battle for Chastity and Monastic Identity." In *Holiness and Masculinity in the Middle Ages*, edited by Patricia H. Cullum and Katherine J. Lewis, 24–42. Cardiff: Cardiff University Press, 2004.

Murray, Jacqueline. "One Flesh, Two Sexes, Three Genders?" *Gender & Christianity in Medieval Europe: New Perspectives*, edited Lisa M. Bitel and Felice Lifshitz, 34–51. Philadelphia: University of Pennsylvania Press, 2008.

Muslu, Cihan Yüksel. *The Ottomans and the Mamluks: Imperial Diplomacy and Warfare in the Islamic World*. London: I.B. Tauris, 2014.

Muth, Robert. "Kastration." In *Reallexikon für Antike und Christentum*, edited by Franz-Joseph Dölger, Theodor Klauser et al., 20: 285–342. 26 vols. Stuttgart: Hiersemann, 1950–2015.

Nakashian, Craig M. "The Political and Military Agency of Ecclesiastical Leaders in Anglo-Norman England." *Journal of Medieval Military History* 12 (2014): 51–80.

Naqvi, Ali Raza. "Adoption in Muslim Law." *Islamic Studies* 19, no. 4 (1980): 283–302.
Nath, R. *Medieval Indian History and Architecture*. New Delhi: APH Publishing Corporation, 1995.
Neal, Derek G. *The Masculine Self in late Medieval England*. Chicago: Chicago University Press, 2008.
Neal, Derek G. "What Can Historians Do with Clerical Masculinity? Lessons from Medieval Europe." In *Negotiating Clerical Identities: Priests, Monks and Masculinity in the Middle Ages*, edited by Jennifer D. Thibodeaux, 16–36. Basingstoke: Palgrave Macmillan, 2010.
Necipoğlu, Gülru. *Architecture, Ceremonial, and Power: The Topkapı Palace in the Fifteenth and Sixteenth Centuries*. New York: Architectural History Foundation; Cambridge: MIT Press, 1991.
Necipoğlu, Gülru. *The Age of Sinan: Architectural Culture in the Ottoman Empire*. London: Reaktion Books, 2005.
Nelson, Janet L. "Carolingian Royal Ritual." In *Rituals of Royalty: Power and Ceremonial in Traditional Societies*, edited by David Cannadine and Simon Price, 137–180. Cambridge: Cambridge University Press, 1987.
Nelson, Janet L. "Literacy in Carolingian Government." In *The Uses of Literacy in Early Medieval Europe*, edited by Rosamond McKitterick, 258–296. Cambridge: Cambridge University Press, 1990.
Nelson, Janet L. "Nobility in the Ninth Century." In *Nobles and Nobility in Medieval Europe: Concepts, Origins, Transformations*, edited by Anne J. Duggan, 43–51. Woodbridge: Boydell, 2000.
Nelson, Janet L. "Charlemagne the Man." In *Charlemagne: Empire and Society*, edited by Joanna Story, 22–37. Manchester: Manchester University Press, 2005.
Nelson, Janet L. "Law and its applications." In *Early Medieval Christianities c.600–c.1100*, vol. 3 of *The Cambridge History of Christianity*, edited by Thomas F. X. Noble and Julia M. H. Smith, 299–326. Cambridge: Cambridge University Press, 2008.
Neue Deutsche Biographie. 26 vols. Berlin: Duncker & Humblot, 1953–2016.
Newman, Martha G. *The Boundaries of Charity: Cistercian Culture and Ecclesiastical Reform 1098–1180*. Stanford: Stanford University Press, 1996.
Newman, William Mendel. *Le domaine royal sous les premiers Capétiens (987–1180)*. Paris: Librairie du Recueil Sirey, 1937.
Nienhauser, William H. Jr., ed. *The Grand Scribe's Records, Volume 5.1: The Hereditary Houses of Pre-Han China, Part I, by Ssu-ma Ch'ien*. Bloomington: Indiana University Press, 2006.
Nightingale, John. *Monasteries and their Patrons in the Gorze Reform, c.850–1000*. Oxford: Clarendon Press, 2001.
Niklesová, Eva. "Frauen und Männer im Dialogus miraculorum des Caesarius von Heisterbach." *Graeco-Latina Brunensia* 15, no. 1 (2010): 65–85.
Noailles, Pierre and Alphonse Dain. *Les Novelles de Léon VI le Sage*. Paris: Les Belles Lettres, 1944.
Northedge, Alastair. *The Historical Topography of Samarra*. London: British School of Archaeology in Iraq, 2007.
Obata Tatsuo. "Jinsakugun no seiritsu." *Tōyōshi kenkyū* 18 (1959): 35–56.
O'Brien, Patrick. "Historiographical Traditions and Modern Imperatives for the Restoration of Global History." *Journal of Global History* 1 (2006): 3–39.

O'Hanlon, Rosalind. "Issues of Masculinity in North Indian History: The Bangash Nawabs of Farrukhabad." *Indian Journal of Gender Studies* 4, no. 1 (1997): 1–19.

O'Hanlon, Rosalind. "Kingdom, Household and Body: History, Gender and Imperial Service under Akbar." *Modern Asian Studies* 41, no. 5 (2007): 889–923.

Oikonomides, Nicolas. *Les listes de préséance byzantines des IXè et Xè siècles*. Paris: Editions du Centre National de la Recherche Scientifique, 1972.

Oldenburg, Veena Talwar. *The Making of Colonial Lucknow: 1856–1877*. Princeton: Princeton University Press, 1984.

Olsen, Glenn Warren. *Of Sodomites, Effeminates, Hermaphrodites, and Androgynes: Sodomy in the Age of Peter Damian*. Toronto: Pontifical Institute of Mediaeval Studies, 2011.

Ortenberg, Veronica. "Archbishop Sigeric's Journey to Rome in 990." *Anglo-Saxon England* 11 (1990): 197–246.

Ott, John S., and Anna Trumbore Jones, eds. *The Bishop Reformed: Studies in Episcopal Power and Culture in the Central Middle Ages*. Aldershot: Ashgate, 2007.

Ott, John S. "'Both Mary and Martha': Bishop Lietbert of Cambrai and the Construction of Episcopal Sanctity in a Border Diocese around 1000." In *The Bishop Reformed: Studies of Episcopal Power and Culture in the Central Middle Ages*, edited by John S. Ott and Anna Trumbore Jones, 137–160. Aldershot and Burlington: Ashgate, 2007.

Ouyang Xiu. "Biographies of Eunuchs." In *Historical Records of the Five Dynasties*, edited by Ouyang Xiu and translated by Richard L. Davis. New York: Columbia University Press, 2004.

Owen, Stephen. "The Manuscript Legacy of the Tang: The Case of Literature." *Harvard Journal of Asiatic Studies* 67, no. 2 (2007): 295–326.

Pacaut, Marcel. *Louis VII et les elections épiscopales dans le royaume de France*. Paris: Librairie Philosophique J. Vrin, 1957.

Palmer, James T. *Anglo-Saxons in a Frankish World, 690–900*. Turnhout: Brepols, 2009.

Palmer, Nigel F. "Exempla." In *Medieval Latin: An Introduction and Bibliographical Guide*, edited by Frank A. C. Mantello and A. G. Rigg, 583–588. Washington, DC: Catholic University of America Press, 1996.

Papaioannou, Stratis. *Michael Psellos: Rhetoric and Authorship in Byzantium*. Cambridge: Cambridge University Press, 2013.

Parish, Helen. *Clerical Celibacy in the West: C.1100–1700*. Farnham: Ashgate, 2010.

Parisse, Michel. *La noblesse lorraine XIe–XIIIe siècle*. 2 vols. Lille and Paris: Université Nancy-II, 1976.

Partner, Nancy. "No Sex, No Gender." *Speculum* 68 (1993): 419–443.

Patterson, Orlando. *Slavery and Social Death: A Comparative Study*. Cambridge: Harvard University Press, 1982.

Patzold, Steffen. "L'épiscopat du haute Moyen Âge du point de vue de la médiévistique allemande." *Cahiers de civilisation médiévale Xe–XIIe siècles* 48 (2005): 341–358.

Patzold, Steffen. *Episcopus: Wissen über Bischöfe im Frankenreich des späten 8. bis frühen 10. Jahrhunderts*. Ostfildern: Jan Thorbecke Verlag, 2008.

Patzold, Steffen. "Zur Sozialstruktur des Episkopats und zur Ausbildung bischöflicher Herrschaft in Gallien zwischen Spätantike und Frühmittelalter." In *Völker,*

Reiche und Namen im frühen Mittelalter, edited by Matthias Becher and Stefanie Dick, 121–140. Munich: Wilhelm Fink, 2010.

Patzold, Steffen. "Bischöfe, soziale Herkunft und die Organisation sozialer Herrschaft." In *Chlodwigs Welt: Organisation von Herrschaft um 500*, edited by Mischa Meier and Steffen Patzold, 523–544. Stuttgart: Franz Steiner, 2014.

Peirce, Leslie. *The Imperial Harem: Women and Sovereignty in the Ottoman Empire.* Oxford: Oxford University Press, 1993.

Peltzer, Jörg. *Canon Law, Careers and Conquest: Episcopal Elections in Normandy and Greater Anjou, c. 1140–c. 1230.* Cambridge: Cambridge University Press, 2008.

Pentcheva, Bissera V. "Containers of Power: Eunuchs and Reliquaries in Byzantium." *Res* 51 (2007): 109–120.

Penzer, Norman Mosley. *The Harem: An Account of the Institution as It Existed in the Palace of the Turkish Sultans, with a History of the Grand Seraglio from Its Foundations to Modern Times.* Philadelphia: J. B. Lippincott, 1936. 2nd ed. London: Spring Books, 1965; repr. New York: Dover Press, 1993.

Pernau, Magrit. *Transnationale Geschichte.* Stuttgart: Vandenhoeck & Ruprecht, 2011.

Peterson, Charles A. "Court and Province in Mid- and Late T'ang." In *The Cambridge History of China, Volume 3: Sui and T'ang China, 589–906, Part 1*, edited by Denis C. Twitchett, 464–560. Cambridge: Cambridge University Press, 1979.

Phillips, Kim M., and Barry Reay. *Sex Before Sexuality: A Premodern History.* London: Polity Press, 2011.

Phipps, William E. *Clerical Celibacy: The Heritage.* New York: Continuum, 2004.

Pirngruber, Reinhard. "Eunuchen am Königshof. Ktesias und die altorientalische Evidenz." In *Die Welt des Ktesias: Ctesias' World*, edited by Josef Wiesehöfer, Robert Rollinger and Giovanni B. Lanfranchi, 279–312. Wiesbaden: Harrassowitz, 2011.

Pixton, Paul B. *The German Episcopacy and the Implementation of the Decrees of the Fourth Lateran Council, 1216–1245: Watchmen on the Tower*. Leiden: Brill, 1995.

Pökel, Hans-Peter. *Der unmännliche Mann. Zur Figuration des Eunuchen im Werk von al-Ǧāḥiẓ (gest. 869).* Würzburg: Ergon, 2014.

Poonawala, Ismail K. "al-Ẓāhir wa'l-Bāṭin." In *Encyclopaedia of Islam*, 2nd ed, online version. Accessed December 2, 2016, http://referenceworks.brillonline.com/entries/encyclopaedia-of-islam-2/al-zahir-wa-l-batin-SIM_8078?s.num=0&s.f.s2_parent=s.f.book.encyclopaedia-of-islam-2&s.q=al-%E1%BA%92%C4%81hir+wa%E2%80%99l-B%C4%81%E1%B9%ADin (print version: vol. 11, Leiden: Brill, 2002).

Pototschnig, Franz. "Priester." In *Lexikon des Mittelalters*, 7: 204. 9 vols. Munich: Artemis, 1995.

Poulhol, Pascal, and Isabelle Cochelin. "La rehabilitation de l'eunuque dans l'hagiographie antique (Iie–VIe siècles)." In *Memoriam Sanctorum Venerantes: Miscellanea in onore de Monsignor Victor Saxer*, 49–73. Vatican City: Pontificio Istituto di archeologia cristiana, 1992.

Powell, Avril A. "Indian Muslim Modernists and the Issue of Slavery in Islam." In *Slavery & South Asian History*, edited by Indrani Chatterjee and Richard M. Eaton, 262–286. Bloomington: Indiana University Press, 2006.

Powers, David S. "Adoption." In *Encyclopaedia of Islam*, 3rd ed., online version (2007). Accessed December 1, 2016, http://referenceworks.brillonline.com/entries/

encyclopaedia-of-islam-3/adoption-SIM_0304?s.num=0&s.f.s2_parent=s.f.cluster.Encyclopaedia+of+Islam&s.q=Adoption.

Preiser-Kapeller, Johannes. *Der Episkopat im späten Byzanz. Ein Verzeichnis der Metropoliten und Bischöfe des Patriarchats von Konstantinopel in der Zeit von 1204 bis 1453*. Saarbrücken: Verlag Dr. Müller, 2008.

Prudlo, Donald S., ed. *The Origin, Development, and Refinement of Medieval Religious Mendicancies*. Leiden: Brill, 2012.

Purkis, William J. "Crusading and Crusade Memory in Caesarius of Heisterbach's *Dialogus miraculorum*. " *Journal of Medieval History* 39 (2013): 100–127.

Qureshi, Hamid Afaq. *The Mughals, the English and the Rulers of Awadh From 1722 A.D. to 1856 A.D.* Lucknow: New Royal Book Co., 2003.

Rapp, Claudia. *Holy Bishops in Late Antiquity: The Nature of Christian Leadership in an Age of Transition.* Berkeley: University of California Press, 2004.

Reuter, Astrid. "Charting the Boundaries of the Religious Field: Legal Conflicts over Religion as Struggles over Blurring Borders." *Journal of Religion in Europe* 2, no. 1 (2009): 1–20.

Reuter, Astrid. *Religion in der verrechtlichten Gesellschaft: Rechtskonflikte und öffentliche Kontroversen um Religion als Grenzarbeiten am religiösen Feld.* Göttingen: Vandenhoeck & Ruprecht, 2014.

Reuter, Timothy. "Episcopi cum sua militia: The Prelate as Warrior in the Early Staufer Era." In *Warriors and Churchmen in the High Middle Ages: Essays Presented to Karl Leyser*, edited by Timothy Reuter, 79–94. London: Hambledon Press, 1992.

Reuter, Timothy. "Ein Europa der Bischöfe: Das Zeitalter Burchards von Worms." In *Bischof Burchard von Worms 1000–1025*, edited by Wilfried Hartmann, 1–28. Mainz: Gesellschaft für mittelrheinische Kirchengeschichte, 2000. Translated into English as "A Europe of Bishops: The Age of Wulfstan of York and Burchard of Worms." In *Patterns of Episcopal Power: Bishops in Tenth and Eleventh Century Western Europe*, edited by Ludger Körntgen and Dominik Waßenhoven, 17–38. Berlin: De Gruyter, 2011.

Reuter, Timothy. "Gifts and Simony." In *Medieval Transformations: Texts, Power, and Gifts in Context*, edited by Esther Cohen and Mayke de Jong, 157–168. Leiden: Brill, 2001.

Reynolds, Roger E. "The Subdiaconate as a Sacred and Superior Order." In *Clerics in the Early Middle Ages: Hierarchy and Image*, 1–39. Variorum Collected Studies 669. Aldershot: Ashgate, 1999.

Van Rhijn, Carine. *Shepherds of the Lord: Priests and Episcopal Statutes in the Carolingian Period.* Turnhout: Brepols, 2007.

Riché, Pierre. *Education and Culture in the Barbarian West: From the Sixth Through the Eighth Century.* Translated by John J. Contreni. Columbia: University of South Carolina Press, 1976 [or. ed. 1962].

Rideout, John Kennedy. "The Rise of the Eunuchs during the T'ang Dynasty: Part One (618–705)." *Asia Major,* New Series 1 (1949–1950): 53–72.

Rideout, John Kennedy. "The Rise of Eunuchs during the T'ang Dynasty: Part II." *Asia Major,* New Series 3 (1952): 42–58.

Ringrose, Kathryn M. *The Perfect Servant: Eunuchs and the Social Construction of Gender in Byzantium.* Chicago: University of Chicago Press, 2003.

Rio, Alice. *Legal Practice and the Written Word in the Early Middle Ages: Frankish Formulae, c. 500–1000.* Cambridge: Cambridge University Press, 2009.

Roberts, Edward. "Flodoard of Rheims and the Tenth Century." PhD diss. University of St Andrews, 2013.
Roberts, Edward. "Flodoard, the Will of St Remigius and the See of Reims in the Tenth Century." *Early Medieval Europe* 22, no. 2 (2014): 201–230.
Robinson, James Harvey. *Readings in European History.* Boston: Ginn, 1905.
Rolker, Christof. "The Two Laws and the Three Sexes: Ambiguous Bodies in Canon Law and Roman Law (12th to 16th Centuries)." *Zeitschrift der Savigny-Stiftung für Rechtsgeschichte. Kanonistische Abteilung* 100 (2014): 178–222.
Roller, Lynn E. "The Ideology of the Eunuch Priest." In *Gender and the Body in the Ancient Mediterranean*, edited by Maria Wyke, 118–135. Oxford: J. C. Gieben, 1998.
Roscoe, Will. "Priests of the Goddess: Gender Transgression in Ancient Religion." *History of Religions* 35 (1996): 195–230.
Rosenthal, Franz. "Ar-Rāzī on the Hidden Illness." *Bulletin of the History of Medicine* 52, no. 1 (1978): 45–60.
Rubin, Miri. *Charity and Community in Medieval Cambridge.* Cambridge: Cambridge University Press, 1987.
Ruggiu, François-Joseph, ed. *The Uses of First Person Writings: Africa, America, Asia, Europe.* Comparatism and Society 25. Brussels: PIE Peter Lang, 2013.
Rumble, Alexander R. "From Winchester to Canterbury: Ælfheah and Stigand – Bishops, Archbishops and Victims." In *Leaders of the Anglo-Saxon Church from Bede to Stigand*, edited by Alexander R. Rumble, 165–182. Woodbridge: Boydell & Brewer 2012.
Runciman, Steven. *The Emperor Romanus Lecapenus and His Reign: A Study of Tenth-Century Byzantium.* Cambridge: Cambridge University Press, 1st ed. 1929, repr. 1963.
Rydén, Lennart. "The Portrait of the Arab Samonas in Byzantine Literature." *Graeco-Arabica* 3 (1984): 101–108.
Sabapathy, John. *Officers and Accountability in Medieval England 1170–1300.* Oxford: Oxford University Press, 2014.
Sachsenmaier, Dominic. *Global Perspectives on Global History: Theories and Approaches in a Connected World.* Cambridge: Cambridge University Press, 2011.
Salimbeniana. Atti del convegno per il VII centenario di Fra Salimbene, Parma 1987–1989. Bologna: Radio Tau, 1991.
Salisbury, Joyce E. "Gendered Sexuality." In *Handbook of Medieval Sexuality*, edited by Vern L. Bullough and James A. Brundage, 81–102. New York, London: Garland Publishing, 1996.
Sanders, Gabriel. "Kybele und Attis." In *Die orientalischen Religionen im Römerreich*, edited by Maarten Vermaseren, 264–297. Leiden: Brill, 1981.
Sanders, Paula. "Gendering the Ungendered Body: Hermaphrodites in Medieval Islamic Law." In *Women in Middle Eastern History. Shifting Boundaries in Sex and Gender*, edited by Nikki R. Keddie and Beth Baron, 74–95. New Haven: Yale University Press, 1991.
Sanders, Paula. *Ritual, Politics, and the City in Fatimid Cairo.* Albany: State University of New York Press, 1994.
Sauer, Michelle M. *Gender in Medieval Culture.* London, New York: Bloomsbury, 2015.
Saxer, Victor. "Die kirchliche Organisation im 3. Jahrhundert." In *Das Entstehen der einen Christenheit (250–430*, vol. 2 of *Geschichte des Christentums*, edited by Charles and Luce Piétri, 23–54. Freiburg: Herder, 1996.

Schäbler, Birgit, ed. *Area Studies und die Welt: Weltregionen und neue Globalgeschichte*. Vienna: Mandelbaum Verlag, 2007.

Schacht, Joseph. *An Introduction to Islamic Law*. Oxford: Clarendon Press, 1964.

Scheibelreiter, Georg. *Der Bischof in merowingischer Zeit*. Vienna: Böhlau, 1983.

Schlinkert, Dirk. "Der Hofeunuch in der Spätantike: Ein gefährlicher Aussenseiter?" *Hermes: Zeitschrift für klassische Philologie* 122 (1994): 342–359.

Schlotheuber, Eva. "'Nullum regimen difficilius et periculosius est regimine feminarum.' Die Begegnung des Beichtvaters Frederik van Heilo mit den Nonnen in der Devotio Moderna." In *Spätmittelalterliche Frömmigkeit zwischen Ideal und Praxis*, edited by Berndt Hamm and Thomas Lentes, 45–84. Tübingen: Mohr Siebeck, 2001.

Schlumberger, Gustave Léon. *Un empereur byzantine au dixième siècle, Nicéphore Phocas*. Paris: Firmin-Didot, 1890.

Schmidt, Paul Gerhard. "Die misogyne Tradition von der Antike bis ins Frühmittelalter." In *Comportamenti e immaginario della sessualità nell'alto medioevo*, 419–432. Settimane di studi sull'alto medioevo 53. Spoleto: Centro Italiano di Studi sull'Alto Medioevo, 2006.

Schmidt-Glintzer, Helwig. "The Scholar-Official and His Community: The Character of the Aristocracy in Medieval China." Translated by Thomas Jansen. *Early Medieval China* 1 (1994): 60–83.

Schneider, Olaf. *Erzbischof Hinkmar und die Folgen: der vierhundertjährige Weg historischer Erinnerungsbilder von Reims nach Trier*. Berlin: De Gruyter, 2010.

Scholten, Helga. *Der Eunuch in Kaisernähe: Zur politischen und sozialen Bedeutung des praepositus sacri cubiculi im 4. und 5. Jahrhundert n. Chr.* Frankfurt: Peter Lang, 1995.

Scholz, Piotr O. *Der entmannte Eros: Eine Kulturgeschichte der Eunuchen und Kastraten*. Düsseldorf, Zürich: Artemis & Winkler, 1997.

Schottenhammer, Angela. "Einige Überlegungen zur Entstehung von Grabinschriften." In *Auf den Spuren des Jenseits: Chinesische Grabkultur in den Facetten von Wirklichkeit, Geschichte und Totenkult*, edited by Angela Schottenhammer, 21–60. Frankfurt: Peter Lang, 2003.

Schrörs, Heinrich. *Hinkmar, Erzbischof von Reims. Sein Leben und seine Schriften*. Freiburg im Breisgau: Herder, 1884.

Schulz, Knut. "Das Wormser Hofrecht Bischof Burchards." In *Bischof Burchard von Worms 1000–1025*, edited by Wilfried Hartmann, 251–278. Quellen und Abhandlungen zur mittelrheinischen Geschichte 100. Mainz: Gesellschaft für mittelrheinische Kirchengeschichte, 2000.

Schürer, Markus. *Das Exemplum oder die erzählte Institution. Studien zum Beispielgebrauch bei den Franziskanern und Dominikanern des 13. Jahrhunderts*. Vita Regularis. Ordnungen und Deutungen religiosen Lebens im Mittelalter 23. Berlin: LIT, 2005.

Schweckendick, Helga. *Claudians Invektive gegen Eutrop (In Eutropium): Ein Kommentar*. Hildesheim: Olms-Weidmann, 1992.

Scott, Joan W. "Gender: A Useful Category of Historical Analysis." *American Historical Review* 91 (1986): 1053–1075.

Sellheim, Rudolf. "al- Khaṭīb al- Baghdādī." In *Encyclopaedia of Islam*, 2nd ed., online version. Accessed December 1, 2016, http://referenceworks.brillonline.com/entries/encyclopaedia-of-islam-2/al-khatib-al-baghdadi-SIM_4235 (print version: vol. 4, Leiden: Brill, 1978).

Serjeant, Robert Bertram. "Haram and Hawtah, the Sacred Enclave in Arabia." In *Mélanges Taha Husain*, edited by 'Abd al-Raḥmān Badawī. Cairo: Dār al Ma'ārif, 1962. Reprinted in Francis E. Peters, ed., *The Arabs and Arabia on the Eve of Islam*, 167–184. Aldershot: Asghate, 2010.

Serper, Arié. "L'influence de Guillaume de Saint-Amour sur Rutebeuf." *Romance Philology* 17 (1963): 391–402.

Sewell, William. "Marc Bloch and the Logic of Comparative History." *History and Theory* 6 (1967): 208–218.

Sharpe, Richard. "The Use of Writs in the Eleventh Century." *Anglo-Saxon England* 32 (2003): 247–291.

Sickert, Ramona. "Qui toz art dou feu de luxure. Zur Tradition der Keuschheitsvorstellungen und zum Vorwurf der Unkeuschheit gegenüber Franziskanern und Dominikanern in der Dichtung des 13. Jahrhunderts." In *Studia Monastica. Beiträge zum klösterlichen Leben im christlichen Abendland während des Mittelalters*, edited by Reinhardt Butz and Jörg Oberste, 303–323. Vita Regularis. Ordnungen und Deutungen religiosen Lebens im Mittelalter 22. Münster: LIT, 2004.

Sickert, Ramona. *Wenn Klosterbrüder zu Jahrmarktsbrüdern werden: Studien zur Wahrnehmung der Franziskaner und Dominikaner im 13. Jahrhundert*. Vita Regularis. Ordnungen und Deutungen religiosen Lebens im Mittelalter 28. Berlin: LIT, 2006.

Sidéris, Georges. "'Eunuchs of Light': Power, Imperial Ceremonial and Positive Representations of Eunuchs in Byzantium (4th–12th Centuries AD)." In *Eunuchs in Antiquity and Beyond*, edited by Shaun Tougher, 161–175. London: Classical Press of Wales and Duckworth, 2002.

Signes Codoñer, Juan. "The Corpus of Leo's Novels. Some Suggestions Concerning Their Date and Promulgation." *Subseciva Groningana* 8 (2009): 1–33.

Signes Codoñer, Juan. "Las Novelas de León el Sabio." In *Introduzione al diritto bizantino. Da Giustiniano ai Basilici*, edited by Jan H. A. Lokin and Bernard H. Stolte, 267–321. Pavia: IUSS Press, 2011.

Silvestri, Angelo. *Power, Politics and Episcopal Authority: The Bishops of Cremona and Lincoln in the Middle Ages (1066–1340)*. Cambridge: Cambridge Scholars Publishing, 2015.

Skaff, Jonathan Karam. *Sui-Tang China and Its Neighbors: Culture, Power, and Connections 580–800*. Oxford: Oxford University Press, 2012.

Smirnova, Victoria. "'And nothing will be wasted': Actualization of the Past in Caesarius of Heisterbach's *Dialogus Miraculorum*." In *The Making of Memory in the Middle Ages*, edited by Lucie Doležalová, 253–265. Leiden: Brill, 2010.

Smith, Julia M.H. *Europe after Rome: A New Cultural History 500–1000*. Oxford: Oxford University Press, 2005.

Smith, Julia M.H. "Une société de ville capitale: Les eunuques dans la Constantinople byzantine (Ive–XIIe siècle)." In *Les villes capitales au moyen âge*, edited by the Société des historiens médiévistes de l'enseignement public, 243–274. Paris: Publications de la Sorbonne, 2006.

Smith, Katherine Allen, and Scott Wells, eds. *Negotiating Community and Difference in Medieval Europe: Gender, Power, Patronage and the Authority of Religion in Latin Christendom*. Leiden: Brill, 2009.

Smith, Katherine Allen. *War and the Making of Medieval Monastic Culture*. Woodbridge: Boydell and Brewer, 2011.

Snowden Jr., Frank M. *Blacks in Antiquity: Ethiopians in the Greco-Roman Experience*. Cambridge: The Belknap Press of Harvard University Press, 1970.

Sot, Michel. *Gesta episcoporum, gesta abbatum*. Typologie des sources du Moyen Âge occidental 37. Turnhout: Brepols, 1981.

Sourdel, Dominique. "Hilāl b. al-Muḥassin b. Ibrāhīm al- Ṣābiʾ." In *Encyclopaedia of Islam*, 2nd ed, online version. Accessed December 1, 2016. http://referenceworks.brillonline.com/entries/encyclopaedia-of-islam-2/hilal-b-al-muhassin-b-ibrahim-al-sabi-SIM_2862 (print version: vol. 3, Leiden: Brill, 1971).

Spear, David. *The Personnel of the Norman Cathedrals during the Ducal Period, 911–1204*. London: Institute of Historical Research, 2006.

Spengler, Oswald. *Der Untergang des Abendlandes: Umrisse einer Morphologie der Weltgeschichte*. 2 vols. Munich: Beck, 1922–1923.

Sreenivas, Mytheli. *Wives, Widows, and Concubines: The Conjugal Family Ideal in Colonial India*. Bloomington: Indiana University Press, 2008.

Sreenivasan, Ramya. "Drudges, Dancing Girls, Concubines: Female Slaves in Rajput Polity, 1500–1850." In *Slavery & South Asian History*, edited by Indrani Chatterjee and Richard M. Eaton, 136–161. Bloomington: Indiana University Press, 2006.

Stauffer, Hermann. "Art. Polemik." In *Historisches Wörterbuch der Rhetorik*, 6: col. 1403–1415. Tübingen: Max Niemeyer, 2003.

Steckel, Sita. "Professoren in Weltuntergangsstimmung. Religiöse Debatte und städtische Öffentlichkeit im Pariser Bettelordensstreit, 1252–1257." In *Pluralität – Konkurrenz – Konflikt. Religiöse Spannungen im städtischen Raum der Vormoderne*, edited by Jörg Oberste, 51–74. Forum Mittelalter Studien 8. Regensburg: Schnell & Steiner, 2013.

Steckel, Sita. "Ein brennendes Feuer in meiner Brust. Prophetische Autorschaft und polemische Autorisierungsstrategien Guillaumes de Saint-Amour im Pariser Bettelordensstreit (1256)." In *Prophetie und Autorschaft: Charisma, Heilsversprechen und Gefährdung*, edited by Christel Meier and Martina Wagner-Egelhaaf, 129–168. Berlin: de Gruyter, 2014.

Stehkämper, Hugo. "Über das Motiv der Thronstreit-Entscheidungen des Kölner Erzbischofs Adolf von Altena 1198–1205: Freiheit der fürstlichen Königswahl oder Aneignung des Mainzer Erstkurrechts?" *Rheinische Vierteljahrsblätter* 67 (2003): 1–20.

Steingass, Francis Joseph. *A Comprehensive Persian–English dictionary, Including the Arabic words and Phrases to be met with in Persian Literature*. London: Routledge & K. Paul, 1892.

Stevenson, Walter. "Eunuchs and Early Christianity." In *Eunuchs in Antiquity and Beyond*, edited by Shaun Tougher, 123–142. London: Classical Press of Wales and Duckworth, 2002.

Stone, Rachel. *Morality and Masculinity in the Carolingian Empire*. Cambridge: Cambridge University Press, 2011.

Stone, Rachel. "Gender and Hierarchy: Archbishop Hincmar of Rheims (845–882) as a Religious Man." In *Religious Men and Masculine Identity in the Middle Ages*, edited by Patricia H. Cullum and Katherine J. Lewis, 28–45. Woodbridge: Boydell and Brewer, 2013.

Stone, Rachel, and Charles West, eds. *Hincmar of Rheims: Life and Work*. Manchester: Manchester University Press, 2015.

Störmer, Wilhelm. *Früher Adel: Studien zur politischen Führungsschicht im fränkischen-deutschen Reich vom 8. bis 11. Jahrhundert.* Stuttgart: Hiersemann, 1973.

Stratmann, Martina. *Hinkmar von Reims als Verwalter von Bistum und Kirchenprovinz.* Sigmaringen: Thorbecke, 1991.

Swanson, Robert N. "Angels Incarnate. Clergy and Masculinity from Gregorian Reform to Reformation." In *Masculinity in Medieval Europe*, edited by Dawn M. Hadley, 160–177. London, New York: Longman, 1999.

Szittya, Penn R. *The Antifraternal Tradition in Medieval Literature.* Princeton: Princeton University Press, 1986.

Tackett, Nicolas. *The Destruction of the Medieval Chinese Aristocracy.* Cambridge: Harvard University Asia Center, 2014.

Tackett, Nicolas. *Tang Wudai renwu zhuanji yu shehui wangluo ziliaoku.* Prosopographic and Social Network Database of the Tang and Five Dynasties, version 1.0, tbdb010.mdb. Accessed July 17, 2015, http://history.berkeley.edu/people/nicolas-tackett.

Takase Natsuko. "'Tō Ri Hosō boshi' shakudoku." *Meidai Ajia shi ronshū* 13 (2009): 211–223.

Talbot, Alice-Mary, and Denis F. Sullivan. *The History of Leo the Deacon: Byzantine Military Expansion in the Tenth Century.* Washington DC: Dumbarton Oaks, 2005.

Tamrat, Taddesse. *Church and State in Ethiopia, 1270–1527.* Oxford: Clarendon Press, 1972.

Tang Changru. "Tangdai huanguan jiguan yu nankou jinxian." in *Tang Changru wenji* 8: *Shanju cungao xubian*, 359–366. Beijing: Zhonghua Shuju, 2011.

Tang Yijie. "Gongde shi kao – du *Zizhi tongjian* zhaji." *Wenxian* 2 (1985): 60–65.

Tani, Yutaka. "Two Types of Human Interventions into Sheep Flock: Intervention into the Mother–Offspring Relationship, and Raising the Flock Leader." In *Domesticated Plants and Animals of the Southwest Eurasian Agro-Pastoral Culture Complex*, edited by Yutaka Tani and Sadao Sakamoto, 1–42. Kyoto: The Research Institute for Humanistic Studies, Kyoto University, 1986.

Tanındı, Zeren. "Topkapı Sarayı'nın Ağaları ve Kitaplar." *Uludağ Üniversitesi Fen-Edebiyat Fakültesi Sosyal Bilimler Dergisi* 3, no. 3 (2002): 41–66.

Taparia, Swapna. "Emasculated Bodies of Hijras: Sites of Imposed, Resisted and Negotiated Identities." *Indian Journal of Gender Studies* 18, no. 2 (2011): 167–184.

Thibodeaux, Jennifer D. "Man of the Church, or Man of the Village? Gender and the Parish Clergy in Medieval Normandy." *Gender & History* 18, no. 2 (2006): 380–399.

Thibodeaux, Jennifer D., ed. *Negotiating Clerical Identities: Priests, Monks and Masculinity in the Middle Ages.* Basingstoke and New York: Palgrave Macmillan, 2010.

Thibodeaux, Jennifer D. "From Boys to Priests: Adolescence, Masculinity and the Parish Clergy in Medieval Normandy." In *Negotiating Clerical Identities: Priests, Monks and Masculinity in the Middle Ages*, edited by Jennifer D. Thibodeaux, 136–158. Basingstoke: Palgrave Macmillan, 2010.

Thibodeaux, Jennifer D. "The Defence of Clerical Marriage: Religious Identity and Masculinity in the Writings of Anglo-Norman Clerics." In *Religious Men and Masculine Identity in the Middle Ages*, edited by Patricia Cullum and Katherine J. Lewis, 46–63. Woodbridge: Boydell and Brewer, 2013.

Thibodeaux, Jennifer D. *The Manly Priest: Clerical Celibacy, Masculinity, and Reform in England and Normandy, 1066–1300*. Philadelphia: University of Pennsylvania Press, 2015.

Thomas, A. H., ed. *De oudste constituties van den dominicanen. Voorgeschiedenis, tekst, bronnen, ontstaan en ontwikkeling (1215–1237)*. Bibliothèque de la Revue d'histoire ecclésiastique 42. Leuven: Bureel van de R.H.E., 1965.

Thomas, Hugh M. *The Secular Clergy in England, 1066–1216*. Oxford: Oxford University Press, 2014.

Tobias, Norman. *Basil I, Founder of the Macedonian Dynasty: A Study of the Political and Military History of the Byzantine Empire in the Ninth Century*. Lampeter: The Edwin Mellen Press, 2007.

Tollerton, Linda. *Wills and Will-Making in Anglo-Saxon England*. Woodbridge: Boydell & Brewer, 2011.

van der Toorn, Karen. "Female Prostitution in Payment of Vows in Ancient Israel." *Journal of Biblical Literature* 108 (1989): 193–205.

Török, László. *The Kingdom of Kush: Handbook of the Napatan-Meroitic Civilization*. Leiden: Brill, 1997.

Toru, Miura, and John Edwards Philips, eds. *Slave Elites in the Middle East and Africa*. London and New York: Kegan Paul International, 2000.

Tosh, John. *Manliness and Masculinities in Nineteenth-Century Britain: Essays on Gender, Family and Empire*. London: Pearson Longman, 2005.

Tougher, Shaun. "Byzantine Eunuchs: An Overview, with Special Reference to Their Creation and Origin." In *Women, Men and Eunuchs: Gender in Byzantium*, edited by Liz James, 168–184. London: Routledge, 1997.

Tougher, Shaun. *The Reign of Leo VI (886–912): Politics and People*. Leiden: Brill, 1997.

Tougher, Shaun. "Ammianus and the Eunuchs." In *The Late Roman World and Its Historian: Interpreting Ammianus Marcellinus*, edited by Jan Willem Drijvers and David Hunt, 64–73. London: Routledge, 1999.

Tougher, Shaun. "Images of Effeminate Men: The Case of Byzantine Eunuchs." In *Masculinity in Medieval Europe*, edited by Dawn M. Hadley, 89–100. London, New York: Longman, 1999.

Tougher, Shaun, ed., *Eunuchs in Antiquity and Beyond*. London: Classical Press of Wales and Duckworth, 2002.

Tougher, Shaun. "Holy Eunuchs! Masculinity and Eunuch Saints in Byzantium." In *Holiness and Masculinity in the Middle Ages*, edited by Patricia H. Cullum and Katherine J. Lewis, 93–108. Cardiff: University of Wales Press, 2004.

Tougher, Shaun. "Social Transformation, Gender Transformation? The Court Eunuch, 300–900." In *Gender in the Early Medieval World: East and West, 300–900*, edited by Leslie Brubaker and Julia M. H. Smith, 70–82. Cambridge: Cambridge University Press, 2004.

Tougher, Shaun. "In or Out? Origins of Court Eunuchs." In *Eunuchs in Antiquity and Beyond*, edited by Shaun Tougher, 143–161. London: Routledge, 2008.

Tougher, Shaun. *The Eunuch in Byzantine History and Society*. London: Routledge, 2008.

Tougher, Shaun. "Cherchez l'homme! Byzantine Men: A Eunuch Perspective." In *The Byzantine World*, edited by Paul Stephenson, 83–91. London: Routledge, 2010.

Tougher, Shaun. "Imperial Families: The Case of the Macedonians (867–1056)." In *Approaches to the Byzantine Family*, edited by Leslie Brubaker and Shaun Tougher, 303–326. Farnham: Ashgate, 2013.

Toynbee, Arnold. *A Study of History*. 10 vols. Oxford: Oxford University Press, 1934–1979.

Toynbee, Arnold. *Constantine Porphyrogenitus and His World*. Oxford: Oxford University Press, 1973.

Tracy, Charles, and Andrew Budge. *British Medieval Episcopal Thrones*. Oxford: Oxbow Books, 2015.

Trampedach, Kai. "Kaiserwechsel und Krönungsritual im Konstantinopel des 5. bis 6. Jahrhunderts." In *Investitur- und Krönungsrituale: Herrschaftseinsetzungen im kulturellen Vergleich*, edited by Marion Steinicke and Stefan Weinfurter, 275–290. Cologne: Böhlau, 2005.

Traver, Andrew G., ed. "William of Saint-Amour's Two Disputed Questions *De Quantitate Eleemosynae* and *De Valido Mendicante*." *Archives d'histoire Doctrinale et Littéraire Du Moyen Âge* 62 (1995): 295–342.

Traver, Andrew G. "Rewriting History? The Parisian Secular Masters' Apologia of 1254." *History of Universities* 15 (1999): 9–45.

Traver, Andrew G., ed. *The Opuscula of William of Saint-Amour: The Minor Works of 1255–1256*. Beiträge zur Geschichte der Philosophie und Theologie des Mittelalters N.F. 63. Münster: Aschendorff, 2003.

Traver, Andrew G. "The Forging of an Intellectual Defense of Mendicancy in the Medieval University." In *The Origin, Development, and Refinement of Medieval Religious Mendicancies*, edited by Donald S. Prudlo, 157–196. Leiden: Brill, 2012.

Trimingham, J. Spencer. *Islam in Ethiopia*. London: Frank Cass, 1965.

Ts'ai, Shih-shan Henry. *The Eunuchs in the Ming Dynasty*. Albany: State University of New York Press, 1996.

Ts'en Chung-mien. "The T'ang System of Bureaucratic Titles and Grades." Translated by Penelope Ann Herbert. *T'ang Studies* 5 (1987): 25–31.

Tuchel, Susan. *Kastration im Mittelalter*. Düsseldorf: Droste, 1998.

Tucker, Judith. *Women, Family and Gender in Islamic Law*. Cambridge: Cambridge University Press, 2008.

Twitchett, Denis C. *Financial Administration under the T'ang Dynasty*. 2nd ed. Cambridge: Cambridge University Press, 1970.

Twitchett, Denis C. *The Birth of the Chinese Meritocracy: Bureaucrats and Examination in T'ang China*. London: The China Society, 1976.

Twitchett, Denis C. "Varied Patterns of Provincial Autonomy in the T'ang Dynasty." In *Essays on T'ang Society: The Interplay of Social, Political, and Economic Forces*, edited by John Curtis Perry and Bardwell L. Smith, 90–109. Leiden: Brill, 1976.

Tyler, Jeffrey J. *Lord of the Sacred City: The Episcopus Exclusus in Late Medieval and Early Modern Germany*. Leiden: Brill, 1999.

Uzunçarşılı, İsmail Hakkı. "Gāzī Orhan Bey Vaḳfīyesi." *Belleten* 5 (1941): 277–288.

Van Dam, Raymond. "Merovingian Gaul and the Frankish conquest." In *The New Cambridge Medieval History 1: c.500–c.700*, edited by Paul Fouracre, 193–231. Cambridge: Cambridge of University Press, 2005.

Van Dam, Raymond. "Bishops and society." In *Constantine to c. 600*, vol. 2 of *The Cambridge History of Christianity*, edited by Augustine Casiday and Frederick W. Norris, 343–366. Cambridge: Cambridge University Press, 2007.

Vauchez, André. *Sainthood in the Late Middle Ages*. Cambridge: Cambridge University Press, 1997.

Veccia Vaglieri, Laura. "Ghadīr Khumm." In *Encyclopaedia of Islam*, 2nd ed, online version. Accessed December 1, 2016, http://referenceworks.brillonline.com/

entries/encyclopaedia-of-islam-2/ghadir-khumm-SIM_2439?s.num=0&s.f.s2_parent=s.f.book.encyclopaedia-of-islam-2&s.q=ghadir+khumm.

Verger, Jacques. "Coacta ac periculosa societas. La difficile intégration des réguliers à l'Université de Paris au XIIIe siècle." In *Vivre en société au Moyen Âge: Occident Chrétien VIe–XVe siècle*, edited by Claude Carozzi, Daniel Le Blévec and Huguette Taviani-Carozzi, 261–280. Aix-en-Provence: Publications de l'Université de Provence, 2008.

Vleeschouwers-Van Melkebeek, Monique. "Mandatory Celibacy and Priestly Ministry in the Diocese of Tournai at the End of the Middle Ages." In *Peasants and Townsmen in Medieval Europe: Studia in Honorem Adriaan Verhulst*, edited by Jean-Marie Duvosquel and Erik Thoen, 681–692. Ghent: Snoeck-Ducaju and Zoon, 1995.

Vogt, Albert. *Basile Ier, Empereur de Byzance (867–886) et la civilisation byzantine à la fin du IXe siècle*. Paris: A. Picard et fils, 1908.

Von Franz, Rainer. *Die chinesische Innengrabinschrift für Beamte und Privatiers des 7. Jahrhunderts*. Stuttgart: Steiner, 1996.

Vykoukal, Ernest. "Les examens du clergé paroissial à l'époque carolingienne." *Revue d'histoire ecclésiastique* 14 (1913): 81–96.

Wagner, Fritz. "Studien zu Caesarius von Heisterbach." *Analecta Cisterciensia* 29 (1973): 79–95.

Walker, Paul P. *Exploring an Islamic Empire: Fatimid History and Its Sources*. London, New York: I. B. Tauris, 2002.

Wallerstein, Immanuel. *The Modern World-System*. Vols 1–3: New York, London, San Diego: Academic Press, 1974–1989; vol. 4: Berkeley: University of California Press, 2011.

Wang Jilin. "Tangdai de shuofang jun yu shence jun." *Di yi jie guoji Tangdai xueshu huiyi lunwenji* (1989): 914–922.

Wang Ming-yu. "The Involvement in Recurrent Power Struggles of the Han, T'ang, and Ming Eunuchs." Ph.D. diss. St. John's University New York, 1974.

Wang Shoudong. "Lun Tang zhonghouqi nanya dui beisi de yifu." *Ha'erbin Xueyuan xuebao* 24, no. 9 (2003): 102–105.

Wang Shoudong. "Tangdai 'quanyan si gui' kao xi." *Qiusuo* 9 (2007): 204–206.

Wang Shoudong. "Tangdai shence jun zhongwei kao." *Dezhou Xueyuan xuebao* 19 (2003): 65–68.

Wang Shounan. *Tangdai huanguan quanshi zhi yanjiu*. Taibei: Zhengwu Shuju, 1971. Reprinted as *Tangdai de huanguan*. Taibei: Taiwan Shangwu Yinshuguan, 2004.

Weber, Max. *Wirtschaft und Gesellschaft: Grundriß der verstehenden Soziologie*. Edited by Johannes Winckelmann. Tübingen: Mohr, 1972.

Weiler, Björn. "The *Rex renitens* and the Medieval Idea of Kingship, ca. 900–ca. 1250." *Viator* 31 (2000): 1–42.

Weiler, Björn. *Kingship, Rebellion and Political Culture: England and Germany, c. 1215–c. 1250*. New York: Palgrave MacMillan, 2011.

Weiler, Björn. "Bishops and Kings in England, c. 1066–c. 1215." In *Religion und Politik im Mittelalter / Religion and Politics in the Middle Ages*, edited by Ludger Körntgen and Dominik Waßenhoven, 157–203. Berlin: de Gruyter, 2013.

Weinstein, Stanley. *Buddhism under the T'ang*. Cambridge: Cambridge University Press, 1987.

Wendehorst, Alfred. *Das Bistum Würzburg, 1: Die Bischofsreihe bis 1254*. Germania Sacra Neue Folge 1. Berlin: De Gruyter, 1962.

Werner, Michael, and Bénédicte Zimmermann. "Beyond Comparison: *Histoire croisée* and the Challenge of Reflexivity." *History and Theory* 45 (2006): 30–50.

West, Charles. *Reframing the Feudal Revolution: Political and Social Transformation Between Marne and Moselle, c. 800–c. 1100*. Cambridge: Cambridge University Press, 2013.

West, Charles. "Lordship in Ninth-Century Francia: The Case of Bishop Hincmar of Laon and his Followers." *Past and Present* 226 (2015): 3–40.

Westenholz, Joan. "Tamar, *Qĕdēšā, Qadištu*, and Sacred Prostitution in Mesopotamia." *Harvard Theological Review* 82 (1989): 245–266.

Wickham, Chris. *Framing the Early Middle Ages: Europe and the Mediterranean, 400–800*. Oxford: Oxford University Press, 2005.

Wittfogel, Karl August. *Oriental Despotism: A Comparative Study of Total Power*. New Haven: Yale University Press, 1957.

Wood, Ian. *The Merovingian Kingdoms, 450–751*. London: Longman, 1994.

Wood, Susan. *The Proprietary Church in the Medieval West*. Oxford: Oxford University Press, 2006.

Woodhead, Linda. "Gender Differences in Religious Practice and Significance." In *The Sage Handbook of the Sociology of Religion*, edited by James A. Beckford and N. Jay Demerath, 570–575. Los Angeles: SAGE, 2007.

Wormald, Patrick. "The Strange Affair of the Selsey Bishopric, 953–963." In *Belief and Culture in the Middle Ages: Studies Presented to Henry Mayr-Harting*, edited by Richard Gameson and Henrietta Leyser, 128–141. Oxford: Oxford University Press, 2001.

Wormald, Patrick. "Archbishop Wulfstan: Eleventh-Century State-Builder." In *Wulfstan, Archbishop of York*, edited by Matthew Townend, 9–27. Turnhout: Brepols, 2004.

Wünsch, Thomas. "Der heilige Bischof. Zur politischen Dimension von Heiligkeit im Mittelalter und ihrem Wandel." *Archiv für Kulturgeschichte* 82 (2000): 261–302.

Xing Tie. *Tang Song fenjia zhidu*. Beijing: Shangwu Yinshuguan, 2010.

Yan Yaozhong. "Tangdai zhonghouqi neishisheng guanyuan shenfen zhiyi." *Shilin* 5 (2004): 77–81.

Yano Chikara. "Tōdai ni okeru karikosei no hatten ni tsuite." *Nishi Nihon shigaku* 6 (1951): 86–97.

Yano Chikara. "Tōdai kangan kensei kakutoku inyu kō." *Shigaku zasshi* 63 (1954): 920–934.

Yarrow, Simon. "Prince Bohemond, Princess Melaz, and the Gendering of Religious Difference in the *Ecclesiastical History* of Orderic Vitalis." In *Intersections of Gender, Religion and Ethnicity in the Middle Ages*, edited by Cordelia Beattie and Kirsten A. Fenton, 140–157. London: Palgrave MacMillan, 2010.

Young, Spencer E. "More Blessed to Give and Receive: Charitable Giving in Thirteenth- and Early Fourteenth-Century *Exempla*. " In *Experiences of Charity, 1250–1650*, edited by Anne M. Scott, 63–78. Farnham: Ashgate, 2015.

Yuan Gang. *Sui Tang zhongshu tizhi de fazhan yanbian*. Taibei: Wenjin Chubanshe, 1992.

Yuan Gang. "Tangdai de shumi shi." *Shandong Jiaoyu Xueyuan xuebao* 3 (1994): 68–76.

Ze'evi, Dror. *Producing Desire. Changing Sexual Discourse in the Ottoman Middle East, 1500–1900*. Berkeley, Los Angeles: University of California Press, 2006.

Zhang Guogang. *Tangdai fanzhen yanjiu*. Changsha: Hunan Jiaoyu, 1987.

Zhang Guogang. *Tangdai zhengzhi zhidu yanjiu lunji*. Taibei: Wenjin, 1992.

Zhang Wenbin. "Tangdai huanguan yangzi zhidu tan lüe." *Yunmeng xuekan* 23 (2002): 42–43.

Zhao Mingyi. "Zhongguo gudai jianjun zhidu tantao." *Fuxinggang xuebao* 84 (2005): 105–128.

Zhao Pei. "Chuantong zongfa wenhua yu huanguan yangzi xijue zhi feng." *Langfang shizhuan xuebao* 1 (1994): 16–20.

Zhao Pei. "Han–Tang shiqi de huanguan yangzi yu huanguan shijia." *Dongyue luncong* 26, no. 4 (2005): 116–119.

Zielinski, Herbert. *Der Reichspiskopat in spätottonischer und salischer Zeit (1002–1125)*. Stuttgart: Steiner Franz, 1984.

Index of eunuchs

Page numbers in bold refer to tables

China, Tang-Empire

Cheng Yuanzhen **113**

Dou Wenchang **113**

Gao Lishi **113**

Han Quanhui **113**
Huo Xianming **113**

Jia Mingguan **113**
Ju Wenzhen **113**

Li Fuguo **113**
Liu Jishu **113**
Liu Xixian **113**
Liu Zhenliang **113**
Luo Fengxian **113**

Ma Cunliang **113**

Qiu Shiliang **113**

Tian Lingzi **113**
Tutu Chengcui **113**, 119

Wang Shoucheng **113**

Yang Fugong (d. 894) **113**, 115
Yang Fuguang **113**
Yang Sixu **113**
Yan Zunmei **113**
Yu Chao'en (722–70) 6, 111, **113**, 117, 120

Zhang Yanhong **113**
Zhao Gao (Qin dynasty, d. 207) 118

Islamic empires (without India)

ʿAlī Pasha (Ottoman grand vizier, d. 1511) 15

Barjawān (Fatimid, r. 997–1000) 6

Fulful (Abbasid, tenth c.) 69

Gazanfer Ağa (Ottoman chief eunuch, sixteenth c.) *cover*, 216

Habeşi Mehmed Ağa (Chief harem eunuch, appointed in 1574) 23–4, 216
Hacı Beşir Ağa (Ottoman chief harem eunuch 1717–54) 23–4, 219–23
Hacı Mustafa Ağa (Ottoman chief harem eunuch 1605–20, 1624) 24, 222f

Ismāʿīl Ağa (Ottoman chief eunuch 1621–23) 16
al-Jawdhar (Fatimid, tenth c.) 21–2, 256–7, 262

Jaʿfar (Fatimid, tenth c.) 255–7, 262

Kāfūr (Egypt, r. 946–68) 6
Khādim Süleyman Pāşā (Ottoman, sixteenth c.) 215

Mābūr (seventh c.) 264n38
al-Manṣūr (Fatimid, tenth c.) 256
Māzij al-Khādim (Abbasid, tenth c.) 69
Mufliḥ (Abbasid, tenth c.) 72–5
Muʾnis al-Muẓaffar (Abbasid, d. 933) 6, 29–30, 65, 69, 71, 73–5, 80–90

Muqbil (Ottoman, fourteenth c.) 214
Muṣāḥib Beşir (Ottoman, seventeenth c.) 219

Naḥrīr (Abbasid, tenth c.) 69
Ṣāfī al-Ḥuramī (Abbasid chief eunuch, d. 911) 65, 68, 71–5

Uzun Süleyman Ağa (Ottoman, seventeenth c.) 217

Yusuf Ağa (Ottoman, seventeenth c.) 219

Moghul India (including Awadh)

Almās ʿAlī Khān (d. 1808) 6, 156–61
Ambur (sixteenth c.) 99

Bahār ʿAlī Khān (eighteenth c.) 160–2
Bakhtāwar Khān (seventeenth c.) 168n17
Basant ʿAlī Khān (eighteenth c.) 153
Bashīr al-Dawla (nineteenth c.) 163–4

Dārāb ʿAlī Khān (eighteenth c.) 151, 153
Dianut (nineteenth c.) 164

Fīrūz al-Dawla (nineteenth c.) 163
Ḥājī ʿAlī Sharīf (nineteenth c.) 163

Iʿtimād Khān (sixteenth c.) 99–100

Jawāhir Khān (sixteenth c.) 100–1, 105
Jawāhir ʿAli Khān (eighteenth c.) 151, 155, 160–2

Khwāja Ṭālib/Khidmatgār (eighteenth c.) 105

Nadīm (sixteenth c.) 100–1, 105
Nāẓir al-Dawla (nineteenth c.) 167n17
Niʿamat (sixteenth c.) 99

Phul Mālik (sixteenth c.) 99

Qulī Khān Maḥram, Shāh (sixteenth c.) 101–1

Roman and Byzantine Empire

Antiochus the Praepositus (fifth c.) 186n4

Basil Lekapenos (tenth–eleventh c.) **230**, 231–7

Constantine (eleventh c.) 231
Constantine Gongylios (tenth c.) 237, 239
Constantine the Paphlagonian (tenth c.) **230**, 231–2, 234

Eusebius (fourth c.) **230**, 233
Eutherius (fourth c.) 183
Eutropius (fourth c.) 177, **230**

George (eleventh c.) 231

John the *Orphanotrophos* (d. 1043) 6, **230**, 231–2, 234, 238–9
Joseph Bringas (tenth c.) **230**, 233–6

Melito of Sardis (bishop and eunuch) 189n23

Narses (ca. 490–574) 6, 25, **230**, 233–4
Nikephoritzes (eleventh c.) 239

Orestes (eleventh c.) 239

Peter „Phokas“ (tenth–eleventh c.) **230**, 234, 237, 239

Samonas (9–tenth c.) **230**, 233–4
St Achilleus (late antiquity) 181–2
St Azat (late antiquity) 189n30
St Boethazat (late antiquity) 189n30
St Calocerus (late antiquity) 181
St Dorotheus (late antiquity) 189n30
St Gorgonius (late antiquity) 189n30
St Hyacinthus (late antiquity) 181
St Indes (late antiquity) 189n30
St Nereus (late antiquity) 181–2
St Parthenius (late antiquity) 181
St Peter (late antiquity) 189n30
St Protus (late antiquity) 181
St Tigrius (fifth c.) 184, 189n30

Theophanes (tenth c.) **230**, 233

Index of bishops

Abbo of Auxerre (r. 857–60) 137
Adalard of Ghent (eleventh c.) 55
Adalbero I of Metz (r. 929–62) 50–1
Adalbero II of Metz (r. 984–1005) 50–1
Adalbero (III) of Metz (bishop elect 1005) 51
Adalbero of Verdun (r. 985–8/89) 51
Adalbert I of Mainz (r. 1111–37) 51–2, 54
Adalbert II of Mainz (r. 1138–41) 51, 54
Adaldag of Hamburg-Bremen (r. 937–88) 53
Adolf of Altena (archbishop of Cologne 1193–1205) 194
Adventius of Metz (r. 858–75) 145n52
Ælfsige of Winchester (r. 951–9) 54
Æthelmaer of Elmham (r. 1047–70) 54
Æthelred the Unready (r. 978–1013, 1014–16) 58n26
Æthelwold of Winchester (r. 963–84) 54
Agilberto of Dorchester (r. until 660) 53
Aldric of Le Mans (r. 832–9) 52
Angelelm of Auxerre (r. 812–29) 50, 53, 137
Angilramn of Metz (r. 768–91) 53
Arnold of Toul (r. 872–94) 53
Arnulf of Metz (r. 614–29) 132, 138
Arsenius of Orte (r. 855–68) 134
Athelm/ Æthelhelm of Canterbury (r. 923/5–926) 55
Audoenus (Ouen) of Rouen (r. 641–84) 48

Barnuin of Verdun (r. 925–39) 145n52
Bernard of Verdun (r. 870–9) 53, 145n52
Brihtheah of Worcester (r. 1033–8) 50
Bruno of Speyer (r. 1107–23) 54
Burchard of Worms (r. 1000–25) 46

Chrodegang of Metz (r. 742–66) 53
Clodulf of Metz (r. ca. 657–ca. 693) 132, 138
Cynesige of Lichfield (r. 949–63/4) 55

Dado of Verdun (r. 880–923) 53, 145n52
Dido of Poitiers (r. ca. 628–67) 52
Dunstan of Canterbury (r. 959–88) 54

Ealdhun of Durham (r. 990–1018) 54
Ebo of Rheims (r. 816–35, 840–1) 62n79
Eligius of Noyon (r. 641–59) 48
Epiphanius of Salamis (fourth c.) 180
Erchanbert of Freising (r. 835–64) 136
Erlung of Würzburg (r. 1106–21) 53, 62n79
Eusebius of Caesarea (ca. 313–339/40)

Franco I of Le Mans (r. 794–816) 145n52
Franco II of Le Mans (r. 816–32) 145n52
Fredrick of Salzburg (d. 991) 63n99

Gallus of Clermont (525–51) 50, 52
Gelasius (pope, r. 492–6) 20
Geoffrey of Auxerre (r. 1052–76) 54
Gerard II of Cambrai (r. 1076–92) 53
Gewilib of Mainz (d. 758) 132
Gibuin I of Châlons-sur-Marne (r. 947–98) 63n95
Gibuin II of Châlons-sur-Marne (r. 998–1004) 63n95
Godo of Metz (r. ca. 641–ca. 652) 138
Goericus of Metz (r. 629–43) 138
Gregory of Tours (r. 573–94) 48, 50, 52, 184

Gregory the Great (pope, r. 590–604) 182, 197
Gregory VII (pope, r. 1073–85) 134

Hadrian II (pope, r. 867–72) 134
Halinard of Sombernon (archbishop of Lyon 1046–52) 62n72
Herard of Tours (r. 855–71) 137
Heribald of Auxerre (r. 828/9–857) 50, 53, 137
Herifrid of Auxerre (r. 887–909) 52
Hildigrim of Châlons (d. 827) 51
Hildigrim of Halberstadt (d. 886) 51
Hincmar of Laon (r. 858–71) 12, 46–7, 50, 134, 137
Hincmar of Rheims (r. 845–82) 12, 46–7, 50–1, 53–4, 131–40
Honorius III (pope, r. 1216–27) 276
Hubert Walter of Canterbury (r. 1193–1205) 194
Hugh I of Nevers (r. 1016–69) 54, 63n95
Hugh II of Nevers (r. 1074–96) 54, 63n95
Hugh of Vermandois (archbishop of Rheims 925–31) 139

Imad of Paderborn (r. 1051–76) 50, 61n60
Innocent III (pope, r. 1198–1216) 200
Isidore of Seville (r. 600–36) 276

John of Antioch (patriarch r. 429–41) 250
John of Lisieux (twelfth c.) 52
John of Sées (twelfth c.) 52

Latro of Laon (r. 550–70) 132, 134, 138
Leopold of Worms (r. 1196–1217) 200–1
Letbald II of Mâcon (r. 993–1016) 63n95
Leudegar of Autun (r. ca. 662–76) 52
Leudwin (Liutwin) of Trier (r. 705–715) 133
Leuthere of Winchester (r. 670–76) 53
Libentius of Hamburg-Bremen (r. 988–1013) 53
Liborius of Le Mans (r. until 397) 132
Lietbert of Cambrai (r. 1051–76) 53
Lupus of Soissons (sixth c. 138

Meinhard of Würzburg (r. 1085–8) 53, 62n79
Meinwerk of Paderborn (r. 1009–36) 50, 61n60
Melito of Sardis (second c.) 189n23
Milo of Trier (r. 715–53) 133

Nicholas I of Constantinople (patriarch, 912–25) 231

Oda of Canterbury (r. 942–58) 50, 52
Oswald of Worcester (archbishop of York 972–92) 50

Philipp of Ravenna 273
Pilgrim of Passau (r. 971–91) 63n99
Poppo I of Würzburg (r. 941–61) 53
Poppo II of Würzburg (r. 961–84) 53
Principius of Soissons (sixth c.) 138

Rather of Verona (d. 974) 18
Reolus of Rheims (r. ca. 672 – ca. 689) 144n33

Salomo I of Constance (r. 838/9–71) 53–4, 63n92, 139
Salomo II of Constance (r. 875/6–89) 53–4, 63n92, 139
Salomo III of Constance (r. 890–919/20) 53–4, 63n92, 136, 139
Sergius of Ravenna (r. until ca. 769) 134
Sidonius Apollinaris (bishop of Clermont, r. ca. 470–85) 191n48
St Ambrose of Milan (339–97) 9, 181, 282
St Augustine of Hippo (r. 395–430) 187n10, 276
St Basil the Great (bishop of Caesarea, r. 370–9) 25, 183, 250, 253
St Chrodegang of Sées (d. 770) 137
St Dunstan (archbishop of Canterbury 959–88) 54–5
St Engelbert of Cologne (r. 1216–25) 18–19, 194–6
St Genebaudus of Laon (r. ca. 499–550) 132, 134, 138
St Liudger of Münster (r. 805–9) 50–1, 53, 136
St Martin of Tours (r. 371–97) 18, 132, 138
St Nicolas of Myra (fourth c.) 18
St Remigius of Rheims (d. 533) 132, 134, 138
St Severus of Ravenna (ca. 342 – ca. 346) 144n33
Stigand of Winchester (r. 1043–70; archbishop of Canterbury 1052–70) 54

Tetricus of Langres (539/40–72) 50
Thierry (Dietrich) I of Metz (r. 965–84) 50–1

Thierry of Verdun (r. 1046–89) 51
Thietmar of Merseburg (r. 1009–18) 49–50, 53

Udoalrich of Augsburg (r. 923–73) 50–1, 53

Victurius I of Le Mans (r. ca. 397–421) 132, 138
Victurius II of Le Mans (r. ca. 422–90) 132, 138

Waldo of Chur (r. 920–49) 54
Waldo of Freising (r. 883–906) 54, 136, 139
Walter of Autun (eleventh c.) 62n72
Walter of Mâcon (r. 1031–61) 63n95
Walter of Orléans (nineth c.) 52
Winither of Worms (bishop elect 1085–8) 54
Wulfstan of York (r. 1002–23) 50
Wulfstan the Homilist (Lupus) (archbishop of York 1002–23) 58n26

General index

Abbasid empire (750–1258) 29, 67–75, 79–90, 213, 246–8, 255
al-ʿAbbās b. al-Ḥasan, Abbasid vizier 68
al-ʿAbbās b. ʿAbd al-Muṭṭalib b. Hāshim, uncle of the prophet 266n56
ʿAbdul Ḥalīm Sharar, historian (1860–1926) 154–5, 167n5, 170n67
ʿAbd al-Jabbār b. Aḥmad al-Hamadhānī, judge (d. 1024) 65
ʿAbd al-Qādir Badāʾūnī, historian (1540–ca. 1605) 99–100
ʿAbd Allāh b. Ḥamdān, Abbasid official 81
ʿAbd Allāh, Fatimid missionary (tenth c.) 255
Abraham (bible) 22, 98
Abū ʿAlī Muḥammad Abū al-Shalaghlagh, Fatimid imam (nineth c.) 255
Abū Ayyūb al-Anṣārī, standard bearer of the prophet 24, 221–3
Abū Bakr, caliph (r. 632–4) 218, 253
Abū Ḥanīfa, jurist (699–767) 221
Abū l-ʿAbbās, son of caliph al-Muqtadir 71, 73, 88
Abū-l-Agharr Khalīfa b. Mubārak al-Sulamī, Abbasid knight 83
Abū l-Fażl, Mughal historian (1551–1602) 93–7, 99, 101–2
Abysinnia 15, 25, 249
Achaemenid empire (550–330 BC) 212
Acre 258
adab 151, 248
Adam (bible) 181, 254
Adham Khān, foster brother of Akbar 99
adoption 154
Afghanistan 213
Africa 211; East 152, 213, 215–16, 218; North 255, 258; sub-Saharan 16, 212
Afżal Khān, Mughal governor 104
Aga Khan IV (b. 1936) 265n53
Agathias, historian (sixth c.) 237
Agnellus of Ravenna, historian (nineth c.) 134
ahl al-bayt 96, 247, 253, 257, 261
Aḥmad Khān Bangash, Nawwāb of Farrukhābād (r. 1749–71) 167n5
Ahmed I, Ottoman sultan (r. 1603–17) 217
Ahwās 83
ʿĀʾisha, wife of the prophet 252
Akbar, emperor (r. 1556–1605) 92–4, 97, 99, 100–4
Alexander the Great (r. 336–323 BC) 212
Alexander, Byzantine emperor (r. 912–13) 230
Alexandria 180, 264n38
Alexios I Komnenos, Byzantine emperor (r. 1081–1118) 239
ʿAlī b. al-Ḥusayn, Shiʿite imam (d. 713) 254
ʿAlī b. ʿĪsā, Abbasid vizier 84–6
ʿAlī ibn Abī Ṭālib, caliph (r. 654–61) 218–19, 253–4, 265n50
Altmann of Hautvilliers, hagiographer (nineth c.) 144n33
Ambrose of Milan 9, 181, 282
Ammianus Marcellinus, historian (fourth c.) 183
Anatolia 183, 213–14, 216, 220, 232; East 16
angels 182, 189n28
An Lushan, rebel (755–63) 111, 115–16, 120
anointment 45

Antichrist 272
Antioch 237
Aphrodite 178
apostles 44, 270–1
Aqmar mosque 260
Arab-Byzantine Frontier 73, 82, 86–7, 232
Arabia 80, 85, 96, 213
Arabs 83
Arcadius, Roman emperor (r. 395–408) 177, 233
ʿArīb b. Saʿd al-Qurṭubī, scholar (d. 980) 68–9, 72, 80, 88
Armenia 84–5
Āṣaf al-Dawla, Nawwāb of Awadh (r. 1775–97) 149, 151, 154, 156–7, 159–62
Āṣaf Khān, brother of empress Nūr Jahān 100
ascetism 7, 23, 130, 135, 179–85, 269–70, 272, 283
Aserbaijan 265n52
Asia: Central 81, 93, 116, 212; Northeast 112
Aṣmaʿī, scholar (d. 828) 71
Attigny 140
Attis, consort of Cybele 178
Augustine of Hippo, theologian (354–430) 187n10, 276
Auxerre 50, 137
Awadh 6, 16–17, 92, 149–66
Awqāf al-Ḥaramayn 215–16, 218, 220, 223
Awrangzēm, Mughal emperor (r. 1658–1707) 103, 105, 168n17
Ayyūbid dynasty (1171–1250) 258
Azerbaijan 84–5
Azhar mosque 23, 221
al-ʿAzīz, Fatimid caliph (r. 975–95) 258

Bābur, Mughal emperor (r. 1526–30) 92, 96, 101–2
Babüssaade 16, 215
Badr, general of caliph al-Mutaʿḍid 86
Badr al-Jamālī, Fatimid vizier (1015–94) 258
Bagdhad 6, 29, 65, 68, 70, 73, 82–9, 221, 248
Bahādur Shāh Awwal (Muʿaẓẓam), Mughal emperor (r. 1707–12) 105
Bahat, river 100
Bahrain 265n52
Bahū Begam, mother of Āṣaf al-Dawla 151, 153, 156–162, 168n25
Bai Juyi, poet (772–856) 119
Bālā Ḥiṣṣār (citadel) 93
Balkans 15, 214
baraka 21, 105, 247, 256, 259
Bardas Phokas, Byzantine commander 239
Bardas Skleros, Byzantine rebel 232, 239
Bashār b. Burd, poet (714–83) 71
Basil I, Byzantine emperor (r. 867–86) 229, **230**
Basil II, Byzantine emperor (r. 976–1025) **230**, 231–6, 238
Basil the Great, theologian (330–379) 25, 183, 250, 253
Basilides, gnostic teacher (second c.) 180
Bavaria 133
bayʿa 71
Beauvais 131, 135
Bedouins 258
Benares 157
Benares rebellion 161
Benedictines 55, 269, 279
Bengal 30, 99, 102–4, 154
Bhakkar, Mughal province 99
bible 270; book of Acts 179, 212; book of Isaiah 179; book of Job 200; Gospel of Matthew 180; Hosea 6.10 273; Matt. 19.12 8–9; Prov. 6.17 275, 278
Bihār, Mughal province 104
bishops: criticism and polemics 18, 194–5, 200–1; designations 44–5; diocese/bishopric 5–7, 44, 46, 139, 201; education 47, 52–3, 137; episcopal dynasties 12–13, 43, 49–54, 131, 136–7, 139; episcopal ideals 194, 198–203; episcopal marriage 10, 12, 31, 54; episcopal republics 126; episcopal saints 18–19; father-son-succession 12, 31, 54–5, 129–36, 139; fosterage 12–13, 47, 51–2; nobility 4, 11–13, 135, 146n75; secular versus ecclesiastical office 18–20, 30, 136–9, 194–5, 199, 200–1; uncle-nephew-succession 12, 49–54; *see also* clergy
Black Sea 230–1
Bon, Ottavio, Venetian ambassador (sixteenth c.) 225n29
Boniface, missionary (d. 754) 133
Brāhmaṇs 149
Bristow, John, British Resident in Awadh 158

Britain 49
British East India Company 6, 149–52, 156–66
Brittany 49, 133
Buddhists 121n1
Buddhist temples 24, 117–18, 218
Burgundy 59n32, 59n34, 271
Butilinus, Alamanni leader (sixth c.) 237
Būyid dynasty (945–1055) 79, 213
Byzantine-Roman empire (sixth c.–1453) 2, 6–7, 15, 17, 20, 65–7, 79–80, 214, 229–40, 249; *see also* Arab-Byzantine Frontier

Caesarius of Heisterbach (ca. 1180–1240) 18–19, 27–8, 193–203, 279
Cairo 6, 16, 22–3, 215, 219, 247, 258–9
Calcutta 161
caliphate 253
caliphs, four rightly guided (632–61) 79, 218, 253
Cambrai 53
Candace /Kandake (royal title) 212
Canon law 10, 12, 44, 46, 55, 56n3, 130, 204n5, 212
Canons Regular of Saint Augustine 13
Cao Cao, Chinese warlord and Chancellor (155–220) 121
Carolingian empire (751–911/987) (*see also* Francia, France, Germany) 12, 44–6, 129–141, 247
castration 7, 9, 10, 15, 28–30, 65–6, 70, 101, 249; forbidden by law 30, 102–4, 183, 190n44, 212, 251; as punishment 111; techniques 8, 126n59, 186n7, 251–2; spiritual 7, 9, 10, 11, 182–3, 191n47; by oneself 178–81, 188n19; by angels 182, 190n38; by family members 231
Caucasus 15, 215
celibacy 10–12, 27; in the early medieval West 11–13, 48–9, 55–6, 129–35; in the Eastern church 10, 43; in the Gregorian reform 10–11, 13; in late antiquity 10-12, 48–9, 179–85; in the late medieval West 13, 283–4; monastic 26–8, 201, 283–4; not as primordial clerical identity 5; practice 13, 55–6
ceremonial 7, 68, 74, 76n20, 93, 259–61
Chang'an 116–17
Charlemagne, Carolingian emperor (r. 768–814) 52, 131, 133, 136–7
Charles the Bald, Carolingian king (840–77) 47, 52, 54
chelā 98, 154, 164
China 2, 6, 25, 43, 212; *see also* Tang empire
Chur 136
Cistercians 13, 18, 27, 193, 196, 198–201, 269, 271, 279
Clairvaux, monastery 197
Claudian, poet (ca. 370–ca. 404) 186n4
clergy: chaste marriage 12, 48–9, 55–6, 134, 142n8; chastity 7–11, 133, 139, 180, 184, 268–86; clerical marriage 10, 12–13, 31, 43, 48–9, 54–5, 129–34, 139–40, 142n21; conflicts between secular and monastic clergy 10, 18–19, 27, 194–202, 270–85; laity versus clergy 11, 136–9, 193, 199, 201; masculinities 26–31, 135, 193, 199, 202–3, 268–86; parish priests 269; pastoral care 269, 274, 277; spiritual knighthood 27, 198–9, 202–3, 208n51
Clement of Alexandria (d. 215) 9, 188n19
Clermont 50
Cluniacs 13
Cnut I the Great, king of Denmark and England (d. 1035) 58n26
Confucian officials 116
Confucian scholars 113, 119
Confucius (551–479 BC) 121n1
Constance (Germany) 53
Constantine I, Roman emperor (r. 306–37) 229
Constantine VII, Byzantine emperor (r. 913–59) **230**, 231–4
Constantine VIII, Byzantine emperor (r. 1025–28) **230**, 231, 239
Constantine IX Monomachos, Byzantine emperor (r. 1042–55) **230**
Constantinople 9, 184, 214–15, 221–2, 220, 231–2
Constantius II, Roman emperor (r. 337–61) 233
Cordoba 80
coronation 17; *see also* anointment
cura monialium 276
Cybele 178

Daizong (Li Yu), Tang emperor (r. 762–79) 116
Dalhousie, British governor-general in India (1848–56) 163
Daoists 121n1
Dār al-Khilāfa, Baghdad 68–9, 79, 82
Darüssaade 216
da'wa 255
Decius, Roman emperor (r. 249–51) 181
Delhi Sultanate (1206–1526) 92
Delhi 99, 150
devşirme 15, 214–15
Dezong (Li Kuo), Tang emperor (r. 779–805) 115
Di, celestial emperor 118
Diocletian, Roman emperor (r. 284–305) 230
Dome of the Rock 22, 98
Dominic Hispanus, Dominican Friar 278
Dominicans 27–8, 268–86
Domitian, Roman emperor (r. 81–96) 181
Du Mu, scholar (803–52) 117

Egypt 16, 21, 23, 84–5, 97, 182, 212–3, 219–20, 247, 249, 258
elephants 100, 104
Elliot, Charles Alfred, colonial offical 160
England 11, 12, 43, 46, 51–2, 54–6, 59n32, 135
Equitus, abbot of Valeria (sixth c.) 182
Etawa 157
Ethiopia 16, 179, 212–13, 249
Eucharist 45
Eunuchs: adoption 14, 16–17, 31, 118–120, 159; ascetism 21; black and white 15–16, 29, 75, 215–16, 249; burial places 15, 115–16, 221–3; *castrati* 10; corporeal appearance 81, 184, 191n48, 238, 249–50, 252; designations 8, 67, 73, 77n28, 81, 90n9, 118, 124, 152, 190n40, 250–1; dynasticism 114–21; guardians of the prophet's tomb in Medina 22–3, 217–19; hybrid gender 25, 118, 150, 155, 178, 187n10, 220, 236–7, 249–52; intermediaries between the mundane and the sacred 20–4, 220, 222, 248, 260–2; *khwāja-sarā'ī* 16, 99, 149–66; marriage 14, 28, 251, 262; masculinities and gender 26–31, 118–19, 151, 155, 178, 235–40, 248–9, 256, 262; military commanders 6–7, 29, 80–9, 119, 215, 233–4, 236–7, 240; monastery St Lazarus 232; *muḥannakūn* 22, 258–61; numbers 79, 185, 216, 218; origins 15–16, 152–3, 212–15, 230–2, 242n9, 249; physical paternity 28, 251, 262; polemics against 25, 119, 155, 164, 183, 236–9, 249–50; priests and bishops 10; saints 20, 181–5, 189n30; *ṣaqāliba* 65, 213, 249, 256, 264n16
Eunuchs, offices 7, 16, 20–4, 66–73, 212–14; Abbasid empire 66–73; Awadh 169; Byzantine empire 7, 177, 229–35; Fatimid empire 22, 257–61, 267n79; Mamluk empire 22, 213; Mughal empire 99–100; Ottoman empire 214–17; Roman empire 177, 229–30; Tang China 111, 116–17; *see also* castration
Euphrates, river 85–6
Eve (bible) 181
exempla 199, 268, 278–80
Eyüb Cemetery, Istanbul 24, 211, 221–3

faḥl (pl. *fuḥūl*) 26, 249
Faizābād 150–1, 153, 155, 161
Fan Ye, scholar (398–445) 112
Farrukhābād 92, 167n5
Fārs *see* Persia
Fateḥpūr-Sīkrī 95, 102
Fāṭima, daughter of the prophet 253
Fatimid empire (909–1171) 6, 14, 21–2, 76n20, 80, 84, 213, 246, 252–63
Fā'iz Bakhsh, Muḥammad, historian (eighteenth c.) 151–3, 155, 160, 162
Fīrūz Shāh Tughlaq, Sultan of Delhi (1351–80) 103
fitna 69
Five Dynasties (907–60) 119
France 12, 46, 52, 135, 269
Francia 45–6, 51, 54–5
Franciscans 27–8, 268–86
Frederic II, Roman-German emperor (r. 1198–1250) 18
Freising 136
Friday prayer 259

Gabriel (angel) 190n38
galli, eunuch priests of Cybele 8, 178
gender 11, 24–30, 71, 181, 202, 252, 274, 290n33; *see also* clergy and eunuchs, masculinities

Gerard of Frachet, hagiographer (1205–71) 278
Germany 18, 46, 52, 53, 55, 139
Ghadīr Khumm 265n50
Gharīb, brother of the Abbasid queen Shaghab 82
Ghaznavid dynasty (977–1186) 213
ghilmān (pl. *ghulām*) 81
gnosis 180
Godfrey, Count of Verdun (963–1002) 51
Goṇḍa district 155
Goths 237
governmentality 17, 154
Gratian, jurist (twelfth c.) 204n5
Great Seldjuk dynasty (1037–1194) 213
Gregorian Reform 10–11, 49, 194, 285
Gregory of Nanzianz, theologian (d. 390) 9
Guillaume de Lorris, poet (thirteenth c.) 283
Gulbadan Begum, princess 93–4
guru 154
ḥadīth 66, 68, 76n8, 220–1, 252

Hadiya kingdom (thirteenth–fifteenth c.) 213
ḥajj 69, 85, 94, 220
al-Ḥākim, Fatimid caliph (r. 995–1021) 258
Ḥāmid, Abbasid vizier 72
Han dynasty (25–220) 112, 118–19
Ḥanafī law 23–4, 220–1
ḥaram 219, 222–3
Herard of Tours, hagiographer (nineth c.) 137
harem 6, 68–71, 79–82, 250; Abbasid empire 68–71; concept 68, 96–7; Fatimid empire 14, 256, 262; Mughal empire 93–5, 97–105, 154; Ottoman empire 15–16, 214–17, 222; *see also zanāna*
Hārūn b. Gharīb, Abbasid prince 87
Hastings, Warren, governor-general of India (1772–85) 161
Hebron 22, 98
Henri de France, brother of Louis VII 198
Henry, abbot of Heisterbach (1208–44) 196
Heribert, Count of Rheims (d. 943) 139
hermaphrodites 29, 104, 251, 262
Herodotus, historian (fifth BC) 212
Herul Fulcaris, Alamanni commander (sixth c.) 244
Hesse, Germany 133
Hijaz 79, 218
hijrās 105, 166
Hilāl al-Ṣābi', scholar (969–1056) 69–70
Hindustan 103
Hippolytus of Rome 188n19
ḥisba 6
Hoey, William, scholar (1849–1919) 168n25
Hohenstaufen dynasty (r. 1138–1268) 200
homosexuality/same sex love 38n89, 101, 285
Huainan 117
hujja 22, 257
Humāyūn, Mughal emperor (r. 1530–50, 1555–6) 92
Humbert of Romans, Dominican master general (r. 1254–63) 278–9
Humilis of Milan, Franciscan friar 277
Huns 186n4
Huosi, episcopal dynasty in Freising 136
Hürrem Sultan (Roxelane), wife of sultan Süleyman I 215–16
Hyder Beg Khān, minister in Awadh (nineteenth c.) 161–2
Hyderabad 92

Ibn Abī al-Sāj, ruler of Armenia and Azerbaijan (tenth c.) 84–5
Ibn al-Furāt, Abbasid vizier 68, 72, 82–5
Ibn al-Mu'tazz, 'Abd Allāh, Abbasid prince 71–2, 82
Ibn al-Ṭuwayr, Fatimid court official (1130–1220) 258–9
Ibn Baṭṭūṭa, traveller (1304–ca. 1368) 218
Ibn Muqla, Abbasid vizier 89
Ibn Rā'iq, Abbasid commander 86–8
Ibn Taghrī Birdī, historian (ca. 1409–70) 259
Ibn Ṭāhir, Abbasid governor of Khurasan (825–44) 87
Ibrāhīm Khān Fatḥ Jang, governor of Bengal (seventeenth c.) 104
Ifrīqiya 84
imamate 253
India 16–17, 25, 43, 92–105, 118, 213; North 16

Indian Ocean 152–3
Indus 264n16
Iran *see* Persia
Iraq 81, 83, 85, 211, 213, 218, 265n52
Ireland 12, 43, 49
Irenaeus of Lyon, theologian (second c.) 188n19
Iṣfahān 83
Isḥāq al-Nawbakhtī, Abbasid offical 89
Isis, goddess 178
Islām Khān, governor of Bengal (seventeenth c.) 103–4
Islām Shāh Sūr, sultan of Sur (r. 1545–53) 99
Islamic law 17, 66, 225n46, 251; *see also* Hanafi and Shiʿi law
Ismāʿīl b. Jaʿfar al-Ṣādiq, Ismaʿili imam (eighth c.) 254
Ismaʿili Shiʿites 85, 254–63, 265n52
Istanbul 23–4, 219–20; *see also* Constantinople
Italy 6, 59n32, 134–5, 157, 182, 200, 234, 269

Jagdīshpur 157
Jahāngīr, Mughal emperor (r. 1605–27) 30, 92, 100, 102–5
al-Jāḥiẓ, polymath (ca. 776–869) 25, 65, 248–50
Janissaries 217
Jawhar al-Ṣiqillī, Fatimid general (tenth c.) 258
Jazīra 85
Jaʿfar al-Ṣādiq, Shiʿite imam (d. 765) 254
Jean de Meun, scholar (thirteenth c.) 283–4
Jerome, theologian (347–420) 9, 10, 130, 178, 184
Jerusalem 22, 98, 212
Jesus (Islam) 254
Jesus Christ 7, 9, 24, 44, 137, 178, 180–1, 199, 247, 270
Jews 24, 75, 179, 183
John Cassian, theologian (ca. 260–435) 182, 186n7
John I Tzimiskes, Byzantine emperor (r. 969–76) **230**, 233–7, 239–40
Jordan of Saxony, Dominican master general (r. 1222–37) 278
Joseph (bible) 183
Julian, Roman emperor (r. 360–3) 183
Julius Cassian, gnostic teacher (second c.) 180, 188n19
Justin Martyr, Christian writer (second c.) 180
Justinian I, Byzantine emperor (r. 527–65) 6, 177, 233

Kabades *see* Kavadh I 236
Kabul 99
Kandake *see* Candace
Kavadh I, Sasanian ruler (r. 488–497, 499–531) 236
Kazakhstan 81
Kaʿba 22, 85, 96, 98, 217
Kedrenos, George, historian (eleventh c.) 235
Khāndēsh 99
al-Khāqāni, Abbasid vizier 84
al-Khaṣībī, Abbasid vizier 86
al-Khaṭīb al-Baghdādī, scholar (d. 1071) 68
Kirghizstan 81
Komnenian dynasty (1057/1081–1185/1461) 239
Kora 157
Korea 218
Kösem Sultan, Ottoman regent (r. 1589–1651) 217
Kutāma Berbers 258
Kuwait 265n52

Lal family, Awadh (nineteenth c.) 165
Laon 132
Lateran council (1215) 273, 285
Layth b. ʿAlī, Ṣaffārid ruler (r. 909–10) 83
Le Mans 132
Lebanon 265n52
Leo Phokas, Byzantine general (tenth c.) 231
Leo the Deacon, historian (tenth–eleventh c.) 234–9
Leo VI, Byzantine emperor (r. 886–912) **230**, 231f
Leutharis, Alamanni leader (sixth c.) 237
Li Jiaxun *see* Shang Kegu
Li Kuo *see* Dezong
Li Longji *see* Xuanzong
Li Shimin *see* Taizong
Li Xilie 120
Li Yu *see* Daizong
Lincoln 18
Liuthar, Count of Nordmark (r. 983–1003) 50
London 54

Lotharingia 50–1
Louis the German, Carolingian king (r. 843–76) 136
Louis the Pious, Carolingian emperor (r. 781–840) 52, 136
Louis VII, French king (r. 1137–80) 197
Lucknow 150, 157, 159, 164–5
Luoyang 114
Luther, Martin (1483–1546) 9

Macedonian dynasty (867–1056) 233–5, 238, 240
madrasa 221
Magdeburg 53
Maghrebins 258
Magna Mater, goddess 8, 178–9
Mahābat Khan, Mughal general 100
Mahadaji Shinde, Maratha ruler (r. 1768–94) 157
al-Mahdiya 257
al-Mahdī (Saʿīd b. al-Ḥusayn ʿAbd Allāh), Fatimid caliph (r. 909–34) 255–6
Mainz 200
Malatya 16
Mamluk empire (1250–1517) 22–4, 97, 213–15, 218, 259
al-Manṣūriya 257
Mang Mountains 114
al-Manṣūr, Fatimid caliph (r. 946–53) 21, 257
al-Maqrīzī, historian (1364–1442) 23, 259
Maria the Copt, concubine of the prophet 264n38
marriage 65, 101–2, 159, 181, 220, 232
marriage, incestuous 60n52
martyrdom 179, 181–2, 195
al-Masʿūdī, historian (ca. 985–956) 68–9
Maura, wife of Bf. Victurius 132
al-Māwardī, jurist (972–1058) 253
Mecca 16, 22, 73, 85, 96–8, 213, 217, 221; *see also* Awqāf al-Ḥaramayn
Medina 16, 23–4, 85, 96–8, 213, 219–21, 247; *see also* Awqāf al-Ḥaramayn; Muḥammad, prophet, tomb
Mehmed II, Ottoman sultan (r. 1444–46, 1451–81) 214–15
Mehmed III, Ottoman sultan (r. 1595–1603) 216
Mehmed IV, Ottoman sultan (r. 1648–87) 215, 217
Mekece, Anatolia 214
Melitene 232
Melkites 264n38
Merovingian empire (fifth c.–751) 11, 45, 48–9, 130, 134–6; *see also* Francia, France, Germany
Mettlach, abbey 133
Metz 50–1
Mian Ganj 156–8, 160
Michael IV, Byzantine emperor (r. 1034–41) 6, **230**, 231, 234, 238
Michael V, Byzantine emperor (r. 1041–42) 6, **230**, 231, 238
Michael VII Doukas, Byzantine emperor (r. 1071–78) 239
Mīrān Mubārak, king of Khāndēsh (sixteenth c.) 99
Mishnah 183
Miskawayh, scholar (932–1030) 68, 70–1, 73, 80, 87
misogynist tradition 276–7, 280
missi 46
Mughal empire (1526–1858) 16, 92–108, 149, 152
Mongols 112
Montpellier 52
Moses (bible) 254
Mosul 88
Muḥammad al-Bāqir, Shiʿite imam (ca. 676–ca. 736) 254
Muḥammad al-Mahdī, Shiʿite imam 254
Muḥammad b. Ismāʿīl, Ismaʿili imam (eighth c.) 254–5
Muḥammad b. Yāqūt, Abbasid commander 89
Muḥammad, brother of caliph al-Muqtadir 87, 89
Muḥammad, prophet (ca. 570–622) 16 , 21–4, 79, 96–8, 105, 221, 247, 251–5, 260, 265n50; tomb in Medina 16, 22–3, 211, 217–23, 246–7
Muḥammad, son of caliph al-Muktafi 89
al-Muḥassin, son of vizier Ibn al-Furāt 85
al-Muʿizz, Fatimid caliph (r. 953–75) 258
al-Muktafī, Abbasid caliph (r. 902–8) 65, 67, 71, 82, 86
al-Muqaddasī, Abbasid caliph (ca. 945–91) 249
al-Muqtadir, Abbasid caliph (r. 908–32) 65, 67–8 , 70–4, 80–6
Murad III, Ottoman sultan (r. 1574–95) 215–16

Murad IV, Ottoman sultan (r. 1623–40) 219
Murshidābād 154
Mūsā al-Kāẓim, Shiʿite imam (d. 799) 254
al-Mustanṣir bi-llāh, Fatimid caliph (r. 1036–94) 258
al-Muʿtaḍid, Abbasid caliph (r. 892–902) 81–2, 86, 89
al-Mutawakkil, Abbasid caliph (r. 847–61) 77n41
Muʾnis al-Khāzin, Abbasid official 82
Muʾnis al-Muẓaffar 6, 29–30, 65, 69, 71, 73–5, 80–90
Muʿaẓẓam *see* Bahādur Shāh Awwal
Muʿtamad Khān, Mughal commander (seventeenth c.) 101

Najaf 218
Naqshbandis 221
Naṣr al-Qushūrī, Abbasid chamberlain 80–1, 85–6
Nawwāb Begam 161
Nāẓir ʿAmbar, Mughal offical (sixteenth c.) 92
Nāzūk, Abbasid chief of police 86–7
Neo-Assyrian empire (911–612 BC) 211
Nicaea, council (325) 10, 43, 180
Nikephoros II Phokas, Byzantine emperor (r. 963–69) 230, 232–3, 235–7, 240
Nikephoros Ouranos, Byzantine offical 234
Nizārīs 265n53
Noah (bible) 254
Normandy 12, 49
Northern Wei dynasty (386–534) 119
Northern Zhou dynasty (557–81) 119
Notker the Stammerer, monk and scholar (ca. 840–912) 136
Nubia 15, 249
nuns 269, 271
Nūr al-Dīn ibn Zangī, ruler in Syria (r. 1146–74) 217
Nūr Jahān, Mughal empress (1577–1645) 93, 100–1, 105

occultation (Shiʿa) 254
Orhan, Ottoman sultan (r. 1326–62) 214
Origen of Alexandria, theologian (ca. 185–253) 180
Ostrogoths 6, 25, 234
Otto I, Roman-German emperor (r. 936–73) 53
Otto IV, Roman-German emperor (r. 1198–1218) 200
Ottoman empire (fourteenth ca.–1922) 15–16, 23–4, 211–23
Ottonian empire (919–1024) 46, 53
Oudh *see* Awadh

Pachon of Scetis, late antique saint 182
Pagans 24
Palladius, Christian writer (fifth c.) 182
paṇḍakas 118
Papacy 10, 48, 129, 247, 269, 276
Paphlagonia 231, 242
Paris 52, 194, 270
Paul (apostle) 179–80
Paul the Deacon, monk and scholar (d. 799) 132, 138
Paulus Aegineta, physician (seventh c.) 186n7
Peace of God movement 192
Persia 83, 85, 213, 236, 265n52
Persians 83
Peter Damian, reforming monk (1007–72) 13
Philotheos, Byzantine court official (nineth c.) 66, 230
Philip (apostle) 179
Philipp of Swabia, Staufian king (r. 1198–1208) 200
Philo of Alexandria, philosopher (1st c.) 183
Pippin III the Short, Carolingian king (r. 751–68) 45, 131
Poitiers monastery 184
Potiphar (bible) 183, 190n38
poverty 269–70
Premonstratensians 13
Procopius, historian (ca. 500–62) 25, 177, 230, 236
prophethood 253
prostitution, sacred 178–9, 187n11
Prudentius, poet (fourth c.) 179
Psellos, Michael, historian (ca. 1017–87) 232, 234–5, 237–6
Ptolomaic dynasty (305–30 BC) 212
Punjab 99, 104
purity 11, 129, 131, 182, 271–4, 277, 285
al-Qāhir, Abbasid caliph (r. 929, 932–34) 87–9
al-Qāʾim, Fatimid caliph (r. 934–46) 21, 257
al-Qalqashandī, jurist (1355–1418) 258–9

Qarāmiṭa (Carmathians) 80, 85–6
Qaṣr al-Jiṣṣ, palace in Samarra 88
Qin dynasty (212–206 BC) 118
Quran 66, 96–7, 221, 260

Rahmut, brother of Almās ʿAlī Khān 158
Rahmutgunge, city 158
Rājā Bhagmul, deputy of Almās ʿAlī Khān 159
Rājpūts 94, 98, 100–1, 149
Ramadan 259–61
rape 10, 277, 281
Raqqa 85–6
Raqqāda 255
al-Rāzī, physician (ca. 865–925) 252
Rāʾiq, Abbasid official 81, 87–8
Repton 28
Rhea (goddess) 178
Rheims 52, 62n79
Roman empire (27 BC–sixth c.) 8, 44, 177–85, 299–300
Roman law 8, 15, 183, 190n43, 232
Romanos I Lekapenos, Byzantine emperor (r. 920–44) **230**, 231
Romanos II, Byzantine emperor (r. 959–63) **230**, 231–3
Romanos III Argyros, Byzantine emperor (r. 1028–34) **230**, 231, 234
Rome 44, 134, 137
Ruqayya Begum, Mughal empress consort (r. 1557–1605) 103
Rus 236–7
Rutebeuf, poet (ca. 1250–85) 271–4, 284, 286

Saarbrücken 54
Sabaeans 249
Safavid empire (1501–1736) 97
St Arsenius (350–445) 269
St Bernard of Claiveaux (ca. 1090–1153) 271–3, 286
St Clare of Assisi (1194–1253) 276
St Dominic (1179–1221) 274
St Elisabeth of Thüringen (1207–31) 196
St Eugenia (late antiquity) 182
St Francis of Assisi (1181–1226) 272, 274–6, 278
St Gall monastery 139
St Guthlac (673–714) 48
St Paul, apostle 282
St Theodor oratory, imperial palace 21
St Paul's Cathedral, London 54
Saint-Rémy abbey 62n79
al-Sakhāwī, scholar (1427–97) 218
Ṣalāḥ al-Dīn, Ayyubid sultan (r. 1171–93) 218, 247
Salamiyya 255
Salian empire (1024–1125) 46
Salīm Chishtī, Sufi saint (d. 1572) 102
Salīma Sulṭān Begum, wife of emperor Akbar (r. 1539–1613) 103
Salimbene of Parma, Franciscan scholar (1221–88) 268–70, 272–4, 276–8, 280–1, 286
Salomonids, episcopal dynasty in Constance 53–4, 63n92, 136, 139
Sāmānids (819–1005) 81
Samarqand 81
Samarra 88, 90n4
Samsat 85
Sarajevo 15
Sasanid empire (224–651) 212
Sawsan, Abbasid chamberlain 65–6, 72
Sayyid Aḥmad Khān, philosopher (1817–98) 166
Saʿādat ʿAlī Khān, Nawwāb of Awadh (r. 1722–39) 149, 152
Saʿīd ibn al-Ḥusayn ʿAbd Allāh *see* al-Mahdī
Saʿīd Khān Chaghatāʾī, Mughal aristocrat (sixteenth c.) 104
Scythians 237
Selim II, Ottoman sultan (r. 1566–74) 216
Sens 137
Serenus, symbolically castrated monk (late antiquity) 182
sexuality 7–11, 275, 283–4, 286
Shaghab, Abbasid queen (d. 933) 65, 70–1, 80–1, 86–7
Shāh ʿAbbās, Safavid ruler (r. 1588–1629) 96
Shams al-Dīn Muḥammad Atkeh Khān, foster-father of Akbar 99
Shang Kegu, adopted son of eunuch Yu Chaoʾen 120
Sharah 157
Shi Siming, Chinese rebel (703–61) 120
Shiʿi law 169n52
Shiʿites 97, 148, 218, 221, 247, 253–4, 259; *see also* Zaydīs, Ismaʿilis, Nizārīs and Twelver Shiʿites
Shujāʿ al-Dawla, Nawwāb of Awadh (r. 1754–75) 149, 156, 160–1, 167n5, 170n67

Shun, Han emperor (r. 125–44) 118
shurṭa 6, 86–8
Sicily 239, 258
Sijilmāsa 255
Sīkrī, village 102
Sima Qian, historian (ca. 145–90) 119
Sind 249
Sixteen Kingdoms (304–439) 119
Skylitzes, John, historian (eleventh c.) 235, 239
slaves and slavery 4, 16, 56n3, 72, 75, 93, 103, 150, 152–4, 160–2, 179, 213, 215, 232; law 169n52; slave nobles 14, 151, 166; slave-trade routes 213; *see also* eunuchs
Sleeman, William, British colonial official (1788–1856) 158, 163–5
Song dynasty (960–1279) 113–14, 119
Sozomen, historian (d. ca. 450) 184
Stephanie, wife of Pope Hadrian II 134
al-Subkī, jurist (1284–1355) 25
Subkarā, Abbasid governor 83
Sudan 15, 212, 249
Sufis 102, 214, 221
Süleyman I, Ottoman sultan (r. 1520–66) 215–16
al-Ṣūlī, Abū Bakr, Abbasid court official 71–3
Sunnites 23, 97, 218–21, 225n46, 247, 253–4, 259
Sylhet 30, 102–3
Symeon the Logothete, hagiographer (tenth–eleventh c.) 234–5
Syria 72, 84–5, 211, 213, 255
al-Ṭabarī, historian (839–923) 68

Taiwan 113
Taizong (Li Shimin), Tang emperor (r. 626–49) 115
Talmud 183
Tang empire (618–907) 14, 111–21
al-Tanūkhī, judge and secretary (941–94) 70
Tarsus 82
Tertullian, theologian (second–third c.) 179, 187n7
Theodora, Byzantine empress (r. 1028–56) 229, 230
Theodora, Roman empress (d. 548) 177
Theophanes Continuatus, Byzantine collection of historical writings 234–6
Theophano, wife of Romanos II 233
Thomas Aquinas, Dominican theologian (ca. 1225–74) 272
Thomas of Cantimpré, Dominican theologian (ca. 1201–ca. 1272) 280–2
Thomas of Celano, Franciscan historian (ca. 1190–1260) 275
Thomas of Pavia, Franciscan historian (d. 1280) 276
Thrace 237
Thuringia 133
Tigris, river 79, 82
ṭirāz 257
Topkapı Palace, Istanbul 15, 214–16, 220–2
Transoxiana 213
Tunisia 84, 255
Turhan Sultan, mother of Mehmed IV 217
Turks 81, 112, 120, 258
Twelver Shiʿites 254
Typhenia, wife of Decius 181

Uighurs 116
ʿulamāʾ 219
Ulpian, jurist (ca. 170–223) 8
Umayyad empire (661–750) 79, 82, 212, 247, 264n17
ʿUmar ibn al-Khaṭṭāb, caliph (r. 634–44) 218, 253
umma 253–4
universities 270, 286
university of Paris 270, 278, 283
Unnāo district 156
ʿUthmān ibn ʿAffān, caliph (r. 644–54) 87, 253

Valesians 180
Victorids, episcopal dynasty in Chur 136
vita apostolica 270, 275
Vulpecula, daughter of St Genebaudus 138

Wājid ʿAlī Shāh, Nawwāb of Awadh (r. 1847–56) 163–5, 167n17, 170n67
walāʾ 75
Walbeck 49
Wang Chengzong, rebell 119
Washilu 213
Wazīr ʿAlī Khān, Nawwāb of Awadh (r. 1797–8) 154
Wei dynasty (220–65) 118
Welf dynasty 200

Wen (Yuwen Tai), Emperor of Northern Zhou (534–56) 120
wen and *wu* 115
Wessex 53
Western Wei dynasty (535–56) 119–20
William de Montibus, theologian (d. 1213) 18
William of Saint Amour, theologian (d. 1272) 270–2, 281–6
Winchester 54
women: disguised as eunuchs 184; male attitudes towards 27, 172n105, 271–85; religious authority 185, 209n70; *see also* misogynist tradition
Worcester 50
Worms 143n25
Würzburg 53

Xianbei 119–20
Xiaowen, emperor of Northern Wei (r. 471–99) 119
Xi'an 114
Xuanzong (Li Longji), Tang emperor (r. 712–56) 115

Yahweh 179
Yalbaq, *ghilmān* of Mu'nis al-Muẓaffar 88–9
Yāqūt, Abbasid official 81, 87–8
Yemen 215, 246, 249
yin and *yang* 115
Yin-Shang dynasty (sixteenth–eleventh c. BC) 111
York 50
Yu Zhide *see* Shang Kegu
Yuwen Tai *see* Wen 120
ẓāhir and *bāṭin* 254
zanāna 154, 160, 166

Zanj rebels 81
Zayd ibn ʿAlī, Zaydī imam (d. 740) 254
Zaydī Shiʿites 218, 254, 265n51
Zhou dynasty (ca. 1045–221 BC) 212
Zoe Karbonopsina, Byzantine empress (r. 914–20) 231, 234
Zoe, Byzantine empress (r. 1028–50) **230**, 231